Personal Construct Psychotherapy
Advances in Theory, Practice and Research

Personal Construct Psychotherapy

Advances in Theory, Practice and Research

Edited by

DAVID A WINTER PhD
University of Hertfordshire and
Barnet, Enfield and Haringey Mental Health NHS Trust

and

LINDA L VINEY PhD
University of Wollongong

W
WHURR PUBLISHERS
LONDON AND PHILADELPHIA

© 2005 Whurr Publishers Ltd
First published 2005
by Whurr Publishers Ltd
19b Compton Terrace
London N1 2UN England and
325 Chestnut Street, Philadelphia PA 19106 USA

British Library Cataloguing in Publication Data

A catalogue record for this book
is available from the British Library.

ISBN 1 86156 394 9

Typeset by Adrian McLaughlin, a@microguides.net
Printed and bound in the UK by Athenæum Press Limited, Gateshead, Tyne & Wear

Contents

The editors   ix
List of contributors   x
Foreword *Fay Fransella*   xiii
Preface *David A Winter, Linda L Viney*   xv

PART ONE   **General principles of personal construct psychotherapy**   **1**

Chapter 1   Personal construct psychotherapy meets
constructivism: convergence, divergence, possibility   **3**

Jonathan D Raskin, Kristian David Weihs, Laurie Ann Morano

Chapter 2   Psychological disorder and reconstruction   **21**

Beverly M Walker, David A Winter

Chapter 3   Kellian invalidation, attachment and the construct
of 'control'   **34**

Sandra Sassaroli, Roberto Lorenzini, Giovanni Maria Ruggiero

Chapter 4   The psychotherapeutic relationship from a
personal construct perspective   **43**

Gabriele Chiari, Maria Laura Nuzzo

Chapter 5   Encountering an other: experiential personal
construct psychotherapy   **54**

*LM Leitner, AJ Faidley, Donald Dominici, Carol Humphreys,
Valerie Loeffler, Mark Schlutsmeyer, Jill Thomas*

Chapter 6 A personal construct approach to narrative and
post-modern therapies   **69**

*Luis Botella, Sergi Corbella, Tary Gómez, Olga Herrero,
Meritxell Pacheco*

Chapter 7 Personal construct psychotherapy: epistemology
and practice   **81**

Greg J Neimeyer, Jocelyn Saferstein, Wade Arnold

Chapter 8 Techniques of personal construct family therapy   **94**

Harry Procter

PART TWO   **Specific clinical problems**   **109**

Chapter 9 Growing through grief: constructing coherence in
narratives of loss   **111**

Robert A Neimeyer

Chapter 10 Deliberate self-harm and reconstruction   **127**

David A Winter

Chapter 11 Resolution of dilemmas by personal construct
psychotherapy   **136**

Guillem Feixas, Luis Ángel Saúl

Chapter 12 From constriction to experimentation: personal
construct psychotherapy for agoraphobia   **148**

David A Winter, Chris Metcalfe

Chapter 13 Constructivist trauma psychotherapy: a framework
for healing   **165**

Kenneth W Sewell

Chapter 14 Personal constructions in therapy with child sexual
abuse survivors   **177**

Christopher R Erbes, Stephanie Lewis Harter

Chapter 15   Personal construct group psychotherapy for
borderline personality disorder   **189**

Ian Gillman-Smith, Sue Watson

Chapter 16   Eating disorders   **198**

Eric Button

Chapter 17   Working with people who hear voices   **212**

Diane Allen

Chapter 18   Issues in forensic psychotherapy   **226**

James Horley

Chapter 19   The experience of anger   **239**

Peter Cummins

Chapter 20   Kids' stuff   **256**

David Green

Chapter 21   Personal construct group work with troubled adolescents   **271**

Deborah Truneckova, Linda L Viney

Chapter 22   Towards a personal construct sex therapy   **287**

David A Winter

Chapter 23   Looking forward towards the end –
working with older people   **296**

Sally Robbins

Chapter 24   Group work with women living with breast cancer   **310**

Lisbeth G Lane, Linda L Viney

Chapter 25   Personal construct workshops for women
experiencing menopause   **320**

Heather Foster, Linda L Viney

PART THREE   **Evidence base**   **333**

Chapter 26   A process and outcome study of personal
                  construct psychotherapy   **335**

            Sue Watson, David A Winter

Chapter 27   The effectiveness of personal construct psychotherapy:
                  a meta-analysis   **347**

            Linda L Viney, Chris Metcalfe, David A Winter

Appendix   An introduction to personal construct theory   **365**

References   371
Author index   413
Subject index   425

The editors

David Winter is Professor of Clinical Psychology and Programme Director of the Doctorate in Clinical Psychology at the University of Hertfordshire, and Head of Clinical Psychology Services for Barnet in Barnet, Enfield and Haringey Mental Health NHS Trust. He has applied personal construct psychology in clinical research and practice in the British National Health Service for some 30 years, and is the author of *Personal Construct Psychology in Clinical Practice: Theory, Research and Applications* (Routledge, 1992/1994) and of about 100 other publications on personal construct psychology and psychotherapy research. He is a Chartered Clinical Psychologist and Fellow of the British Psychological Society, and has chaired the Society's Psychotherapy Section. He is also registered as a Personal Construct Psychotherapist with the UK Council for Psychotherapy, and has chaired the Council's Experiential Constructivist Section and Research Committee.

Linda Viney is an Associate Professor in Clinical Psychology at the University of Wollongong, where she directed the Clinical Postgraduate Program for 15 years. She has applied personal construct psychology and published in the areas of clinical, counselling and health psychology, with 175 book chapters and articles with an emphasis on evaluation. She has more recently been applying this approach leading a research project funded by the Australian Research Council with mental health consumers to evaluate mental health services. This project has just received the Gold Medal for the best Mental Health Research in Australia and New Zealand for 2004.

Contributors

Diane Allen, Coventry Teaching Primary Care Trust

Wade Arnold, University of Florida, Gainesville, Florida

Luis Botella, FPCEE Blanquerna, Ramon Llull University, Barcelona

Eric Button, Leicester Partnership NHS Trust and Leicester University

Gabriele Chiari, Centro Studi in Psicoterapia Cognitiva, Florence

Sergi Corbella, FPCEE Blanquerna, Ramon Llull University, Barcelona

Peter Cummins, Coventry Teaching Primary Care Trust

Donald Dominici, Miami University, Oxford, Ohio

Christopher R Erbes, Douglas County Hospital and Minneapolis
Veterans Affairs Medical Center

AJ Faidley, Miami University, Oxford, Ohio

Guillem Feixas, University of Barcelona

Heather Foster, University of Wollongong

Ian Gillman-Smith, Barnet, Enfield and Haringey Mental Health NHS
Trust

Tary Gómez, FPCEE Blanquerna, Ramon Llull University, Barcelona

David Green, University of Leeds

Stephanie Lewis Harter, Texas Tech University, Lubbock, Texas

Olga Herrero, FPCEE Blanquerna, Ramon Llull University, Barcelona

James Horley, Augustana University College, Camrose, Alberta, Canada

Carol Humphreys, Miami University, Oxford, Ohio

Lisbeth G Lane, Westmead Hospital and University of Wollongong

LM Leitner, Miami University, Oxford, Ohio

Valerie Loeffler, Miami University, Oxford, Ohio

Roberto Lorenzini, Studi Cognitivi, Postgraduate Cognitive Psychotherapy School and Research Centre, Milan

Chris Metcalfe, University of Bristol

Laurie Ann Morano, State University of New York at New Paltz

Greg J Neimeyer, University of Florida, Gainesville, Florida

Robert A Neimeyer, University of Memphis, Memphis, Tennessee

Maria Laura Nuzzo, Centro di Psicologia e Psicoterapia Costruttivista, Rome

Meritxell Pacheco, FPCEE Blanquerna, Ramon Llull University, Barcelona

Harry Procter, Consultant Clinical Psychologist, Taunton

Jonathan D Raskin, State University of New York at New Paltz

Sally Robbins, Coventry Teaching Primary Care Trust

Giovanni Maria Ruggiero, Studi Cognitivi, Postgraduate Cognitive Psychotherapy School and Research Centre, Milan

Jocelyn Saferstein, University of Florida, Gainesville, Florida

Sandra Sassaroli, Studi Cognitivi, Postgraduate Cognitive Psychotherapy School and Research Centre, Milan

Luis Ángel Saúl, Universidad Nacional de Educación a Distancia, Madrid

Mark Schlutsmeyer, Miami University, Oxford, Ohio

Kenneth W Sewell, University of North Texas, Denton, Texas

Jill Thomas, Miami University, Oxford, Ohio

Deborah Truneckova, Department of School Education, New South Wales

Beverly M Walker, University of Wollongong

Sue Watson, Barnet, Enfield and Haringey Mental Health NHS Trust

Kristian David Weihs, State University of New York at New Paltz

Foreword

In his work *The Psychology of Personal Constructs* (Kelly, 1955/1991a/1991b), George Kelly used psychotherapy to exemplify how his theory might be applied. He was at pains to point out that it would apply as much to those who read his book as to those with psychological problems described in it. Perhaps because he used psychotherapy as his example of how his theory might be used, this has been a major focus for those working with personal construct theory in the years since Kelly's *magnum opus* was launched into the psychological arena.

The contributors to *Personal Construct Psychotherapy: Advances in Theory, Practice and Research* demonstrate both the quality and the breadth of application of personal construct psychotherapy as well as the influence it has had on the development of other therapeutic approaches. There is much to discuss arising from the extensive coverage in this book, so I would like to dwell on just two issues that seem important to me. One is the growth of the philosophy of 'constructivism' and the opportunity this offers for the integration of the 'psychotherapies' and the other is the increasing demand for evidence of effectiveness of personal construct psychotherapy itself.

George Kelly's own philosophy of *constructive alternativism* underpins the whole of his theory of personal constructs and hence his psychotherapy. Many are of the opinion that this has played a major part in the increasing importance given to the philosophy of *constructivism* in psychotherapy and in psychology itself. Several authors here give readers in-depth insights into the importance of this development and the advantages it offers for integrating many psychotherapies under the constructivist umbrella.

My personal interest is whether increased focus on constructivist philosophy may result in the *theory* of personal constructs increasingly taking a back seat. That may, of course, be no bad thing. Kelly himself said: 'Our own theory, particularly if it proves to be practical, will also have to be considered expendable in the light of tomorrow's outlooks and discoveries. At best it is an ad interim theory' (Kelly, 1955/1991a, p. 14/p. 11). So the issue is not so much whether it will hasten the demise of personal construct theory itself but whether one can conduct effective psychotherapy solely from a philosophical standpoint. I would argue that psychotherapists need the structure of a theoretical system to guide their day-to-day work. This book plays a major role in highlighting the issues involved in keeping personal construct psychotherapy alive as an identifiable therapeutic system as opposed to constructivism providing the main focus as an integrative approach to psychotherapy as a whole. Of course, there may well be room for both. This book helps us understand more clearly the issues involved.

My second interest is in the value of seeking research evidence to demonstrate the effectiveness of personal construct psychotherapy. Many people from many therapeutic persuasions consider the search for evidence of effectiveness is doomed to failure, the main reason being the number of variables that can never be controlled. Who decides what 'depression' is, for instance? Diagnosis of many problems tends to be unreliable except in their most severe form. Even when it is agreed that people in a certain group are definitely 'depressed', the individual variation within that group is usually very great. Then there are the therapist variables, which again are numerous. In fact, the editors cite me in their preface as saying in 1972 that personal construct psychotherapists may show very little in common in their practice. They go on to say that this book emphasizes the diversity of the therapy and that that is particularly apparent in Part Two, 'which does not attempt to be comprehensive (neither could it be, for there are as many different forms of the therapeutic approach as there are individuals seeking therapy)'. This all adds up to the possibility that psychotherapy in general and personal construct psychotherapy in particular cannot be treated like soap powders showing which washes whitest. This book adds weight to that argument by reporting the effectiveness of a wide range of specific personal construct therapeutic approaches that have been used with specific problems in specific contexts.

I have raised just two issues that are addressed in this comprehensive work. There are many others. Without doubt this is a major work in the field of psychotherapy in general and of personal construct psychotherapy in particular. It will be of value to anyone interested in the many approaches that are subsumed under the general title of 'psychotherapy' as well as those who specialize in the application of the theory of personal constructs to psychotherapy.

Fay Fransella

Preface

Half a century has passed since George Kelly (1955/1991a/1991b) published *The Psychology of Personal Constructs*, setting out what he considered an alternative to existing psychologies. It therefore seems timely to present the developments of the therapeutic approach derived from his theory. Personal construct theory was first applied in a clinical setting and, although extensively applied in other fields (Fransella, 2003), it is in this setting that it has been most extensively elaborated. The theory has also influenced a range of other forms of psychotherapy that have been developed subsequently, the originators of which have in many cases acknowledged a debt to Kelly (for example, Beck et al., 1979; Ellis, 1979; Mahoney, 1988a; Mischel, 1980).

Being based on a theory that emphasizes the multiplicity of constructions of the world, it is not surprising that there are numerous alternative approaches to personal construct psychotherapy. Indeed, Fay Fransella (1972, p. 231) remarked that 'if one observed a dozen people who say they are doing "personal construct psychotherapy", they will seem to have very little in common.' This book captures this diversity, which is regarded not as a weakness of this form of therapy but as an indication of its flexibility and the creativity with which it has been applied to a very wide range of clinical problems across the full age range. The different approaches to personal construct psychotherapy are unified by a common commitment to the basic principles of personal construct theory. However, as will be apparent in the chapters that follow, a distinction can be made between those approaches that are 'purist' and those that attempt some integration of personal construct with other approaches or use personal construct theory as a framework for an integrationist approach to psychotherapy (RA Neimeyer, 1988a). This integration is most comfortably achieved with therapies within the constructivist tradition (although it has been argued that even integration with other constructivist therapies may lead to a dilution of the personal construct approach (Fransella, 2000)), but it has not been limited to these therapies. Indeed, as we shall see, whereas some authors stress the contrasts between personal construct psychotherapy and traditional psychoanalytic and cognitive therapies, others attempt to integrate personal construct psychotherapy with apparently constructivist variants of these approaches.

A further issue on which these authors express contrasting views is 'evidence-based practice'. Some argue that the notion of evidence is incompatible with a constructivist approach but others have carried out investigations of the process and outcome of personal construct psychotherapy using either traditional research designs or, as might be expected in an approach that emphasizes the personal nature of construing, intensive single-case studies. Our own position is that it is as incumbent on personal construct psychotherapists as on therapists of any other persuasion to examine the effectiveness of their approach, and indeed this book was initially conceived following a symposium on the evidence base for personal construct psychotherapy, which we convened at the Twelfth International Congress on Personal Construct Psychology in Seattle. As we shall see, this evidence base is now impressive.

We are delighted to have been joined in this venture by authors from three continents. Most of them have made a long and distinguished contribution to the field of personal construct psychotherapy but some newer 'recruits' have also joined them. This range of contributors, and the diversity and freshness of their writing, indicates to us the continuing vitality of Kelly's theory and therapy 50 years on.

Part One of this book considers the general principles underlying personal construct psychotherapy, highlighting how these have been elaborated since George Kelly's original presentation of his theory. In Chapter 1, Jonathan Raskin, Kristian David Weihs and Laurie Ann Morano consider this form of therapy within the broader context of constructivism. Although there has been some debate concerning the degree of commonality between personal construct and other construcivist approaches, Raskin et al. highlight the similarities between them. As well as outlining the fundamental features of personal construct theory and therapy, they describe three other forms of constructivist therapy that they consider to be convergent with the personal construct approach.

Chapter 2, by Beverly Walker and David Winter, focuses on the personal construct view of psychological disorder and its opposite — optimal functioning. Revisions to Kelly's original formulation of disorder are proposed, elaborating on the notion that this involves a failure to test out construing adequately. Implications for optimal and non-optimal therapeutic processes are discussed.

In Chapter 3, Sandra Sassaroli, Roberto Lorenzini and Giovanni Maria Ruggiero attempt to integrate personal construct theory, and in particular the notions of validation and invalidation of construing, with both cognitive concepts and attachment theory. This is illustrated by case examples and by research on the role played by stress in eating disorders.

In Chapter 4, Gabriele Chiari and Maria Laura Nuzzo also examine convergences between personal construct psychotherapy and developments in both psychoanalytic and cognitive therapies as well as noting divergences between these perspectives. Their focus is on the therapeutic relationship and this is central to the 'experiential' form of personal psychotherapy described in Chapter 5 by Larry Leitner, April Faidley, Donald Dominici, Carol Humphreys, Valerie Loeffler, Mark Schlutsmeyer and Jill Thomas. Unlike the authors of some of the more integrationist chapters, they are concerned to highlight the features of personal construct theory that distinguish it from cognitive-behavioural perspectives but have similarities to existential approaches. As well as discussing the process of experiential personal construct psychotherapy they outline a diagnostic system derived from this approach.

In Chapter 6, Luis Botella, Sergi Corbella, Tary Gómez, Olga Herrero and Meritxell Pacheco identify themes that are common to narrative and postmodern approaches to psychotherapy. Personal construct psychotherapy is considered to be consistent with these approaches, to which, in the authors' view, the systematization of personal construct psychology may make a major contribution.

Chapter 7, by Greg Neimeyer, Jocelyn Saferstein and Wade Arnold, considers how epistemological allegiances are reflected in the theoretical positions and therapeutic approaches adopted by psychotherapists. Relevant research is reviewed, some of which indicates the commitment of personal construct psychotherapists to a constructivist epistemology.

Chapter 8, by Harry Procter, although presented as a list of therapeutic 'techniques', is included in this section because it clearly outlines the basic principles of a personal construct approach when this is extended to work with families. In this chapter, we learn what guides the originator of personal construct family therapy in his work.

Part Two consists of chapters on the application of personal construct psychotherapy to specific clinical problems. Although this section indicates the wide 'range of convenience' of this form of therapy in the diversity of problems that are considered, it does not attempt to be comprehensive (and neither could it be, for there are as many different forms of the therapeutic approach as there are individuals seeking therapy).

Each chapter in this section considers how the problem may be understood in terms of personal construct theory. It outlines the principal features of therapeutic practice derived from such a formulation, illustrates the approach with case examples (with details altered to ensure client anonymity) and reviews any relevant research. In Chapter 9 Robert

Neimeyer describes an approach to working with grief that represents a radical departure from more traditional, stage models of bereavement and that draws upon personal construct theory as well as a broader array of constructivist narrative and social constructionist approaches. A taxonomy of disruptions of life narratives following loss is outlined, and therapy is vividly presented as a process of meaning reconstruction.

In Chapter 10, David Winter elaborates George Kelly's taxonomy of suicidal acts by extending this to different types of deliberate self-harm. A psychotherapeutic intervention derived from this perspective is described and the findings of research indicating its effectiveness are presented.

Chapter 11, by Guillem Feixas and Luis Ángel Saúl, considers the dilemmas that underlie symptoms, and the techniques that may be employed in personal construct psychotherapy to resolve these dilemmas. Preliminary results from a multi-centre research project on this approach are presented.

In Chapter 12, David Winter and Chris Metcalfe indicate how agoraphobia may be viewed from a personal construct perspective. A group therapy approach derived from this perspective is described, research evidence concerning its effectiveness is presented, and a treatment manual for the approach is provided.

Chapter 13, by Kenneth Sewell, describes how traumatic events disrupt the construing of the traumatized person and outlines a framework for psychotherapy based upon this perspective. He emphasizes the centrality of 'therapeutic love' to such an approach.

In Chapter 14, Christopher Erbes and Stephanie Harter consider one particular type of trauma, childhood sexual abuse, in terms of the meaning system of the survivor of abuse. They illustrate a therapeutic approach that works within this meaning system, rather than imposing the therapist's views, and review research on this approach.

In Chapter 15, Ian Gillman-Smith and Sue Watson explore how the psychiatric diagnosis of borderline personality disorder may be reframed in terms of personal construct theory, and describe a group psychotherapy approach derived from this model. Indications of the value of this approach are provided by client feedback and data from process research.

In Chapter 16, Eric Button considers eating disorders and their treatment in terms of clients' construing and reconstruction of themselves and others. A distinctive feature of this chapter is that it includes an account, by one of Button's clients, of her therapy.

Chapter 17, by Diane Allen, demonstrates that personal construct theory concepts may be usefully applied to understand the experiences of the person who hears voices. An innovative therapeutic approach based on these concepts is described and evidence is provided of reconstruing over the course of therapy.

Jim Horley, in Chapter 18, argues that there is an emerging forensic personal construct psychology. His own therapeutic approach employs both personal construct techniques and those derived from other theoretical perspectives. The need to adapt the personal construct approach for work in the forensic setting is highlighted.

In Chapter 19, Peter Cummins contrasts a personal construct approach with a cognitive-behavioural approach to treating problems involving anger. He conducts his therapy in a group setting and pays particular attention to the significance of problems with literacy and verbal fluency in his clients.

David Green, in Chapter 20, considers how personal construct theory may allow an exploration of 'young people's struggles to make sense of their existence'. This chapter draws particularly on Kelly's individuality, commonality and sociality corollaries.

Deborah Truneckova and Linda Viney consider a particular subgroup of young people, troubled adolescents, in Chapter 21. This chapter describes a group psychotherapy approach based on personal construct theory, explores helpful and unhelpful forces in the group process, and presents some research evidence of the effectiveness of this approach.

Chapter 22, by David Winter, contrasts personal construct psychotherapy for psychosexual problems with the more mechanistic approach that is commonly adopted in sex therapy. The holistic view of the person taken in personal construct psychotherapy and its technical eclecticism are considered to make it particularly suited to the treatment of such problems.

Sally Robbins, in Chapter 23, describes how a personal construct approach to working with older people has been elaborated in recent years. She indicates the axes along which such work may differ from that with young people and focuses in particular upon the elaboration of both the client's and the therapist's construing of old age as a major component of therapy with older people.

In Chapter 24, Lisbeth Lane and Linda Viney consider the emotions likely to be faced by women who receive a diagnosis of breast cancer and the importance of role relationships in adjustment following such a diagnosis. They describe a personal construct approach to group work with such women and present research findings suggesting the effectiveness of this approach.

Chapter 25, by Heather Foster and Linda Viney, illustrates how the menopause may face women with a need for reconstruction. Personal construct workshops that have been developed to facilitate such reconstruing are described and evidence of their effectiveness is presented.

Part Three considers the evidence base for personal construct psychotherapy. Chapter 26, by Sue Watson and David Winter, presents findings from one of the largest studies of this form of therapy, which compared it with cognitive-behavioural and psychodynamic therapies. Areas addressed, as well as therapy process and outcome, include predictors of therapeutic change and relationships between measures of construing and of psychological distress.

Chapter 27, by Linda Viney, Chris Metcalfe and David Winter, uses the statistical technique of meta-analysis to evaluate the results of 17 independent data sets from comparative outcome research on personal construct psychotherapy. The findings are encouraging and support the continued use of this form of therapy.

Finally, although we assume that most readers of this book will have some familiarity with the concepts and methods of personal construct theory and psychotherapy, we have included a short appendix giving an introduction to them. More detailed accounts may be found in Kelly (1955/1991a/1991b), Epting (1984), Bannister and Fransella (1986), Fransella and Dalton (1990), Dalton and Dunnett (1992), Winter (1992a) and Viney (1996).

As well as thanking our authors for the very high quality of their contributions, we wish to acknowledge the help of Alex Clarke and Heather Mason in the preparation of the manuscript. David Winter is also indebted to the Psychology Department of the University of Wollongong and the Illawarra Institute of Mental Health for supporting his Visiting Scholarship in 2002.

David A. Winter
Linda L. Viney
April 2005

PART ONE

GENERAL PRINCIPLES OF PERSONAL CONSTRUCT PSYCHOTHERAPY

Personal construct psychotherapy meets constructivism: convergence, divergence, possibility

JONATHAN D RASKIN, KRISTIAN DAVID WEIHS, LAURIE ANN MORANO

It has been 50 years since George Kelly published his seminal two volumes, *The Psychology of Personal Constructs* (Kelly, 1955/1991a/1991b). In those volumes Kelly outlined personal construct psychology (PCP) in detail, emphasizing its psychotherapeutic implications. However, unlike many other clinically oriented theorists, Kelly did not tie PCP to an explicit therapeutic regimen. He did introduce one important clinical approach with fixed-role therapy, but the subsequent development of PCP has generally followed Kelly's lead by eschewing blind adherence to specific therapeutic strategies and techniques and instead tending to look at therapy in a more metatheoretical manner, seeing all theories and techniques of psychotherapy as constructive alternatives for understanding how to assist those experiencing problems in living. The advantage of this theoretical openness has been a willingness on the part of PCP therapists to make use of a disparate array of clinical approaches and strategies while avoiding the intellectual limitations of an unreflective theoretical eclecticism (Winter, 1992a). The disadvantage has been that, while PCP therapists have provided some stimulating and important discussions of therapy with a variety of client problems (for example Landfield, 1971; Epting, 1984; Landfield and Epting, 1987; Winter, 1992a; Faidley and Leitner, 1993; Leitner and Dunnett, 1993; Viney, 1996; Fransella, 1995, 2003), they simply have not produced the same impact as approaches willing to market more specific therapeutic programmes to practising therapists in search of explicit clinical techniques and strategies.

Concurrently, recent years have seen the rise of psychotherapeutic approaches dubbed 'constructivist' (for example Hoyt, 1994, 1996; RA Neimeyer and Mahoney, 1995; Sexton and Griffin, 1997; Mahoney, 2003). These approaches have been of interest to personal construct psychologists because they emphasize many of the same presuppositions on which PCP therapy is based. They also offer some very concrete clinical strategies that seem consistent with PCP. However, despite their shared focus on meaning as central to therapy, there has often been an uneasy relationship between personal construct therapists and their constructivist cousins (Raskin, 2004). This is unfortunate, as they share much in common and can enrich one another's work deeply. Building on this sentiment, we examine connections between personal construct therapy and other constructivist therapies.

Basics of personal construct theory and therapy

Fundamentals of theory

Postulate and corollaries

Central to PCP is the fundamental postulate, which states that people's psychological experiences are structured according to how they anticipate life events (Kelly, 1955/1991a/1991b). People expect certain things from the world based on how they meaningfully make sense of their past experiences. They anticipate by construing, which involves the lifelong development and evolution of a set of hierarchically interconnected bipolar dimensions of meaning. These dimensions of meaning, or constructs, allow people to anticipate through contrast. For example, one person may construe the opposite of 'happy' as 'unemployed', while for someone else an individual who is not 'happy' is 'responsible'. Every one of us creates a unique set of constructs, each consisting of some thing or idea that we identify and define in terms of its perceived opposite. Thus, constructs are conceptualized as bipolar mental structures used to understand ongoing experience. People continually revise and expand their construct systems.

Constructive alternativism

There can be an infinite number of ways to construe the world according to PCP's seminal notion of *constructive alternativism*. All people filter the world through a set of unique personal constructs of their own making, so there are as many ways to construe circumstances as there are people to do the construing. Importantly, what is experientially true for a person is at least as dependent on that person's constructs as it is on the world itself. That is, people construe life in unique and idiosyncratic ways, only getting at the way things are indirectly through their constructs. In this regard, PCP is in keeping with rationalistic and romantic philosophies, which stress – despite their differences – how the mental structure of an active knower is crucial in influencing what is known (Winter, 1992a; Chiari and Nuzzo,

1996a, 1996b; Warren, 1998; Raskin, 2002). By contrast, one could argue that PCP is not as consistent with empirical philosophical approaches and their emphasis on people as passively responding to sensory data. Perhaps this explains why both cognitive (rational) and humanistic (romantic) psychologists often lay claim to Kelly's theory (Winter, 1992a; Raskin, 2002). It also offers clues as to why Kelly and other PCPers have often criticized psychotherapeutic approaches traceable to a more empirical philosophy (such as behaviourism) (Kelly, 1955/1991a/1991b; Winter, 1992a). Some basic therapeutic implications of PCP are examined next.

Fundamentals of therapy

Diverging from the medical model

Kelly's magnum opus, *The Psychology of Personal Constructs,* does not read like an especially radical text. However, its formal and often stodgy style masks a conception of therapy that moves away from seeing therapy clients as victims of mental impairments that render their behaviour meaningless and incoherent. Instead, client problems are seen as meaningful, albeit often less than successful, efforts to navigate life. That is, PCP therapy moves away from the medical model of abnormality (Kelly, 2003). Currently, the medical model influences psychotherapy a great deal (Wampold, 2001). Those espousing it hold that psychological problems can be organized into concrete categories, each of which can be remedied via specific clinical interventions. The most prominent example of the medical model in current mental health practice is the Diagnostic and Statistical Manual of Mental Disorders, currently in its sixth incarnation (American Psychiatric Association, 2000). Though the authors of DSM remain neutral about the causes of particular categories listed in the manual, the manual itself is clearly structured according to a medical model. That is, behaviours are conceptualized as coherent syndromes or disorders over which those afflicted have little control – and each of these disorders requires systematic and specific treatment.

Meaning construction as agentic process

Kelly (1969a) was dismissive of the medical model's 'treatment-based-on-objective-diagnosis' approach because it ran counter to the PCP notions of (1) people as forever in process, and (2) people as active participants in how they construe events and live their lives. Unlike the static and deterministic medical model view of people afflicted with DSM disorders, personal construct therapists tend to see people (even those experiencing great emotional anguish who currently are likely candidates for diagnosis of a mental disorder) as permanently in motion, continuously encountering new experiences, and actively employing their respective construct systems to deal with such experiences (Epting, 1984; Winter, 1992a; Faidley and Leitner, 1993; Viney, 1996; RA Neimeyer and Raskin, 2000). As a result, personal construct therapists often question the utility of conceptualizing their clients' ways of construing self and relationships as disordered, even when their clients' ways appear to have extensive drawbacks. Several authors have written about the contradiction between traditional medical model conceptions of people as passive sufferers of universally similar disorders and PCP's process-oriented view of people as active meaning makers continually struggling to devise life-enhancing ways of understanding themselves and their world (Faidley and Leitner, 1993; Raskin and Epting, 1993; Honos-Webb and Leitner, 2001; Leitner and Faidley, 2002; Raskin and Lewandowski, 2000). More simply, to the personal construct therapist, psychotherapy is not an undertaking in which medical specialists cure passive persons of disorders or repair their dysfunctional mental states but rather it is about helping agentic individuals evolve new and more personally effective ways to make sense of life experiences meaningfully. Several concepts PCP therapists use in thinking about therapeutic change are described below.

Experience

Growth through experience. Personal construct psychotherapists' emphasis on process is best captured according to the *experience corollary,* which holds that people develop their constructions based on ongoing experience. That is, a person encounters something in the course of living, makes meaningful and organized sense out of it by construing it in a particular manner, and uses the resulting constructs to anticipate what might occur in future encounters; the person learns from experience by imposing an orderly structure upon it (Kelly, 1955/1991a). Experience implies both regularity and innovation as key to the ongoing process of construing. Consequently, experience can be both liberating and imprisoning. It is liberating when one uses it as an opportunity to revise one's constructions – after all, 'a person's construction system *varies* as he successively construes the replication of events' (Kelly, 1955/1991a, p. 72/p. 50, italics added). The psychologist who, after years of laboratory training in deterministic research methodologies, has come to view herself as intellectually shallow for indulging notions of human agency may find experience a great liberator after encountering a colleague who endorses total determinism stammering to explain how he can hold students responsible for missing class. On the other hand, because '[t]o construe is to hear the whisper of recurrent themes in events that reverberate around us' (Kelly, 1955/1991a, p. 76/p. 54), experience can also be confining.

The case of Emily
For example, when 'Emily' – an 18-year-old still living at home with her parents – began therapy she saw herself as a neglectful daughter. This assessment was based on her ongoing experience with her parents, who diagnosed her avoidance of them as suggesting she did not care about them. Emily saw her encounters with her parents the same way they did. She found dealing with them stressful and each time she actively avoided them she construed herself as neglectful. Thus, by imposing regularity and orderliness on experience, Emily's negative view of self was confirmed. Therapy involved assisting Emily to consider alternative ways of imposing order on her experience. Recasting her parental avoidance as a means of warding off long-term patterns of parental scorn for her feelings was one such way that ultimately proved liberating to her. Through encountering experiences in the consulting room in which her feelings were accepted rather than scorned, Emily came to distinguish between more nurturing versus judgmental relationships. This allowed her to stop seeing herself as neglectful in those relationships where she felt criticized; instead she began to see her behaviour as adaptive and protective. Further, she began to experiment with being more attentive and open with those she came to see as accepting of her. In other words, Emily varied her constructions of ongoing experience as a result of her experience in therapy.

Individuality

Unique construing. In the *individuality corollary*, Kelly (1955/1991a) stated that individuals differ from each other in how they construe things. This is therapeutically important because it fosters psychotherapy as a process in which therapists try to understand the unique constructions of each client. It may sound commonsensical that therapists need to understand the meanings of every client individually. However, in a professional climate dominated by the use of general diagnostic categories that are often presumed to share common underlying processes (such as those contained in the DSM), the individuality corollary's idiographic emphasis cannot be overstated. The ease with which psychiatric diagnoses are bandied about in lieu of efforts to understand the personal meanings that clients bring to the consulting room is both remarkable and unsettling.

The case of Jamie
For example, a hospital admissions report about a recent client ('Jamie') who was experiencing psychotic symptoms indicated that the client's mother was 'Munchausen by proxy' because she refused to see her daughter as schizophrenic. Instead, Jamie's mother clung to alternative medical

opinions suggesting her daughter's emotional and cognitive problems were due to untreated Lyme disease. Never mind that the clinician diagnosing Jamie's mother (1) had not interviewed her and was presenting his diagnosis in a report ostensibly about Jamie, (2) downplayed that there were indeed multiple reports from a plethora of specialists, with little consensus among them as to the origin of Jamie's troublesome behaviour, and (3) used the Munchausen by proxy diagnosis incorrectly (there was no evidence the mother had physically tampered with her daughter to get medical attention; rather, she simply insisted her daughter was not schizophrenic). Across all the various medical reports about Jamie, there was no effort to try to understand either her or her mother's individual constructions of the situation (beyond that, many details of Jamie's case were incorrect in the psychological report her therapist received; clearly, the hospital staff were not listening carefully). It does not surprise us that a mother might try to extort validation, in a hostile way, to bolster her view that her daughter's problems did not result from mental illness (and, by implication, bad mothering?). While terms like 'schizophrenia' and 'Munchausen by proxy' may provide general ideas about the kinds of behaviours a clinician is referring to in a client (and, as in this case, her mother), they tell us nothing about the individual meanings – the personal constructions – of the people at hand. In personal construct therapy, such meanings are critical. The individuality corollary, in all its simplicity, is vitally important to PCP therapy because of how it stresses the need for therapists to move beyond general labels for client problems and towards a detailed understanding of each client's unique and personal experiential meanings.

Sociality

The therapeutic role relationship. When two people work to understand and empathize with one another's ways of construing thoroughly, they potentially create a meaningfully rich interpersonal relationship with one another. Kelly (1955/1991a) referred to such a relationship as a role relationship, and it is the major theoretical idea springing from his *sociality corollary*. Sociality and role relationships are important aspects of personal construct therapy, particularly for those who approach it from humanistic and experiential perspectives (Faidley and Leitner, 1993; Leitner and Pfenninger, 1994; Leitner and Faidley, 1995, 2002; Leitner, Faidley and Celentana, 2000). By establishing role relationships with their clients, therapists are better able to understand the world as their clients do. Often, this involves adopting a *credulous approach*, whereby what clients say is accepted as experientially true for them rather than dismissed as the product of dysfunctional thinking. The ongoing relationship between therapist and client becomes the basis for therapeutic change. In this regard, personal construct therapists who stress sociality have a great deal in common with interpersonal and object relations therapists by emphasizing how therapist and client collaboratively process their respective feelings about their ongoing relationship as a primary tool in fostering therapeutic progress (Mahoney and Marquis, 2002). That is, transference and countertransference become important aspects of the therapy.

Transference in PCP terms. When considered in personal construct terms, transferences occur when clients generalize their commonly employed constructions about relationships to their interactions with their therapists. Countertransferences occur when therapists (1) credulously comprehend how clients meaningfully construe and conduct interpersonal relationships, and (2) attend to and share the feelings they experience in response to how clients construe and conduct relationships with them. As in object relations therapy (Cashdan, 1988), personal construct therapists can share their countertransference feelings in order to encourage conversations about the ways clients inhibit the establishment of genuine role relationships with others. Clients often do this by perpetually employing rigid interpersonal constructions that prevent sociality from occurring. After all, clients need to construe how others construe relationships in order to establish genuine role relationships. Within the safe confines of a trusting therapeutic relationship, clients can experience how they pre-empt that process by imposing a ready-made set of relational constructions on others. This can be quite powerful therapeutically and can lead to clients experimenting with new styles of relational engagement.

The case of Diana
Creating a role relationship was key to my (JDR) therapeutic work with 'Diana', a single 30-something woman seeking therapy after receiving a black eye from her longtime boyfriend. Diana initially worried that her problems were not especially severe and that by coming to session she was denying a more worthy individual an hour of therapy. She also repeatedly expressed concern that I had better things to do than spend an hour working with her because her problems just were not very important; yes, her boyfriend had belted her in the eye, but she insisted it was not a big deal. Diana clearly tried to establish a role relationship with me but the only kind she knew how to create involved her as dependent, weak, and deferent. Because she construed relationships in such a manner, a genuine role relationship did not initially develop. That is, Diana failed to construe my construction processes and therefore failed to understand that, unlike her, I did not construe relationships as requiring her to be deferent and dependent on my opinions and needs lest she get me angry and I abandon

her. Diana was surprised when I shared how her deferent behaviour created discomfort in me. After all, such behaviour suggested that I did not need to attend to – or even respect – her needs. A series of interesting conversations surrounding our relationship and how each of us construed it ensued. Through this conversation, Diana realized that it was OK to express what she felt because I valued that, even if what she felt might not always please me. Thus, over time a role relationship developed in which we both came to construe the other's construction processes without Diana pre-emptively engaging me in dependent ways. Even better, as therapy progressed Diana began to generalize this process to other areas of her experience. She began to assert her needs while more carefully attending to the ways others construed relationships. This allowed her to begin developing genuine role relationships in a variety of life settings. She stopped adopting a dependent and deferent role automatically every time she met someone and began to make distinctions between relationships that would enhance her personal growth and those that would not.

Transitive understanding

Diagnosis as meaning comprehension. Kelly (1955/1991b) presented a unique approach to psychological evaluation and diagnosis. It is an approach that diverges substantially from what occurs when using DSM assessment. He called it *transitive diagnosis*. When engaged in transitive diagnosis, the therapist moves through several steps. Put simply, these steps are as follows: (1) formulating the problem; (2) understanding the client's construction of the problem; (3) evaluating the client's construct system; and (4) helping the client to address the problem. Several fine overviews of transitive diagnosis and its application in the consulting room have been published (Winter, 1992a; Faidley and Leitner, 1993; Leitner and Pfenninger, 1994; Johnson, Pfenninger and Klion, 2000). In many respects, transitive diagnosis is unlike diagnosis as it is often conceptualized. Rather than an expert clinician reaching pre-emptive conclusions about client functioning that dictate ensuing treatment (an unfortunate definition of 'diagnosis' that one might argue has become reified in current mental health practice), transitive diagnosis involves the ongoing collaborative effort between client and therapist to understand the evolving system of personal meanings that clients use to manoeuvre through everyday life (Raskin and Epting, 1995). It has been suggested that personal construct therapists use the term 'transitive understanding' rather than 'transitive diagnosis' in order to move away from the medical model connotation that the word 'diagnosis' all too often implies (Raskin and Epting, 1995).

The case of Steve

Honos-Webb and Leitner (2001) presented the fascinating but somewhat disheartening case of 'Steve', a 27-year-old man who had been in and out of psychiatric treatment (and had experienced several hospitalizations) from the age of 7 years. Steve's difficult family background (neglectful alcoholic mother, father who abandoned the family when Steve was 6 years old) led to his construing many things in ways that probably inhibited his psychological functioning. However, by assigning Steve a variety of diagnostic labels over the years (obsessive-compulsive disorder, generalized anxiety disorder, major depression, bipolar disorder, attention-deficit hyperactivity disorder, intermittent explosive disorder, and paranoid personality disorder), the psychiatric establishment may have ended up doing him more harm than good. Steve was stigmatized, taught to see himself as disturbed, and locked into a pathologized identity. More disturbingly, little effort was made to understand things credulously from Steve's point of view. Honos-Webb and Leitner collaborated with Steve to develop a transitive understanding of Steve's difficulties. Unlike the many mental health professionals, who all too readily fell back upon a startling array of DSM diagnoses (none of which generated interventions leading to therapeutic change), Honos-Webb and Leitner – in the spirit of transitive understanding – recognized that even Steve's most severe behavioural and psychological difficulties grew out of his efforts to make sense of extremely harrowing and emotionally distressing life experiences: 'Steve's "excessive" fears reflect the degree to which his environment was threatening while he was growing up, not his degree of "craziness." Steve's paranoia may be seen as his way of making meaning out of an otherwise incomprehensibly threatening environment' (Honos-Webb and Leitner, 2001, p. 47).

Fixed-role therapy

Though he was clinically eclectic to the degree that he encouraged clinicians to use whatever therapeutic strategies they found helpful, one might say that fixed-role therapy is *the* psychotherapeutic technique created by George Kelly. This form of therapy allows clients to take an experimental approach to exploring their relationships and experiences; that is, the therapist, in accordance with the client, develops hypotheses that may be tested for validity in the client's everyday life. Fixed-role therapy was originally meant to be quite brief and rather intense; to be carried out over a two-week period in which the client is asked to take on a different role or, in other words, assume a new identity. Kelly intended for this alternative role to be so pervasive that clients would be asked to forget who they were for the entire two weeks and to act, think, talk, eat, dream and approach all relationships and every aspect of life the way the fixed-role character would (Epting, 1984; Kelly, 1955/1991a).

The case of Melanie

Melanie came to therapy feeling socially isolated and anxious. She had few friends and rarely went out socializing. In therapy, she was encouraged to collaborate with the therapist in developing a fixed-role sketch. The sketch she developed was of 'Confidence Woman', a person like her in many ways but different from her in at least one significant respect: 'Confidence Woman' did not always enjoy socializing, but felt comfortable enough around other people to seek out social situations actively because she knew that such situations were the best way to make new friends. Melanie agreed to enact the 'Confidence Woman' character for a few weeks to see what ensued. At her next therapy session, Melanie reported attending a party as 'Confidence Woman'. While at first she felt awkward at the party, she tried to behave as 'Confidence Woman' would and stayed despite her anxiety. As a result of her staying, several acquaintances began talking to her and – to her great surprise – she wound up the hit of the party! Within days of the party, she had already attended a second party and had made extensive social plans for the following week with some of her new-found friends. To her great surprise, many aspects of 'Confidence Woman' quickly became part of her new-found identity. Her social wariness, a problem that had long plagued her, dissipated within a very short time as her fixed-role experience allowed her to experiment with new ways of being. Not all fixed roles are as immediately as effective as Melanie's but her case provides a good example of fixed-role therapy in action.

Personal construct psychology and constructivism

Types of constructivism

There is no clear consensus on where and how PCP fits into the larger constructivist movement in psychology. Some PCP therapists have embraced constructivism (Mahoney, 1988a, 1991; RA Neimeyer and Mahoney, 1995; Chiari and Nuzzo, 1996a; RA Neimeyer and Raskin, 2000; Raskin and Bridges, 2002, 2004). These therapists have identified similarities between PCP and other 'constructivisms', including but not limited to social constructionism (Burr, 1995; Gergen, 1985, 1994; McNamee and Gergen, 1992; Shotter, 1993), radical constructivism (Maturana, 1988; Von Glaserfeld, 1984, 1995; Maturana and Varela, 1992), and narrative-oriented psychotherapy (White and Epston, 1990; Guidano, 1991; Eron and Lund, 1996; Gonçalves, Korman and Angus, 2000). However, other PCPers – although aware of areas of convergence between PCP and constructivism – have expressed concern that if PCP too readily embraces constructivism as a metatheory, the unique aspects of Kelly's theory and their clinical implications may fall by the wayside (Fransella, 1995; Warren, 1998).

Chiari and Nuzzo's (1996b) distinction between *epistemological constructivism* and *hermeneutic constructivism* becomes useful here, as it bridges divisions between PCP and constructivism by placing PCP and other constructivist theories within a larger framework. Epistemological constructivist theories hold that there is an independent real world but this world can only be known indirectly through one's constructions. Hermeneutic constructivist theories reject the notion of an observer independent reality; instead, they maintain that a community of observers inevitably produces the reality people know by way of discourse, language, and social coordination. The epistemological–hermeneutic distinction is helpful because it provides a means to compare and contrast constructivist theories, including PCP. It allows examination of PCP in its own terms (without reference to other types of constructivism) while simultaneously locating PCP within a larger constructivist framework (Raskin, 2004). The epistemological–hermeneutic distinction allows for pre-empting a single philosophical premise as central to defining what makes a psychological theory constructivist, namely, a focus on the structure of and relationships between human knowers as the central factors in shaping what is known. Constructivist approaches attempt to transcend the classic realism–idealism debate by arguing that the structural and relational engagement of the knower is always critical to what we know and how we know it.

The epistemological–hermeneutic distinction is simply a general rubric for classifying PCP and other constructivist theories. Personal construct psychology strikes many as fitting comfortably into the epistemological constructivist mould (Raskin, 2004). However, some PCPers have begun to develop clear arguments for why PCP, like social constructionism and some forms of radical constructivism, can be productively construed in more hermeneutic terms (Botella, 1995; Chiari and Nuzzo, 2004; Paris and Epting, 2004). The more persistent controversy does not involve whether PCP should be classified as either an epistemological or hermeneutic constructivism, but whether it should be classified as a constructivism at all. For those who see PCP as a version of limited realism (Walker, 1992; Warren, 1992a; Stevens, 1998; Warren, 1998), Chiari and Nuzzo's (1996b) move to use the epistemological–hermeneutic distinction as a way to transcend the realism–idealism debate is troublesome because 'whereas epistemological constructivists emphasize the viability of knowledge structures, limited realists believe that some correspondence can be established between constructions and external reality, even if it is imperfect' (Raskin, 2004, p. 10). Despite its authors' awareness of tension over limited realism versus epistemological constructivism, this chapter nevertheless tries further to elucidate connections between PCP therapy approaches and their constructivist brethren. Three constructivist therapeutic methods identified as having points of convergence with PCP are examined below.

Constructivist therapies and PCP: three examples of convergence

Many recent therapies that can be classified as constructivist share much in common with PCP. Three of these therapies are outlined and related to important PCP concepts and methods. The therapies discussed do not constitute a complete, or even comprehensive, overview of constructivist therapies. They are intended as a sampling, with the goal of highlighting similarities between these therapies and PCP. The approaches highlighted are narrative therapy, narrative solutions therapy, and depth-oriented brief therapy.

Narrative therapy

Basics. Narrative therapy has origins in the work of Michael White and David Epston (1990) and shares a number of commonalities with PCP. Narrative therapists assume that people have difficulties when their life stories no longer account for lived experiences. People are seen as living their lives along a narrative continuum, shaped and defined by the stories they use to make sense of experiential reality. Rather than viewing 'people as having problems', White and Epston (1990) view 'problems as having people'. In this respect, narrative therapy attends to how social and familial interaction patterns sustain problematic behavioural configurations. Whereas PCP begins with the person-as-scientist metaphor, narrative therapy begins with the person-as-author metaphor. Therapy in both domains is collaborative and privileges the individual's lived experience, focusing on the meaning each person ascribes to events.

Externalizing the problem. Therapy within the narrative milieu starts with *externalizing the problem,* or identifying the problem as 'other' rather then an inherent or fixed quality of the individual. Externalization frees clients from 'problem saturated' (White and Epston, 1990, p. 16) perspectives, allowing them to engage in a process of 're-storying' (p. 17) their experiences with more personally satisfying and functional alternatives. Externalizing the 'problem-saturated story' begins by 'asking persons about how *the problem* has been affecting their lives and their relationships' (White and Epston, 1990, p. 16, italics in original). From there, clients consider strategies for re-storying problems in new ways. This often involves specifying alternative behaviours that resist, or fail to give in to, the requirements of the problem.

The case of Jason

Consider 'Jason', a client diagnosed with depression, whose narrative casts him in a role as someone suffering from a debilitating mental illness. Jason came to therapy after several weeks of sleeping in and skipping work. Instead of seeing Jason as afflicted with clinical depression – a self-conceptualization that, in classic DSM manner, posits depression as an internal dysfunction within Jason (a disorder he 'has') – his therapist encouraged Jason to identify depression as something outside of him that 'gets the best of him'. Depression was 're-storied' as an independent entity whose directives and desires Jason could resist. Therapeutic conversation focused on how 'Jason's Depression' effectively talked Jason into skipping work. It also focused on exceptions – times Jason did not give in to 'Depression'. Externalizing the problem moved Jason away from a pathologized identity and also helped him to recognize ways to out-smart and resist 'Depression'. For example, in therapy Jason discovered that 'Depression' lost much of its influence over him when he regularly arranged social activities with other people, set aside time each day for a relaxing evening walk, and adopted a work schedule that ensured he got 'up and out' in the morning.

Experimenting via behaviour. Re-storying one's life through externalizing the problem is similar in certain respects to fixed-role therapy. In both, behaviour is an experiment. Clients are encouraged to behave differently based on the premise that in so doing they may very well come to experience things in new and potentially liberating ways. In fixed-role therapy, the client acts 'as if' she was the person in her fixed-role sketch. In narrative therapy, the client acts 'as if' the problem was external to him and could be resisted. In both instances, when successful, these methods lead to clients trying out alternative behaviours that hopefully lead them towards new ways of construing themselves and their relationships.

Client as expert. White and Epston's narrative approach is also similar to PCP therapy in its emphasis on clients as experts on their own problems. Like Kelly and his credulous approach, White and Epston cleverly see clients – not their therapists – as the sources for possible solutions. By asking clients to ponder exceptions (times when their problem did not win out over them), White and Epston overcome a common therapeutic problem, namely 'resistance' on behalf of clients who realize on a logical level that their therapists' suggestions for change are reasonable but who experientially know these suggestions will not work because they do not account for the unique contours of the clients' personally lived experiences. Therapists all too often construe resistance as a problem with their clients rather than a mismatch between their clients' particular ways of construing and the generic therapeutic solutions being proposed. Consistent with PCP's credulous approach, White and Epston's therapy navigates around this problem by encouraging therapists credulously to entertain and solicit the solutions clients already have at their disposal, but of which clients may not be aware.

Narrative-solutions therapy

Basics. Joseph Eron and Thomas Lund (1993, 1996, 2002) have developed an approach to therapy very much in keeping with PCP. Described as an integration of concepts and techniques from strategic, solution focused, and narrative therapy, narrative solutions therapy seeks to help people solve their problems through the art of helpful conversations. The narrative solutions approach begins with the philosophical assumption that 'how people feel and how they act in a situation depends on how they construe the situation' (Eron and Lund, 1996, p. 42). In this way, the narrative solutions approach emphasizes the personal and interpretative nature of human experience in quite the same manner as PCP.

The gap. Narrative solutions therapy proposes that people encounter psychological difficulties when their behaviour, as well as how others respond to it, deviates from their preferred ways of viewing themselves. This discrepancy, or 'gap', is often the heart of the relational problems people carry into therapy. The therapeutic process begins by having clients elaborate what their preferred views of self are. Clients discuss times in the past when they acted more in accord with their preferred ways of being. These times, during which life was often better, are contrasted with a client's current negative circumstances. The therapist then collaboratively and credulously joins with and speaks to that preferred view. Therapy focuses not on what is currently wrong with clients but on past successes clients have had in living according to their preferred views and how these past successes can be incorporated more fully in the present.

Preferred view as guide to solutions. In working with clients, Eron and Lund's narrative solutions therapy stresses clients' preferred views of themselves. Eron and Lund accept their clients' preferred views as legitimate. For example, with a client whose preferred view is that of a 'good son', Eron and Lund might wonder aloud how such a 'good son' came to be seen as selfish by his mother. The goal is not to discredit the client's preferred view. On the contrary, the goal is to accept the client's preferred view and to help the client bridge the 'gap' between said preferred view and everyday behaviour, usually with an eye towards times when the client successfully lives out preferred views of self. Thus, the 'good son's' preferred view is accepted at face value (à la Kelly's credulous approach), with specific interpersonal goings on that violate it cast as unfortunate and alterable transactions that get in the way of the client being the kind of son that down deep he knows himself to be. Familiarity with a client's preferred view can help therapists from blundering, as they do all too often when they presume to know what solutions are best for their clients but fail to consider what their clients intend when engaging in troublesome behaviours.

The case of Don

Eron and Lund (2002) present the case of 'Don', a former businessman hospitalized for a long term after descending into seemingly psychotic behaviour. Don's refusal to take the drugs prescribed for him was taken by the hospital staff as a sign of resistance to treatment, something further evidenced by his generally disobedient and argumentative behaviour on the ward. Eron and Lund discovered that Don's preferred view entailed self-discipline when it came to taking drugs into his body; apparently he had stopped drinking alcohol several years before and readily saw himself as someone who did not need to rely upon drugs of any kind. Don's refusal to take prescribed drugs was reformulated as a product of his preferred view rather than simply resistance to treatment. When Eron and Lund shared Don's feelings with the hospital staff, the staff began giving Don more say about his drug regimen and Don's behaviour changed. The ongoing conflicts he was having with the staff ended. Don's refusal was, in the end, not productively viewed as resistance to treatment or, even worse, as a symptom of a 'psychotic personality'. Instead, his behaviour was more effectively seen as an effort to live in accordance with his preferred view. By credulously accepting his preferred view as a guide to possible life solutions (not just to his medication problem, but also to other more long-standing issues in his life), Eron and Lund helped Don rebuild his life.

Construal, roles, and relationships. In stressing preferred views of self, Eron and Lund can be seen as using the credulous approach to develop role relationships with their clients, much like a personal construct therapist might. Narrative solutions therapy, following PCP, holds that emotions and behaviour are linked to how a person construes. In this way, narrative solutions therapy, like PCP, pays special attention to the meanings people derive from events. The concept of self-image becomes central to the meaning-construction process. A person is said to have a preferred view of self and sets out to relate to others in accordance with this view. Interpersonal problems occur when there is a mismatch between a client's preferred view and how others view and, consequently, interact with the client in the course of daily life. The therapeutic process becomes one in which therapists attend to clients' preferred views and in so doing assist them in finding their own inner resources and solutions. Understanding and accepting clients' preferred views appears rather similar to PCP therapists' emphasis on developing role relationships through the credulous acceptance of client narratives.

Depth-oriented brief therapy

Depth-oriented brief therapy (DOBT) springs from the clinical work of Bruce Ecker and Laurel Hulley (1996, 2000). It combines a constructivist emphasis on individually created meanings with a psychodynamic accent on the importance of unconscious, or tacit, processes. In other words, DOBT practitioners postulate that not only do people construct meaningful realities that govern their interpersonal relationships and life positions but also that these constructions unconsciously govern behaviour and emotional experience. The symptoms clients bring to therapy are 'constrained and shaped by a deep structure of more abstract, unconscious, and nonlinguistically held constructs' (Ecker and Hulley, 2000, p. 64).

Symptom coherence. Because presenting problems are tied to the ways clients construe, DOBT posits that even the most dumbfounding symptoms are coherent and meaningful – although this meaningful coherence may be initially difficult to spot. Client presenting problems are seen as tied to their ways of tacitly construing themselves and their relationships, so when clients lack conscious awareness of their own most core ordering processes, they too are befuddled by their own symptoms. Therapy becomes a means to assist clients in gaining insight into those constructions that they have created for themselves. These constructions are so implicit and taken for granted at a basic level that clients cannot consciously articulate or identify them, even though these constructions are of the clients' own making. While clients usually enter therapy vocally advocating the 'anti-symptom position' (all the reasons why the presenting symptoms are undesirable), depth-oriented brief therapists are interested in helping clients articulate the 'pro-symptom position' – the unconscious constructs that the symptoms unwittingly help sustain. Therapy is successful when these constructions are made conscious and changed so that the symptoms no longer serve any purpose.

Functionless versus functional symptoms. Ecker and Hulley draw a clever distinction between functionless and functional symptoms. The former are not required in order to sustain the underlying constructions central to a client's psychological predicament, whereas the latter are part and parcel of the problem. For example, Ecker and Hulley (2000) discuss a case of functionless panic in which a client experiences panic attacks; the unconscious construction is elaborated, 'I am a dangerously harmful, even lethal, presence' (p. 71). This construction does not require the occurrence of panic attacks in order to be sustained, even though the panic attacks help the client avoid situations in which her perceived lethality is unleashed. By contrast, Ecker and Hulley (2000) also describe a case of functional panic, wherein a client's unconscious construction holds, 'The universe requires intense suffering . . . and will actively inflict it if not enough suffering occurs' (p. 71). In this instance, the client experiences panic attacks in situations where she feels suffering is necessary to forestall even worse suffering from occurring. For example, she has panic attacks when in the car with her spouse because suffering via a panic attack is preferable to the suffering that might otherwise be imposed – namely, a terrible car wreck. In this case, the panic attacks are a functional component of the unconscious construction governing the client's life; they are one way she suffers to prevent the universe from imposing an even worse fate.

Personal, hierarchically structured meaning. Ecker and Hulley's approach converges nicely with PCP in several respects. Ecker and Hulley stress the personal nature of human meaning making. That is, therapists cannot presume that the meaning of the same kind of symptom (such as panic attacks) is similar across clinical scenarios. Meaning is idiographic, personal, and needs to be understood by the therapist on a case-by-case basis. Not only is meaning personal, but also one's constructs are hierarchically interrelated. Unconscious constructs are usually those that are most core and tend to be superordinate. Ecker and Hulley's attention to the interrelated hierarchy of constructions is likely to resonate deeply with personal construct therapists.

Preverbal constructs and levels of awareness. Ecker and Hulley's emphasis on unconscious constructs that cannot be readily verbalized has some similarity to Kelly's (1955/1991a) notion of *preverbal constructs,* which cannot be verbalized because they evolved prior to one's acquisition of language capable of encapsulating them. Leitner's (1999) recent attention to levels of awareness seems pertinent; rather than simply using the term 'unconscious' in the traditional Freudian manner (wherein unconscious ideas are uncovered), we can also talk about constructs dwelling at different levels of awareness. During therapy, as one elaborates a construction at a low level of awareness, that construction is created as much as it is discovered – the process of raising one's awareness of a construction inevitably impacts the construction recalled.

Conclusion: sociality and enrichment

Fifty years after its initial formulation, personal construct therapy remains a powerful therapeutic approach. It combines a focus on meaningfully understanding the individual experience of the client with the practical benefit of encouraging clients to try out new behaviours in everyday life. In both these respects, PCP therapy has much in common with concomitant developments in constructivist therapy. In this chapter, we have highlighted some of these similarities. In the spirit of sociality, PCP therapists are encouraged to peer through the lenses of their constructivist colleagues in order to grasp better the exciting possibilities for expanding their clinical repertoires. We encourage constructivist therapists to do the same in relationship to PCP, for a multitude of mutually enriching opportunities may result. We see many prospects for convergence between PCP therapists and other constructivist practitioners and – in the spirit of constructive alternativism – we believe this holds many enticing and generative possibilities for the next 50 years of personal construct therapy.

CHAPTER TWO

Psychological disorder and reconstruction

BEVERLY M WALKER, DAVID A WINTER

When Kelly (1955/1991a/1991b) proposed his psychology of personal constructs he described processes that were characteristic of all of us; he outlined a *general* theory of personality. As he stated, 'the psychology of personal constructs is designed around the problem of reconstruing life, but it is not a system built upon psychopathology' (Kelly, 1955/1991b, p. 830/p. 192). However, he explicitly considered his theory in its application to clients, and in this context formulated a definition of disorder, as well as broad guidelines for clinicians about the goals they would pursue.

Kelly's position enables us to gain an understanding of people's functioning in the broad sense, both those seeking therapy as well as those who are not. It also gives us a conceptual framework and tools to intervene effectively to facilitate change when needed, and goals to aim for when conducting such interventions. Nevertheless, we shall argue that Kelly's formal definition of disorder is problematic in several respects. Recent papers (Walker, 2002; Winter, 2003a) have moved to overhaul his definition and elaborate a position that, while remaining consistent with the overall philosophy and theory, better reflects the problems confronting clinicians and the solutions that personal construct practitioners have sought for them. This chapter will integrate the issues and solutions raised to clarify an approach to understanding disorder from a personal construct perspective. We shall then go on to consider the implications of such a view for the therapeutic process.

Kelly's use of the term 'disorder'

In *The Psychology of Personal Constructs* (1955/1991a/1991b), Kelly specifically devoted over 100 pages to disorder, distinguishing between disorders of construction, how we apply our construing systems in our day-to-day living (Chapter 16), and of transition, how we deal with change whether it be self-initiated or thrust upon us (Chapter 17). He defined disorder as 'any personal construction which is used repeatedly in spite of consistent invalidation' (Kelly, 1955/1991b, p. 831/p. 193) and then subsequently, but not necessarily consistently, 'it represents any structure which appears to fail to accomplish its purpose' (p. 835/p. 195). In elaborating this view he regarded the way disorder was viewed as integral to the goals of psychotherapy. Here he proposed that '. . . the goal of psychotherapy is to alleviate complaints – complaints of a person about himself and others and complaints of others about him' (Kelly, 1955/1991b, p. 830/p. 193).

Note that he did not propose that these definitions cover everything about disorder. Rather, they were statements within the range of the theory and, pragmatically, the range of influence of therapists. With regard to this range, he was distancing his position from psychoanalysis by suggesting that the latter's focus on the past as an explanation of disorder does not readily allow forward movement. The past cannot be erased – but it can be reconstrued: 'a man may not now choose his past but he may select his future' (Kelly, 1955/1991b, p. 833/p. 194). This led Kelly to the conclusion that 'the proper question is not *what* is disorder but *where*, and the therapist's question is not *who* needs treatment but *what* needs treatment' (Kelly, 1955/1991b, p. 835/p. 196, italics in original).

In answer to these new questions Kelly gave some examples using the processes central to his theorizing. Under disorders of construction he wrote about problems involving the broadening of one's perceptual field known as dilation, such that so much is involved in all matters that even the simplest things of life become overwhelming. He included the problematic use of both tightening and loosening, the former illustrated by obsessional behaviour and the latter by frequent variation in conclusions drawn from occasion to occasion, making predictability by both self and others difficult. Finally, he gave examples involving core constructs, those most central to our survival, as when we fail to develop constructs that can enable us to sustain ourselves and be safe, such as when we seek all-embracing dependency relationships rather than more specialized ones tailored for differing needs.

With regard to transition, he included problematic aggression and hostility, anxiety, constriction (regarded as central to depression), guilt, dependency, 'psychosomatic' and 'organic' problems, and control including impulsivity. He finished, almost as an addendum, with a brief section on disorders 'arising out of the content rather than the form of personal constructs'[1] (Kelly, 1955/1991b, p. 935/p. 264), but the emphasis of these chapters is on the problematic use of processes. What he makes clear in his discussion is that their use is not, in and of itself, problematic. Dilation, for example, may be the cause of, or solution to, the client's problem. It is how they are applied that is critical.

Limitations of Kellian disorder

There are two principal issues we want to raise in discussion of the utility of Kelly's explicit consideration of disorder. One concerns the limitations of Kelly's formal definition of disorder, with its lack of close relation to his illustrative examples and general theoretical thrust. The other is the general issue of the contradiction between the connotations of disorder per se and the philosophy and spirit of Kelly's theory.

With regard to Kelly's definition of disorder as 'any personal construction which is used repeatedly in spite of consistent invalidation', we have several observations. We suggest that there would be very few constructions that are 'consistently invalidated' – or indeed validated. The process of validation is one that is largely interpersonal. Others provide us with the feedback, both direct and indirect, to extend and define our constructions as we test and retest them (RA Neimeyer and GJ Neimeyer, 1985). This places the locus of defining disorder in part in the constructions others have of our actions and interpretations. Many problematic ways of being may be validated by others, even relatively consistently, such as the concentration of a person's dependencies on someone willing or eager to be depended upon. And unproblematic, even laudable, beliefs and actions may be invalidated by those around their advocate, but prove to be desirable developments in retrospect, such as the beliefs of the suffragettes, fighting for equality. Kelly's alternative definition of disorder, focusing on the purpose of the action, bears no clear relation to the invalidation definition and raises all sorts of problems concerning how a structure's purpose is determined. Besides, we could provide many examples where problematic structures exist consistent with their purpose. Finally, and very importantly, if one looks at the examples Kelly gave of

---

[1] Oddly, disorders of content are included as a subsection of control. This would appear to be a misnumbering. Indeed, there are several questions one can raise about the chapter differentiation (Why does dilation link to disordered construction and constriction to disorders of transition? Why are some processes such as dependency discussed in both sections? And so forth.) However, they seem irrelevant to any substantive issue, so this distinction between construction and transition has been ignored in this chapter. Given the layout, it is possible that Kelly's formal definition of disorder, which is the first section in the construction chapter, may apply only to construction, but if that is the case no definition is provided that relates to transition. Overall, these chapters are full of rich clinical examples, but lack the clear, incisive theoretical structure of earlier chapters.

disorder, most do not correspond to the definitions presented. The definitions focus on the construction or structure per se, whereas Kelly's examples centre on the problematic use of processes, not the faulty construction.

With regard to the second issue, the inconsistency between disorder per se and the theory, Kelly was concerned with the ways in which our language traps us into theorizing in particular ways, so that, for example, once we have made an observation about someone's behaviour (for example, 'she is behaving aggressively'), this commonly becomes transformed into an assumption about their nature (for example, 'she is aggressive'). In other words, the problem of reification of behavioural and other processes was at issue. The central reason for his objection was related to his focus on the importance and encouragement of change. A behaviour can be readily modified, but an identity may not. Further, once someone has been pigeonholed in some way, it is a small step to treating them pre-emptively, as 'nothing but' an aggressive person or a schizophrenic, and so forth, a view that others have also put forward (Laing, 1960; Szasz, 1961; Raskin and Lewandowski, 2000). Labelling of disorder is readily confused with explanation, as many critiques of the *Diagnostic and Statistical Manual of Mental Disorders* have proposed (Johnstone, 1989). And, of course, when dealing with negative terms, the likelihood of discrimination and neglect may be a consequence. Indeed, the whole notion of disorder carries connotations of the mechanistic, medical model view of the person, and hence seems antithetical to the thrust of Kelly's theorizing.

Overall then, this analysis would suggest that the notion of disorder as outlined by Kelly (1955/1991b) needs reconsideration. Do we need a construct of disorder at all? Some might argue, consistent with a relativist interpretation of personal construct psychology, that such a notion is inappropriate, a remnant of mechanistic theories and contrary to its central philosophy, which focuses on considering alternative perspectives. However, we do not believe that all constructions are as 'good' as each other, a position that Kelly also adopted. Indeed, we do not see how therapists can proceed in therapy without some broad aims, however much the specifics arise from the particular collaborative relationship with the client.

In order to elaborate this issue further, it is useful to discuss what personal construct therapists consider to be optimal functioning, as well as what they consider to be problematic, setting aside the notion of disorder for the time being. In so doing we shall be focusing in part on implications that flow from some of the main themes Kelly put forward, rather than his formal definitions – themes that have been elaborated in recent post-Kellian personal construct theorizing.

What is optimal functioning?

A variety of processes have been noted by Kelly and post-Kelly theorists as being conducive to optimal functioning. These include:

- completion of both the creativity and circumspection–preemption–control cycles (Kelly, 1955/1991a/1991b);
- the employment of hierarchies of meaning (Epting and Amerikaner, 1980; Landfield, 1980);
- a capacity for propositional construing (Landfield, 1980);
- tolerance of anxiety and uncertainty (Landfield, 1980);
- propensity to place alternative interpretations on events (Landfield, 1980);
- egalitarianism, the seeing of others as equal partners (Warren, 1992b);
- construal of the construction processes of others, with a resulting capacity for and engagement in, intimate relationships (Leitner and Dill-Standiford, 1993);
- appropriate dispersion of dependencies (Kelly, 1955/1991b; Walker, 1993).

What is striking is the diversity of this list. But is there something that links the items? Is there some more general theme that is superordinate to these more specific examples?

At a more general level, Kelly himself wrote about optimal functioning in terms of two cycles. The first of these he termed the 'validational cycle' (Kelly, 1955/1991a, p.160/p. 112), the testing out of construing, which is linked to the well-known metaphor of the scientist. With regard to the latter it is less commonly recognized that Kelly did not consider that people *were* scientists, but that they were *incipient* scientists, *potential* scientists. That is, he was proposing that optimal functioning was associated with a cycle that involves the testing out of construing, with appropriate revision dependent on the outcome of the experiment. In two later papers, Kelly (1970a, 1977) wrote about the experience cycle, the process of experimentation whereby people anticipate an event, invest themselves in this anticipation, and so actively encounter the event, assess whether their anticipations have eventuated or not, and revise their construct system if needed.

It is unclear if Kelly thought that the experience cycle was a better way of outlining the process of the testing out of construing than the scientist metaphor. Both have their advantages and disadvantages, highlighting different aspects of the testing out and revision of construing. The scientist metaphor could be interpreted as consistent with a more cognitive emphasis to the theory but being more specific about the processes involved. The experience cycle has the advantage of bringing in the passion of the person's investment in their experimentation, but gives us less detail because it does not have the additional connotations that flow from a metaphor.

The generic term 'validation' is used to cover the general issue referred to by these cycles, the testing out and revision of construing. But there are several additional issues that are noteworthy in the elaboration of Kelly's original views.

Button (1996) has highlighted the importance of seeing validation in terms of the strengthening or weakening of a way of construing, rather than any absolute confirmation or disconfirmation. One can readily see the importance of this if one looks at a practical example. We might test out our view that the ground is solid by walking on it. What is being tested is the construct that there are things that take our weight, and others that cannot, with the element here being the ground we are about to walk on. But what if while conducting this experiment we sink slowly downward? This invalidation of our prediction does not invalidate our construct. It merely at this point invalidates the prediction of the pole under which the element is construed. The ground here does not take our weight. Considerable variation in the same piece of land taking our weight and not taking our weight would need to occur over time and for other bits of land for this *construct* to be thoroughly invalidated. Of course occasionally there are decisive experiments, such as when people discover that their partner has been cheating on them, but the evaluation of everyday construing is more cumulative.

A second issue is the recognition that the process of validation is very centrally an interpersonal one. This is not just the case of it being through the reactions of others to what we say and do that we fine-tune our own sense-making system, although that is clearly important. Vicarious learning would also be relevant. But Kelly stressed the importance of our capacity to understand the ways others make sense of the world, what he termed 'sociality', and by which we can hone our own system and explore alternative ways of making sense of things. This, of course, does not mean that we end up with identical discriminations to others, but the overlap may be considerable for some individuals, facilitating communication between them.

A third issue is that validation is more complex than the unidimensional scientist metaphor suggests. It is a multi-layered process in that, at one and the same time, several different things are being tested (Walker et al., 2000). There is the particular prediction we have made, and its associated discrimination. But there is also the structure of our construing, the extent to which we value the discriminations we make. And most importantly there is a more general issue of our efficacy as construers. Others communicate that our sense making is, or is not, understandable and valued, and this is central to our sense of identity, self-esteem and belongingness.

Finally, it is important to recognize that the place of validation varies in its importance developmentally. Clearly childhood is a period when many discriminations are in their early formulation. Children are almost full-time experimenters. Inconsistent and confusing feedback, if widespread, has the potential to affect seriously the development of their sense making, resulting in much anxiety, confusion, and lack of a sense of being understood or even understandable. Neither validation nor invalidation is intrinsically problematic – both may be essential to the development of an effective system. Nevertheless, widespread invalidation can be a major impediment to the development of our construing and particularly our understanding of ourselves as effective. 'Serial invalidation' is the term that Bannister (1963) used to refer to this kind of personal history. He linked this with schizophrenic thought disorder. Problems in childhood have the potential to compound, so that the capacity to use the experience cycle or to be a good scientist as an adult, may be seriously impaired. This decreases our capacity to cope with change and makes the elaboration of ourselves as a sense-maker fragile and precarious.

In conclusion, we want to suggest that the seeming diversity of accounts of what constitutes optimal functioning from a personal construct perspective can be viewed as parts of the testing out process of our construing. Effective testing, whether conceived of in terms of the scientist metaphor or the experience cycle, is contingent on a number of processes, including interpersonal ones. Let us now return to the issue of the opposite of optimal functioning.

Non-optimal functioning

While the notion of disorder, as discussed, is in certain respects antithetical to the philosophy and theorizing of personal construct psychology, nevertheless interventions, whether clinical, organizational or social, need goals, at least at the level of change in a process. While this relates to what we have just discussed, optimal functioning, what is problematic must also be articulated. At its simplest we might regard this as the opposite of optimal functioning. That is, it is the failure adequately to test out our construing; Walker (2002) has termed this 'non-validation'.

Walker and colleagues have recently elaborated this notion more extensively, relating non-validation to problems at different stages of the scientist metaphor (Walker, 2002), as well as the experience cycle (Walker et al., 2000). Non-validation can be considered a protective strategy for avoiding revision of construing, a process that may lead to threat or the conglomeration of negative emotions Leitner (1988) terms terror. Its consequence is that we remain stuck, immobile, unable to move forward, and unable to reconstrue. In RA Neimeyer's (1985) view, the earlier in the experience cycle a blockage occurs, the more severe is the resulting disorder.

Winter (2003a) has pointed out that the major way in which non-validation is accomplished is by imbalance. He focused on the pairs of processes that Kelly considered central to our construing, for example, loosening versus tightening and dilation versus constriction, viewing these as strategies that an individual may use to cope with or avoid invalidation. Optimally, there is a cyclical and balanced interplay of contrasting strategies, as for example reflected in Kelly's notion of the creativity cycle, but disorders may be considered to be characterized by the virtually exclusive use of a particular strategy.

Much of the early personal construct clinical literature focused on clients for whom the predominant strategy is loose construing, in which constructions are so vague and inconsistent that they are highly invulnerable to invalidation. In such individuals, the experience cycle is blocked at its very first stage because they are unable to frame any coherent anticipations of their world. As was demonstrated by Bannister's (1960, 1962) classic work, clients who adopt this strategy exclusively tend to be labelled as thought-disordered schizophrenics. Loosening is also evident in some other client groups, and the extent and persistence of the loosening may determine the nature of the problems presented by the client (Winter, 1992a).

People who adopt the converse strategy of consistently construing tightly have been described by Kelly (1955/1991b (p. 849/205)) as developing a construct system that is designed to be 'anxiety-tight'. This strategy might be effective if they were to live in an unchanging world, but a tight construct system is very vulnerable to invalidation by new events and there is evidence that the effects of invalidation may be far-reaching in the tight construer, reverberating from the invalidated construct to others that are related to it (Lawlor and Cochran, 1981). The superordinate constructs of such an individual may not be sufficiently permeable to accommodate changing events and there is some research support for Kelly's view that this is the predicament of the person who is likely to be diagnosed as suffering from a disorder within the 'neurotic' spectrum (Winter 1985a, 1992a). The experience of invalidation may itself be invalidating for the self-constructions of some tightly construing individuals, who may therefore find themselves spiralling into a cycle of recursive self-invalidation (Semerari and Mancini, 1987; Gardner, Mancini and Semerari, 1988). For such people, their view of the self as a construer has essentially been invalidated (Walker et al., 2000). The threat posed by invalidation to the tight construer may result in him or her exhibiting hostility, in Kelly's sense of attempting to extort evidence for constructions. Such a person's experience cycle is blocked at the 'confirmation or disconfirmation of anticipation' phase.

The strategies of dilation and constriction may also be used in an imbalanced way, and this may be manifested in a disorder. In the former strategy, the person who is faced with incompatible constructions extends his or her perceptual field in an attempt to reorganize it at a more comprehensive level, but in disorders involving dilation 'the person's exploration has outrun his organization' (Kelly, 1955/1991b, p. 846/p. 203) and a diagnosis of manic or paranoid may result. In using a constrictive strategy, the person deals with incompatibilities by drawing in the outer boundaries of the perceptual field. While this may provide some temporary relief from anxiety, 'it may let issues accumulate which will eventually threaten a person with insurmountable anxiety' (Kelly, 1995/1991b, p. 908/p. 246). The person's experience cycle is essentially blocked at the 'encounter' phase, and this is the predicament of many individuals who receive diagnoses of anxiety or depressive disorders.

A further cycle that may not be completed in disorder is the circum-spection–pre-emption–control cycle, as indicated in Kelly's (1955/1991b, p. 927/p. 258) statement that 'all disorders of construction are disorders which involve faulty control'. This may be manifested in either prolonga-tion or foreshortening of the circumspection phase of this cycle, which may be reflected in ruminative or impulsive behaviour respectively.

Strategies involving covert construing, in which the person is not fully aware of all of his or her constructions, may also be employed to avoid anx-iety and reconstruing, and may be manifested in disorders. One such strategy is submergence, in which one pole of a construct is relatively inac-cessible, thus preventing the construct from being tested out: for some clients, such as those diagnosed as agoraphobic (see Chapter 12 in this vol-ume), the construct poles concerned may relate to negative views of others. Suspension is another strategy that may be used to hold in abeyance a con-struction that poses a threat to the person's construct system.

The block in the process of experimentation that is manifested in a dis-order may have various potentially negative consequences. One may be the development of an idiosyncratic pattern of construing, such as change-inhibiting dilemmas (Ryle, 1979), which may be derived from experiences of parents or other people who served as 'prototypes' of the constructions concerned. There may also be difficulty in construing other people's con-struction processes, and hence in the development of role relationships, as has been found by Widom (1976) in individuals diagnosed as psychopath-ic. There may be undispersed or undifferentiated dependency, which Walker, Ramsey and Bell (1988) have related to pre-emptive and imperme-able construing, and to vulnerability to invalidation. There is also likely to be the experience of the 'negative emotions' that, according to McCoy (1981, p. 97), 'follow unsuccessful' construing, although this definition is not without its problems.

The symptoms by which a disorder is expressed would not be regarded by the personal construct theorist as manifestations of a disease process of which the client is a passive victim but rather as 'urgent questions, behaviourally expressed, which had somehow lost the threads which lead either to answers or to better questions' (Kelly, 1969b, p. 19). Indeed, the individual may be viewed as, to some extent, 'choosing' a particular symptom, this choice often being explicable in terms of the individual's validational experiences and the construct subsystems which are in consequence most highly elaborated. Thus, for some people social constructions of a particular symptom (as reflected, for example, in media portrayals) may provide a ready-made, elaborated role of sufferer from the symptom concerned. Similarly, the individual who is raised in a family that tends to communicate by means of physical illness is likely to develop an elaborated 'somatic' construct subsystem, unlike the 'psychological' subsystem likely to be developed by the individual whose family openly expresses emotions. As Mancuso and Adams-Webber (1982) have indicated, the experience of persistent invalidation is one that involves a high level of arousal, with both physiological and psychological components. People who are exposed to such a situation are likely to focus pre-emptively on different aspects of this experience depending upon whether their 'physical' or 'psychological' construct subsystems are better elaborated, and to present with somatic or psychological symptoms respectively. There is research evidence of relationships of symptom choice with such features of the construct system, as well as with whether the client is predominantly concerned with his or her outer or inner world (Winter, 1992a). Whatever the client's symptom, it can be considered, as Kelly described, to involve both gains and losses for the individual. The gains may include the 'way of life' (Fransella, 1970) offered by a highly elaborated symptom, particularly for the individual who has no other well-structured role. Other purposes served by symptoms are that they may allow clients to avoid the terror involved in role relationships (Leitner, 1985); and, in those cases where they carry some positive implications for the individual, may have the 'payoff' of allowing the self to be construed in a favourable light (Tschudi, 1977).

The therapeutic process

If optimal functioning is a question of balance of contrasting processes, so too is an optimal experience of psychotherapy, the balance in this case being between validation and invalidation. For change to occur during therapy, it is necessary for the client to experience a certain amount of invalidation. However, for this to be a reconstructive experience rather than one that leads the client to resist therapy or that has adverse effects, this invalidation must occur within an overall climate of validation. As Kelly (1955/1991b) put it, the client 'needs a broad base of confirmation, often at the rather generalized level of value or dependency constructs, in order to trust himself to make major revisions of his system'. Leitner and Guthrie (1993) have pointed out the particular importance of core role validation in this regard, and Cummins (1993), similarly, has noted that clients often enter therapy after suffering core role invalidation and that the first two or three sessions are particularly crucial in determining whether the therapist can be trusted with this invalidated core structure. In these early stages, the therapist may be particularly concerned to lay some groundwork of validation, perhaps by providing support and reassurance, demonstrating acceptance of the client; attempting to use the client's constructions, and taking a credulous attitude to these. In so doing, the therapist is conveying an attitude of respect, or what Leitner (1988) terms reverence, for the client. A similar message is conveyed by therapy being conducted in an invitational, rather playful mood rather than in terms of the prescription of better ways of behaving or thinking. It is also conveyed by a therapeutic relationship in which client and therapist are collaborative coexperimenters rather than the therapist adopting the role of the expert with privileged access to rationality and truth.

Even when the client's constructions are challenged by the therapist, the latter's approach is generally not one of denying the validity of these constructions but rather of suggesting that they be suspended while alternative constructions are explored. This may be achieved in various different ways. In time-binding, for example, the client is helped to discover the time or situation within which a particular construction was originally developed and to view the construction as having been useful for the anticipation of events at that time but not in current circumstances. This neatly allows the therapist to facilitate exploration of alternative constructions while not invalidating the original problematic construction, merely suggesting that it is now somewhat anachronistic. The use of humour, which generally involves some interplay and coexistence of apparently incompatible constructions, may also allow a new construction to be explored while not dispensing with some cherished old construction, and it is of interest in this regard that Epting and Prichard (1993) regard personal construct psychotherapists' liking for humour as possibly one of their greatest contributions to psychotherapy. Metaphors can serve a similar purpose: for example, the client who adopts some constellatory construction of the self may be encouraged to experiment with Mair's (1977) notion that he or she could be seen as a community of selves, and to play with the relationships between these different selves using whatever metaphors they find most meaningful. The client's original self-construction need not be discounted in this process but instead is viewed as one of several alternatives. Variations on Kelly's (1995/1991a) self-characterization may similarly be employed to explore alternative self-constructions. Enactment techniques, including the Gestalt empty chair procedure, may also be used to allow a particular construction to be suspended while the client experiments with alternatives with the protection of make believe and the knowledge that he or she is only playing a role and not totally dispensing with some particular way of construing in favour of another. The classical example of this is Kelly's (1955/1991a) fixed-role therapy, various aspects of the procedure of which exemplify the delicate balance within personal construct psychotherapy between facilitating experimentation with alternative constructions and not invalidating aspects of the client's core construing.

'Resistance' to therapy

When the therapist fails to achieve an appropriate balance between validation and invalidation such that therapy faces the client with the terrifying prospect of profound core role invalidation (Leitner, 1988), most clients will have the good sense to display 'resistance'. From the personal construct theory viewpoint, as Fransella (1985, p. 300) has described, such clients are 'behaving perfectly reasonably from their own perspective'. This exemplifies what Liotti (1987) has termed the exploratory approach to the resistant client, in which resistance is seen as a normal, self-protective process that provides a valuable opportunity to explore in a collaborative relationship the client's core structures and processes. By contrast, the pedagogical approach to the resistant client may, in Liotti's view, have the unfortunate effect of validating a client's construction, perhaps developed from childhood experiences of indoctrinating parents, that others can, but he or she cannot, understand the true meaning of his or her feelings. In such an approach, the therapist's relationship with the client will tend to become adversarial, with the therapist 'heroically' persevering in attempting to persuade the client of the truth of the therapist's view of the client's predicament. This runs the risk of precipitating much more detrimental reactions than resistance (Leitner and Dill-Standiford, 1993), and these adverse effects of therapy may be viewed, just as in our earlier discussion of disorder, in terms of the client making an imbalanced use of such strategies as loosening, tightening, dilation and constriction in an attempt to deal with the invalidation with which he or she is confronted in therapy (Winter, 1996).

Conclusions

Optimal functioning involves effective testing out of construing, including the revision of invalidated constructions, while in disorder there is a failure to do this. This is because, in disorder, the process engaged in cannot lead to the testing out and revision of the invalidated constructions, most commonly because the individual is stuck in the repeated use of one or other of the strategies described by Kelly by which people engage with, and live in, the world. Thus, the disorder (which may perhaps alternatively be termed 'imbalance') is likely to be reflected in the exclusive use of a particular strategy, as opposed to the cyclical interplay of strategies that characterizes optimal functioning. The strategy adopted may depend upon the persistence of the invalidation experienced by the individual; its extensiveness; the availability of alternative sources of validation; the nature of invalidated constructs (for example, whether they are core or peripheral); the degree of elaboration of the construct system at the time of invalidation; and the strategies to which the individual has been most exposed.

An optimal therapeutic process also involves balance, this time between experiences of validation and invalidation. When an imbalanced therapeutic process leads the client to experience core role invalidation, he or she will generally resist therapy. The therapist who fails to heed this message and adjust his or her approach accordingly is likely to be faced with a 'therapeutic casualty', manifested, as in disorder generally, by imbalance in the use of strategies.

CHAPTER THREE

Kellian invalidation, attachment and the construct of 'control'

SANDRA SASSAROLI, ROBERTO LORENZINI,
GIOVANNI MARIA RUGGIERO

'Invalidation' and its links with later cognitive conceptualizations

Kelly's psychopathology is based on the cornerstone concept that 'all disorders can be considered to represent strategies by which the individual attempts to cope with invalidation and avoid uncertainty' (Winter, 1992a, p. 15). The term 'invalidation' is derived from Kelly's conceptualization of the human mind as a hierarchical architecture of constructs (Kelly, 1955/1991a/1991b). What is peculiar about Kelly's theory is that the author goes beyond a trivial definition of constructs as the cognitive counterpart of folk concepts of 'character' and 'personality' and stresses that basically they are the person's style of producing hypotheses about the world and how to interact with it to achieve personal goals. It is the well-known metaphor of the person as a scientist.

Of course, hypotheses can be confirmed or rebutted. In Kelly's terminology, confirmation is 'validation' and disconfirmation is 'invalidation'. During daily life people deal continuously with validations and invalidations, and all the Kellian theories of psychopathology depend on how people manage these phenomena, above all invalidation. The human mind functions at its best when the person is able to manage flexibly the invalidations coming from reality which disconfirm the person's hypotheses. 'Good' mental functioning is the capacity to use invalidation to increase complexity. Invalidation, far from distorting the system of personal constructs, provides a possibility of growth of knowledge (Mancini and Semerari, 1985).

Optimal functioning is between the two opposite extreme poles of psychopathology, which are 'literalism' and 'fragmentalism'. 'Literalism' is the repeated and rigid use of a construct in spite of consistent invalidation, whereas 'fragmentalism' is a relative disorganization of complexity and consequently of actual predictive power of the personal constructs (Landfield, 1980). In 'literalism' the person does not attempt to integrate the invalidation in his or her system of personal constructs and reacts by avoiding and controlling the invalidating situations. Basically, 'literalism' corresponds to anxiety and depression, whereas 'fragmentalism' corresponds to schizophrenia and any formal psychopathology of thought.

Some Kellian concepts are productively applicable to disorders such as anxiety and eating disorders. In fact, Kellian 'literalism' has points in common with later conceptualizations of anxiety. In particular, Kelly defined anxiety as a form of literalism in which the constructs of weakness and danger are rigidly linked to certainty, detailed knowledge of the future and the capacity to master and control reality. These concepts have much in common with later cognitive psychopathological concepts like 'catastrophic thought', 'intolerance of uncertainty', 'perfectionism' and 'need for control'.

'Catastrophic thought' is a disproportionately threatening appraisal of the environment. Anxiety disordered individuals have elevated expectations of negative events (Tomarken, Cook and Mineka, 1989), wider predictive webs than controls (Vasey and Borkovec, 1992), and a higher tendency to interpret neutral stimulation negatively (Butler and Mathews, 1983; Mathews, Richards and Eysenck, 1989; Richards and French, 1992; MacLeod and Cohen, 1993; Calvo, Eysenck and Estevaz, 1994; Winton, Clark and Edelman, 1995; Calvo, Eysenck and Castillo, 1997). The tendency for negative predictions is correlated to the severity of anxiety (Butler and Matthews, 1983, 1987; McNally and Foa, 1987). 'Intolerance of uncertainty' is the incapacity to tolerate the uncertainty of events and the potential existence of risks and negative events (Dugas, Gosselin and Ladoucer, 2001). The person worries about the fact that he or she does not know exactly what will happen and that negative events do exist. Intolerance of uncertainty is positively correlated with the severity of anxiety (Dugas, Freeston and Ladoucer, 1997). According to Frost et al. (1990), concern over mistakes is the cognitive distinguishing feature of pathological 'perfectionism'. Pathological perfectionists allow little room for making mistakes and perceive even minor ones as likely to lead to a future final failure. Thus, pathological perfectionists never feel anything is done completely enough or well enough and their actions are always accompanied by feelings of self-criticism and a sense of ineffectiveness. 'Need for control' is a contingent relationship between a response and a consequent outcome (Seligman, 1975). The need for control is underlined in cognitive literature as a feature of both normal and anxiety disordered people (Seligman, 1975, 1991; Bandura, 1977). The normal person needs control but judges it as mostly sufficient (Langer, 1975). In the anxiety disordered person the level of exerted control is considered to be insufficient (Suls and Fletcher, 1985; Roth and Cohen, 1986; Barlow, 1988, 1991; Mineka and Kelly, 1989; Basoglu and Mineka, 1992; Foa, Zinbarg and Olasov-Rothbaum, 1992; Mineka and Zinbarg, 1996; Rapee et al., 1996; Shapiro and Astin, 1998). Sanderson, Rapee and Barlow (1989) have shown that a perception of increased control is linked to a decrease of anxiety. 'Control' could be defined as the anxious person's need for certainty to avoid all the negative and aversive events he or she continuously imagines, fears and predicts as possible during his or her worry. Such a person tries to control negative events by monitoring some aspects or parameters of the external or internal world (Sassaroli and Ruggiero, 2002). In the case of people with eating disorders, the goals of control are weight, fat and food (Fairburn, Shafran and Cooper, 1998). For this reason they conceive control as obligatory and lacking any alternative solution (Crosina, 1994–2002; Lorenzini and Sassaroli, 2000).

Of course, there are differences. The four above-mentioned constructs are more oriented towards the informative content, whereas Kellian 'literalism' is focused on the formal structure of thought. On the other hand, there are many commonalities. Presumably, anxious people might have a general feeling of the world as a highly dangerous environment and justify their fears using the construct of intolerance of uncertainty ('I know that dangers are not highly probable, but I do not accept even the low probability of negative events') or in terms of fear of fear ('I fear that I am not able to cope with even minor feelings of fear') or in terms of negative self-evaluation ('I judge myself as incapable of coping with any danger or negative event'), and so forth. All these statements are good examples of rigid constructs in which people strictly link the concept of security and self-confidence to absence of uncertainty and unforeseen events in the future, and non-predicted events are confused with dangerous events. Kelly uses the term 'permeability' in the 'modulation corollary'. This corollary states that 'permeability' is the construct's capacity to admit new elements into its range, which were not originally construed within its framework. For example, a student who rigidly applies the construct 'intensive/superficial' to psychodynamic and cognitive therapies respectively, the first one being 'intensive' and of course the other 'superficial', does not use a permeable construct (Winter, 1992a). In conclusion, if the construct of 'control' may be defined as the absolute certainty of avoiding all the threatening events continuously predicted by anxious, worrying and perfectionistic people (Sassaroli and Ruggiero, 2002), in Kellian terminology there is a 'literalistic', 'impermeable', 'tight', and rigid link between 'control' and 'security' and' 'self-confidence'.

Invalidation and the construct of 'control': clinical vignettes

Giovanna is 25 years old and asked to follow a course of psychotherapy because she 'can't bear to control everything, and all of the time, any more'. She began to suffer from anorexia when she was 14 after her father left the family to go and live with his secretary and all contact with him ceased. Her mother had a serious reaction to this and attempted suicide by taking an overdose of prescription drugs, which left her in a coma for 3 days. The client had had rapid weight loss and a loss of her menstrual cycle within three months. She weighed 39 kilos after being hospitalized in the final year, having reached a minimum weight of 34 kilos. During her illness she took a degree in engineering but can only manage work in the mornings as an office clerk.

She declares herself as desperate because

> For almost 10 years I spend all of my time controlling food and what I eat, this control devours all of my other thoughts, I worry about it all through the day and I'm terrified to stop. I don't know what else to do, my life has lost all sense. I'm 25 years old and this control has never given me the time to have a boyfriend, kiss a boy, go out for dinner like other normal people of my age. Then when I do gain some weight I find myself controlling other things like washing the dishes or cleaning the bathroom. I'm very scared of starting therapy because this disgusting control has kept me alive and if I reduce it or reduce the worry, there will be nothing left.'

Francesco P is a 30-year-old man who asked to start therapy for serious affective insecurity. He constantly fears not being loved enough by his friends, parents and above all by his girlfriend. Until a few weeks before he started therapy Francesco managed to calm his insecurity through the continuous reassurances that he asked of his girlfriend. Unfortunately, since his girlfriend left for Brazil to visit her relations, it has been difficult to obtain this reassurance. He says, 'I realize now that I can't control the affection of others as I once believed, or even have the certainties that I once had.' An interesting case of invalidation.

Attachment as an informative relationship

Kelly thinks that every human activity is basically a learning activity, a continuous construing of hypotheses and their validation or invalidation. This explains the limited interest he showed in child developmental processes. Lorenzini and Sassaroli (1995) tried to find out the learning and informative components in attachment relationships. Their general goal was to integrate a developmental aspect into Kelly's theory. In particular, they proposed a conceptualization of attachment as the context in which the child learns the rules of knowledge in the sense of assimilation and rejection of invalidation coming from reality. A 'good' attachment relationship is not only a secure base, but also a sort of learning laboratory in which the child learns not to be afraid of invalidations and develops the capability to integrate them in the system. On the other hand, an insecure attachment is also a context in which the child tends to conceive any invalidation as a threatening event. It is clear that this concept of insecure base parallels the cognitive constructs of 'catastrophic thought', 'intolerance of uncertainty' and 'control'.

Attachment is the central relationship where the child learns about two different domains of knowledge. He or she learns his or her own internal working models and those of others and the favourite strategies to obtain and maintain the attachment – the physical proximity of the parents. The different strategies to obtain these goals are those considered in attachment patterns research. The attachment patterns correspond to internal beliefs regarding the lovability of the self, and the accessibility of social and affective relationships with others. These beliefs produce expectations and behaviours that in turn can influence the initial beliefs.

The other great domain concerns knowledge strategies – beliefs not regarding the self, others and the world, but regarding knowledge itself: the rules to obtain and increase knowledge and explore the world. The child learns to learn, to integrate invalidations in the construct system. In our original hypothesis there are four growth knowledge styles (GKS), the strategies of knowledge (Lorenzini and Sassaroli, 1995, 2000) corresponding to the four attachment patterns. The four GKS are exploration, elusion, hostility and immunization. The GKS can be both adaptive when used flexibly and pathogenic when they become pervasive and impermeable to alternatives (Shapiro, 1965).

This chapter focuses on the GKS related to anxiety: elusion. Elusion is a strategy of narrowed attention and exploration, which permits the person to avoid invalidating events. Basically this cognitive avoidance can be carried out following three paths (Miceli and Castelfranchi, 1995):

- *Scotomization* relates primarily to the present and consists in diverting attention from the relevant event (Ciuffi, 1989; Krohne, 1993). Normally, unexpected news captures our attention. To divert attention from the new stimulus it is necessary to direct it toward something else.
- *Repression,* a term widely used in psychoanalysis, relates primarily to the past and consists in putting away the appraisal of invalidating events in hard access memory where attention is rarely focused (Bagnara, 1984; Goleman, 1985; Ciuffi, 1989; Weiner, 1992).
- In *Avoidance* the anxious person tends to switch attention far from situations, places and events that may test and invalidate his or her internal beliefs.

The choice to explore or to elude an unknown event depends also on the individual's self-perception. A person who perceives himself or herself as weak and unable to cope efficaciously with unforeseen events would probably judge that event as threatening and tend to avoid the feared situation. The fact that none of the manifold feared events has ever happened in the past is evaluated by the anxious person as a confirmation that his or her strategy is valid, and not as an invalidation of the hypothesis of the world as a dangerous place. Summing up, the person prone to develop an anxiety disorder may have developed the belief to be weak – dependent on support and love from others – and that the exploration of the world is dangerous in an insecure attachment relationship. An invalidating event – a situation even partially difficult if not dangerous – could have definitely confirmed such beliefs. Finally, for such a person, the idea of the world as a dangerous place is protective in that it creates a relative feeling of security. Any attempt to disconfirm this hypothesis is in turn a really problematic possibility that could maintain the disorder.

Control and invalidation in research

The hypothesis of invalidation as a situation in which the rigidity of the architecture of constructs is tested and, if present, revealed can be investigated studying the role played by stress in the psychopathology of eating disorders. Stress situations and major life events negatively affect eating both in human and in animal models (Connan and Treasure, 1998). Stress situations may trigger abnormal eating and even eating disorders in a perfectionistic personality, and in turn perfectionism may function in eating disorders by increasing the painful impact of distressing environmental and developing events (Hewitt and Flett, 1993a; Hewitt, Flett and Ediger, 1995). In a perfectionistic personality even minor shortfalls are tantamount to significant failures, so perfectionists have an increased probability of experiencing a painful perception of failure in stress situations. Thus, a perceived failure after a performance may reveal a parallel tendency to worry about and to feel dissatisfied with perceived eating mistakes and imperfections of body shape and weight.

The constructivist interpretation of the interplay of perfectionism and stress in eating disorders is that the person tends to have a tight, impermeable and rigid link between 'perfection' and 'absence of mistakes', and between 'self-esteem' and 'avoidance of mistakes'. A performance in which the person's skills are tested could be a good experimental situation to investigate the correlation between fear of mistakes, control, possible invalidations (failure or fear of failure of the performance) and emergence of symptomatological attitudes.

We can find good examples of stressful (and invalidating) situations in the school context. A school examination is a stress situation involving the whole person's perception of his or her sense of competence and efficacy. Research has shown that perfectionism is related to students' perceptions of greater course difficulty and higher anxiety prior to examination (Brown et al., 1999) and to female students' higher drive for thinness, thoughts of dieting and body dissatisfaction prior to examination and prior to receiving results of the examination (Ruggiero et al., 2003). The results of the latter study were that in the stress situation (the day the students received the examination results) the constructs of perfectionism and parental criticism showed a significant association with the drive for thinness and body dissatisfaction. On the other hand, this association was absent on an average, non-stressful day of school.

Plausibly, a stress situation is a situation in which the person experiences a condition of lack of control. Perfectionistic people can be defined as a subgroup of anxious people, who are in turn those with a strong tendency to overestimate the probabilities of negative events and to over-predict threatening events, dangers and damage (Rachman, 1998; MacLeod, 1999). In perfectionism, the over-prediction of threatening events is linked to a highly intense fear of failure after important performances. Pathological perfectionists never feel anything is done completely enough or well enough, always experience feelings of self-criticism and a sense of ineffectiveness, and perceive even minor mistakes as likely to lead to a future final failure. The perfectionistic over-concern for mistakes may be relevant to eating-disordered individuals because they interpret any perceived shortfall and any bodily or weight imperfection as catastrophic failures of their strong desire for a faultless, impeccable and dazzling social and self image (Hewitt and Flett, 1993b).

Consequently, as any clinician knows from daily experience, eating-disordered people often look for 'control' (Bruch, 1973; Button, 1985; Katzman and Lee, 1997). The sense of control is often obtained by the continuous monitoring of a certain parameter, such as bodily perception in panic, intrusive thought in obsessionality, and so on. In the case of eating disorders, such a parameter appears as concerns over eating and body weight and shape (Fairburn, Shafran and Cooper, 1998). As explained by Slade (1982), dietary restrictions enhance the subjective sense of being in control. Hence, eating disorders could be described as disorders of the sense of self-esteem and self-worth, which are, without remedy, pervasively negative, if not lacking in such individuals. The need to feel self-control would be the final-level coping goal pursued by eating-disordered people to fight their major and final fear, which is the fear of being insufficiently worthy. They are oppressed by a pervasive, generic and vague feeling of being insufficiently qualified, competent or suited for the demands of life, and they spend a lot of time worrying about these negative feelings. This general self-schema is the second core characteristic of eating disorders from a cognitive perspective and has been called 'long-standing negative self evaluation' (Vitousek and Hollon, 1990).

The hypothesis of 'control' may well explain why only in the stressful situations of the study did perfectionistic dimensions correlate with the drive for thinness. It is possible that on those occasions people experienced a situation of lack of control. In the stressful situation they conceived themselves as passive, because they were waiting for their results. They may have actually felt that the notification of their examination results was a highly threatening situation of possible failure and out of their control. They probably spent that day worrying about the possible negative consequences of a failure. The correlation of perfectionism with drive for thinness may be explained as an attempt to recover 'control' in another field, the field of eating and body weight.

The correlations of the construct 'parental criticism' with other constructs give us further information and suggestions about the familial facet of perfectionism in that they indicate the typical conceptions of perfectionistic people regarding their relationships with parents. In fact, perfectionistic people tend to conceive their parents' love as conditioned by satisfaction of parental expectations and by their critical evaluations (Hollander, 1965; Hamachek, 1978; Burns, 1980; Patch, 1984). Parental criticism can be defined as the parents' attitude to blame their children with the goal to control their behaviour and thoughts. The autonomy of the children is not respected or even recognized. Parental love is strictly linked to the child's obedience. Subsequently, the familial form of failure intensively feared by the perfectionistic person is the loss of parental love. This study confirms that eating restraint may be associated with dysfunctional family relationships (Humphrey, 1988; Råstam and Gillberg, 1991; Thienemann and Steiner, 1993).

The pathological correlates of criticism could be related to characteristics of the blamer parent: his or her higher status (with related anger of the child), over-involvement and over-protectiveness, lack of confidence in the child, and induction of guilty feelings in the child (Apparigliato, Ruggiero and Sassaroli, 2003). The critical attitude can generate or reinforce different constructions in children. In a perfectionistic child, there may be beliefs of the self as weak, prone to mistakes and failures, and even guilty. In turn, these beliefs can stimulate an over-controlling coping style. In other cases, the child would radically reject the criticism with feelings of anger and distrust towards parents. Another possible scenario is depression, self-distrust, and feelings of abandonment and withdrawal from the world.

A distrustful and directive parenting style is deeply connected with a traditional cultural representation of human nature, viewed as a blend of good and evil tendencies. Specimens of such a cultural phenomenon are present in ancient text. For instance, Pilch (1993) describes in detail two instances in the Bible: Sirach's familiar poem on raising boys, and the Proverbs. The traditional parent thought that human evil tendencies were difficult to control, always present in any human being, unforeseeable and likely to erupt at any moment into evil deeds. For this reason the traditional parenting style was highly directive and did not reject physical punishment as a good strategy both for controlling the youngster and teaching self-control. The child is perceived as a selfish and demanding being who probably desires more satisfaction and gratification than he or she actually needs. Traditional parents seek to control and direct the child and think that children must conform to a predetermined pattern and learn to accept authority and discipline. Parents often ignore a child's point of view and disregard a child's feelings and capacities. Hostility and negativity are aggravated, and unless repressed, they require force to control.

Conclusions

This chapter is an attempt to integrate Kelly's classical view of invalidation with contemporary 'standard' cognitive research on constructs and beliefs. Invalidation represents an important clinical concept coming from Kelly, which ought to be introduced and valued in cognitive 'standard' theory. Only the Kellian hypothesis of the failed integration of invalidation can account for the transformation of potentially rigid expectations about reality to manifest symptomatology. The above-mentioned research on the emergence of psychopathology from a stress situation could be considered as a confirmation of the invalidation theory. In turn, attachment theory can account for both the shaping of expectations during childhood and the functional or dysfunctional styles of integration of invalidations within the construct system.

CHAPTER FOUR

The psychotherapeutic relationship from a personal construct perspective

GABRIELE CHIARI, MARIA LAURA NUZZO

The different psychotherapeutic schools of thought may vary considerably in theory and methodology. Coherently, they seem to imply different kinds of relationship between therapist and client.[1]

Notwithstanding the differences, a great many of the psychotherapeutic perspectives agree that the relationship that develops between therapist and client is of great importance to the success of treatment. This is the case, in particular, for the perspectives that acknowledge the role of interpersonal processes in the development of personality and the genesis of personal disorders. Of course, how to define a 'successful' client–therapist relationship, how exactly the psychotherapeutic relationship influences process and outcome, what are its various components, and which are most important to the healing process, all are questions whose answers depend on the specific conceptions of the nature of interpersonal processes and of personal disorders.

In a paper presented in 1965 at a symposium on 'Cognitive and analytic conceptions of the therapeutic relationship', Kelly (1969c) chose to differentiate the personal construct theory view by resorting to the different ways devised to understand the relationship between the person and the environment. In elaborating the differences, Kelly made obvious reference to his understanding of the cognitive and psychoanalytic perspectives of that time. Thus, the cognitive perspective is equated to a S-O-R psychology, and the psychoanalytic perspective is anchored in Freud's drive theory.

---

[1] Bannister and Fransella (1980, p. 133) listed some of them in the ironic and provocative style of their introduction to the psychology of personal constructs, *Inquiring Man*:

The most traditional imply a 'doctor–patient' relationship which tends to encourage passivity in the allegedly ignorant patient while he or she waits for the ministrations of the expert doctor. A psychoanalytic approach to psychotherapy suggests a relationship more akin to that of priest and penitent, with absolution from the original sin of the Id as the ultimate goal. Some forms of client-centred psychotherapy adopt a stance that is reminiscent of that of an indulgent parent towards a child, while some cognitive therapists seem rather like authoritarian teachers in relation to their pupils. In behaviour therapy, the relationship seems to be broadly that of trainer–trainee. The relationship between psychotherapist and client envisaged by Kelly was essentially that of co-experimenters.

In our opinion, the developments of both psychoanalytic and cognitive psychotherapies in the direction of more and more attention to the interpersonal processes involved in the emergence of disorders as well as in psychotherapeutic process are resulting in a progressive convergence between the two perspectives and between both of them and personal construct psychotherapy. The differences are still important, but the spreading of object relations theories in psychoanalysis (see, for example, Bacal and Newman, 1990), and the elaboration of interpersonal-developmental approaches within the cognitive perspective (see, for example, Safran and Segal, 1990) are favouring the opening of a domain of conversation that personal construct psychotherapists can at long last begin to join, thus putting an end to their isolation.

We shall outline what we regard as the most important elements of both convergence and divergence among the psychoanalytic, cognitive and personal constructivist perspectives, before addressing the elements of specificity of the personal construct view on the psychotherapeutic relationship.

The psychotherapeutic relationship in psychoanalytic, cognitive and personal constructivist perspectives

Elements of convergence

Indications of a relative convergence are represented by the acknowledgement of the importance attached to early relational experiences, by the role given to some kind of collaborative alliance between client and therapist, and by the attention to transference and countertransference phenomena.

The importance of early relational experiences

The psychoanalytic literature on the child's tie to the mother is extremely rich and variegated (Bowlby, 1958). Such an interest is due to the role that early relational experiences is supposed to have for the successive development of personality, as well as to the influences that they have on the transference relationship with the analyst. Freud's notion of transference shows that he viewed the clinical situation as structured in interpersonal terms according to the patient's early relational experiences. However, it is object relations theorists who consider social relationships to be of primary importance for the development of personality and their clinical significance has been extensively explored (Greenberg and Mitchell, 1983).

As cognitive therapies have begun to give importance to interpersonal processes, some of them found in Bowlby's (1969) attachment theory an understanding of the role of early relational experiences suitable for an integration with the epistemological and theoretical assumptions of cognitivism. In fact, even though attachment theory has its historical references in the traditional psychoanalytic models, particularly in object relation theories, it is characterized by combining the ethological study of the child's behaviour with system control theory. The clinical applications of attachment theory (Bowlby, 1988) consist in the understanding of emotional disorders in terms of specific patterns of attachment, and in the consideration of the role of the same patterns in the patient–therapist relationship (Guidano and Liotti, 1983).

The personal construct understanding of early relational experiences lies in its original elaboration of the notion of dependency. However, Kelly's invitation 'to look at psychology in a new way, more particularly at counselling in a new way, and especially at interpersonal dependency' (Kelly, 1966) has not been properly followed. Maybe due to its abandonment of a consideration of clinical disorders in terms of disease entities and to its emphasis on anticipation rather than on the past determinants of disorders, the role of early relational experiences has been disregarded by personal construct psychologists and psychotherapists. Only recently has there been a renewed interest in an understanding of our dependence on others and its role in the clinical setting (Walker 1993, 1997).

We have proposed (Chiari et al., 1994) that many people, in the course of their ontogenic development, have their possibility of adequately dispersing their dependencies limited by their early relationships with their parents. This happens whenever the child–caregiver relationship, rather than allowing aggressiveness in the child, is characterized by prevailing transitions of threat or guilt. The developmental paths traced by threat and guilt are supposed to be unfavourable to the elaboration of role constructs in the child, and more likely to result in disorders in the adult. In our experience, many people referred for psychotherapy show disorders involving undispersed dependency.

The collaborative alliance between client and therapist

Within the orthodox psychoanalytic tradition, two kinds of alliances have been described: the therapeutic and the working alliance. Though often used interchangeably, they actually designate distinctly different dimensions of the analytic relationship.

The concept of *therapeutic alliance* dates back to Zetzel's (1956) seminal paper, in which she refers to a relationship between analyst and patient that provides an atmosphere of basic acceptance, understanding and safety. Zetzel had in mind the early mother–infant object relationship. She emphasized that developing the therapeutic alliance is a mutual and reciprocal process. In fact, not only does it require that the patient identifies with the analyst, but also that the analyst is able to identify with the patient. By contrast, Greenson's (1965) concept of the *working alliance* refers to the more circumscribed and rational phenomenon in which the patient comes to identify with the 'work ego' of the analyst and gradually becomes an analytic collaborator. Developmentally, the working alliance can be regarded as sequential to, and made possible by, the therapeutic alliance (Rather, 2001).

A main source of debate within the psychoanalytic community is represented by the question whether the concepts of therapeutic and working alliance are classifiable as transference or non-transference phenomena. In fact, a 'real' relationship between the patient and the psychoanalyst has been described (Greenson, 1978) and conceived of in contrast to transference. The prevailing view is that one may conceptualize several relational dimensions in the analytic dyad:

• the transference;
• the therapeutic and/or working alliance; and
• the non-transference relationship.

That is, the concepts of therapeutic alliance and working alliance would occupy an intermediate ground in which elements of transference and non-transference commingle.

Cognitive therapists require from the client an active and conscious collaboration in the therapeutic task more similar to the working than to the therapeutic alliance. This collaboration is regarded as crucial to the success of the therapeutic process. In its most systematic description, Beck's (1976) *collaborative empiricism*, the shaping of the alliance between patient and therapist goes through distinct steps: the communication to patients of a first conceptualization of their problem in terms that appear plausible for them, and the consequent formulation of a therapeutic contract; an explanation of the central role of cognitive processes in determining emotional states and behaviours; and a formulation of the aim of therapy and of the techniques designed for its achievement. Through collaborative empiricism the alliance between patient and therapist is continually monitored and adjusted.

Kelly also described the client–therapist dyad as a sort of alliance: more precisely, as a team, or a partnership:

> In this undertaking the fortunate client has a partner, the psychotherapist. But the psychotherapist does not know the final answer either – so they face the problem together. Under the circumstances there is nothing for them to do except for both to inquire and both to risk occasional mistakes. So that it can be a genuinely cooperative effort, each must try to understand what the other is proposing and each must do what he can to help the other understand what he himself is ready to try next. They formulate their hypotheses jointly. They even experiment jointly and upon each other. Together they

take stock of outcomes and revise their common hunches. Neither is the boss, nor are they merely well-bred neighbors who keep their distance from unpleasant affairs. It is, as far as they are able to make it so, a partnership'. (Kelly, 1969d, p. 229)

The team of client and therapist can go about their task in a variety of ways. (Kelly, 1969d, p. 231)

. . . the client and his therapist embark together as shipmates on the very same adventure. (Kelly, 1969d, p. 235)

The personal construct psychotherapist dismisses the role of expert typical of so many helping professions to join the client in the exploration of a personal world of meanings, in a journey where they walk forward, not following a path, but 'laying down the path in walking' (Varela, 1991, pp. 48–64).

Kelly's consideration that the whole therapeutic process is subordinate to the task of 'teaching the client how to be a "patient"' by giving him/her specific instructions' (Kelly, 1955/1991b, pp. 643–9/pp. 61–5) can appear dissonant with the above. However, the task 'involves much more than the recitation of a formal charge [and] it may take months to teach the client how he should respond to the therapeutic situation in order to get the most out of it' (Kelly, 1955/1991b, p. 644/p. 62). In other words, the partnership between client and therapist is the progressive result of a social process based on each member's understanding of the other.

The role of transference and countertransference

The acknowledgement of the role of interpersonal processes implies a different way of considering the relationship between client and therapist: as an experience having a central role in the therapeutic process, rather than as the means for the application of the techniques provided to the therapist by his/her approach.

The way personal construct psychotherapy deals with the therapeutic content of the psychotherapeutic relationship is so similar to the psychoanalytic one that Kelly (1955/1991b, pp. 662–86/pp. 75–90) chose to make use of the psychoanalytic terms of transference and countertransference. Even though without a systematic treatment of these notions, the recent developments of some cognitive approaches seem to share the view that the client's relationship with the therapist favours the change of central beliefs about self in interaction with others. Moreover, they attach to the emotions of the psychotherapist the value of important sources of information as to the patient's way of relating with others.

Elements of divergence

The differences among the psychoanalytic, cognitive and personal constructivist perspectives lie at a metatheoretical level and imply specific theories about personal and interpersonal processes, change, and disorder.

Broadly speaking, the psychoanalytic perspective applied to psychotherapy is aimed at facilitating a change in intrapsychic or relational conflicts by means of the interpretation of those same conflicts as expressed in the psychotherapeutic relationship through transference. Interpretation, in its turn, is aimed at increasing clients' understanding of themselves and of their symptoms, thus allowing a greater mastery of their relational problems (Luborsky, 1984).

The cognitive–relational perspective directs its efforts towards the correction of maladaptive interpersonal schemata and the recovery of a sense of integration of experience, mainly by means of the 'good quality' of the relationship between client and therapist and the consequent development of metacognitive abilities (Liotti, 1999). Alexander's notion of 'corrective emotional experience' applies to the understanding of the role of the client–therapist relationship in many cognitive-relational approaches. The corrective experience encourages the client toward 're-experiencing the old unsettled conflict, but with a new ending' (Alexander and French, 1946, p. 338).

Lastly, the personal constructivist perspective is aimed at the reactivation of an elaborative motion through the *reconstruction* of the client's experience. The purpose of personal construct psychotherapy, to use Kelly's expression, 'is not to produce a state of mind but to produce a mobility of mind that will permit one to pursue a course through the future' (Kelly, 1955/1991b, p. 649/p. 65). It is not a question of increasing consciousness of the interpersonal pattern the client uses in order to prevent it from being repeatedly used (what is the alternative?), nor of letting the client experience a fixed, 'positive' type of relationship (as if it was the only alternative). Rather, it is a question of helping clients in inventing and experimenting with some viable, alternative ways of relating with other people within the experimental field of the psychotherapeutic relationship, so as to give back meaning to their social world and to their role in it. It is in this very sense that the relationship between client and therapist can be regarded as a reconstructive relationship.

A reconstructive relationship

Constructive alternativism: man the scientist

The view of the psychotherapeutic relationship as a reconstructive relationship is implied by the metatheoretical assumption of personal construct psychology – that is, constructive alternativism: 'We assume that all of our present interpretations of the universe are subject to revision or replacement' (Kelly, 1955/1991a, p. 15/p. 11). Its meaning can be easily understood when one adopts the most usual way of presenting personal construct theory: that is, moving from the analogy of man the scientist (Kelly, 1955/1991a).

All people are scientists in the sense that they all have their own views (that is, elaborate theories) of the world, and their views allow them to have their own expectations (to formulate hypotheses) about what will happen in given situations. It is on this basis that they act and at the same time, through their very behaviour, they put their hypotheses to the test (make experiments), and revise their constructions (that is, modify their theories) in the light of the outcomes.

This continuous cycle of experience (Kelly, 1970a) implies a specific understanding of what other perspectives regard as psychopathology. A disorder, in fact, is seen as 'any personal construction which is used repeatedly in spite of consistent invalidation' (Kelly, 1955/1991b, p. 831/p. 193), and as 'any structure which appears to fail to accomplish its purpose' (Kelly, 1955/1991b, p. 835/p. 195). In other words, disordered people use constructions that are not able to give a proper meaning to their experience, but that in spite of this they keep using for lack of anything better. The person is no longer able to conserve an adaptation with the environment through recursive changes. His/her processes become repetitive instead, as if the person tried to maintain the old, no-longer-meaningful kind of adaptation (Chiari and Nuzzo, 2004).

Usually, a clinically relevant disorder corresponds to an arrest of elaborative motion in a core part of a person's construction system: the person as scientist is no longer able to revise his or her most basic constructions notwithstanding the negative outcomes of his or her experiments. Of particular importance are the failures of experiments in the social domain, given their close relationship with the person's construction of his or her core role, that is, his or her self-identity.

Given the above, the healing process consists in the constructive elaboration by clients of that part of their construction system 'which appears to fail to accomplish its purpose', as stated earlier, and the task of the psychotherapist is to facilitate such elaboration by acting as a co-experimenter.

Acceptance: psychotherapist as supervisor

The client and the therapist enter into relationship with each other in different ways. Clients will usually try to construe therapists by applying to them some of their own constructs, which have other people as elements in their range of convenience, whereas psychotherapists are interested in understanding just what are the constructs clients apply to other people –

to themselves, and to the therapist. In fact, if therapists want to act in a therapeutically effective way, they have to relate to the client on the basis of their understanding of the client as a person (a personal construct system), subsumed in its turn by the professional constructs provided by the theory. This twofold process is what Kelly means by 'acceptance':

> The accepting therapist tries earnestly to put himself in the client's shoes, but at the same time seeks to maintain a professional overview of the client's problems. This means that in accepting the client the therapist makes an effort to understand him in his – the client's – own terms, and that, also, he subsumes a major portion of the client's construction under his – the therapist's – own professional constructs. (Kelly, 1955/1991b, p. 649/p. 65)

Kelly goes so far as to assert that 'one might even say that the psychology of personal constructs is, among other things, a psychology of acceptance'. In fact

> since the psychology of personal constructs lays great stress upon the interpretation of the regnancy of the constructs under which acts may be performed, rather than upon the mere acts themselves, and since it lays great stress upon *personal* constructs rather than *formalistic* constructs, it does demand of the psychologist that he have an acceptance of other persons. (Kelly, 1955/1991a, p. 373/p. 277)

Kelly illustrates the personal construct therapist's role by the analogy of the psychotherapist as supervisor in relation with a research student. Research supervisors must subsume crucial aspects of students' research interest if they want to help students to design the optimal methodology through which to answer their questions. The supervisor's talent lies in the methodology of how to ask a good experimental question. The student's level of expertise lies in his or her specialist knowledge of the subject matter. Clients are their own subject matter but they have become clients because they are no longer in a position to learn from their experimentation. The therapist's task is to help clients to formulate the questions they need to ask themselves to put in motion again their incomplete cycle of experimentation. It is in this sense that this model of the psychotherapeutic relationship is one of active co-experimentation.

However, the analogy of the psychotherapist as supervisor does not put enough emphasis on the central role of acceptance. It is acceptance that differentiates personal construct psychotherapy from other psychotherapies, even from those cognitive therapies defined as constructivist in opposition to the rationalistic cognitive approaches (Mahoney, 1991).

Acceptance does not imply a distancing from the other, or a fusional empathy with the other: it is something transcending both of them. Acceptance is 'a precondition to the intentional adoption of role relationships' as implied by the sociality corollary, and hence a precondition to a deep personal change. Acceptance is an attitude that characterizes the role of constructivist psychotherapists and that consists in their striving to understand the construction processes of another person, and in their employing them to see how the world appears from that point of observation. This is the only access to the otherwise unconstruable experience of the other.

We shall come back to this feature of the psychotherapeutic relationship in connection with the notion of orthogonality.

Personal identity and sociality

The importance of the psychotherapeutic relationship emerges from a consideration of the person as a socially embedded network of processes, as a person-in-relation with other people, and from the ensuing consideration that the process of socialization involves the development of different social selves, or a 'community of selves' in the words of Mair (1977).

Such a view – shared by the social constructionist movement (Gergen, 1985) and by the therapeutic approaches based upon it (McNamee and Gergen, 1992) – is coherent with Kelly's thought not only in the sense that other people are important for the testing of one's construing system and its resulting development, but also in the sense of Bateson (1976) when he writes that

> conventional epistemology . . . boggles at the realization that 'Properties' are only differences and exist only in a context, only in relationship. We abstract from relationship and from the experiences of interaction to create 'objects' and endow them with characteristics. We likewise boggle at the proposition that our own character is only real in relationship. We abstract from the experience of interaction and difference to create a 'self' which shall be 'real' or thingish, even without relationship.

Buber's (1958) 'I–Thou philosophy' appears extremely relevant in this connection. Buber writes that personality is neither simply an individual matter nor simply a social product, but a function of relationship happening in the 'sphere of between' (Chiari and Nuzzo, 2001).

Personal change and the psychotherapeutic relationship

We agree therefore with Leitner (1985) when he affirms that 'psychotherapy may be defined as the attempt to change pathological ways of organizing experience through the use of an interpersonal relationship'. The psychotherapeutic relationship is not a means to the end of a change, but the social medium in which a personal change happens. It follows that there are not particular personal problems that better than others can be dealt with by working on the psychotherapeutic relationship. It is our opinion that every disorder can be understood as a personal difficulty in relating with other people and therefore can be dealt with in the ambit of the client–therapist relationship, even those complaints presented by clients as determined by something wrong in their character rather than linked to the sphere of interpersonal processes.

Orthogonal psychotherapeutic relationships

Clients – consistently with Kelly's choice corollary – usually seek to structure their relationships with therapists by resorting to the tried dimensions they use in relationship with other people. The notion of transference arises from such observations. Whether they succeed in this endeavour or not also depends on whether therapists can lend themselves to be construed in such a way. If this is the case, clients can easily anticipate their relation with therapists, but change is not facilitated because the very same relationship that implies problems for them is reproposed. Sometimes inexperienced psychotherapists are eager to make and maintain a relationship with their clients and thus favour such a therapeutically ineffective relationship.

Rather, therapists' ability consists in their capability of understanding clients' tried constructions in order to extricate themselves from them and present themselves to their clients so as to encourage the pursuit of new ways of relating. In Kelly's (1955/1991b, p. 664/ p. 76) terms, 'the therapist enacts a series of carefully chosen parts and seeks to have the client develop adequate role relationships to the figures portrayed'. In other words, 'through the construal of the therapist, the patient has an opportunity for in vivo experimentation with alternative ways of construing other people in her life' (Soldz, 1993, p. 191).

The therapist's construction of the client's transference is a necessary starting point. However, the general framework is represented by the view that an interpersonal relationship is a reality that cannot be reduced to what takes place independently within each of its members. When personal construct psychotherapists construe their clients' processes, they are aware that those processes are such within the clients' relationship with them: they assume a reflexive attitude and regard themselves as an integrating and fundamental part of the relationship. The client and the therapist bring their own structures into the psychotherapeutic relationship, and the realities that are co-constructed there bear the stamp of those structures. Incidentally, a similar understanding of the shared responsibility in the shaping of the psychotherapeutic relationship is one of the principles of Hoffman's (1998) dialectical-constructivist view of the psychoanalytic process.

A careful and continuous consideration from therapists of their relationship with the client as a relation of complementarity resulting in a co-constructed reality can allow them to relate with the client by assuming an orthogonal position, and hence can facilitate the making of a relationship that is likely to make the client's problem-related constructs not applicable to the therapist. By orthogonal position we mean the therapists' ways of proposing themselves to the client so that clients cannot adequately construe them under the poles of the constructs they usually apply to other people and that are implied in the disorder, nor under the contrasting poles: clients have to resort to different constructs, the axes of reference of which are perpendicular to the first ones.

On the basis of such understanding the personal construct psychotherapist can hope to facilitate a relationship that at the same time allows the client to elaborate new construct dimensions and permits both the client and the therapist to maintain an optimal therapeutic distance. The attainment of an optimal distance concerns the whole relationship, not only one of its members (that is, the therapist). Within a psychotherapeutic relationship characterized by an optimal therapeutic distance, the client's core role constructs are not directly involved in the relationship with the therapist and are more likely to be explored and worked out.

In this connection, the personal construct psychotherapist can draw from a repertoire of techniques, most of which fit into the conversational flow between client and therapist. The question of whether psychotherapeutic change derives from the client–therapist relationship or from the utilization of specific techniques becomes meaningless in the light of the awareness that all techniques derive their efficacy in the context of the psychotherapeutic relationship and, at the same time, contribute to its shaping.

CHAPTER FIVE

Encountering an other: experiential personal construct psychotherapy

LM LEITNER, AJ FAIDLEY, DONALD DOMINICI,
CAROL HUMPHREYS, VALERIE LOEFFLER,
MARK SCHLUTSMEYER, JILL THOMAS

> Those who wish to be
> Must put aside the alienation
> Get on with the fascination
> The real relation
> The underlying theme
>
> From the song *Limelight* by the band Rush

The above lines from Rush's song about the superficiality of the relationships that often accompany fame speak to some of the key tenets of experiential personal construct psychotherapy (EPCP): this approach is rooted in the idea that the fabric of meaning in our lives is woven in the deeply intimate and meaningful relationships we cultivate with others. These close relationships, or ROLE relationships (described below), are developed through the sharing and mutual understanding of those aspects of ourselves that we hold most dearly – those most central to our view of who we are. EPCP involves working with ROLE relationships. The therapist and client form a unique ROLE relationship, through which they experientially explore the client's process of engaging in and/or retreating from ROLE relationships. EPCP postulates that, at one and the same time, ROLE relationships are a source of joy and awe and involve great risk and potential terror. After all, if we open ourselves deeply to others and feel the awe of caring for them and being cared for by them, we also are deeply open to having the depths of our being disconfirmed by the other (Leitner, 1985; Leitner and Faidley, 1995). It is this terror of undertaking such a deep personal risk that makes (in the words of Rush) putting aside 'the alienation' and embracing 'the fascination' of connecting with another person such a difficult endeavour.

This chapter is an overview of EPCP, including clinical aspects of the approach that are important in its practice. First, we will summarize the theoretical background and philosophical assumptions that underlie EPCP. Next, we will discuss the nature and structure of diagnosis from the EPCP framework. The following section will explore the use of symbolism in EPCP and explain the concept of levels of awareness. Transference, countertransference, and the validation and invalidation of the therapist's interventions will be discussed. We conclude with a discussion of the importance of creativity and therapeutic artistry in the practice of EPCP. Each of these facets of EPCP is essential to paint a vivid picture of this perspective and how it is put into clinical practice.

Theoretical and philosophical background of EPCP

The theoretical underpinnings of EPCP stem from George Kelly's (1955/1991a/1991b) personal construct psychotherapy. In particular, EPCP underscores the relational, experiential, and existential aspects of Kelly's theory, which distinguish it from more cognitive-behavioural approaches (Leitner, 1995). In its emphasis on understanding human beings in the context of their relationships, EPCP shares similarities with Buber's (1958) notion of I–thou relationships and Surrey's (1991) self-in-relation model of women's development. It deals with the very core of clients' meaning-making processes and clients' understanding of their existence in the world. Thus, it shares similarities to existential approaches to psychotherapy (for example, Yalom, 1980). Since EPCP is an elaboration of Kelly's work, we will focus on the underlying assumptions of his theory.

Kelly's (1955/1991a/1991b) psychological theory is rooted in the philosophical standpoint of constructive alternativism: there are an infinite number of ways in which a person may construe the world and a person's constructs are always subject to revision. In other words, Kelly explains, no one has to paint him or herself into a corner by the way he or she construes the world. We construe the world through anticipation or prediction of future events. These predictions then are tested against the actual events that occur, and are either found to be consistent with these events (validated) or inconsistent with them (invalidated). With the sociality corollary, Kelly adds to his basic theory the idea that a person may play a role in another person's social process by construing the other's construction process. Stated simply, this means that the more completely you understand the core meanings and experiences of another person, the more extensive the role is that you play in your relationship with that person (see Leitner, 1985, for a more complete discussion of this idea.) Thus, Kelly's definition of a ROLE (as in a ROLE relationship) involves actively construing the construction process of another person. In EPCP, the word ROLE is capitalized when used in this way, to distinguish Kelly's use of the word from its other common meanings.

One important implication of the sociality corollary is that the 'awe-ful' (Leitner and Faidley, 1995) joy found in ROLE relationships brings essential meaning to our lives. Similarly, when one's core meanings, those that are the very foundation of being alive, are invalidated, the anxiety, fear and threat involved in feeling pressured to change can be an experience of 'terror' (Leitner, 1985). Thus, the wonder and beauty of intimate, meaningful connection comes only at the risk of the invalidation of the constructs that are the core structure of experience. The alternative to taking this risk is to retreat from ROLE relationships. In so doing, one avoids the potential terror by choosing safety, emptiness and alienation. Experiential personal construct psychotherapy asserts that all of our experiences and actions reveal both the need to connect and the need to retreat from connection.

A major goal of therapy in EPCP is helping the client understand how he engages in and retreats from ROLE relationships. One way this is accomplished is through an awareness of the process of the client–therapist relationship as it unfolds. For example, a client may retreat from a ROLE relationship with the therapist through physical or psychological distancing (for example, not showing up for sessions, not fully engaging with the therapist in the session). Retreating protects the client from the terror of disconfirmation that may occur should she get too close to the therapist. In this way the client–therapist relationship becomes a useful model for exploring how the client handles engaging in ROLE relationships. We will discuss other aspects of the client–therapist relationship later. First, however, we turn to the diagnostic features of EPCP.

Diagnosing human meaning-making

Theoretical basis for the EPCP diagnostic system

According to experiential personal construct theory, a good diagnostic system has several important characteristics. First, it is *theoretically based*. That is, it is derived from a theory of human nature and pathology. The fundamental tenet of EPCP is that all people struggle with negotiating a balance between the terror and richness of engaging in meaningful personal relationships (ROLE relationships) versus the safety and emptiness of retreating from them (Leitner and Faidley, 1995). Pathology is conceptualized as an impoverishment in the meaningfulness of life caused by excessive retreating from ROLE relationships. Therefore, the EPCP diagnostic system distinguishes the ways people deal with the complex dilemma of engaging versus retreating from these essential relationships.

Second, a good diagnostic system is *transitive* in nature (Kelly, 1955/1991a). It not only describes where clients are now, but also suggests ways in which they can grow in the immediate future. In other words, it has treatment implications. Because of its constructivist (as opposed to realist) assumptions, the EPCP diagnostic system does not aim to diagnose clients 'correctly' or discover the 'true' essence of their pathology. Rather, it provides a framework by which therapists can develop whatever professional constructions might be useful in their work with an individual client (Leitner and Faidley, 1999). If those constructions do not prove useful, they can be discarded in favour of new ones. Similarly, as clients evolve, their 'diagnosis' is allowed to evolve with them.

Third, a good diagnostic system helps therapists understand their clients better. It assists therapists to form an empathic construal of the clients' meaning systems. The very process of diagnosis is often used by therapists to disengage from meaningful interactions with their clients. For example, basing diagnoses on symptoms (as is currently done in the DSM-IV-TR) and basing treatment on diagnoses can be a retreat from knowing and connecting with clients (Leitner, 1985). No diagnostic system can prevent therapists from using it as a means to disengage from their clients, but the EPCP diagnostic system is designed to facilitate therapists' construal of their clients' construction processes (Kelly, 1955/1991a/1991b), the essential ingredient in forming ROLE relationships.

Fourth, instead of summarizing clients as a list of disparaging traits, a good diagnostic system allows for a description of strengths as well as struggles. While this helps the therapist to be more empathetically attuned to the client, it also helps the client by avoiding stigmatizing labels and the dehumanization that results from being reduced to a disorder. When clients can recognize themselves in a diagnostic description and feel both understood and empowered by it, they learn to value themselves and their experience – an important ingredient in successful psychotherapy (Leitner and Faidley, 2002). An EPCP diagnosis is one that therapists should feel comfortable sharing with their clients – or even constructing with them.

The role of symptoms in EPCP theory

Traditional symptoms (e.g. anxiety, depression, and hallucinations) play a different role in EPCP conceptualizations than they do in other systems. While some theoretical orientations view symptoms as problems to be eliminated, EPCP views symptoms as important messages to us, from us, about us. Symptoms often are ways that clients communicate their struggles with ROLE relationships to themselves and others (Leitner and

Faidley, 1995). This symptomatic signal is important because it directs attention to injuries in our relational life and resultant retreats from meaningful connections. Unfortunately, it is possible for symptoms to be eliminated without actually enabling the client to engage in true ROLE relating with others (Leitner, 1985). When this happens, the client acts in more socially appropriate and apparently 'healthy' ways without experiencing any lessening of the internal emptiness that comes from a life lived without meaningful connections. Experiential personal construct psychotherapy aims to help clients form ROLE relationships, and considers the reduction of symptoms that often accompanies meeting this goal an added bonus – but only if it does not impair one's ability to listen to internal experience.

Experiential personal construct psychotherapy diagnostic system

Experiential personal construct psychotherapy uses a three axial diagnostic system to describe and distinguish ways that people engage in ROLE relating, successfully and unsuccessfully (Leitner, Faidley and Celentana, 2000). The first axis describes developmental/structural arrests that can occur in response to traumatic experiences in the formative years. The second axis describes several common interpersonal styles that are used to reduce a person's experience of the emptiness of non-ROLE relating. The third axis describes ways a person can facilitate or retreat from ROLE relationships.

Structural arrests – axis 1

The notion of developmental/structural arrests is founded on the premise that the fundamental task of childhood is to develop the very basic constructs that are essential for later ROLE relating. If a person is traumatized during these formative years, the process of meaning-making may be arrested so that the person continues to experience the world in simplistic and concrete ways instead of developing more abstract and complex meanings. The three basic constructions essential for the formation of ROLE relationships are *self versus other, self–other permanence,* and *self–other constancy.* People who have not developed the *self versus other* distinction can experience a variety of problems, including the inability to recognize a clear separation between themselves and others, 'psychotic' terror around connection, and the inability to assess the impact of their being on others. *Self–other permanence* is the experience of the self and other remaining intact and enduring despite physical distance. Without a sense of another's permanence one may become extremely fearful of any separation and feel absolutely alone when the other is absent. *Self–other constancy* is the experience of self and other as stable despite variations in mood, personality and behaviour. Without *self–other constancy* an angry other may be experienced as completely rejecting or uniformly bad. Similarly, any experience of the self as less than wholesome results in convictions of one's absolute wickedness.

Interpersonal components – axis 2

The second axis of the EPCP diagnostic system describes the interpersonal styles that people often use in their attempts to dispel the emptiness of a life without ROLE relationships. Connections sought for the sake of reducing one's sense of emptiness (instead of from a true sense of caring for the other) are not true ROLE relationships because the other is used as a means to an end. There are several interpersonal styles associated with this kind of relating. People with *undispersed dependencies* place their dependencies on a limited number of others, leaving them open to the devastating feeling of abandonment that results when the other cannot meet all of their needs. People with *excessively dispersed dependencies* allow many people access to the most central aspects of their lives without evaluating the other's potential to invalidate that core. People who *avoid dependencies* do not allow others access to their core and view their own needs for affirmation as signs of weakness. People can also *physically distance* themselves from others (for example, by literally fleeing from others when connection is imminent), or *psychologically distance* themselves from others (for example, by objectifying others or denying their basic human rights).

Experiential components – axis 3

The nine experiential components of the EPCP diagnostic system are descriptions of ways that people can construe others' construction processes – the essential ingredient in ROLE relating. As such, each is an elaboration of empathy or an action taken to test the accuracy of one's empathy (Leitner and Pfenninger, 1994). Assessing an individual on each of these nine components will reveal areas of strength and areas of limitations. *Discrimination* is the ability to construe differences between people and evaluate the impact of those differences on the potential for a ROLE relationship. *Flexibility* is the ability to apply different constructions to different relationships, and simultaneously to hold one's own meanings and those of another in awareness. *Creativity* is the ability to create new ways of seeing self and other as relationships evolve. *Responsibility* is the willingness to examine one's own meanings and their implications for others. *Openness* is the willingness to reconstrue when invalidated. *Commitment* is the willingness to validate another's meanings over time. *Courage* is the ability to act in spite of fear. *Forgiveness* is the process of reconstruing self and other so that major injuries do not hinder one from developing future ROLE relationships. *Reverence* is the experience of awe that results from the awareness that one is affirming another's core meanings (Leitner, Faidley and Celentana, 2000).

Using the diagnostic system in psychotherapy

One particularly important premise of personal construct psychology is that people engage life in ways that make the most sense to them. Therefore, this diagnostic system is not intended to elaborate the ways that people maladaptively or illogically engage in relationships with others. Rather, it is designed to help the therapist recognize the ways that people who have been terribly injured in relationships can, often very creatively, make their own worlds as tolerable as possible. For example, behavioural choices that may look odd or maladaptive to the therapist may be excellent ways in which clients protect themselves from devastating invalidation. It is only as therapists truly empathize with clients' creative constructions of their worlds that clients will allow their therapists the moral authority to work with them toward change.

Therapist–client ROLE relationship, symbolism and levels of awareness

Ideally, encountering an other in the therapy room involves coming to understand the process of the other, thus creating an intimate and power-ful relationship (a ROLE relationship) with the other. In experiential personal construct psychotherapy, as in other forms of therapy, the thera-peutic relationship is at the core of the work of therapy. However, unlike some other therapies, in EPCP the relationship is not viewed solely as a means to an end but also as an end in itself. In EPCP the ability to form ROLE relationships is an indication of optimal functioning (Leitner and Pfenninger, 1994) as it signals a fulfilling richness and depth to life that encompasses both the awful and the awe-ful (Leitner and Faidley, 1995) nature of human connectedness.

Although developing the ability to engage in ROLE relationships is a goal for the client in EPCP, the encounter in the therapy room is decided-ly *not* one sided. Just as the therapist hopes clients will risk the terrors of engaging in ROLE relationships by opening up their most central process-es, the therapist must also be willing to be open in this way to the client. While therapists and clients play different roles in the relationship, such that therapists are not sharing of themselves in the same way as clients, the therapist, in order to engage in the relationship, must be fully present in the room. As this presence requires one's most central processes to be exposed, the therapist also is risking in the relationship. By taking the risk, both are open to the experience of joy, reverence and healing inherent in ROLE relating.

The therapist invites the client into a ROLE relationship using a credulous approach (Kelly, 1955/1991a; Rigdon, Clark and Hershgold, 1993). With this approach, the therapist momentarily suspends his own ways of understanding the world so that he may see the validity of the ways the client understands things. Further, the therapist accepts these understandings as the client's personal truth. If the therapist is able to accomplish this shift in perspective, the client may then feel understood, and thereby freer to explore further these meanings and their implication as well as to test alternative meanings. However, in order to adopt this credulous approach, in order to engage in an EPCP process of coming to know the meanings of another, one must first understand what is meant by the notion of a construct or personal meaning.

According to Kelly, a construct is a bipolar unit of meaning inherent in which are both the similarities and contrasts of experience. This is often expressed in words (for example, 'good' versus 'terrible'; 'lovable' versus 'hateful'), but Kelly is careful to state that constructs are not the same as ideas, concepts or words, and that construing should not be 'confounded with verbal formulation' (Kelly, 1955/1991a, p. 51/p. 35). Constructs are meanings, not literal or verbal but experiential. Therefore, words symbolize constructs but are not the constructs themselves. This is an important distinction as it has significant implications for the therapeutic encounter.

For instance, when a therapist approaches the client in a manner consistent with the notion of construct as concept or idea, the therapy easily can become a cognitive one. This cognitive orientation toward the client, while possibly allowing for in-depth exploration of one aspect of the client, misses other fundamental pieces of the client's existence. A cognitive focus ignores the more felt aspects of the client's experience and tends to downplay the contextual, or lived, nature of human experience. Similarly, if the client were to see the therapist through these same cognitive lenses, the client also would have a very limited understanding of the therapist, thus missing out on the intimacy and power associated with knowing a person more fully.

Also problematic, when the therapist approaches the therapy without making the distinction between constructs and the words used to symbolize them, the focus of the therapeutic work tends to shift to surface content versus underlying process. When words are mistaken as the meanings themselves, the words begin to take on primary importance. Much attention is then placed on understanding exactly *what* the client is saying rather than grasping *how* the client is communicating fundamental aspects of the experience of being in the world. While content is not irrelevant, a content-focused therapy is ultimately limiting to the development of a therapeutic ROLE relationship that can be used as a living experiment for wrestling with issues that also are present in outside relationships.

To exemplify the restricted perspective resulting from not appreciating the difference between words and constructs, one might make the comparison to viewing a piece of visual art. If one views a piece of art attending to only one surface level of the work (for example, the forms on the canvas), one sees only soup cans or a girl in a purple dress, for example. Ideally one recognizes that there is more to a painting than the literal forms on the canvas, that the work carries a message that cannot be understood simply by identifying the subject as 'can' or 'girl'. Then, instead of Warhol's 'cans', one might see disgust with American commercialization and capitalism. Likewise, through Klimt's girl in purple, one might appreciate a calm, entrancing innocence. The restricted view of the artwork, like the restricted view of the client, misses the more powerful, deeply felt meanings that are revealed through symbols.

To aid in understanding the crucial distinction between concept and construct it is helpful to explore how constructs can be symbolized non-verbally. There are many meanings that are more accurately captured in symbols other than words. Some meanings do not take the form of discursive symbolism, which involves a linear arrangement of symbols (words) that have fixed meaning independent of context (Guthrie, 1991; Faidley, 2001). Rather, the meaning only can be fully expressed by the whole of an experience or a person, or by a poem or a painting. This is an example of presentational symbolism, which involves loose, non-linear, contextually bound, integrated wholes and is often experienced as intuition or insight (Guthrie, 1991; Faidley, 2001).

Presentational symbolism also may be a sign of structural arrest, or a freezing of the meaning-making process referred to earlier (Faidley, 2001). People who have experienced great injury or trauma, especially early in life, may halt the process of meaning-making in some areas. The person continues to interact with the world and is thus engaged in the process of meaning-making, often with implications for the arrested meanings. New meanings are not experienced at the verbal level, but many of the meanings resulting from the person's ongoing experience with the world do exist but are symbolized presentationally rather than discursively. These meanings may also exist at a lower level of awareness (Kelly, 1955/1991a; Leitner, 1999). The EPCP concept of levels of awareness addresses the fact that much of the construing process occurs on a tacit level, outside of conscious awareness.

With structural arrest, a major role of the EPC psychotherapist is to come to understand the meanings being symbolized and to help the client create some kind of alternate symbolization in order to thaw the meaning-making process (Faidley and Leitner, 2000; Faidley, 2001). Moreover, as some of these meanings exist at lower levels of awareness, an essential aspect of therapy is to provide the relational context that helps raise the level of awareness of these meanings. In so doing, the therapist eventually may help clients to understand more explicitly the meanings that form the foundation of the ways they engage in and retreat from relationships. Although here we are specifically referring to therapy with clients with severe disturbances, the role of the therapist in EPCP is consistent across therapeutic contexts. The therapist engages the client with the credulous approach, inviting the client to engage with the therapist in a deeply meaningful ROLE relationship. In the context of this relationship, the therapist and client seek to appreciate the ways the other understands the world by seeing through the symbols, verbal and non-verbal, to the meanings they represent. In the context of coming to know one another in this way, clients are then more able to understand and explore their personal meanings and to raise previously tacit constructions to higher levels of awareness so to allow for future elaboration, change and growth. The therapist, being deeply engaged in this process and in the relationship as well, will also be changed by the experience of having this encounter with the client.

Transference and countertransference

The client's experience of the therapist, like all experiences, manifests the struggle over creating or avoiding ROLE relationships. During the development of the therapeutic relationship, the client makes predictions about the therapist based on previously held constructions of past relationships. Quite often, predictions are born of relational wounds from the past that are transferred to the therapeutic relationship (Leitner, 1997). In so doing, the client is retreating from relational intimacy (by believing the therapist will respond in the injuring ways others have) and moving toward relational intimacy (by bringing the wound into the here-and-now relationship where it can be encountered and explored).

A primary goal of EPCP is to engage and use the client's experience of transference within the therapy relationship as a way to transform the client's current relational experiences (Leitner and Thomas, 2003). The therapist enters the relationship with the intent of recognizing potential transference and begins by eliciting the client's relational history as well as a history of past therapy. Histories allow the current therapist to speculate about the ways the client may relate to the therapist. For example, the therapist might worry about a client's willingness to commit to a ROLE relationship with the therapist if, in the past, the client has started therapy enthusiastically only to terminate in disappointment after a few sessions. The therapist might engage the transference material by predicting its presence ahead of time (for example, 'it will be interesting to see what you do when you are disappointed in me as time goes by') and inviting the client to explore the experience of the therapist (for example, 'You seem disappointed in me as you have been with other therapists. The temptation might be to terminate therapy as you did those other times. I wonder if, rather than doing that, can we talk some about the experience of disappointment. What might happen, do you think, if you were to openly tell me why you're disappointed in me?').

Therapists are also active members of the therapeutic dyad and have also suffered relational wounds. They bring their own struggles over relational connection into the therapy ('countertransference') and need to recognize, engage, and take responsibility for their countertransference. If they do not, they will experience either excessive distance ('therapeutic strangers') or excessive fusion ('therapeutic unity'). Experientially, 'therapeutic strangers' occurs when the therapist is unable to experience the world the way the client does. In contrast, 'therapeutic unity' is experienced when the client's struggles become the therapist's.

Both stances are deviations from experiencing an optimal therapeutic distance with a client (Leitner, 1995). Optimal therapeutic distance is a blend of connection and separation that Leitner (1995) describes as the therapist being close enough to experience the client's experience yet separate enough to recognize that it is the client's experience and not the therapist's. Ideally, therapists monitor themselves to recognize deviations from optimal therapeutic distance. If they can explore, personally, the painful issues underlying their retreat from the client, their experience of countertransference can facilitate greater connection (Leitner, 1997).

A clinical vignette will illustrate optimal therapeutic distance, transference and countertransference.

During early sessions, Sydney and his therapist, Julie, explored Sydney's inability to sustain intimate relationships with women. They identified Sydney's pattern of desperately seeking an intimate connection with a woman but then pulling back in fear by objectifying the woman rather than relating to her as a whole person, with desires, thoughts, experiences and feelings of her own. Before long Julie and Sydney saw the pattern in action. While Sydney repeatedly mentioned that he wished his girlfriend was more like Julie, he began arriving late or failing appointments. When Julie addressed his feelings about therapy, Sydney broke down in tears. He shared his fears about the closeness they were developing and his concern that she would be angry and reject him. He added that he had never opened up like this to a woman before. In the following sessions Sydney expressed his deepest feelings of fear and shame regarding childhood abuse. He occasionally compared the women in his life to Julie, always idealizing Julie. He fantasized about dating Julie and told her she was 'the one' for him. Julie was threatened by the intensity of Sydney's idealizations of her. She retreated from him, thinking of him as someone to fix, to change, to work on, to teach. Her withdrawal resulted in their becoming 'therapeutic strangers'. Not surprisingly, Sydney withdrew as before, missing a session and being late.

The therapy did not change until Julie identified her countertransference. She admitted to herself that she was resentful and angry over what felt like objectification by the client. She requested additional supervision, discussed the countertransference in her personal therapy, and looked more deeply at her experiences with men who had objectified her. Finally, Julie readdressed the subject with Sydney, inviting him to relate his experience of her during the past few weeks. Sydney shared deep feelings of betrayal. They discussed how distancing from each other had harmed the ROLE relationship. In the following sessions, they worked together to engage the transference while Julie worked to remain aware of her countertransference.

Creative artistry

Experiential personal construct psychotherapy offers few prescribed techniques or therapy 'tricks'. Creativity is therefore an essential aspect of the therapy process and an important therapist attribute.

The creativity cycle

Kelly (1955/1991a/1991b) viewed therapy as a cycle of creativity that involves moving between loosened and tightened construing. The process is moderated by the ongoing validation and invalidation of existing constructs. For example, a father who rigidly construes his daughter as a 'helpless child', despite visible evidence of her growing independence, likely will encounter a significant power struggle with her. In order to help him in therapy, the therapist must be flexible enough both to engage with the father at the tightened point of his creativity cycle, and also embark with him in a process of exploring how he might safely construe his daughter in other ways.

Just as client changes in therapy can be understood in terms of movement within the creativity cycle, therapists' engagement in the therapy process involves continual creative movement. In the early phases of therapy, the therapist may take an open and exploratory approach in relating to the client. As therapy progresses, the therapist's constructions of the client will probably tighten. Therapists can preserve the flow of the creativity cycle by maintaining an open attunement to clients' validation or invalidation of interventions. Failure to do so may stifle therapy.

For example, if a client is very invalidating, the therapist might interpret the behaviour as 'resistance' or 'hostility' and see therapy as hopeless (see Leitner and Dill-Standiford, 1993 for a more complete discussion of resistance in therapy). Alternatively, a therapist may be 'snowed' by a client who validates every word that falls from the therapist's mouth, and may fail to understand the client's desperate need to please others. In both cases, the therapist might instead view these validations and invalidations as an invitation from the client to be construed differently. Attention to such feedback from clients assures that the creativity cycle continues and the therapy relationship is preserved in spite of apparent 'blocks' in the treatment process.

Another way therapists can maintain creative reconstrual in therapy is by attending to how their own construction of the therapy is affecting the process. If a therapist too rigidly construes the therapy process, therapy may have a rote, clichéd flavour. If a therapist too loosely construes the process, therapy may feel directionless, off-the-cuff, or inappropriately touchy-feely. The former problem may be more common in the current practice of therapy given the zeitgeist of manualized and empirically validated treatments. On the other hand, continuing the flow of creativity may at times require the therapist to tighten her construal of therapy in ways that seem counterintuitive to creativity. For example, a therapist might experiment by increasing structure, trying out prescribed techniques, more clearly articulating therapy goals, or developing a more distinct vision of his model for therapy. Leitner and Faidley (1999) have discussed several ways to foster creative engagement in therapy, such as making time for aloneness, fantasizing, loving one's work, trying on roles, exposing oneself to literature and the arts, leading a balanced life, reducing time pressures, focusing on process, and seeing client growth.

The art of therapy

Maintaining creativity in therapy includes being open to a wide variety of possible interventions in the therapy room as clients symbolize central aspects of their experience in a variety of verbal and non-verbal ways (Faidley and Leitner, 2000). For example, a client's discomfort with others may be verbally hidden, but may find expression in body positioning or physical pain. While verbal attempts to access such core meanings in therapy may fail, clients may address these meanings through involvement in more body-focused activity, such as Gestalt exercises, sensate focus, or Tai

Chi (Leitner, Celentana and Faidley, 1998). Similarly, client and therapist expressions in therapy may take a variety of artistic forms, such as drawings, poems or performance art (Thomas and Schlutsmeyer, 2002, discuss factors to consider in using such art forms in therapy).

It is not necessarily relevant whether the creative work in therapy leads to tightened or loosened construing, or whether it involves verbal or nonverbal construing. It is also not necessarily relevant whether the client or the therapist have artistic skill in poetry, dance, or the fine arts. The real importance of creativity is that it touches and validates the client's core constructs. These core meanings can be reached and avoided in a variety of creative ways. For example, a therapist encouraged a client to share his artistic expressions during therapy. One day the client brought a guitar and performed a song he had written. While the work initially focused on the meaning of the song and the creative process, the pair later discussed the more central issue of the client's process of sharing his music. When the client discussed feeling a deep need to be liked and admired by others, the therapist wondered aloud whether sharing his art in therapy afforded a chance to feel that kind of admiration. They were then able to discuss the deeper implications of the client's relationship to the therapist. In this case, the creative exchange fostered movement toward core meanings.

Creativity in ROLE relationships

A part of all creative endeavours in therapy is deepening the process of forming a ROLE relationship. This happens when a client can access profoundly personal aspects of experience, face the risk involved in sharing that experience with the therapist, and emerge with a sense of core validation. A therapist who is sensitive to ways that a client is retreating from ROLE relationship material can play a part in creating a safe atmosphere for such material to emerge. Leitner (2001) has referred to this process as 'evoking experiential truths'. The therapist credulously and sensitively attends to the client's experience and speaks to those aspects of that experience that seem most central to the client's struggle. Leitner suggests that listening and responding in this way is more similar to creative artistry than technical application. Gifted therapists create a safe atmosphere for ROLE material by using poetic language, metaphors, and symbols, and by making attempts to connect past traumas to present experiences.

Creatively attending to ROLE material in this way may be as simple as maintaining a focus on issues that clients have alluded to but directed attention away from.

A therapist met with a client who early in a session vaguely referred to a troublesome past relationship but spent much of the rest of the session attributing her stress and anxiety to 'bad nerves'. The therapist made a comment that sometimes it is hard for someone to have 'good nerves' if they have been through difficult relationships and seen horrible things. The client then began to talk about frequent domestic violence that she witnessed in her home as a child. At the end of the session the client commented that she was amazed at what she had said during the session, as she had never before told anyone about what she had seen as a child. She also remarked that she felt a great burden had been lifted off her. Helping the client address ROLE relationship material involved choosing words that validated her initial sense that her nerves had 'had it' and helping her draw links between this feeling and past horrors she had experienced.

The challenge of evoking experiential truths can place the highest of demands on a therapist's creativity. Core experiences may lie at a low level of awareness or are very difficult for the client to address because they are associated with major invalidation. Unless the therapist is able to anticipate the potential discomfort that may arise for the client, the therapist may collaborate with the client in retreating from ROLE material. If this happens, the therapist may perpetuate the very process that leads the client into distress during daily life. It is all too easy for an entire session or even course of therapy to take place on a completely peripheral level. The therapist's job, then, is more like that of a poet than a storyteller. The poet is cautious not to be caught up in thick descriptions but attempts to travel straight to the heart of matters and present the world as it is experienced, often in its most troubling and deeply felt forms. The creative experiential personal construct therapist seeks these same ideals and attempts to touch the very core of the living process that is the other.

CHAPTER SIX

A personal construct approach to narrative and post-modern therapies

LUIS BOTELLA, SERGI CORBELLA, TARY GÓMEZ,
OLGA HERRERO, MERITXELL PACHECO

Common themes in narrative and post-modern therapies

What is a narrative therapy about?

According to Combs and Friedman (2004, p. 137), 'narrative therapy takes its name from the post-structuralist notion that meaning is carried in the retelling and re-enacting of stories'. Every school of psychotherapy has always worked with client narratives in its preferred way. In fact, if *narrative* is equated to *storytelling*, it is hard to conceive of any form of human meaningful conversation that does not involve the telling of some form of story – let alone a personally, emotionally and biographically rich conversation such as a therapeutic one. In recent decades different psychotherapeutic approaches became increasingly aware of such a 'narrative turn'. Contemporary *psychodynamic psychotherapists* work explicitly with patient narratives by means of the *core conflictual relational theme* approach (Luborsky, 1984; see Book, 2004, for a review). Family therapists are also turning to narrative and social constructionist notions instead of the more mechanistically oriented ones – derived from general systems theory or cybernetics – which used to be the dominant cornerstone of *systemic therapy*. Some forms of *cognitive therapy* have also evolved from their originally rational and intellectual emphasis to an explicitly narrative focus (see, for example, Gonçalves, Henriques and Machado, 2004). Also, the contribution of client narrative expression in *experiential therapies* has been highlighted both in clinical practice and by means of research studies (see Angus et al., 2004). Our own approach to *constructivist therapy* (see Botella, 2001; Botella and Herrero, 2000; Botella et al., 2004), which will be briefly discussed later in this chapter, explicitly incorporates the significance of narrative processes in the construction and reconstruction of identity and psychological distress.

However, *working with client narratives* in psychotherapy does not necessarily entail that one is practising a form of *narrative therapy* – in the same sense that, for instance, working with client behaviour in psychotherapy does not necessarily entail that one is practising a form of behaviour therapy, because behaviour can be approached in a host of different ways. Thus, a more restrictive definition is needed in order to avoid the extreme looseness of equating narrative therapy to any form of therapy. In the remainder of this section we will briefly sketch and synthesize two such definitional attempts.

First, according to one of the pioneers of narrative therapy *strictu sensu* (White, 1995, p. 75), a narrative therapy is about, among other things:

(a) Options for the telling and re-telling of, for the performance and re-performance of, the preferred stories of people's lives.

(b) Rendering the unique, the contradictory, the contingent, and, at times, the aberrant events of people's lives significant as alternative presents.

(c) Rich description in that alternative stories of people's presents are linked with the alternative stories of people's pasts, a linking of stories across time through lives.

(d) Rich description in that it provides for the linking of the alternative stories of people's pasts and presents with the stories of the lives of others – a linking of stories between lives according to shared themes that speak to purposes, values and commitments in common.

A second and compatible synthetic definition of the main themes in narrative therapy is discussed by Polkinghorne (2004), and includes the following:

- emphasis on client strengths;
- a view of clients and therapists as partners;
- adaptation of a constructionist approach to meaning;
- emphasis on the narrative or story form of meaning.

White's and Polkinghorne's lists of themes in narrative therapy resonate with parallel attempts to define the main themes in the so-called *post-modern psychotherapies*, which are the main focus of the next section.

What is a post-modern therapy about?

Polkinghorne's (1992) already classical definition of *post-modern thought* differs from more nihilistic ones in including neopragmatic criteria for choosing among knowledge claims. Thus, Polkinghorne's notion of post-modern epistemology includes the following four basic themes:

- foundationlessness;
- fragmentariness;

- constructivism;
- neopragmatism (see Botella, 1995 for a more detailed discussion).

Foundationlessness, according to Polkinghorne (1992), refers to the notion that we human beings have no direct access to reality, but only to the product of our constructions. Thus, human knowledge is inevitably speculative, since we have no definite epistemic foundation on which to build it.

Fragmentariness refers to the post-modern emphasis on the local and situated, instead of the general and totalizing. According to Polkinghorne (1992, p. 149), 'knowledge should be concerned with these local and specific occurrences, not with the search for context-free general laws.' The post-modern notion of the self as a polyphonic narrative (see Hermans, Kempen and van Loon, 1992; Hermans, 2004) is a good example of this local emphasis.

Constructivism as Polkinghorne (1992) uses the term is closely related to foundationlessness, and refers to the notion that:

> Human knowledge is not a mirrored reflection of reality, neither the reality of surface chaos nor that of (if they exist) universal structures. Human knowledge is a construction built from the cognitive processes (which mainly operate out of awareness) and embodied interactions with the world of material objects, others and the self. (Polkinghorne, 1992, p. 150).

Polkinghorne aptly notes that the three themes of foundationlessness, fragmentariness, and constructivism may generate a relativistic epistemology. So far, it is possible to assert that no knowledge claim can be privileged, but this radical relativism leaves one unable to act upon the world, to make choices, to take stands. Thus, a fourth theme should be included if post-modern thought is to avoid solipsism and nihilism: the theme of *neopragmatism.*

Neopragmatism, according to Polkinghorne (1992), concentrates on local and applied knowledge. Polkinghorne's emphasis on pragmatic and situated knowledge is common to other proponents of a post-modern psychology, such as Gergen (1992) and Kvale (1992). The neopragmatic question is not whether a given proposition is true (is it an accurate representation of reality?) but whether accepting it as if it were true leads to the anticipated outcome.

The influence of the above mentioned post-modern themes is noticeable in Friedman's (1996) proposal of what a post-modern therapy is about:

- reality is considered a social construction;
- client and therapist co-construe meaning in conversation;
- attempts are made to disintegrate hierarchies and respect the differences;
- the power of conversations to liberate oppressed voices or narratives is recognized;
- the client is considered an expert in the sense that client and therapist co-construe therapeutic goals in a negotiated way;

- the therapist focuses on discovering the client's resources and strengths instead of a rigid diagnosis or pathology;
- the therapist uses a language that is accessible to the client instead of technical jargon;
- therapy is oriented towards the future and the promotion of change;
- conversationally contingent processes are emphasized.

Synthesis

Table 6.1 presents a synthesis of the three proposals discussed so far (White,

Table 6.1 Common themes in Polkinghorne's, White's and Friedman's proposals

Common Theme	Polkinghorne (2004)	White (1995)	Friedman (1996)
i. Constructivist/constructionist approach (*vs. realist/objectivist approach*).	Adaptation of a constructionist approach to meaning.	Rich description in that it provides for the linking of the alternative stories of people's pasts and presents with the stories of the lives of others – a linking of stories between lives according to shared themes that speak to purposes, values, and commitments in common.	Reality is considered a social construction.
ii. Collaborative stance (*vs. authoritarian stance*).	View of clients and therapists as partners.	Options for the telling and re-telling of, for the performance and re-performance of, the preferred stories of people's lives.	Client and therapist co-construe meaning in conversation.
			Attempts are made to disintegrate hierarchies and respect the differences.
			The client is considered an expert in the sense that client and therapist co-construe therapeutic goals in a negotiated way.
			The therapist uses a language that is accessible to the client instead of technical jargon.
			The power of conversations to liberate oppressed voices or narratives is recognized.
			Conversationally contingent processes are emphasized.

iii. Focus on strengths, resources and the future (*vs. focus on weaknesses, limitations and the past*).	Emphasis on client strengths.	Rendering the unique, the contradictory, the contingent, and, at times, the aberrant events of people's lives significant as alternative presents.	The therapist focuses on discovering client's resources and strengths instead of a rigid diagnostic or pathology.
iv. Focus on creative connections between past, present and future (*vs. focus exclusively on the past, or on the here-and-now*).	Emphasis on the narrative or story form of meaning.	Rich description in that alternative stories of people's presents are linked with the alternative stories of people's pasts, a linking of stories across time through lives.	Therapy is oriented towards the future and the promotion of change.

1995; Friedman, 1996; Polkinghorne, 2004). Our point is that the three of them can be organized around four overarching themes that are common to narrative and post-modern approaches to psychotherapy: (a) the adoption of a *constructivist/constructionist approach* (versus a realist/objectivist one); (b) a *collaborative stance* (versus an authoritarian one); (c) an *explicit focus on clients' strengths, resources and the future* (versus clients' weaknesses or limitations); and (d) an explicit focus on helping the client establish *creative narrative connections between his or her past, present and future* (versus an exclusive focus on the past, or on the here and now).

The remaining sections of this chapter will focus on a discussion of the extent to which these themes are also shared by personal construct psychotherapy and on the potential contributions of personal construct psychotherapy (PCP) to an approach to psychotherapy organized around such overarching themes.

Personal construct psychotherapy, constructivism and constructionism

As we discussed in a previous work (Botella, 1995), PCP can be defined as a constructivist theory to the extent that one accepts the characterization of constructivist theories as defined by

- an approach to knowledge that assumes that it is a hypothetical (anticipatory) construction instead of an internalized representation of reality and

- a set of non-justificationist epistemic values (for example, the pragmatic value of knowledge claims, or their coherence, internal and external consistency, and unifying power).

Kelly's theory of personal constructs was the first attempt to devise a theory of personality and psychotherapy based on a formal model of the organization of human knowledge. Kelly's philosophy of constructive alternativism asserts that reality is subject to many alternative constructions, because it does not reveal to us directly but through the templates that we create and then attempt to fit over the world (Kelly, 1955/1991a).

The constructivist conception of knowledge as an anticipatory construction is explicit in PCP's fundamental postulate: a person's processes are psychologically channelized by the ways in which he or she anticipates events. Personal construct psychotherapy also shares the constructivist notion of predictive efficiency as an epistemic value. Adams-Webber and Mancuso (1983) noted how, in PCP terms, the question is not whether our constructions are true or false, but whether they are useful dimensions for tracing alternative courses of action and then making sense of feedback from experience.

When placed upon the ground of other constructivist theories, PCP stands out as a historical forerunner. Mischel (1980) and Mahoney (1988a), among others, acknowledged the pioneering contribution of Kelly, and noted that he was able to anticipate in the 1950s many of the major directions of contemporary psychology.

However, PCP differs from social constructionism in some important points – for example, their relative emphasis on the social versus personal origin of construing. Being well aware of such divergences, and motivated by what we consider potential benefits of bridging them, during the last 10 years of our academic and therapeutic work we have been developing an attempt to press the dialogue between constructivism and social constructionism further and to enrich it with the voice of narrative and post-modern approaches (see Botella, 1995; Botella and Herrero, 2000; Botella, 2001; Botella et al., 2004). What we call *relational constructivism* constitutes a set of related theoretical assumptions, and its applied implications inform and inspire our own practice as psychotherapists at the Servei d'Assessorament i Atenció Psicològic Blanquerna (Blanquerna Psychotherapy Unit) in Barcelona as well as our research programs at the Constructivism and Discourse Processes Research Group at Ramon Llull University (see http://recerca.blanquerna.edu/constructivisme). It is based upon the following 10 interrelated propositions, all of them sharing the aforementioned set of constructivist metatheoretical principles:

1. Being human entails construing meaning.
2. Meaning is an interpretative and linguistic achievement.

3. Language and interpretations are relational achievements.
4. Relationships are conversational.
5. Conversations are constitutive of subject positions.
6. Subject positions are expressed as voices.
7. Voices expressed along a time dimension constitute narratives.
8. Identity is both the product and the process of self-narrative construction.
9. Psychological processes are embedded in the process of construing narratives of identity.
10. Psychotherapy can be equated to a collaborative dialogue addressed to transform the client's narratives of identity.

(Since the focus of this chapter is not relational constructivism in psychotherapy we will not discuss each one of these points in detail; interested readers can refer to the works mentioned above.)

PCP and therapy as collaborative dialogue with a proactive client

There are many potential ways to approach psychotherapy from a collaborative and proactive position: constructivism, constructionism, post-modern and narrative therapies. However, what is common to all of them is a move away from medical or drug metaphors. Rather, psychotherapy is addressed at helping clients regain a feeling of agency and movement, and it is construed as the activity of generating meanings that might potentially transform experience through collaborative dialogue (Kaye, 1995).

This stance towards the encouragement of the client's agency and involvement (instead of seeing him or her as the passive recipient of a medical intervention) is supported by an impressive amount of research evidence on client factors that contribute to positive therapy outcome (see Bohart and Tallman, 1999, for a review).

In their detailed review of well controlled and executed studies the members of the Institute for the Study of Therapeutic Change (see http://www.talkingcure.com) found that, contrary to the popular idea, such studies often fail to find a difference favouring drugs over psychotherapy or even an additive benefit from combining drugs with psychotherapy. Moreover, data from the National Institute of Mental Health Treatment of Depression Collaborative Research Project (Blatt et al., 1996) showed, again, that the variance attributable to the therapist overshadows any difference between the forms of treatment that are offered (IPT, CBT, pharmacotherapy and placebo for the treatment of depression). This large-scale study once again found that differences in outcome were more 'related to differences among patients and therapists than to types of treatment.' Effective therapists: (1) had more experience treating depression prior to the study; (2) were more likely to treat with psychotherapy alone; and (3) rarely used medication either alone or in combination in their treatment of depression. In conclusion, more effective therapists (in this study) had a psychological rather than a biological orientation in their treatment approach.

A different source of critiques of this or any other approach can be based on the positions it invites – on the relational possibilities it opens (or closes) once one is 'making sense' in terms of that given form of intelligibility. If a collaborative stance were useless, then it could be expected that therapists be positioned as experts, treatment as the main factor in the patient's cure, and patients as not responsible either for the problem or its cure. None of these positions has received support from psychotherapy research on factors contributing to client change (see Bohart and Tallman, 1999).

In an oft-quoted paper dating back to 1969 Kelly anticipated the notion that the therapeutic relationship is far more important than the techniques the therapist uses:

> Personal construct psychotherapy is a way of getting on with the human enterprise and it may embody and mobilize all of the techniques for doing this that have been yet devised. Certainly there is no one psychotherapeutic technique and certainly no one kind of interpersonal compatibility between psychotherapist and client. The techniques employed are the techniques for living and the task of the skilful psychotherapist is the proper orchestration of all of these varieties of techniques. (Kelly, 1969c, p. 222)

In fact, throughout the paper just mentioned (in which he discusses the psychotherapeutic relationship from a PCP standpoint), Kelly (1969c, p. 222) is eager to state that the goal of therapy when seen in this light is 'not to produce behaviour, but rather to enable the client, as well as the therapist, to utilize behaviour for asking important questions.' This position is clearly and coherently derived from Kelly's attempt to differentiate PCP from the 1950s rigours of both behaviourism and psychoanalysis by incorporating the active nature of human beings as a point of departure of his theory, and not as something that needed to be explained by means of such mechanistic constructs as 'reinforcement' or 'drive' (see Kelly, 1955/1991a).

PCP and the (re)construction of self-identity

In its original formulation, PCP endorsed the metaphor of man the scientist and, consequently, an approach to self-identity based on the metaphor of the self as a personal theory. In contrast, narrative psychology prefers the metaphor of the self as a narrative and, thus, of therapy as a narrative reconstruction. The metaphors are different but they are reconcilable. In fact, Miller Mair (1989, p. 5) tentatively rewrote PCP's fundamental postulate as follows: 'Persons' processes are psychologically channelized by the stories that they live and the stories that they tell.'

Regarding psychological processes underlying the construction of self theories and self narratives, and according to PCP, the basic psychological act in the construction of meaning is the abstraction of a personal construct. This abstraction depends on the process of noting features that characterize some events and are uncharacteristic of others; that is, on the process of noting similarities and contrasts between events.

According to narrative approaches, and particularly to Sarbin's (1986) elaboration, the basic psychological act in the construction of meaning is the creation of a metaphor. The creation of metaphors and the abstraction of personal constructs are strikingly similar in Sarbin's terms. According to him:

> When a person confronts a novel occurrence for which no ready-made category or class is available, the occurrence remains uninstantiated, unclassified, or unassimilated until a class or category is located or invented. The recognition of partial similarity on some dimension or construct provides the basis for analogy, and if linguistic translation is necessary, the partial similarity is expressed as a metaphor. (Sarbin, 1986, p. 76)

In the realm of self-identity, it is easy to note the metaphoric qualities of many personal constructs. For instance, applying constructs such as *competent, hard working, ambitious,* and *aggressive* to oneself suggests the metaphor of life as a competition. On the other hand, describing oneself as *fun loving, easy to get along with, enjoying life,* and *relaxed* suggests the metaphor of life as an enjoyable party.

In summary, to the extent that one accepts the notion of metaphor creation as the recognition of partial similarity in some dimension, the psychological processes underlying the construction of self theories and self narratives can be viewed as essentially the same.

Regarding the basic structure of self-theories and self-narratives and according to PCP, the building blocks of a self theory are personal constructs related to each other as hypotheses (or anticipations).

According to Hermans' elaboration of the narrative approach to self-identity (see, for example, Hermans, 2004), the basic building block of a self-narrative is a *valuation*. In Hermans' terms, a valuation is any unit of meaning that has positive, negative or ambivalent value in the eyes of the individual. Such meaning units are temporally organized and emplotted in a self-narrative form.

Again, the similarities between the self-theory and self-narrative approaches are obvious. Both constructs and valuations are personal meaning units with cognitive, emotional and behavioural implications attached to them. However, as Hermans himself notes, self-narratives are more explicitly structured along a time dimension – particularly as far as the past is concerned. Self-theories in PCP terms give primacy to the future orientation, implicit in the positively valued poles of personal constructs.

As for the main function of self-theories and self-narratives, and according to Berzonsky's (1990) elaboration of a PCP approach to self-identity, the main functions of a self-theory are essentially pragmatic:

- Does it offer an adequate basis for adapting, coping with life problems, and interpreting self-relevant information?
- Does it enable the individual to organize personal experience, maintain a sense of self-consistency over time and situations, maximize self-esteem, and maintain a positive ratio of pleasure and pain?

A useful self-theory, then, should be capable of helping us to understand and predict our thoughts, emotions and behaviour. It should contribute to our general feeling of being a whole person, with a sense of core biographical continuity despite specific changes.

According to Gergen and Gergen (1986), this meaning-making function is essentially the same one in self narratives. By means of self-narratives, 'rather than seeing one's life as simply "one damned thing after another" the individual attempts to understand life-events as systematically related. Such creations of narrative order may be essential in giving life a sense of meaning and direction' (Gergen and Gergen, 1986, p. 23).

Again, there are obvious similarities between the two approaches. Both of them adopt as a basic assumption the notion that human beings are best understood along a time dimension, and that our present self-identities are personal ways to link our past with our anticipated future. This feeling of personal continuity seems to be lost, for instance, in cases of paranoia, as Keen (1986) discussed. In such cases, self-narratives become cataclysmic in the sense of portraying no future, no redeeming social value, and a total loss that will not be remembered. Also, depressive self-narratives and self-theories depict a negative anticipation of the future, as cognitive therapists have traditionally highlighted.

Regarding the processes of change and development of self-theories and self-narratives, according to PCP, self-theories change and develop by means of recurrent cycles of validation and invalidation of their predictions. Generally speaking, a prediction is validated when its results are compatible with what was expected, and invalidated if they are not.

According to narrative approaches to self-identity, self-narratives are validated or invalidated by means of the social context in which they take place. That is to say, one's self-narratives typically require that significant others play a supporting role.

So, while PCP emphasizes the role of direct personal experience in the validational process, narrative approaches emphasize social processes as a source of validation or invalidation. In our opinion these differential emphases are not incompatible. Kelly probably emphasized personal experience because of the clinical (and chiefly individual) original context in which he developed his theory, while the narrative approach emphasized social consensus because of its primarily social focus. However, social consensus can easily be subsumed as one particular case of personal experience: one that does not rely on direct action on physical reality but on social and interpersonal processes. Besides, the very nature of social validation requires the personal qualification of significant others as validational agents – and so it becomes a form of personal experience.

Finally, the authorship of self-theories and self-narratives is probably the most controversial point. Apparently, PCP and narrative psychology (particularly when interpreted from a social constructionist approach) take opposite stands in this issue. On the one hand, Kelly was at pains to reiterate that personal constructs are essentially personal, individual and even idiosyncratic – the sociality corollary notwithstanding. On the other hand, social constructionists such as Gergen have repeatedly asserted that even self narratives are not essentially private, since they are linguistic products, and language is a social act. According to Gergen (1985, p. 270): 'The individual is limited at the outset to a vocabulary of action that possesses currency within the culture. One cannot compose an autobiography of cultural nonsense. One is also constrained by the demands for narrative coherence.'

In our opinion, however, both extremes (individual authorship versus social authorship) represent two ends of a continuum. Certainly, from within PCP there have been attempts to take *corporate constructs* and *family constructs* into account. These promising lines of research help render PCP more sensitive to the social and family context of our construing. While the use of personal constructs and self-theories may be a highly idiosyncratic one, this need not always be the case since many dimensions of meaning are forged in the social and cultural matrix of human life.

On the other hand, self-narratives have been used to advance the understanding of mainly individual processes, such as self-deception. They have also been used as an assessment and intervention device in individual constructivist therapy. So, in spite of the social authorship of self narratives, their individual significance is not denied. Again, Gergen himself accepted the possibility that

> the process of social negotiation need not be solely a public one. People appear generally to avoid the threat of direct negotiation by taking prior account of the public intelligibility of their actions. They may select in advance actions that can be justified on the basis of an intelligible or publicly

acceptable narrative or may privately justify questionable acts when they suspect that they have to account for behaviour. (Gergen and Gergen, 1986, p. 259)

This kind of self-conversation becomes, then, an interface of private processes and public ones, because the voices of one's validational agents are introjected – as when a client in therapy catches him or herself thinking, 'what will my therapist have to say about this?' So, in a sense, the issue of personal versus social authorship of self-theories and narratives seems to be more of a theoretical artefact than a meaningful contrast. Most people neither construe a world totally of their own nor are they totally confined to social expectations about them. The relationship between personal and social constructs is likely to be a dialectical one in which the person adapts his or her self-theory or self-narrative to social feedback and, at the same time, selects what will count as relevant feedback.

Final comments: what can PCP contribute to narrative and post-modern therapies?

Narrative and post-modern approaches to psychotherapy constitute a refreshing and liberating voice in a context that seems otherwise dominated by the rigours of cognitive-behavioural therapies, so-called empirically supported treatments, and more-or-less disguised attempts to turn psychotherapy into the equivalent of a psychological pill.

The level of systematization of PCP is still unparalleled by any other theory of personality and psychotherapy. The formal structure of Kelly's original formulation, the assessment techniques it inspired, and the amount of research studies validating them are simply impressive. In our opinion, it is precisely this systematization that constitutes the main contribution of PCP to the realm of narrative and post-modern psychotherapies.

Two examples taken from our own work can illustrate such contributions. First, in the realm of *psychotherapy research*, we have developed a form of narrative analysis that we have repeatedly applied to clients' self characterizations, thus combining notions from narrative psychology with other ones from PCP (see Botella et al., 2004 for a review). Also, in the realm of *psychotherapeutic practice*, we find PCP concepts increasingly useful in order to translate the sometimes elusive ideas of narrative and post-modern therapies to clinical practice.

CHAPTER SEVEN

Personal construct psychotherapy: epistemology and practice

GREG J NEIMEYER, JOCELYN SAFERSTEIN, WADE ARNOLD

Personal construct psychology (Kelly, 1955/1991a/1991b) is participating in an epistemological movement that may constitute a highly significant contribution to the practice of psychotherapy. Together with proponents of structural-developmental approaches (Guidano, 1995), narrative therapy (White and Epston, 1990), selected family therapies (Efran, Lukens and Lukens, 1990; Feixas, Procter and Neimeyer, 1993), and other 'meaning-making' approaches to human change (Carlsen, 1988; Mahoney, 1991), personal construct psychotherapists have rejected objectivist positions, instead emphasizing the human capacity to 'actively create and construe their personal realities' (Mahoney and Lyddon, 1988, p. 200). Signposts signalling this shift are posted throughout the intellectual landscape that marks the practice of psychology. Mahoney and Albert (1996), for example, have traced significant shifts in our discipline's published vocabulary as one indication of this sea of change in psychological tides. Across the 20-year period of their review, they documented substantial declines in the use of mechanistic metaphors and corresponding increases in terms reflecting personal agency, meaning and interpretation. Terms such as 'operant', 'reinforcement', and 'contingency' showed marked declines across time, whereas significant increases were registered in the frequency of terms such as 'systems', 'constructivism' and 'construct'. This significant shift in what Mahoney and Albert (1996, p. 22) call the 'world of words' may signal the shifting epistemologies that support the science and practice of psychology.

The purpose of this chapter is to address the role of epistemologies in guiding theoretical developments and preferences, and their translation into clinical practice. Contemporary psychotherapeutic practices owe allegiance to their epistemological premises and can be viewed within the historical traditions that have spawned them. This chapter further explores the correspondence between therapists' epistemological positions and the theories and interventions that mark their practice, and examines the potential interaction of these positions with those of the clients they serve. In reviewing current work at the intersection of epistemology and practice in psychotherapy, the boundary becomes blurred between personal and professional domains, with deeply held convictions about the nature of knowledge informing the intimate enactments that constitute psychotherapy.

The nature of knowledge

Epistemology, or theory of knowledge, is coincident with the origins of philosophy itself. Three Ancient Greek epistemologies flowed from the writings of Democritus, Plato and Pyrrho. Democritus held that the surest path to knowledge was through the senses. Plato, however, believed that what is real is the essences of phenomena, accessible only through the mind or the use of reason. Pyrrho introduced scepticism, emphasizing the elusive and uncertain nature of knowledge, whether it was obtained through the senses or through reason.

The clearest contemporary expression of Democritus' position is empiricism, with its emphasis on the senses, privileging knowledge accessed through sight, sound, smell, touch and taste. Progenitors of modern empiricism, Bacon and Lock, translated these epistemological convictions into an image of science with verification at its heart, an image that became central to the position of logical positivism that remains dominant in contemporary expressions of psychological science and practice. Within twentieth-century psychology, behaviourism constitutes the most enduring expression of this empiricist epistemology.

The genesis of modern rationalism, by contrast, can be traced to the ideas of Plato. The founder of the modern rationalist traditions, Rene Descartes, argued that the senses could be deceived, advocating instead for the rational powers of the mind as a firmer foundation for the creation of knowledge. The rapid proliferation of cognitive therapies stands testament to the attractiveness of this position within contemporary psychology (see Mahoney and Lyddon, 1988; Mahoney, 1988b; Mahoney, 1988c).

Pyrrho's death ended the formal development of scepticism as an independent school of thought, but undercurrents of scepticism have continued to hold an important place across time. Among the many places where the seeds of scepticism have found fertile soil are the constructivist and constructionist literatures, where both empiricism and rationalism are viewed with jaundiced eyes. The important role of context in scaffolding meaning is highlighted through attention to language games (Wittgenstein, 1921/1988), power relations (Foucault, 2000), deconstruction (Derrida, 1967/1997), and, of course, psychotherapy (Kelly,

1955/1991a/1991b), each of which has contributed to what has become a rapidly evolving post-modern movement.

Post-modernists challenge traditional notions of foundationalism, essentialism and realism. Foundationalism is the belief that there are fundamental facts from which knowledge can be inferred. For instance, Descartes' expression *cogito ergo sum* forms the foundation upon which all other knowledge claims are built. Essentialism is the philosophical position that 'objects have essences and that there is a distinction between essential and non-essential or accidental predications' (Loux, 1999). Expressions of essentialism in psychology include traditional notions of the 'true self' as an entity to be discovered, rather than constructed, over the course of psychotherapy (Berzonsky, 1994). Realism, by contrast, holds that there are real objects in the world that exist independent of our experience, and that their existence is separate from our efforts to understand them. That is, an object's ontological status is not subject to our perception of that object. Psychoanalysis, behaviourism and many cognitive therapies all retain varying levels of adherence to foundationalism, essentialism and realism, while post-modern approaches actively challenge these positions (Gergen, 1992).

As exemplars of a post-modern position, constructivist approaches like personal construct psychology (Kelly, 1955/1991a/1991b) emphasize viability over validity, and highlight the critical role of context (historical, cultural, social) in the generation, continuation and interpretation of meaning. Because neither our perceptions nor their utility are tied directly to features of the external world, constructivists hold that any event is subject to a variety of alternative constructions. Kelly's concept of constructive alternativism remains the earliest and clearest expression of this position within the contemporary field of psychotherapy. As Kelly (1970a, p. 1) observed

> Howsoever the quest for truth will turn out in the end, the events we face today are subject to as great a variety of constructions as our wits will enable us to contrive. This is not to say that one construction is as good as any other . . . But it does remind us that all our present perceptions are open to question and reconsideration and it does broadly suggest that even the most obvious occurrences of everyday life might appear utterly transformed if we were inventive enough to construe them differently.

Practical epistemology

Practically speaking, what differences do these epistemological distinctions make in the conduct of psychotherapy and what implications do they carry for the people, processes and procedures that are collectively enjoined in efforts towards human change? Conceptual answers to this question can be found in Mahoney and Lyddon (1988), GJ Neimeyer and RA Neimeyer, (1993), RA Neimeyer (1993) and Lyddon (1993), among others (Mahoney, 1988b, 1988c; RA Neimeyer, 1995a). In each case these authors trace the translation of epistemological differences into probable differences in therapeutic practices. So, for example, rationalists tend to view negative emotion as a problem in correspondence, a dysfunctional discontinuity between the perception of an event or experience and the reality of that event or experience. The goal is to control this emotion through logical analysis aimed at disputing or modifying dysfunctional cognitions in an effort to better see things 'as they really are'. By contrast, constructivists tend towards a developmental perspective, conceptualizing 'affective experiences as primitive and powerful forms of knowing' (Mahoney and Lyddon, 1988, p. 219) that are integral to the process of meaning making. One direct expression of this difference in psychotherapy, then, might be the tendency for emotional expressions to be excluded or minimized in a rational form of therapy, whereas they may play a more central role in constructivist therapies, such as personal construct therapy, where they are attended to, encouraged, amplified, or incorporated into broader meaning-making efforts. In practice, however, this differential attention to emotional processes is one of a select set of conceptual distinctions that have received research attention (Viney, 1994). A much broader range of strategic and technical differences have been outlined in relation to differing epistemological positions than have been documented in research literatures (Mahoney and Lyddon, 1988; RA Neimeyer, 1993). These include conceptual distinctions regarding the functions and forms of assessment in psychotherapy (GJ Neimeyer and RA Neimeyer, 1993), the characteristic style of therapy, the different levels of intervention associated with different epistemological positions (Lyddon, 1990), and differences in the nature of the therapeutic relationship and approaches to therapeutic resistance, among others (RA Neimeyer, 1995a). Despite the rich array of differences that have been outlined at a conceptual level, relatively few of these have received careful empirical attention. At a broader level, however, the role of epistemological differences in guiding theoretical and therapeutic preferences has been addressed. This literature provides a glimpse into the potential power of epistemology in the selection and evaluation of psychotherapeutic perspectives.

Epistemic style and therapeutic orientation

A longstanding literature addresses the relationship between epistemological differences and therapeutic preferences and persuasions. Much of this work has been guided by the early work of Royce and his colleagues that spans nearly four decades (Royce, 1964; Royce and Powell, 1983). A central theme of Royce's (1964) model of personal epistemologies is the notion that individual differences in how people construe reality and test the validity of their beliefs are a function of their relative commitments to rational, empirical and metaphorical styles of knowing. Broadly speaking, the rationalist is a logical conceptualizer, the empiricist is a perceiver, and the metaphorist is a symbolizer.

More specifically, the rational style of knowing is based on conceptual cognitive abilities, entails a commitment to relating to the world using one's rational and analytic skills, and involves testing the validity of personal beliefs in terms of their logical consistency. By contrast, the empirical style of knowing involves a commitment to relating to the world through using one's senses, and entails evaluating the validity of personal beliefs in terms of one's reliable correspondence to observation. The metaphorical style of knowing depends on the capacity for symbolic representation, and involves testing the validity of personal beliefs in terms of one's pragmatic ability to generalize to other realms of experience. Although all forms of knowing encompass aspects of rational, empirical and metaphorical epistemic styles, these processes are hierarchically organized within Royce's system, with individuals tending towards the use of one predominant form of knowing (Royce and Powell, 1983). Exemplars of contemporary psychotherapies that owe primary allegiance to each of these forms of knowing are easy to nominate. Rational emotive therapy reflects a rational epistemology; behavioural therapy represents strong empirical leanings; and personal construct psychotherapy represents a stronger adherence to a metaphorical way of knowing.

The broadest support for the utility of this 'epistemic styles' framework stems from the development and application of the Psycho-Epistemological Profile (PEP), a self-administered questionnaire developed by Royce and Mos (1980) to assess an individual's differential epistemological commitments. The relevance of these epistemic styles in psychotherapy has been demonstrated in a series of studies that link epistemic styles to psychotherapists' preferred theoretical orientations. Schacht and Black (1985) were among the early researchers to find that therapists of different theoretical persuasions reported significantly different epistemic styles. Compared to psychoanalytic therapists, for example, behavioural therapists were disproportionately dedicated to an empirical epistemic style, while psychoanalytic therapists evidenced a greater commitment to a metaphorical orientation.

Mahoney's (1991) more recent distinction between rationalist and constructivist epistemologies underscores some of the distinctions outlined by Royce and his colleagues, and has served as a platform for additional work aimed at studying the correspondence between epistemic style and psychotherapeutic orientation. Mahoney and Gabriel (1987), Mahoney and Lyddon (1988) and Mahoney (1991) suggest that contemporary cognitive-behavioural therapies can be distinguished by their differential commitments to these two positions. In general, rationalism (a) argues for the distinction between thinking and feeling, (b) favours thinking as a superior vehicle for validating knowledge, and (c) adheres to a realist version of ontology in which there is a single, stable and potentially knowable external reality. The translation of these beliefs into therapeutic practice tends to favour a greater emphasis on instruction, education and direct intervention designed to correct, rectify or restructure faulty or dysfunctional cognitions or cognitive processes.

Constructivism, by contrast, (a) argues for the artificiality of the distinction between thinking and feeling, (b) regards feelings as primitive knowing systems, and (c) challenges the assumption that reality is singular, stable and knowable. The translation of these beliefs into therapeutic practice tends to favour a more metaphorical, symbolic and exploration-oriented therapy that conceptualizes psychological disorders as challenges to personal knowing systems and seeks to understand or transcend these limitations through developmental reorganization.

Using this distinction, GJ Neimeyer and Morton (1997) recruited 49 practising psychotherapists to explore the relationship between psychotherapeutic orientation and underlying epistemic leanings. Two samples of therapists were included, one group of rational-emotive therapists drawn from the membership of the Institute of Rational Emotive Therapy, and one group of personal construct therapists drawn from the International Network of Personal Construct Theorists. Therapists from both groups were asked to complete the Therapist Attitude Questionnaire (TAQ) developed by DiGuisseppe, Raymond and Linscott (1993) to measure Mahoney's distinction between rationalist and constructivist orientations. Second, they were asked to compare their own therapy orientations to six prominent psychotherapists known for their predominantly rationalist orientations (Aaron Beck or Albert Ellis, for example) or constructivist orientations (George Kelly or Michael Mahoney, for instance). Third, they were asked to rate their therapeutic style along adjectives aligned with a rationalist orientation (for example, logical, directive, educational) and with a constructivist orientation (for example, symbolic, metaphorical, meaning oriented).

The pattern of results was generally consistent with the translation of epistemic commitments into psychotherapeutic practice. Compared with rational-emotive therapists, personal construct therapists showed a significantly higher commitment to a constructivist epistemology, and a lower commitment to a rationalist perspective. In addition, practising personal construct therapists showed a stronger identification with notable constructivist therapists, and tended to describe their therapeutic styles along dimensions more closely linked with constructivist psychotherapy.

Related work by Winter, Tschudi and Gilbert (2005) extends these findings in a sample of seasoned psychotherapists of widely varying orientations, including personal construct therapists. From their administration of repertory grids to these therapists, they were able to discern patterns that support the consistency of epistemic commitments on the one hand, with therapeutic perceptions, on the other. For example, the personal constructs elicited from cognitive-behavioural therapists reflected greater attention to technical aspects of therapy, whereas the personal construct therapists showed greater attention to personal meaning. When asked to nominate their own therapy preferences for themselves, if they were to go to therapy, different psychotherapists reacted differently. Whereas psychodynamic therapists were most likely to remain within their own ranks for psychotherapy, constructivist therapists (neurolinguistic and personal construct psychotherapists) were most likely to embrace alternative orientations. Overall, the work by Winter and others in this area supports the claim advanced by Arthur (2000, p. 235) that 'psychotherapists' theoretical orientations reflect certain characteristic personality traits and cognitive epistemological styles.'

The translation of these theoretical differences into concrete distinctions at the level of intervention has been the subject of further inquiry. This developing work has begun to emerge despite a number of specific challenges. These include the significant differences that occur among theories in relation to their levels of abstraction and flexibility, as well as the extent to which they have attracted the attention of researchers in the field.

Epistemic style and therapeutic practice

In contrast to the relative clarity and simplicity of rationalist forms of psychotherapy, for example, the processes and procedures of constructivist psychotherapy have long suffered a reputation as diffuse, indistinct or even absent. Anderson (1990, p. 137) noted that 'Constructivist therapy is not so much a technique as it is a philosophical context within which therapy is done', an understanding that places severe constraints on efforts to effect direct comparisons of the concrete enactment of psychotherapy from the two schools of thought. O'Hara and Anderson (1991, p. 25) echo the frustration of many researchers in the field in this regard, noting that post-modern practitioners have been 'short on practical ideas about [what] is to be done. The task of therapists is to turn some of postmodernism's vague celebrations of multiplicity and change into lived experience.'

The technical eclecticism that characterizes many constructivist therapies has no doubt contributed to this perception. As the progenitor of constructivist therapies, Kelly's (1955/1991a/1991b) personal construct therapy illustrates this concern. In noting that 'the relationships between therapists and clients and the techniques they employ may be as varied as the whole human repertory of relationships and techniques', Kelly (1969c, p. 223) seems to suggest that his approach could embrace an infinitely broad range of therapeutic processes and procedures and, by extension, may have little distinctive contribution to make in this regard.

However, a closer read of personal construct theory and other constructivist therapies suggests otherwise. Both at the level of therapeutic method and relationship, constructivist therapies have had a range of distinctive contributions to make. Concerning methods, Feixas, Procter and GJ Neimeyer (1993) have detailed a number of distinctive contributions such as interview methods, circular questioning, cognitive marital therapy, the bow-tie technique, and a range of writing interventions, self- and family characterization approaches, and novel repertory grid modifications. Likewise, GJ Neimeyer, Hagans and Anderson (1998) reviewed a variety of distinctive constructivist interventions ranging from individual and interpersonal methods, through systemic and cultural ones. Mahoney's (1991) 'mirror time' and 'streaming' techniques, Guidano's (1995) 'moiviola technique', Clarke's (1993) 'meaning symbolization' process, and Hermans' (1995) 'self-confrontation method' all represent further examples of distinctive constructivist contributions to the practice of psychotherapy. The dedication of entire volumes to constructivist methods of assessment and intervention (see GJ Neimeyer, 1993 and Taylor, Marienau and Fiddler, 2000) stands testament to the field's effective response to earlier outcries that constructivist psychotherapists 'have produced almost nothing about how to put these theories into practice' (Minuchin, 1991, p. 48).

As in the case of methods, personal construct and constructivist approaches to psychotherapy have developed clear expressions regarding the nature of the therapeutic relationship that distinguish them from their rationalist counterparts. For the rationalist psychotherapist, a therapeutic relationship is oriented more towards the delivery of guidance, technical instruction, and behavioural rehearsal regarding the role of cognitions in the development and maintenance of emotional distress. The use of therapist-directed exercises, structured interventions, and directed homework assignments illustrates the relative emphasis placed on the development of technical skills trumping the therapeutic relationship as a primary means of generating change.

Constructivist therapies, including personal construct therapy, tend towards a greater developmental focus, often conceptualizing the therapeutic relationship as a critical factor in personal change. Serving as a kind of safe harbour or secure home base, the psychotherapeutic relationship provides the effective workbench for experimenting with the construction of new meanings and novel enactments. Faidley and Leitner's (1993) distinctive description of the psychotherapy relationship within personal construct psychology is characteristic in this regard. In contrast to the more instructional mode of the rationalist therapist, they view both the client and the therapist as embarking 'on an uncharted journey that will require them to enter unknown territory, to struggle, to bear fear and pain and, hopefully, to grow' (Faidley and Leitner, 1993, pp. 6–7).

The translation of rationalist and constructivist epistemologies into the concrete technical and relational operations in psychotherapy has been the subject of some recent attention. Viney (1994), for example, studied the transcripts of psychotherapy sessions conducted according to five different theoretical orientations. Consistent with epistemological commitments, she found that personal construct and client-centred therapies were characterized by greater acknowledgment of the client's distress, which was followed by further expressions of distressed emotion on the part of the client. Rational-emotive therapy, by contrast, tended to minimize the expression of emotional distress, viewing it instead as an expression of irrational thinking.

Vasco's (1994) work represents another effort to articulate the distinctive features of psychotherapeutic practice that follow from a constructivist orientation. He studied a group of 161 Portuguese psychologists, assessing their degree of commitment to a constructivist epistemology and aspects of their therapeutic style and practice. His findings indicate that stronger constructivist leanings were inversely related to the degree of therapeutic structure and direction, as well as to a focus on current concerns or problems, to confronting clients in relation to issues of resistance, and to a variety of behaviours related to emotional expression. The only characteristic that was positively associated with constructivist commitments was greater technical eclecticism, which recalls Kelly's (1969c) observations about the breadth of techniques and the relationships that can be embraced within the framework of personal construct psychotherapy. From his overall pattern of findings, Vasco (1994, p.12) concluded 'these results suggest that, at present, and possibly as a consequence of the neophyte status of constructivist therapy, strongly constructivist therapists find it easier to state what they do not do than to state what they do.'

Perhaps the most ambitious research along these lines has been conducted by Winter and Watson (1999). They studied the work of four personal construct therapists and six rationalist therapists across a range of clients in an outpatient mental health context. Both forms of therapy were conducted on the basis of a 12-session renewable contract. Results from audiotaped recordings of the sessions provided an intriguing glimpse into the differing procedural and relational components of these two orientations. Overall, the rationalist therapists demonstrated a more negative attitude towards their clients, while the personal construct therapists demonstrated greater regard for them, although the two did not differ in terms of perceived warmth or friendliness. In addition, clients receiving personal construct therapy demonstrated greater overall involvement in psychotherapy. These differences are consistent with the credulous and collaborative nature of the therapeutic relationship outlined by Kelly (1955/1991a/1991b) in his original discussion of personal construct psychotherapy.

Possible interactions between client and therapist orientations were suggested from this work, as well. Tentative evidence suggests, for example, that the rationalist therapists showed greater regard for their more tightly construing clients and were, in turn, perceived by these clients to be more empathic. There was also provisional evidence that linked the 'internality' or 'externality' of clients' orientations to differential preferences for the two therapies. These findings were consistent with the work of Vincent and LeBow (1995), who found that clients with an internal locus of control tended to rate a constructivist therapist more favourably, whereas those with a greater external locus of control favoured the rationalist therapist.

The interaction between world views echoes Lyddon's (1989, p. 428) observation that clients, like counsellors, 'may also hold different encapsulated images of reality and . . . these world views, in turn [might] predispose them to prefer counseling theories and approaches that are congruent with their own particular epistemic styles.' This possibility has been the subject of an ongoing line of research dedicated to exploring the possible role of 'epistemic match' in the evaluation of psychotherapy.

Epistemic match and psychotherapy preferences

Much of the work that addresses the impact of epistemic match in psychotherapy has followed Lyddon's (1989) lead in providing individuals with descriptions of psychotherapy ostensibly crafted by different therapists. These one-page descriptions include relevant theoretical and practical aspects, and are presented to individuals as transcripts of three different therapists who have been asked to describe their orientations to therapy. These therapists, identified only as Counselor A, Counselor B, and Counselor C, represent rational-emotive, empirical/behavioural, and metaphorical/constructivist perspectives on therapy. For example, the transcript for the rational-emotive approach begins as follows:

> My approach to counseling focuses on the way people think about certain life events and situations. In particular, it is my contention that most problems people experience stem from their own irrational and illogical thinking patterns. As a result, the main task of therapy, as I see it, is to correct certain thought patterns and rid people of their irrational ideas.

The transcript for the empirical (behavioural) approach begins with the following statement:

> Fundamental to my view of therapy is the idea that all behavior is lawful and can be explained through systematic observation and study. In other words, I believe problem behaviors are learned just like non-problem behaviors, and thus can be unlearned. As a result, my approach to therapy tends to rely upon a systematic method of examining your behavior and your environment and, together with you, developing specific interventions or strategies designed to alter your behavior and life circumstance.

The transcript of the metaphorical (constructivist) approach begins:

> My approach to counseling is based on the idea that we all experience a unique history of development which leads us to view the world in a very personal way. For example, through interactions with significant people in our lives, each of us has learned to organize in a meaningful fashion our own internal experience of what we see, hear and feel. In short, we have come to construct personal representations of ourselves and of our worlds which serve as maps or guides for our everyday actions and decisions.

After assessing individuals' epistemic styles using Royce's Psycho-Epistemological Profile (PEP), Lyddon (1989) asked a group of undergraduate students to evaluate each of these three therapies in relation to their own preferences for therapy. Results indicated that participants preferred therapy approaches that represented an epistemic match between their own epistemic style and the underlying epistemological framework of the therapeutic orientations. Participants with dominant rational, empirical and metaphorical epistemic styles preferred rational-emotive, behavioural and constructivist counselling approaches, respectively.

GJ Neimeyer et al. (1993) replicated and extended this finding in a series of four studies exploring the relationship between epistemology and therapeutic preferences. Study 1 replicated Lyddon's (1989) findings, and found additional evidence in support of them from a listing of participants' thoughts in reaction to their reading each of the transcripts. Studies 2 and 3 noted the different approaches to information processing that were related to the different epistemic styles, with rationalist orientations reflecting high levels of information seeking, and metaphorical orientations being linked to greater openness to experience (see also Berzonsky, 1994). The fourth study in the series provided an exploratory look at the relationship between epistemic style and preferences for different theoretical orientations among counsellors in training. Results presaged subsequent work in this area (GJ Neimeyer and Morton, 1997) by suggesting 'the intriguing possibility that epistemic style guides or channels preferences regarding one's own therapeutic orientation' (GJ Neimeyer et al., 1993, p. 520).

Recent work by GJ Neimeyer and Saferstein (2003) has extended this work to a group of practising psychotherapists. Their work included a sample of 23 therapists who were assessed in relation to their rationalist or constructivist leanings. These therapists were then asked to read descriptions of rational-emotive and metaphorical orientations to therapy, and to rate them in relation to their preferences. Consistent with predictions, therapists aligned with a rational epistemic style preferred the description of the rational-emotive therapy whereas those with stronger constructivist leanings showed a greater preference for the metaphorical description.

Importantly, therapists were then asked to listen to an audiotape of two different therapy sessions. Both therapy sessions were conducted by the same therapist in relation to the same client with the identical presenting problem (social anxiety). One session was conducted according to a rational-emotive therapeutic orientation, and the other was conducted according to a personal construct orientation. The rational-emotive session described the A-B-C model, identified each of these components within the context of the client's presenting problem, and then enjoined the client in applying the model to restructure her thoughts to minimize her emotional distress. The personal construct session first attended to embodied emotion, and then used Hinkle's (1965) laddering technique and a metaphorical intervention to understand better the meaning of the anxiety for the client. Sessions were independently judged to be equally effective portrayals of their respective approaches, and they were presented to therapists in counterbalanced order. Results again supported expectations based on 'epistemic matching'; therapists with a rational epistemic style expressed a stronger preference for the rational-emotive therapy session, whereas those with a more constructivist orientation preferred the personal construct therapy session. As with related work, these findings again support the relationship between epistemic commitments and the differential evaluation of various psychotherapies.

Conclusion

The examination of the relationship between personal epistemology and psychotherapy represents an ongoing line of work with a range of important expressions and implications. The current stage of this work provides strong evidence for the interdependence of epistemological commitments and psychotherapeutic preferences. Available evidence suggests that the epistemological leanings of psychotherapists are linked to their preferred theoretical orientations and translated into their therapeutic practices. In the case of personal construct psychotherapists, the current research suggests their allegiance to a constructivist epistemology, which is translated, in turn, into distinctive attitudes, preferences and enactments in relation to the practice of psychotherapy. Although the current research remains limited and tentative, provisional findings suggest the likelihood that epistemological differences are translated into concrete differences in the nature of the relationships, processes and procedures that define the practice of psychotherapy.

As work continues in this area, it may also turn to examine the relationship between different epistemological positions and the personal impact, challenges and satisfactions experienced by psychotherapists who adhere to them. Personal construct psychology is a participant in a broader epistemological movement, for example, which questions the primacy of thought over feeling, that challenges the permanence of all our constructions, and that invites the continual deconstruction and revision of all we know. It recognizes the dynamic tension that necessarily exists between our efforts to retain and to relinquish our current constructions in an ongoing process of development and growth. It follows from this that a commitment to constructive alternativism carries with it a wide range of distinctive entailments for its practitioners, as well as its clients. Mahoney (1988b; 1988c) has sketched an outline of these entailments (Mahoney, 1995), observing

> The psychological demands of constructive metatheory are unsurpassed by those of any other contemporary perspective. No other family of modern theory asks its adherents to maintain such a degree of self-examining openness, to so painstakingly tolerate and harvest (rather than eliminate) ambiguity, or to so thoroughly question both the answers and the questions by which they inquire. (Mahoney, 1988c, p. 312)

And yet the special burdens that are borne by practitioners of constructivist traditions have not yet attracted the attention of researchers. It seems likely that each epistemology etches somewhat different lines in the lives of its practitioners. However, the distinctive marks worked across time by these divergent practices remain largely unknown and unexamined. Future work that continues to articulate the entailments of different epistemological positions in psychotherapeutic practice may advance ongoing efforts to understand the complex and evolving interplay between epistemology and practice.

CHAPTER EIGHT

Techniques of personal construct family therapy

HARRY PROCTER

Differences in viewpoint constitute a resource for the family

Personal construct psychology (PCP) evolved with the practice of individual therapy as its focus, but when working with families it becomes especially vibrant and alive as we help the members negotiate their unique takes on reality. Kelly (1955/1991a) said, in his basic philosophy, 'constructive alternativism', that there are many valid ways of construing the world. This principle is the cornerstone of the theory and practice of this approach to family therapy both at the level of understanding the struggles and politics of family life and in the way it translates into a technique or method of engaging with the family in daily practice. The individuals in any group are unique (even identical twins) but within the family in its many forms, biological relatedness (or lack of), gender and differences in life-cycle stage all result in similarities and differences being thrown into stark relief. The family is also always wider than those sitting in the therapy room. Other members of the family, both immediate and extended, provide a context and can exert their influence, even from beyond the grave. Even when working with individuals with the many 'voices' of others in their heads, one is, in a sense doing family therapy.

Because of its reflexivity (Bannister, 1975), PCP can be shared and discussed openly with clients. Bannister insisted that any psychology applied to other people should be equally open to looking at oneself. We can say then in the family session, 'Everyone is basically trying to make sense of their circumstances. Each person does this in their own unique way. I am really pleased that you have all been able to come because it allows me to understand everyone in the family's point of view. In putting all those different views together, it helps me get a deeper and richer understanding of your situation.' This last point was inspired by Gregory Bateson's (1972) metaphor that in having two eyes, or binocular vision, perception in three dimensions is possible. By putting two or more viewpoints together, a quantum leap of extra understanding is enabled. This kind of statement is worth making towards the beginning of the work and at times of conflict and strife in the session. It is supportive and helps family members feel that they will be heard and taken seriously. In families some points of view are typically dominant whereas other – for example, those of children, girls, or a member with disabilities – may be subjugated, driven underground or so disconfirmed that individuals 'forget' their own viewpoint. Many children whom I see, particularly those with behaviour problems, have never had the experience of their own views being listened to and taken seriously. Yet the human being has remarkable resilience and perspicacity, with unexpressed individual need for validation being expressed in oppositional resistance, destructive violence, encopresis, stealing and so on.

Unique preferences, interests and elaborative choices

Therapy is enhanced if one has managed to build a unique relationship with each family member. This may be achieved by knowing something of where their 'growing edge' is, what their spontaneous choices and values are, and what constructs are governing their lives currently at both superordinate and subordinate levels. In the latter, the more specific one can be the better, especially with children. Thus, to know of a boy that Patrick is his best friend, and that they like to go to Jesmond Park to play 'Bench ball' on a Saturday afternoon, is better than only knowing 'he saw his friend' in general. Therapists often pass over the little 'gems' that they are offered too readily, instead of dwelling on them and going into them further. It is helpful to write these details down unless one's memory is unusually good! (Doing so will usually be taken as the therapist taking the trouble to help them thoroughly.) This will allow a continuing conversation communicating that one is really interested in them as people. One gauges from non-verbal communication whether the material really is elaborative for them or if one is overdoing the detail. We are on the right track when things are offered spontaneously rather than everything said being merely as a response to questioning. This may indicate that the therapist is being construed as a friendly ally who is seen as somebody with whom the members could collaborate to move things forward.

One can, of course, ask members about each other's lives and interests, indicating the levels of and enhancing sociality (see p. 105). If a person is unwilling or unable to talk, for example in catatonia (Procter, 1985, 1987), selective mutism or just plain unwillingness to participate, this becomes particularly potent. Figure 8.1 shows a visual metaphor of a jigsaw puzzle for this. One can establish what Jonathan's likes and dislikes are, what he would think and say, and 'reconstruct' him as a person in the family via information from the others, of course emphasizing the caution that the others' constructions may be wrong and are only guesses. He remains psychologically present therefore, making it much easier for him to re-enter at a later date.

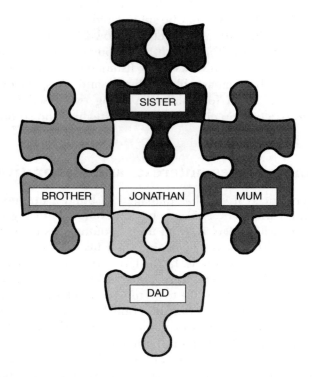

Figure 8.1 Building up a picture of Jonathan's world by asking other family members about him.

A great deal could be written about the use of names in family work. Needless to say, it is important to understand correctly what members like to be called both in terms of familiar or first names and also surnames, being careful that the latter may entail issues of central emotional significance such as paternity. Names may signify what Kelly called whole-figure constructs such as 'he's just like Jim, as a son should be' or 'she's totally different to Mary'. It is common for these to be operating powerfully in family construing, with even babies being identified at birth: 'he's just like his Uncle Vernon.' Asking for similarities and differences between relatives may reveal these constructs.

Members' concerns and worries and changes that would address them

The problem instigating referral to the therapist is likely to originate from the conversation between referrer and one particular complainant inside or outside the family. This needs to be acknowledged but it is often better to go back a step and find out in general *who* in the family is worrying about *what* and *whom* and to look at the referred complaint in this context. Often there will be other even more pressing concerns. Construing is very influenced by current social context and the conversations will go differently according to who is participating at the time. Supplying the construct of worry can be useful: 'Who do you think is worrying most at the moment? Who is most worried about you?' Very negative construing may be best addressed by going to the contrast pole: 'How is it that you would like him to behave?' 'How have you been trying to help her do that?' 'What do you think would be required to achieve that?'

The meaning and affect of particular constructs

Personal construct psychology provides us with an integrated or holistic view of human functioning. Thus, the 'construct' covers cognition, emotion and action all in one. If a girl is choosing to construe her father as 'an unfair bastard' (versus 'fair, like my friend's dad') the associated anger, physiology and behaviour are, in this approach, all part of the construct, which governs her whole approach in relating to him. A choice is always involved, a choice to see him that way, and a choice to act accordingly, hence the importance of bipolarity. A construct may be more enduring, shaping the dyadic relationship, or very transient, used to govern specific choices in the ongoing interactional sequences.

We are continuously monitoring the session, the conversation, the interaction, and reported conversations and episodes to learn how the members are construing their circumstances. If the constructs have verbal labels we can hear them as adjectives and phrases, or we can elicit them using formal PCP methods, for example the triad method: 'Of you, your mother and your sister, in what ways do you see two as similar and the other as different?' The Perceiver Element Grid (PEG) (see Figure 8.2) is a pencil and paper task for families in which each member draws or writes how they see themselves and the others, perceivers down the left and as perceived along the top (see Procter, 2001; Fransella, Bell and Bannister, 2004). The PEG in Figure 8.2 gathers material from one interview with the four members. The blank cells give us food for thought too. Giles (2004)

	ELEMENTS		
	MOTHER	**ANDREW** (13)	**GEMMA** (9)	**TOM** (STEPFATHER)

PERCEIVERS		MOTHER	ANDREW	GEMMA	TOM
	MOTHER		He is aggressive I wish he was less aggressive They are *my* kids!	They are *my* kids!	Tom is too heavy and restrictive with Andrew.
	ANDREW				Tom moans all the time He's a twat! I hate him I wish he'd commit suicide!
	GEMMA			(Gemma draws a picture of herself as an angel saying 'be happy!')	
	TOM		He's a rude, cheeky, aggressive, disrespectful lad. He spoils *my* (sic) house.		I blow up sometimes. It is my DUTY to bring them up as *respectful* (and not be *soft* like my wife is)

Figure 8.2 Perceiver-element grid (PEG) in a stepfamily.

has used art work with families to explore their construing. Using drawings is enormously helpful in flattening power hierarchies between the generations because children are often more confident with art materials than their parents. More detailed discussion of construct elicitation methods with families can be found in Feixas, Procter and Neimeyer (1993).

The chief values and views that each holds in particular scenarios

According to Kelly, construct systems are pyramidal structures with core or superordinate constructs at the top, which tend to shape and govern construing subsumed beneath. For example, in the area of beliefs about child rearing, couples will come together and agree, synthesizing values and philosophies that have evolved in each of the families of origin, possibly at quite a low level of cognitive awareness. Alternatively, the values of one parent will predominate, the other being subjugated, or the couple will remain in chronic conflict about how best to bring up or reprimand their child. Issues may only emerge when children arrive or when a young person reaches a new stage such as adolescence and she is beginning to challenge parental values in the light of new construing arising from peer group contact. Issues invoking core values are likely to involve strong emotions as old loyalties and memories arise. A wide range of issues across long time periods may arise as structure subsumed by the superordinate is questioned.

Adapting Kelly's original dictum, if you want to know people's core values: *ask them*. They may tell you! Asking about what beliefs were encouraged in childhood, how much the parents' sibling group agree or disagree and in what way may be helpful. One can discuss religious faith, belief in God, death and the afterlife and so on. When there is an issue one may use the laddering technique: 'Which of the two alternatives, being strict or being laissez-faire, would you prefer, is more you? Why would you prefer that?' Doing this with family members together constitutes a core therapeutic process that can enable long-standing issues to be resolved as members negotiate and revise construing at this level. Christine Padesky (1994), writing in the cognitive-behavioural tradition, uses the term 'core schemata' to describe an almost identical concept to Kelly's superordinate constructs. She even sees them as dimensionally bipolar in form. One wonders whether Kelly influenced her significantly. She suggests the following questions: 'What does this (internal or external event) say about you? What does this say about how your life or the world operates?'

Enhancing commitment to the process by negotiating agreed therapy goals

Often families have become 'stuck' because different members are trying to move in different directions towards contradictory goals. Conflict then escalates or a member becomes discouraged and wants to opt out. Symptoms or problems arise and the family's energies are then focused on this secondary scenario. Major polarization may develop along a family construct such as 'he can't help it, he's ill' versus 'you're treating him too gently, it's deliberate behaviour'.

Asking what goals they would want to achieve is a core technique designed to return the family to an agreed mutual path, like a magnet aligning them in one direction. (If this has not been possible we may agree on a goal of working towards agreement.) Commonly, it is useful for goals to be *concrete, positive* and, obviously, *achievable*. Genuine change may not be detected if the family are hoping for her 'just to behave all the time!' By positive, I mean going towards something rather than away from it, for example 'I want her to learn to control her moods' rather than 'I just want her tempers to stop'. Such techniques are now commonplace in brief therapy and behavioural work. However, in this approach, we do not necessarily do much with the goal. Its main purpose is to define the therapeutic work as *being about change*. Change typically occurs in spontaneous and unpredictable rather than planned ways. Too much focus on the process can become an impediment. Nevertheless, having a defined goal at the back of the mind is probably helpful in generating the creative process towards change.

Understanding agreements and disagreements and enhancing 'agreement to differ'

In various papers (for example, Procter, 1996) I have argued that the *family itself* develops a construct system that governs family functioning and interaction. Individual construing seems to be sacrificed in favour of adherence to sometimes even only one *family construct* with members taking up one or the other of the two poles (for example, 'he's got autism' versus 'there's nothing wrong with him'). All the family may have taken up positions at one end of the construct, seeing professionals or others as occupying the other pole. In single parent or stepfamilies, the family may see the child's other parent in very negative pre-emptive terms, leaving the child, whose natural tendency is to identify with the parent, in a dilemma of divided loyalties.

Forming a *credulous* and *accepting* stance towards family members who are themselves locked in apparently irreconcilable disagreements allows the therapist to begin a process of ameliorating and modifying family construing. Antagonistic positions are often maintained by the members drawing on separate sets of *validational evidence* to prove their own position. Having the antagonists consider just one or two episodes and making sense of them from the two positions may allow new similarities and differences to emerge, which allows progress. If conflict begins to arise in the session, one can say, 'John, you're saying so-and-so and Mary, you're saying such-and-such, is this a typical way you tend to disagree?' Sometimes people think it is essential to agree on an issue when, in fact, the differences can be reconstrued as complementary, as in the first technique that we discussed in this chapter. For example, with warring parents, one can say, 'in a child's development it is essential to have both *firm structure* and *warm nurturance*'. Acceptance of this will probably result in a de-escalation of the polarization. Such work is the stuff of working with children whose parents have gone their separate ways in anger.

Extending the range and scope of individual and group construing

Even the most deprived families will usually have a richness of tradition and construing that contains sufficient resources for therapeutic progress to be attained. However, sometimes the family construct system is so *constricted* in its range that a broadening of knowledge and understanding is required. This is a great challenge. By definition, a person cannot understand something that lies outside the construct system's range. Families will often seek 'advice', but when given it, will immediately reject it or fail to sustain its implementation (see Tom Ravenette, 1999, on advice). This rejection may be of two types:

1. it lies outside the construct system range; or
2. it is interpreted within the system as invalid – for example, the advice just given is what the client's mother has been saying and mother's opinion is regarded as wrong.

Hopefully the earlier careful exploration of family construing will have enabled the therapist to understand how to present information in a way that is acceptable. In type 1, what is required includes what is now called a *psychoeducational* approach. For example, one might offer knowledge based on developmental psychology to explain that the child is still too young to understand certain concepts. Often families are willing to accept the new constructs, but one might ask first if they would welcome some new ideas that might throw light on the situation. In type 2, more understanding of the rejection is required. For example, if a psychological account of chronic pain is being offered, it will certainly be rejected if the suggestion is interpreted as 'the pain is just in the mind and is being imagined'. Appropriate metaphors and explanations will be needed to extend the range but it may be necessary to work within the existing construing system.

Lighting up different areas of the family's universe

Constructs remain active because they are useful for making sense of and anticipating a range of experiences, indeed they *shape* the very way such experiences are apprehended and *select* what is seen as significant versus irrelevant. The members and the family as a whole are therefore concerned with a range of events and elements (each other, problems, memories, and so forth), which validate their set of constructs, which in turn recursively keep this range of experience central to consciousness. The therapist may therefore actively steer the conversation to topics that the family may not have seen as relevant to a discourse about the 'problems'. The therapist should show an interest in *anything* in the family conversation. I find myself talking about all sorts of abstruse topics, for example about carburettors and fuel injection systems (from father's work), Egyptian archaeology (from mother's course), about 'Robot Build' and 'Yu-gi-oh' trading card games. Why? Because they are a source of constructs and metaphors, they are part of functional life and, if I show a *willingness genuinely to learn something new from them,* they are more likely to *open to new learning from me.* The next two techniques are important examples of this general approach.

Steering the conversation to the constructive and functional and to topics containing therapeutic lessons

There is a strong tendency for family members to wish to discuss the problems that face them at great length, to offer the therapist further examples, to explore the apparent historical causes and so on. There is a danger that the problem expands to fill the family's entire universe, leaving the member who is complained about or worried about feeling blamed, helpless, defensive or guilty. The atmosphere of the session becomes tense, children bored and angry and wishing to leave. This is not a good recipe for resolution of problems and creative reconstruing of the situation.

Personal construct psychology comes to us with the optimistic notion that everything is open to being construed in a different and more functional way. The person is said to be a 'form of motion' (Kelly, 1955/1991a), to which I add, 'The family is a form of motion.' Any negative construct always has its contrast pole, although there is not always a convenient word in the language to summarize the opposite to the myriad words describing human suffering and complaint. As Fransella (1972) showed in relation to stuttering, the problem constructs are often highly elaborated, but the constructs governing absence of the problem are sparse. We need to encourage the family to consider times when the problem is *least noticeable,* and to consider *improvements* and *exceptions* (Berg, 1994) and elaborate these: what was happening at this time, how did the person manage to keep his or her temper, what were other people doing to help, how do others control their temper when provoked, and so forth. More generally we need to encourage the development of constructs about the member functioning happily and being OK. This counters the tendency to construe the person's *identity* in essentially problematic terms. They move, for example, from 'He's aggressive, like his father was' to 'Ryan can be thoughtful, helpful and funny but can be impatient.'

Establishing wider and historical interpersonal contexts

It is common in family therapy to draw up a *family tree* or *genogram* to look at how members are related, to look at the wider extended families and consider past experiences. It is important to understand that the family tree is potentially an extremely powerful therapeutic tool, which should be used judiciously, and only when the time is right. Doing a genogram effectively forces the consideration by the family of vital and central experiences such as paternity, losses and bereavements, separations and divorces, familial 'mental illness', abuse and trauma. If it is done before therapeutic rapport and trust have developed, or with inappropriate people in the room to hear about certain experiences, the result will be superficial and censored accounts, which may preclude the possibility of further exploration later. At the right time, however, hugely rich accounts of what people were like, how they saw things, relationships and stories will be evoked. In PCP terms, the family tree can be used both as a *loosening* device, bringing in new material which will extend and loosen over prescriptive constructs, and as a means of tightening, by helping members with diffuse identity constructs to further define their origins and connectedness.

Rudi Dallos (2003) has developed the use of attachment theory and research which links security of attachment to the coherence and style of narratives about attachment experiences. He uses the Adult Attachment Interview (George, Kaplan and Main, 1996) in a family therapy context. The parent is asked to list 'five adjectives which best describe the relationship and attachment that you had with each of your own parents'. This is very similar to eliciting constructs, but it is not only the *content* of childhood episodes that is then evoked but the *coherence of reporting* is also of interest: insecure attachments seem to be associated with much more hesitant and disrupted accounts.

This leads to interesting comparisons between PCP and the currently popular narrative approaches in family therapy (White, 1995). There is a tradition within PCP emphasizing stories, which predates the narrative school (see Mair, 1989). However, Adroutsopoulou (2001) takes PCP to task for focusing more on constructs rather than whole narratives. These, of course, are not contradictory but complement each other. The way I see it is that *constructs subsume narratives* and *narratives communicate constructs*.

When people tell stories they are communicating a construction of the characters, their relationships and how the teller values these. Likewise when a construct is voiced, subsumed under it are not just further constructs, but episodes and validational evidence in the form of narratives structured in time. We only understand the construct to the extent that we know these stories. The construct is like the handle of a suitcase and the stories are inside the suitcase. The construct is a name or summary of the stories which comprise it. A story will be listened to and remembered to the extent that it validates or revises a construct in the listener's repertory.

Again, when we hear stories about the wider family and past experiences we will be steering towards a balanced account that sees the positive or elaborative aspects too. Procter and Dallos (2005) recount the story of an angry boy who is transformed when he hears something good about his father ('brilliant at football'), when the only thing he had known about his father was that he had been violent to the boy's mother. The past does not cause effects in the present: it no longer exists. However, through having shaped construing that is still being applied, it does affect the present although these constructions are always open to modification.

Working towards involving different subsystems and subgroups

Offering choice about dividing up the session and seeing people separately is fundamental in this work, although it is likely to be advantageous to negotiate first how to do that with the wider group. This enables the therapist to get to know the family as a whole and explain his or her role and hopefully build good working relationships with all members. If the family as a whole accepts the therapist as a friendly and helpful figure it will go a long way to enable effective work. Early on in the sessions I usually say 'Only talk about what you feel like saying at any particular time, if you don't want to answer a question you don't have to. I often see children by themselves, or parents or any smaller group. I may suggest that, and you can too.' To the child: 'Would you like to see me by yourself later on?' To the parents: 'Would you like to talk to me without the children?' I explain, 'Each part of the meeting is confidential, so you can say what you like and I won't be a communication "bridge" between one and another of you, although I might suggest you talk and help you do that. I will use the information and the overall understanding I gain to help the situation in the best way I can think of.' I have rarely found difficulties with this approach.

One might typically work with subgroups when dealing with adolescents, who will talk more freely and without interruption from their parents. Why not just work individually with them? One may choose to, of course, but usually more can be done by working with parent and young person together and helping them negotiate new shared understandings. If the parent is the complainant, one will also learn far more about what situations are occurring. Parents need to be given time to explore hypotheses that may only worry their children or make them more difficult to collaborate with. Children may wish to share difficult or abusive experiences at the hands of their parents. It is common to talk with parents alone in order to move towards dealing with marital or couple issues, which may be associated with child problems. One may even move on to seeing each person in a couple separately to address issues about the other. There are too many situations to address adequately here. It is eminently possible to work with families using a combination of whole family, subgroup and individual sessions and, indeed, in my experience, this is a highly effective format of work. In general, we will separate into subgroups if the associated positions have become so polarized and intolerable for the other to hear that credulous exploration becomes impossible.

Developing interpersonal understanding, empathy and sociality

Perhaps the fundamental way in which family therapy helps is by increasing the level of interpersonal understanding between intimates. Family members of course know each other extremely well and yet systematic misperceptions and mutual stereotyping can only too easily develop. Members may rarely get the chance for their voice to be heard. Parents have often said to me, 'he's said more today than he has in months'.

Kelly's sociality corollary argues that relating is based on mutual construction of each other's constructs. This has recently been made topical with the 'theory of mind' work in which low sociality or ability to understand others' viewpoints has been shown to be associated with autistic spectrum disorders (see Procter, 2000, 2001) as well as other difficulties including eating disorders, conduct problems and offending in young people. Working with the family is an ideal way to address this issue. The chance is there over a period of time to help a person become more aware of systematic misperception of others' intentions and to learn to construe the signals and cues that we all give out when we communicate. If a person is impaired in this area, it is helpful to have other family members become more aware of this in day-to-day communication and to find ways of compensating for it by providing additional cues, simplifying language, using written signs, and so forth. Difficulties of generalization from one context to another (for example, from school to home) make it particularly apposite to work directly in the natural environment of the family.

Moving from individual to relational construing

Gregory Bateson (1972) argued that we are continuously communicating at two levels, the *content* level and the *relational* level. Even animals will pretend to fight in a playful way, giving the message 'this is play'. We are continuously communicating about our role relationship through gesture, posture, facial expression, and voice tone as well as linguistic messages. The constructs governing this communication are not necessarily given verbal labels. Encouraging an awareness and discussion of how the family members are construing their relationships often gives the opportunity to resolve issues and conflicts that may be long-standing.

In relating to each other people are often using *individual constructs*, for example 'lazy' applied to his son by a father, or 'useless' applied to himself by the son (see Figure 8.3). These constructs govern and shape action towards the other, which all too easily can become caught in recursive and repeating patterns of interaction. Critical and pathological labels can become self-perpetuating, with the person complained about reacting in the very way that confirms the label. Moving gently from *individual* to *relational* construing (see Procter, 2002) is helpful in ameliorating this tendency. One can ask one of the two (or a third observer) 'How do you see the relationship between you and your son?' If an episode of less strife is described, we may ask, 'Were you closer during that afternoon? How were you getting on?' Relational construing leads to entirely different outcomes and mirrors the move in psychology away from personality trait approaches.

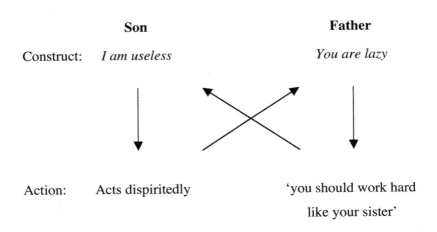

	Son	**Father**
Construct:	*I am useless*	*You are lazy*
Action:	Acts dispiritedly	'you should work hard like your sister'

Figure 8.3 'Bow-tie' diagram of construing between father and son.

Hierarchy and power are central issues in nearly any family. In family construct terms (Feixas, 1995; Procter, 1981, 1996) we can define power in terms of *whose construing tends to predominate in the family*. Roles defined hierarchically may cease to be functional or appropriate as the family moves into new stages. Viney, Benjamin and Preston (1988) give some good examples of this in family therapy work with older adults. A man whose wife suffered a stroke was defined by a family construct: 'the father is the boss'. Conflicts arising from his being controlling were modified when this construct was revised when he admitted that having to 'take all the responsibility' was actually a significant burden to him.

Reflecting on changes in construing and making sense of the original concerns

A lot of work revising constructions can occur in the hypothetical. Kelly (1955/1991a) stressed rehearsing and enacting situations including the well-known 'fixed role therapy'. 'If' questions are very useful in situations of apparent impasse. Thus, I asked an angry seven-year-old boy who hates his stepfather David, 'If you and David could get along better and be friends, would you be interested?' He nodded and this led to it being possible to admit that they *had got on better* the previous week when David had helped him make a 'flick' book. Essex and Gumbleton (1999) have adopted a whole approach for working with denied sexual abuse. The family are encouraged to consider a 'similar but different' family where abuse had occurred, and what steps they would make to ensure the continued safety of the child.

Later on in therapy, when changes are occurring, one can begin to make sense of the original concerns in a new way. Once the family construing has revised sufficiently, it is possible to look back with much less threat. 'What sense are you making now of what was going on when he used to get so angry?'

Conclusion

This is necessarily only a brief tour of these techniques but I hope it shows that PCP can provide a comprehensive method of intervening in families, a mode of therapy relevant to many areas of human difficulty. I have used the word 'technique' perhaps provocatively as it is so out of fashion in these days of post-modern critiques of the old interventionist, strategic 'first-order' therapies. I wish to emphasize that the family will be hardly aware of these techniques – therapy should be like an ordinary conversation. Not even the experienced therapist is very aware. This chapter was born of a question to my students, 'what do I do when I work with families?' I was not sure myself as, after many years of practice, I am simply being myself with families and my thoughts are dwelling almost entirely on *their lives*. Nevertheless, interviewing families well is a challenging business. How does one learn to do it? Lots of practice and experience is the answer but I hope that this chapter will prove useful for students and more experienced workers alike. A jazz improviser will learn by spending a great deal of time learning scales and arpeggios. This list of techniques may also provide the basis for a manual of personal construct family therapy, which could be used in psychotherapy research studies.

PART TWO
SPECIFIC CLINICAL
PROBLEMS

CHAPTER NINE

Growing through grief: constructing coherence in narratives of loss

ROBERT A NEIMEYER

Case example

Joanne W.'s pursuit of therapy was prompted by a number of recent but frightening physical symptoms, which included dizziness, rapid heartbeat, and racing pulse, accompanied by seemingly inexplicable spirals of 'nervousness'. When thorough medical testing disclosed no organic basis for these reactions, she was referred for psychotherapy with a diagnosis of 'panic attacks of psychogenic origin', although Joanne herself was hard put to explain the reasons for her paralysing anxiety in terms that were convincing to her or to others. Presenting for her first session attractively attired in a conservative, well-tailored suit, Joanne noted that her symptoms first appeared when she prepared to leave the eastern city that had been 'her only home' some 5 months earlier to follow her husband's 'call' to take a position as the pastor of a southern African-American church over 1,000 miles away. Now, distant from her mother, sisters, and friends in the community that had shaped and sustained her, she found herself becoming increasingly reclusive lest members of the new congregation discover her 'emotional problems' and label her as 'crazy'. Over the past several weeks, Joanne confided, she had even begun to 'pull away' from her husband, George, and 12-year-old daughter, Leitha, deepening her concern that she not only was failing as the 'first lady' of her church, but also was 'losing herself' and those she loved.

After spending a few minutes exploring Joanne's understanding of her problem in more detail, I then inquired about any previous experiences she might have had with therapy, as a way of seeking her consultation on what therapeutic styles or methods had worked especially well – or poorly – for her. Joanne responded that her only previous exposure to therapy had been in the context of a brief training programme for pastoral counsellors a few years before, part of which focused on the participants' own issues and their possible impact on their interactions with parishioners.

The major issue at the time, she recalled in a controlled fashion, had been her father's death two years before, the stress of which had been compounded by the long illness that preceded it, and for which she and her mother had been the primary caregivers. Tears rolled down Joanne's cheeks in response to my empathic inquiry about the trembling in her lip as she recounted her father's passing, and she noted that she had only in the past year begun to cry for him, as his uncharacteristic meanness during his illness left her more with a sense of numbness and relief, than with clear grief over his passing. Now, she realized, she really missed him, and speaking quietly but unevenly through the haze of tears, added that, 'He would have been able to give me advice about moving, if only he were here.'

Alerted to the emotional vividness of this material for Joanne some six years after her father's death, and struck by her spontaneous linkage of his absence with the problems in her relocation that had precipitated the anxiety attacks, I gently asked Joanne if she would like to invite her father to join us in the therapy room, to reopen a relationship with him that had been interrupted by his illness and death. Intrigued, she accepted the suggestion, and with guidance began a conversation with her father, who we symbolically offered an empty chair positioned across from his daughter. Sobbing, Joanne recounted to her father the outlines of her current problems, and, after a few seconds of silence, deepened her disclosure to include her feeling of guilt for having abandoned him by leaving the city in which he had lived for his whole adult life, to return to the South he had known only as a boy.

Accepting my suggestion that she take her father's place and respond to what she had said, Joanne changed chairs, dried her tears, and offered reassurance, concluding with, 'Don't worry, baby, I'll come visit you', words that rung strangely hollow in view of the poignant sense of loss Joanne had shared only moments before. Again taking her own seat at my gesture, Joanne repeated the words I tentatively offered to her: 'You can't visit me, Dad. You're dead.' Joanne then poured forth both her grief and self-doubt, punctuated by wracking sobs. As she grew quiet, I again invited her into her father's chair, where, unprompted, Joanne (as her father) provided loving and genuine reassurance, affirming that, despite his death, he would always be with her, always believe in her. This interaction triggered a startling insight for Joanne. In her words, 'I realize now that I *can* keep him, that he *can* be with me, and that I can even come to know him more through the South that he loved.' Buoyed up by the new-found reconnection with her father, Joanne then went on to place her own sense of uprootedness and disloyalty in the context of her relationship with the surviving members of her family of origin, who, like her, were 'struggling together to make sense of this new transition'. As our first session neared its end, Joanne somewhat sheepishly shared her wish to pursue advanced schooling despite her 'first lady' status, but serving as a cultural inter-preter, described for my benefit as a Caucasian therapist the implicit social expectations that constrained this potentially 'selfish' goal within African-American faith communities. Eager to pursue the 'fresh ideas' generated in the session, Joanne closed by requesting another appointment.

In her remaining three bi-weekly sessions, Joanne deepened her explo-ration of both her history of loss, revisiting the death of an infant son early in her marriage, and renewed her effort to 'find her voice' as a woman in her own right in her family and church community. As she did so, she remarked with some surprise that life was starting to seem some-how 'more real', and she related with pride several concrete instances in which she had negotiated important family decisions with her husband, played a more active role in providing guidance to her pre-teen daughter, and 'stood up' for innovative church programmes that she believed in. In all of this, she continued to feel a strong sense of her father's presence and pride in her, and the feeling that something had 'lifted' for her in the pivotal 'conversation' with him in the opening session. In Joanne's own words, she no longer felt 'held back' and was gratified by George's sup-port for her being her own 'outspoken' self, even to the point of wearing neat but casual clothes to both church committee meetings and therapy sessions. Perhaps most remarkably, she had been entirely freed of the panic symptoms from the point of her 'conversation' with her father onward, despite these symptoms never having been made the specific tar-gets of therapeutic intervention. Our therapy concluded by reflecting on the 'changed narrative' of Joanne's life, which re-established a sense of continuity with who she had been (as anchored in an ongoing relation-ship with her supportive father), while also permitting her to 're-author' aspects of her identity in critical living relationships. Follow-up indicated that these changes were consolidated over coming months.

Theory and research

This opening case vignette not only hints at fresh conceptualizations of grief that are beginning to revitalize the once tradition-bound field of bereavement theory (RA Neimeyer and Gamino, 2003), but also illustrates features of constructivist therapy that have particular relevance to helping people integrate experiences of loss into the larger stories of their lives. My goal in this chapter will be to review this growing edge of constructivist grief theory and therapy, and then extend it modestly by describing a ger-minal taxonomy of disruptions in life narratives that can be occasioned by loss, and suggest something of how they might be addressed in therapy or counselling informed by a constructivist or narrative spirit. Throughout, I

will attempt to anchor the discussion in both concrete clinical case material and the burgeoning research literature, each of which sheds light on the
struggle for coherence in the aftermath of loss.

The new landscape of loss

Popular and professional models of mourning have long depicted it as a relatively predictable series of stages of adjustment following a profound loss,
which begins with some form of shock or denial, progresses through various phases of distressing emotions, and eventuates in a state of acceptance,
recovery, or the like (Kubler-Ross, 1969). Even the most scholarly and well-
grounded of such models (Bowlby, 1973) tend to focus attention on the
immediate aftermath of bereavement, seeking presumably universal patterns of adaptation as the survivor moves from psychic disequilibrium
toward ultimate emotional stability as healing progresses. Of course, pathological variants are acknowledged and indeed diagnosed (Lindemann,
1944), including such seemingly sinister syndromes as delayed grief, in
which the bereaved show little visible psychological distress following the
loss while remaining vulnerable to emergence of later symptomatology, and
chronic grief, which fails to remit satisfactorily over time. Accordingly, in
keeping with influential psychodynamic formulations (Freud, 1957), the
goal of therapy is to promote appropriate 'grief work', which requires the
withdrawal of emotional investments in the deceased in order to permit
reinvestment in new relationships. The pursuit of 'closure' thereby becomes
the chief aim of therapy, as the bereaved is helped to 'say goodbye' to his or
her loved one and 'move on' to fresh opportunities. Because this process
typically meets with considerable unconscious resistance, progress is predicted to be slow, as the therapist helps the client call up and painfully
de-cathect or withdraw all libidinal energy from the deceased (Freud, 1957).
Viewed in this perspective, a lingering 'identification' with the loved one is
seen as pathognomic, suggesting the incapacity of the living to 'emancipate'
the self from psychic 'bondage' to the dead (Lindemann, 1944).

Significantly, nearly every feature of this widely accepted model has been
called into serious doubt by recent research and scholarship. Gone is the
reliance on stage models of grief, in view of mounting clinical and empirical evidence that the actual responses of bereaved persons lack the
predictable progression they implicitly prescribe (Corr, 1993). Likewise, the
early focus on the immediate emotional sequelae of loss has been complemented by the study of the cognitive and behavioural means by which the
bereaved cope with their changed lives across an extended period of time
(Stroebe and Schut, 1999), a process that in some cases has been found to
extend decades beyond the actual point of the death (Malkinson and Bar-
Tur, 1999). Furthermore, patterns of adaptation once held in suspicion

such as 'delayed grief' have been challenged by data suggesting that bereaved persons who show minimal perturbation in the early months of loss virtually always continue to function well, even years later (Middleton et al., 1998; Davis et al., 2000). Perhaps most fundamentally, there is growing scepticism about whether 'grief work' works, that is, whether the arduous task of reviewing and relinquishing ties to the deceased does indeed lead to improved functioning (Stroebe, 1992; Wortman and Silver, 1987). In place of the traditional suspicion regarding continued emotional 'bondage' to the deceased, a growing number of theorists and researchers are exploring the potentially sustaining role of continuing bonds with those we have loved and lost, which can take the form of holding them close in memory, inspiration, conversation and ongoing ritual recognition of their roles in our lives (Klass, Silverman, and Nickman, 1996; Klass, 1999; Attig, 2000). As this implies, this form of active adaptation has a social as well as a psychic dimension, taking place as much in the external world as in the internal world of the grieving person (Walsh and McGoldrick, 1991).

A constructivist perspective

My own response to this intellectual ferment has been to further the exploration of the new landscape of loss by drawing on a broad repertory of constructivist, narrative and social constructionist concepts and methods. In this, a personal construct view (Kelly, 1955/1991a/1991b) of persons as attempting to attribute significance to the thematic recurrence of events provides an important point of departure, underscoring the human quest for viable personal theories of life and detailing the sense of threat, anxiety, and guilt that can attend their actual or imminent invalidation. Kelly's work also draws attention to the social embeddedness of our sense-making efforts and the hopeful prospects for transcendence of traumatic circumstances through bold experimentation with new life scripts, as in the process of fixed-role therapy (RA Neimeyer, 1987).

Joanne's therapy highlights some of the implications of this emerging constructivist view for the conceptualization of loss and the practice of grief therapy. As I listened to her account of her puzzling panic attacks, I did so with the conviction that her symptoms had significance, and that her anxiety signalled a breakdown in her ability to make sense of her present circumstances in terms of her previously sustaining construction of life (Kelly, 1955/1991a/1991b). Evidence supporting this hypothesis was not long in coming. As Joanne described the geographic dislocation that preceded her symptomatology, she also touched on the emotional dislocation from a validating relationship with her beloved father that was anchored in her previous community, and fresh tears of grief suggested the continued relevance of this old wound. Alerted by her passing reference to the advice that her father would give her if he were present, I checked with Joanne on her willingness to invite him to join us symbolically in the room, not with the goal of seeking 'closure', but instead to reopen a conversation that had been interrupted by death. The ensuing discussion 'between' them, performed evocatively by Joanne, provided surprising and powerful experiential validation of their continuing bond, a bond that she subsequently strengthened in her daily life between sessions. Thus, in stark contrast to the slow and anguishing work of relinquishing her attachment suggested by traditional grief theory, Joanne quickly and spontaneously affirmed her deep connection to her deceased father, and recovered in their renewed 'relationship' the resources needed to validate and elaborate a more adequate sense of self.

In the remainder of this chapter I shall build on this general constructivist framework for understanding the inter-braiding of self and other and its potential unravelling by bereavement by summarizing an emerging narrative formulation of loss, and hinting at its usefulness in case conceptualization and grief therapy.

Loss and narrative disruption

As human beings, we are defined by the stories that we live and the stories that live us (Mair, 1988). At the most individual level, this implies that the narration of life experiences can be viewed as an 'effort after meaning' (Bartlett, 1932), an attempt to establish a sense of lived continuity in our experience over time (RA Neimeyer, 1995b). On the broadest level, the 'culture tales' (Howard, 1991) formulated by tribes or whole societies can offer ways of addressing the perennial questions 'Who are we? Where do we come from? And where are we going?' As such, they provide discursive resources (and concomitant constraints) for the self-definitions of individuals living within the culture's matrix of meaning (Harré and Gillett, 1994). At intermediate, interpersonal levels, storytelling may involve various ways of 'positioning' oneself within the story (for example, as clown, hero, victim, or supporting actor), while at the same time assigning complementary roles to other characters (Winslade and Monk, 2001).

Viewed from this perspective, all three levels of narrative activity – intrapersonal, cultural and interpersonal – can be viewed as concerned with the construction and co-construction of identity. That is, all three entail processes contributing to or challenging the development of a self-narrative, defined as 'an overarching cognitive-affective-behavioral structure that organizes the 'micro-narratives' of everyday life into a 'macro-narrative' that consolidates our self-understanding, establishes our characteristic range of emotions and goals, and guides our performance on the stage of the social world' (RA Neimeyer, 2004a). As such, the self-narrative is (typically) both more stable and coherent than our moment-to-moment performances in discrete social episodes, and more fluid and shifting than is implied by the 'essentialist' terminology of traits, personality or character. At times, however, the meaningful assimilation and direction of experience provided by the self-narrative are severely challenged. Three such disruptions that have special relevance to the phenomenon of loss concern narrative disorganization, dissociation and dominance. Here I shall consider each in turn, summarizing and extending a germinal taxonomy of narrative disruption developed elsewhere (RA Neimeyer, 2000, 2004a) and illustrating this framework through the use of brief case studies.

Disorganized narratives

Disorganized narratives commonly result from traumatic loss, in which life events that are radically inconsistent with the person's prior self-narrative profoundly challenge its form and function (RA Neimeyer, 2000). The resulting disruptions can be felt on virtually every level of narrative activity, from the organization of a coherent plot structure for life experiences (RA Neimeyer and Stewart, 1996), through the underlying themes of the person's assumptive world (Kauffman, 2002), to those overarching goals that conferred on the earlier self-narrative its distinctive teleology and direction (RA Neimeyer, 2000). When the trauma is associated with a human cause (such as the murder of a loved one, violent assault or torture, sexual abuse by a member of the family), the characterization of specific actors in one's life narrative – or even of people in general – can also be deeply affected (Sewell, 1997). Finally, even seemingly benign features of the setting of one's life story can be contaminated by the trauma, as previously neutral sights, sounds, smells and sensations associated with the loss event become 'triggers' for subsequent traumatic re-experiencing (Horowitz, 1997). The unique biology of traumatic memories (Van der Kolk and Van der Hart, 1991), being encoded under conditions of high neurophysiological arousal, results in a fragmented, intrusive and ruminative recall of the relevant events, fused with the intensive emotions (for example, anxiety, helplessness, despair) that initially accompanied them. Consequently, catastrophic events can remain in this sense 'pre-narrative', persisting as fragmentary and affectively charged perceptual 'modules' that are difficult to integrate into a consistent 'micro-narrative' of the traumatic experience, much less into the broader 'macro-narrative' of the survivor's life story.

As Hermans (2002) observes, this struggle to integrate conflictual emotional episodes may be especially acute for persons whose relationships with caregivers during development provided insufficient empathic attunement to stimulate the maturation of brain centres necessary for the transcendence of distressing experience. As a result, the traumatized individual is handicapped in shifting from immersion in the problematic experience to alternative internalized perspectives or 'I-positions' that offer the prospect of 'self-solace' (as Joanne was ultimately able to do in accessing and enacting internalized images of her father). Unable to construct transitions or 'meaning bridges' between highly negative and positive states of mind, the individual's sense of self-continuity is jeopardized, contributing to the disorganization of the self-narrative. This view is compatible with the general argument that insecure attachment during critical developmental periods complicates later adult efforts to construct a coherent self-representation in the face of conflictual experience (Schore, 1994). It also accords with the specific argument that the traumatic disorganization of the self-narrative following the loss of a loved one is especially likely for bereaved persons with problematic developmental histories, predisposing them to complicated grief following the loss of a stabilizing attachment (RA Neimeyer, Prigerson and Davies, 2002).

An example is provided by the case of Wanda who, at 62, consulted a therapist with a significant worsening of the intermittent low-grade depression with which she had struggled for much of her life.

Wanda's downward spiral began some 6 years earlier, when she was employed as a successful executive in a large financial firm. She could identify a specific precipitating event: a call from her husband telling her to leave work immediately and meet him at home because of an unspecified family crisis. Pressing him for details, Wanda learned that her father, who had been living with her mother several hours away in another state, had died suddenly of a massive heart attack. Wanda recalled a sense of disbelief as she dashed home to pack hurriedly and drive to her parents' home. The next several days were a blur of making funeral arrangements, holding a memorial service, and – most problematically – trying to support a needy and bereft mother who, she said, 'had never been there for her' when she was growing up. When her mother, 2 months later, decided to sell her home in attempt to escape the memories it held and move in with Wanda despite her daughter's feeble protests, the situation worsened dramatically. Within weeks Wanda was vacillating between depressive avoidance of her mother and suicidal/homicidal fantasies of ending their fights in a burst of violence. Alarmed, Wanda's husband arranged for her psychiatric hospitalization, which effectively terminated her professional career. Although Wanda stabilized and was discharged to her home following the residential placement of her mother, she remained in tenuous adjustment 2 years later when she received a second fateful phone call: her only daughter, Kim, had been hospitalized at age 31 in a serious but unspecified condition. Rushing to the emergency room with her husband, she arrived just in time to be escorted by a nurse to her daughter's room, where a doctor announced that he had been powerless to stop the cerebral aneurism that took Kim's life. Glancing in panic from the doctor's face to her daughter's lifeless expression, mouth and eyes frozen partly open in death, Wanda lost consciousness.

Wanda described the 4 years that followed as filled with unmitigated suffering. As she phrased it, it was as if 'everything in [her] life was broken by these deaths', and she 'had not been the same person since'. Although frequent intrusive images of her daughter on the hospital gurney were particularly traumatic, the death of her somewhat distant, but clearly favoured parent two years before, compounded by a deeply resented responsibility for a mother to whom she had never been close, had already deeply disrupted a life script that was for the most part organized around independence and professional success. Thus, the losses had undercut the plot structure of a progressive career narrative that had served as a bulwark against her periodic depressions, and the loss of her job following her hospitalization decimated the goals that had given a hopeful direction to her life story. The sudden death of her daughter profoundly worsened Wanda's predicament, and added a new and still darker dimension to her crisis: the apparent invalidation of long-sustaining beliefs in the power of self-determination, and even the existence of a caring God. Bereft of father, daughter, work, church and a familiar assumptive world, Wanda clearly met criteria for complicated grief (Prigerson and Jacobs, 2001), a condition to which bereaved individuals with problematic models of attachment, like Wanda's to her mother, might well be predisposed. The result was a profound crisis of meaning (RA Neimeyer, Prigerson and Davies, 2002), in which separation distress and traumatic distress were inextricably woven together with the breakdown of her self-narrative at levels ranging from its plot, through theme, to goals. In the face of this anguishing disintegration of a personal world of meaning, Wanda was inconsolable, either by others or by herself.

Although Wanda's case provides a particularly dramatic illustration of a conflicted and disorganized narrative following profound loss, it is worth emphasizing that even more normative and less concentrated experiences of loss can have a substantial disruptive effect on the self-narratives of survivors, representing jarring micro-narratives that can be hard to integrate into one's larger macro-narrative of identity. The consequence can be a significant perturbation of self-coherence, making it harder to envision future life chapters that flow meaningfully from those past.

Dissociated narratives

Dissociated narratives are 'silent stories', accounts of loss or trauma unvoiced to others, and often even to the self (RA Neimeyer, 2004a). As such they commonly involve dissociation in two senses, disrupting the link between narrator and audience, as well as the communication between 'I-positions' within the self (Hermans, 2002). The result is a breakdown in sociality, as well as subtle or profound dissociation in the classical psychodynamic sense, such that critical incidents in one's self-narrative are segregated and compartmentalized in an attempt to control the pain or guilt that would come with their fuller integration into the public or conscious story of one's life. As in Stiles' (1999) assimilation theory, dissociated experiences can be seen as ranging from those that are warded off from conscious acknowledgement, through those that are acknowledged, but actively avoided, to those that are painfully known, but denied expression. Incongruous micro-narratives that threaten an individual's image in the eyes of relevant others are particularly likely to be held in this silent, unvoiced fashion, such as histories of sexual abuse, marital infidelity and hidden addiction. But even the losses of loved ones through stigmatizing death (such as the death of a son through AIDS) can be dissociated in this manner, depriving the bereaved of the social support – but also safeguarding him or her from the social censure – that might come from an unabridged account of the circumstances of the death (RA Neimeyer and Jordan, 2002).

An illustration of this arose with Denise, a professional woman who returned home late one night, expecting to find an irritated husband who had been holding dinner for her for 2 hours. Instead, Denise entered a house that was strangely quiet, with no sign that dinner had been started. Calling her husband's name, she walked down the hall toward the bedroom, when she noticed a light shining from beneath the door leading to the basement. Denise opened the door, called 'Bill?' with a questioning intonation once more, and then started down the wooden steps. The sight that greeted her at the bottom of the staircase immersed her in a horror she had never known, as she froze screaming before her husband's gently swinging body, his purple head titled at an odd angle, as he dangled from a cord lashed to a drainpipe in the ceiling. Compounding her incomprehension, Bill was naked from the waist down, and pornographic magazines lay scattered at his feet around a tumbled footstool. Denise could scarcely recall the next half-hour, as she sobbingly and frantically dressed his body and removed the magazines before calling emergency services. Thus began a carefully 'edited' story of Bill's death, pronounced by the coroner a suicide, rather than the still more unsettling and accidental act of auto-erotic asphyxiation that she understood it in her heart to have been.

Denise's subsequent story of Bill's death thus qualified not only as a disorganized narrative, one that massively disrupted her prior story of their relationship on both the level of plot and theme, but as a dissociated one as well. Socially, Denise rarely spoke about the death except with her closest confidants, and even then remained silent about its actual nature, colluding with the story that his death was a straightforward, if incomprehensible, suicide. As a result, Diane ironically ensured that her grief would be 'disenfranchised', in the sense that it would be met with 'empathic failure' by even those who tried to offer her support, but whose words necessarily fell short of relevance to a silent plot that remained unarticulated (RA Neimeyer and Jordan, 2002). Internally, Denise also struggled with a dissociative 'walling off' of the death as she partly consciously and partly non-consciously attempted to avoid and 'erase' the disturbing images, emotions, and meanings triggered by the untold story of his death. Integrating this dimension of the loss into her account of her relationship to Bill, and particularly into her characterization of him, was simply too threatening to the macro-narrative of their (partly) shared life, and so it remained fragmented and isolated, with her personal and interpersonal avoidance of the story reinforcing each other.

Denise's case introduces a social dimension to the narration of loss, illustrating the disruption of processes of account-making that typically promote transcendence of trauma (Harvey, 1996). It also emphasizes the delicate dance between interpersonal and intrapersonal narration, as the silencing of a story at one level also disrupts meaningful (internal or external) dialogue about the experience at the other. However, narrative dissociation in this instance focuses largely on the more tangible sphere of relationships with particular others, rather than on the sphere of broader social processes. It is to this larger context, and its unique implications for narrative disruption, that I now turn.

Dominant narratives

Dominant narratives, as the term implies, can disempower and marginalize alternative accounts of self, conferring problem-saturated self-narratives on those subject to them (White and Epston, 1990). As such, they typically have their roots in larger societal or cultural discourses, such as professional discourses of psychopathology that subordinate an individual's unique challenges and resources to the dominant narrative of his or her psychiatric diagnosis, or narratives of ethnic, gender or racial inferiority that 'colonize' the individual's self-narrative and that justify oppression.

However, dominant narratives represent more than simply the heavy-handed inscription of a cultural text on an individual's experience. This is because one's most personal sense of self is appropriated from the social world (James, 1890). Moreover, even an oppressive dominant narrative can serve legitimate functions for the person-in-social-context, while nevertheless obscuring other features of his or her life or experience that are inconsistent with or irrelevant to the broader themes or goals of the dominant story. As a result, the individual can experience a complex form of allegiance to the dominant narrative, but at the cost of living within a constricted account of self that limits his or her sense of authorship in life, and forecloses future possibilities.

An illustration of this arose in the case of Carlos, a man in middle age who had fled political persecution in his native country in his youth and had lived in exile for some 25 years. On many levels he had made a satisfactory adjustment to his new culture, developing impressive competence in his new language and ultimately beginning both a career and family in his adopted land. However, on other levels he remained deeply engaged in the plight of his homeland, whose government continued to make halting steps toward genuine democracy, only to suffer setbacks and the resurgence of a 'police state'. Outside the domain of his work and family, Carlos was most committed to the expatriate community in the city in which he lived, many of whose members had been tortured, as he had been, and many of whom had had loved ones 'disappeared' as retribution for their families' involvement in political opposition movements.

Not surprisingly, political discourses about the injustices of the ruling regime in their homeland, its seeming immunity from prosecution even when abuses were brought to light, and the need to overthrow it to make way for more liberating ideologies permeated Carlos's passionate conversations with his expatriate peers, as well as with family members and friends in his homeland whom he had not seen for many years. In this way the dominant narrative of injustice provided a frame of intelligibility and shared purpose for both exiles and residents of his country, casting them as actors within a broader narrative of political and social change. But the dominant political narrative also had its constraining features, as the individual losses Carlos sustained over time – from his torture as a young man to the death of his father thousands of miles away in Carlos's middle adulthood – were given no place in his self-narrative, except as minor and seemingly self-indulgent instances of a broader political oppression affecting all the citizens of his country. Thus, Carlos had difficulty voicing or

accrediting the micro-narrative of his torture or its after effects as significant in their own terms, and quickly subsumed all subsequent losses as
the direct or indirect result of repressive political forces, such as those
that blocked his attendance at his father's funeral. The result was a dominant self-narrative that legitimized his anger, but not his grief; his
revolutionary zeal, but not his vulnerability. Moreover, Carlos came to
realize that the same narrative domination held sway in the lives of his
expatriate colleagues, in a way that had 'real effects' (Foucault, 1970) by
reinforcing a one-dimensional preoccupation in their relationships.

Carlos's case suggests the role of larger social and cultural processes in
our narration of loss, which necessarily draws on the terms and discourses
of our historical place and time as we strive to attribute meaning to our own
life experiences (RA Neimeyer, Prigerson and Davies, 2002). When such discourses are pre-emptive and hegemonic, they can eclipse alternative
accounts of the person submerged in them, such that all loss is assimilated
into a 'grand narrative' that makes totalizing claims on the experiences of
people subjected to it. Thus, dominant narratives (a) often arise within
broad social systems, (b) structure the self-narratives of individuals, and (c)
confer a good deal of meaning on experience, at the expense of (d) obscuring more personal accounts of the individual's life and identity.

Therapeutic practice: psychotherapy as meaning reconstruction

What implications does this narrative conceptualization hold for psychotherapy, and how might particular change strategies be used to address
the problems of narrative disorganization, dissociation, and dominance?
Although answers to these questions have been pursued at length elsewhere (RA Neimeyer, 2001; RA Neimeyer and Mahoney, 1995; RA
Neimeyer and Raskin, 2000), I will summarize here a narrative framework
for intervention and apply it to each of the above brief case studies.

A tenet of constructivist therapy is that problems are defined, lived and
resolved at the level of meaning, not at the level of behaviour alone (RA
Neimeyer and Bridges, 2003). In narrative terms this implies that stories
can be experienced as problematic or pathological from the standpoint of
their primary protagonists, from that of an observer or member of the
'audience', or both. In some instances (for example, in the case of silent,
dissociative narratives), the sense of narrative disruption and loss of coherence might be most evident to the principal subject of the story, while in
other cases, problematic identities can be imposed on the main characters

of a given account, who may then be constrained to perform in accordance with the dictates of the dominant narrative. In both cases, however, the constructions of meaning that shape the self-narrative represent both the immediate locus of the experienced difficulty and the ultimate set of resources that must be drawn on for its solution.

Case examples

Although a constructivist therapy can have several foci and make use of a great variety of interventions (as other chapters in this volume demonstrate), the general thrust of therapy will depend on the nature of disruption that is targeted. Thus, I will close by offering some thoughts on distinctive therapeutic goals associated with the preliminary taxonomy of narrative forms sketched and illustrated above, concentrating on different patterns of disruption in the client's meaning-making.

In the case of Wanda, the massive disorganization of her self-narrative by a succession of anguishing losses both presented her with traumatic micro-narrative sequences (for example, her daughter's death) and fundamental invalidation of the overall thematic and goal structure of her self-narrative. The result was a sense of personal incoherence in a life trajectory interrupted by loss, and a painful fixation on intrusive memories of experiences that seemed to make no sense in light of the life she had lived before. Accordingly, therapy with Wanda might appropriately adopt as its goal the integration of the trauma narrative(s), at two levels: seeking a meaningful account of each disorganizing micro-narrative, and then working to grasp its significance for the overall macro-narrative of the life in which it was embedded. Several specific strategies might assist with this process, including 'plot work' to help Wanda tell an orderly story of the events themselves, 'setting work' to draw fresh meaning from vivid contextual details of accounts, 'characterization work' to deepen her understanding of the feelings and motives of the relevant actors in the story, including the self, and 'theme work' to examine the invalidation of her assumptive world that now requires reaffirmation, revision or replacement. Finally, 'goal work' might also be in order, to help Wanda envision new short- and long-term objectives consonant with her changed circumstances (RA Neimeyer, 2000). Many specific constructivist techniques have been developed to implement these therapeutic strategies, ranging from experientially vivid chair work similar to that employed with Joanne (Greenberg, Watson and Lietaer, 1998) to the 'moviola' method (Guidano, 1991) of panning or focusing the camera of therapeutic attention across or within critical scenes associated with the problem narrative. Likewise, 'jigsaw memory' tasks can help clients reassemble initially chaotic accounts of trauma narratives (Stewart and RA

Neimeyer, 2001), and various reflective exercises can promote the meaningful integration of loss into the clients' life stories (RA Neimeyer, 2004b). The overarching objective of many of these interventions is to help clients like Wanda to discern greater coherence in their lived experience (RA Neimeyer and Mahoney, 1995), and in this way transcend some of the massive disorganization of their life stories occasioned by loss.

Denise's struggle with the horrific imagery of her husband's self-inflicted (if unintentional) death shares features with Wanda's story, but adds a level of dissociation related to her strenuous attempts to edit the hardest plot elements out of her public (and perhaps private) version of the account. For this reason, personal assimilation (Stiles, 1999) and selective disclosure of the story might become relevant therapeutic goals, seeking an audience to the telling that could provide support for Denise as she shares the silent story. One witness to her disclosures could, of course, be the therapist, who could then join her in seeking answers to the difficult 'why' questions that are often raised by tragic deaths (Davis, 2001). In Denise's case, this effort at meaning reconstruction is likely to be particularly daunting, as she faces the task of wholesale post-mortem identity reconstruction of her spouse in light of her traumatic discovery. This task might be approached through chair work inviting her to reopen the dialogue with 'Bill' in individual sessions, but discussions of his death in a safe and caring group therapy environment might also support her in acknowledging and making sense of the trauma, as it has been demonstrated to do with survivors of sexual abuse (Alexander et al., 1989). Ultimately, constructing and conversing with a 'community of concern' that can appreciate and affirm one's therapeutic progress can play a crucial role in helping clients span the social schism that silences their narration of their experience (Monk et al., 1996).

Finally, Carlos's predicament illustrated the extent to which a dominant narrative of a compelling loss experience can 'crowd out' alternative readings that could affirm other, more personal features of a client's life story, and suggest healing alternatives. Narrative domination therefore suggests the relevance of narrative elaboration as a therapeutic goal, in the sense of assisting the client to create or discover new accounts of familiar events so as to open new possibilities for the self and others. Narrative therapists of the Australian/New Zealand school (White and Epston, 1990; Monk et al., 1996) specialize in working in this fashion, first 'externalizing' the dominant narrative to help the client distinguish it from the self, and then noticing and amplifying the client's spontaneous attempts to live outside its dictates.[1]

---

[1] It is interesting in this regard that the New Zealand Association of Counsellors is called in the native Maori language Te Ropu Kaiwhiriwhiri O Aotearoa, or 'Weavers of Stories in the Land of the Long White Cloud'. Indeed, an indigenous awareness of the importance of narratives in the counselling process seems to animate many of the innovative developments in therapy originating in this region.

Conclusion

We are currently witnessing a sea change in grief theory, as older models of mourning, such as those of a stage-like adaptation to loss or an effortful breaking of attachment bonds, are challenged by more active, individualized and relationally respectful models. To this change constructivist concepts are making important contributions, shedding light on the review, revision and replacement of disrupted self-narratives as bereaved individuals grow through grief. I hope that this chapter extends this effort, and that other constructivist theorists and therapists will find in it encouragement for their own efforts to grasp more fully the lessons of loss.

CHAPTER TEN

Deliberate self-harm and reconstruction

DAVID A WINTER

Every year, in the UK, approximately 150,000 people engage in deliberate self-harm (NHS Centre for Reviews and Dissemination, 1998). Every day, worldwide, approximately 3,000 people kill themselves. These people's actions may appear incomprehensible, even to health professionals, who have often been found to display negative attitudes towards people who harm themselves (NHS Centre for Reviews and Dissemination, 1998). Such reactions are of particular concern because a history of self-harm is the best predictor of eventual suicide: at least 1% of people who harm them-selves will kill themselves within a year, and approximately 5% will do so within five years. Any approach that provides greater understanding of the behaviour of people who self-harm, and a basis for therapeutic interven-tion, may therefore be anticipated to contribute to a reduction of the suicide rate. Personal construct theory provides such an approach.

Theory

From the personal construct theory viewpoint, acts of self-harm are no less comprehensible than any other behaviour, when seen from the perspective of the individual concerned (RA Neimeyer and Winter, 2005). Thus, like any behaviour, they may be viewed as experiments directed towards the better anticipation of the individual's world, or as 'validating acts' (Stefan and Von, 1985). This was illustrated by George Kelly's (1961) classification of different types of suicidal acts, which may be extended to encompass acts of non-fatal deliberate self-harm.

One of Kelly's (1961) categories of suicide was the *dedicated act*, which is 'designed to validate one's life . . . to extend its essential meaning' (p. 260) rather than to terminate it. In such suicides, individuals anticipate that their death will encourage core beliefs, which may be under threat, to be elabo-rated by others. In some cases, such as kamikaze pilots or suicide bombers, such acts may involve the death of others as well as the individual concerned. For example, Pierre Riviere, who killed his mother, sister, and brother but then did not go through with his original plan to commit suicide, wrote that 'I thought . . . that by my death I should cover myself with glory, and that in time to come my ideas would be adopted and I should be vindicated' (Foucault, 1975, p. 108).

Kelly contrasted suicide as a dedicated act with *mere suicide*, which may occur under conditions of realism or indeterminacy; or certainty or chaos (Stefan and Linder, 1985; Stefan and Von, 1985). In *deterministic suicide*, when the individual's experience is of realism and certainty, 'the course of events seems so obvious that there is no point in waiting around for the outcome' (Kelly, 1961, p. 260). For example, George, who marked his fiftieth birthday by taking 50 sleeping tablets, said that 'I can't see the point of being alive . . . No romance, the kids couldn't care two monkeys, my relatives don't see me any more.' A major factor in a deterministic view of the world may be a failure to disperse dependencies across a range of people. For example, if individuals focus all of their dependencies on one other person, they may feel faced with the certainty of a future of isolation if the person concerned dies, leaves or betrays the individual's trust. Sylvia Plath, who killed herself following the breakdown of her marriage to fellow poet Ted Hughes, had written in her journal that she could not 'conceive of life without' her husband because 'my whole being has grown and interwound so completely with Ted's that if anything were to happen to him, I do not see how I could live. I would either go mad, or kill myself' (Kukil, 2000, p. 274).

Chaotic suicide is in marked contrast to deterministic suicide in that it occurs when 'everything seems so unpredictable that the only definite thing one can do is abandon the scene altogether' (Kelly, 1961, p. 260). From a personal construct theory perspective, such uncertainty would be associated with considerable anxiety. A good description of chaotic suicide was provided by Antonin Artaud, who wrote

> If I commit suicide, it will not be to destroy myself but to put myself back together again. Suicide will be for me only one means of violently reconquering myself . . . of anticipating the unpredictable approaches of God. By suicide, I reintroduce my design in nature. I shall for the first time give things the shape of my will. (Hirschman, 1967)

In some cases of chaotic suicide, the individual's interpersonal world may be particularly unpredictable as a result of a limited capacity for sociality, or for construing the other person's construction processes. Whatever the basis of the unpredictability, chaotic suicide may be regarded as the ultimate expression of a process of constriction (Kelly, 1955/1991a), in which a person, confronted by 'the apparent incompatibility of his construction systems' (p. 477/p. 352), draws in the boundaries of his or her world. Deliberate self-harm may also reduce inner chaos even if it is not committed with suicidal intent, in that it may be the person's 'way of life' (Fransella, 1970), providing an island of structure and certainty at times when life appears particularly unpredictable. This was the case with Fred, whose history of self-harm involved swallowing not only tablets but also an impressive array of other objects, ranging from razors to starter motors, and who said that 'I don't really want to stop. It doesn't harm me. It's just part of me, going to hospital and getting better.'

As well as reducing the anxiety associated with a chaotic world, self-harm may also serve to reduce guilt. For example, in the person whose core role is structured around being a victim of abuse, any departure from this role, as by finding oneself in a loving relationship, may occasion guilt, which may be relieved by acts of self-abuse.

As Stefan and Linder (1985) have indicated, two further processes of construing are particularly relevant to suicidal gestures. One, which is characteristic of impulsive acts of self-harm, is *foreshortening of the circumspection phase of the circumspection–pre-emption–control cycle*. Here, individuals act without weighing up the issues involved in their actions. For example, John described how 'I was thinking about a person I worked with who cut himself and killed himself. I thought that if he can do it I can do it . . . I ran to the kitchen, grabbed a knife and started cutting myself out of sheer depression.' A second process often evident in suicidal gestures is *hostility* (Lester, 1968), in that they involve the attempted extortion of validational evidence for some construction. An example is provided by Aldridge (1998, p. 131), who describes how the self-harm of psychiatric inpatients enabled them to obtain evidence for constructions of staff as 'unsympathetic, uncaring and unable to help'.

Therapeutic practice

A personal construct formulation of a client's self-harm will indicate which of a range of therapeutic strategies are most likely to be effective with the individual concerned. Those that might be appropriate with the person whose self-harm is deterministic are, for example, likely to be diametrically opposed to those that might be useful with the chaotic self-harmer. Such an approach is possible in personal construct psychotherapy because it is technically eclectic (Norcross, 1986), using a variety of techniques, some borrowed from other therapeutic orientations. Hughes and RA Neimeyer (1990) make a similar point in relation to their model of suicidal behaviour, which draws upon personal construct theory, and which in their view 'could provide a more coherent rationale for intervention efforts, by specifying a relevant set of "targets" for psychotherapy or primary prevention programs' (Hughes and RA Neimeyer, 1990, p. 24).

The personal construct psychotherapy intervention for self-harm that we have developed is provided on a six-session renewable contract, commencing within a few weeks of the act of self-harm (Winter et al., 2000). In the first session, the meaning of this act for the client is explored by discussing its antecedents, anticipated outcomes, and whether these were validated or invalidated by its actual outcomes. A principal aim of this session is to bind in words the non-verbal communication expressed in the act of self-harm. As Stefan and Linder (1985) have indicated, this process of 'encoding' may enable the client to view self-harm as a strategy that was used in particular circumstances but may be replaced by alternative strategies. According to these authors, this is of crucial importance since 'if alternative reconstruction of the issues surrounding the suicidal act does not occur, the client may well attempt suicide again' (p. 204).

In the first session, clients are also asked to consider how their significant others may have been affected by the act of self-harm, and are invited to bring a significant other to the next session to explore how that person actually construed the self-harm. The third session usually commences with the presentation of a formulation of the client's difficulties, in some cases with the aid of results of a formal assessment procedure such as a repertory grid. The therapeutic strategies employed in this and subsequent sessions are determined by the principal features of this formulation. For example, if the self-harm is considered to have occurred in the context of abnormally or persistently tight construing and a deterministic view of the world, techniques aimed at loosening construing are used. These may include brainstorming of alternative ways of construing and behaving; guided imagery; relaxation; discussion of dreams; the use of metaphor, as in considering the self as a community of selves, each with their particular role (Mair, 1977); free association; and the use of open-ended questions. If undispersed dependency is evident, there is a focus upon the dispersion of dependencies. If the self-harm is considered to have occurred in the context of chaotic and loose construing, tightening techniques are employed, and Hughes and RA Neimeyer (1993) consider that they may be particularly useful with seriously suicidal clients. These include the use of formal construct assessment techniques, challenging inconsistencies in the client's construing, keeping diaries or self-monitoring charts, task assignments, asking clients to give summaries at the end of each session, and the use of closed questions. If a low degree of sociality appears to be a relevant factor, the primary therapeutic focus is on construing the viewpoints of significant others, enactment of interaction with these others, and elaboration of construing of others in psychological terms. If self-harm seems to be the individual's 'way of life', attempts are made to develop an alternative way of life that will offer at least as much structure as does self-harm. If guilt is considered to be a major issue, therapy might focus upon reconstruction of the client's core role. If foreshortening of the circumspection–pre-emption–control cycle is apparent, exercises in the use of this cycle are employed. If clients are displaying hostility, they may be encouraged to experiment in circumscribed areas. However, whatever the formulation, therapy tends to include the facilitation of experimentation, especially with alternative ways of approaching situations which might in the past have led to self-harm, or with a view to the testing and revision of negative constructions of the self and the future (Hughes and RA Neimeyer, 1993).

As Stefan and Von (1985) have described, group therapy may be particularly useful in encouraging experimentation in people who have self-harmed. In their view, those who have difficulty in describing their experiences may be helped to verbalize these by hearing the accounts of others. By hearing a range of views, they will also be enabled to take a less pre-emptive view of events. A sense of 'universality' (Yalom, 1970/1975/1995), or of not being alone, may be engendered by being in a group with others who have had similar experiences. For similar reasons, it has also been argued that group therapy may be appropriate with depressed people (Winter, 1985b). Personal construct group psychotherapy tends to employ structured exercises, and amongst those used by Stefan and Von in their groups is an invitation to members to describe their ideal house. This provides a fairly non-threatening context for consideration of anticipations of the future and possible experimentation. Hughes and RA Neimeyer (1993) also suggest that group-brainstorming techniques may help the suicidal client to generate alternative solutions to problems.

As Brogna and D'Andrea (2000) have indicated, therapists who work with suicidal clients are likely to be faced with transitions, including anxiety, when the client appears unpredictable; guilt when the therapists feel inadequate in their professional role; and threat, when a client's suicide is anticipated to have far-reaching personal implications for the therapist or when the therapist has a high level of death threat (RA Neimeyer et al., 1983). Therapists' reactions to these transitions, including constriction and hostility, may be less than helpful, but in the view of Brogna and D'Andrea (2000), the therapist may to some extent be protected from transitions by the use of professional constructs to anticipate the possibility of suicide.

Case example

Sarah's presentation at an Accident and Emergency Department followed an incident in which she had put her children to bed and then taken an overdose of tranquillizers. This was not her first overdose and, as on previous occasions, she said that she did not know why she had acted in this way. A personal construct diagnostic assessment suggested four factors that may have been relevant. A repertory grid completed prior to treatment indicated that her construct system was extremely tightly organized, essentially consisting of a single dimension of construing that differentiated her view of herself from that of her ideal self and virtually all of her significant others. However, her life seemed to be largely organized around drinking, with little structure apart from this. It appeared that she tended to foreshorten the circumspection–pre-emption–control cycle and to act impulsively. Finally, her account of her marital relationship suggested that she and her husband had considerable difficulties in construing each other's views of the world.

Following from this assessment, therapy included the use of some loosening techniques. An attempt was made to elaborate with her an alternative structure to her life to drinking, incorporating new leisure activities. Exercises were also conducted in following the circumspection–pre-emption–control cycle: for example, she was persuaded not to act immediately on an impulsive decision to emigrate but instead to consider the alternatives in therapy. There was also a focus on understanding her husband's construing.

When interviewed following therapy, Sarah said that she 'found the therapist a great help, she helped me see a lot of things . . . made me very aware of things I needed to deal with, especially the drink, she was marvellous.' The positive outcome of therapy was reflected in changes in her questionnaire scores, presented in Table 10.1. This table also indicates that such changes were matched by those in her construing, as assessed by the repertory grid. The considerable reduction in the percentage of variance accounted for by the first component from principal component analysis of this grid indicated a loosening of her construing. There was also a reduction in the percentage of the variance accounted for by the construct 'self-destructive – not self-destructive', suggesting that self-destructiveness was a less superordinate, or salient, concern for her. Distances between elements in the grid, where high distances indicate dissimilarity in construing of the two elements concerned, revealed that she came to construe herself as much more similar to her ideal self and much less like her stereotype of someone who would self-harm. She imagined that her husband came to see her as more similar to his ideal wife, and there was a reduction in her idealization of how she had been prior to engaging in self-harm. Angular distances between elements and constructs, where the higher the distance the less a particular construct pole is viewed as describing the element concerned, indicated that she saw herself as less 'self-destructive', 'controlled', and 'unable to make sense of anything' following therapy. The changes on some of these measures were less marked at 6-month follow-up assessment than immediately post-therapy, but on all measures there was still a considerable difference from her pre-therapy position.

Table 10.1 Changes in Sarah's questionnaire and repertory grid scores following therapy

	Pre-treatment	Post-treatment	Follow-up
Beck Depression Inventory	25	11	17
Beck Hopelessness Scale	7	2	3
Beck scale for Suicide Ideation	3	1	0
Repertory Grid:			
% Variances			
Component 1	90.19	68.02	69.08
Self-destructiveness	8.33	6.54	3.63
Element distances			
Self-ideal self	1.46	0.57	0.73
Self- someone who would self-harm	0.56	1.54	1.72
Husband's view of his ideal wife	1.63	0.67	1.03
Self before self-harm – ideal self	0.00	1.13	1.07
Element – construct pole distances			
Self – 'self-destructive'	15.7	140.4	75.6
Self – 'controlled'	24.1	145.9	117.3
Self – 'can't make sense of anything'	24.1	141.1	84.4

Research evidence

There has been some evidence of features of construing associated with aspects of deliberate self-harm. Landfield (1976) found serious suicide attempts to be related to disorganization of the construct system and constriction, whereas Dzamonja-Ignjatovic (1997) provided evidence that suicidal people are particularly constricted in their view of themselves in the future, and that those who have attempted suicide have a less constricted view of their own death. The latter finding indicated that, for these individuals, death offered more certainty than did life. Winter et al. (2000) reported that high symptom levels in people who deliberately self-harmed were related to negative construing of the self and significant others, and that high levels of hopelessness and suicidal ideation were associated with a constricted view of the future self. However, Hughes and RA Neimeyer (1993) found that, although negative self-construing was a predictor of suicide risk, such risk was predicted by low levels of constriction. They explain the latter, surprising finding as indicating that high suicide risk is associated with a reduction in subjective uncertainty, which they relate to a pattern of cognitive rigidity (Neuringer, 1964) and stable attributions for negative events (Abrahamson, Seligman and Teasdale, 1978). Hughes and Neimeyer also reported that clients who were most at risk of suicidal behaviour were characterized by high levels of differentiation and polarization in their construing, indicating that 'conceptual disorganization and all-or-nothing thinking may provide an instigating context for suicidal or parasuicidal behavior' (Hughes and RA Neimeyer, 1993, p. 104). This represents a modification of their previous model (Hughes and RA Neimeyer, 1990), in which they had suggested a progression of suicidal risk from the relatively stable construct systems of non-suicidal people, in which the self and the world are viewed largely positively, to the more disorganized systems of people who have experienced invalidations resulting in some negative construing, and finally, with continuing invalidation, the stabilization of a predominantly negative view of the self and the world. The finding in the later study that stress was a very weak predictor of suicide risk, compared to cognitive factors and processes of construing, suggested to them that the most productive focus of therapy would be on the latter areas rather than on the impact of external stressors.

Another repertory grid study, by Parker (1981), investigated the choice of suicidal behaviour as compared to other alternatives. Clients with low suicidal intent who take overdoses were found to be more likely than those with high intent to construe overdosing as an escape from tension, similar to getting drunk or crying, and less likely to view it as related to death.

There is a growing evidence base for personal construct psychotherapy (Winter, 2003b), including studies indicating its effectiveness with depressed clients (Sheehan, 1985). However, only one study has specifically investigated its outcome with clients presenting with deliberate self-harm, and this examined the therapeutic approach employed by Winter et al. (2000). Serial assessments with questionnaires and a repertory grid were carried out on clients who had presented to an Accident and Emergency Department following self-harm, 24 of whom were allocated to the personal construct psychotherapy intervention and 40 to a 'normal clinical practice' condition. The latter involved assessment by, and possible follow-up appointments with, a mental health team. Participants in the intervention condition showed significantly greater reduction in scores on the Beck Scale of Suicidal Ideation, the Beck Hopelessness Scale, and the Beck Depression Inventory from pre- to post-therapy assessments than did those in the normal clinical practice condition. The relevant effect sizes were 0.52, 0.48, and 0.73 respectively. Significant changes on these measures occurred in the intervention condition but not in the normal practice condition. On the repertory grid, participants in the intervention condition showed a greater increase in favourable construing of the present and future selves, and a greater reduction in perceived self-destructiveness and perception of being controlled than did those in the normal practice condition at the second assessment. The effect sizes concerned were 0.63, 0.82, 0.76, and 0.69 respectively. Their perceptions of the world, and of themselves in the future (effect sizes 0.81 and 1.09) also became less constricted, as reflected in a reduction in the number of midpoint ratings on the grid, than did those of participants in the normal practice condition. Post-treatment interviews with clients in the intervention condition indicated a high level of satisfaction with therapy.

There were no significant differences between the two conditions on the questionnaire measures at 6-month follow-up assessment, but there was considerable sample attrition at this point. However, at this assessment, participants in the intervention condition showed a greater increase in their perceived ability to make sense of their worlds and in favourable construing of their partners, now and in the future (effect sizes 0.67, 0.83, and 0.97).

Accident and Emergency Department records were also examined to trace further episodes of self-harm in the participants. Although the percentages of clients repeating self-harm in the normal practice condition within 1 and 3 years following the initial episode were 1.5 times those in the intervention condition, the differences between the two conditions were not statistically significant. That this is a common finding is indicated by a review by House et al. (1992) of outcome research on interventions for clients who deliberately self-harm, which concluded that 'none of the studies has shown the benefit of intervention on reducing repetition rates' but that the interventions are not necessarily ineffective. Hawton et al. (1998) reached similar conclusions, and suggested that further treatment approaches should be developed and large research trials should be conducted on interventions that have been shown in small trials to be of possible benefit. Personal construct psychotherapy would appear to be one such intervention.

Conclusions

Personal construct theory offers a way of comprehending the actions of the person who self-harms by taking that person's perspective. Furthermore, it allows a therapeutic intervention to be targeted at the particular features of construing that appear to underlie the individual's self-harm. Evidence for the effectiveness of such an approach is sufficiently encouraging to suggest that it should be developed further and evaluated in larger trials with a particular view to examining whether, for some individuals, it may help to prevent them taking the path from non-fatal deliberate self-harm to suicide.

CHAPTER ELEVEN

Resolution of dilemmas by personal construct psychotherapy

GUILLEM FEIXAS, LUIS ÁNGEL SAÚL

Theory

Like other constructivist approaches, personal construct theory (PCT) views human activity as a meaning-creating process. What human organisms do is informed by the way they construe events, and in turn assign meaning to those events. Symptoms are a rare, but legitimate part of their activity. They challenge our everyday conceptions regarding human behaviour. From a personal construct perspective, however, they are not an exception to the laws of behaviour, or an error of nature, but activities embedded in a meaning-making process.

Personal construct theory has elaborated several hypotheses for understanding symptoms as related to the construing process. For example, Fransella (1970), in her study with individuals who stutter, suggested that symptoms could end up being a way of life for clients by becoming a central structure in their construct systems or identities. In this situation, abandoning the symptoms would involve abandoning a core meaning structure that could be essential for making sense of oneself and the world. Lack of predictability within the construct system would be experienced as anxiety by the person. In terms of Kelly (1995/1991b), 'Even an obviously invalid part of a construction system may be preferable to the void of anxiety which might be caused by its elimination altogether' (p. 831/p. 193).

Another type of hypothesis derived from PCT for the understanding of symptoms as related to meaning focuses on the threat that a change would involve. For some clients, symptom loss, while desirable, may carry negative implications. That is, construing the self with a symptomatic pole of a construct is a way of maintaining their present position on positive poles of other, more core, constructs. This is because the symptomatic construct for which the change is desirable is linked in their construct system to other constructs for which change is not desirable. For example, Winter (1988a, 1989a) studied clients with social anxiety problems for whom social competence carried negative implications, and the more pronounced these implications, the more negative the outcome in social skills training groups. He suggests that improvement or symptom reduction may confront these clients with guilt (Winter, 1989a), which Kelly described as the experience of dislodgement from one's core role (our way of relating to others).

In previous studies (Feixas, Saúl and Sánchez, 2000; Feixas et al., 2001), we described a way of identifying implicative dilemmas from the repertory grid that has been implemented in the GRIDCOR (version 4.0) programme (Feixas and Cornejo, 2002). For this purpose, two different types of construct are differentiated: discrepant and congruent constructs. The former type refers to those constructs for which the person rates the self now and the ideal self at different poles of the construct. For example, on a seven-point Likert scale, the difference would have to be greater than 3 points to meet the criteria for a *discrepant construct*. A difference of less than 2 would be considered as indicating a *congruent construct* – the person rates the self now and ideal self elements similarly.

Discrepant constructs (for example, timid versus sociable) indicate areas of dissatisfaction for the individual, areas in which he or she would like to experience substantial change. Often, they represent symptomatic aspects of the person. Conversely, congruent constructs (for example, modest versus arrogant) reveal areas of satisfaction for the individual. They refer to personal qualities (such as modesty) that are not felt to require change, and of which the person may even be proud. The dilemma appears when the desired change in a discrepant construct (becoming sociable) implies an undesired change (i.e. becoming arrogant) in a congruent construct (as measured by a correlation between these two constructs, set at the minimum level of 0.2, for clinical practice, or at the level of 0.35 in our research studies). We used the term *implicative dilemmas* (see Figure 11.1 for a graphical presentation of it) to refer to this type of conflict.

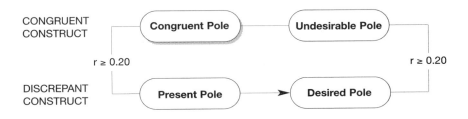

Figure 11.1 Basic Structure of an implicative dilemma derived from repertory grid data.

As far as we know, Hinkle (1965) was the first to employ the term 'implicative dilemma'. However, he was using it in a different sense from ours. For Hinkle, this term referred to a particular form of implication between two constructs (A–B, and X–Y), one that he named 'ambiguous':

> A and B imply X, and B implies Y; also A implies X and Y, and B implies X and Y. One subject, for example, when relating desirable–undesirable and realism–idealism, said that realism and idealism both implied desirable and undesirable aspects for him. Conflict theory and double-bind theory relate to these *implicative dilemmas*. (Hinkle, 1965, pp. 18–19, emphasis in the original).

Although this definition also focuses on the conflictual relationship between two constructs, our definition is different. Our use of the term retains the dilemmatic nature of the phenomena described by Hinkle (1965), but we consider the location of the self now and the ideal self elements as central to the concept. In his definition, Hinkle considered the types of implication between two constructs regardless of where the self and other elements were located. Later, however, he based his laddering and implication methods upon the preferred pole of a construct for a given individual, which is a way of taking into account the ideal self. In light of his method, we think that our use of the term 'implicative dilemma', although not exactly as Hinkle defined it, is legitimate within PCT.

Ryle (1979) defined the term 'implicative dilemma' in a way that is more commonly understood nowadays, and the one we use in our present work:

> Dilemmas can be expressed in the form of 'either/or' (false dichotomies that restrict the range of choice), or of 'if/then' (false assumptions of association that similarly inhibit change). Two common dilemmas could be expressed as follows: 1) 'in relationships I am *either* close to someone and feel smothered, *or* I am cut off and feel lonely' . . . 2) 'I feel that *if* I am masculine *then* I have to be insensitive.' (Italics in the original.)

Another author who expresses even more clearly what we mean by a dilemma is Rowe (1971) with the case of a chronically depressed client embracing a construction whereby her choice was either to be depressed and humane or to be a destructive and unpleasant person. In general, dilemmas occur when the apparent alternatives available in the construct system are both seen as undesirable. In this vein, Tschudi's (1977) ABC technique is based on this very same idea, that is, that change, although desirable from the viewpoint of a given set of constructs, becomes undesirable from the perspective of another set of constructs.

Therapeutic practice

By understanding the symptoms as a part of a meaning-making process, PCT allows both client and therapist to look at distress from an alternative perspective. Often clients present their symptoms in a way that suggests that they do not carry any meaning for them, except for the inconveniences that they cause in their lives, as if the part or aspect of their functioning that is wrong is not related to their sense of identity. Accordingly, mainstream therapists are inclined to consider the problem in terms of its external manifestations, associate them to a clinical diagnosis, and struggle to eliminate the symptoms as quickly as possible. Rather, constructivist approaches direct their efforts to searching for the meanings involved in the problem, that is, to understanding the constructions the client erects for him or herself and the problem and how these relate to the problem itself. In particular, the therapy method we propose is addressed to those cases where the problem poses a particular dilemma for the client, from the perspective of his or her construct system.

The first step in our personal construct approach for dealing with dilemmas begins with *reframing the problem in terms of the dilemma*. Thus, the client's problem is reformulated as a conflict between the desire for change and the difficulty to do that, which results in a blocking of the client's development with considerable suffering and symptoms. In our experience, it is useful to show to the client that his or her 'impasse' reflects a coherence, an internal logic, rather than being a sign of incompetence, stupidity or madness, as many clients (and some therapists) believe.

The problem is presented to the client as related to the way of being, or the type of person that the client has chosen to be. Thus, a connection is suggested between the symptoms and the client's self image or personal style. It is suggested also that the 'impasse' is a coherent and wise position that clients choose to uphold, because a change (for example, becoming social) might involve the abandonment of some of their own self-definitions (such as modesty) and a shift to their opposite poles (arrogance), which would be undesirable for the clients' core structure. In fact, it may be the case that every time clients explore (in actions or fantasy) the possibility of allocating themselves to the desired pole (social) they might experience guilt. They may begin to construe themselves outside their core role structure (for example, modesty). Retreat to timidity is the easiest way to alleviate the guilt by returning to their 'usual' self. In the therapy session, examples of that process are highlighted to help clients realize how this issue constitutes a dilemma in their lives.

Some clients, after understanding the dilemma, pose a question of the type 'Would it be possible to become social without having to be arrogant?', to which the therapist replies: 'Mmmm . . . it seems an interesting question, maybe a project to be implemented. What would you do in the following days to be social without being arrogant?' The latter question constitutes in itself a therapy programme for the following sessions without pursuing further work on comprehending the dilemma. On the other hand, for some clients the formulation of the dilemma appears as a truth that they already knew but one that was never spelled out before; for others it appears as a new construction about their problem, a new perspective that needs to be explored.

Once many clients recognize the existence of the dilemma, and the constructs involved, it is convenient to explore the implications of each of these constructs. For that, we can explore their ascending and descending implications using *laddering procedures*. Exploring the implications of the dilemma in terms of other, related, constructs allows for a wider understanding of it. It also makes it possible to identify new constructs related to the dilemma (other than those obtained during the repertory grid elicitation), and explore new 'advantages' in keeping the present position and not changing.

Another central aspect of this work for the elaboration of the dilemma involves identifying the *prototypical figures* that occupy the two positions of the dilemma. On the one hand, there are the figures who are construed using the undesired pole of the discrepant construct but the preferred pole of the congruent construct (for example, timid and modest). On the other hand, there are the figures who are construed according to the desired pole of the discrepant construct but under the undesirable pole of the congruent construct (for example, social and arrogant). Thus, the dilemma can be phrased in terms of the type of person that each prototypical figure represents.

In one of our cases,[1] Laia, a 24-year-old girl presenting with problems of insecurity and lack of confidence in engaging in Master level courses, she recalled that in her family it was commonly assumed that her brother Josep was bright in school whereas she was 'a good person'. Her family (including herself) did not expect her to have good grades at school. Instead, they expected her to take care of her younger sister while their mother was at work, or even to join her father for an excursion day during the weekend. For Laia, achieving good success in the university was equated to resembling her brother Josep, who was also described by her as an 'uncaring' and 'selfish' kind of person.

The exploration of the dilemma stimulated in the client memories and narratives about the dilemma and its prototypical figures, which is a common process in other cases as well. Then, when these figures were identified, the therapist asked, 'Do you think that if you would become successful in your studies you would also become similar to your brother as a person?' Laia replied that that was probably so although she never

[1] The therapist for this case was Guillem Feixas.

thought of it in that way. At this point, the dilemma can be phrased in terms of a change that would involve a change in the type of person one has always been to becoming a different type of person, one who is not preferred because the prototypical figure that represents it (for example, the brother) is disliked in many senses.

One interesting development that might follow is finding out whether the client can think of figures situated both on the congruent and the desired poles of the dilemma (for example, people who are social and also modest). This exploration may lead to a realization that that path has already been walked, and to a discussion of whether that is a viable option for the client.

All this work with the dilemma is carried out in a way that underlines the coherence of the symptom by clarifying its function of validating the client's values and sense of identity. Tschudi's (1977) ABC technique can be of great help in this process because in it the disadvantages of change are also made evident, and it may serve to clarify the symptom's function. With that, new constructs related to the dilemma, unforeseen advantages, or previously undetected constructs may also appear. These conversational procedures allow us to go beyond the construct universe delimited by the repertory grid.

Once the client accepts the dilemma as a new construction about the problem, and its implications have been explored, *controlled elaboration* can be a useful option. Suggested by Kelly (1955/1991b), it can be defined as the attempt to make consistent and communicable one part of the client's construct system to make it possible to explore its validity. To use controlled elaboration to work with dilemmas we suggest to begin by focusing the conversation on the dilemma's theme, accompanying the client on the experience cycle, phase by phase (for example, noticing which constructs are being validated or invalidated, and so forth). This will involve weighing up each construct of the dilemma with the client, exploring the conditions in which it is being validated or invalidated, and working with the ascending and descending implications of those constructs. This process may help clients to elaborate their thoughts and feelings related to the dilemma with more care and precision than in the normal flow of life – that is, to promote the observer role, the client's self-observation (Guidano, 1991).

Although in many cases it is not necessary to promote change, in some it might be useful to explore the origins (the primary focus of convenience) of the dilemma in order to erect an *historical reconstruction* of it. For this the client and therapist can search for past episodes that exemplify the dilemma across the client's life. This process can be exemplified by the case of Laia (see above), whose memories of the family's construction (Procter, 1981) of her as a 'good person' and her brother Josep as 'bright' refer to the time when she was 8 or 9 years old. Often, this exploration of past events, many of them back in infancy, provokes intense emotional expressions.

This historical perspective on the dilemma permits clients to contemplate themselves from a different position that both facilitates understanding of their personal evolution and allows the envisioning of new alternatives. At this point, it is useful to acknowledge that the dilemma was structured in that way according to a given historical, emotional and relational context. However, in the present, things can be seen differently (Kelly's, 1955/1991b 'time binding').

At different moments of this process, *generation of alternatives* is promoted to explore non-dilemmatic solutions. In sum, this process is aimed at creating a life without the dilemma. For this it is convenient for the client to be aware of the existence of possible alternatives to dilemma construction and that these alternatives are not better or worse than others. They are simply other possible alternatives. As with the brainstorming technique, it is a good idea not to evaluate these new alternatives too quickly. Rather, they can be explored using imagination or role playing.

Finally, an optional phase in the dilemma resolution work is engaging the client in a *fixed role of the solved dilemma*, an adaptation of Kelly's (1955/1991a) original technique. The client is asked to represent a role, designed by the therapist, which includes among other characteristics, the congruent and desired poles of the dilemma. So in this role the dilemma is not present. With this, it is intended to provide the client with a lived experience, in his or her habitual environment, of him or herself living without the dilemma.

The case of Teresa

This client was in the final year of her degree in chemical sciences. She was treated by the psychological care services of the University of Salamanca. At the initial assessment she displayed somatization, depressive symptoms, and a high level of interpersonal sensitivity according to the scales of SCL-90-R (Derogatis, 1977). Although Teresa proved to be an excellent student, she revealed serious doubts about her self worth. She cried frequently, and had great difficulty in meeting others, even though she had a boyfriend who was extremely supportive. Her relationship with her parents was very strained, and she described her mother as a very dependent person who put a great deal of pressure on her. Her parents lived 80 km from the city. At the time of the consultation, Teresa lived with her brother, but the two of them had not been on speaking terms for 3 months.

The first time that I interviewed her,[2] she explained to me that in a few weeks time she would be travelling 600 km. from home to work in a firm that would allow her to gain work experience in a field related to her studies. Teresa displayed great insecurities regarding her departure, and questioned whether or not she should go, but she was aware that it was necessary for her to go ahead with her plans. We had two support sessions before her departure where I focused on preparing her to realize the benefits of this upcoming experience.

After analysing the client's grid we identified two implicative dilemmas related to her depressive symptoms (see Figure 11.2).

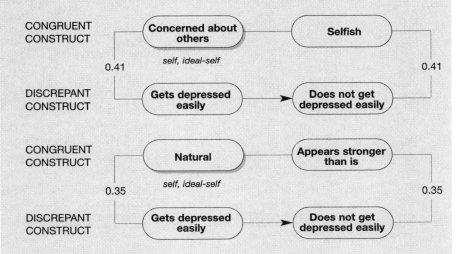

Figure 11.2 Implicative dilemmas identified in the initial grid of Teresa.

Teresa associated the construct pole 'does not get depressed easily' with two construct poles that she considered opposite to her self-definition:

- to be 'selfish' (versus concerned about others);
- to be the kind of person who 'pretends to be stronger than one is' (versus natural).

The aim of therapy was to sever these associations because they were preventing Teresa from forming alternative definitions of her self as a person who does not get depressed easily. As a consequence of implicative dilemma resolution, it was expected that her depressive symptoms would be alleviated.

According to our therapeutic hypothesis, we should help the client to elaborate in alternative ways the implications of her core constructs and

---

[2] The therapist for this case is Luis Ángel Saúl.

facilitate a wider perspective in which to view herself. Loosening the implications of her core constructs would help Teresa to see herself as a person who is natural, concerned about others (the opposite of a 'selfish' person and one who pretends 'to be stronger than one is') while at the same time she 'does not get depressed easily'.

The period of time between the first and the last grid was only 4 months. The therapy had to end just before the academic holidays, so we did not have much time to work. However, the client began to show signs of elaboration of some of her core constructs. She started to appreciate that 'concern about others' also implies concern about oneself. Thus, the construct became more permeable so as to include the self among the range of its elements. Probably as a consequence of this reconstruction, the client's psychological wellbeing was enhanced and therefore her depression reduced as denoted by the assessment at the end of therapy.

We can observe the changes in Teresa's construing by looking at the correlations among the constructs forming the dilemma at the end of therapy (Figure 11.3) and comparing them to those at the initial assessment (Figure 11.2).

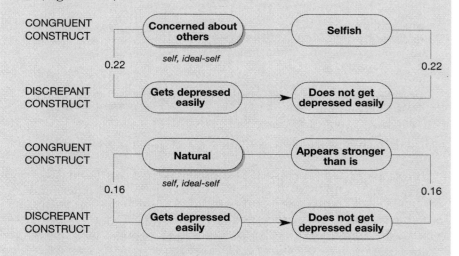

Figure 11.3 The implicative dilemmas of Teresa's post-therapy grid.

As can be seen, a reduction was achieved in the degree of association between those constructs that formed dilemmas. These correlations are still positive after therapy but the reduction of their intensity is noticeable. It was also found that reduction in the intensity of the dilemmas was accompanied by symptom reduction. Although variations in the SCL-90-R scales were not substantial, her Beck Depression Inventory score changed from 26 (at the start of therapy) to 9 (at the end of therapy).

Research

A multicentre research project was launched in 1999 to investigate the role of dilemmas in different mental and physical health problems, and also to devise and implement therapeutic methods focused on resolving those dilemmas (see more details in Feixas, Saúl and Sánchez, 2000, and on the Internet at www.usal.es/tcp). Currently, various universities and clinical centres, mainly from Spain but also from the UK, Portugal, Italy and South America are involved, at different levels, in this project.

A preliminary data report (Feixas and Saúl, 2003) indicates that dilemmas can be identified in grids of one-third (34%) of a non-clinical sample of 321 subjects recruited by psychology students after some training in grid administration and analysis. In a clinical sample of 286 psychotherapy clients presenting with a wide variety of clinical problems (excluding psychosis), dilemmas appear in more than one-half (52.4%) of the sample. This difference proved to be significant using a chi-squared test.

To further investigate the number of dilemmas appearing in each sample (amongst those subjects who presented at least one), we computed the percentage of implicative dilemmas (PID) measure.[3] The mean score of the clinical sample on this measure (4.37%) was double that of the non-clinical sample (2.11%), a significant difference.

This first exploratory result indicates that

1. The presence of dilemmas as captured by repertory grids is a usual, natural, situation in humans at least to some degree.
2. People consulting for clinical problems are more likely to present dilemmas than people who do not.
3. Grids of people presenting with psychological symptoms yield a greater number of dilemmas.

Points 2 and 3 suggest that dilemmas are related to psychological distress but point 1 cautions us against considering dilemmas necessarily as a

---

[3] Although the number of dilemmas in a given grid would seem an obvious measure, we have found, in a pilot study, that the amount of dilemmas may increase with grid size. Therefore, as grid size is not standardized, grids cannot be reliably compared.

$$\frac{d}{n!/2[(n-2)!]} \times 100$$

d = number of dilemmas
n = number of constructs in the grid

As indicated above, a method was devised to counteract for this difficulty which takes account of the number of constructs in the grid. The number of possible pairs of constructs was calculated and used as the denominator in the formula. The result of this equation is multiplied by 100, in order to establish the percentage.

pathological sign. Altogether, our research seems to suggest that dilemmas are part of life but when not addressed or excessive in number (and possibly in intensity) they can be associated with suffering and pathology. This can be seen as an argument in favour of the idea that there is not a discrete line distinguishing between 'normal' and 'pathological' individuals. Maybe we, as humans, develop symptoms (among many other reasons) when the dilemmas we face are excessive, 'in over our heads' (Kegan, 1994).

With respect to therapy and its influence in resolving dilemmas, Feixas and Saúl's (2003) preliminary report discusses another study with 87 clinical clients, including a reanalysis of 46 neurotic clients who were part of the sample used by Watson (1998). We examined the presence or absence of implicative dilemmas before and after therapy. From the data, it can be observed that clients who do not present with implicative dilemmas at the start of therapy are unlikely to exhibit them when therapy ends; only 7.9% of the patients who did not exhibit implicative dilemmas at the start of therapy did so at the end. More than two-thirds (69.4%) of the sample who presented with implicative dilemmas at the start of therapy did not present with implicative dilemmas at the end. These data suggest that psychological therapy, even when it is not specifically addressed at resolving previously identified dilemmas, produces a statistically significant reduction in the number of clients' implicative dilemmas ($p < 0.001$).

Overall, we find that the percentage of clients who present with implicative dilemmas after the therapeutic process is 20.7%. In comparison with 34% found in the non-clinical sample mentioned above this is a lower profile of dilemmas for clients who completed a psychotherapy process. This finding suggests that therapy decreases the number of implicative dilemmas to a level below that of the general population. So, psychotherapy does not merely return clients to a normal level of conflict within their construct system but actually serves to enhance or facilitate their construing to a level that is more resolved and dilemma free than average.

Obviously, more research is needed to explore differences among psychotherapy approaches and their influence in decreasing the number of dilemmas and, more important, to assess whether a brief therapy protocol focused on resolving previously identified dilemmas produces good outcomes both in terms of symptom reduction and the resolution of dilemmas.

Conclusions

Conceptualizing the problem presented by the client in terms of a dilemma is a way of understanding it in terms of a meaning-making process consistent with a constructivist perspective. Thus, by inhabiting the symptom pole the client is validating other core constructions about his or her identity that are associated with it. Change to the opposite pole, the desired pole, would also imply abandoning part of the client's identity, which would involve a central change in the client's construct system.

Implicative dilemmas can be identified using repertory grid technique, and assessed for each individual's grid in terms of their presence (or not) and also the proportion of dilemmas found.

The results so far obtained from the Multicentre Dilemma Project indicate that one third of a non-clinical sample present with implicative dilemmas, which suggests that dilemmas (even those detected using repertory grids) are part of tensions of 'normal' life. However, they are more common (and more numerous) for people asking for help in psychotherapy services. Further data with therapy clients show that psychological therapy, even when it is not specifically directed at resolving previously identified dilemmas, produces a statistically significant reduction in the number of implicative dilemmas.

These results suggest that more attention should be paid to implicative dilemmas in the therapy process. Personal construct therapy provides a number of useful clinical techniques (reframing, laddering, ABC, controlled elaboration, historical reconstruction, generation of alternatives, fixed role, and so forth) that can be adapted to work with these dilemmas and resolve them. In this way, the person can feel that change can be consistent with his or her identity and, thus, be more easily attainable.

CHAPTER TWELVE

From constriction to experiment-ation: personal construct psychotherapy for agoraphobia

DAVID A WINTER, CHRIS METCALFE

Theory

From the personal construct theory perspective, agoraphobia might be considered to reflect a clear expression at the behavioural level of the process that Kelly (1995/1991a) termed constriction, in which people draw in the outer boundaries of their perceptual field to exclude from awareness material which their constructs are ill-equipped to predict and which therefore generates anxiety and confusion (Winter and Gournay, 1987). As Lorenzini and Sassaroli (1988, p. 333) have stated, agoraphobic avoidance behaviour 'aims at defending the predictive skills of the subject who gives up predicting any further because he runs the risk of not successfully predicting anything at all'.

The nature of the unpredictable, anxiety-provoking events that agoraphobia may help an individual to avoid has been indicated by work from other theoretical perspectives as well as that of constructivists. For example, Goldstein and Chambless (1978) linked the onset of agoraphobia to interpersonal conflict and used an attributional framework to explain the avoidance of anger and conflict, which are experienced instead as anxiety. Other workers, such as Hafner (1977a, 1977b, 1983, 1984; Hafner and Ross, 1983), have made use of such psychodynamic concepts as repression and denial to explain the agoraphobic predicament in terms of their marital situation. Consistent with such views is Fisher and Wilson's (1985) demonstration that people diagnosed as agoraphobic show little emotional reaction to scenes of marital conflict.

Guidano and Liotti (1983), approaching the subject from a constructivist perspective, have also associated agoraphobia with difficulties in situations of interpersonal conflict and intense emotion. In their view, clients with this diagnosis 'do not possess articulate cognitive structures capable of dealing with emotions' (Guidano and Liotti, 1983, p. 225). They also consider agoraphobia to involve an organization of personal meaning in which there is oscillation between the need for protection and that for total independence (Guidano, 1987). A similar view has been taken in some personal construct theory accounts of agoraphobia. For example, both Frazer (1980) and Lorenzini and Sassaroli (1987) have suggested that the family background of the person diagnosed as agoraphobic was one in which exploratory behaviour was inhibited and the child was protected from invalidation. Lorenzini and Sassaroli, using repertory grid technique, found that agoraphobics construed situations of exploration and change as anxiety provoking and as not associated with attachment; and that they had poorly elaborated subsystems of emotional constructs. O'Sullivan (1985) also carried out a repertory grid study of agoraphobics, finding them to construe expression of negative feelings and assertion unfavourably and to use relatively few constructs concerning change. Hopkins (1996), employing both repertory grids and self characterizations, demonstrated that agoraphobics viewed themselves as more characterized by tender feelings towards others than do non-agoraphobic clients, as well as being distinguished by various other features of construing. Finally, Jackson (1992) has explored the dilemmas that may underlie agoraphobic symptoms.

A programme of repertory grid investigations of agoraphobia over a period of nearly 20 years has provided evidence, consistent with the findings of some of these other personal construct studies, that in both agoraphobics and their partners there is a low level of cognitive awareness, and a poorly elaborated subsystem of constructs in the area of interpersonal conflict and emotion (Winter and Gournay, 1987; Winter, 1989a; Winter, Gournay and Metcalfe, 1999). Specifically, we have found agoraphobic symptoms to be associated with a tendency not to construe people as angry, selfish and jealous and to show little discrimination between people in terms of the latter two characteristics. However, there were indications that a construct concerning infidelity was superordinate for both agoraphobics and their partners, and, in one study, that agoraphobics associated the ability to go out with possible infidelity. Their phobia may therefore allow some agoraphobics to avoid the guilt that might be provoked by increased awareness of such possibilities. Apart from the implication of possible infidelity, agoraphobics and their partners in our studies tended to hold an idealistic fantasy of how their lives would be if the agoraphobics could go out. This perhaps reflects what Fransella (1972) has termed the 'if only syndrome', and may provide an additional maintaining factor for the agoraphobia in that this allows avoidance of the testing out of their fantasies. Agoraphobics and their partners also both tended to contrast the agoraphobic's low self-esteem and weakness with the partner's high self-esteem and strength. In general, their construct systems were very similar, and it appeared that the greater this degree of commonality the more severe were the client's symptoms. In effect, agoraphobia seemed to allow clients to limit their interpersonal worlds to a partner who was likely to be a constant source of validation.

Therapeutic practice

The most commonly employed treatment methods for agoraphobia have been derived from the cognitive-behavioural tradition. A personal construct theory perspective would not necessarily be inconsistent with a behavioural component to treatment, in which the agoraphobic is exposed to previously avoided situations, because such an approach may encourage experimentation and dilation of the construct system (Kelly, 1970b). In McFadyen's (1989) view, it may also invalidate clients' anticipations of the harmful consequences of panic attacks. The finding that the symptom tends not to be integrated with the remainder of the construct system in agoraphobics (Metcalfe, 1997) also suggests that a symptom-focused intervention may be likely to be beneficial for such clients as it may be relatively unthreatening. Indeed, there is evidence that behaviour therapy may be accompanied by reconstruing, not only in agoraphobics but also in their partners (Winter and Gournay, 1987; Hopkins, 1996). However, in one of the studies concerned (Winter and Gournay, 1987), at follow-up the clients appeared to be becoming increasingly aware of the possible negative implications of their growing independence, suggesting that behaviour therapy did not result in any fundamental, lasting change in the patterns of construing that seemed to underlie their symptoms. Any reconstruing in these clients may only have been at a peripheral level.

It is not altogether surprising, therefore, that a purely behavioural approach has been found to be inadequate both in its explanation of agoraphobia (Hallam, 1978) and its effectiveness (Gournay, 1989; Fava et al., 2001). However, the addition of a cognitive component to such treatment has not been found to enhance effectiveness to any great extent (Emmelkamp et al., 1978, 1986; Emmelkamp and Mersch, 1982; Williams and Rappoport, 1983) and, when cognitive-behavioural therapy has been found to be effective, the role of cognitive processes in treatment outcome has not been clear (Oei et al., 1999). The cognitive treatment methods investigated have mostly involved attempts to modify 'surface structures', such as beliefs and self-statements regarding the consequences of going out, whereas it has been argued that fundamental changes in the agoraphobic require the modification of core structures (Biran, 1988).

On the assumption that such 'core structures' might involve the features of construing that our theoretical analysis and research investigations have associated with agoraphobia, a personal construct therapy approach to agoraphobia focusing upon these areas has been developed, with the aim of facilitating reconstruing. This approach is combined with graduated exposure treatment (Hand and Lamontague, 1974), to encourage experimentation, which may be usefully provided in six 3-hour group sessions. We alternate these sessions with six 2-hour personal construct group psychotherapy sessions, the first three of which are in an interpersonal transaction group format (Landfield and Rivers, 1975), in which the members initially interact in dyads on themes provided by the therapist, rotating from one dyad to the next until each member has interacted with every other. The focus of these sessions is on:

- elaboration of construing of interpersonal conflict and of associated emotions;
- exploration of negative implications of independence and of the ability to go out, and reconstruction of these implications;
- elaboration of a favourable yet realistic construction of the non-phobic self (following a homework assignment of completion of a characterization of the self without agoraphobia).

The two subsequent personal construct psychotherapy sessions also include clients' partners, and focus upon identification and modification of shared constructions held by clients and their partners that might have contributed to the maintenance of agoraphobic symptoms. The major focus of the final session is on clients' constructions of how they have changed over the course of therapy, the results of their experimentation during this time, and their anticipations of the future, including possible further experimentation. The sessions are conducted according to a manual, which is included as an appendix to this chapter.

Alternative approaches to the treatment of agoraphobia have been adopted by other constructivist therapists. Guidano (1991) uses a 'moviola' technique in which the client is trained in self-observation by 'zooming in' on particular scenes in his or her life and viewing these from both a 'subjective' and 'objective' perspective. This in itself may promote reconstruing by helping clients to view their beliefs as hypotheses. The therapist's reformulation of the client's problem in terms of an underlying personal meaning organization is likely to continue this process. Capps and Ochs (1995) focus upon the narratives of agoraphobics, which they have found to elucidate both the clients' explicit theories of panic and alternative theories at a lower level of awareness. For them, 'the therapeutic process involves a blending of the client's story with a story line adopted by the therapist' (Capps and Ochs, 1995, p. 177).

Case example

In the first session of Janet's personal construct psychotherapy group, the theme of which was interpersonal conflict, she described a year in her life during which she had felt constantly angry, leading her to commence therapy focusing upon anger control. Although this achieved its stated aim, the reduction in her anger was associated with the development of panic attacks. Describing the most important event in the first personal construct psychotherapy session, she wrote that 'it was important for me to realise that not all panic was anxiety, but could in fact be anger misinterpreted.' In the second session, focusing on the advantages and disadvantages of being able to go out, she realized that 'there is actually a good side and a bad side to being agoraphobic – becoming independent wasn't a completely good thing.' She also became aware that her agoraphobic symptoms had allowed her, without having to take responsibility for this decision, to leave a job with which she was dissatisfied and to take a 'breathing space' during which she reassessed the direction of her life. In a subsequent session, she described how she had transformed from being an extravert to becoming agoraphobic after meeting her partner, on whom she had become very dependent. She began to realize that their relationship would probably not survive her recovery from agoraphobia because her partner would be likely to become very insecure if she were to resume her social outings. At the next session, she began to elaborate a future self without agoraphobia, writing that 'it's good to talk about the future in a positive way, realising that the agoraphobia should, one day, be out of my life altogether'. This prospect became increasingly apparent during the exposure sessions, when she was able to confront situations that she had previously avoided, such as travelling on an underground train. Describing these experiences, she wrote that 'If I can achieve this much feeling anxious then what can I achieve in the future?'

Janet's positive account of her therapy is reflected in changes in her scores on a range of questionnaire measures, which showed a marked reduction in the severity of her symptoms (see Table 12.1) over the course of therapy, although follow-up questionnaires were not returned. There were also indications of reconstruing, particularly in the six months following therapy, when there was evidence of resolution of dilemmas underlying her agoraphobia. Thus, whereas while on the waiting list (it was not possible to complete a grid immediately pre-therapy) she construed people who are able to go out as 'uninterested', 'manipulative', 'full of themselves', and 'not understanding', this was no longer the case at the six-month follow-up. The variance in her repertory grid accounted for by a construct concerning the ability to go out reduced considerably, suggesting that it may have become less superordinate (Bannister and Salmon, 1967), whereas the reverse occurred for constructs relating to interpersonal conflict.

Table 12.1 Changes in Janet's scores on symptom and repertory grid measures

	Assessment point			
	waiting list	pre-therapy	post-therapy	6 month FU
Symptom measures				
Problem rating	–	8	1	1
Fear Questionnaire Agoraphobia	34	36	3	
Agoraphobia Scale Anxiety	71	57	11	
Mobility Inventory Alone	4.96	7.65	1.65	
Mobility Inventory Accomp.	3.13	5.28	0.88	
Mobility Inventory Panic	4	2	0	
Agoraphobic Cognitions	2.79	2.21	1.57	
Beck Depression Inventory	21	24	6	
STAI Trait Anxiety	61	56	45	
HDHQ Total Hostility	22	–	16	
HDHQ Direction of Hostility	+8	–	-3	
Repertory grid				
i) Construct correlations				
Able to go out – helpful	-0.32		-0.15	0.22
manipulative	0.36		0.38	0.01
full of self	0.58		0.56	0.13
understanding	-0.30		-0.16	-0.09
selfish	0.30		0.24	0.25
jealous	0.27		0.27	0.06
ii) % Sum of squares of constructs				
able to go out – unable	7.98		3.16	1.22
selfish – unselfish	10.29		11.08	14.98
angry – not angry	5.53		9.15	6.59
jealous – not jealous	8.19		4.00	10.25
could be unfaithful – would not	6.22		10.77	11.89

Research on personal construct psychotherapy for agoraphobia

To evaluate our personal construct psychotherapy approach for agoraphobia, we have compared it with supportive therapy, conducted in exactly the same group format but with sessions not focusing upon aspects of construing relevant to the personal construct theory model of agoraphobia. Thus, the themes for the supportive interpersonal transaction groups were:

• situations in which phobic anxieties are experienced;

- difficult and easy aspects of the exposure sessions;
- clients' self-constructions (following a homework task of writing a characterization of the present self).

The aims of these sessions were to provide a cohesive and supportive group experience and to facilitate discussion of the experience of agoraphobia and of the exposure sessions. Sessions involving partners largely focused on their perceptions of the clients' problems, how these affected them and on partners' views of the clients' response to the exposure sessions. The final supportive therapy session was largely concerned with reviewing clients' experience of therapy and considering the state of their agoraphobic symptoms.

Both types of therapy were combined with graduated group exposure therapy, conducted by a nurse behaviour therapist, and both were manualized. They were both conducted by personal construct psychotherapists, who were instructed not to use personal construct interventions in the supportive groups.

Eighty-five clients were recruited for the research from a National Health Service Clinical Psychology Department, and 74 of these attended pre-treatment research assessments. Only 54 of these clients eventually attended for therapy, and 27 were allocated to each treatment condition. They underwent research assessments on a range of symptom measures and a repertory grid while on the waiting list, immediately pre- and post-treatment, and at 6-month and 18-month follow-up, although there was some sample attrition at each assessment point.

As in our previous research, Spearman correlations indicated significant relationships at pre-treatment assessment between symptom and repertory grid measures. Specifically, severe agoraphobic symptoms were associated with tendencies not to construe people as selfish or jealous; with super-ordinancy of the construct of infidelity; and with tight construing.

In addition to the symptom and grid measures, three measures of the treatment process were completed after each therapy session. On one of these, the Session Evaluation Questionnaire (Stiles, 1980), group sessions were found to be perceived as 'smoother' in personal construct psychotherapy than in the supportive therapy condition. On the Group Climate Questionnaire (Mackenzie, 1983), personal construct psychotherapy clients gave their group sessions, particularly at the beginning and end of the group, significantly lower scores on the Avoidance Scale than did supportive therapy clients, suggesting that supportive therapy sessions were more likely to be characterized by group members 'avoiding a significant encounter with themselves and their problems as well as with other group members' (MacKenzie, 1983, p. 166). What clients regarded as the most important events in group sessions were coded in terms of categories of therapeutic factors provided by Bloch and Crouch (1985), and it was found that a factor considered highly important by all clients was what Yalom (1970/1975/1995) has termed the experience of 'universality', of finding that one is not alone. However, personal construct psychotherapy clients mentioned more experiences of self-understanding than did supportive therapy clients.

With regard to the outcome data, due to the large proportion of participants who agreed to be allocated to therapy but then did not complete any of the post-treatment assessments, a pure intention-to-treat analysis was not conducted because the resulting conclusions would have been unacceptably dependent upon the model for the missing data. The procedure that was adopted in analysing the outcome data was to include in the analysis all participants who had completed at least one post-treatment assessment. A conservative model was chosen for substituting missing data in that the participant's pre-treatment scores on the measures concerned replaced them. An analysis of covariance was performed for each measure with the mean of the three post-treatment assessments as the outcome variable and the pre-treatment score as the covariate. With the agoraphobic symptom measures, the pre-treatment Beck Depression Inventory score was an additional covariate because there was a significant pre-treatment difference between the groups on this inventory.

This method of analysis revealed no significant differences between the two group treatment conditions.

Paired t-tests were also conducted to compare change on the outcome measures in the personal construct psychotherapy condition during the waiting list period with that during treatment. For this analysis, where post-treatment data were missing for an individual, they were replaced by the mean of the two pre-treatment assessments. The number of supportive therapy clients completing the waiting list assessment was insufficient to allow a similar analysis. Significantly greater symptom reduction was found to occur during personal construct psychotherapy than during the waiting list period on the primary outcome measure, the Fear Questionnaire Agoraphobia Scale (Marks and Mathews, 1979) ($t = 2.26$; $p < 0.05$), as well as on some other measures of agoraphobic symptoms (Mobility Inventory/Alone (Chambless et al., 1985): $t = 3.25$; $p < 0.01$; Mobility Inventory/Accompanied: $t = 2.35$; $p < 0.05$; Behavioural Avoidance Test: $t = 2.46$; $p < 0.01$). On two grid measures, the percentage of variance accounted for by a construct concerning anger and that accounted for by the first principal component, there was greater change in the direction associated with more optimal functioning (an increase in the former, and decrease in the latter, percentage) during treatment than during the waiting list period ($t = 2.06$; $p < 0.05$ and $t = 2.58$; $p < 0.05$ respectively), when change was in the opposite direction.

To examine the ability of the non-agoraphobia measures to predict change on the Agoraphobia Scale of the Fear Questionnaire from pre- to post-treatment, analyses of covariance were conducted with adjustment for baseline scores on the Agoraphobia Scale. Available data from both treatment conditions were pooled in this analysis, which made no attempt to 'correct' for missing data but was corrected for clustering due to groups by using robust standard errors. Clients who improved more over the course of treatment in terms of scores on the Agoraphobia Scale were found to be less depressed pre-treatment ($F = 9.18$; $p = 0.01$). On the repertory grid, they perceived more anger ($F = 5.06$; $p < 0.05$) and somewhat more jealousy ($F = 4.24$; $p = 0.06$), and showed less idealization of their fathers ($F = 5.76$; $p < 0.05$).

Spearman correlations were also carried out between change scores on symptom and grid measures over the treatment period. These indicated that clients who showed greater symptomatic improvement tended to differentiate between people more in terms of anger, to increase their perception of selfishness, to view themselves as closer to their ideal selves, and to loosen their construing. All relationships were checked for linearity by inspection of scatter-plots.

This study provided some support for the personal construct theory model of agoraphobia in that high levels of agoraphobic symptoms were again associated with a tendency not to construe others in terms suggestive of interpersonal conflict, and also with superordinacy of a construct of infidelity. Furthermore, when clients' symptoms reduced in severity over the course of treatment, there was evidence of increasing awareness of interpersonal conflict, and their construing loosened.

Some evidence was also provided of a more facilitative treatment process in the personal construct group condition for agoraphobia that we have developed; and of a greater degree of positive change on some measures of symptoms and construing during exposure plus personal construct psychotherapy than while clients were on the waiting list for therapy. However, it is disappointing that there was no evidence of greater change in the personal construct psychotherapy than in the supportive therapy condition. This may have been due to various factors. A conservative method of data analysis was employed, combining post-treatment scores and substituting for missing data, and this has removed some of the differences in favour of the personal construct psychotherapy condition which were apparent in a previous analysis of the same data (Winter, Gournay and Metcalfe, 1999). Sample sizes may have been insufficient to allow detection of significant differences between the treatment conditions, since sample attrition caused these to fall below the levels that power calculations had indicated would be required. The fact that personal construct psychotherapists conducted both the personal construct and

supportive therapy groups, although allowing control of therapist variables, might also have obscured differences between the conditions.
Despite the manualization of the treatment conditions and the instructions
to therapists not to use personal construct psychotherapy interventions in
the supportive groups, they might not have been able to resist doing so!
Finally, it may be that the limited number of treatment sessions employed
in this study was insufficient to lead to significantly greater change in the
personal construct condition.

Conclusions

Agoraphobia may be viewed as a constrictive strategy allowing avoidance
of: anxiety associated with situations of interpersonal conflict; guilt associated with implications of going out; and/or testing out of idealistic
fantasies concerning the ability to go out. It may also allow the maintenance of mutual validation of construing by the agoraphobic and their
partner. A group personal construct intervention developed on the basis of
this model has been found to facilitate the treatment process and to be
associated with greater improvement than while clients were on the waiting
list. Although a research study has failed to provide evidence that the intervention is more effective than supportive therapy, this may be due to
limitations of the study. Nevertheless, the reports of individual clients in
the personal construct psychotherapy condition have been sufficiently
encouraging to suggest that further exploration of a personal construct
approach to the treatment of agoraphobia would be merited in a study
with a larger sample size.

Appendix: A manual for personal construct psychotherapy for agoraphobia[1]

Aims:

The major aims of this component of treatment are:

i   elaboration of clients' and their partners' construing of interpersonal conflict and of associated emotions;
ii exploration, and reconstruction, of negative implications of independence and of the ability to go out for the client and his/her partner;
iii elaboration of a favourable yet realistic construction of the non-phobic self.

Timing and content of sessions

All personal construct psychotherapy (PCP) sessions are of 90 minutes duration and alternate with exposure sessions, the first PCP session being held between exposure sessions 1 and 2. The therapist's interventions during these sessions are guided by the personal construct theory model of agoraphobia (Winter, 1989b).

PCP sessions 1 to 3:

These follow an interpersonal transaction group format (RA Neimeyer, 1988b):

i   initial didactic input by the therapist explaining the possible relevance of the topic of the session to agoraphobic clients;
ii consideration of the topic in rotating dyads, such that each group member is paired consecutively with every other member;
iii plenary group session with feedback from the dyads and further exploration of the topic.

PCP session 1

i) The therapist begins the session by reminding the group that this is the first of six sessions that will focus upon the discussion of issues relevant to clients' agoraphobic problems, and that such discussion is as important as the more 'practical' exposure sessions if lasting relief of their symptoms is to be achieved. The therapist indicates that the sessions will focus upon areas that research has shown to be particularly pertinent to

---

[1] Nicole Rossotti contributed to the development of this manual.

agoraphobia, and also tells them that they should invite their partners to the fourth and fifth PCP sessions, but that clients without partners may bring any close friend who is involved in their problem to these sessions or may attend them alone. The therapist then asks group members to state the sensations that they experience in the situations of which they are phobic, and lists these situations on a flipchart. Next, the therapist asks members in what other situations they experience any of these same sensations, and the situations concerned are again listed on the flipchart. This material is then used to introduce the notion that the sensations experienced in phobic situations are manifestations of physiological arousal no different from those experienced in any other arousal-producing situation, e.g. interpersonal conflict. All that differs is how the person construes, or labels, the sensations concerned. The diagram in Figure 12.1 is presented on the flipchart to indicate the normal pathway of events when a person is in a situation of interpersonal conflict:

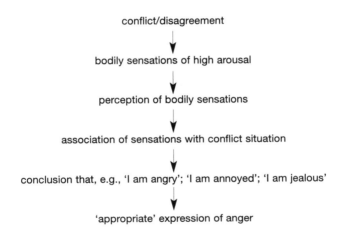

Figure 12.1 Normal sequence of events when a person is in a conflict situation.

Members are informed that there is evidence that people with agoraphobic symptoms tend to be less likely to admit to negative feelings towards, and conflict with, others than do people in general. There is no evidence, however, that agoraphobics are any less likely to be in conflict with others, and to experience the physiological sensations associated with this, than is anyone else. The sensations are merely labelled differently, namely as indicating anxiety rather than, for example, anger or conflict. The diagram in Figure 12.2, presented on a flipchart, summarizes this situation:

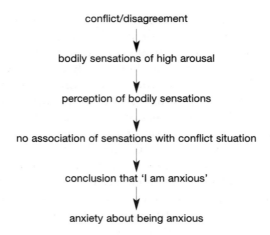

conflict/disagreement

↓

bodily sensations of high arousal

↓

perception of bodily sensations

↓

no association of sensations with conflict situation

↓

conclusion that 'I am anxious'

↓

anxiety about being anxious

Figure 12.2 Agoraphobic labelling of the sequence of events when they are in conflict situations.

Therefore, if the person can become more aware of feelings of anxiety or conflict, he or she will be less likely to experience these as anxiety. A helpful example may be to ask group members to imagine how a person who does not suffer from agoraphobia might feel when in a long supermarket queue; to indicate that such a person might often feel considerable irritation, for example with queue members with heavily laden trollies, with crying children, or with slow checkout assistants; and to point out that the sensations experienced by this person may not be essentially different from those experienced by the agoraphobic, the only difference being how they are construed.

ii) Members are told that for the above reasons the session will focus upon their experience of interpersonal conflict. They are then introduced to the format of this and of the following two PCP sessions, namely that the first part of each session will involve each member being paired with every other for a six-minute interaction. One member will be the main speaker in the first three minutes of each interaction and the other primarily a listener; they will then reverse roles. Members are told that they should listen carefully to each other, and that the emphasis is on non-confrontative sharing of experiences, perceptions and points of view but not to the point of excessive discomfort. They are also told that the final part of the session will involve the group reconvening as a whole to explore further the disclosures made during the dyadic interactions.

Before commencing these interactions, group members are reminded of the topic, namely 'situations leading to disagreement or conflict with other people, and how I feel in such situations; situations in which other people are in disagreement or conflict with me, and how they might feel in such situations'. The therapist then assigns each group member a number and allocates them to pairs according to a pre-arranged plan. The therapist times interactions and indicates the end of the first 3 minutes of each interaction, the end of the second 3 minutes and the pairings for the next set of interactions, and so on. In the event of the group consisting of an odd number of clients, the therapist becomes part of the interactions.

iii) The plenary phase of the group aims to elaborate themes and issues apparent in the disclosures made during the dyadic phase, with particular reference to the model introduced by the therapist during the didactic phase of the group, and to the consideration of feelings which members find difficult to express or to receive. Useful general questions in facilitating the plenary phase may be taken from RA Neimeyer (1988b, p. 187), namely:

- What sorts of things did you find out about other group members during your conversations?
- Whose experience did you most identify with?
- In what ways did you and other group members differ?
- Did you hear anything that surprised you?
- Did you find out that what you had to say changed or developed in any way over the course of the conversations?
- How did the conversations influence the way you think about the topic?
- Is there anything you would like to explore further?
- What questions do you have at this point for other group members?
- How did the things discussed relate to the problem that brought you here?

PCP session 2

i) The session commences with the therapist introducing the notion that while it might seem obvious that being better able to go out, and the greater independence associated with this, would offer numerous advantages to group members, it is possible that they might also see it as carrying some disadvantages for them or for people close to them. Such perceptions, and the conflict associated with them, may help to perpetuate members' agoraphobic symptoms.

As in Tschudi's (1977) ABC Procedure, members may be asked to brainstorm a few examples of:

- possible advantages of being able to go out and independent;
- possible disadvantages of being unable to go out and dependent;

- possible advantages of being unable to go out and dependent;
- possible disadvantages of being able to go out and independent.

These are listed on the flipchart.

ii) Dyadic interactions are then organized as in PCP session 1, but with the topic being 'advantages for me of being better able to go out and more independent; disadvantages for me of being better able to go out and more independent'.

iii) The plenary phase is also organized as in PCP session 1. The therapist focuses upon the validation of positive implications of the ability to go out and independence, and may find it helpful to ask group members to consider people they know who manage to combine the ability to go out and independence with positive qualities, and to attempt to elaborate their construing of these people.

At the end of the session, members are given the homework exercise of writing a character sketch of how they would be without agoraphobia. They should be told that they may find it helpful to write this sketch in the third person just as if they were the principal character in a play, and as it might be written by a friend who is sympathetic towards them and knows them very intimately, perhaps better than anyone else ever really could know them. They should also be told that the topic of the sketch will be the focus of the next PCP session, at the end of which they will be expected to hand it in to the therapist.

PCP session 3

i) Members are asked how they found the homework exercise. It is probable that at least some of them may not have found it particularly easy, and this will allow the therapist to introduce the notion that it may be very difficult to lose one's agoraphobic symptoms if one does not have a clear view of the self as a person who is able to go out, or indeed if one appears to have nowhere to go out to. For such a person, agoraphobia may be viewed as their way of life, and one that is more meaningful than its alternative.

Other members may have found the exercise easy in that they consider that their life would be perfect if they could go out. This will provide an opportunity for the therapist to introduce the notion of the 'if only' fantasy (Fransella, 1972), namely that an idealistic view of life without agoraphobia may only be maintained if clients retain their agoraphobia. For some members, then, their phobic symptoms may be seen as allowing them to avoid testing out such idealistic fantasies.

ii) The dyadic interaction phase, organized as in previous sessions, focuses upon 'me as I would be without agoraphobia'; 'me as I definitely would not be without agoraphobia'.

iii) The plenary phase is also organized as in previous sessions, with the additional element that members are invited to read their character sketches to the group. The session focuses upon elaboration of positive but realistic constructions of the non-phobic self, and the therapist may find it useful to ask members to consider positive aspects of themselves before their symptoms developed and how these features might be built upon in future.

PCP session 4

Members' partners are welcomed to the group, all of which is held in the 'large group' format, and the therapist indicates that they have been invited to this and the following session because the nature of agoraphobia is such that they will inevitably be very much involved in the clients' problems. They are asked to indicate how these problems have affected them, and the therapist takes any opportunities presented to interpret this material in terms of the various components of the model of agoraphobia on which the previous groups have focused. Ways in which clients and their partners share a view of the world that may contribute to the maintenance of the client's symptoms are identified, and an attempt is made to facilitate reconstruing in these areas. The therapist also takes any opportunities to draw attention to relationships in which the client's incapacity allows the partner to construe himself or herself as strong and confident. Such partners may be invited to consider ways in which this necessity to be strong can at times be a burden, and to reveal ways in which they feel less strong. They may also be introduced to the notion that by revealing more of their weaknesses, they may allow their phobic partners to reveal more of their strengths. A further area that may be worthy of consideration is clients' and their partners' construing of ways in which they and their families differ from people outside the family. If it appears that a sharp contrast is made between family and non-family members, the latter being construed more negatively, an attempt is made to validate more favourable constructions of people outside the family.

The therapist should resist any attempts to make the session focus upon the nature of clients' symptoms and practical advice concerning these.

PCP session 5

This session, also attended by partners as well as clients, focuses upon aspects of the personal construct model of agoraphobia that have not been explored fully in the previous session in the context of partners' construing and client–partner relationships. Particular attention is paid to partners' anticipations of the clients, themselves, and their relationships if the clients lost their phobic symptoms, and to reconstruction of these anticipations if they do not appear to be conducive to symptom loss.

PCP session 6

This, the final PCP session, is attended by clients only and is held in the 'large group' format. The therapist first invites clients to share their views of attending sessions with their partners, and of meeting fellow members' partners, and draws attention to aspects of their accounts that are consistent with the personal construct model of agoraphobia. It may be of value, during this discussion, to ask members what surprised them in how their partners responded to the group, and what surprised them about other members' partners. However, the major focus of the session is on clients' constructions of how they have changed over the course of therapy, the results of their experimentation during this time, and their anticipations of the future. The experimentation in which they will engage in the future is discussed, and concepts of personal construct theory (for example, constructs of transition) that may help them to construe their experiences are stressed.

CHAPTER THIRTEEN

Constructivist trauma psychotherapy: a framework for healing

KENNETH W SEWELL

Theory

Defining trauma

Traumatic experiences come in many forms. Clearly, the Western professions of psychiatry and psychology have grappled with the range of convenience of 'trauma' from their very inception (for example Freud, 1897, 1914), often arguing along an objective-subjective dimension. The dichotomy of defining trauma along the objective-subjective dimension has moderated in recent years. The current diagnostic manual, DSM-IV (American Psychiatric Association, 2000), has loosened Criterion A for Post-traumatic Stress Disorder from its more objectivist predecessor, DSM-III (American Psychiatric Association, 1980) to include vicarious experience (e.g. learning that something life-threatening occurred to a loved one). This moderation has occurred with a concomitant shift in theoretical predomination via the influence of constructivist frameworks. Extreme events sometimes happen to otherwise adjusted persons such that their functioning is seriously compromised. Some persons, owing to their experiential histories, their worldviews, or even their idiosyncratic momentary circumstance can experience an event as *traumatic* even though a panel of expert reviewers might rate the event itself as trivial. Constructivist theories have no problem integrating these two claims. Indeed, the conceptual maturity and common-sense moderation instantiated by personal construct theory account for its steady influence on both the fields of psychopathology and psychotherapy. Because it transcends the objective-subjective distinction, the constructivist position described here is unlikely to strike anyone as 'revolutionary'. Instead, its utility should strike many open-minded practitioners as self-evident.

Traumatic experiences disrupt the psychosocial world of the survivor in two fundamental ways. First, the traumatic experience introduces a sense of chaos and catastrophe into the person's sense of the flow of time. Thus, the person's perception of cause and effect can be impaired – specifically as it relates to perceiving the self as a causal agent. Thus, a traumatic experience disrupts the survivor's sense that good outcomes can be *caused* (anticipated as likely and predictable). Second, the traumatic experience invalidates at least some preferred ways of understanding and experiencing the self and self-in-relation-to-other. Stated differently, traumas disrupt the construing of the social world.

If the client's world now seems chaotic and unpredictable, and if the client's social construal of the self and others has been breached, then this model of post-traumatic stress would suggest that the person has been traumatized. Whether the event was a parental divorce, a world war, or a broken promise is of little consequence to this conceptualization.

Elsewhere, I have laid out the above-summarized and related theoretical positions, along with their research support, in considerable detail (Sewell, 1996, 2003; Sewell et al., 1994, 1996; Sewell and Taber, 2001; Sewell and Williams, 2001; also see Cromwell, Sewell and Langelle, 1996). Furthermore, other constructivist authors have described narrative reconstructive approaches consistent with the one presented here (for example, RA Neimeyer, 1995b; Viney, 1996). The major purpose of the present chapter is to build a theoretical framework within which a constructivist therapeutic approach to post-traumatic stress can be described.

Therapeutic practice

I have proposed elsewhere that a traumatized person 'needs to be loved *within* her trauma' (Sewell, 2002, p. 123). The traumatized person needs to experience that love from a valued other who she believes can endure and share her horror and pain. As a group, we psychotherapists tend to be fearful of framing our relationships to psychotherapy clients in terms of love, due to our simplistic association of 'love' with 'sexuality'. Nonetheless, much of what goes on in the therapy rooms of diligent and effective clinicians could be described as genuine attempts to love clients within their pain, and honest efforts to convince clients that they are loved. However, rather than conceptualize therapy in such a taboo-laden way, we often focus on diagnostic formulations, therapeutic *techniques* and treatment plans. If we are being effective psychotherapists, all of these standard foci are alternative labels for experiencing and communicating love for our clients, albeit with an ostensibly safe, impersonal distance.

Make no mistake, a loving psychotherapist is exercising a complex set of skills. Being an effective psychotherapist with a traumatized client certainly requires more than affection and good intentions. Thus, it is essential that these emotional and interpersonal skills be grasped and articulated in verbally communicable ways. Pure intuition may work wonderfully in a specific instance, but it cannot comprise the basis of a legitimate therapeutic approach without the ability to scrutinize, teach and expand it reliably. The following sections of this chapter will outline a model of post-traumatic stress psychotherapy that casts the loving psychotherapeutic relationship squarely in an articulable constructivist frame.

Defining therapeutic love

From an evolutionary biological perspective, Maturana and Varela (1992) defined love as the desire of one organism to exist in close physical proximity to another. This definition might lack sufficient breadth to capture all that we want to say about human love. Nonetheless, it does convey a felt desire for closeness – an aspect that is crucial to the kind of love we must exercise in psychotherapy. McCoy (1981) viewed love as the valuing of another person's construct system. In merging these two definitions, I have argued that 'Love is treasuring another's entire existence' (Sewell, 2002, p. 124). 'Treasuring' implies more of the organismic desire-for-closeness in Maturana's definition than McCoy's 'valuing'. Thus, love is simultaneously psychological and embodied. Likewise, treasuring another person's 'entire existence' also subsumes the notion of holding the other's 'construct system' in high regard. The other person's experiences, strengths, weaknesses, and attributes (physical, psychological, and otherwise) are worthy of adoration and nurturance. When a client reveals valued self-aspects, he experiences his therapist's treasuring of those same aspects and comes to feel closer to the therapist as a result. On the other hand, when the client feels safe enough to reveal self-aspects that he despises, he likewise experiences his therapist's treasuring response. This is the loving moment at which healing can begin – when the client feels treasured in his fears, pains and inadequacies . . . not simply tolerated or accepted in his difficulties and flaws, but utterly treasured. Leitner and Faidley (1995, p. 291) called this process the 'awful, aweful nature of ROLE relationships'.

Why love is psychotherapeutic

I would argue that the experiential valence of feeling loved is inherently positive. On the other hand, the often-present 'strings attached' to expressions of love can complicate the experience such that its overall valence can become a complex calculus. But when love is experienced and communicated without demands for performance or reciprocation, the client's attention can turn away from her perceived flaws and toward the positive resources she possesses. The therapist's love (a positive experience by definition) comes to be experienced as reliably predictable, leading to the more global anticipation that at least some positive outcomes are predictable. Of course, this predictable experience of being treasured occurs in the context of a social relationship. The client truly *belongs* in loving connection with the therapist, even if other aspects of her social construing lack coherence and comfort.

Because therapeutic love is dually connected with (1) an increased sense of personal agency and (2) an increase in social connectedness, it works in direct opposition to the timeless chaotic fear and social dislocation provoked by the trauma.

Why love from a therapist?

Unlike a typical peer/partner/friend relationship, a therapeutic relationship is structurally unidirectional and non-reciprocal. Not that information flows in only one direction, or that only one person might change as a result of the relationship, but rather there is an explicit contract that the help giving is to be from therapist to client and not vice versa. Of course, clients may love their therapists intensely. However, the effective psychotherapist does not make therapeutic decisions based on whether or not the client seems (or is likely) to love him. Instead, therapeutic love is given freely and without demand for affection or protection in return.

Love in non-therapeutic relationships (those that are bi-directional and mutual) is almost never unconditional – not even for brief periods of time. That is not to diminish the importance of familial, romantic or fraternal love; it can be life changing, intensely moving and meaningful, and even spiritually profound. Nonetheless, reciprocal love always demands attention to the needs of the other (either directly or by implication). By contrast, in the loving therapeutic relationship, demands to earn the love of the therapist are not only absent, but they are systematically invalidated by the therapist if they are assumed by the client to be in force.

As quoted above, a traumatized person needs to be loved *within* the trauma. Paradoxically, the person closest to and most loved by a traumatized person (the daughter of the bereaved wife, the spouse of a rape survivor, the mother of a combat veteran) is often in the very worst position to provide this healing love. This is because the 'other' is too highly invested . . . in the recovery of the survivor, sometimes in the very events that were traumatizing, and almost certainly in the ability of the traumatized person to continue loving them. Given the professional, uni-directional, and non-mutual nature of the defined relationship, a loving therapist does not need the client's love and protection. Thus, the therapist can love the client out of the simple desire to be of help.

Constructivist framework for post-traumatic psychotherapy

There are several 'steps' to the framework to be described herein. However, I do not mean to suggest that psychotherapy occurs in distinct phases. Rather, I mean that some aspects of a relationship must develop as building blocks for deeper processes of therapeutic love to be experienced and communicated. The steps would best be conceived as ingredients in a recipe that have separate functions and interactive potentials. They have an order of entry into the preparation, but all must remain present and continue to interact in the creation of the completed product.

The first step in loving a traumatized client is to meet him at the level of his pain and show a willingness to be of help. I have referred to this as 'symptom management' (Sewell, 1997, 2003; Sewell and Williams, 2001, 2002). The primary function of symptom management is to gain the client's trust by helping to alleviate distress. This serves the function of 'enrolling' the therapist as an important social figure in the client's life. Furthermore, relieving some of the client's debilitating anxiety and/or social dysfunction can mobilize the client's anticipations toward change and growth (as opposed to mere survival). A variety of technical tools from many therapeutic traditions (discussed under the concept of 'techniques' below) can be employed in the service of symptom management. Symptom management never cures – rather, working to reduce initial distress will provide the basis for a healing psychotherapeutic relationship.

The next step is gently to elicit the client's life story, or 'life review'. In a life review, the therapist guides the client in sharing her past personality development, experiences and memories both before and after the trauma. This creates a shared narrative so that the therapist and client jointly know the story of the life that was disrupted by the traumatic experience. As Kelly (1955/1991a) asserted, construing the construction process of another (sociality) is the foundation for playing a social role with that person. Sociality is a necessary but not sufficient condition for a loving therapeutic relationship. Therapeutic love involves affection/desire and efforts towards closeness. Knowledge is a type of closeness; open acceptance and appreciation of this knowledge communicate the affection and warmth characteristic of a loving therapist. This closeness further enrols the therapist as an important audience (Sewell and Williams, 2002) to the story the client is seeking to tell and recompose. With the therapist now present with the client in her life story (not simply in the therapy room), the relational basis exists for the client to endure the next step, 'trauma reliving'.

Trauma reliving involves the client bringing the therapist *into* the memory and experience of his trauma. Trauma reliving is not simple repetition; instead it is a literal re-membering of the traumatic experience, open to transformation given the new skills, resources and co-narrator (the therapist) now available to the client. During trauma reliving, the therapist becomes acutely aware of the crucial value of her valued co-narrator and audience status nurtured via symptom management and life review. When a client relives his most painful experiences in this shared and connected way, he brings the therapist's love into the trauma and its memory. This transforms the power of the memory, from potentially overwhelming to patently survivable. Clients takes on new courage from the therapist's loving willingness to share and endure their pain.

Once the therapist and client are jointly facing the horror of the client's traumatic experience, the therapist can begin juxtaposing the client's various psychological layers of experience (also known as 'constructive bridging'). This process can actually begin during the trauma reliving, but certainly extends into other therapeutic interactions that have no reliving content (in a relational sense, once the trauma is effectively relived with the therapist, the client and therapist are always in joint psychological contact with the relived trauma). In constructive bridging, the therapist places the past next to the present, the catastrophic fears of disclosure next to the actual experience of sharing the trauma with the therapist, and so forth. The client and therapist then weave meanings between these juxtaposed elements that build a viable sense of self for the client. Bridging the dimensions of time (past, present, future, before, after and so forth) and social connectedness (alone, connected, worthy and so forth) in relation to the trauma allows the client and therapist to co-construct a new experience of the trauma, and thus a new experience of the self.

The next treatment aspect involves the active and collaborative anticipation of the client's future (also termed 'intentional future metaconstruction'). Traumatized persons often have no clear sense of their own future. Some envision a future only in terms of yet more trauma and chaotic fear. Intentional future metaconstruction involves creatively co-composing possible future scenarios and selves. The process is intended to open clients up to their future, not to predict or select a singular trajectory.

Through intentional future metaconstruction, new layers of experience are formed that can provide the basis for yet more constructive bridging. This process continues (including additional life review and trauma reliving as clients' new development opens other aspects of their experience to the therapy relationship) until the trauma experience exists within the client's life as a perhaps important but integrated component of the overall story. Successful psychotherapy results in clients experiencing the trauma as an event that has influenced but has not singly determined the content, quality and trajectory of their life.

The psychotherapeutic posture

For love to be psychotherapeutic, it must be experienced by the therapist *and* effectively communicated to (felt by) the client. This is most directly achieved by adopting a gentle, healing spirit. A gentle spirit is characterized by several identifiable qualities. The therapist must embody a sense of *calmness;* the client should sense a soothing presence when with the therapist. The therapist must be reasonably *self-assured,* conveying that nothing the client says or does can devastate the therapist. The therapist's *acceptance* must extend to all aspects of the client – to his predicament, his desire for healing, and his fear of change. Acceptance values change, but never demands it. A gentle therapist actively practises *forgiveness,* giving the client permission to be human, to have faults, to struggle, and to share this frailty with the forgiving therapist. A therapist with a gentle, healing spirit is *humble,* nurturing a sense of awe in the capacity of humans to endure and overcome hardship. Finally, a gentle therapist has *confidence* – in her client's potential and in her own skills as a therapist.

Developing and embodying a gentle, healing spirit is sufficient to communicate love to a client. Merleau-Ponty (1964) posited that humans perceive emotions *directly* in the interpersonal realm. Tompkins (1992) and other affect theorists (for example, Nathanson, 1992) supported that emotions are perceived directly as feeling states when in social connection. Thus, a therapist who adopts and fosters a gentle, healing spirit and who risks putting himself in caring contact with a hurting client will very likely be perceived as loving.

Finally, psychotherapists use the power of direct statements of love and affection. Even in Western cultures conflicted about love in the therapy room, it is perfectly permissible, and often profoundly impactful, to say

> I truly admire you for having the courage to face these problems. I feel very deeply for you in your pain. I sometimes find myself wishing I could just wave a magic wand and make all these things go away. But we both know that I can't. So I will be as close to you in your pain as you will let me be. I care for you and I hope you know that I want to be helpful.

Such direct statements of love and affection can reach even the most frightened and numb clients, even if their ability to perceive emotions directly and effectively has been debilitated by their pain and social disconnection.

Techniques

I believe that 'techniques' are often more for the benefit of the therapist than for the client. They can serve as props to allow the self-doubting therapist to feel he is 'doing something' while the relationship is developing into one that can support loving collaboration. Nonetheless, techniques have a place in constructivist therapy for post-traumatic stress. Symptom management can often be achieved via technical tools (cognitive-behavioural techniques such as self-talk analysis, thought-stopping, and relaxation skills training; social engineering; judicial use of medicine; interpersonal support, and so forth). A variety of gestalt and art therapy techniques (such as empty chair, journaling, poetry, painting, letter writing, and so forth) can assist the life review, constructive bridging and intentional future metaconstruction. Indeed, even the overall structure of the therapeutic process outlined above can be viewed as an example of 'exposure and response-prevention' therapy. The intentional processing of the traumatic content (as well as its social and life-course context) could be considered 'exposure', then 'response-prevention' is achieved by using the therapeutic relationship (via the gentle, healing spirit) to prevent the client from fleeing the pain and retreating into isolation. It would be difficult, if not impossible, to create a session-by-session 'manual' for the type of therapy described here. Nonetheless, there is considerable room and respect for established therapeutic techniques.

Case example

In providing any clinical case example, there is a delicate balance between providing ample detail to present the case realistically and keeping the description simple enough to illustrate the pedagogical points. The following example may lean toward the latter in that the emphasis is clearly on the aspects of the case that illustrate the treatment model described above. Suffice it to say that Frank's psychotherapy was full of the rich humanity that characterizes any experience of personal change.

Frank came to therapy at the insistence of his primary care physician. At the age of 78, Frank had never viewed psychology as relevant to his life and had certainly never considered himself the 'type of person' who would go to a psychotherapist. Frank had been modestly successful in his career as a personnel manager with a large trucking company. His wife of 51 years died approximately 18 months prior to his beginning therapy. Frank was living alone in a house owned by his son, who lived in an adjacent town. Frank was fairly active at a nearby senior centre, where he would frequently play board and card games with a group of men and women he considered friends.

Frank was experiencing episodes of overwhelming negative emotions; he would find himself crying uncontrollably, even in the midst of his friends. These episodes would often be accompanied by vague somatic symptoms of heaviness in his chest and headache. He had consulted his physician about the episodes. The physician was satisfied that systemic ill-nesses had been ruled out as likely causes and queried about the content of his thoughts preceding the episodes. Frank would not discuss his thought content. When psychotherapy was suggested, Frank insisted that he would only see a doctor who was a military veteran. The physician con-vinced him to see me for a consultation, explaining that I had worked with many military veterans and might be able to understand his situation.

In his initial consultation, Frank was clearly interviewing me. He seemed satisfied that I had adequate experience dealing with military vet-erans. He described his physical symptoms in some detail and included behavioural details of his emotional distress (for example, crying, inabili-ty to engage in his recreational activity) as if they were yet additional physical symptoms. He expressed a desire to have me 'get this figured out' so I could tell his physician how to treat it.

For symptom management, I began to search for ways to interrupt his mental focus at the onset of his episodes. Given that he was not yet ready to share the details of this focus, we shifted our attention to his general mental hygiene (eating and sleeping patterns, exercise regimen, religious observances, frequency and nature of his interactions with his children, grandchildren, and siblings). He seemed intrigued and energized by the possibility that these unpleasant episodes might simply be a result of an unfortunate combination of situational factors. He volunteered to begin keeping records of his eating, sleeping and exercise so that we might match these patterns against the occurrence of his episodes. As soon as Frank saw me as willing to join with him as detective in sleuthing the ori-gin and potential alleviation of his symptoms we were ready to begin the life review.

Frank's early, middle and later life were shared with the therapist as if he were reporting his life's details to be placed in a record never to be read by anyone important. Even his wife's decline and death as a result of rapidly deteriorating Alzheimer's disease was discussed to his apparent satisfaction in a mere 15 minutes. Only Frank's experiences and relation-ships in the military generated a sense of relevance and importance. Our sociality was developed enough for me to apprehend his sense of impor-tance but our commonality lacked the experiential depth to make the relevance clear. So, my therapeutic stance was one of great intrigue and interest in every detail that seemed important to Frank. I asked him to bring items that he had kept from his wartime experience, including pho-tographs of himself and his buddies, photographs of battle-damaged cities, monetary currencies he had collected, and commendations he had received. I expressed awe at his experiences and asked permission to pho-tocopy some of the paper currency and post-battle photographs. He seemed to take a sort of fatherly pride in being able to show me things that were obviously important to him and have me find them important as well. I asked him to detail how he felt about relationships with particular buddies he mentioned. This particular query (in the context of our deepened relationship) was the thread that led us into trauma reliving.

In trying to relate to me just how important a particular buddy had been to him, Frank changed his posture in his seat and said, 'Do you really want to know what it was like over there?' At this point, he was able to walk me through two different horrific experiences that involved losing comrades to mortar fire and land mines. Then Frank changed his posture again. Tears welled as he related an incident in which he and several others were ordered to proceed through an urban area that had been shelled to the point that buildings were reduced to rubble. Walking past a building that had four walls but no roof, he and his buddies noticed something moving by a window. They took cover and prepared to defend against sniper fire. When none commenced, they yelled for the occupant to show himself. After several seconds of silence, a male voice began screaming inside the building. Finally, the screaming man showed himself at the window. Frank shot his weapon three times; the screaming and gunfire turned to silence. Frank's buddies then rushed to the window and peered in, leaving Frank under cover (still somewhat shaken from the incident). Frank's comrades then ran back to him and insisted that they proceed as ordered. When Frank asked about the screaming man, they changed the subject and insisted they proceed. Frank complied. For more than 50 years, Frank was haunted by the possibility that he had shot an unarmed civilian or, worse yet, an American soldier through that window.

Now that I was on the inside of Frank's traumatic memory, he was able to let me know that his worry about this incident had become a focus of rumination. With the death of his wife and his concomitant loss of the nearly consuming caretaker role, he was left with his own thoughts more accessible. He had told no one of this incident prior to telling me, not even his wife. 'I just need to know for sure', he would say. 'Then I can . . .' He could never quite finish that sentence.

Constructive bridging with Frank went in a variety of directions, the clearest of which involved bringing those important relationships from the past into the present. Of the two buddies with him on that fateful day, one had been an extremely close friend; he referred to him by his last name: Templeton. Frank was aware that Templeton had died some years later (he learned this from Templeton's widow, who located Frank). The other man had been a good friend, but Frank could not recall his name – a fact that bothered Frank immensely. I encouraged Frank in his attempt to find the name of this man. Frank found his name via a company roster maintained by a veterans group: Tommy Carpenter. With my encouragement, Frank began to have silent conversations with Templeton and

Carpenter. He knew that they were acting in his best interest when they protected him from knowledge that might have overwhelmed him in the context of war. He would now ask them to help him deal with his uncertainty and the distress it was causing. Frank found these internal conversations extremely helpful. Three shots through a window had robbed Frank of a sense of continuity to his life before and after the war. The bridging of past with present via the intensely positive wartime friendships built a new continuity, based at least in part in his new-found relationship with a loving therapist.

Intentional future metaconstruction was relatively simple with Frank. Now freed from his isolation in his pain (he had not only me, but Templeton and Carpenter as well), Frank could reclaim his identity as being a 'man who can handle things' and extend that into the challenges that were before him in his final years (death included). Because Frank knew several people who died over the course of our work together he would process his feelings about their deaths as a clear method of preparing for his own. Frank told several people how a psychologist had helped him with just a few simple suggestions. 'I never thought it could, but it really works!' he would say, clearly as proud of me as he was of his own improvement.

It . . . the relationship . . . the love . . . really does work.

Research

The particular therapeutic approach described here has not been subjected to straightforward, nomothetic, empirical research. The theoretical concepts underlying the approach have been studied extensively (Cromwell, Sewell and Langelle, 1996; Sewell, 1996; Sewell et al., 1994, 1996; Sewell and Taber, 2001) with considerable validation and empirically informed theoretical developments along the way. However, I am hesitant to offer the research cited above as even indirect support for my therapeutic approach. Similarly, I am hesitant to suggest the sort of nomothetic research that would best demonstrate its effectiveness. Would process research be most appropriate? If so, tools do not currently exist to operationalize many of the interpersonal and intrapersonal constructs proposed as important to this approach. If nomothetic outcome research were pursued, to what should this method be compared? Should a DSM approach to diagnosis be considered the standard, even though the treatment approach does not fully espouse the DSM as its pathology model? If client reports of symptom improvement are to be considered the standard of proof, then case examples such as those reported above should, in conglomerate, be all that is necessary. But I can certainly list a variety of reasons why a client might report improvement that is either (a) not concordant with the client's actual experience, and/or (b) not a result of what is considered (by the therapist) to be the active components of that treatment.

Conclusions

Given the concerns outlined above, how can we proceed as scientist practitioners? On the one hand, we need to be innovative and creative in designing and inventing assessment tools and research methods that will address our questions about psychotherapy in useful ways. On the other hand, we need to be integrative and pragmatic in using treatment models that rest upon coherent and empirically grounded theories, and that simultaneously offer an approach to therapy that is sensible, communicable and capable of embracing the totality of a client's experiences (rather than treating symptoms as isolated germs). Finally, we need to try out such approaches and continue to use them if they appear effective, until other more coherent treatment methods emerge. I believe the approach outlined herein meets these broad criteria as worthy of judicious use by practitioners who are willing and able constantly to evaluate the viability of their work with clients.

CHAPTER FOURTEEN

Personal constructions in therapy with child sexual abuse survivors

CHRISTOPHER R ERBES, STEPHANIE LEWIS HARTER

Over the past few decades the field of psychology and mental health has undergone a virtual revolution in terms of its conceptualization and treatment of trauma (Yehuda and McFarlane, 1995). This is perhaps most evident in the way that mental health professionals now view and deal with childhood sexual abuse (CSA). Childhood sexual abuse has gone from being something seen as almost non-existent, and unimportant, to something that is seen as disturbingly common and potentially devastating (Finkelhor, 1990; Herman, 1992; Briere, 1996). From the inception of the current surge of research and clinical interest in the area, personal construct psychology has added its voice to the important and at times contentious discussion of how to make sense of the presence and consequences of CSA in our society and the lives of those we work with (for reviews see Harter and RA Neimeyer, 1995; Erbes and Harter, 2002).

Research has now confirmed what clinical observation suggested years ago, that CSA is both common and harmful. Studies have shown that about one-third of women and one-fifth of men in the general population report some form of sexual abuse occurring in their childhood (Finkelhor et al., 1990). Reviews of the literature have also demonstrated empirical links between the experience of sexual abuse during childhood and a host of negative long-term difficulties in adulthood. These include, but are not limited to, troubles labelled as depression, generalized anxiety, post-traumatic stress disorder (PTSD), dissociation, personality disorder (particularly borderline personality disorder), substance abuse, vulnerability to repeated traumas later in life, interpersonal difficulties, and suicide (Browne and Finkelhor, 1986; Beitchman et al., 1992; Briere and Runtz, 1993; Polusny and Follette, 1995). This research on the long-term effects of CSA has been invaluable as it has made us more aware of the potential consequences of CSA and the difficulties that survivors of CSA can face. However, it has also indicated an enormous diversity of reactions to CSA. Theory and treatment of CSA must acknowledge that not all survivors of

CSA suffer from all (or even any) of the problems listed above. A failure to acknowledge this risks perpetuating a narrative in which sexual abuse survivors are seen as being inevitably damaged or flawed. Such a view may be harmful in its own right (Durrant and Kowalski, 1990; Erbes, 2004).

Empirical research has also begun investigating possible moderators and mediators for the long-term effects of CSA. Studies have examined whether the severity or type of abuse, the perpetrator of abuse, the family context within which abuse occurs, the disclosure of abuse and cognitive/constructive interpretations of the abuse are related to long-term outcome. There is a great deal of heterogeneity in the results, but some more consistent findings emerge. Abuse that is performed at the hands of a parental figure, particularly violent or forceful abuse involving penetration, is typically linked with more severe outcomes (Browne and Finkelhor, 1986; Beitchman et al., 1992). However, meaning-making processes and the family environment in which those processes develop are even more closely related to outcome than objective aspects of abuse events (Harter, 2004; Harter and RA Neimeyer, 1995).

Theory

Construing the trauma of sexual abuse

Kelly (1955/1991a) taught that events are known only through the lenses of personal constructs. As events are experienced, their constructions also influence the construal of future events in an evolving process. The corollary is that an event is not construed in a random, capricious fashion, but instead in a way that fits within the existing construct system. Traumatic events, such as some instances of CSA, invalidate or stand outside the range of convenience of societal and personal construct systems and thus disrupt the ongoing anticipations of future events (Harter and RA Neimeyer, 1995; Harter, 2001; Sewell and Williams, 2002). Not only may the victim be unable to make useful meaning of the abuse itself but the abusive experience may disrupt the previous systems of meanings that constituted the person's constructions of self and of important others.

Sexual abuse survivors have been presented with all-too-convincing proof that the world is not a just, benevolent, or predictable place. In particular, constructions of core relationships, of trusted adults, and of the child's own self may be shattered. In the absence of personal meanings for the abuse experience, victims may be particularly vulnerable to cultural myths that attempt to preserve 'just world' assumptions by blaming those without power for their own victimization (Janoff-Bulman, 1992). Empirical research has demonstrated that child victims and adult survivors are at risk for constricted, abuse saturated, and/or fragmented constructions of self as markedly different from others and from their own ideal (Harter, Alexander and RA Neimeyer, 1988; Harter, 2000, 2001; Freshwater, Leach and Aldridge, 2001). Closely related to constructions of self and close others, they may have particular difficulty making meaning of emotional aspects of experience (Harter, 2004; Harter, Erbes and Hart, 2004).

A traumatic event such as sexual abuse may be construed only on very basic, physiological or non-verbal levels (Harter and RA Neimeyer, 1995; Harter, 2001; Stewart and RA Neimeyer, 2001). If so it can have profound emotional consequences, as replications of the event (with accompanying emotional distress) are anticipated with little verbal understanding of why such anticipations are made. Even when an event is construed in more verbally mediated, conscious ways it may end up being construed using poorly elaborated, extreme constructs that are poorly equipped to make flexible, useful meanings from the event and to integrate the event into ongoing personal experience (Sewell, 1997; Sewell and Williams, 2002). A traumatic event can be so 'poignant and isolated' in a person's construct system that it leads to the development of a new system of meaning that is blatantly coloured by the traumatic experience and that is isolated from previous, non-trauma saturated systems of meaning (RA Neimeyer and Stewart, 1996).

Familial and social context

To the extent that individuals are able to integrate their experiences of sexual abuse into their existing meaning-making system, and to adapt their system in flexible and useful ways to construe sexual abuse, it may be possible to avoid many of the negative correlates described in the sexual abuse literature. Unfortunately, the family and social environments many abuse survivors must deal with do not foster flexible meaning construction. While the types of families in which abuse occurs may be as varied as the types of sexual abuse themselves, research has consistently demonstrated that such families are prone to abuse of power, emotional invalidation of children, and related difficulties (Draucker, 1996; Harter, 2004). There is ample research demonstrating that the family environments of abuse survivors have serious implications for their later functioning (Nash et al., 1998; Harter and Vanecek, 2000).

In many ways a sexually abused child's efforts at meaning construction occur in isolation from supportive social resources. Often the child is unable to disclose the abuse to important others within and outside of the family. The child can be faced with only the perpetrator's constructions for what is happening and why it is occurring. Such constructions often include minimizing the seriousness or consequences of the abuse and blaming the child for its occurrence (Finkelhor, 1979; Rush, 1980; Herman, 1981). When the abuse is occurring within the family, the child can be confronted with irreconcilable disparities between the family's spoken values and public presentation and the child's own experiences. For example, a child can be raised in a family in which, on the one hand, family values and the innocence and sacredness of children are touted, and on the other, they are being frequently and secretly violated and harmed. Even when the abuse is disclosed, a child can be told to 'get over it and put it in the past'. Sometimes when abuse is disclosed, an opposite reaction occurs and the child can be seen as irrevocably damaged, in desperate need of 'fixing' by mental health professionals.

These responses not only isolate the child in efforts to construct adaptive meanings from the experience of abuse but they may also invalidate the child's basic meaning-making processes (Harter and RA Neimeyer, 1995). Such invalidating processes are not limited to families in which abuse is perpetrated by a family member but can also occur in families struggling to cope with abuse perpetrated by an outsider. A child (and then adult) who is repeatedly invalidated in this fashion can have a hard time trusting his or her own constructions, even when the alternative constructions offered by others are quite harmful.

A person's meanings about sexual abuse occur in a familial context, of course, but they also occur in a social context. Popular and professional culture has become saturated with narratives of abuse survivors as being irrevocably scarred by their events. While such narratives can serve to validate the pain and suffering of abuse survivors, they can also perpetuate a feeling of isolation, difference and damage in survivors both as children and as adults. In the mental health field, for example, there are stereotypes that abuse survivors cannot be proficient psychotherapists or even researchers (Harter, 2004). Such societal narratives, which are sometimes perpetuated by the mental health profession, can further increase the isolation and the enforced secrecy that some survivors continue to face.

Research and therapy are only beginning to acknowledge the huge diversity that is present not only in terms of types and circumstances of abuse but also in terms of reactions to abuse and ways of coping with it. Survivors are active creators of meaning, as are all people, and they can come up with remarkably resilient ways of dealing with past events (Draucker, 1992; Morrow and Smith, 1995). Although some families can oppose efforts to create flexible meanings about the self and the world, others can work very hard to provide opportunities for children who are abused simply to be children, rather than problems or patients. The preceding discussion highlights some of the difficulties and challenges that abuse survivors can face. However, it should not be seen as describing an inevitable or insurmountable course of events. Flexibility in terms of our conceptualization and treatment of abuse survivors is essential (Erbes, 2004).

Therapeutic practice

Central to a personal construct approach to work with sexual abuse survivors is that the therapist work within the meaning system the survivor has established, rather than imposing his or her own preconceived professional notions about the problems or resiliency of sexual abuse survivors in general (Erbes, 2004). Therapists must position themselves not only in terms of the constructs that the client is using regarding the abuse but also in terms of the familial, social and societal narratives within which the client's and therapist's meaning making occurs (Erbes, 2004; Harter, 2001, 2004). For example, some well-meaning therapeutic approaches can play into dominant and harmful narratives that hold that sexual abuse is shameful, that it is the fault of the survivor, and that it is irreparably harmful. A therapist who conceptualizes and treats sexual abuse as something that is always a unique and almost Herculean obstacle can emphasize a survivor's feelings of isolation, difference and damage. On the other hand, a therapist who refuses to acknowledge or discuss the implications that sexual abuse has had for a particular client can unintentionally take part in a narrative in which sexual abuse is shameful and secret, not to be mentioned or explored.

The personal construct therapist takes a credulous approach, seeking to learn the client's personal experience, including personal experience of abuse – not only what has happened but also how the client makes sense of what has happened. The abuse is not assessed in isolation but in the context of a life narrative potentially comprising many experiences, relationships and meanings. Clients can be asked about what they were like before the abuse occurred, if they have had a chance to talk about their abuse with others, whether it is something that they feel affects them now, whether it is something they find themselves thinking of very often, how they are different from who they might have been as a result of the abuse, how they have resisted the effects of the abuse, and whether there are current relationships or experiences that remind them of the abuse. The goal is to try to assess what sorts of meaning clients, and others in their lives, have made of this event and how clients locate the event within a larger life story.

The course of therapy with sexual abuse survivors will be dictated to a great extent by answers to the questions outlined above. There seems to be little benefit, and some potential harm, in trying to convince clients that they have been 'traumatized' if they do not feel that they have been. At the same time, there is a potential for gross invalidation of a client's constructs if the therapist is unable to hear or accept the experiences and problems that sexual abuse survivors can face. Some clients have had ample opportunity to discuss and make meaning of sexual abuse. They may have been able to get support immediately after it happened, or they may have had prior therapy experiences. Others may not feel a need to discuss their experiences because they do not perceive them as continuing to affect their present lives as much as other issues. Still others will feel profoundly affected by their experience, while at the same time feeling very confused and overwhelmed when they try to make sense of it.

Therapeutic questions may open space for the creation of some meanings about resilience and fortitude (Durrant and Kowalski, 1990; Mann and Russell, 2002). A clinician has an opportunity to enquire gently about how an abuse survivor has managed to deal with whatever consequences of the abuse they have experienced. If a person feels they have not been adversely affected, it may be helpful to invite them to construct some meanings around what it is about them that has allowed them to live beyond the experience. Although enquiries along these lines can be invaluable, they must follow the client's own constructions carefully. If clients do feel devastated by what has happened, too much emphasis on their resiliency or strength, especially early on, can serve to invalidate their constructions. A therapist must also be attentive to possible non-verbal constructions. If a client claims to have no problems at all with an experience of abuse but shows visible distress about it, it may not be appropriate to invite too much in terms of constructions of resiliency and 'overcoming the abuse' because that may invalidate implicit, but important, constructions.

There are some specific techniques that are often, although not always, useful when they are integrated into the respectful stance we have outlined above. Techniques are presented to clients in a hypothetical, experimental manner, as potentially useful tools. They are not offered as an ultimate cure or a required strategy.

Provision of 'coping tools', especially early on in therapy, can be a useful way of reducing symptom distress and increasing clients' confidence in themselves and in the therapy (Sewell and Williams, 2002). Techniques taken from the cognitive-behavioural literature are often useful in this regard – for example, diaphragmatic breathing as a relaxation technique (Foa and Rothbaum, 1998); grounding techniques for dealing with intrusive memories and acute distress (Najavits, 2001); distress tolerance skills for dealing with overwhelming emotions and crises (Linehan, 1993). These techniques serve an ameliorative function (Harter and RA Neimeyer, 1995) but are not generally sufficient for more restorative or elaborative tasks.

Narrative strategies may be helpful in deconstructing oppressive meanings attached to the abuse or other aspects of the survivor's life story and in identifying alternative constructions. The therapist assists the client to construct a coherent narrative of the abuse that locates it within a life story that provides a sense of authorship and future possibilities. This includes an acknowledgment of multiple alternative meanings that continue to unfold over time, rather than correction of a singular narrative of events. The therapist provides an audience for the client's performance of new meanings and assists the client to identify other potential audiences (Adams-Westcott and Dobbins, 1997; Harker, 1997; Harter, 2004).

The prescriptive and inflexible use of exposure therapies (therapies that require that a client recount abuse experiences in great detail) is inconsistent with a constructivist stance. However, it is often very important, though difficult, for abuse survivors to discuss their abuse experiences. Discussing what a client has been through gives him or her an opportunity to create new meanings about the event and its implications. Not the least of these meanings can come from being able to relate the event to a therapist who is able to listen in an empathic, non-judgemental manner. Some clients may have developed a story of the abuse, and their life, that is all too coherent but limited in possibilities. Other clients may have been unable to make any coherent meanings. When clients are able to talk about their past experiences of abuse, they may be able to 'put together the pieces' of what happened into a new story of the event and also a more coherent or elaborative story of their lives (Stewart and RA Neimeyer, 2001).

Often a client may never have disclosed the abuse experience before revealing it in therapy. The lack of a safe context in which to voice the experience may have limited available meanings to those ascribed by the abuser or available social stereotypes. Meanings constructed through voicing the experience in a safe, therapeutic context are not limited to the verbal level but include an enactment of new ways of relating as an adult who can own one's own experience. Subtle and at times profound changes can take place over time in such discussions.

The context of safety, respect and choice that the therapist co-constructs with the client is pivotal to resisting the re-enactment of oppressive relationships that survivors can experience in therapy (Harter, 2001, 2004). If a client chooses to tell the story of the abuse, the therapist and client should work together to monitor the client's emotional reaction to the discussion. Clients need to be able to feel and express their feelings about the abuse, but also to enact choice and self-protection. It is not helpful if they are overwhelmed by distress that is experienced as uncontrollable (Briere, 1996). Because such conversations can be potentially very painful, it is sometimes helpful for a therapist to guide a client's discussion with gentle questions or encouragement. This also reassures the client that the therapist can tolerate the painful material offered by the client. However, questioning should be done with the client's permission and with the understanding that questions can be halted at any time the client requests it.

Case example

To illustrate a constructivist approach to work with an adult CSA survivor, we shall briefly discuss a client whom we shall call Jane, whom one of us worked with on an outpatient basis. Identifying information about this individual has been changed to protect her identity. We shall also not identify which of the authors served as her therapist to further ensure confidentiality.

Jane is a divorced Caucasian female, in her mid-thirties at the time she was referred for psychotherapy by her treating psychiatrist. She came to therapy because she was concerned about the types of relationships in which she tended to get involved. She had just ended a 7-year relationship that was emotionally invalidating and at times physically abusive. Jane was dealing with strong feelings of depression, which included some powerful thoughts of suicide. While Jane did inform the therapist in the first session that she had suffered sexual abuse at the hands of a family member, her initial concerns were about her present relationships and feelings.

Following Jane's lead, the first half of therapy focused on how she was striving to regain some independence in her life. In that phase of treatment the therapist used narrative techniques (White and Epston, 1990; Freedman and Combs, 1996) to highlight some of the ways that Jane was already achieving her independence and to invite her to form meanings (narratives) about those flashes of independence.

After 6 months of bi-weekly sessions Jane had made considerable progress in addressing current safety issues and relationship concerns. She was more independent and less depressed. She informed the therapist that she wanted to look more closely at long-term patterns in relationships, particularly why she tended to blame herself for so many things, including paradoxically for when other people would hurt her. Jane began, on her own, to relate this to her experiences of abuse in her past. The therapist consulted with Jane about how they might best be able to talk about such experiences. The therapist pointed out that talking in detail about abuse experiences could be very painful and made it clear that Jane could choose to discuss them or not. The therapist offered to help Jane discuss them but only if Jane would agree to let the therapist know if things were too difficult or if she wanted to stop at any point. Jane agreed, and the focus of therapy shifted.

Jane found it very difficult to talk about her abuse experiences. She had been molested and raped by a paternal figure, and molested by some siblings as an adolescent, as well as being raped by an acquaintance as a young adult. She experienced a great deal of shame in relating these experiences to the therapist. The therapist would, with her permission, ask questions about what happened, when, and in what context to help her tell her story. As often occurs during detailed disclosure of abusive experiences, Jane felt a profound increase in guilt and depression. She began to drink excessively and to drive while intoxicated after drinking. This was an old way of dealing with pain and guilt that Jane had used for many years but she had gradually stopped doing it in the earlier phases of therapy. The therapist gently informed Jane that a focus on sexual abuse in therapy could not continue if it was going to put Jane's life at risk. Over several sessions the therapist and Jane discussed whether she wished to continue to talk about the abuse, whether she wished to curtail her drinking, and whether she wished to receive a referral for specific treatment for alcohol use. This was something of a turning point in the therapy as Jane was confronted with a choice between caring for herself or hiding and potentially harming herself.

Jane chose to continue talking about the abuse while not using alcohol as a shield against her emotions. The therapist offered several kinds of grounding and coping skills for Jane to try (especially as discussed by Najavits, 2001) but Jane did not find them to be helpful. Instead, she developed her own ways of dealing with and facing her emotions without alcohol. She greatly reduced her drinking. Continued discussion of abuse experiences alternated with focus on more current issues, titrating Jane's self-exposure to painful memories and encouraging constructive bridging between past and present experiences. The therapist used the last part of each session as a kind of 'winding-down' period so that Jane could calm herself and refocus in the present before she had to leave.

Discussing the abuse experiences remained very painful, but Jane started to form some new meanings as she did so. She started to question whether she was entirely to blame for what happened to her and she started to feel more justified in her anger towards those who had abused her. As Jane questioned some of her older constructions of her experience she began to develop newer constructions from the present perspective of an adult in a supportive context that validated her ability to make meaning of her own experience. Therapy with Jane ended when the therapist moved out of the area. Jane chose not to continue therapy with another provider, despite the recommendations of her therapist. When asked what had been helpful about the therapy, Jane spoke about the trust in the relationship and the ability to open up about her feelings and experiences.

The preceding example illustrates several points about how one can approach CSA issues in therapy. The first and most important is that of the stance of the therapist, respecting the client's authorship of her experience, including her participation in the therapy relationship. It is doubtful that Jane would have been willing or able to discuss her experiences of childhood abuse if she had not formed a strong sense of trust for her therapist through the earlier phase of therapy. When Jane decided to discuss her abuse, many specific techniques were used (including narrative techniques, some skills training from a cognitive-behavioural treatment manual, and retelling of traumatic material). However, none of these seemed as important as the therapeutic relationship within which the work occurred. Indeed, some of the techniques simply were not helpful and Jane and the therapist worked flexibly to pick what was and was not useful. Talking about the abuse with the therapist offered a new experience that others could hear about the abuse without seeing her with judgement, revulsion, or rejection. This allowed Jane to begin reconstruing her roles in past and current relationships.

Research

The previous sections on theory and therapeutic practice have cited empirical literature from which the constructivist psychology of abuse has evolved (see Harter and RA Neimeyer, 1995; Harter, 2001, 2004; Erbes and Harter, 2002 for more extensive reviews). Development of a personal construct theory of abuse and related therapeutic approaches has proceeded hand-in-hand with research on meaning making processes. The present section will focus on research specific to psychotherapy with sexual abuse survivors, which has been less extensive.

The first controlled outcome study of treatment for sexual abuse survivors was conducted from a personal construct therapy perspective (Alexander et al., 1989). This study also examined process variables related to therapeutic outcome (RA Neimeyer, Harter and Alexander, 1991). The two treatment conditions, a process group (Alexander and Follette, 1987) and a more structured interpersonal transaction group derived from personal construct theory (RA Neimeyer, 1988b), were both conducted from a constructivist stance. Both were effective, in contrast to a wait-list control condition, in reducing symptom distress, with symptom reduction maintained at 6-month follow-up. Participants in the process group made more improvement in social adjustment, perhaps because the focus on less structured, more naturalistic interpersonal interactions more easily generalized to social relationships outside the therapy context. The interpersonal transaction group was more helpful to more severely distressed participants in reducing their levels of fear. This group was more structured, with a period of rotating dyadic discussions in each group meeting, followed by group processing of topics discussed in the dyads. The one-to-one dyadic discussions may have provided a less threatening context for more anxious members to share issues related to their abuse (Harter and RA Neimeyer, 1995).

The process analysis of these groups highlighted the importance of developing constructions of self, fellow members and the group therapists. More positive outcomes were associated with perceptions of oneself as similar to other members and to the group therapists early in treatment and also to less polarized perceptions of group members and the therapists early in treatment. More positive perceptions of the therapists, both early and late in treatment, were also associated with positive outcomes. Perceptions of the therapists, relative to perceptions of other group members, became more important later in treatment. Positive changes during treatment and continued at 6-month follow up were particularly related to seeing oneself as similar to the therapist and to seeing the therapist in a less polarized and more positive manner (RA Neimeyer, Harter and Alexander, 1991).

These process analyses highlighted the importance of the therapeutic relationship as a context within which clients may reconstrue themselves in relation to others. The therapists may have represented both nurturing authority figures and representatives of a larger social system. Both treatment conditions focused on participants' experiences, with little therapist disclosure of issues outside the therapy relationship. Thus, the evolving identification with the therapists was unlikely to have been based on recognition that therapists' life experiences or meaning-making systems were similar to the clients'. Rather, the clients appeared to develop a differentiated perception of commonality with the therapists from the validation of the clients' own meaning-making ventures. The safety and mutual validation encouraged in the group provided a context within which clients could experience themselves as valuable and as able to connect with others to share common universal issues (Harter, 2001).

Westbury and Tutty (1999) demonstrated the effectiveness of a feminist approach to group therapy that is similar to personal construct approaches described above in emphasis on a safe, supportive context for survivors to be heard and believed. This model also addresses multiple levels of meaning, cognitive, emotional, physical, and spiritual, including body-focused relaxation, personal boundary exercises, guided visualization, and discussion of personal, family and cultural meanings around issues relevant to abuse. It diverges from the personal construct approaches in its stated goal to move women survivors toward a particular narrative of survival, becoming a 'warrior'. While survivors in personal construct therapy may construct a warrior self, this is only one possible narrative of healing.

Within the child-abuse literature generally, treatment studies have been rare. Most studies have focused on documenting potential long-term effects, while fewer have addressed processes through which those effects occur or might be ameliorated. However, there is a slowly emerging literature on treatment outcome, generally concurring that interventions addressing meaning-making processes are beneficial.

Most of the studied therapies have drawn from cognitive-behavioural theories, more than from constructivist theory, and have targeted abuse survivors diagnosed with PTSD. Psychoeducation concerning the effects of trauma, training in affect management and interpersonal skills, cognitive restructuring, imaginal exposure and imagery rescripting, and symbolic confrontation of the abuse perpetrator have appeared to be potentially helpful (Apolinsky and Wilcoxon, 1991; Zlotnick et al., 1997; Wolfsdorf and Zlotnick, 2001; Cloitre et al., 2002; Fallot and Harris, 2002; Smucker et al., 2002). Consistent with the stance taken in this chapter, many of these therapy researchers caution that sexual abuse survivors are more likely to experience increased distress, retraumatization and treatment failure or dropout if exposure treatments, often used with PTSD, are not carefully contained. Development of a strong therapeutic relationship and emotional regulation skills are probably necessary before clients can tolerate or benefit from exposure (Zlotnick et al., 1997; Wolfsdorf and Zlotnick, 2001; Cloitre et al., 2002).

Conclusions

Personal construct therapy with adult survivors of sexual abuse emerges from a burgeoning empirical and clinical literature both within and outside of constructivist circles. It is characterized by a collaborative stance that privileges the client's experience (Erbes and Harter, 2002). The therapist avoids authoritarian or directive approaches that could re-enact the coercion and invalidation of the client's experiencing that occurs in abusive environments. The therapist works with the client to co-create a context in which the client feels valued and validated as a decision-maker and creator of meanings. This stands in stark contrast to approaches that view the abuse survivor as a 'damaged' patient who must be repaired by a wise and powerful therapist. The therapist negotiates activities with the client that invite experimentation with new meanings, rather than prescribing didactic 'facts', cookbook exercises, or challenges to 'faulty' beliefs or 'distorted' perceptions. The specific activities are less important than the co-construction of a healing relationship within which the client can voice new, previously silent, or unheard meanings.

CHAPTER FIFTEEN

Personal construct group psychotherapy for borderline personality disorder

IAN GILLMAN-SMITH, SUE WATSON

Personal construct group psychotherapy has been a focus of interest for some time (for example, Dunnett and Llewelyn, 1988; Winter, 1997; Foster and Viney, 2001; Lane and Viney, 2001a, 2001b) and the authors are of the opinion that this is an area of research and clinical endeavour that has much to offer. Our clinical work in a psychological therapies service has involved developing a personal construct group psychotherapy approach for working with people with a principal psychiatric diagnosis of borderline personality disorder.

Theory

The meaning of diagnosis within the medical model differs from the personal construct perspective. It is, however, important that personal construct practitioners do not thereby alienate themselves from others working within mental health settings in which are used what, in personal construct terms, may be considered pre-emptive labels. Kelly (1955/1991a) used the term 'dimensions of diagnosis', suggesting that this was not a reference to disease entities, types of people or traits and that it was important not to pigeonhole observations of human behaviour. The label of 'borderline' itself has been repeatedly criticized as pejorative and inadequately descriptive (Harter, 1995).

Within our group psychotherapy intervention, clients were selected according to the DSM-IV (American Psychiatric Association, 2000) criteria for borderline personality disorder and the outcome of the Millon Clinical Multiaxial Inventory (Millon, Davis and Millon, 1997). A personal construct model of borderline personality disorder based on the DSM-IV diagnostic criteria is shown in Table 15.1. This reframing of these criteria in personal construct terms assisted the group psychotherapists in planning the structure of the group and anticipating and identifying possible commonalities between group members and emerging themes within the group. It also allowed the therapists to ask questions and make assumptions that were in themselves propositional and open to revision and reconstruction, this approach being, in the authors' view, the spirit of personal construct interventions. As Kelly (1955/ 1991a, p. 453/p. 335) stated, 'the human personality . . . is not well adapted to receptacles' – the 'receptacle' in this instance being the diagnostic label of borderline personality disorder. Harter (1995) suggested that it remains 'vital' that in working with clients who have been diagnosed as 'borderline', the therapists adopt a hypothetical stance within their professional and personal constructions. This must also be with the awareness that our theories, which allow us to see, can also blind us to the unique stories of our clients. As Mair (1988) suggested, it is our stories that inform life and can hold us together or keep us apart.

Table 15.1 A personal construct model of borderline personality disorder (Winter et al., 2003)

DSM Diagnostic Criteria	Possible Characteristics of Construing
i) A pattern of unstable and intense relationships characterized by alternating between extremes of overidealization and devaluation.	Tendency to pre-emptive construing; slot rattling; superordinacy of constructs concerning valuation of self and others; fragmentation; low sociality
ii) Impulsiveness in at least two areas that are potentially self-damaging.	Foreshortening of CPC cycle.
iii) Affective instability.	Slot rattling; loose construing.
iv) Inappropriate intense anger or lack of control of anger.	Dearth of validation and failure to reconstrue following invalidation.
v) Recurrent suicidal threats, gestures or behaviours, or self-mutilating behaviours.	Lack of verbalization of constructions or demands expressed in suicidal behaviour; hostility.
vi) Marked and persistent identity disturbance.	Poorly elaborated or fragmented self-construction
vii) Chronic feelings of emptiness and boredom.	Failure to be aggressive (Kellian) and complete new experience cycles.
viii) Frantic efforts to avoid real or imagined abandonment.	Dependency path characterized by threat; construction of current relationships in the same terms as early relationships.

Therapeutic practice

Following from our previous experiment with personal construct group therapy for clients with a diagnosis of borderline personality disorder (Winter et al., 2003), we co-facilitated a second group which ran for 40 sessions, clients attending the group weekly and simultaneously attending 40 sessions of individual personal construct therapy.

The purpose of group psychotherapy from a personal construct perspective was to create a setting in which the group participants could have role relationships with each other with the eventual aim of experimenting with alternatives about how they saw themselves and how others saw them. Kelly (1955/1991b) suggested that the function of group psychotherapy was broadly the same as that of individual psychotherapy, which was to assist individuals in developing more effective channels through which both they and others could anticipate events.

The group was designed to be exploratory, with respect to 'elaborating the complaint', in the anticipation that the group process may eventually lead to suggestions of alternative constructs. However, such exploration would involve a loosening of individuals' construing, the prospect of which could lead to Kellian anxiety, or indeed other emotions associated with transition. Therefore, group members needed first to focus on construing the group and their role relationships within the group, identifying similarities and differences between themselves and other group members. In order to facilitate this a somewhat tight approach was initially required until members construed the group as 'safe enough', after which further exploration of personal construing could be considered. The consequent loosening needed to proceed with due caution to protect group members from the threat resulting from their awareness that they may have emotionally exposed themselves.

Once individuals were able to identify areas of construing where they felt psychologically 'stuck', or unable to complete full experience cycles, this was made explicit, as were the associated patterns of behaviour. Role relationships and interactions were also viewed in relation to transference and this too was made explicit with the propositional suggestion that some interactions within the group could also reflect scenarios and situations in which group members all too often found themselves in their daily lives.

The Kellian idea of constructive alternativism was introduced and the notion of experiential experimentation to try out alternative constructs was outlined by the therapists. The group setting provided a safe forum to try out new experiments, report experimental results and hear from other group members of potential propositional adjustments to individuals' experiments, or changes and adaptations to the initial hypotheses. The rationale for taking on such experiments was explained in terms of aggressive elaboration and that this could be a way in which one may recon-strue or begin to retell a story. Kelly (1955/1991b) described group psychotherapy as being like a well-equipped social laboratory, containing a variety of figures as compared to individual psychotherapy. The group set-ting can therefore allow for a comparatively greater variety of social experiments.

A personal construct approach can be an empowering one, and one function of the group was to consider ways of dispersing dependencies and identifying potential for further and future reconstruction. Emphasis was placed on facilitating group members to be their own agents for recon-strual and change. It was important for group members to be able to regard themselves as resources and agents of change rather than constru-ing any psychological movement or indeed psychological immobility as being purely dependent on the therapists, others or external factors. Group psychotherapy can be a rich and fertile ground for identifying vali-dational evidence with respect to individual group members' new endeavours. It can provide a forum where clients can tell their stories and eventually be able to retell aspects of these stories (or at least consider the potential for the retelling of these stories in the future).

In terms of group structure and process, there were four distinct phas-es. In planning a personal construct group intervention, we considered the potential problems posed by the difficulties of borderline clients with inter-personal relationships, impulsivity and anger control and their tendency to transgress boundaries. It was hypothesized that a formal, structured thera-peutic approach such as that offered by the interpersonal transaction format (Landfield and Rivers, 1975) might be used advantageously, partic-ularly while the group was in an early stage of its development. Thus, the first phase was the interpersonal transaction format, which, we considered, corresponded to the circumspection phase of the CPC cycle. Interpersonal transaction groups are designed to focus on the improvement of social rela-tionships. The format is highly structured and involves the use of rotating dyads in which each group member briefly discusses a predefined bipolar topic with every other group member. The resulting experience is then shared and processed by the group as a whole in a plenary part of the ses-sion. The emphasis is on non-confrontational sharing of selected information without fear of invalidation. The interpersonal transaction for-mat is considered to promote controlled self-disclosure, empathy, group cohesion and equal participation (RA Neimeyer, 1988b). Examples of bipo-lar topics set for discussion in this phase included 'hopes and fears of being in group therapy', 'how I am now and how I would like to be in future', 'pros and cons of sharing emotional difficulties', and 'when and when not to trust others'. The structure imposed by the use of rotating dyads and the subsequent plenary seemed to contain potential threat and anxiety and facilitate increasing familiarity and ease of interaction between group members. The interpersonal transaction format was abandoned after 10 sessions since group members now seemed to be developing role relationships within the group. It was predicted that they might now feel sufficiently contained to explore their construing within a less tight structure.

The second phase, still located in the circumspection stage, involved elaboration of the complaint and the formulation of propositional hypotheses. It was now up to the group to suggest and agree on the content covered in each session, such material usually emanating from group members' experiences during the week since the last session. The absence of a defined structure and the consequent elaboration of personal stories sometimes induced a 'free for all' atmosphere leading to the emergence of conflict between group members as personal styles clashed and role relationships were reconstrued. This resulted in the generation of group ground rules to assist in the maintenance of appropriate boundaries, thus providing some containment and minimizing potential threat and anxiety. A major focus of this phase was the elaboration of 'how I am now' for each group member in terms of the production of a written self-characterization, followed by consideration of 'how I would like to be' and examination of the implications of personal change.

The third phase was characterized by aggressive experimentation both within and outside the group, regarded as representing the pre-emption phase of the CPC cycle. To facilitate sociality, group members were encouraged to experiment with testing their construing on the group. Members were asked to provide feedback and, where helpful, to generate alternative constructions of events, often using role play. The emphasis was on the validation of shifts from pre-emptive to propositional construing. Possibilities for tentative experimentation were devised, agreed and conducted, members reporting outcomes to the group at the following session. During this phase, experimentation focused first on peripheral constructs, gradually moving to more core levels, once more in an attempt to minimize threat. The concept of time binding of constructs acquired in early life and applied indiscriminately and possibly unhelpfully in the present was introduced, giving some group members new insight into their situations, which they reported finding empowering. Using material taken from group members' self-characterizations, fixed role sketches were developed and agreed.

The fourth phase was largely concerned with consolidation and tightening, construed as the control phase of the CPC cycle. Group members were asked to consider and describe ways in which they and other group members had changed over the course of group therapy. The members each gave and received feedback in terms of their own and others' progress.

Potential difficulties in sustaining new, alternative construing were identified and how such difficulties might be overcome was explored. In invitational mode, it was proposed to group members that the outcomes of their experimentation indicated that, as Kelly (1955/1991a) argued, they did not have to be victims of their own biographies and there is always the potential for reconstruction in the future. This led to the identification by each member of further areas of desired personal change. Ideas for future experimentation to facilitate such change were generated by the group. Finally, time was allowed for group members to feed back to us in terms of what they had regarded as helpful and not helpful in the group structure and process.

Case example: the group

The group members were five women aged between 19 and 43 years. Two were single although three lived with partners, and one was unemployed but four were employed. All had suffered disordered attachment and regularly self-harmed by cutting. Three regularly binged and vomited, four had a history of illicit drug use and one was a recovered problem drinker. Four had no previous experience of psychotherapy, but one had participated in many different therapies.

The first interpersonal transaction phase of the group saw the emergence of a number of common themes. These concerned anger and aggression (directed both towards the self and others), fear of being judged by others, self-harm (particularly self-cutting), invalidation from significant others (this included childhood experiences), issues of self-worth versus worthlessness, and self-respect versus self-hatred. The group had the common experience of conflicting internal dialogues. For example, one group member spoke of her 'two nutters', who would argue self-destruction versus a logical objective stance, with her feeling like a passive onlooker and then acting according to which 'nutter' had won the argument.

The second phase, which still represented circumspection and the elaboration of the complaint, was a time when personal stories and the way in which members saw their difficulties were further elaborated. There was now the emergence of some conflict between group members as personal styles clashed. Members attempted to establish their own and others' membership by identifying themselves with the elaborated problems such as self-harming (including suicidal attempts), eating disorders, externalized rage, sexual excesses, and trusting everyone versus trusting no one. This perhaps represented a polarization in relation to how problems were construed in the group during this phase and served to establish alliances and alienate others in regard to those who are 'like me' and those 'not like me'. It was towards the end of this phase that group members were encouraged to elaborate 'how they would like to be in the future' and begin to explore the implications of such goals. Some members questioned the prospect of change in relation to the threat of failure and invalidation and considered how remaining the same could at times seem relatively appealing.

The third phase saw the beginning of experimentation to re-examine issues highlighted in the first and second phases. For example, one group member who had been identified as slot-rattling in relation to anger (passive victim of others' anger versus vengeful rage), sexual behaviour (celibacy versus going to S&M clubs and being promiscuous) and trust (absolute trust versus complete rejection) was encouraged by the group to experiment with 'shades of grey' and note what this meant and how it felt. This group member was also supported in constructing experiments that involved features of self-preservation and personal protection.

Another member had identified herself as a victim of her mother's emotional neglect from a child's perspective in her adult life. She was able to consider the possibility of reconstruing herself as mature and separate from her mother and also to use the concept of sociality in construing some issues from her mother's perspective. This led to her experimenting with different ways of relating to her mother and also, significantly for her, accepting that although she could not change her mother, she could change the experience of her interactions with her. Similarly, another member had issues in relation to her father, by whom she felt dominated and invalidated since childhood. She was able to consider experimenting with setting limits on her father's verbal abuse and recognizing this as a problem for him in his interaction with others rather than it becoming her problem.

Another group member pre-emptively predicted that others construed her in negative terms, because this was how she construed herself. She was encouraged to consider and enter into social situations in a more propositional manner. After doing so, she was able to entertain the notion that the way she construed herself did not necessarily correspond with others' constructions of her, and accept that this would be dependent on others' individual construction processes.

The fourth and final phase involved group members consolidating the work they had done and receiving feedback from other group members. Group members were encouraged to acknowledge their potential for reconstruction in the future and how this might evolve with time. Generally, members were positive about the group experience and felt that they had moved some way towards achieving their therapeutic goals. At this end point of group psychotherapy, members were encouraged to brainstorm and consider what they would take away from the group experience, leading them to generate the list below:

- the knowledge that I am not alone in how I feel;
- new friends;
- the realization that life is worth living;
- stuff I've learnt about myself;
- the ability to challenge myself;
- coping techniques;
- our lunacy, or 'accepting how mad I am';
- accepting that some things cannot change.

Research

Perhaps not surprisingly, given its idiographic emphasis, personal construct psychology has not featured heavily in the literature as a theoretical rationale informing group therapeutic interventions. Kelly's (1955/1991b) stage model of group psychotherapy has been little used (Winter, 1992a), and was reported to be of limited value by some of those employing it (Morris, 1977). The view has been expressed that personal construct theory is useful only when applied to individuals and is less helpful than alternative theoretical approaches when used in group therapy (Dunnett and Llewelyn, 1988).

However, other theorists have reported favourable outcomes in research involving personal construct group therapy using the interpersonal transaction format. These include clients with problem drinking (Landfield, 1979), eating disorders (Button, 1987), childhood sexual abuse (Alexander et al., 1989), agoraphobia (Winter, Gournay and Metcalfe, 1999), and adolescents with problems (Truneckova and Viney, 1997). The recent Winter et al. (2003) preliminary report on the ongoing comparative study of personal construct therapy and dialectical behaviour therapy for clients with a diagnosis of borderline personality disorder, of which the present study is a part, provides some interesting findings regarding differences in process. Clients in the personal construct therapy group regarded their sessions in terms of group climate as characterized by more conflict and avoidance of significant issues by the group than did clients in the dialectical behaviour therapy group. However, clients in the personal construct therapy group described the most important in-session events as self-disclosure. As Winter et al. (2003) speculate, high levels of self-disclosure might enhance opportunities for conflict and avoidance of significant issues. Thus the sessions seemed 'not so much an interpersonal laboratory as an interpersonal crucible' (Winter et al., 2003, p. 351). This is in marked contrast to dialectical behaviour therapy clients, whose most important event was guidance and whose construction of their therapeutic setting seemed more akin to a classroom. Comparative outcome in the two groups has yet to be evaluated, but Winter et al. (2003) hypothesize that their approach may offer greater opportunities for personal construct aggression.

Conclusion

It would appear from our own experience of referrals to our service that there is an ever-increasing demand for service providers to offer effective interventions for clients who present with difficulties that lead them to receive a diagnosis of borderline personality disorder. We have now co-facilitated two personal construct psychotherapy groups for clients with this distressing diagnostic label. The anecdotal feedback provided by our clients, together with preliminary results from analyses of process data, indicate that this type of group therapeutic intervention is of potential value in helping these clients to function more effectively in their lives.

CHAPTER SIXTEEN

Eating disorders

ERIC BUTTON

My interest in eating disorders goes back to 1973. As a young clinical psychologist inspired by the publication of *Inquiring Man* (see Bannister and Fransella, 1980, 1986), I was fortunate enough to obtain a post as research assistant to Fay Fransella at London's Royal Free Hospital. The research was concerned with perceptual and conceptual change in the treatment of anorexia nervosa and obesity. My doctoral research at the Royal Free Hospital (Button, 1980) was to provide the platform for the development of my own ideas about eating disorders and my subsequent role as a clinical psychologist specializing in eating disorders. Some 30 years later, I am still involved in this field and it is a pleasure to be able to share my clinical and research experience with you.

The format for this chapter is a familiar one and in many ways echoes previous publications, such as my book *Eating Disorders: Personal Construct Psychotherapy and Change* (Button, 1993). There is a broad theoretical position, an approach to therapeutic practice and some research evidence. At the outset, however, I have to declare that there is no panacea, but hopefully a guide to those who choose to explore this path.

Theory

The term 'eating disorders' has come to be used to describe the experiences and behaviour of people (predominantly, but not exclusively, female) who are excessively concerned about their body shape and size to the point that they indulge in extreme forms of behaviour in their efforts to achieve thinness and avoid fatness. The most obvious and well-known manifestation of this is anorexia nervosa, where the pursuit of thinness becomes the central preoccupation and the prospect of becoming fat becomes the number one thing to avoid. Strategies for seeking this out centre mainly on food restriction (usually little in quantity and low in energy content), but rigorous exercise regimes, self-induced vomiting and laxative abuse may also be part of the armoury of the sufferer in her desperate attempts to stay ahead of the game and feel in control. The end result can in some cases be lethal and in up to around a third of cases the disorder becomes very long-term and debilitating, although some people do make some degree of recovery (see, for example, Button and Warren, 2002).

Although the pursuit of thinness and avoidance of fatness has become almost normative in young women, very few people can sustain such persistent deprivation and most people with eating disorders present with other variants on the above theme. Bulimia nervosa describes a pattern of behaviour in which individuals (usually of average size) strenuously aim to eat very little, but they are unable to keep it up and they succumb to frequent episodes of so-called 'binge eating'. The latter is very hard to define but clinical definitions emphasize a sense of loss of control and the great volume of food typically eaten in such episodes. Following a binge, a common response is to induce vomiting, but laxatives, diuretics, exercise and not eating may all follow, as well as feelings of guilt, shame and low mood. Both anorexia nervosa and bulimia nervosa are subject to international definition in clinical circles, but inevitably rather more clients with problems in this area fail to meet the criteria than those who do. Nowadays, the favoured term to capture this wider spectrum of eating problems is eating disorder not otherwise specified (EDNOS). This encompasses a range of problems of clinical severity, including those who binge but do not purge (binge eating disorder), people who only binge occasionally, and those with anorectic behaviour and attitudes whose weight is suboptimal but not life threatening.

Looking at such behaviour from a personal construct theory perspective, the most useful concept seems to me to be that of *constriction*. No one who has worked with these sad individuals will fail to recognize the extent to which their perspective on the world has become narrowed. Matters of relationships, work, play, even life and death tend to come second place to the two big and inextricably linked issues of weight/size and eating. Although the sufferers may have a job, be engaged in study or bringing up a family, they are generally more preoccupied with trying to fend off the temptations of food and not surprisingly other aspects of life end up suffering – partners, children, jobs and study may all begin to fall by the wayside. Indeed, it is often pressure from these areas that leads to people seeking help. Given the choice they would probably prefer to carry on unhindered.

So why do some people engage in such extremes of constricting their world? Maybe because this makes life almost manageable. Typically, clients will acknowledge that in other areas of life they are struggling and feel a lack of ability to control. This generally centres on *people*, who arguably provide the biggest challenge for all of us. Most people like to have some control of their world, to achieve some degree of predictability, to make things the way we want them to be. But there are other people, like parents, teachers, employers, friends and acquaintances, who have other ideas. Indeed, these people may actively be seeking to impose their own view of the world on us because of their own need for control. Parents who want to be good parents with happy, healthy and successful children; bosses who have their own goals and targets; friends who have their own needs and other relationships to develop. Amazingly most people seem to be able to negotiate these many perspectives and agendas and lead a life in which they can be themselves and also feel loved and part of something. Sadly, however, some people just feel lost and find other people a threat and a source of *invalidation*. This leads me to the second big concept. Invalidation and validation is at the heart of personal construct theory and it is central to my theoretical position on eating disorders.

People with eating disorders often experience considerable invalidation in their experience of other people. This may centre just on certain specific relationships or may be more widespread. They are often deficient in their ability to construe other people. This leads them to have difficulty understanding, controlling or interacting with other people. Their constructs about other people may be very limited or they may have restricted expectations of other people, the resulting effect of which is that they are unable to engage successfully in other than limited relationships with others. It seems to me to be no coincidence that the process of entrenchment of eating behaviour is often accompanied by restriction in social activity, staying at home more, keeping to familiar places and people and gradually withdrawing from socializing.

The response to this invalidation, usually accompanied by very low self-esteem, is to focus narrowly on getting thinner. This may initially be very attractive and earn considerable admiration from peers as well as an enhancement of confidence. Naively, perhaps, sufferers assume that this will solve the underlying difficulties, but weight loss alone is insufficient to tackle the underlying interpersonal issues. Sufferers, however, have nowhere else to go psychologically and can only dig their heels in further by more strenuous efforts to control weight and eating. After a while, other people tend to lose interest and the pursuit becomes increasingly solitary and the die may be cast towards an eating disorder becoming a way of life. Such a life and identity may seem distinctly unattractive to most of us but to the sufferer it may at least offer some area of life that is reasonably predictable and under their control. The alternative prospect, of eating just being a *part* (albeit pleasurable) of life, may be hard to imagine and intolerable.

Therapeutic practice

My approach to trying to help people with eating disorders derives directly from the above theoretical position. The overall aim is to improve
people's ability to function in the interpersonal domain by (a) developing
a more positive construction of self which does not centre primarily on
weight or body size and (b) improving their ability to construe other people's varying constructions of people. The emphasis of this approach is
thus more on people than weight and eating.

Agenda for change?

People with eating disorders often feel under considerable pressure when
they first come for professional help. They may be very afraid that their
control of their eating is going to be taken away from them and indeed
that the whole rationale for their recent being is to be undermined. In
such circumstances, the individual presenting for help is likely to be somewhat on the defensive and may quickly run away if they sense that they are
about to be taken over by others who do not understand them. For these
reasons it seems important to focus on the client's agenda. What are their
expectations and what is their position on change? It is not uncommon for
clients initially to be quite adamant that they don't want to change but
once they discover that the clinician or therapist respects their choice and
is not going to push them, their stance will *loosen* somewhat and they can
move to a more balanced position of ambivalence. For those with eating
disorders, this ambivalence usually takes the form of knowing how damaging their behaviour is but being scared by their expectation that any
change will result in the ultimate horror of fatness. It seems important for
the helper to convey an understanding of such ambivalence and to emphasize that they have a *choice* as to whether to explore the possibility of
change.

Developing a therapeutic alliance

In the case of individual psychotherapy, a lot depends on the nature of the
relationship between the client and therapist. The personal construct
model of *co-collaborators* is one to which I subscribe, but this will not necessarily be an easy form of relationship for all clients. Many clients have little
idea of what to expect and may be very fearful of what may lie in store. For
some clients, there will also be rather negative expectations of therapy and
of the therapist. Depending on the stage of development the client has
reached in interpersonal relationships there may need to be a fair amount
of time spent on developing a therapeutic alliance. There is no easy way to

achieve this, but above all the therapist needs to expect that the clients may need time to discover whether they can trust the person sitting alongside them sufficiently to be able to engage fully in this collaborative process. For those who have had a series of invalidating experiences of other people, this may take some considerable time, but others may be able to slot into the process quite quickly.

Experimenting with change in eating

Clinicians who work with people with eating disorders generally agree that change in both eating and wider psychological issues is necessary but there are differences of emphasis as to which should be seen as the priority. In cases of low weight anorexia nervosa where the client's very life is under threat, it is usually the case that medical practitioners will be involved and that the initial therapeutic effort prioritizes reversing the starvation process. Some would argue that psychotherapy cannot commence until a certain amount of weight is regained and the nutritional crisis is relieved. The position taken in this chapter is that both are necessary but there are no hard and fast rules about the sequence of change.

Eating disorders services generally recommend three meals a day with adequate amounts of carbohydrates and one or two snacks in between, a horrifying prospect for many clients. I am less interested in exactly what and how much they eat than the constructs that surround food and eating. In clients with eating disorders, such constructs are rather limited to whether the food is likely to cause weight gain or not, so that they have 'good' and 'bad' foods. Rather than prescribing menus, my initial approach is to encourage *experimentation* with eating, which may include changing amounts, type of food and the context of eating. Getting the client to begin by recording their food intake in a diary, with comments about associated thoughts and feelings, might be a useful starting point. This may suggest the need to work on a particular time of day. For example, one or two pieces of toast or a bowl of cereal might be suggested for breakfast, emphasizing the importance of setting aside some time for this before embarking on the events of the day. Although I am generally a bit uneasy about imposing my constructs on clients, some new constructions of eating may be offered, for example eating will improve my *health,* I need food for *energy,* and if I eat enough it will stop me feeling hungry and help me to *think about other things.* For those who binge eat there is also the likelihood that eating more regularly and substantially will reduce binge eating and associated distress. In the spirit of what Kelly called the 'invitational mood', I also encourage experimentation with new foods that may just open a door to something new.

Eating in front of others and going out for meals is often avoided and the source of much fear. Exploration of the contexts in which the person does or does not eat may reveal that eating with some people is more acceptable than with others. Encouraging the client to try eating with someone they feel comfortable with may be easier than trying to force the issue in less comfortable eating situations (for example, a family meal). Eating with a friend, for example, can help to put eating into context where the interaction with the friend can become the main focus rather than having just to focus on what one is eating and what other people may think of one's eating. Practice in social eating can also help to highlight the diversity of eating preferences and choice.

Some degree of change in eating can usually be achieved early on but this will inevitably confront the underweight client with the possibility of weight gain. For those who are bulimic and of normal weight, improved eating doesn't usually lead to weight gain. Construction of body image (Damani, Button and Reveley, 2001) can take a lot longer to change, particularly if dealing with someone with a long history of anorexia nervosa, in which a very low weight has been maintained for many years. It is important, therefore, to explore the kinds of construction that surround being of normal weight. The client may, for example, anticipate that people might see her as fat and think badly of her. Another possibility is that being normal weight may make the person more attractive to the opposite sex, something that the client may choose to avoid. They may also think that others will expect more of them, having preferred to hide behind the image and role of a frail and fragile being. In exploring such issues with clients, I would seek to de-emphasize the importance of weight and size and encourage people to experiment with being themselves. One of my favourite lines goes something like 'There are thousands of people who weigh 8 stone (112 lbs/ 51 kg), but there is only one of you – you are unique.' It seems important in psychotherapy to help clients discover and construct their own identity and role in society, rather than fall into the trap of thinking they have to fit into a stereotype.

This leads nicely into the second and more important aspect of therapy, which concerns construing people.

Reconstruing self and others

At the heart of my approach to therapy is the view that eating disorders have something to do with people's ability to understand, predict and control other people, including themselves. Whether therapy achieves something will depend a lot on whether it opens up new ways of understanding self and others.

Exploration of self-construing, using a form of repertory grid or self-characterization, can be a useful starting point. Detailed clinical examples of the use of such methods in eating disorders can be found in Button (1993). Although such methods are best thought of as tools for exploration, it is also possible to derive formal measures which can be clinically useful. For example, my procedure known as SELFGRID (Button, 1994) allows derivation of a personal construct self-esteem (PCSE) score. This does not depend on complex statistics and simply involves calculating the average rating difference between self and ideal self across all ratings in SELFGRID. This measure has been shown to correlate highly with the Rosenberg Self-Esteem Scale (Rosenberg, 1965) and there is some evidence to suggest the personal construct measure allows finer discrimination of level of self-esteem than the Rosenberg (Button and Warren, 2002). The measure can also be used to chart progress during therapy, on the assumption that more positive self-construing is usually a desirable outcome. Knowing something of how clients construe themselves is important, but it is equally important to understand how they construe others. Indeed the two are inextricably linked. SELFGRID includes both self and non-self elements (for example, mother, father, and most liked person), so that one could also compute similar measures for others as for oneself. This can highlight problems with particular significant others (for example, mother or male figures) and also whether there are more generalized problems, such as high levels of polarization between self and others.

Once one has gained some idea of how the clients construe themselves and others, one has to consider whether there are aspects of such construing that need working on. For example, if the client presents with predominantly negative self-construing then one needs to explore the potential for identifying and building areas of more positive self-construing. I usually seek out some areas of positive self-construing (however small) and aim to help the client to 'elaborate' or build on such construing, such as by engaging in more behaviour which can validate it. More adventurously, one might seek to introduce new constructs, which open up new avenues for development of the person's identity in a more positive sense, rather than concentrating on the negatives. For example, rather than focusing on whether one is too *fat* (a negative self-construction), the client might become more interested in whether she is *comfortable with the people around her*.

The biggest problems I find with clients with eating disorders are the difficulties they encounter with other people. In some cases, this may be an understandable result of experiencing negative reactions from others (such as bullying at school, sexual abuse or a very critical parent). In other cases, the client has not suffered at the hands of anyone, but engages in repeated unfavourable comparisons with others. In all such cases, using therapy as an opportunity to understand better the construing of others and our relationship with them can be very fruitful. In this regard, one's role as a therapist is often crucial. Clients will construe *you*, and their relationship with you is likely to influence the course and outcome of therapy in no small measure. For example, the client may be quick to construe you as *critical* because they are used to seeing themselves as worthless and likely to be criticized. The therapist can help the client to reconstrue such events by explaining something of his or her construing. The client thus may learn that events in which criticism is perceived do not have to provide validation for the worthless self-construction, but may alternatively provide an opportunity to understand another person, for example, the therapist may be overanxious for change.

Most of the problems with people, however, are likely to be in the person's everyday life, and clients usually have no shortage of examples of where the problems lie. A particularly common problem is where clients repeatedly become upset by other people, which acts to fuel eating control and/or binge-eating. Often clients suffer in silence and hold on to their negative assumptions about people. In order to break such cycles, it is important to try and understand the other better *and* communicate better to others. All too often assumptions are made about the other and perhaps vice versa. By being more open with each other and sharing one's feelings (arguably the result of invalidation) about difficult interpersonal events, a small step may be taken towards reducing the potential for such interpersonal triggers for problem eating.

Although improved shared understanding with another person is often a possibility, with some people it may be unrealistic. For example, it is unlikely that such rapprochement would be feasible with major sexual abuse from an adult perpetrator during childhood. Similarly, there may be limits to how far one can go in achieving mutual understanding where a disturbed parent has repeatedly inflicted their psychopathology on their child. In such cases, it may be as much as one can achieve to help reconstrue the events as not their fault. In the long term, the way ahead may be to encourage the client to concentrate more on building relationships with people who share similar perspectives with them.

If one succeeds in helping clients to develop a more positive construction of themselves, which doesn't rely primarily on weight and eating issues, and they are generally more comfortable with others, then one is heading for a conclusion to their therapy. This in itself needs careful handling, particularly if the client has had limited or bad previous experience of endings. This could be the subject of another chapter but it suffices to say that the best kind of endings are probably where there has been a proper goodbye, with a chance to air unfinished business and move on to something new. Endings are also not always for ever and the option to come back for more seems entirely consistent with a personal construct approach to therapy as it is in real life.

Case example - Eleanor

This case example is a joint effort between Eleanor and me. I have known her for almost 6 years, following her referral for specialist help with her eating problems. When I recently approached her about this chapter she was keen to contribute and what follows includes both of our perspectives on her problems and the therapeutic work we have been engaged in.

When I first met Eleanor she was age 27 and told me she had had eating problems since around age 18, when she went away to study at university, although she also reported depressive symptoms as young as age 16 and had seen several psychiatrists and psychologists over the years. At initial assessment she presented with fairly typical features of anorexia nervosa, with a very restricted eating pattern, low weight and fear of weight gain. As well as controlling her eating, she had various 'obsessional' symptoms, such as counting things, checking the lights, and hand washing. She was also moderately depressed and did not feel very connected to people, mostly interacting at a superficial level. It was clear that things were pretty bad and she was keen for help.

My initial therapeutic work with Eleanor was on a weekly basis but, gradually, as her eating became more 'manageable', this moved to monthly and we now only meet on an occasional basis, in which she can ring me up when she feels it would be helpful to meet. It is difficult to try and summarize concisely this quite extensive therapeutic work spread out over 5 or 6 years. We will begin with Eleanor's account:

> Some of my memories of my eating disorder are hazy and some are painfully clear; there are times when I feel as though it is part of my past and yet other times when I know that parts of it may always be with me. I first developed behavioural signs and symptoms of an eating disorder in my first year at university, during a relationship which was at best destructive and, at worst, abusive. Over the next four years I entered a series of relationships with unstable, bullying men and by the age of 24, with my self-esteem in shreds and being utterly unable to function in personal relationships any longer, I was diagnosed with anorexia nervosa.
>
> My main course of therapy along personal construct lines began when I was 28 years old. Reading the rest of this chapter, there are many things that strike a chord with me. The idea of constriction is still a strong thread in my life, not just in my diet but at work [always taking a safe option so as not to fail], in relationships [seeking people who do not expect too much, but who also give too little] and at play [at one point I hardly left my house for six months, preferring to be alone rather than risk forming bonds with others].
>
> Luckily I was able to undertake therapy with an experienced clinical psychologist and, with time and patience, formed a trusting and reliable working relationship with him. This therapeutic alliance gave me a safe environment in which I could try out the possibility of being truly myself, good and

bad, something which I believe is of critical importance to eating disorder sufferers, who seem to believe that they are simply not good enough human beings. Over the years my eating disorder has become manageable and now I co-exist with it; sometimes I think that of all my relationships, the one that I have with food is still the most important, but undoubtedly my experiences of personal construct therapy have enabled me to develop the tools to deal with the problems that arise without allowing them to grow to damaging levels.

One of the areas in which I still struggle is that of personal relationships. I am certainly a very good friend and in return have many people I can count on to support me when I am feeling alone. However, it seems likely that the years spent with an eating disorder have held me back from developing the skills that I need to become a successful partner; I am still single and struggling with this aspect of adulthood. I would certainly say I have difficulty 'construing' other people and thus my expectations of them can be wildly unreasonable – for example, my friends constantly tell me to slow down when I have just met a potential partner as I am prone to getting upset when, a week into the relationship, the new person has not declared their feelings for me! It's quite laughable when I see it written down, but very difficult to live with and continues to be the cause of great anxiety. I understand that my desire for immediate intimacy in a relationship is connected to low self esteem – I am desperate for the person to like me [regardless of the voice in the back of my head that's asking me whether I even like them or not] – and it is also my attempt to regain control in an area in which I feel vulnerable. I would dearly love to be in a long-term relationship but often struggle to believe that I will attain this goal.

I try to take one day at a time, but sometimes get overwhelmed as I blame myself for what I see as a very out of control past and a very uncertain future. As with everyone, each day is different; however, on the bad days my mood can change from minute to minute and I hate this unpredictability. I crave peace of mind and spirit and believe that my therapy to date has provided the best basis upon which to build the life I have yet to live.

It seems to me that Eleanor's account very clearly illustrates many of the themes with which this chapter has been concerned and I don't feel it leaves me with too much more to say, but I will add a few thoughts from my perspective as therapist.

The control theme

The experience of feeling out of control is a prominent theme in Eleanor's account and her need for control is a recurrent theme. Indeed, I would see that as something we all need to some degree and my efforts with Eleanor have been directed at helping her to explore a wider range of ways of feeling in control, with particular reference to relationships with people. Her need for control of eating is heightened when she feels out of control in her relationships with others. This is particularly the case with men and when that becomes particularly bad she digs her heels in with her eating because that's what she knows best. Although we have worked on eating behaviour and situations, particularly in the early stages of therapy, the main emphasis has been on the relational context of her eating.

Relationships versus being alone

Eleanor emphasizes her struggle with relationships and difficulty in becoming 'a successful partner'. At times in the past, she has dealt with things by avoidance, but more recently she has been troubled by being alone and feels peers who have partners and children are leaving her behind. Difficulties arise, however, when she tries to play a part in line with what she imagines a man wants, whereas I have been encouraging her to see it as a two-way process in which both parties face inevitable uncertainty or excitement as they explore each other and test out their assumptions on each other. Although I don't necessarily use personal construct theory language during our meetings, I point out that both parties need to modify their construing if they are to do more than hold on to their individual worlds.

Ups and downs

It is perhaps a cliché to say that life is full of ups and downs and Eleanor is no stranger to this principle. Intermittent 'invalidation' from people seems inevitable unless one can tolerate the life of a hermit. When we met weekly there would be weeks when things seemed to be going well when she felt more in control but times when she would retreat into herself. Nowadays, the nature of our contract is such that I only see her when she is particularly struggling. At such times, when we explore recent issues together, she often leaves in a positive frame of mind, having been enabled to see things in a wider perspective.

My role as therapist

I have tried to remain true to the principle of being a co-collaborator and I think I have offered Eleanor the opportunity to gain other perspectives (or constructs) on her situation often at times when she has become blinkered and very negative about how she views herself. When we moved to an open contact, she said that I had helped her see how life works and how other people live without promising that everything will be OK when you eat better. She didn't need to have regular appointments because my voice was in her head. It seems that I have increasingly become a kind of mentor to her, someone who knows, accepts and validates her as a person. Maybe the time will come when she can find that validation elsewhere but I anticipate that like many people with eating disorders she may need occasional support for some time.

Research

Anorexia nervosa

My first piece of personal construct research on anorexia nervosa was for my doctoral thesis (Button, 1980). The original stimulus for this work derived from Fay Fransella's research on stuttering (Fransella, 1972), in which she found a relationship between fluency of speech and the 'meaningfulness' of life as a fluent speaker. Working in a specialized inpatient unit for the treatment of anorexia nervosa, we began by using implications grids to measure the meaningfulness of life as an anorectic as opposed to being at normal weight, monitoring changes in meaningfulness during therapy. The results of this initial research did not work out entirely according to prediction, in that we did not find that thinness was more meaningful than normal weight. We did, however, find some interesting relationships between our measure of meaningfulness and clinical variables. In particular, it emerged that more meaningfulness of life at normal weight was predictive of a better outcome from treatment. Conversely, lower degrees of meaningfulness were found in those patients who had longer treatment histories. Clients who did well following treatment tended to start therapy with less unidimensional construing and went through a process of tightening and loosening of construing, whereas resistant clients tended to stay with more unidimensional/tighter construing.

A further study was conducted on the same population using conventional rated grids repeated during and after therapy. There were many significant findings from this research, but I would like to highlight the results pertaining to the *structure* of construing, which I think may be at the heart of the anorectic's difficulties. Those clients who did poorly at follow-up had more unidimensional construct systems and more fixed construing of self.

Bulimia nervosa

At the time of the above research, bulimia nervosa had not been identified as a disorder. Given the clinical similarities and differences between anorectics and bulimics, I became intrigued by the degree of similarity and difference in their construing in the interpersonal context. Using a form of rated grid known as SELFGRID (Button, 1994), four groups of participants (anorexia nervosa, bulimia nervosa, general non-psychotic psychological disorder and healthy controls) were compared. All three clinical groups showed similar levels of negativity of construing of self nowadays, but anorectics had a much more favourable construing of self when younger than bulimics. This is consistent with another repertory grid study by Weinreich, Doherty and Harris (1985), who suggested that anorectics may suffer from a 'plummeting identity crisis' whereas bulimics have a more 'prolonged identity crisis'. Taken together with my finding that anorectics showed more unidimensional construing than bulimics, this suggests that the anorectic's problem is rather more structural in nature.

Anorexia nervosa revisited

More recently, Button and Warren (2002) carried out an in-depth study of a group of sufferers of anorexia nervosa, on average 7.5 years after presentation for treatment. This study focused rather more on the *content* of construing than structure. We were able to compare varying levels of therapeutic progress with aspects of self-construing. There was a close relationship between the positivity of construing of self and a number of clinical variables. Using their own personal constructs, more positive construing was closely related to better functioning. Once again quite strong relationships were thus found between measures of personal construing and outcome.

The main limitation of such research is that it is based on relatively small samples but the results do provide some evidence to support the theoretical position that deficits in self and interpersonal construing play a part in the etiology and course of the eating disorders. The main unanswered question is whether anything can be done about this. It remains to be demonstrated whether such deficits in construing can be changed for the better and there is a need for more research into the efficacy of personal construct psychotherapy in eating disorders.

Conclusions

It is argued that people with eating disorders *constrict* their world such that issues of weight and eating become their primary source of validation as a person. Although this initially offers the attraction of some degree of manageability and control, it can eventually drive them into an isolated and unhealthy existence in which they are clinging on to life rather than living it. It is my contention that underlying problems in construing people are what lead people in this direction, and research using repertory grids provides some evidence for disorders of both content and structure in vulnerable individuals. Psychotherapy may help some sufferers eventually to move away from their constricted world, and I have outlined a personal construct therapy approach to such change. The emphasis is on developing alternative and more positive forms of self-construction and aiming to improve the individual's ability to function in an interpersonal context by learning to construe other peoples' construing more effectively. The case example of Eleanor illustrated how one person was able to make use of such therapy as a basis towards building the life she had 'yet to live'.

CHAPTER SEVENTEEN

Working with people who hear voices

DIANE ALLEN

> Life . . . is characterized by its essential measurability in the dimension of time and its capacity to represent other forms of reality, while still retaining its own form of reality. (Kelly, 1955/1991a, p. 8/ p. 7)

The phenomenon of hearing voices that are not part of consensual reality has been studied in many different ways. The medical model views the experience as part of a pathological process that needs to be corrected by medication. Here the experience is described as an auditory hallucination, a cardinal feature of schizophrenia. Auditory hallucinations are also sometimes present in severe depression and where there are organic changes to the brain through substance misuse, trauma or tumour (American Psychiatric Association, 2000). The cognitive psychology approach focuses on voice hearing as a distortion in the way the individual processes information and attributes the source of the information they receive (McKenna, 1994; Rankin and O'Carroll, 1995; Bentall, 1996). The social psychiatry perspective (Romme and Escher, 1993; Romme, 1998) makes use of evidence from samples of people in clinical and non-clinical populations (Pennings and Romme, 1998) of voice hearers to assert the importance of examining the experience from the perspective of the voice hearer. They advocate taking into account past and present factors that may help to explain the content of the person's experience. This focus on the experience of the individual is central to the personal construct psychology perspective on working with people who hear voices.

Theory

This chapter will explore some proposals for the ways in which Kelly's (1955/1991a) theory can be applied to an understanding of the processes involved in working with people who hear voices.

212

The fundamental postulate

Kelly (1955/1991a) argues that we should acknowledge that there are multiple ways of construing events and that people's construction of an experience will influence their anticipation of future events. In the fundamental postulate he maintains that 'A person's processes are psychologically channelized by the ways in which he anticipates events' (Kelly, 1955/1991a, p. 46/ p. 32). These processes are a form of motion which directs the person towards anticipating and interpreting events (Kelly, 1955/1991a), but the constructs for that interpretation do not necessarily have 'specific predictive efficiency' (Kelly, 1955/1991a, p. 15/p. 11) when the events are faced. With regard to the predictive efficiency of the constructs of people who hear voices, the whole construing system will be exposed to one or more channels of communication from the voice(s). This may compromise the person's ability to anticipate events in an effective manner, because some voice hearers view the voices as being elements at the 'not me' pole of the 'me versus not me' construct. So the predictive efficiency of the constructs selected from their system will be influenced by constructs presented by voices that are construed as not belonging to their system. In this way Kelly's view of people's processes being psychologically channelized has to take into account the possibility that the construers may believe that there is more than one network of pathways through which their processes are operating.

The organization corollary

An alternative interpretation could be that the voice hearing construer is operating with one system but not accepting ownership of the poles of the constructs expressed by the voices. The organization corollary (Kelly, 1955/1991a) maintains that there is a hierarchical relationship between constructs, so the non-preferred pole of a construct expressed in extreme terms by a voice may be a superordinate version of a non-preferred pole of a construct further down the system. For example, the voice might say, 'You are worthless' as an extreme expression of a subordinate pole expressed as 'You can't do anything right at the moment'. Kelly (1955/1991a, p. 136/pp. 94–5) maintains that

> . . . constructs may be used as viewpoints for seeing other constructs, as in the hierarchical relationship of constructs within a system. In that sense the superordinate constructs are versions of those constructs which are subordinate to them. This makes the subordinate constructs a form of reality which is construed through the use of the superordinate constructs.

Therefore one of the main difficulties experienced by voice hearers is that they are exposed to an exaggerated form of reality which is non-consensual and leads to communication and behavioural problems when in contact with other people. This supports Romme's (1998, p. 53) view that '. . . it is not the experience (of voice hearing) itself that is a sign of mental illness but that the way of coping with the experience may lead to or can be the expression of mental illness.'

The role of metaphor and construct organization

It could be further argued that some of the apparently unintelligible extreme forms of expression used by the voices could be interpreted as metaphors at the superordinate level of construing, which give clues to the semantic links with subordinate constructs representing the person's reality. For example, the phrase 'the devil's eye is poisoning your brain' could be viewed as superordinate to 'you know you are being watched by powerful people who want to influence your mind with medication'. The person listening to the voice hearer may dismiss the superordinate view of reality as bizarre, yet treating the view as exaggerated and metaphorical enables listeners to adopt a credulous approach when trying to understand the underlying meaning of the voice hearer's attempts to explain their distress. In this way the voice hearing experience can be considered similar to using a foreign language which needs translation to enable meaningful communication between a voice hearer and a non-voice hearer to take place.

Core constructs

Watkins (1998) maintains that some common existential themes such as life, death and sexual identity are expressed by people's voices. In personal construct psychology terms these themes represent core constructs that govern a person's maintenance processes. Kelly (1955/1991a, p. 482/ p. 356) maintains that

> . . . a healthy person's mental processes follow core structures which are comprehensive but not too permeable . . . if his constructs are too permeable . . . he is likely to see too many new events as having deeply personal significance. He tends to be less detached and objective. He may become paranoid, as he interprets each new event as intimately related to himself.

Paranoia can be part of the presentation of schizophrenia, especially in response to messages conveyed by the voices. People who hear voices may also complain that the television or the radio is talking about them or personal information is being revealed in the newspapers. This information is sometimes held to be about issues that are associated with their identity, such as their sexuality. It could be argued that people who hear voices have highly permeable core constructs that take in information about events from a wide variety of sources, for example, the media. The events then take on a high degree of personal significance when absorbed into the core constructs and are verbalized by the voices in such terms as 'you are gay', 'I know you masturbate', or 'the people in the street can see you have sex through the TV screen, like you watch sex on TV.' The voices may even express a submerged pole of the core construct in which the person does not want to be included as an element, for example gay versus straight. As Kelly (1955/1991a, p. 470/p. 358) argues, 'submergence may be a handy way of keeping a construct from being tested', and this may be why voices are construed as presenting material that is separate from the individual, having a 'not me' quality.

Invalidation

The accuracy with which people who hear voices can anticipate events may be impaired by the attribution of responsibility for the prediction. The bias of attribution may be influenced by whether the voices or the person's own thoughts are experienced as being the most powerful at the time. For example, the voices may say 'she is going to hit you' and, even though the hearer is aware of the contrasting position, the one adopted by the voices is experienced as more powerful and accepted as the appropriate anticipation of the event. This anticipation then influences the choice of constructs applied to the situation on an emotional and behavioural level. This means that the individual can be exposed to the invalidation of their construct system when the voices are active and powerful.

Bannister (1963, 1965a) argues that people with schizophrenic thought disorder have experienced serial invalidation of their construct system and they receive some protection from this by loosening the associations between constructs. This is held to make the system less likely to be invalidated because the predictions will be too vague. Kelly (1955/1991b, p. 856/p. 210) argues that this leads the individual to have 'less access to validational material of an interpersonal nature' because their constructions are too loose to be formulated and tested and they withdraw from social interaction. Loose thinking is also difficult to follow in conversation and people tend to abstain from interaction with a loose thinker.

Dilation

It could be argued, from an alternative viewpoint, that people who hear voices are not construing in a loose manner but that the powerful presence of voices has led to a dilation of the person's perceptual field. The chaos experienced by the voice hearer may be due to having a dilated field without the framework offered by an effective superordinate structure (Kelly,

1955/1991b). The thought disorder seen in schizophrenia may be a response to the voices having opened up a new area of construing to the person such as being in control of the universe, being the Chosen One, or being the devil, in the absence of a containing framework. The presentation of a secondary delusion may then be an attempt to develop a superordinate framework and impose some meaning on the chaotic experience.

Commonality and sociality

Hearing voices can mean that the individual has difficulty accessing consensual reality. Since commonality requires a 'construction of experience which is similar to that employed by another' (Kelly, 1955/1991a, p. 90/p. 63) and sociality requires 'one person (to) construe the construction processes of another' (Kelly, 1955/1991a, p. 95/p. 66), hearing voices could interfere with the communication processes necessary to play a social role in relation to other people. The voices add a different dimension to the process of communication because the voice hearer may have competing constructions operating simultaneously and may feel obliged to accept the interpretation of the situation conveyed by powerful voices at the expense of their own interpretation. For Kelly (1955/1991a, pp. 177–8/p. 124) 'a role is a course of activity played out in the light of one or more other person's construct systems . . . when one plays a role one behaves according to what one believes another person thinks.' In this respect the voice hearer may have the experience of what he or she believes the other person thinks versus what the voices believe the other person thinks. The voices may be expressing the non-preferred pole of a construct in a powerful, exaggerated, superordinate form, whereas the voice hearer may be struggling to access the preferred pole of the construct in subordinate form.

The self and the community of selves

Earlier on in this section it was argued that people who hear voices sometimes experience the voices as being subsumed as elements under the 'not me' pole of the construct 'me versus not me', a split between the self and the voices. Kelly views the self as 'a construct . . . a group of events which are alike in a certain way and, in that same way, necessarily different from other events . . . The way in which the events are alike is the self' (Kelly, 1955/1991a, p. 131/p. 91). This means that the self is not construed in isolation but in comparison with other elements and is built up as abstractions of similarity and difference. In this way the voices heard by a voice hearer are themselves a source of information which can be used to develop constructs. Although this chapter has focused on examples of voices expressing the non-preferred pole of constructs, voice hearers can have the experience of voices expressing the preferred pole of a construct. Some voice hearers use their voices to help with the circumspection phase of their decision-making cycle, thereby using voices to help them make decisions.

The work of Mair (1977), who employs the metaphor of the 'self as a community of selves' (Mair, 1977, p.142), allows for a further development of this argument. A voice hearer could be described as having voices that represent a community of selves, a community of voices. Mair's description of the community of selves points out that the self is not a unitary concept but a complex grouping of different aspects of the self that contribute to the whole person. These different aspects emphasize qualities that the person possesses that are useful in certain role relationships and also offer differing perspectives on events. If the voices were viewed as a community then the voice hearer may be able to develop and accept a relationship with them and acknowledge the bipolar nature of the constructs being employed.

Therapeutic practice

Before therapy begins it is worthwhile building up a picture of the client's voice-hearing experience. It is important to bear in mind that any exploration of this experience can create difficulties for the client since it brings the 'me versus not me' aspects of voice hearing into sharp focus. This can be associated with an increase in the intensity and frequency of the experience, potentially leading to anxiety and depression that is difficult to control. It is therefore up to the therapist to ensure that clients are not placed under too much pressure and have a strong enough 24-hour support network to ensure that they are safe. Since exposure to invalidation is a frequent experience of people who hear voices it is also important to ensure that clients have access to either a support group for people who hear voices or a wider network such as the Hearing Voices Network (see the contact details at the end of this chapter, p. 225).

A basic picture of the client's experience can be built up using the following guidelines based on an overview of the work of Chadwick, Birchwood and Trower (1996); Haddock and Slade (1996) and Romme (1998):

- General information: home life; social support; current problems that create tension; individuals who have helped the client with their voices in the past.
- History of the voices: incidents that took place prior to the onset of the voice-hearing experience; qualities possessed by the voices such as the number of voices, their identity, the location of sound, the frequency with

which the voices presented, the context in which they presented, how the voices presented and perceived control over the voices.

- Changes in the voice hearing experience over time.
- General questions about voices, looking at why the client thinks he hears voices; the client's views on changes in his life since he started hearing voices; consideration of what life would be like without the voices; current coping strategies and their effectiveness.
- A brief overview of when the voices are most likely to be experienced as intrusive, for example, time of day, day of the week, association with events or people.

The above information provides a background for therapeutic work and during therapy the content of what the voices say is explored in more depth. The relationship between the self and the voices can also be explored by eliciting constructs based on a variety of elements, for example, different views of the self, the worst self, how the client would like to be, how the client would describe himself at the moment, how other people might describe the client, how the voices would like the client to be. Alternatively elements could be represented by the different voices, including the client's. It is often less confusing for the client to elicit constructs based on individual elements (Spindler Barton et al., 1976) rather than using dyadic or triadic methods, bearing in mind that most voice hearers who are referred for this work will be taking medication that can affect their capacity for processing information.

One of the key therapeutic tasks involves working with the client to break down a voice-hearing episode into its component parts. This includes the identity of the voice and what was said; precipitating factors and how they relate to past events; and response to the episode through verbal and non-verbal construing. The client then examines a range of alternative constructions of the episode as a way of identifying how it could be managed in the future. Breaking down a voice-hearing experience is an attempt gently to loosen and then tighten an individual's construing in readiness to learn how to make use of an experience cycle (Kelly, 1970a). Before therapy clients often do not realize that voice hearing could be managed by methods other than medication and therefore do not construe it as part of experiencing that could be changed in any way. While clients engage with the anticipation of voice hearing on a daily basis they tend not to enter into the phase of commitment to experiment with different ways of approaching the experience. After breaking down a voice-hearing episode clients are then ready to look at different ways of experimenting with the experience. This then encourages individuals to have a full encounter with voice hearing and the way they propose to manage it. They can then make use of the confirmation or disconfirmation of the expected outcome of the experiment with their voices and make a constructive revision about their experience that would then have an impact on their anticipation of the next voice hearing experience.

If the client finds it difficult to focus on breaking down the voice-hearing experience, then adapting Bannister's approach to working with people who have delusions would be useful. Bannister (1985) argues that it is sometimes easier to work with the theme of a delusion rather than its content. He cites the example of a client who believed that the doctors in the hospital had made arrangements with lorry drivers to kill him. The successful interpretation of the delusion as an underlying belief that the hospital doctors disliked him formed the basis of the therapeutic work. This approach is supported by Kelly (1955/1991a, p. 8/p. 7), who argues that a 'fictitious perception will often turn out to be a grossly distorted construction of something which actually does exist.' Further, Leitner and Celentana (1997) maintain that auditory hallucinations represent an existential truth for the person who is hearing voices. They imply that the truth is expressed in the form and content of the experience and it is up to the therapist to work alongside the client to unravel the truth and its implications for anticipating events. In this sense, working with the underlying theme represented by what the voices say may well reduce the distress experienced by the client.

Case example

The following case example explores aspects of the material covered in this chapter and, in the interests of confidentiality, is an adaptation of work undertaken with a client, using a different name.

Beth was referred by her psychiatrist for therapy to help her manage her voice-hearing experiences. She was a 50-year-old unemployed single woman who has been involved with the local psychiatric services since late adolescence. She had a history of termination of a teenage pregnancy arising from sexual abuse by her father, depression and anxiety with psychotic features, alcohol abuse and deliberate self-harm. The medical diagnosis was borderline personality disorder.

During the first weeks of the therapeutic relationship Beth examined her experiences of voice hearing in more depth. We first examined what she could realistically expect from managing her intrusive voice with a psychological approach and concluded that, while it would be helpful for her to lose the voice completely, the most reasonable expectation would be to reduce its impact on her life. This would then enable her to have more confidence in social interactions and give her the opportunity to think about meeting her needs rather than the needs of the voice.

There was also an educational component to these early sessions as Beth requested information about her diagnosis and treatment. Although she was given the information she required, a more useful intervention proved to be looking at ways in which she could ask the hospital staff to supply the information she wanted. We practised a role play to enable Beth to work out a safe and non-confrontational way of managing the interaction during her clinical review. She had always found it hard to get her opinions across in the reviews because she assumed that her opinions were worthless. The voice would also become more intrusive and make it difficult for her to pull her ideas together, express them clearly and process the response without becoming paranoid later on in the day when she was alone. After discussion she decided to attend the clinical reviews with a note containing all the questions she wanted to raise and asked a nurse to write down the replies if she was unable to write them down herself.

We explored Beth's first voice-hearing experience and identified the intrusive voice as that of her father. She realized that the critical voice could be associated with guilt at the termination, guilt at being sexually abused by her father, and the impact such a disclosure could have on the family. We looked at how her construct of guilt contrasted with uncertainty because she could not remember what it was like not to feel guilty. This tied in with her childhood experiences of being construed by others as being an attention seeking and difficult person. Her construction of the way other people continued to think of her in adulthood reflected these experiences as she used the terms 'attacking, guilty, damaging, vicious, pushy, intolerant, depressed, evil and tight-lipped' to denote their opinion. During the sessions we explored the ways in which people's construction of her could be altered and she decided to experiment with different types of behaviour to see how members of her family responded. One experiment was to attend a family gathering at her parents' house and imagine that an army major had come to control her father and shoot his voice out of her mind so that she could behave in a less fearful way. This worked well as she found she could sit in the middle of the room and chat to the people nearest to her in the knowledge that her father's presence was not going to be experienced as intrusive.

The sessions went on to look at other ways in which Beth could manage her voice-hearing experience. We reviewed the material gathered from the initial assessment about the location of the voice, precipitant factors for the experience, and existing coping mechanisms. In the assessment she mentioned that her voice was easier to manage when it was outside her head, compared with being inside her head. She also mentioned that she could cope better when the voice was inside her head at night if she slept with the light on. She had discovered in the past that when she responded to the commands of the voice by self-harming she got some relief from its intrusion for a while. The voice was also described as being more intrusive when she was under stress. She was also more likely to hear the voice in the evening when her mood was low, if she saw a television programme about abortion, or if she saw a baby in the street. The assessment therefore indicated that Beth would need to look at methods of reducing stress, managing a low mood, and coping with the voice if she refused to respond to its commands.

The most useful methods of reducing stress that Beth found included listening to music and getting comfort from feeling something soft and warm. For the latter method she considered the use of a hot water bottle in a soft cover or a soft blanket. Although these were comforting they did not meet her needs directly. She also found talking to someone helped her feel less isolated and on one occasion was able to reduce her level of stress and the intensity of the voice in her head by telephoning the Samaritans.

A series of positive statements were also an effective way of reducing stress and managing a low mood. These statements were: 'I'm OK really, I can allow myself to be me. I am not responsible for the sins of others.' The most useful statement was 'I can stay with my feelings and move forward.' This meant that Beth could accept herself as someone with feelings that did not necessarily overwhelm or harm her. This was an effective statement because the intrusive voice would often tap into distressing feelings and make them worse, or say words that were a contrast to her content or happy feelings and invalidate the experience. The statement also encouraged the ownership and acceptance of her feelings and the anticipation that she could move through a negative feeling or build on a positive feeling. She was allowing herself to access, rather than deny, her emotions.

As time went on Beth realized that loneliness was one of her greatest problems and, with the help of a canine charity, was able to get a small dog. The dog made the greatest difference to her life. She gave Beth a sense of comfort and companionship; and meeting the dog's daily needs in a gentle and caring way gave her the opportunity to distract her attention away from the intrusive voice as well as elaborate the construction of herself as good, rather than evil. Beth was able to meet new people when she took the dog out for exercise and this meant that she developed a new social role: dog owner and carer, rather than being confined to the role of person with mental health problems. So she was able to see herself less as someone who was always being cared for and more as someone who did the caring for the dog. She began to realize that people did not necessarily construe her as a problem and she started to experience positive interactions that began to challenge her previous perception of the way she was construed by others. The dog also helped Beth to resist the intrusive voice's commands to harm herself. When the voice made commands she was able to challenge what was being said by telling herself and the voice that she would not be able to look after her dog if she was injured.

The final intervention was the use of a structured method of breaking down a voice-hearing episode into its component parts. The following example shows how the process was applied. The voice came from the corner of the television screen and said 'I am going to get you!' in an angry tone in response to an image on the television of someone being interviewed. Beth thought 'he will get me'; she felt distressed, her action was frozen; she wanted to get rid of the television image but couldn't. As we worked through the episode Beth considered that she would have felt better if she challenged the thought by saying out loud 'he won't get me – he is on the television', and tried to clean the corner of the television screen or turn the programme over and then switch back to the original channel to see if the voice had gone. We then reflected on precipitating events during the day that might have generated feelings of vulnerability. Beth recalled going to see her doctor, who had been angry with her when she had not been able to respond to his questions because she could not understand what he was saying. We considered how this could have been managed differently and Beth thought that she could ask a nurse to act as advocate for her when she saw the doctor or that she could ask the doctor if he could speak more clearly or rephrase the question.

Non-preferred pole of construct Scored 1-3	Hearing the voice a year ago		The voice now		I would like the voice to be		When I am at worst I am		I would like to be		At the moment I am		Other people think I am		The voice would like me to be		Preferred pole of construct scored 5-7
	A	B	A	B	A	B	A	B	A	B	A	B	A	B	A	B	
Attacking	2	1	1	3	7	7	1	3	5	6	1	4	1	5	1	1	Amusing
Guilt	1	1	1	3	6	6	1	3	5	5	1	5	1	4	1	1	Uncertainty
Damaging	1	2	1	2	6	7	1	4	7	7	1	4	3	4	1	1	Carefree
Vicious	3	2	3	3	7	7	1	3	7	7	1	4	1	4	1	1	Friendly
Pushy	4	3	4	4	7	7	1	4	7	7	1	4	1	5	1	2	Patient
Intolerant	2	1	2	4	6	7	1	2	7	7	1	5	1	5	2	1	Content
Depressed	3	1	1	4	7	7	1	4	7	7	1	3	2	3	1	1	Happy
Evil	1	1	1	4	7	7	1	2	7	7	1	3	1	4	1	1	Good
Tight-lipped	3	2	2	4	7	7	1	3	7	7	3	3	3	4	1	3	Humorous

KEY: A = Grid 1: Pre-therapy
     B = Grid 2: Post-therapy

Figure 17.1 Beth's raw grid scores.

As the raw repertory grid scores (see Figure 17.1) show, by the end of therapy Beth described other people's constructions of her as amusing rather than attacking, patient rather than pushy, and content rather than intolerant. Although she thought they still construed her as somewhat depressed they no longer viewed her as being guilty, damaging, vicious, evil and tight-lipped. Beth's construction of herself was still tight-lipped but less evil and depressed. She did not construe herself as attacking, damaging, vicious or pushy. She construed herself as having uncertainty, rather than guilt, and being content, rather than intolerant. The contentment was associated with feeling more in control of the intrusive voice and putting a stop on the paranoia that often arose from the voice distorting her perception of events. Beth also said that she had not abused alcohol or self-harmed for a while and was less ashamed of being a voice hearer.

Research

Research in the field of working with people who hear voices has largely come from the social psychiatry perspective (see the review in Davies, Thomas and Leudar, 1999; Leudar and Thomas, 2000; Romme and Escher, 2000) and the cognitive-behavioural approach (Wykes, Tarrier and Lewis, 1998; Paley and Shapiro, 2002; Shapiro and Paley 2002; Tarrier et al., 2002). In terms of published research into hearing voices the personal construct psychology perspective is less well developed.

I undertook a small-scale evaluation study with the members of the Hearing Voices group that included Beth as a member. The participants used supplied elements to elicit personal constructs, and then rated the elements on the constructs. Figure 17.1 shows the constructs that Beth elicited from the following elements: hearing the voice a year ago; the voice now; I would like the voice to be; the voice would like me to be; when I am at my worst I am; I would like to be; at the moment I am; other people think I am. The aim was to look at constructions of the voice, the self and the view of others. The grids were completed before and after therapy and at each point all the participants in the group consistently scored the elements 'I would like to be' and 'I would like the voice(s) to be' towards the preferred poles of their constructs. The elements 'when I am at my worst I am' and 'the voice(s) would like me to be' were consistently rated at the non-preferred poles of the constructs. This suggested that there was a link between the voice(s), the ideal self and the worst aspects of the self. The relationship between the pairs of elements went in opposite directions. The ideal self was associated with a choice in the way the hearer would like to experience their voice(s) and the worst aspects of the self were associated with the choices made by the voice(s). The latter link may also imply that these voice hearers considered that the voice(s) were either responsible for their worst behaviour or that their worst behaviour coincided with the least preferred message of their voice(s).

An eyeball analysis of Beth's raw grid results (see Figure 17.1) shows her rating of the element *hearing the voice a year ago* changed during the course of therapy. At the end of therapy the voice was recalled as being more attacking, pushy, intolerant, depressed and tight lipped, but less damaging and vicious. This may have been related to her contact with other people who heard voices, giving her a source of comparison for her own experiences. Change was also evident in her construction of the voice-hearing experience after therapy. Scoring of the element *the voice now* indicated that the voice's approach to Beth had become less attacking and damaging and less associated with guilt. The voice continued to be vicious but had ceased to be construed as intolerant, depressed, evil and tight-lipped. In contrast her scoring of the element *the voice would like me to be* indicated that at the end of therapy the voice continued to want Beth to be attacking, guilty, damaging, vicious, depressed, evil, more intolerant and less pushy and tight lipped. Overall, at the end of therapy, there was a move away from rating the constructs at the extreme of the non-preferred poles for the following elements: *the voice now, at the moment I am, other people think I am and when I am at my worst I am*. The move on these four elements contrasts with little change in Beth's scoring of the element *the voice would like me to be*. This implies that Beth's reconstruction of herself meant that she could resist the voice's influence on her behaviour. She had also recognized that there was a difference between the voice hurting Beth directly and influencing her to hurt others.

The Hearing Voices Group members also evaluated the impact of the group through contrasts made between their construction of the medical model approach to working with their voices and the membership of the symptom focused group. The medical model was described as one in which the voice-hearing experience was ignored, denied, overmedicated and separated from life history issues. The model gave the group members the impression that they had to spend their lives waiting for the voices to go away before they could begin to live again. Membership of the group allowed them to talk about their experiences and develop personal coping strategies.

The realization that they did not have to be alone in their experiences and could learn to live with their voices became part of their framework of understanding. They described themselves as using the sense of support from the group as a way of validating the development of their personal construction of the experience. This sense of validation of experience and personal involvement in the structure and process of change is central to the personal construct perspective.

Conclusion

This chapter has reflected the creativity that is the hallmark of personal construct therapy by exploring theoretical proposals for explaining voice hearing and how constructivism can be used as an approach to therapy. It has demonstrated how the experience may be described and understood by considering the organization corollary, metaphor and access to core constructs; the role of invalidation, dilation, commonality, sociality and the community of selves. There has been a consideration of how to build a structured picture of the voice-hearing experience and how to use a repertory grid to evaluate the process of therapy. The grid used in the example of Beth's experiences has shown how constructions of the voice, the self and the views of other people represent the complex nature of the process of change. It is this complexity that generates the need for therapy based on the requirements of the individual. Just because voice hearers have experiences that are not part of consensual reality, it does not mean that they should not have the opportunity to work on their construction of reality. As Kelly (1955/1991a, p. 8/p. 7) writes, 'Any living creature, together with his perceptions, is a part of the real world; he is not merely a near-sighted bystander to the goings-on of the real world.'

Hearing Voices Network, 91 Oldham St, Manchester M4 1LW
tel: 0161 834 5768
email: hearingvoices@care4free.net
website: hearingvoices.org.uk

CHAPTER EIGHTEEN

Issues in forensic psychotherapy

JAMES HORLEY

Although concerned with aspects of police work and the courts, forensic psychology deals especially with the assessment and rehabilitation of criminal offenders (Bartol and Bartol, 1999; Hess, 1999). Psychotherapeutic interventions with offenders have increased significantly over the past decade or two (see Cordess and Cox, 1996; Mobley, 1999). This followed a period of pessimistic 'nothing works' (Martinson, 1974) in offender rehabilitation, especially within North America. A number of treatments assumed under the generic title of 'cognitive-behavioural' appear effective with offenders (Andrews et al., 1990; Gendreau, 1996). These cognitive-behavioural therapies include a wide range of techniques with bases that range from cognitive-rationalist to strict behaviouristic. Some theorists (for example, Marshall and Barbaree, 1990) have attempted to develop a more central approach – territory that I (Horley, 2000) suggested is occupied already by a number of well-established theories such as cognitive-social learning theory (Bandura, 1986) and personal construct theory (PCT) (Kelly, 1955/1991a/1991b). Contributions to forensic psychotherapy within PCT, while limited at present, are developed to the point that we have an emerging forensic personal construct psychology (Horley, 2003a, 2003b).

This chapter will outline some of the approaches to psychotherapy compatible with PCT that have or could be used with criminal offenders. Some, such as fixed-role therapy (FRT), were developed by Kelly (1955/1991a) or later personal construct therapists, but other techniques (to be presented) were developed by other therapists but appear consistent with the tenets of PCT. Problems encountered while delivering these therapeutic services to offenders will be discussed briefly, and cases will be presented to illustrate some forensic problems. Although relatively recent, PCT-based forensic psychotherapy offers promise to offender rehabilitation.

Theory

Personal construct theory emphasizes experience and choice. According to Kelly (1955/1991a, p. 64/p. 45), 'a person chooses for him or herself that alternative in a dichotomized construct through which he or she anticipates the greater possibility for extension and/or definition of his/her construct system.' What Kelly is concerned with here, and more generally with his theory, are the psychological reasons for particular acts. Although Kelly eschewed the term 'motivation', the importance of asking and examining responses to motivational questions for offenders has been suggested by many investigators in various disciplines (for example, Taylor, 1972; Scully and Marolla, 1984) but examined by relatively few.

'Extending a construct system' is one main reason for selecting one act or behaviour, and Kelly (1970b) viewed all behaviour as experimental, or a tentative trial to observe whether an outcome was acceptable or not. Having sex with a young boy or killing a rival gang member could allow individuals, as normatively unappealing or repulsive as they may seem, to experience power or status through self-understanding as 'attractive' or 'tough'. The extension to an individual's construct system does not require any degree of social acceptability, although social demands undoubtedly shape an individual's likely construal of an act before, during, and after the experience. Definition, for Kelly and PCT, refers to more explicit and clear self-definition. The act of murder or rape could lead to a more refined sense of self. Whether the self-referent includes a 'negative' label such as 'diddler' or 'sick bastard', or whether it would lead to a 'positive' label such as 'dominant' or 'brave', probably is a function of the actor's thinking at the time and the immediate social input that they receive.

One problem that arises concerns the question of limits on freedom, many placed by lack of awareness and conditioning. Certainly when Kelly uses the term 'choice' he is not suggesting that all individuals have access to all pertinent information before choosing a course of action. There are limitations on cognitive processing – we simply cannot know everything about ourselves and the world around us to state categorically and correctly why we choose one act over another (Nisbett and Wilson, 1977). Also, once chosen, we must accept the consequences of an act, which clearly limit freedom. An individual does appear free, for conscious or less-than-conscious reasons, to enact and to re-enact a wide variety of behaviours, offensive ones included. Why would an individual choose the actions of a 'pervert', say, or why would a person act in a manner that appeared to be both self-injurious and injurious to others? The answer may be ultimately an individual one – it depends on the person's own experience and past efforts to construe personal experience, but it can also be a simple, shared one – it depends on perceived construct extension and definition. Pain, whether through physical injury or humiliation, can be self-confirming and hence very positive. Being physically injured and/or humiliated during what one construes as a sexual act can confirm one's identity as a sexual masochist. Pain, in other words, can be pleasure. In the same way, a painful or negative label like 'heartless killer' can, when reinforced by the experience of homicide, or even being told that one is such a creature, provide the reassurance of self-knowledge or identity.

Kelly (1955/1991a/1991b) and other personal construct theorists say little about the origins of constructs, especially self-constructs. The origins of these constructs, both positive and negative, lie in personal experience, but it is probable that the social environment (for example, family, peer groups) is responsible for the initial application of these descriptions (see Mead, 1934/1977). Offenders often recall, perhaps because of the emotional impact, an incident in which a parent or school mate called them 'fucking loser'. The acceptance of such labels may be instantaneous or very gradual, but their impact can be profound. Even well-intentioned formal labels, such as 'antisocial personality disordered', can lead to negative behaviour. Many offenders accept personal labels quite freely in an attempt to interpret their own bewildering and harmful acts.

Although experience, choice, labelling, and meaning making might explain offensive actions in general terms, PCT-based explanations of specific offensive acts (such as sexual offending) require elucidation and examination. A number of specific explanations of homicide (Winter, 2003c), sexual offences (Horley, 2000, 2003c), and mentally disordered offences (Houston, 1998, 2003) have been offered, at least as preliminary statements about the nature of particular criminal acts. What these authors and others appear to argue in common is that there is no single explanation within PCT to account for offending, however specific, because the final actor is the individual. What does seem accepted is that there may be common features at the base of many offenders' actions that will provide at least some general thinking and approaches to addressing change.

Therapeutic practice

Forensic institutions present a special challenge to clinicians hoping to assist offenders in altering construction processes. First and foremost, forensic institutions, especially maximum-security prisons, are not very therapeutic settings. One possible exception includes programmes based on therapeutic community principles (see Cullen, 1997), but even these programmes generally exist within a larger, brutal environment that is a prison. Months of therapeutic progress with offenders in treatment can be erased quickly by intentional or unintentional comments or acts. As one client of mine serving a lengthy penitentiary sentence for a series of armed bank robberies opined rather well, prisons are full of 'vultures', including both guards and inmates, who prey on any sign of weakness, and simply attending therapy sessions makes you appear weak. Development of settings where freedom can be restricted without the brutalizing effects of typical contemporary correctional institutions might be suggested as a major social priority in many countries. Milan, Chin and Nguyen (1999, p. 581) have argued that 'the creation of a more humane prison environment may prove to be one of the most significant components of corrections professionals' efforts to ensure that prisoners are not harmed by the prison experience.' Until such time that we can claim to have caring prison environments, the best that most forensic clinicians can hope is for a microcosm that at least does not punish those who attempt to address personal demons via therapy.

Prison settings can also be brutalizing and dehumanizing settings for therapists. The danger may be subtler than that presented to inmates, but it is present nonetheless. Remaining optimistic in a pessimistic place requires the resilience that social support and frequent 'escapes' (secondment, sabbaticals) can help to provide. Too many prison therapists fall victim to the effects of their work environments and provide less-than-adequate assistance to clients in dire need. Fortunately, not only are most offenders on probation or parole rather than incarcerated, but the most effective offender rehabilitation appears offered by community-based correctional programmes (Andrews et al., 1990). While there may be few community-based forensic treatment programmes based exclusively on PCT, there are some that are consonant with PCT (Eccles and Walker, 2003; Horley and Francoeur, 2003).

Fixed-role therapy (FRT)

The principles and practice of FRT are well established (Kelly, 1955/1991a; Epting, 1984; Winter, 1992a). Use of FRT with offenders has been reported by Horley (2005) and Houston (1998). It appears that FRT should be examined in more forensic treatment settings, especially involving more complex and difficult cases. The ability to help a client address various problems at once, as opposed to dealing with each separately then combining the outcomes to examine possible interactions, is important. Dramaturgical approaches like FRT may not suit all clients, but many forensic clients are experienced in 'confidence games' and may well accept a role-playing approach to therapy. This approach might be advantageous in that it emphasizes the development of existing strengths, versus the elimination of personal weaknesses, of forensic clients (Roesch, 1988).

The emphasis in FRT is placed on a thematic shift rather than the correction of minor personal problems. By acting a new and more functional role, important change to the client should be manifested over time. Developing an acceptable personality sketch is the task of the therapist only after assessment of the client, which includes some understanding of the nature of the person that the client would like to become. The sketch, rarely if ever representing an ideal individual, is presented to the client with 'the full protection of "make-believe"' (Kelly, 1955/1991a, p. 373/p. 277). This means that clients engage in a creative endeavour, an attempt to become what they believe is possible, rather than what the therapist desires.

One difficulty with FRT for offenders comes in developing effective fixed-role sketches (ones that the client can relate to in terms of a workable alternative to present self). Standards for many offenders – perhaps less so for sexual offenders, who do not express the antisocial sentiments that other offenders typically do (Horley, Quinsey and Jones, 1997) – are difficult to relate to for therapists insofar as they may involve drug abuse, sexual variation, aggression or other antisocial aspects. To write an effective sketch, however, the client's alternative needs to be considered seriously. The sketch writer must avoid unworkable roles (those construed as 'square Johns' or simply 'not me, never could be'). If a very prosocial character with no 'rough edges' is foisted on the client, rejection of the sketch by the client will result.

Another difficulty with FRT in a prison setting, or even certain community-based forensic settings (for example, half-way houses), is limitation of experimentation with the new role. The social and physical environmental conditions of most prisons do not permit the range of experiences that allow for 'behavioural try-outs' of new actions based on new ways of construing. Often, poor substitutes are all that would be available for a client in a prison (for example, talking to a female guard in an appropriate manner in place of asking a female love interest for a date). In many cases where only poor substitutes were available, I have relied on imaginary encounters and substantial discussion of how the new role would respond or think.

A related, critical point to consider when developing and presenting a fixed-role sketch is the forensic setting. Some sketches could result in a client's death if enacted in the wrong place, and some prisons are completely the wrong places for clients attempting to become more sensitive to others, concerned about a neighbour's well-being, and so forth. The 'inmate code', or the unwritten yet prescribed set of acceptable behaviours for prison inmates, demands consideration. This code varies somewhat from facility to facility but offenders in any institution, including many forensic or special hospitals, need to conform to it. A prudent approach would be to go over the new sketch in extreme detail with the client about possible negative outcomes of implied behaviours from the sketch, expressing warnings wherever necessary. On more than one occasion, I have found it necessary to send a sketch 'home' (to the community on release) with a client. Feedback can then be provided through telephone conversations, letters, or contacts through community-based probation/parole officers or therapists. This situation is far from ideal, but dealing with the frustration on both sides is better than dealing with the death or severe injury that may result from trying to be too therapeutic in an extremely non-therapeutic setting.

Cognitive restructuring

One popular, contemporary form of psychotherapy provided to offenders is cognitive restructuring. This term was used in part because offenders see it as non-threatening. One problem with the term is connection with rationalist forms of psychotherapy (for example, Ellis, 1962) but it can be construed as constructivist. Cognitive restructuring, in either an individual or a group format, is useful in situations where FRT is limited by setting or client objections to enactment-based approaches.

Cognitive restructuring as I practise it is very much an elaborative technique as described by Winter (1992a). A client is invited to identify and to explore his or her own construct system by way of 'talking about yourself, your past, and how you think about things'. This process inevitably involves addressing a client's inconsistencies, construct system fragments or subsystems, and personal concerns with the intent of allowing him or her to resolve inconsistencies and to elaborate meanings. Clearly, some slot-rattling (viewing a person or event in terms of the opposite pole of a construct to that which was previously used to describe it) can be involved but altering the use of a particular construct might be significant for an offender client.

Challenging accounts or understandings of one's life and actions is part of the process of cognitive restructuring but, because this is not a rationalist therapy, there is no 'name calling' or 'finger pointing' with respect to a client's account of events. The client must be left to tell his or her story and express his or her perspective but anti-social sentiments and statements cannot go unchallenged lest silence be construed as validation, and many offenders are adept at finding or extorting validation. As described by a number of authors (for example, Andrews and Bonta, 1998), the most effective forensic counsellors appear to be firm in accepting only pro-social comments. This may seem to compromise a complete acceptance of a client's perspective that PCT accepts (Winter and Watson, 1999), but the therapist must also consider the 'other', whether a victim or any potential victim (all members of society), in a therapeutic encounter. Challenges do not have to be abrupt verbal assaults but can be requests to examine particular statements.

Much of my work in cognitive restructuring is spent examining the many constructs applied to self by the client. Use of guilt in the Kellian sense, and even displacement from negative core roles (for example, 'solid con'), can be an important tool in getting an offender to reconstrue self and relationships with others. In general, success depends on respect for the client's views and providing the individual with hope for change, keeping in mind that most offenders experience respect and hope all too seldom.

Problem identification

Developed as a general first step for offenders interested in some help with psychological problems, problem identification is intended to provide a supportive environment for sex offenders to discuss their lives, personal difficulties, and construct systems in order to receive feedback from therapist(s) and peers. As such, it has been operated as an open, process-oriented group that is a first step rather than an end in itself. The main intent of this group is to allow individuals to examine and to 'troubleshoot', usually in very preliminary ways, their construct systems. A very comfortable environment is required because trust of all participants is a key to group success. Clients, usually six to eight per rotation in a closed group, are allowed to speak without fear of attack (there are no 'hot seats', insults, physical contact), although questioning and challenge is encouraged. Each group member is permitted over 2 weeks, or 8 hours of group time, to 'tell his or her story' through an autobiographical account or simply recounting specific episodes that are construed as meaningful for some reason. The group composition that seems to work best is a homogenous one with respect to offence – in fact, the more homogeneity the better (for example, all child molesters with offences involving male victims) – and client background. The pitfall that has been noted with this arrangement is 'alliances' where individuals band together to support each other and to validate each others' deviant perspectives. While this is a real danger, it can be countered by challenges to all potential allies when encountered.

Relapse prevention

Relapse prevention, borrowed from the alcohol treatment area, has been used by various forensic therapists, including those who work with sex offenders (see Laws, 1989), in a group format. Relapse prevention attempts to help clients recognize why problem behaviours occur and how to avoid repetition. The language or jargon of relapse prevention can be extensive, but it is not necessary.

The relapse prevention group that I have offered to offenders in a prison setting involved bi-weekly meetings over a 12-week period. A number of topics for discussion were presented including the notion of offence chains, the role of negative emotion in offending, victim impact/ empathy, developing helping networks, informed decision-making, and avoiding high-risk situations. Homework in the form of mock letters to victims and decision-making exercises was included. Most individuals became involved in this group just prior to release; hence, it was viewed often as an attempt to consolidate gains made throughout other aspects of treatment.

My emphasis in relapse prevention is not on behaviour per se or on the didactic information to prevent reoffence. Rather, the discussions about thoughts and feelings relevant to offences are highlighted and form a central theme throughout the group meetings. The key to relapse prevention is allowing individual offenders to examine how their own constructions of the world can lead directly to inappropriate actions. One major problem with this approach can occur if insufficient time is spent exploring the connections between how views of people and life lead to behavioural experiments – often relapse prevention becomes a harangue about the obvious cues that offenders are unable or unwilling to notice in order to avoid negative behaviours. Lecturing and berating offenders, whether in a group or individually, is not therapeutic and is unlikely to lead to personal change.

Case examples

Fixed-role therapy with a violent drug offender

When I first met 'Doug', he was a 26 year-old male with a violent past, including almost 30 adult criminal convictions involving assaults and drug possession and sales. He worked occasionally as a home renovator – his early exit from high school limited occupational options – but most of his livelihood was derived from illicit drugs, either selling or enforcing the collection of drug-related debts. He was a serious drug consumer, mostly methamphetamine, and his skeletal appearance betrayed a long-term addiction, although he was very proud of his recent 'beating' of alcohol abuse. He was divorced with a young son. It was, he claimed, his relationship with his son that compelled him to seek intensive individual psychotherapy.

Although extremely taciturn, with a perpetual icy stare and sullen facial expression, Doug argued compellingly that, while he had no concern for others and seemed to hurt everyone he became involved with, he needed 'someone who can understand the pain I live with everyday . . . I feel myself slipping into a void where I block out the rest of the world.' He needed 'desperately', to quote him, to leave his violent, criminal life behind in order to be a good father to his son.

Doug's prior involvement in therapy was limited to institutional anger-management group therapy, which he characterized as 'useless', and regular visits to a psychiatrist in the community. He was prescribed chlorpromazine because of diagnoses that included antisocial and borderline personality disorders. Although he found that the medication did provide some relief for violent outbursts, it 'dulled and slowed' him and was no long-term solution. Because our time was relatively brief – he was only 2 months short of sentence completion when he came to me in the maximum secure prison where he was incarcerated – I suggested FRT. He was somewhat cool to the suggestion at first, but claimed to be 'willing to try anything' in order to make meaningful, personal change. Our meetings over the next 2 months, scheduled weekly, were infrequent because of his refusals to leave his cell and his brief stays in solitary confinement. Even in maximum security, or perhaps because of it, he confronted inmates and prison staff violently.

Doug was back behind bars within 2 months of his release. He was sentenced to 9 months for a conviction involving firearms possession, and he immediately began FRT with me. Our early sessions during his earlier incarceration had produced a brief but revealing self-characterization sketch, and he now completed a role construct repertory grid. He saw himself very clearly as a violent and vengeful person, who felt 'betrayed because I've never been given a fair chance in life'. He described himself as 'dead inside', yet someone who was 'like a time bomb', able to go off at anytime. He admitted that he gained pleasure from the pain he inflicted on others, recognizing that 'I always come out the winner and loser at the same time'.

His repertory grid results were both interesting and disturbing. Doug saw the social world in two fairly distinct camps, law-abiding versus criminal. The 10×20 grid, only half completed, consisted of a single factor that could be easily recognized as antisocial–prosocial. His role elements, including his son, were comprised of people who were 'convicts' who had 'done time', 'give up', 'temperamental', 'drunk', 'not helpful', and 'like a time bomb' or not. While he classified himself generally as antisocial, he did describe himself as a helpful person who was no longer a drunk.

My work with Doug over the next 5 months focused on elaboration and acceptance of the character sketch, developed together, that was presented to him as a viable alternative to his current self. The new role included some aspects of Doug's current self-identified strengths (for example, loyalty, helpfulness, ability to 'defeat demons') as well as some rather new aspects (for example, respect for authority, forgiveness, ability to express feelings). Doug maintained his 'tough con' role during his incarceration but I was at least allowed glimpses of a softer, caring side of this violent individual. The extent of his acceptance of the new role was unclear but, because I viewed our efforts as an extended project, I anticipated more opportunity to work with Doug on his next incarceration. Unfortunately, the opportunity was unavailable because, within 2 weeks of his release for the firearms offence, Doug was shot and killed by an unknown assailant.

Cognitive restructuring with a sexual offender

'Zenon' was a very bright and articulate man, a confirmed bachelor in his early 50s. He was born in Europe, but raised and educated in Canada. He earned four university degrees, including two graduate degrees, and worked as a teacher in a public school system. We met during his incarceration – he was classified to a maximum secure prison because of the notoriety of his case – following convictions for a number of charges, most notably sexual assault involving young males. These were not his first sexual convictions involving minors. He had been convicted twice in the past for indecent acts and sexual interference with pre-pubescent males. Zenon approached me initially because of anxiety, a fear based on the view that many people wanted to hurt him. Although segregated from most inmates, his current fear was not unfounded. We began therapy with an intention to address anxiety issues, but I suggested that other issues (for example, his sexual involvement with pre-pubescent males) might be examined. Zenon was adamant initially that his problems concerned 'society' rather than any personal difficulties. He believed that, rather than being an abuser or an exploiter, he was a lover of all people, especially boys. He revealed that he had spent roughly 2 months every year for the past decade in south-east Asia where he had developed a network of 'friends', mostly pre-pubescent males and their families but including several men with similar sexual interests.

Zenon completed a number of psychological assessments. Interestingly, despite complaints about anxiety, he revealed little social anxiety and, when observed with others including inmates, seemed very comfortable around people. While his attitudes, as reflected by responses to the Criminal Sentiments Scale (Andrews and Wormith, 1990), could be described as very pro-social, his beliefs about adult–child sex on the Cognition Scale (Abel, Becker and Cunningham-Rathner, 1984) appeared very aberrant. He reported, for example, that adults show affection for children via sexual involvement. Interestingly, he described himself in rather negative terms physically and sexually, although perhaps this was not unexpected given his short, stout and balding appearance.

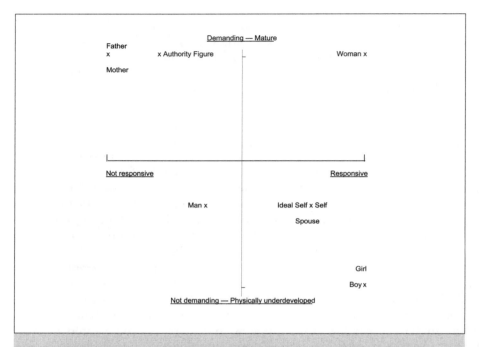

Figure 18.1 Graph of Zenon's rep grid results (non-parametric factor analysis).

His repertory grid results were most fascinating and helpful (see Figure 18.1). In completing a 10 × 20 rep grid, Zenon used detailed descriptions of each construct pole. Two dominant factors emerged. The first factor, accounting for 50% of the overall variance, seemed to be concerned with responsiveness. 'Comforting and caring' versus 'emotionally distant', 'physically nurturing' versus 'more cerebral', and 'able to give and receive affection' versus 'unable to deal with affection' were just some of the constructs that loaded on this factor. The second factor, accounting for 15% of the variance, seemed concerned with a theme of dominance. This factor included the constructs 'physically mature' versus 'physically undeveloped', 'hard to please' versus 'easy to satisfy', and 'demanding needs' versus 'less demanding of others'. Overall, the grid graph of elements seems to group the emotionally attractive (children, Zenon) and the less than attractive individuals (most adults). We discussed these results in individual sessions, and Zenon appeared both intrigued and mystified by these findings. He admitted that he seldom considered the specific reasons why children were attractive to him, and accepted that it probably had much to do with their accepting and loving expressions toward him. In recounting some early life experience, he recalled one incident when he was reaching puberty (about age 12) and was playing with a same-age female friend of the family, which involved an assertion from his domineering father to the effect that he would marry the girl someday. He remembers thinking at the time 'not on your life', and construed this as a recognition of latent homosexuality rather than psychological reactance and an attempt to establish freedom and independence. On the surface, throughout the course of individual psychotherapy, Zenon was open to my reinterpretation of his accounts. While he would frequently argue his position and his interpretation as if in an intellectual debate – he was a consummate intellectualizer – he appeared to consider alternative constructions. In the end, he appeared to accept, rather reluctantly, that his sexual expression involving prepubescent males might indeed hurt rather than help the boys.

Zenon, just prior to release, also participated in a relapse prevention group. He proved to be a keen observer of others and, while he focused on the content of their stories rather than any non-verbal cues, he was very insightful and challenged other group members helpfully. He also appeared much less defensive than he had earlier when others challenged him. The impact of the psychotherapy that he received while incarcerated is difficult to assess but, in the 9 years since his release, Zenon has not been charged with, let alone convicted of, further criminal offences. Whether he continues his previous lifestyle beyond Canada is very difficult to know.

Research

Research into the efficacy of PCT-based psychotherapy for offenders has been relatively limited and, like the situation in personal construct psychotherapy more generally (see Winter, 2003b), often based on case studies. There is a paucity of formal, systematic evaluations of psychotherapeutic programmes, but there is reason to believe that this situation is changing.

Some of the forensic case studies reported in the clinical literature to date are difficult to interpret in terms of therapeutic result. Skene's (1973) report of the treatment using FRT of a 'homosexual' is a good case in point. From Skene's description of the client, it is impossible to know whether the teenager being treated was sexually aggressive with young males at least five years his junior – hence, hebephilic to use current, psychiatric terminology – or was simply engaged in consenting sexual relationships with similar aged peers. Shorts' (1985) interesting report of PCT psychotherapy with an adult male who assaulted adult females is rather unclear as to the result of therapy insofar as identifying with rapists at the termination of treatment is not necessarily the mark of success that many clinicians would accept. Case studies do suggest that various PCT-based treatments, especially FRT, can and have been used with some efficacy with arsonists (Fransella and Adams, 1966; Landfield, 1971), exhibitionists (Landfield and Epting, 1987; Horley, 1995), complex sexual deviations (for example, Horley, 2005), and mentally disordered offenders (Houston, 2003), among others.

Among the more formal evaluations of PCT-based offender therapies, Cummins (2003) has described a programme that he offers for those with anger problems. Anger, although not necessarily a forensic issue per se, can clearly lead to criminal outcomes such as assault. Cummins reports on the qualitative indices, such as client feedback, that he has gathered post-treatment, and they suggest success in terms of personal insight gained from participation in his group therapy.

Horley and Francoeur (2003) have offered a PCT-based therapy group to men convicted of spousal assault, or at least self-reported domestic abusers. Preliminary data (n = 14 from the first three groups) from a number of indices (for example, repertory grid, semantic differential) suggest treatment efficacy. A significant increase in self-esteem – an outcome considered crucial by a number of specialists in domestic violence (for example, Woolfus and Bierman, 1996) – was found from pre- to post-treatment for group completers.

Conclusions

Clearly more theoretical and empirical investigation of offenders is required in order to improve psychotherapeutic services. A problem with the limited literature on both violent offenders and sexual offenders is the tendency to view them as having common constructions. In fact, Prentky and Knight (1991) have demonstrated that there are many different subtypes of rapists and child molesters, while Winter (2003c) has argued convincingly that there are many constructivist roots to violence.

Much more research is required on treatment efficacy. One important avenue of further psychotherapeutic practice and research concerns multifaceted or multimodal programmes. A multimodal approach to treatment programming has been advocated not only within psychotherapeutic circles broadly (for example, Lazarus, 1971) but within the treatment of offenders narrowly (for example, Marshall and Barbaree, 1988). Although treatment resources are scarce in most forensic settings, it appears worthwhile to provide a range or choice of services to offenders.

CHAPTER NINETEEN

The experience of anger

PETER CUMMINS

Theory

There is little written in the personal construct literature directly about anger and its treatment. For me the key reference was McCoy's (1977) paper entitled 'A reconstruction of emotion'. There is also a provocative paper by Don Bannister (1977), 'The logic of passion', in which he challenges the whole way in which emotion is dealt with within personal construct psychology (PCP). Viney's (1983b) *Images of Illness* discriminates between images of anger that 'take the form of mild irritation which encourages those who experience it to deal promptly with some annoyingly discrepant aspects of their lives' and a second kind of anger that 'take[s] the form of wild outbursts against the people and events of one's world' (Viney, 1983b, p. 37). Davidson and Reser (1996) look at the cultural nature of construing. In looking at the experience of aboriginal youth they note that where social links break down the 'emotional state appears to have elements of extreme anger and loss' (p. 119). Kirsch and Jordan (2000) quote Catina and Schmitt (1993) as stating that 'emotional behaviour is seen as an indicator of the state of a person's construct system' (p. 291). They go on to use a system of categorizing constructs into categories of emotion. The most common construct category at the beginning of treatment was that of rage/anger. There is also an interesting book on emotion from an existential perspective, written by Strasser (1999), which has a chapter on anger. In this Strasser describes a clinical case where anger originated in the person's childhood experience of being disregarded as a person. This view fits very well with my previous suggestion (Cummins, 2003) that the most useful definition of anger is that anger is *an* emotional expression of invalidation. Emotion and invalidation, then, are at the heart of understanding anger.

The language here is difficult, as Kelly was quite explicit about the need to abandon the emotion – cognition construct dichotomy in favour of trying to understand 'emotion as forms of transition'. The underlying argument is that change or resistance to change is the place where we can see most clearly constructs expressed in a way that would be called 'emotional'. As Bannister (1977, p. 27) describes it, 'At such times we try to nail down our psychological furniture to avoid change or we try to lunge forward in answer to some challenge or revelation by forcefully elaborating our experience. It is at such times that our conventional language most often makes reference to feeling.' Bannister goes on to point out that Kelly's definitions of transition try to make us recognize that we can only understand the person from within, in terms of the why, from their point of view. To understand my anger you have to understand my understanding of *why* I get angry. The first step in doing so is to remind ourselves that constructs are not verbal labels. A construct is an act of discrimination. Some acts of discrimination may not have a verbal label. Most of us will have had the experience of trying to decide which of two actions to take, for example shall we go to the cinema or the pub. We cannot decide, saying we do not care which we go to. We toss a coin to decide. The coin says cinema; we then realize that we really want to go to the pub. The construct was there but had not been capable of being verbally realized until the forced choice made this possible. This experience of 'not verbally realized constructs' is at the heart of working with anger. The most common statements made by people when I first meet them are:

- there is no reason for my anger;
- I just get angry about silly things;
- it just happens.

What they are often saying is that they do not have verbal labels for their particular constructs around anger. This reliance on verbal labels is one that can also be seen in much of the personal construct literature. Because we rely so heavily on verbally labelling constructs, PCP itself has been labelled a cognitive theory. As Bannister (1977, p. 33) points out

> It may be that our failure to argue about 'experience' using construct theory has impoverished the theory . . . If this is true then it is only when we seriously undertake explorations of our own and other peoples' experience and behaviour in terms of constructs like guilt, aggression, anxiety, hostility that we will begin to understand their meaning and their content.

In this chapter I intend to elaborate two main themes:

- the contrast between the cognitive behavioural therapy (CBT) and the PCP approach to anger – in particular the distinction between first and second order change (Ecker and Hulley, 1996);
- the significance, for their construing, of the extent of illiteracy/dyslexia/lack of verbal fluency in people referred with anger.

Personal construct psychotherapy and CBT

Mr X has been in trouble with the law since childhood. The psychiatric assessment concluded, 'He has no emotion as emotion is a sign of weakness. I believe he poses a significant risk to others and he openly stated that he is naturally inclined to violence.'

The conclusion of this report was that the best answer was anger management in a community outpatient setting. Our conclusion was that (as a significant risk to others) he belonged in the forensic services! This referral sums up a common current perspective on anger; that even at the extreme it can be treated by an anger management program in an outpatient setting.

This management framework is based on the CBT approach. Anger has been the almost exclusive preserve of CBT. A colleague commented to me recently that anger management has become the new anxiety management. (In the 1970s, anxiety management training, using relaxation, was one of the core roles of clinical psychologists.) The key figure in the CBT literature has been Raymond Novaco. He defines anger as: 'A negatively-toned emotion, subjectively experienced as an aroused state of antagonism towards someone or something perceived to be the source of an aversive event' (Novaco, 1998).

Alternatively, Meichenbaum (2001, p. 19) suggests that 'Anger is a feeling an individual may have when he thinks he cannot get something he wants to obtain or to do and believes that he deserves it and is being blocked from obtaining it.'

In general the cognitive behavioural literature told me that feeling anger is usually the result of feeling out of control of your life and the situations that affect your life. 'Anger is a problem because of the effects that it has on the person and on others with whom he or she interacts' (Novaco, 1998).

While acknowledging that there is a positive side to anger, the cognitive behavioural position seems to slip almost seamlessly into seeing anger as a major problem that requires management. 'The goal of anger management is for you to avoid acting out your anger in the non-productive and/or destructive ways you have used in the past. In managing your anger, you work toward NOT having anger outbursts, temper tantrums or violent reactions' (Cullen and Freeman-Long, 1996). This position is linked to an essentially negative perception of anger.

'People with anger problems do not feel good during and after their angry experiences. Most people dislike feeling anger' (Cullen and Freeman-Longo, 1996).

This statement does not match up with my clinical experience. Many of our clients will acknowledge that they actually enjoy the experience of being angry, and sometimes even the experience of expressing it. While angry they experience a sense of power and validation that is often lacking in the rest of their lives. What they do not like are the consequences of their anger, such as broken relationships, frightened children, loss of friends and jobs, court appearances, fines and even jail.

Having attended one of Novaco's workshops it became clear that all his work has been carried out within the confines of high security hospitals. This may be why his work is so focused on the negative consequences of anger. The people he deals with are at the extreme end of the scale where anger has led to their long term incarceration. By contrast, the people I work with are all living within the local community. I am frequently struck by the lack of connection between the degree of crime and the extent of incarceration. Many of the people I have worked with have been involved in extreme acts of violence that have never been the subject of police action. A high proportion of them have already been to 'anger management'. They have two distinct reactions to this, either 'it was a bit helpful but it didn't change anything' or 'it was a load of C**P'.

I was intrigued to read a description of a study by a sociologist of the effects of teaching one particular group to control their anger. Hochschild (1983) looked at airline stewardesses who were trained to control their anger even in the face of infuriating passengers. The result was that they not only mask their unpleasant emotions in flight but have difficulty sorting out their emotional responses elsewhere (quoted in Stearns, 1995). In a recent study Hosie (2001) suggests that suppressing anger could just be storing up trouble for an emotional rebound. Participants who were instructed to inhibit their expressions of anger during the first of two anger eliciting film clips both reported and showed more anger during the second one, relative to 'expressers'. This helped to confirm my doubts about the conventional CBT approach to anger management. This model talks about the cycle of anger: there is a trigger, followed by thoughts and feelings, followed by physical symptoms, followed by behaviour, followed by consequences, followed by beliefs. Meichenbaum (2001, p. 219) summarizes this approach as being a 'problem solving approach'.

The role of anger management is to teach people to recognize trigger points and so to recognize what lights the fuse. People are encouraged to keep anger diaries and thus to develop self-awareness. Thinking errors are thus identified, for example selective perception, minimization, overgeneralization. These are then challenged. Behavioural techniques such as relaxation, exercise and silly humour are taught to avoid overarousal.

Like all such programs they work well if they fit within the range of convenience of the person's construing (first order change). The person is able to accept the set of ideas/constructs and incorporate them into their existing construing system. The problem comes with those people who do not have the capacity to integrate the provided set of ideas and constructs.

There is also a problem with those people for whom anger is a core part of their construing. For many of them their aggression is a 'genuine protest against hardship in life' (Fonagy, 2003).

The pain of change

The importance of anger to each person often means that the process of change is extremely painful. In my opinion anger management does not give enough weight to the fear/pain/ difficulty of changing emotional constructs. Kelly (1955/1991a) called these 'constructs of transition'. This description is to the point. The essence of being in transition is that we have left a safe place but have not yet reached our destination. Once we do reach it, it usually takes time for us to feel at home in the new surroundings. This metaphor of travelling has been creatively explored by Walker (2000). It is a metaphor that resonates with people who stop being angry. The difficulty of transition can be seen clearly in one of my patients who has been extremely violent. The first time he did not respond to an insult with violence but instead walked away he was physically sick. He later chopped his finger tip off to punish himself for being a wimp who walked away. The pain of transition could not be more clearly seen. This pain is not acknowledged in conventional anger management.

Interestingly Novaco himself has developed his ideas beyond the concept of 'management'. At the workshop I attended in 1999 he suggested that there are three levels:

1. general clinical care for anger;
2. anger management;
3. anger therapy.

1. General clinical care is the level required by all staff to deal with people, for example, the receptionist dealing with an angry person or the ward staff dealing with everyday anger.
2. Anger management is a fixed length group, which is run along psychoeducational lines. People are taught the model and encouraged to integrate it into their daily lives.
3. Anger therapy acknowledges that there can be more to anger than management.

The problem is, however, that the wider world and in particular the criminal justice system has adopted the idea of anger management. This comes up in all parts of the justice system. People often attend anger management courses in prison. Family courts have become keen on insisting that people complete anger management courses before they are allowed access to their children or their partner where there are no children. Doctors who lose their temper at work in stressful situations are told by their disciplinary hearing that they should attend an anger management programme. We now have Hollywood in on the act in the film called *Anger Management*.

As indicated in Table 19.1, RA Neimeyer (1993, p. 11) offers a very useful contrast between CBT and constructivist approaches to assessment.

In some ways I think that this is unfair to CBT. Not all CBT practitioners are as passive as implied, for example: 'From a CBT perspective Assessment and Treatment are highly interdependent processes' (Meichenbaum, 2001, p. 132). This hardly represents a neutral, non-

Table 19.1 Cognitive behavioural therapy vs. Constructivist assessment

Feature	CBT approach	Constructivist approach
Intended effect of assessment	Neutral, non-'reactive'	Change generating
Target	Isolated thought unit, self statements, beliefs	Construct systems, personal narratives
Characteristic Focus	Frequency of thought, degree of belief	Implicative relations between constructs
Temporal Focus	Present	Present but more developmental emphasis
Form of cognition studied	Proposition, e.g. 'I am worthless'	Fundamental distinction or bipolar construct
Assumed relations between cognitions	Associationist, (para) logical	Hierarchical: emphasis on core ordering processes
Level of analysis	Individualistic	Individualistic to systemic
Diagnostic emphasis	Disorder-specific	Comprehensive, general
Mode of administration	Self-administered questionnaire	Interactive interview or program, personal 'diary'
Format of instrument	Highly structured and standardized	Less structured, idiographic
Scoring	quantitative	Both quantitative and qualitative
Criteria for adequacy	Psychometric	Both psychometric and hermeneutic

reactive approach. However, for my purposes what is interesting about Neimeyer's chart is that it can be used to represent the expectations of the wider world about anger management, as indicated in Table 19.2.

The anger management approach can be clearly understood as being underpinned by a rationalist approach. The rationalist approach sets out to change people's thinking styles and to 'take the therapist's voice with them' (Meichenbaum, 2001, p. 312).

Table 19.2 Anger management expectations

CBT approach	Popular expectation	Constructivist approach
Neutral, non-'reactive'	We will do an assessment of your anger	To give an understanding of anger, invalidation
Isolated thought unit, self statements, beliefs	Anger is separate from rest of the person, and can be managed	To understand implications of anger, construing systems
Frequency of thought, degree of belief	Reference is usually made to things getting worse	Laddering of provoking situations
Present	My anger just happens	Understand where invalidation comes from
Proposition, e.g. 'I am worthless'	I am violent	Constellatory/pre-emptive
Associationist, (para) logical	Road rage without any insight into why	Idea of a construct system with a hierarchy of construing e.g. regnancy
Individualistic	My anger is my problem	Sociality
Disorder-specific	I have an anger problem	An emotional expression of invalidation
Self-administered questionnaire		Interactive interview or programme, personal 'diary'
Highly structured and standardized		Less structured, idiographic
Quantitative		Both quantitative and qualitative
Psychometric		Both psychometric and hermeneutic

Once we understand the background assumptions each approach becomes clear. The background assumptions are developed by GJ Neimeyer and Morton (1997, p. 110), who elaborate the useful distinction between rationalist and constructivist orientations made by Mahoney (1991).

Rationalism:

- argues for the distinction between thinking and feeling;
- favours thinking as a superior vehicle for validating knowledge;
- adheres to a single stable known universe.

Constructivism, by contrast:

- argues the artificiality of the distinction between thinking and feeling;
- regards feeling as primitive knowing systems;
- Challenges the idea of a stable knowable universe

As Winter and Watson (1999) have described, rationalist cognitive approaches, such as those used in anger management programs, are usually 'active, directive, commanding, forceful, scientific and psycho educational' (Grieger, 1989, pp. 99–100). They require from the therapist what RA Neimeyer (1993) described as 'to be persuasive, analytical and technically instructive'.

This approach is what Ecker and Hulley (1996, p. 8) call 'first order change', which aims to 'work directly on the symptoms in order to diminish them and produce more agreeable, less symptomatic conditions within the SAME view of reality.'

For obvious reasons I rarely see people who have had a successful experience of anger management. What I do see are people like Sam, who told me that 'I have had anger management and it was crap.' When I asked him about this he described a day programme that he had attended in prison. I asked him what made him think it was crap and he replied, 'I knocked a screw out the following day.' This may be a reasonable assessment of limited success in anger management.

Therapeutic practice

Constructivist approach to running an anger group

In our early stages of running an anger group we used most of the CBT-derived approaches already described. We initially tried a 10-session format, with handouts for each session. We came to realize that over 60% of our population was illiterate. I often get complex psychological reports about someone who it transpires cannot read. These reports usually include a range of self-report questionnaires as well as more formal psychometrics. How can they be completed by people with real reading problems? When asked about this they usually replied, 'I guessed the answers.' This situation was highlighted in a recent report in the British *Observer* newspaper (5 October 2003, p. 25) on the very limited progress in Britain of a model (developed in Canada) that uses psychological techniques to reduce offending behaviour. A probation union spokesman was quoted as saying that 70% of interviewees were no more able to fill out the questionnaires used in this model than to read Homer in the original.

We quickly discovered three important things:

- Anger diaries and self monitoring did not initially work as the majority of our attendees were not comfortable with reading and writing. We would give out handouts only to see them being quietly folded up half way through the presentation. They were irrelevant to the people concerned.
- Self administered questionnaires were unrealistic.
- Much of the underlying construing was not immediately available in the way that appeared to be assumed by cognitive approaches. Where we did access controlling beliefs it was often to find that these were seen as justified, for example 'he deserved the assault'. This was often within the context of violent lives. As Fonagy (2003) put it, 'violence ultimately signals the failure of normal developmental processes to deal with something that occurs naturally.'

First order change – to 'produce more agreeable, less symptomatic conditions within the SAME view of reality' (Ecker and Hulley, 1996, p. 8) – became an increasingly difficult proposition.

The contrast is to change the view of reality; second order change. In Ecker and Hulley's (1996, p. 8) words: 'Second order change' aims to 'usher the client into an alternate view of reality that does not include producing the symptoms.'

But how would I go about achieving that? I returned to the PCP literature to see if I could work out a better approach. I have previously outlined the central themes of this approach (Cummins, 2003). In writing this chapter I could find no other constructivist research on anger. Research on anger has been almost entirely within CBT. I did find an interesting constructivist literature on emotion. I took the suggestion of McCoy (1977) and used it to develop the idea of anger as representing invalidation. This idea is then developed using the key PCP concepts of regnancy and sociality. If we can understand what has been invalidated then we can begin to understand the anger. In other words if we understand anger as a symptom of a particular form of construing then understanding the construing will begin to alter the anger construing process.

Almost all our group members have histories of fairly extreme physical abuse, usually by parents. This often leads to forms of construing which can be best understood using Leitner, Faidley and Celentana's (2000) framework of structural arrest. A further consequence of childhood abuse was usually that they had not had a good educational experience. As already mentioned, many of them are functionally illiterate. I have recently begun to get more and more interested in the implications of this for people's construing.

The extent of illiteracy/dyslexia in people referred with anger/the forensic population

Over half of the people we are referred for 'anger management' have problems with literacy. As I have already described, when we first began running the anger group, over time (we were slow to realize the significance) we noticed that again and again group members were not using written material we provided. It was clear that the written word had little significance for them.

We have gradually developed different ways of working within the group which do not rely totally on the written word.

We now use three main techniques:

- drawing scenes on flipchart;
- repetition;
- constant use of examples within the group using more experienced members to validate this.

I was intrigued to discover from a neuropsychological colleague (Ruth Telfer) that these are the techniques for dealing with people with brain injury and developmental learning problems (Telfer and Cummins, 2003). This use of similar techniques makes perfect sense if we accept Fonagy's (2003) proposal that 'the primary developmental role of early attachment is neurocognitive in character'. Telfer describes using:

- rephrasing;
- repetition;
- image ability, for example use of mind maps.

When I began exploring this similarity of technique with her she introduced me to her neuropsychological understanding of why she uses these techniques. This relies heavily on Baddeley's (1994) idea of working memory. Working memory is a 'cognitive function that helps us keep track of what we are doing or where we are moment to moment, that holds information long enough to make a decision, to dial a telephone number, or to repeat a strange foreign word that we have just heard' (Logie, 1999).

We jointly developed a model of verbal processing that suggests what happens when verbal working memory is restricted, as described in Figure 19.1 (Telfer and Cummins, 2003).

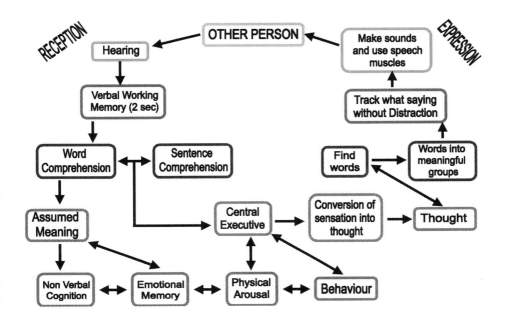

Figure 19.1 Working memory and emotion.

From the above model I began to think about the implication of having a poor working memory. The idea is that each of us has a different working memory capacity. A healthy working memory has a capacity of up to two seconds. It is like the control tower for language based information coming in to be processed by our brains. The suggestion is that we subvocalize when people talk to us; we do this by temporarily storing the sounds (phonemes). Differences in capacity can then be related to differences in performing complex tasks such as verbal comprehension or verbal problem solving (as capacity is related to speed). You cannot comprehend incoming information if it comes in quicker than you can process it.

If you cannot process it then it drops out of the verbal working memory and enters the 'emotional, non-verbal loop'. Here it is matched against assumed meanings, which are derived from emotional memories. For example, I say 'hello you old bastard, long time since we have met, what are you doing now'. This is too much for the person to construe. The word 'bastard' is matched with its assumed meaning of insult, and this links to other memories of being insulted, leading to physical arousal and violence. As a result I am shocked; I thought I was greeting the person in a friendly manner.

If they can process it then it stays in the verbal loop and is understood by the central executive as it was intended to be understood and the interaction proceeds. The word 'bastard' is seen as an affectionate use of the term and no offence is taken.

Working memory is not related to levels of understanding per se; it is possible to score at the ninetieth percentile for other kinds of intellectual/cognitive tasks and still have a poor working memory. Daneman and Carpenter (1980), using this idea, were able to show that there was a good relationship between working memory span and reading comprehension. Other more detailed studies have shown that subjects with high working memory spans are better able to cope with passages such as the following:

> There was a strange noise emanating from the dark house. Bob had to venture in to find out what was there. He was terrified: rumor had it that the house was haunted. He would feel more secure with a stick to defend himself and so he went and looked among his baseball equipment. He found a bat that was very large and brown and was flying back and forth in the gloomy room. Now he didn't need to be afraid any longer.

Most people reading this passage tend initially to assume that the large brown bat is a baseball bat rather than a flying creature. However, subjects with a high working memory span are able to correct their misapprehension on about 75% of occasions, while low span subjects are correct only about 25% of the time (Baddeley, 1994).

This mirrored very closely the sort of incidents that were reported within the anger group. A situation would be described that to us had several different explanations. As far as the group member was concerned there was only one explanation, the one that led to invalidation and therefore anger. A good example of this is road rage. I drive in front of you because I am late for a meeting. I pay no attention to you at all. As far as you are concerned this is a direct insult to you, and has to be dealt with by ramming me off the road. Just like the people with low working memory span, our group members were likely to misapprehend the link between two pieces of information. As a consequence of this misapprehension they then go on to assault the other person. We spend much time exploring whether this is the only possible response. This response is often linked to a lack of sociality and regnant constructs. This regnancy is often non-verbal. As far as these people are concerned their anger just happens.

This is where the value of PCP approaches really shows. As I have described elsewhere (Cummins, 2003), by laddering, pyramiding and other PCP techniques, anger can be understood and once this happens then the invalidation can be addressed. This then leads to second order change. The anger disappears. The person ends up in our group saying 'it is weeks since I really got angry.' What I think we see within the group is the replacement of the belief that anger is the only way to keep control, be powerful, control fear, and so forth. A critical part of this is the development of a better sociality. This process starts within the group. It facilitates its members in developing the capacity to be aggressive in a Kellian sense and in doing so to replace the central belief about anger. The most important experience within the group has been the clarification of the role that the experience of anger plays for each group member.

Case example

The majority of the cases that we see are men in their late twenties. They usually have a history of offending and have often served at least one prison sentence. They are referred because their family/partner has made it clear to them that their behaviour is unacceptable. This behaviour includes violence, wrecking the house, throwing plates/cups at family members, shouting and other threatening behaviour. They usually have a history of multiple relationships. A key factor in referral is often that they themselves now have children. It is common to be told by them, 'I have started behaving to my kids the way I was treated by my Dad and I do not want to repeat with my kids what was done to me.'

The case example that follows is based on a number of people I have worked with. Jim is 28. He was sent to see the local Community Mental Health Team (CMHT) by his family doctor. He described himself as becoming angry more often and hitting inanimate objects (walls and doors). He has twice trashed the house, destroying the kitchen on the last occasion. He is worried about losing control of his temper. He has been prescribed a variety of antidepressant medication, which he finds helpful, but says that it has not sorted out his problems.

He has had numerous different jobs, usually losing them because of his temper. He has assaulted colleagues in previous jobs but has never been taken to court. He lives with his partner and two children. It is a third relationship and he has three other children from previous relationships. He has no contact with the older three children.

The CMHT suggested that he be referred to the anger group.

When I saw him he told me that he has always had a short temper. He was struggling to control his temper and not to shout at his wife and children. He was keen to come to the anger group as he knew that his relationship with partner and children was suffering. He was worried that he would end up separating from his wife and therefore losing contact with the two youngest children. He was very clear that he had never hit his wife or children, preferring instead to hit the walls and doors.

His father was very violent and he often saw his mother being physically assaulted. When he tried to intervene, aged 7, he himself was badly beaten up by his father. His parents separated when he was seven. He never accepted the stepfather who came to live with his mother when he was 12. He was taken into care because of his aggressive behaviour. He never learned to read and write properly and asks his wife to deal with all written material. He left school and home as soon as he could at the age of 16.

His previous relationships had all ended because of his angry outbursts, but it was only now that he was acknowledging that he had a problem with his anger. He was particularly worried that he was repeating what his father had done to him, in his own treatment of his children. He wanted to give his children a different life to that which he had experienced as a child. He went on to say how puzzled he was as he 'gets angry for silly reasons'. I asked him for an example of a 'silly thing'. He replied that he really got angry when people were critical of England as a place to live.

The laddering that this produced was:

1. Critical of England . . . . . . be grateful for where you are
2. Think other country better . . . . . . not any better than England
3. Don't listen to my view . . . . . . listen to my view
4. Make me feel I am in the wrong . . . . . . accept my opinion
5. Treating me like a piece of dirt on their shoe . . . . . . value me
6. Anger

This is a very typical ladder. I had a struggle to elicit it at the beginning. The critical move comes in line 3 when it becomes clear that what is at stake here is his sense of being listened to. When he feels that he is not being listened to he very quickly jumps to feeling that he is being treated 'as a piece of dirt on a shoe' (line five). As I have described elsewhere (Cummins, 2003), this is the typical invalidation that leads to anger. It is an invalidation experienced by Jim throughout his life. He felt that he was not important enough for his father to care about him. He had never been able to secure a job that challenged him, particularly because of his problems with literacy. Now when his children did not do what he said he was quick to become invalidated.

My assessment of Jim was that he would do well in the anger group. The profile he presented, described above, is typical of many of the people we have had in the group.

A major part of the work in the group is understanding the sources of invalidation, and revalidating people within the context of the group. At the conclusion of a short-term group at least one person has required further therapeutic work and has therefore joined our longer term group. The majority, however, are clear that the group has worked for them, and have maintained this progress over six month follow up.

Research

Pekkola and Cummins (2005) have now evaluated our 10-week program using this framework. Administering mainstream assessment measures, the State-Trait Anger Expression Inventory-2 (STAXI-2) (Spielberger, 1999) and the Clinical Outcome in Routine Evaluation (CORE) (Evans et al., 2000) they were able to demonstrate the efficacy of the group programme.

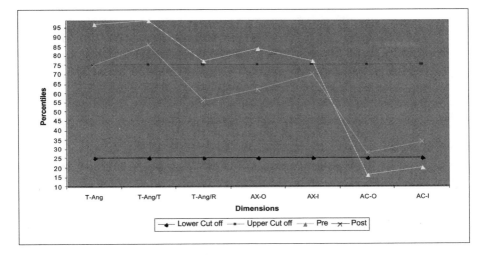

Figure 19.2 Anger group STAXI-2 scores.

Comparison of pre- and post-group STAXI-2 scores (Figure 19.2) indicated that the group's anger trait scores, experience and expression of anger had all reduced from atypically high scores (typical of the people referred to us) to the scores typical of the normal population. In addition, the group's scores on the ability to control the internal experience of anger and the external expression of anger had increased from below the normal population (< 25%) into the normal population.

On the CORE, Pekkola and Cummins (2005) were able to demonstrate (Figure 19.3) that change had not just occurred on the risk subscale. In addition, there had been a reduction on the other subscales, which measure wellbeing, level of mental health problems and level of functioning, with the subscale of functioning showing a clinically significant change.

We interpreted these results as demonstrating the existence of second order change – we had been able to facilitate 'an alternate view of reality that does not include producing the symptoms'. This interpretation was supported by our experiences in the latter stages of the group, when group members relayed incidents that would previously have elicited anger or

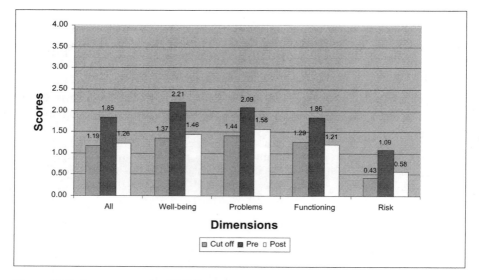

Figure 19.3 Anger group 1 – CORE scores.

violence in them, and conveyed their sense of surprise and pride that they did not have to 'control' their anger, as the situation had not elicited that response within them.

The group members' evaluation of the program was favourable, with all group members referring to the benefits of sharing within a group setting. Evaluation of the different components of the program were rated, with overall scores ranging between 20 and 31 out of a possible 35. Attendance verified the group members' positive experience of the group, with 100% attendance occurring at four of the 10 sessions and no lower than 71% attendance at any session.

Conclusion

In conclusion, I am suggesting that since anger is an emotion we have to keep looking for new ways to reach where words do not. This is particularly true for people who are not used to using language to mediate their emotion. Personal construct psychology gives a clear framework within which an emotional approach can be developed within the limits of a standard health service outpatient setting. It also allows us to acknowledge the pain of reconstruing and to address the implications of major emotional reconstruing.

I began by acknowledging the contribution of Don Bannister. In the 'Logic of passion' (Bannister 1977, p. 35), he comments:

I no longer see myself as the victim of my 'emotion'. My 'emotions' may torment me but I accept them as an integral part of me, as entailed in all that I have 'thought'. I now accept that in my 'emotions' lie the beginnings, endings and forms of my 'thoughts' and it is to what I have 'thought' that I 'feelingly' respond . . .

If I change a crucial word we get:

I no longer see myself as the victim of my 'anger'. My 'anger' may torment me but I accept IT as an integral part of me, as entailed in all that I have 'thought'. I now accept that in my anger lies the beginnings, endings and forms of my 'thoughts' and it is to what I have 'thought' that I 'feelingly' respond.

CHAPTER TWENTY

Kids' stuff

DAVID GREEN

The simple thrust of this chapter is to share some understandings of the way in which personal construct theory can inform and inspire clinical work with young people. These reflections will be structured around three of Kelly's most influential corollaries – those of individuality, commonality and sociality. But first some opening thoughts on the nature of childhood or rather how we have been inclined to construe childhood.

Children's capability

Theory

There is a tradition within a certain strand of developmental psychology of seeing children primarily as immature, imperfect beings en route to becoming proper grown ups. Salmon elegantly summed up this point of view when she noted:

> We think of childhood as essentially entailing incompetence. Children's lack of competence forms the constant basic theme of psychological research, which typically focuses on what a child cannot do rather than on what she or he can. More generally we view the young in the perspective of helplessness, ignorance, neediness – as requiring to be guided, taught, brought up. (Salmon, 1985, p. 25)

Personal construct theory was never intended to be a psychology reserved for fully formed minds. Kelly wrote of human passions and ambitions, and his model of mankind has implications for us all, big or small. So the notion of people as personal scientists who construct and test their evolving theories about themselves and the worlds they inhabit applies to young and old alike.

Our psychologies of childhood also tend to be painted in broad, normative brushstrokes. We talk of developmental milestones (walking,

256

talking) and maturational tasks (starting school, going courting) and can become preoccupied with concerns that our offspring will be able to do the right thing at the right time. It is as if all youngsters are on the same road to an identical destination. But that is not how we remember our own youth or how children experience their everyday lives. It is the special that stands out, not the shared. Salmon again hits the nail on the head: 'Certainly children when asked about their lives, typically tell very personal stories – stories which are far from standardized, stories of unique protagonists each on their unique journey' (Salmon, 1985, p. 32).

Perhaps we have not been inclined to take young people's narratives as seriously as we ought. We even use the expression 'telling stories' as a euphemism for lying when we talk to children as in 'I hope you're not telling stories again, young Frank!' It seems we have some niggling doubts about the trustworthiness of children's accounts of their lives. Ravenette (1997) has linked this suspicion to the dominant influence of psychoanalytic thinking in the child guidance movement in the UK. If you accept the psychodynamic credo that the most powerful determinants of human conduct are unconscious motivations of which the actor is largely unaware, there seems little mileage in opening up a conversation with a fearful 7-year old girl about her theories of where these anxieties come from. What would she know about it? Personal construct theory in contrast is especially interested in exploring young people's struggles to make sense of their existence. So as clinicians we want to find ways to enable children to tell us what they know while realizing that they will likely know a good deal more than they can easily say.

Therapeutic practice

Kelly's (1955/1991a/1991b) writings are somewhat light on technical instruction. Therapists looking for a prescriptive manual to guide their practice should look elsewhere. However, Kelly did lay down a few very helpful maxims about the attitude that psychologists and their like should attempt to strike when working with children. He chose the word 'credulous' to describe the preparedness to believe that he wanted the adult to convey – an unusual adjective to select. It is not generally a compliment to be described as credulous. The word implies a foolhardy faith in other people that lays you open to ridicule or worse. If you were looking for a synonym, 'gullible' might most readily come to mind. It is therefore a vulnerable rather than a powerful position for adults to adopt in their dealings with children. Neither party is likely to be very used to this state of affairs, which is probably just the sort of creatively unsettling experience that Kelly had in mind. If these atypical ground rules can be established in intergenerational conversations then adults just might get a privileged access to the private world of the young people they are seeking to understand and help. If we get some of the 'inside story' then children's seemingly senseless behaviour may make sense from their perspective. If children experience, even fleetingly, the luxury of being understood, then the seeds of a powerful therapeutic alliance will have been sown.

The uniqueness of the individual

Theory

Kelly's (1955/1991a, p. 55/p. 38) individuality corollary states that 'persons differ from each other in their construction of events'. So the first task of the psychologist is to try and appreciate the unique view that each particular child has on its world. While establishing an appropriate interpersonal climate is a necessary first step along that route, we should not anticipate that young people will easily respond to the invitation to 'tell us what *you* think'. They will likely be unused to this focus on their own constructions and may not be able to offer much of an answer in the first instance. They may have instead an implicit awareness of what matters to them that they can only begin to articulate when provided with an enabling exploratory structure. Personal construct psychologists have developed a number of techniques that can provide this sort of conversational scaffolding.

Therapeutic practice

Kelly's (1955/1991a) oft-quoted first principle goes along the lines that if you want to know what's wrong with a person, why not ask them, they might just tell you. This recognition that the individual is the world expert on their own experience applies as much to children as it does to adults. However, whereas psychologists might be all too adept at conjuring up explanations for their own behaviour, their young charges will probably not give an easy or instant account of themselves. A timely question can prove a great help.

Kelly recognized how fond of complaining we all seem to be. Even our most taciturn of colleagues will generally open up a bit if we are prepared to provide an audience for one of their favourite beefs! Kelly guessed that we are drawn to complaint because the themes to which we are inclined to return have personal importance for us. This deeper import may not be immediately obvious to the listener, but it is a meaning that can be investigated by elaborative questioning. A sentence-completion task can be used in either a conversational or written 'quiz' format:

The trouble with . . . is.
They are like that because . . .
It would be better if . . .
The difference that would make is . . .

Case examples

The wording can be adjusted to suit the topic of enquiry, be it brothers, teachers, illness, going to bed, or West Ham United. On occasions this simple style of questioning does seem to provide the 'royal route' to a person's core construing that Kelly envisaged. For example, one young man was able to explain how his aversion to mathematics was linked to his teacher's fondness for getting pupils to solve problems 'out loud' in front of their classmates. He saw these sessions not as opportunities to learn but as opportunities to be publicly humiliated. Another lad was not only able to put into words his dread of receiving regular injections as the worst aspect of being treated for cancer, but also suggest a couple of ways in which the experience could be made more bearable for him (more control and a cuddle from his Mum).

Therapeutic practice

Ravenette (1997) has pioneered the use of drawings when eliciting children's constructs. For example, he developed a series of pen and ink drawings depicting a number of classroom scenarios that he entitled 'trouble in school'. As the example in Figure 20.1 illustrates, these cartoons set

Figure 20.1 Example of 'trouble in school' drawing.

a particular scene without in any way dictating the nature of the exchanges being portrayed. Facial expressions and physical characteristics are kept intentionally ambiguous.

In his work as an educational psychologist Ravenette would invite a young pupil to select a few of these scenes and to construct a story to accompany the picture.

Somebody's feeling troubled here, who?
What's going on in their mind?
How come they got to feel that way?
What would make a difference to them?
Why would that be better?

It is important to appreciate the difference between this style of interviewing and the approach adopted by child psychologists employing projective tests such as the Children's Apperception Test (CAT). The Kellian intention is not to lure children into projecting their own feelings on to the major characters in their stories. Rather, in telling their tales children are employing the constructs that they are likely to use in understanding their own experience of the classroom. That may or may not include having personally suffered in the same way as the pupils in their stories. Ravenette's closing questions to the Trouble in School interview make this distinction clear:

In what ways are you and the person in this story different?
Are there any ways in which you are similar to them?

Over a lengthy career Ravenette developed a number of intriguing ways of inviting children to join him in constructive conversations, and the interested reader is strongly advised to read his original accounts. A couple more examples of his inventiveness will perhaps whet the appetite for further research.

Ravenette appreciated that the questions that adults ask of children can be highly perplexing, for example 'Why did you do this?' or 'What do you think about that?' The young person probably is unsure what the questioner is driving at and how they are supposed to go about framing an answer. Ravenette therefore developed a style of open questioning that retained a spirit of curious enquiry but made the child's task manageable, understandable and even tempting. First he put practical limits on the length of reply he expected from the young person, for example 'Tell me three things that best describe you . . .' There is of course nothing magical about the number three. It's not a daunting request and if the youngster only offers two comments we are in business anyway. Then he expanded the area of enquiry by inviting the child to use his or her imagination a little, for example, 'Can you tell me three things that your mother/teacher/pal might say about you?' Next he might perhaps affect the puzzled demean of the TV detective Columbo and ask the child to help him out by providing some further explanation of what particular words mean for them, for example, 'So how would I know that somebody was trendy/kind/serious?' or 'Tell me about someone you know who isn't trendy/kind/serious?' The conversation might then lead naturally into constructs of change, for example, 'What do you expect to be like in five years time?' 'What difference would it make if you decided to be more like X?'

Case example

This style of questioning, which Ravenette titled 'who are you?' can open up surprising avenues of exploration. I recall trying the approach out with my son Joe when he was 13 years old. I discovered unexpected depths to his thinking – and so did he! The conversation however soon exhausted him. 'Can we stop now please, Dad? This is really hard. You're asking me things I only just know.' Out of the mouths of babes and sucklings . . .

Conclusion

Fortunately, we don't all have to possess Ravenette's creative touch. The techniques that have been developed to investigate adults' constructions of themselves and their world such as self-characterizations and various forms of repertory grid can generally be adapted for use with young people (Butler and Green, 1998). Then let the 'unique protagonists' use the opportunity as they see fit.

Common concerns

Theory

Kelly was interested in perceptions that people share as well as those that are unique to each individual. The Commonality Corollary states that 'To the extent that one person employs a construction of experience which is similar to that employed by another, his or her processes are psychologically similar to those of the other person' (Kelly, 1955/1991a, p. 90/p. 63).

So although in theoretical terms there are no constraints on the number of ways we can make constructive sense of our lives, in practice our imaginations are far from unbounded. Kelly (1955/1991a) almost accidentally acknowledges this limitation in the dichotomy corollary, which states that 'a person's construction system is composed of a *finite* number of dichotomous constructs' (Kelly, 1955/1991a, p. 59/p. 41). Both these corollaries beg an important developmental question – where do we get our constructs from?

The social constructionist movement (Burr, 1995) has laid great emphasis on the cultural determinants of our apparently personal perspectives on the world. The alternative constructions of events that are open to us are seen as governed by powerful social and political forces of which we are, at best, only partially aware. So the cycle of deprivation in which recurrent generations of the most disadvantaged sections of society remain stuck at the bottom of the pile can be understood as a result not only of a poverty of opportunity but also a poverty of ambition. We shall return to this theme of the crucial capacity to 'imagine you're different'.

One implication of the social constructionist critique of the rampant individualism of personal construct psychology is that we might expect that young people who share a common upbringing and cultural heritage will also share some common constructions of themselves and their world.

Research

Butler (2001) has produced a self-image profile for use with young people in the UK that relies on precisely that assumption. He collected a wealth of self-descriptive material from over 1,000 children and adolescents in both clinical and community settings in Leeds in West Yorkshire by asking good Kellian questions such as, 'if you could describe yourself in three ways what would they be?' He then subjected the considerable list of adjectives generated in this exercise to a systematic content analysis. By judiciously grouping synonyms and calculating total frequencies, Butler was able to create a manageable 25 item questionnaire – the SIP (self image profile). There are two published versions of the SIP – one for children aged between 7 and 11 years and one for adolescents aged 12 to 16 years. The two scales contain very similar items (such as kind/unkind, happy/unhappy, friendly/unliked) but the wording reflects the preferred terms in the respective age groups. For example, children chose to describe themselves as 'brainy' whereas the adolescents preferred 'intelligent'. For both versions of the SIP young people are asked to rate 'how you think you are' on an equal number of positively and negatively framed items using a 6-point Likert scale.

Therapeutic practice

There has been a long-standing debate within personal construct psychology about the legitimacy of providing constructs for people to employ rather than eliciting those constructs that are uniquely important for each individual. However, Butler and his colleagues appear to have found a convincing middle route whereby the constructs that are provided for young people completing the SIP have been generated by a substantial group of their peers. The SIP should therefore pose questions that make sense to its users. But why would practitioners employ the SIP rather than elicit constructs from their young clients using some of the methods described in the previous section? It's quicker and easier – at least from the psychologist's viewpoint! There is a growing body of normative data that allow people's views of themselves to be compared with their age-matched peers. These may well prove practical attractions for the hard-pressed professional. However, it is another aspect of the SIP that holds most clinical possibility for me.

Butler recommends that as well as asking young people to rate 'how you think you are', they should also be invited to consider 'how you would like to be'. The discrepancy between these two scores offers a pragmatic index of self-esteem. Broadly speaking, the smaller the gap the higher the young person's self-regard. However, a failure to discriminate between current self and ideal self may be more an indicator of complacency than glowing mental health. As the poet said, 'a man's reach should exceed his grasp or what's a heaven for' (from Robert Browning's poem *Andrea del Sarto*). It is this motivational potential that the SIP administration seeks to unlock. As I have argued earlier in this chapter, young people, particularly those from socially deprived backgrounds that are over-represented in our clinic populations, frequently struggle to articulate the directions in which they would like to develop. They know that they are not currently content with their lot. They know that others, usually complaining adults, are keen that they should change their ways. What they cannot easily imagine is where they would like to get to and how they could be helped to get there. The SIP offers a simple and relevant framework with which to set that process in motion. Butler recommends that the psychometric element of the SIP is followed up by an explicitly change-oriented conversation with the young person when discussing the results. When talking over the current self profile one might ask, 'So how did you get to be like this?' or 'When you are like that what is it that you do?' Then considering the portrayal of the preferred self one might ask, 'What do you think would be the advantages of changing or staying as you are?' or 'How might others treat you differently if you were to move in that direction?' Once young people have found a way to describe in ever thickening detail the person they would like to become, the focus of the therapeutic conversation can switch to strategy and support, for example, 'So what do you need to do to get from where you are to where you want to be?' and 'What can others do to help you on your way?'

Case examples

Butler employed a comparable process of negotiation in his sports psychology consultancy with Olympic boxers and their coaches (Butler and Hardy, 1992), and this athletic analogy can go down particularly well with boys. There is also some intriguing evidence about the rapid changes in the classroom performance of young people who under-achieve educationally once they develop the playful capacity to 'imagine you're clever' (Hartley, 1986). So providing children and adolescents with a commonly held conceptual framework can open up very personal avenues for individual development.

Theory

Kelly's definition of a group also suggests some therapeutic applications of the commonality corollary. Kelly characterized groups not as collections of people who were seen as similar by the world at large, but as collections of people who saw the world at large in similar ways. He therefore defined a group from the inside looking out rather than from the outside looking in. Medical diagnosis is an example of an externally defined group. Doctors categorize folk as suffering from particular diseases depending on the symptoms they report, so their patients are seen to belong to diagnostic groups such as diabetics or asthmatics. Kelly, by contrast, would define his groups not by the disease from which they all suffer but by the shared attitudes group members adopt towards their ill health. So some young people with asthma might share a preferred coping style whereby they seek to get fully informed about their condition in contrast to other sufferers who choose to remain in blissful ignorance (Fritz and Overhoiser, 1989). Some teenage cancer patients may welcome the close attention of their parents during the trials of treatment whereas others may sense that this closing of the family ranks constricts their space for autonomous experiment (Rolland, 1987).

Therapeutic practice

When young people who have taken part in group psychotherapy are asked what profited them most from their sessions together a frequent reply is the sense that they are not alone in their thoughts and feelings – others hold similar views. So self-help groups or peer-tutoring arrangements (where an older child helps a younger partner learn to understand his or her condition better) take advantage not just of the similar circumstances with which a cluster of children are confronted but also of the shared attitudes they are likely to adopt towards their predicament (Shute and Patton,

1990). When healthcare staff support ventures such as these they are also likely to begin to see the experience of illness through their young patients' eyes - which leads us seamlessly into the final section of the chapter.

The growth of sociality

Theory

The sociality corollary states that 'To the extent that one person construes the construction processes of another they may play a role in a social process involving the other person' (Kelly, 1955/1991, p. 95/p. 66).

This ability to read other people is not a capacity with which we are born though there are good reasons to imagine that being 'hard wired' with that potential has had a considerable evolutionary advantage for mankind as a social species. As children grow they tend to become progressively more skilled at 'putting themselves in another's shoes'. Their thinking is less ego-centric and their collaborative capabilities expand. However, this developmental trend is not universal. A few young people find trying to understand other people is a lifelong challenge while many more struggle to make headway in particular developmentally important relationships.

Theory of mind

Within the field of autism research there has been a great interest in the notion of 'theory of mind' as an explanatory model for the particular com-bination of social, cognitive and communication deficits that characterize the condition (Baron-Cohen et al., 2000). Theory of mind is defined as the capacity to infer the mental states of others and has been investigated by the use of scenarios in which children are asked to anticipate what certain characters in a story might be thinking in particular circumstances. For example, the tale might unfold along the following lines. A child finds what he thinks is a tube of Smarties. He picks it up and shakes the contents. Then he opens the tube to discover that it is in fact full of stones not choco-lates. He replaces the top on the tube and puts it back down again. Along comes another child who sees the same Smarties tube. What might he be thinking? Most (but not all) youngsters on the autistic spectrum fail to dis-tinguish between what they know and what the second child in the story knows and so suggest that the character in the story will not pursue any interest in the Smarties tube because it's full of stones. This inability to 'mind read' so convincingly displayed in experimental conditions also appears to have important practical implications in the everyday life of young people diagnosed with autism (Frith, Happe and Siddons, 1994). As

Kelly predicted, the capacity to construe the construction processes of others is central to successful social development (Badanes, Estevan and Bacete, 2000).

Autism is currently viewed as a predominantly social-cognitive disorder that has its neural origins in abnormal development of the dorsal medial-frontal cortex and anterior cingulate system (Mundy, 2003). Further evidence for this biological basis of theory of mind deficits comes from studies of young people who have sustained head injuries and subsequently lost previously acquired social competences. Again frontal lobe damage seems to have a critical effect on social competence and the capacity to see the world through others' eyes (Stuss and Knight, 2002).

It appears, therefore, that a small minority of unfortunate children have major neurological constraints on their ability to learn how to construe the construction processes of those with whom they live and interact. The majority of youngsters in contrast are not handicapped in this way. Is their development of social understanding just a straightforward process of brain maturation?

The sociocultural view of theory of mind development (Dunn, 1988) argues that appropriate life experiences are also necessary if children are to achieve their social potential. A rich environment in which the child experiences positive interactions with families and peers is held to promote the growth of interpersonal understanding (Badanes, Estevan and Bacete, 2000). Not all young people are able to benefit from such optimal training opportunities.

Bullying

There is an ongoing lively debate between child development theorists about whether school bullies should be best understood as oafish thugs with minimal social skills or Machiavellian psychopaths with an exquisite understanding of their victims' weaknesses (Arsenio and Lemerise, 2001; Sutton, Smith and Swettenham, 2001). It makes sense to differentiate between those whose aggression is reactive and defensive (for example, when responding to some imagined slight or threat) and those who planfully use violence for the material rewards it delivers. The former group of bullies probably misread others' intentions and may not be fully aware of the hurt their actions cause to fellow pupils. The latter group can be characterized as being well able to appreciate the pain they inflict on their victims but do it anyway. What light might the sociality corollary throw on this distinction?

A first thought is that Kelly chose to write about playing a role in a 'social process', not a pro-social process. So the capacity to construe the constructions of another can be used for selfish, rather than mutually satisfying ends. A military general might successfully anticipate the strategy of an enemy commander and so inflict a bloody defeat with great loss of life. Chess champions might become so expert at reading their opponents' plays that they win effortlessly. By this reading of the sociality corollary, war, sport and bullying are all social processes in which participants need to be competent mind readers. An alternative reading explores the conceptual differences between theory of mind and personal construct theory. Theory of mind is defined in exclusively cognitive terms as an inability to represent mental states. The autistic child is seen to struggle to work out how other people's thinking differs from his or her own. In contrast, Kelly was adamant that construing is more than a merely intellectual act. He saw emotion and cognition as indivisible. Construing the construction processes of another therefore requires that we appreciate how they feel as much as we understand how they think. So apparently socially skilled bullies are also handicapped in the range of social roles that they can play with other young people by the limited 'extent' to which they are able to empathize with the emotional experiences of their peers. Interestingly, cognitive-behavioural therapeutic interventions with adolescent sexual offenders also seek to promote this empathic appreciation of the victim's experience and challenge self-serving attributions ('she was asking for it') that allow perpetrators to remain cut off from the emotional suffering they have caused (Marshall, Anderson and Fernandez, 1999).

Friendship networks

There seems to be a universal 'like plays with like' principle that governs children's choice of friends. Generally speaking, girls play with girls, and boys play with boys. Black teenagers generally prefer to hang around with other black teenagers, rather than mix with white contemporaries and vice versa (Graham and Cohen, 1997). So from an early age opportunities for mutual understanding are missed and the seeds for a socially separated adult society are sown. Residential living arrangements remain racially segregated in broad terms and men are famously portrayed as living on a different planet from women (Gray, 2002). Schools in the UK have been exhorted to promote transcultural friendships between their pupils and well-intended anti-racist policy statements abound. Nonetheless, the separate clusters of children dotted across every playground bear testament to the continuing power of the 'like plays with like' rule of children's friendships. However, there are some exceptions and perhaps these young pioneers will be able to reveal how they have managed to break the mould. If we were to adapt Kelly's first principle and ask them the secret of their success what might they say? Maybe their replies would reflect the dynamics of a Kellian group in which the members shared a common perspective on the world (Erwin, 1985). Outsiders might note their different cultural backgrounds but the participants themselves would pride themselves on their shared attitude to schoolwork, football, rap music or whatever. Alternatively these pals might be well aware of the variability in their backgrounds and enjoy discovering the unexpected as their friendships deepen. *Vive la différence!* As the sociality corollary asserts, you do not need to share the same take on life with another person to do social business together. You do, however, need to understand and appreciate your different points of view. There is an intriguing experiment here just waiting to be conducted . . .

Therapeutic practice

Sociocultural approaches to theory of mind emphasize the ongoing learning that children acquire through everyday interactions with family and friends. Is there a place for the more orchestrated educational opportunities that formal psychotherapy provides in promoting children's ability to understand others and, in turn, be understood by others? Two independent developments in the fields of family therapy and care for children with profound learning difficulties hold particular promise in this regard.

Interviewing the internalized other

The Canadian family therapist Karl Tomm (1988) shares Ravenette's interest in the power of the well-phrased question and has devised an innovative way of inviting family members to try and see the world through each other's eyes that he called the Internalized Other Interview or IOI (Burnham, 2000). The format is engagingly simple. Two people who are perhaps struggling in their relationship – say a mother and her teenage daughter – are invited to swap identities for the course of a brief conversation lasting perhaps 20 minutes. The therapist checks that each party understands the exercise and proceeds to interview each person as if she were the other (mother becomes daughter and vice versa). So she might ask the Mum-as-Daughter about her taste in clothes or boys; her hopes for the future; or whether there is anything bothering her at the moment. Meanwhile the daughter herself listens in on the conversation (usually intently) but makes no comment. Once the initial interview is completed the therapist might ask the daughter what she thought of her mother's guesses. What answers were spot on? Where was she off beam and how? Then the roles are reversed and the Daughter-as-Mother is put in the hot seat. The questioning might turn its focus towards the pair's own relationship. What makes you feel most proud of your daughter? Did the two of you used to get on better than you do now? Again the mother listens attentively until the conversation closes, and she is invited to comment. Although IOI can sound like a psychological parlour game it has the potential to open up some highly fruitful discussion. Because the conversations are neither planned nor scripted, participants have to rely entirely on their ability to construe the construction processes of the other. What they don't know, they are obliged to imagine and guessing wrong may ultimately prove more helpful than guessing correctly. Tomm locates his ideas within the social constructionist tradition but they also map perfectly on to Kelly's sociality corollary.

Intensive interaction

Interviewing the internalized other takes advantage of our capacity to put our thoughts and feelings into words. However, children with profound learning disabilities have to negotiate their social worlds without that opportunity to exchange meanings with other people. In the UK the intensive interaction movement (Kellett and Nind, 2003) has sought to transfer the non-verbal communication styles that characterize mother and baby interaction to the relationship between young people with major learning difficulties and the adults who care for them such as teachers and classroom assistants. Staff are trained to 'mirror' the sounds and movements of the children and to strike up the kind of conversations that mothers have with their infants. For example, they might attribute communicative intention to a facial expression such as 'Oh you are pleased to see me, are you.' The young person hence receives a high dose of consistent, playful and intimate attention from a sympathetic adult who is determined to find a way of entering their world. This innovative approach has yet to be extensively evaluated but early qualitative studies report that staff can develop a fresh sense of communicating with those in their care at a much more personal level. Experiencing this level of empathic understanding tends to bring out our more altruistic instincts (Batson et al., 2002), which offers the promise of greater job satisfaction for the adult and a better quality of life for the child. The most satisfying outcome of these exchanges is when learning-disabled young people themselves initiate some form of contact by, for example, reaching out to touch their teacher and a pattern of two-way communication begins to be established. Intensive interaction probably has its intellectual origins in attachment theory but, again, seems to sit very comfortably alongside the sociality corollary for two reasons. Firstly, Kelly well understood the importance of pre-verbal and non-verbal construing in human relationships. Secondly, he appreciated the reciprocal nature of our most satisfying social exchanges. There may be some adolescents who are able to make sense of those with whom they live and work while remaining baffling enigmas to their friends and family (Jackson and Bannister, 1985) but the goal of most of our therapeutic interventions will be to enable young people to understand others and be understood themselves in return.

Conclusion

Although Kelly himself worked as a school psychologist at one stage of his career, personal construct theory has not been widely influential as an applied psychology in the care and treatment of children. This chapter represents my attempt to illustrate a few straightforward applications of PCP ideas with young people while also teasing the reader with a sense of the deep well of creative implications Kellian psychology offers to the imaginative clinician. What it cannot provide is an established evidence base for therapeutic practice grounded on large-scale empirical outcome research. Perhaps a first step along the important road of systematic evaluation of the effectiveness of personal construct interventions with children is more widespread reporting of carefully conducted single case studies (Green, 1997). Fortunately both Kelly's theoretical framework and the assessment methods that he pioneered (such as the repertory grid) seem singularly well suited to small-scale research of this nature.

CHAPTER TWENTY-ONE

Personal construct group work with troubled adolescents

DEBORAH TRUNECKOVA, LINDA L VINEY

In recent years there has been increasing interest in group work with adolescents. Group work has been found to be more effective than individual treatment (Tillitski, 1990), and has been found to be a critical aspect of any comprehensive psychological approach to troubled adolescents (Kalogerakis, 1996; Kymissis and Halperin, 1996; Malekoff, 1997; Pollock and Kymissis, 2001). The exploration of personal construct processes in adolescent group work and the implications of the helpful and unhelpful forces experienced by participants will be presented in this chapter, and case examples will illustrate these processes. The efficacy of this approach was investigated by measuring individual outcomes, participants' perceptions of the group work, and group members' evaluations of group processes. Our purpose in this account is to argue the usefulness of personal construct group work as an intervention for troubled adolescents attending school.

Theory

As a forward-looking rather than a reactive approach (Fransella and Dalton, 1990), personal construct theory states, through its fundamental postulate, that 'a person's processes are psychologically channelized by the ways in which he anticipates events' (Kelly, 1955/1991a, p. 47, p. 32). Personal construct psychology is concerned with 'making sense out of the ways in which people make sense of their world' of 'constructions about constructions' (Bannister and Fransella, 1986, p. 19). Construing is the process by which adolescents make sense of their world, as creative interpreters (Faidley and Leitner, 1993).

Adolescents are seen as having the capacity to make choices and invent new solutions and, in so doing, have the power to change the course of life events for themselves and for others. Forming a relationship based on an understanding with another (role relationship) is considered central to interpersonal relationships in personal construct theory. The integration of social with individual psychology makes the role relationship, according to Kelly (1955/1991a), more than a socially prescribed dialogue (Bannister and Fransella, 1986). When discussing the idea of 'role', Kelly pondered '. . . the notion of role that comes out of construct theory, I wonder if we might not develop the notion of man as a society composed of "empathic man" or "inquiring man"' (Bannister and Fransella, 1986, p. 34). For the adolescent, according to personal construct theory, physical, behavioural and social role constructs are increasingly replaced by personality constructs as they become relatively more important in construing role relationships (Duck and Spencer, 1972; Duck, 1973; RA Neimeyer and GJ Neimeyer, 1977; Lea, 1979; GJ Neimeyer and RA Neimeyer, 1981), constructions of others (Adams-Webber and Davidson, 1979), and in defining personal identity (Adams-Webber, Schwenker and Barbeau, 1972; Adams-Webber and Benjafield, 1976; Bannister and Agnew, 1976; Adams-Webber, 1977, 1978), and constructions of self (Bannister and Agnew, 1976; Sewell, Baldwin and Williams, 1998). In personal construct psychology, the concept of personality implies that adolescents are what they psychologically represent themselves to be (Kelly, 1955/1991a), that is, they are what they believe themselves to be. Kelly saw adolescents as creators and testers of their own hypotheses about themselves and others. Adolescents are anticipatory and not reactive beings.

Developing personal construct group work with adolescents

Personal construct group work with adults has proved to be useful with a wide range of clinical problems, and with clients of different ages (Winter, 1985b, 1992b, 1997; Viney, 1998). This form of group work with adolescents was first devised by Jackson (1992), who found that it fostered psychological change in adolescents with emotional and behavioural difficulties. Personal construct group work has been developed for troubled adolescents at school (Truneckova and Viney, 2001, 2002, 2003), and for adolescent offenders (Viney et al., 1999) and non-offenders (Viney et al., 1997). In an investigation of these offending/non-offender adolescents, personal construct group work was found to be effective in increasing maturational processes, such as industry and affinity, and in the reduction of immature modes of psychosocial functioning, especially uncertainty and anger (Viney, Henry and Campbell, 2001; Viney and Henry, 2002).

Therapeutic practice

A model of personal construct group work with troubled adolescents was developed, based on Kelly (1955/1991a/1991b). It proposes that the major roles of group processes are to encourage group members to make sense of each other, for them to establish what they have in common, and to form and develop interpersonal (role) relationships. The model also proposes that adolescent group work can be better understood in terms of the roles, functions and processes of peer groups. As adolescents are involved in the developmental task of identity formation, the peer grouping becomes the vehicle within which the processes of making sense and forming role relationships are played out repeatedly. The model also acknowledges the particular needs of adolescence, of adolescent experiments in independence, in risk-taking behaviour, in feelings of acceptance/non-acceptance, and in identity formations and the role they play in group processes.

The group work goals

The overall goal of the group work is to provide active encouragement and support to the troubled adolescents in order to help them adopt an attitude of enquiry, and from this base undertake experiments testing different ways by which they may meet their development needs. The working goals are developed from the six stages of group work outlined by Kelly (1955/1991b). Therapy groups are seen as passing through varying phases of development, and at each of these stages, Kelly (1955/1991b) considered different therapeutic approaches are needed. The specific group goals at each stages of group development are presented in Table 21.1.

Table 21.1 Goals for the group work

Stages of group development (Kelly, 1991a)	Therapeutic strategies
	1. To provide validation for the construing of each member
1.Initiation of mutual support to the group	2. To develop a sense of belonging
2.Initiation of primary role relationships	3. To develop a sense that others in the group understand
3.Initiation of mutual primary enterprises	4. To develop sufficient trust within the group to allow for the sharing of constructions

Table 21.1 contd.

Stages of group development (Kelly, 1991a)	Therapeutic strategies
4.Exploration of personal problems	5. To explore personal problems and begin to formulate hypotheses and to design experiments leading to change
5.Exploration of secondary roles	6. To explore the similarities and differences in both the group members and significant others outside the group
6.Exploration of secondary enterprises	7. To reconstrue ways of applying the group experiences to everyday situations
	8. To grow in self-validation and self-regard

Themes

Themes, developed for each session, promote exploration and experimentation directing the content and process of each session. The theme for each session is provided in Table 21.2.

Table 21.2 Themes for the sessions

Themes of Construction

Session1	The group/The group and me
Session 2	Advantages and disadvantages of getting close to people
Session 3	Times I feel I belong to my family and times I feel I do not belong My family and me/not me
Session 4	Feeling hurt by others Hurting the feelings of others
Session 5	Feeling angry and being understood Feeling angry and not being understood The different ways we feel angry and the different ways other people feel angry

Table 21.2 contd

Themes of Construction

Session 6	The ways I see myself and the ways others see me
Session 7	What I want in myself and what I do not want in myself
	The ways I am changing and the ways I am not changing
Session 8	Times I feel powerful and times I feel powerless
	Being in control and being out of control
	Ways I control others and ways others control me
Session 9	The meaning of the group
	The meaning of the group to me
Session 10	My experience in the group
	My experience after the group. How will I be different?
	Saying goodbye to the group

The group setting, sessions and structure

The group work was conducted for 10 sessions, of one-and-a-half hours' duration, in schools during school hours. Each group was closed, and its size ranged from four to eight adolescents. The personal construct group work used the Interpersonal Transaction Group format (Landfield and Rivers, 1975), a tested intervention (Rivers, Adams and Meyer, 1978; RA Neimeyer and GJ Neimeyer, 1983; RA Neimeyer, GJ Neimeyer and Landfield, 1983; RA Neimeyer, 1988b; Alexander, RA Neimeyer and Follette, 1991; Winter et al., 2005) with a structured format, structured events playing an important role in group work (Viney, 1996).

While following the guidelines defined by Landfield (1979), the group work structure for each session involves the following eight phases: the group statement, 'taking care of yourself', mood tag, dyadic interactions, the large group, group activity, mood tag and session evaluation. The structure is outlined below. The group statement encompasses the three superordinate constructions of listening, sharing and respecting (Landfield, 1979). It also provides the four rules of the group work: no side conversations are allowed, we must be kind to one another, no physical harm can occur to people or to the room, and when we meet as a group, we all sit together in a circle. The mood tag, developed by Landfield and Rivers (1975), involves group members writing on a self-adhesive paper tag, placed on their shirts, their name and how 'I feel/don't feel at the moment'. The procedure occurs at the beginning and end of sessions.

The themes of the dyadic or paired interactions, while introducing the theme for the session, also provide tools with which the adolescents can explore their meanings about this theme, and those of the other members. The group members are asked to choose a partner, and these pairings are rotated until each member has paired with every other member in the group. The tools involve activities such as discussion points, craft/art activities, worksheets and stories. Following the dyads, the group members come together as a large group in which discussion is supported by activities and role plays. This group encourages further elaboration of the theme by encouraging the members to experiment with other meanings and understandings of the theme, and to develop greater confidence and clarity in their meaning systems. This continuous process of elaboration and experimentation, in which meanings are opened up and clarified, encourages the adolescents not to get stuck in one way of viewing and reacting to the world, and invites them to be flexible, to experiment and to move on through a creative process of change, rather than through prescribed pathways. This large group is also designed to help adolescents' movement through cycles of sharing and understanding of themselves identified by Koch (1985): searching for shared meanings and their confirmation, the clarification of differences in personal meanings and their elaboration by the group members.

The group activity, within the large group, tests revisions in construing through physical activities involving tactile and emotional behaviours, such as the trust walk and family sculpture (Carrell, 1993). The activity also provides a medium for the group to offer support, by reaching out to different members through physical contact. After the second mood tag, the group members are asked to complete the session statement: 'How was today's session?' The adolescents are also asked to rate themselves on eight statements designed to reflect the eight group work goals.

The group work processes

The group work processes, following the guidelines provided by Landfield (1979), focus on the 'here and now' rather than taking an historical focus. These beliefs about working as a group are emphasized throughout the sessions:

- listening and sharing;
- talking about feelings and thoughts rather than acting them out in the group;
- sharing as much as each person chooses;
- listening actively and asking for clarification if needed but not questioning values or statements;

- everyone having their own points of view;
- everyone having their unique views of the world;
- in the group all are trying to understand how everyone else sees their worlds;
- needing to maintain confidentiality.

Working in personal construct groups with troubled adolescents

These experiences of personal construct group work with troubled adolescents provided many experiments in the psychological challenge of identity formation that significantly impact on the group processes. It is argued here that a therapeutic group intervention for such adolescents needs especially to rise to this challenge, and it is the depth of this acknowledgement that will determine the efficacy of the intervention.

The struggle for identity in the personal construct group work appeared to release both constructive and destructive experiences, that is, *helpful* and *unhelpful* forces. In the following account of the group processes, these experiences are described with particular emphasis on the unhelpful experiences. In the personal construct group, these experiences, helpful and unhelpful, are interrelated, and the growth and development of the group work depend on both of these being available in the group work. Helpful and unhelpful forces are bipolar or alternating meaning systems in group processes. In order to understand the helpful forces, it is necessary to understand something of the unhelpful forces.

The nature of the unhelpful forces in this group work are explored by using the concept of the anti-group (Nitsun, 1996). The anti-group is the range of group processes in which the negative experiences and emotions are directed at the *group*, rather than at the group members. The group is then seen as threatening by the members. Recognition and validation of the role of the anti-group with this type of group work has implications for the personal construct leader, as will be described shortly.

There has been a substantial body of writing on group cohesion but there has been very little beyond Bion's (1961) work to account for the instability or disruption experienced in groups (Hawkins, 1986). Nitsun (1996) observes that descriptions of group aggression are generally about aggression in the group in the form of anger, hostility or rivalry between *members,* and there has been very little about the notion of aggression towards the *group*. The general assumption is that the group is a safe, good place to be, and that any problems with it are within the individual members rather than the group itself. Aggression towards the group, Nitsun maintains, creates a problematic setting, triggering withdrawal or unhelpful behaviour ultimately intended to undermine the group. Nitsun sees the anti-group as occupying a complementary relationship with creative, change-seeking group forces. Nitsun sees this conflict between helpful and unhelpful as generative.

Case examples

During the early stages of the personal construct groups, anti-group behaviour begins when the level of anxiety and hostility increases. The unhelpful behaviours are expressed through aggressive comments, with either implicit or explicit sexual overtones, challenging the rules of the group work. When the adolescents' anxieties build, disparaging remarks increase in frequency and intensity. So do statements by the members about withdrawing from the group, keeping distance between themselves and the group, and 'them – not me'. These statements or actions are indiscriminately directed at other members or at the leaders. An overriding sense of distrust and lack of safety then develops. At times it is not possible to experiment with issues of trust and distrust without the anxiety of the adolescents becoming too great. Some members feel increasingly threatened, staring angrily at members describing personal events and experiences. Others then withdraw, choosing not to participate in group activities, such as the 'trust' exercises.

As the group work moves along, interpersonal interactions take precedence. Yalom (1970/1975/1995) has described interpersonal learning as probably the core 'curative factor' in group work. In these groups however, interpersonal learning also brings interpersonal threat. The adolescent is confronted with a basic dilemma: does he or she protect 'the self from the terror of invalidation by revealing less of oneself and lead an empty but safe existence or risk (and invariably also experience) the terror of invalidation to gain the richness and depth that life in a ROLE relationship can bestow' (Leitner, Faidley and Celentana, 2000, p. 176). This sense of threat develops from interpersonal experiences within the group, of rivalry, envy, dominance, criticism, rejection, scapegoating and hostility. When a member became angry after being teased, the members laughed, further communicating their dislike for this member and his differences. As the adolescents try to regain their sense of control, they lash out at the other group members, unleashing their feelings of hurt and anger. These feelings are expressed in the groups by the members being persistently sarcastic to each other, by cutting across the speech of other members, and through the personal verbal abuse of each other, again breaking the rules of the group work.

However, often the blame for this abuse is placed on the setting or group, rather than on the members themselves. This blaming of the group or setting takes the form of indiscriminate disruptive behaviour. The members confront any group talk and try to draw the attention of the group away and onto themselves. Members in one group grabbed at and held onto equipment, such as pens and paper, shouting '(they) did not care about anything or anyone.' This means, at times, the group has all of its members being disruptive for the 'sake of it'.

Troubled adolescents feel that the world in general disconfirms many of their views of it, especially about their identities. Most members described themselves to each other and to the group as 'the bad kids in the school'. So these adolescents are very vulnerable to similar experiences of disconfirmation while in the group. They therefore vent their anger and hostility on the group, seeking to destroy it rather than have their accounts of themselves further disconfirmed. One member was increasingly being very hurtful to other members and wanting to dominate. When other members protested, this member threatened a number of times to disrupt and break all the group rules, boasting that she could then be 'thrown out of the group'. For some members, experiences of disconfirmation in the group often follow the acceptance by most of the group of a member who has previously been scapegoated. These members then in turn feel disconfirmed, and anti-group behaviours follow. They then set out to disrupt the group activities, work against group work rules, and talk directly about wanting to 'destroy' or 'wreck' the group. One member, after being disruptive, challenged the leaders, saying they did not like him and the group. Responses from the leaders or members were savagely interrupted by this member shouting 'you don't like me'. He then continued denigrating the usefulness of the group and the value of the other members.

Often these adolescent groups create those anxieties they seek to allay. With the range of members and potential relationships, there is a constant need for the adolescents to differentiate themselves and others. The possibility of loss of identity evokes threat for some members, leading to hostile feelings, with the adolescents seeing the group as divided into 'good' and 'bad'. The 'bad' part in the group is often scapegoated, becoming that thing outside the group – school, parents and other adults. Then, they, as a group, condemn the school and authority figures, painting these figures as worse than themselves. The group, for example, was seen by some members as caring, while the school was said not to care about them. One member expressed it like this: '. . . the teachers can't be hurt but they hurt us', while in another group the scapegoating of the 'bad' part was forcefully stated as: '. . . we want the group because we can do what we like and shit on the school, which is shit, and nobody can touch us'.

While these processes have the power to weaken the group by increasing anxiety and concerns about safety, they also have the paradoxical effect of uniting the group against authority, such as school and parents. The 'other' in the process of differentiation becomes the authority of adults.

The anti-group can become a helpful force, allowing the adolescents to experiment with their feelings of conflict with the world. This process is seen in their attempts to work through separating self from other. It allows members to unite in their blaming of their parents and families for all things they 'haven't done'. Just as forcefully expressed were statements about how 'the school doesn't care about us so we don't need to care about them (school)'.

As the groups mature, there is generally a reduction in anti-group behaviour. There is greater trust and intimacy and a sense of safety. While the members felt 'uncared for' by the school, they talked about 'our group', wanting the group to continue, adding that they felt safe and valued in the group. Some members were able to articulate these experiences and feelings: 'it allows me to feel angry and show it and let off steam, get rid of my feelings', 'I can trust you (group)', and 'I don't get teased here and I can make friends'. And yet, with that sense of safety comes greater openness and potential for further confrontation and anti-group behaviour, as the adolescents experience the group cohesion and empathy as frustrating, and as difficult to understand and manage. Describing how he had trusted his group, one member then accused other members of breaking confidentiality, shouting 'I can't trust!', and he joined two others in disrupting the group discussion, breaking group rules.

When the groups are coming to an end, ambivalent feelings are expressed and the anxiety arising from this makes it difficult for the group members to work through them. These ambivalent feelings are probably no more apparent than when members in the groups are able to participate together in the group activities but unable to work together as a group during group discussion. The group experience becomes one of members pulling the group apart, while others are actively drawing it together. There is a sense of chaos as feelings about belonging and not belonging vacillate within the group, and within individual members. Anti-group behaviour is then acted out, making the termination of the group a difficult process with many ambivalent feelings still present.

Implications for the leaders of the anti-group

From a reflexive and credulous approach, the group leaders play a pivotal role by developing and maintaining role relationships between the members, between the members and leaders, and between the members and group. They need actively to support, by listening and confirmation, the process of experimenting and hypothesis testing by the adolescents in making new sense of what they feel is their 'good self' and their 'bad self'. Leaders need to be aware that this process of differentiation creates tensions of its own, with the anti-group behaviours, the unhelpful forces, tending to predominate over more positive behaviours, the helpful forces, as the adolescents struggle with these conflicts.

As these groups progress, there can be a suddenness, intensity and amplification of emotions, and these experiences can be disturbing and threatening to the role constructs of the leaders. Their leadership comes under constant invalidation during these sudden and intense changes in group emotions. The crucial integrating function of the leaders becomes one of pulling the group together. This requires the leaders to keep the whole group in mind (Nitsun, 1996), and not to side with any members. It is about making sense of the group as a whole, and the relationship every participant has to the group. Member-to-group relationships in the personal construct group travel through cycles of commonality and sociality, where cohesiveness is initially important, but as creativity of change grows, this is supplanted by more experiences of individuation and role relatedness.

At these stressful times in the groups there is also very strong pressure for the leaders to collude with the group in scapegoating another member, attempting to invalidate developing role relationships. The adolescents attack the leaders' authority through angry challenges, encouraging them to control or criticize an acting-out member and again attempting to invalidate the role relationships with that member. During these processes, the group draws together, seeking allegiance with the leaders by demanding that they do something to stop the disruptions, and blames them for letting it happen. It is necessary for the leaders to distinguish unhelpful from helpful expressions of hostility in order to maintain the role relationships, to identify the anti-group behaviour, to set limits to prevent abusive interactions taking place. After blaming the group for the discipline he received at school, a member then tried to occupy the complete attention of the leaders. When he felt he was unable to get this, he started interrupting and denigrating group discussion, with this anti-group behaviour escalating into angry sexual name calling, the member shouting: 'I want to destroy this (group).'

When such group processes occur, group leaders are apt to experience threat to core role constructs and to be confused about themselves and the group, often feeling powerless and impotent while struggling to contain their own feelings of threat and anger, as they try to keep the whole group in mind. Such challenges can arouse strong negative emotions in their counter-transferences. Winnicott (1949) has described how the hate in the counter-transference is a natural response to the demands made of the leaders, and owning such hatred is an essential part of the therapeutic process. A loosening of construing is needed to allow the leaders to make an elaborative choice in their response when role constructs are threatened.

Challenges to the authority of the leaders may also occur when the group believes that it is able to withstand and survive the confrontations. When the leaders are able to loosen and tighten their construing, the group construing is able to move through the creativity cycle. Within the groups, these confrontations, in the form of anti-group behaviours, are often personal attacks on the leaders, threats to core role constructs. Such attacks may begin with members revealing hurtful experiences where their core constructs have been threatened. In one group, this reaction followed a member discussing his hurtful and violent altercation with his brother. Then the leaders and the members were accused by the member of not caring about him and each other. In another group, a member angrily recounted how he had been recently disciplined at school, and then turned and blamed the leaders and the group for the punishment. On these occasions, the member continued to disrupt the group activity and process for the rest of the session. Such attacks were made possible because the group no longer felt so threatened. The members felt the group was confirmed, the threat to core role constructs had diminished. They also felt the leaders had the capacity to impose limits, cope with their anxiety and maintain role relationships, as anti-group behaviours were acted out.

The anti-group, the pole of the construction of alliance opposed to group cohesion, can become the barometer of group process by measuring the growth and development of the group. It can signal to the leaders whether a group process is a helpful or unhelpful force. The concept of the anti-group enables this group work to explore and elaborate these conflictual struggles of the adolescents and understand the role relationships within this context. It enables the group leaders to validate this struggle, and to offer experimental situations in which further useful meanings can be gained. Importantly, as a clinical process, it allows the leaders to maintain or re-establish the therapeutic distance (Leitner, 1995) in the adolescent group when core role relationships are under threat. An understanding of the role of the anti-group in the group process can be confirming for the group leader, allowing a reduction of negative emotions in the counter-transference by providing a clinical framework in which to reconstrue the adolescents' hostility and maintain group alliance.

This personal construct approach provides a therapeutic practice able to connect the helpful and unhelpful forces in adolescent group work. It provides ways to translate into practice the processes of the anti-group. The emotional experiences of anxiety, threat, aggression and hostility, key players in the anti-group, are confirmed through the group work and well understood in this approach. This approach can provide the conceptual framework and the psychological skills for leaders to acknowledge and work with these emotions in the developmental task of identity formation.

Research

The evaluation undertaken to demonstrate the effectiveness of this group work will now be briefly described. A fuller presentation is available elsewhere (Truneckova and Viney, 2001, 2003). Seventy-six adolescents including 48 troubled adolescents (32 males, 16 females), aged between 12 years and 15 years (M = 13 years and 9 months, SD = 0.95) attending five government secondary schools in New South Wales, Australia took part in the research, along with their parents and teachers. The troubled adolescents were referred by Student Welfare Committees, which were responsible for their pastoral care. These adolescents were described by these committees as highly disruptive in the classroom, and often non-compliant and defiant in both the classroom and playground. Disciplinary actions taken by the schools were considered ineffective, making little impact on the troublesome behaviour. The adolescents were randomly assigned to a treatment ('group-work sample') or control ('control sample') condition, the offer being presented to both the adolescents and their parents as a 'positive way to make some helpful changes'. Three of the five group-work groups had two leaders, whereas, in the other two, there was only one. All leaders were trained psychologists employed as school counsellors with the Department of School Education. The first author was the principal leader for all groups, and was not deployed in any of the five schools.

In Strand 1, the group-work sample was compared with the control sample at the beginning (Time 1) and at the completion of the group work (Time 2). The main effect of personal construct group work on the overall measure of the number of interpersonal constructs was approaching significance (MANOVA) (multivariate $F(1,41) = 3.86$, $p = 0.056$) with medium effect size (Cohen, 1988) $d = 0.43$ on the repertory grid (Time 1, M = 7.50, SD = 3.77; Time 2, M = 9.12, SD = 3.90) and small to medium effect size $d = 0.39$ on the self-characterization (Time 1, M = 2.29, SD = 1.61; Time 2, M = 2.92, SD = 2.28). After the group work, these adolescents increased their use of interpersonal construing (see Figure 21.1). The effect of the group work on the overall rate of abstract constructs by the adolescents was found to be also approaching significance although not so strongly (MANOVA) (multivariate $F(1,41) = 3.04$, $p = 0.089$). There was a moderate effect size for both the repertory grid, $d = 0.47$ (Time 1, M = 8.79, SD = 3.98; Time 2, M = 10.65, SD = 4.71), and the self-characterization, $d = 0.5$ (Time 1, M = 4.71, SD = 2.42; Time 2, M = 5.92, SD = 2.51), with adolescents in the group work increasing their level of abstract construing (see Figure 21.2).

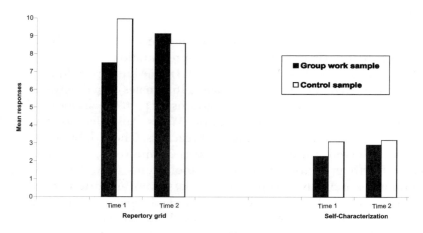

Figure 21.1 The mean responses rated as interpersonal construing in the group work and control samples on the repertory grid and self-characterization.

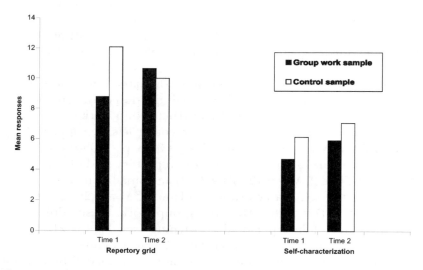

Figure 21.2 The mean responses rated as abstract construing in the group work and control samples on the repertory grid and self-characterization.

Positive changes in behaviour at school and home (see Figure 21.3) were also found for the group-work sample. A significant main effect of treatment was found on the behavioural measures, Conners' Parent Rating Scale-48 (CPRS-48) and Conners' Teacher Rating Scale-39 (CTRS-39), (MANOVA) (multivariate $F(1,39) = 4.45$, $p < 0.05$) approaching medium

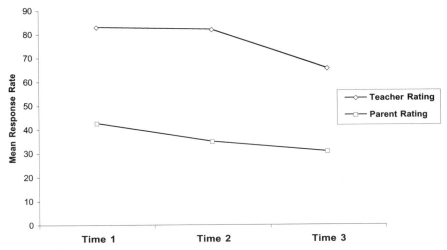

Figure 21.3 The mean ratings of the Conners' parent rating scale-48 and the Conners' teacher rating scale-39 for the group work sample at Time 1, Time 2 and Time 3.

effect size d = 0.4 (CPRS-48) and d = 0.43 (CTRS-39). There were reported decreases in negative behaviours between Time 1 (CTRS-39: M = 83.04, SD = 34.58/CPRS-48: M = 42.46, SD = 19.17) and Time 3, 12 months later (CTRS-39: M = 65.46, SD = 34.86/CPRS-48: M = 30.80, SD = 20.14).

In Strand 2, there was support for the hypothesis that group work would be perceived as effective by the participants: the adolescents, their parents and teachers. There were also reports from the group members at the end of the group work that they felt better understood, more valued, and more willing to experiment with change (Strand 3).

However, although these results are encouraging, they need to be considered in the light of a number of design problems identified in the project. For example, pre-treatment differences of the contrast samples question the representativeness of the samples and limit the power and generalization of the results. Contrast samples now more commonly involve an alternative treatment. Further, a system developed for the content analyses of responses to the repertory grids and self-characterizations remains untested beyond this research.

There are also questions about whether the tools designed for this research were able to maintain the integrity of the participants' meanings (Strand 2). The tools (Strand 3) used to measure the changes in group processes are untested beyond this research, and while hopefully valuable tools, can, however, only provide a window into the meanings of the group processes from the members' and the leaders' perspectives. These tools have tried to quantify very fluid multidimensional processes occurring between and within the members in the group.

Conclusions

Rather than a deficit-based approach (Murphy, 2000), the group processes in our personal construct group work encourage the adolescents to develop a reflective awareness of themselves and others, and to form relationships. These relationships then provide supportive structures for experimentation, allowing the adolescents to generate and facilitate their own self-healing capacities.

In the light of our group work experiences, what would we do differently? A short-term intervention of 10 sessions appears to be too brief for these adolescents. More sessions would allow greater depth and breadth in the experimental processes. We also judged that the rotating dyads, an integral part of the interpersonal transaction format (Landfield and Rivers, 1975), were possibly not as effective with troubled adolescents in promoting trust and intimacy as has been reported with adults (Alexander, RA Neimeyer and Follette, 1991). These adolescents with their fledgling identities felt at times overwhelmed by close relationships with members, and were more comfortable in the larger groupings, retreating from role relationships (Leitner, Faidley and Celentana, 2000). Rather than the dyads, small groupings of three members may be more helpful.

Finally, while there are many more issues on which we would like to reflect, probably the most important development was understanding the bipolar construct, group alliance, where the anti-group forms one pole of the construct, the other pole being group cohesion, that sense of togetherness and the feeling of belonging. It provides a framework that we judge will promote better understanding of group processes with adolescents and lead to more effective therapeutic practice by group leaders of adolescent group work.

CHAPTER TWENTY-TWO

Towards a personal construct sex therapy

DAVID A WINTER

> I have carried out a full series of endocrine investigations and have found no cause for his reduced potency. He did not seem to like the idea of injections into the penile body as a solution to his problems and preferred to have a chat to you to see if anything could be done.

This referral letter demonstrates common features of clinicians' responses to psychosexual complaints: a tendency to view the complaint as a mechanical breakdown, and to apply a mechanistic, and often highly invasive, procedure even when there is no evident organic etiology; failure to consider clients' constructions of their situations, as in this physician's incredulity on finding that his client does not altogether welcome the idea of penile injections; and a view of psychotherapy as a last resort in treatment.

Extreme examples of this mechanistic approach are numerous. Inorgasmic women have been treated by surgically relocating the clitoris (Burt, 1977) and men with erectile problems by implanting a penile prosthesis (Small, 1983). Rowan, Howley and Nova (1962) tried to elicit ejaculation by an anal probe in 35 clients, only nine of whom had sought help for sexual complaints! None could tolerate the pain involved, but the authors, undeterred, suggest that the procedure be used under anaesthetic. Sobrero, Stearns and Blair (1965) applied an electrical vibrator to the penis, proudly noting that 'The device has been extensively used with more than 100 chronic schizophrenic patients, with about 80% success in cooperative patients' (Sobrero, Stearns and Blair, 1965, pp. 765–6). Moan and Heath (1972, p. 28) even describe how septal stimulation of the brain allowed a client to reach orgasm during intercourse with a prostitute 'despite the . . . encumbrance of the electrode wires'.

Such means of treating psychosexual disorders may appear far removed from psychological methods. However, mechanistic assumptions are apparent in many sex therapy approaches, which are also extraspective, the complaint being viewed in terms of constructs imposed by the clinician rather than from the client's perspective (Winter, 1988b). Such approaches tend to aim towards normative goals and may paradoxically, as a result, exacerbate the very performance anxieties that they see as central to the client's problems (Lazarus, 1980). By contrast, personal construct psychotherapy, which has only rarely been applied to sexual complaints, adopts a credulous attitude (Kelly, 1955/1991a), taking clients' constructions seriously.

Theory

Personal construct theory may at first sight seem of limited relevance to problems, such as psychosexual complaints, which have a bodily expression. However, as Epting and Prichard (1993, p. 51) note, 'It is not possible to have a disembodied construction of any aspect of one's life. Every construction has some bodily involvement, and every construction has the accompanying feeling that goes with that construction throughout the body.' Consider, for example, the constructions revealed by the repertory grids of two clients presenting with psychosexual problems. The grid completed by Jill, whose presenting complaint was lack of sexual desire, indicated that she contrasted herself with people who 'have libido', but are 'inconsiderate', 'unkind', and 'unconcerned about the family'. Her lack of libido therefore allowed her to view herself as kind. In the case of John, whose marriage of two years was unconsummated and who lost interest in sex therapy after some degree of penetration was achieved, his grid revealed that affection and sexual attraction were viewed as polar opposites. Therefore, feeling more sexually attracted to his wife would have involved feeling less affectionate towards her. In both these cases, the bodily feelings going along with the clients' constructions seemed evident.

Clients such as Jill and John anticipate that if they were to lose their sexual problems, they might relate to others very differently from their core role. In personal construct theory terms, this experience is one of guilt, the avoidance of which may therefore be central to resistance to sex therapy. Also central may be the threat that therapy could fundamentally change core constructs, or the anxiety induced by confronting largely unconstruable events. One such event may be successful sexual performance, particularly if a 'way of life' (Fransella, 1970) has been built around the sexual problem. For example, Apfelbaum (1980) describes a retarded ejaculator who advertised as a 'stud' in contact magazines and whose resistance to therapy may have reflected a choice to continue this way of life. Even if an alternative way of life seems available, this may be an idealistic fantasy that can only be maintained if change is resisted. Thus, couples who believe that their relationship would be ideal if only they achieved perfect sexual functioning often drop out of sex therapy, so avoiding test-ing out their fantasies (Arentewicz and Schmidt, 1983).

The frequency with which behavioural sex therapy techniques produce resistance to change has also been noted by LoPiccolo (1992, 1994). He considers that such 'first generation' techniques are likely to be inappro-priate for, and ineffective with, clients of today, whose problems are likely to have a more complex etiology than 'simple negative attitudes, lack of information and sexual skill deficits' (LoPiccolo, 1994, p. 6). Instead, he calls for a post-modern approach to sex therapy, which recognizes that clients' sexual problems have an adaptive value for them.

In their 'holonic sex therapy', Zumaya, Bridges and Rubio (1999) have attempted to integrate personal construct theory with the notion that par-ticular 'holons' are central to human sexuality, namely gender, eroticism, interpersonal bonding and reproductivity. Holons are considered by Zumaya et al. (1999, p. 187) to be 'those parts of a larger system that have sufficient complexity in their internal organization to be considered as wholes in and by themselves', and sexual holons to be 'the result of the development and integration of constructs resulting from the experiences that the biological component of the holon leads us to have' (Zumaya et al., 1999, p. 188). Characteristics of clusters of holons that may lead to sexual difficulties include 'integration with conflict', in which there is conflict within or between holons; 'centralized integration', in which one holon takes precedence over the others; and 'lack of integration', in which a holon is underdeveloped or disconnected from others. A case example provided by Zumaya et al. of Maria, a woman suffering from uterine pain, demonstrates all of these characteristics: conflict within the eroticism holon in that sexual arousal was construed as dirty; conflict between the eroticism and gender holons in that her construing of women as pure was incompatible with her feelings of sexual desire; centralized integration of the gender holon, reflected in a macho view of sexual activity, in her ex-partner; and lack of integation of the eroticism holon by Maria.

More recently, Sewell (2005) has mapped the sexual response cycle (Masters and Johnson, 1966) and the experience cycle, in which Kelly (1970a) portrayed the process of construing, onto each other. This allows him, for example, to equate sexual desire with formulation of, and invest-ment in, erotic anticipations and to equate orgasm with validation. Sexual dysfunctions are viewed as disruptions of the cycle.

Therapeutic practice

It follows from the personal construct theory view of psychosexual prob-lems that, in treating clients presenting such problems, the personal construct psychotherapist, rather than turning to sensate focus exercises, surrogate partners, blue movies or mechanical aids, will take care not to plunge them into sexual situations that involve acting in a way inconsistent with their core roles, which challenge core constructs, or that they are ill-equipped to predict. The therapist is likely initially to be concerned to identify the constructions and processes of construing that might underlie the presenting problem, and to this end may make use of formal personal construct assessment techniques such as laddering, Tschudi's (1977) ABC technique or the repertory grid. Amongst the variations on the latter which have been used to explore sexual problems are implications grids (Fransella, 1972); double dyad grids, in which the elements are relationships and the couple, as well as completing their own grid, also predict how their partner would have completed it (Ryle and Breen, 1972); and 'duo grids', in which a couple completes a grid together in addition to their own individual grids (Bannister and Bott, 1973). Following diagnostic assessment of the client's, or couple's, construct system, therapy will be technically eclectic, attempting to facilitate reconstruction by employing techniques selected on the basis of this assessment. These may specifically focus on the sexual problem or, if a couple are being seen together, more generally on their relationship (GJ Neimeyer, 1985; RA Neimeyer and GJ Neimeyer, 1985).

In 'post-modern sex therapy' (LoPiccolo, 1992), there is an emphasis on the positive aspects of the sexual problem for the client, which are explored by means of a functional analysis focusing on the systemic homeostasis of the couple; individual psychodynamic issues; unresolved issues from the family of origin; and external rewards. In addition to direct work on the presenting problem, alternative means are then sought to meet the needs served by the problem. In 'holonic sex therapy' (Zumaya, Bridges and Rubio, 1999), there is also a concern with both the sexual and non-sexual aspects of a couple's relationship, with the focus on understanding of the sexual meaning structures underlying their sexual difficulties. Mapping of these 'holonic' structures, coupled with the use of Kelly's diagnostic constructs, allows the development of a treatment strategy (Bridges and RA Neimeyer, 2005).

The principal feature of the personal construct psychotherapy approach to psychosexual problems, as described by Sewell (2005), is that it 'must replace the tacit construction of problematic sexuality with effortful elaboration and verbally narrated reconstruction of sexual experience as well as the relationship in which it is anticipated and enacted' (p. 10). To illustrate this approach, he describes how sexual performance anxiety can be treated by helping clients to reconstrue sexual situations as involving experimentation and play; to elaborate their range of erotic cues; and to reconstrue the experience of anxiety, for example, as sexually arousing.

Case examples

Stanley, aged 25, complained of erectile difficulties of 4 years' duration. A repertory grid indicated that he imagined that without these difficulties he would be less like his ideal self, for example, less honest and lovable. It also provided a clue to the origin of his negative construal of sexuality, in that he imagined that recovery of his erection would make him similar to his father. He described how, as a child, his view of his father as very moral was invalidated by seeing him flirting with women. Another contrast that he had experienced was between times when his father was 'hard' and unloving and those when he was 'soft and malleable'. It seemed that Stanley might now be expressing this contrast in the state of his penis. Time-binding (Kelly, 1955/1991b) was employed, constructs once applied to his father's behaviour being 'bound' to these events but seen as obsolete in anticipating current events. After six therapy sessions, he reported that he was again obtaining an erection. A second grid revealed a much more favourable construal of the self without sexual problems and of sexual attractiveness.

Rodney, aged 35, presented with an inability to ejaculate. A bipolar implications grid (Fransella, 1972) indicated that sexual responsiveness implied game playing and deceptiveness (see Figure 22.1). As with Stanley, these constructions of sexuality seemed to derive from early experiences, in his case of a hypochondriacal mother. He now construed many of her childhood demands on him as sexual, and remembered that her approach to sex education had been to suggest that he sleep with her. Also significant, given his particular sexual problem, was his recollection that she espoused the principles that 'you yourself must always come last' and 'do everything for others but do not love yourself'.

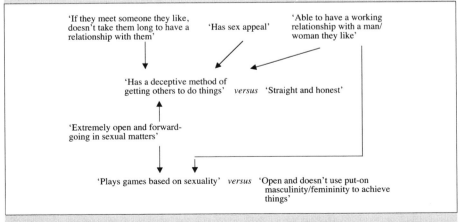

Figure 22.1 Implications of sexual responsiveness in Rodney's pre-treatment implications grid.

Rodney had coped with confusion concerning sexuality by constricting his field of awareness to exclude sexual experiences; as he put it, he had 'dismissed thinking about it'. Therefore, an aim of therapy was to elaborate his construing of, and reduce the anxiety caused by, his sexual responses. He was asked to:

- keep a daily record of the frequency, and degree of pleasure associated with, his sexual urges;
- complete a repertory grid with sexual situations as elements; and
- carry out homework tasks to enhance his awareness of pleasurable bodily situations.

The grid indicated that he construed masturbation as 'tedious', and situations that he 'desired to achieve' as associated with fear and avoidance. Ratings of the degree of cognitive anxiety (Viney and Westbrook, 1976) expressed by him in each therapy session demonstrated that when he described events as unpredictable, he reported significantly fewer sexual urges the following week, perhaps again reflecting the use of a constrictive strategy to limit anxiety.

After 3 months of therapy, Rodney dreamed that he tore off his penis and replaced it with a new one. Two weeks later, he masturbated to orgasm for the first time. A second sexual situations grid (see Table 22.1) indicated that tedium and fear were no longer central to his view of sexual experiences, the variation accounted for by these constructs being much reduced; and a second implications grid (see Figure 22.2) revealed that sexual responsiveness no longer necessarily carried negative implications.

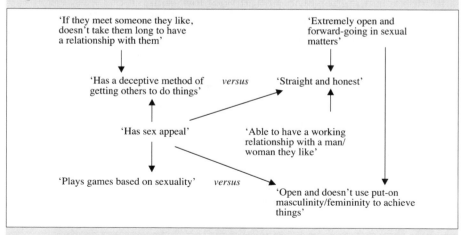

Figure 22.2 Implications of sexual responsiveness in Rodney's post-treatment implications grid.

Table 22.1 Changes in scores on Rodney's sexual situations grid during therapy

	Assessments	
	1	2
Construct correlations		
'afraid of' – 'desire to achieve'	0.61	0.17
'makes me uneasy' – 'desire to achieve'	0.80	0.21
'would feel unreal' – 'desire to achieve'	0.82	0.09
Element – construct relationships (cosines)		
masturbation – 'rewarding'	−0.78	0.14
masturbation – 'tedious'	0.73	−0.17
orgasm during masturbation – 'rewarding'	−0.41	0.34
orgasm during masturbation – 'tedious'	0.80	−0.46
orgasm during intercourse – 'afraid of'	0.61	−0.25
orgasm during intercourse – 'I shy away from'	0.82	0.01
orgasm during intercourse – 'makes me uneasy'	0.80	−0.28
orgasm during intercourse – 'would feel unreal'	0.85	−0.30
% variation		
'tedious – not tedious'	6.31	1.28
'afraid of – not afraid of'	10.65	6.52

Jim, aged 42, presented the rare problem of ejaculating with no sensation of orgasm, and consequently felt unable to contemplate a long-term relationship with a woman. His repertory grid showed that he construed people who are 'able to feel fulfilled sexually' as 'uncertain about how to do their work', having a 'male chauvinist pig sense of humour', and 'not good managers'. Exploring these implications of sexual fulfilment, we discussed how he resisted the seemingly innocuous fantasies that he required for his own fulfilment because he viewed them as demeaning towards women. With a girlfriend's encouragement, he gradually dilated his field of experience to experiment with these fantasies, although characteristically the book that, after much deliberation, he bought to aid this experimentation was not a 'girlie' magazine but a volume of Japanese prints. In allowing him to adopt a strategy consistent with his core role rather than bombarding him with sexually explicit material, I attempted to minimize the guilt that he might experience in therapy. Jim was also eager to talk about his childhood experiences, and, in an account of the most significant features of therapy, he wrote: 'I had failed to realise how strong the example of my parents' relationship-in-action was in the way I behave with members of the opposite sex.' Although such considerations may seem more characteristic of psychodynamic than of personal construct psychotherapy, Kelly (1955/1991a) noted that children who cannot understand the relationship between their parents may fail to elaborate a clear construction of their own relationships with the opposite sex. Jim also writes that 'I have in the last few months started to accept my own sexuality, I've been able to be a bit more selfish and achieve more enjoyable ejaculations'. He has also married. A second grid showed that sexual fulfilment and attractiveness no longer carry negative implications for him.

In the case of Maria, who was described above to illustrate the holonic approach, care was taken not to employ therapeutic techniques that might provoke the threat likely to be associated with a too rapid development of a sexualized identity. The use of repertory grid technique allowed her and her partner to explore their constructions of their relationship and those of other couples. Finally, dilation of her gender holon was attempted by referral to a women's awareness group.

Research

There are no research investigations of personal construct sex therapy apart from single case studies, such as those presented above, which have demonstrated reconstruing during therapy. While changes in construing have also been revealed by repertory grid technique during behavioural sex therapy (Burns, Hunter and Lieberman, 1980), such changes may on occasion be of dubious value. For example, Bannister (1965b) described a woman receiving therapy designed to desensitize her to sexual intercourse, whose grid results indicated that she reconstrued sex as good and weak rather than bad and powerful, but as a result found intercourse 'no longer . . . actively repugnant but merely acceptable and uninteresting' (Bannister, 1965b, pp. 980–1).

Behavioural sex therapy has been found to be less effective than was originally reported (Zilbergeld and Killmann, 1984), whereas there has been some evidence of the effectiveness of a post-modern approach to sex therapy (Schover and LoPiccolo, 1982).

Conclusions

The limited previous use of personal construct theory approaches with psychosexual disorders may reflect a misconception of the theory as cognitive, individually oriented, and unconcerned with the person's history. As we have seen, however, personal construct sex therapy may incorporate behavioural experiments, explorations of the early origins of clients' constructs and of their somatic expression, consideration of emotions and analysis of clients' construing of their partners' constructions. Its holistic position therefore makes personal construct psychotherapy ideally suited for the treatment of psychosexual disorders, and its technical eclecticism allows it to combine techniques on the basis of a consistent theory rather than, as in many sex therapy approaches (for example, Kaplan, 1974; Lazarus, 1980), mixing theoretical models.

CHAPTER TWENTY-THREE

Looking forward towards the end – working with older people

SALLY ROBBINS

Theory

George Kelly's (1955/1991a/1991b) original exposition of personal construct psychology did not concentrate on older people as a separate client group. The theory is universal, applying to people, both therapists and clients, young and old alike. Previously (Robbins, 1993), I have argued that the fundamental postulate itself makes personal construct psychology particularly appropriate for working with older people. The fundamental postulate states: 'a person's processes are psychologically channelized by the ways in which he anticipates events' (Kelly 1955/1991, p. 46/ p. 32).

The image conjured up by Kelly's use of the word 'channelized' in the fundamental postulate is one of movement along personally created channels, or perhaps we might see them as ruts. Most of us have some sense of continuity in our life course, of one phase leading to another. Looking back over a long life one can often discern these channels reaching far back into the past, and for unhappy people seeking therapy they can easily appear as ruts, impeding their attempts to change. Kelly's (1969e, p. 275) description of personal construct psychology as one that 'will turn its attention to man's plastic future rather than to his fateful past' speaks directly to the situation of older people. This emphasis on anticipation rather than looking back means that the amount of past need not be an impediment to change.

Moving on from the fundamental postulate, Ellis and Scheer (1995) identify six of Kelly's original corollaries as having particular relevance for older people. They suggest that the key questions for construing old age are:

- How does a person construe being old? (Construction corollary.)
- How does an old person construe his or her (obviously limited) future? (Construction corollary.)
- How do old persons handle their choices? (Choice corollary.)

- How does the enormous amount of experience influence the construing by old persons? (Experience corollary.)
- How do older persons cope with the changes inevitable in life? (Modulation corollary.)
- How do older persons cope with the diversities and contradictions in life? (Fragmentation corollary.)
- Does equal experience make people similar? (Commonality corollary.)

Thus we can see aspects of the original personal construct psychology theory that merit particular attention when working with older people.

The theory of personal construct psychology as applied to older people was extended greatly by Viney (1993a). Her monograph took a large body of clinical experience with older people and drew from it a number of guidelines and conclusions. The central theme is the notion that older people's stories can be seen as lying on a dimension 'relatively self-limiting – self-empowering'. Through story retelling older people can develop and elaborate their stories to become nearer the 'self-empowering' pole. Viney identifies four common areas of transition for older people that require reconstruing: bodily related changes, self-related changes, interpersonal losses, and changes in social roles. Ways of understanding the effects of the person's construing, as reflected in their life stories, are examined. There are extensive descriptions of the ways in which the stories can then be helped to change, particularly through loosening and tightening.

A relatively recent addition to the theory of personal construct psychology with older people has been an interest in understanding dementia. This work is also relevant to an unfortunate number of younger people, but problems of persistent cognitive deficits become much more frequent with age. Kelly (1955/1991b, pp. 924–6/pp. 256–8) had already presaged this with his 'well documented facts' about 'conditions of organic deficit'. He first said that 'in cases of organic deterioration or injury some broad types of psychological functions are disturbed more than others.' He identified a 'greater loss of memory for recent events' as opposed to relatively preserved vocabulary and certain language skills, even after sharp impairment of problem solving, and 'retention of certain formalised social skills long after social sensitivity has been blunted'. He further noted that 'the physiologically handicapped person tends to constrict his field of spontaneous elaboration' and linked this to rigidity, perseveration and general ineptitude in changing the course of one's thinking.

Kelly (1995/1991b, pp. 924/257) described the task of the 'organically deteriorated person' as reconstruing himself 'in a constricted world, using as his point of departure the constructs which were once richly documented, and gradually substituting them for constructs dealing with new content and with new and limited ranges of convenience.' Conversely, the therapist was to help the client to develop 'constructs that will bridge the past, the present, and the future, even though, for this particular client, the events of these periods may seem markedly different from each other'. He told us firmly:

> The life role must be firmly established . . . It is extremely important that the significance of his earlier life be carefully preserved and enhanced. The therapist must help him to see his life role as something far more than the little daily orbit that he taps out with his cane. (Kelly, 1955/1996b, pp. 925/257)

Essentially, we have Kelly stating the essence of Kitwood's (1996) personhood approach long before the word was coined and the idea became popular.

Morris (2001) suggested that personal construct psychology provides an appropriate framework for understanding dementia because it gives 'a model of the person that can be applied equally to the person with dementia at all stages of the disease; family and formal caregivers; and you and me.' She considers that the framework is also able 'to describe the process of therapy' and to integrate 'the eclectic influences of the cultural revolution in dementia care'.

Robbins and Bender (2001) attempted to develop further a personal construct psychology understanding of dementia by considering the things people said to them when referred because of memory problems and dementia. They identified eight clusters of problems that people reported, such as failing to remember messages and instructions or putting things in very odd places. Reviewing how these seem to operate led them to conclude that a number of changes in the ways in which the person's construct system operates are likely to underlie the observable symptoms. Generally the construing tended to show more looseness, to use less permeable constructs and to be characterized by constriction. They describe the experiences of one particular client in detail, to illustrate how these changes in construing might interact in one individual.

Finally Morris (2004) brings these theoretical advances up to date by giving an overview of the contribution personal construct psychology can make to the care of people with dementia, looking both at theory and at practical applications.

Dalton's (1985, 1992) work on amnesia is also particularly relevant here. Although she was not writing about older people as such, she gave insights into the effect of memory loss on day-to-day life and on personal construing. She noted a continual effort after meaning, which can lead to the sort of reconstructed memories that become written off as 'confabulation'. Amnesic people have large gaps in their accessible memories, which make it difficult to anticipate events in the future as well as to remember those in the past. How can you attempt to anticipate a holiday, for example, if you cannot remember previous ones? Dalton observes that constriction of the perceptual field is a common way of trying to cope with this, and that amnesic people are understandably anxious about future events they cannot construe. Finally, she notes there is often an intensification of feeling about things that can be construed, which might easily be dismissed as 'emotional incontinence' in many medical and care settings. Her advice to those who work with people with amnesia is to respect the person and adopt a credulous approach.

Therapeutic practice

Therapeutic work with older people differs from such work with younger people along three main axes, which I will go on to consider in turn. The axes deal with practical, often physical issues, life-experience issues, and life-stage issues respectively. Both therapists in training and more experienced colleagues frequently express worries about working with older people that they do not feel when contemplating work with other client groups. Viney (1993a, pp.177–87) addressed some of these concerns in her chapter on the stories that therapists tell about older people. Fundamentally, the personal construct solution to these difficulties lies in combining the reflexivity central to the theory with the sociality corollary. We pay attention to our own construing in the same ways that we approach the client's. We also try to understand their construing so as to play a useful role with them. Just as the older people need to elaborate and change their construing to make it more useful, so do the therapists.

Practical considerations

The first axis, concerning practical, often physical considerations, involves things that are often fairly simple objectively but have both subtle and far reaching effects. Older people commonly have hearing problems, for example, and our work with them needs to have sensitivity to this possibility built in. We might find it difficult to achieve an appropriate tone to the therapy if we have to speak loudly all the time, for example, and we might need to work on ways of combining a loud tone with other cues. Older people are also more likely than younger clients to have bodily aches and pains, or concomitant medications, which can make it more difficult to concentrate for long periods of time, or to sit still in lengthy therapy sessions. This affects session length, which in turn poses issues of how to work at sufficient depth and concentration while still preserving the necessary opening and closing phases of therapy sessions. Older people may have mobility problems, which raises the question of whether to offer home-based therapy more frequently with this client group than with a younger client group. If we do work at home we are then open to a wider range of influences than if we stay in the office. We may be interrupted and inspected by family, neighbours or postmen, for example. Physical realities can easily intrude on a home visit. If you arrive at a house and smell a gas leak or find the heating broken, for example, the session is instantly catapulted into the practical realm. The opportunities to move into a more social role are more extensive in the client's home because of the contextual cues around. With home visits the issue of being on time for sessions shifts from being mostly the client's responsibility to being mostly the therapist's. Some of these practical considerations can be addressed by some aggressive elaboration on the part of the therapist. Learning more about the experience of deafness, for example, or of some other physical ailment will help to guide the therapist towards greater sociality with the client. A credulous approach will enable the right adjustments to be made to the therapist's approach by tailoring them to the client's own experience.

Life-experience issues

The second axis for therapeutic consideration involves life-experience issues that will influence the content, if not the process, of therapy. We may worry that the age gap between us and the clients is so great that we cannot hope to build a therapeutic relationship. As therapists we need to be careful to reflect a proper respect for the diverse life experiences of older people and how these differ from our own lives. Although it is now rare to work with someone who remembers the First World War, the privations of the 1930s, the trauma and upheaval of the Second World War, and the challenges of societal change in the last half of the last century are a common context for their stories. Here the personal construct therapist's interest in teasing out similarities and differences to understand personal meaning can come fully into play. Most older clients are fully retired from work and have had to adjust to the different demands and roles this brings. Many will have been bereaved of close family or life partners. Quite commonly they will themselves be struggling with life-threatening diseases, and it is common for the course of therapy to be interrupted or altered by a physical health crisis. Quite sensibly, many of these people will want and need to discuss and review existential issues with their therapist and some of them will have a very real sense of the imminence of death, which will need to be addressed. The extent of the differences in life experience between the therapist and client can lead to doubt on both sides about whether there can be a strong enough therapeutic alliance to work with. Older people are likely to forgive our lack of common experience and trust us to work with them if we show that we can grasp the essence of their construing and treat our differences with respectful curiosity. Personal construct techniques such as the self-characterization, the repertory grid and more recent inventions such as Drawing the Ideal Self (Moran, 2001) give us structured ways of doing this, as will be illustrated below.

Effecting change

The third axis for consideration concerns the perceived challenges for both therapist and client of trying to effect change at this stage of life. Commonly therapists who work with older people have concerns in this area. There are several different but related strands involved, which we will consider in turn.

First, therapists fear that older people have too much past and not enough future either to develop change through therapy or to live out the changes afterwards. It can seem that there is not enough to occasion hope for the future because there is not enough future left. A related concern is about how people will make sense of their past if they change things now; will they regret not changing before? The personal construct psychology emphasis on the future helps us to escape from this therapeutic nihilism, as I have argued before (Robbins, 1993). Kelly's (1955/1991a, p. 15/p. 11) famous quote 'No one needs to paint himself into a corner; no one needs to be completely hemmed in by circumstances; no one needs to be the victim of his biography' addresses these concerns directly. Part of developing and then choosing a way out of one's personal 'corner' is concerned with making sense of past choices, and making some sort of peace with them.

Second, colleagues worry that the whole enterprise of therapy with older people will be so dominated by loss and death that it will be impossible to stimulate healthy growth and exploration. Perhaps this reflects a lack of developed construing about loss and death on the part of the therapist. Personal growth following loss and bereavement is common, but as therapists we need to be able to grasp the issues with clients and to risk feeling some of their pain and despair along the way. This might be seen as another facet of the 'terror' of therapy described by Leitner (1988).

Third, therapists sometimes fear that they will become so bogged down learning about the life that preceded the therapy that it will be impossible to work on current issues. Conversely we might choose to concentrate on the present and then appear crass and uncaring because we ignore the past. Like many things in therapy, the art is to obtain a balance that allows movement from one area to another, elaborating our constructions as we go. Viney (1993a, 1995) has written extensively on reminiscence as a framework for reconstruing with older people. She describes their stories as coherent construct systems that serve to develop and maintain identity, give guidance on how to live, place an order on events and cast the tellers in an active role as they tell their tale. In her 1995 paper she goes on to note the relative dearth of media stories about active older people, which might suggest that their need to tell their own stories might be all the more important. In the paper she gives three illustrative examples of reminiscence-based therapy in which the judicious validation and invalidation of aspects of the clients' stories helps towards healthy reconstruction.

Kelly talks about cycles of experience and creativity, and in the same way issues of the past and of the present need to alternate in a cyclical manner, as the construing linked to them comes under scrutiny in therapy. Techniques aimed at articulating core construing help with this, because they are linked to both past and present experience. Through using something like a self-characterization we can often strike the right balance.

Case examples

Anita's work with me provides a simple example of how a personal construct approach, in this case particularly exemplified by the self-characterization, can help the therapy to keep on track with an older person. For the therapist, the two main problem areas with Anita could be seen first as creating a useful focus for improvement in the midst of multiple problem areas, and second as keeping the focus despite the illness and then death of Anita's husband during the therapy. These refer back to the first and third axes outlined above, with perhaps some second axis issues around the husband's illness. The initial referral suggested work around anxiety and depression. Anita found it very difficult to go out alone and she felt miserable about her life and her relationships. As she told her story it became apparent that she had also felt unwanted and unpopular as a child, that she felt dominated by her husband and that her relationship with her only child was often tense and strained. She had learned some behavioural anxiety management techniques with a local charity, and was able to use these to some extent to guide her actions and gain a sense of self-control. The larger issues, how to manage her relationships and how to understand herself in relation to her history, remained. Her husband's death intensified her anxieties about coping with everyday life alone and brought overwhelming feelings of guilt about their relationship. It would have been easy to become bogged down in any one of these areas and deflected from the work we still agreed needed doing.

The introduction of a current self-characterization and of one for two years' time provided a reference point to which we returned throughout our work together. Anita understood the change constructs that these two together created. They allowed us to identify more specific constructs about changes she wanted to make. The constructs we discussed from the self-characterizations included:

worrier .... placid (well adjusted, calm)
very anxious .... secure, in control of self
afraid of offending .... confident
(doormat, don't like to say no)

Anita felt that her understanding of herself in relationship to these constructs had shifted over the years. To a large extent her struggles with these issues were played out in day-to-day conversations. Through talking about these encounters we developed two constructs that served as a touchstone, encapsulating the sorts of changes she felt were desirable and possible:

hardly ever disagrees .... confident to put my point of view
readily talks to people .... very quiet and shy
(tongue runs away with me) .... (reserved, private)

At intervals while Anita worked through her grief and reworked her roles in life we would return to these two constructs to check where she was with them. This seemed to anchor the therapy and served to show both Anita and her therapist how she was doing with her central concerns.

In contrast to Anita, Julia's story is one of several phases of therapy, each linked with a particular personal construct guided intervention. The issues involved related largely to the third axis described above (the challenge of effecting change this late in life). Julia was referred for problems with depression and anxiety five years after her mother's death. She described herself as feeling tearful but unable to laugh or cry. Before seeing me Julia had worked for nine sessions with a counsellor. The referral came to me because he had 'tried everything' and thought Julia needed longer term and more in depth work. One of our early tasks was therefore to mark some difference between this new work and what had come before to avoid the danger of Julia's feeling that we were just repeating what had failed her before. The self-characterization was introduced in session one and completed by session two, a time scale distinctly faster than the norm for this.

The self-characterization yielded a number of emergent poles, which we went on to consider further in subsequent sessions, including 'salt of the earth', 'dead inside', 'blue-eyed girl', 'not a snob', and 'a knife sticking in her heart'. It emerged that during her childhood Julia had felt herself to be at the emergent end of the construct 'not loved by mother' as opposed to 'loved by mother', while her sister was at the opposite pole. During adulthood this had changed, as a great number of invalidating events occurred to make Julia reconstrue herself as much nearer her sister's position. After the mother's death Julia had found herself catapulted back to her childhood understanding of her relationship with her mother by being neglected in her mother's will.

In the early days a large proportion of each session was concerned with incidents and issues involving just Julia, her mother and her sister. It was hard to hear much about any other characters, and with one of the others dead and the third infrequently in contact there was little opportunity for Julia to experiment with her understanding of her relationships with her mother and sister and to elaborate her construing. In her understanding of life other people seemed to appear rather as 'film extras', part of the scene but rarely intimately involved. In order to dilate from this position Julia was asked to try a 'button sculpt' – to produce her family tree with each person represented by one or more buttons. Although this technique derives from family therapy practice and there is now a wide range of variants of this approach, the idea of using this with Julia was prompted by a personal construct understanding of what might prove a useful therapeutic task. The button sculpt was used in order to foster a non-verbal elaboration of her whole family network, in order to access a wider range of construing of her relationships and to encourage looser construing. It was hoped that this looser and broader style of construing could then be applied to her current predicament as she thought about her immediate family and relationships.

It seemed that Julia felt this change quite quickly. She arrived at the session, having done the button sculpt at home, saying she was 'starting to come to life a bit more'. She began to talk more readily about current relationships with a range of people and to examine different ways of understanding herself. One important construct from this phase of therapy was 'being a martyr' as opposed to 'being uncaring'.

Later in her therapy Julia was wrestling with how to frame her future, whether to keep her home or move in with her partner. It was difficult for her to sort out what to do because of the complexity and importance of the issues involved. It seemed that Finn Tschudi's (1977) ABC methodology might help to elucidate Julia's dilemma. Her work with this allowed her to articulate and then review her views. Having had such a shock over her mother's will, she was still mistrustful of her own judgement. After doing the ABC she announced at the next session that she had 'surprised herself'. She had made an offer to buy a smaller property nearer her partner. This would both remove most of the worries about upkeep that were pushing her to sell her home, and preserve an independent base, should sharing with her partner prove unwise. As she talked about this solution she was buzzing with plans for the new flat, which presented a great contrast to her manner in our early meetings. This spontaneous upsurge in creativity was welcomed by Julia and her therapist alike and was experienced as a great relief by Julia herself.

In all Julia had 20 sessions of personal construct psychotherapy – just over double the number of counselling sessions she had before. It seemed likely, from looking at the process and content of therapy, that it was the level of construing addressed during the therapy rather than the length of time involved that made the contrast between the two.

In the section on therapeutic approaches with older people reference was made to using a new technique introduced by Moran (2001). Moran's paper describes the process of 'drawing the ideal self' as promoting a collaborative approach between therapist and child and helping the child to become actively engaged in the dialogue. My interest in the technique came from attempts to extend the range of ways in which I can encourage tacit construing (RA Neimeyer, 1981) as a way of encouraging movement in therapy. Moran describes how readily children engage in drawing themselves. I suspected that this would not be as easy for older people, drawing on experiences working with an art therapy colleague. Our experiences suggest that some older people will be happy to draw and feel relaxed and confident with it but others are more anxious. Those who are more doubtful about drawing often say they are not good at it, or link the opportunity to some unfortunate experiences at school. The expectation that the client will draw readily therefore has to be adjusted with older people. In order to adapt this approach for use with older people the references to going to school were omitted from the instructions. This technique, with these minor adjustments, has proved a helpful way of engaging the central therapeutic issues of several older people. It provides an alternative approach for people who are not comfortable with writing and helps to explore and articulate non-verbal construing.

Jane was one such older person. Having had her education interrupted by evacuation during World War Two, she was less than keen to do any writing tasks. She had an interest in drawing, and had done some as a younger adult. When we started to work together her spontaneous thoughts on her life tended to use the same phrasing repeatedly, having been repeated to a large number of mental health professionals over the years. The way she talked led more easily to nosological categories of psychiatric diagnosis rather than to opportunities for active experimentation.

Using the 'drawing the ideal self' technique encouraged Jane to imagine how she did not want to be and to imagine her ideal self. She did not do much actual drawing but she was able to give a word sketch for each of the categories sampled by the technique. Her few sketches spoke volumes about the horror of becoming dependent and not caring about herself or her relatives any more. Her responses to the questions in Moran's technique revealed a range of rich constructions about her life and her aims that conventional therapeutic discussion had failed to reveal. This opened up avenues for exploration, which then served to guide the therapy in new directions.

Research

Although work with older people is by no means a popular area for personal construct psychology research there is a growing literature, particularly from Australia and Germany. The areas of enquiry can be loosely grouped as focusing on the experience of ageing and our attitudes towards ageing and the aged, or on more clinically related topics. This review of work is therefore organized into two sections.

Ageing experience and attitudes

Ellis and Scheer (1995) examined ideas about successful ageing among 20 to 25 year olds and among people aged over 60 in Germany and Australia using a repertory grid methodology. The grid elements were a mix of self-elements, examples of successful and unsuccessful coping, and representatives of different age groups. They also added two supplied constructs if they did not emerge spontaneously: healthy – unhealthy, and satisfied – unsatisfied. They reported illustrative results from two grids in particular. The first, from an Australian woman, showed a move along the principal component during life, with self at 8 and 25 at one extreme, self in middle age in the middle, and the ideal self at the other pole. They saw this as an example of successful ageing. The second was from a German woman with significant health problems. On the first component her current self and ideal self were close, and there was again evidence of movement towards the ideal self and away from less preferred elements, such as the saddest person she knew, over time. This too was seen as an example of successful ageing. Both these grids showed what Ellis and Scheer term 'upward development' patterns, with migration of the self towards the ideal over time. As expected, the country of origin had little effect, despite the different life experiences in the two countries.

Scheer, Hundertmark and Ellis (1997) reported on an extension of this research, focusing on data from Germany. They used similar grid methodology and found that both the young and older groups construed themselves at 45 or over 60 as closer to their ideal self than at 8 or 25. The actual construing of satisfaction, however, showed some difference between the age groups. Young people tended to construe satisfaction as being near to openness to experience, whereas the older people saw satisfaction as closer to agreeableness. Young people were likely to construe themselves now as satisfied if the areas of job and study, sexuality and health were satisfactory. For the older people it was satisfaction with their financial status that was most likely to be associated with current self-satisfaction.

Ellis (1996) looked at nursing students' construing of older people, their most numerous client group. She looked at grid data from the students and found five major themes: activity, health status, age, dependency and work situation. Overall the construing of older people by the students covered quite a narrow range. When the grid data were linked with the students' memory work stories of early experience of old age there was a clear and strong link between early experiences of older people and later understandings and anticipations of older people. The influence also extended to their own expectations for old age. In her 1997 paper on nurses' anticipations of older people Ellis (1997) went on to consider the ways in which early construing of caring and of old people influenced student nurses' experience and practice, and to consider ways of effecting change in their attitudes.

Clinical research

An early report of personal construct psychotherapy with an older person was presented by Hill (1988). She pointed out that the quality of life enjoyed by older people depends on their construing rather than on any objective experience, a point confirmed by Ellis and Scheer's (1995) work and noted above. She considered that 'disoriented seniors' had dormant constructs that needed reactivating. In this she seems to be talking about unvisited areas of construing, perhaps unused because of life change or constriction. Her description of the recovery of thought, orientation and mental energy, in what psychiatrists might see as a case of pseudodementia, is recognizably 're-mentia', to use Kitwood's (1996) term. The therapy she described was very intensive, taking 5 hours a day for over 2 months. She noted an increase in reminiscence and creativity as part of the reconstruction process, once sufficient sociality was developed.

There were a number of reports on groupwork with older people using a personal construct psychology approach from Botella and colleagues at about the same time (Botella and Feixas, 1989; Botella, 1991; Botella and Feixas, 1992). They used a psychoeducational style to introduce psychological approaches to older people who attended day centres, stressing enrichment and prevention as the aims rather than alleviation or compensation for losses. They found that approaching these topics through a well-elaborated path of 'education' was more acceptable and more easily incorporated into the older peoples' daily activities than the alien and less well construed 'therapy' approach. They report on autobiographical groups and on a coping skills group, and reported changes in repertory grids for those who attended.

The field of personal construct psychology research on clinical topics with older people has been largely dominated by the work in Australia of Linda Viney and colleagues. They produced the first controlled trial of personal construct therapy for older people, demonstrating its efficacy in comparison with a control (Viney, Benjamin and Preston, 1989). The study involved short-term therapy, between five and 13 sessions with a median of 10, for 30 older people. They do not report the exact length of sessions, but in contrast to Hill (p. 307) it seems likely that these lasted an hour or less. There were two comparison groups. A criterion group of 46 people had good physical and psychological health. The second control group was randomly chosen from people referred for therapy and thus had similar problems to those given therapy. Nine scales were used to give a range of data on psychological functioning. At the end of therapy the treatment group had significantly better functioning than the matched controls on all the scales. They also had better scores for depression and for anxiety about death, loss of bodily integrity and loneliness than the high functioning criterion group.

Viney and colleagues have also worked on a number of physical health topics of relevance to older people and on bereavement and dying. Viney's (1993a) monograph summarizes much of the work to that date and proposes extensions to the theory base, as outlined above.

Rossotti, Winter and Watts (2005) found their interest in trust and dependency stimulated by work with older people who had lost the people they had been accustomed to trust. Using grids to examine the trust-dependency relationship they set out to design an instrument to measure trust among people referred for psychological therapy. Two age groups were involved in the research, 30 to 45 year olds and 65 to 79 year olds. The resultant trust grid could be used alone or in combination with a dependency grid to help in assessment and therapy.

Finally, we must note the burgeoning personal construct psychology research on topics that are not exclusively related to older people but frequently have a bearing on their experiences and on our work with them. Linda Viney's (1990) seminal work on the psychological effects of physical illness and injury is accompanied by research on pain (Drysdale, 1989), the effect of stroke (Skelly, 2002), and the impact of heart attack (Scheer, 2001), to cite just a few examples. RA Neimeyer and colleagues have presented research on death and bereavement (Epting and RA Neimeyer 1984; RA Neimeyer, 1999). Kelly himself gave us a personal construct psychology view of suicide (Kelly, 1961), which has been followed up by later research such as Dzamonja-Ignjatovic's (1997) paper on the relationship between suicide and depression.

Conclusions

Personal construct psychology did not originally focus on older people specifically but a gradually increasing body of work with this client group has shown repeatedly how relevant the theory is for them. The dominant issues in therapy with older people now are to do with the therapist and client creating a relationship within which therapy can proceed. In order to do this, both, but especially the therapist, may need to review and elaborate their construing of old age. Personal construct psychology gives a theoretical base that actively helps with this, and a number of derived techniques that help to guide the process.

CHAPTER TWENTY-FOUR

Group work with women living with breast cancer

LISBETH G LANE, LINDA L VINEY

A diagnosis of breast cancer is a threat to life itself, generating fear and turmoil in the lives of women diagnosed with the disease (Massie and Holland, 1984; Zabora et al., 2001; Deimling et al., 2002; Bowman et al., 2003), as they and their families struggle to define and resolve the series of meanings and decisions that confront them (Weisman and Worden, 1976; Parle et al., 1996). Fear of death, fear of physical imperfection and a fear of recurrence are consistently reported (Carter, 1993; Ferrans, 1994; Polinsky, 1994). Thus, when mortality is 'rendered visible' (Little et al., 1998) by their diagnosis, denial of mortality for women with breast cancer is gone forever, and for many, taken for granted assumptions (Janoff-Bulman, 1989), and the personal and social life goals they had previously constructed will need to be reconstructed. To date, no personal construct therapies developed to work specifically with this population are reported. The aim of this chapter is to describe a personal construct group intervention, developed for women faced with the ongoing uncertainty of their future. The goal of the group work was to encourage interpersonal opportunities for group members to formulate, revise, elaborate and test their meanings of living as breast cancer survivors. Five women's accounts of their experiences of this group work are provided, as well as a brief report of its successful evaluative research findings.

Theory

A basic assumption of personal construct theory (Kelly, 1955/1991a) is that people commit to and invest in their anticipation of the events they experience. These anticipations are then tested against their experiences and either validated/confirmed or invalidated/disconfirmed. When important meanings are invalidated, as often occurs with a breast cancer diagnosis, a conglomeration of emotions that can be characterized as 'terror' (threat, dislocation and loss of hope) may ensue (Leitner and Dill-Standiford, 1993). Personal construct psychology further suggests that, when women diagnosed with breast cancer need to revise meanings relating to their existence and place in the scheme of things, they will turn to their relationships with others to test and elaborate new meanings (Kelly, 1955/1991a). These important 'core role' constructs operate to define people's personal identities, their complex and unique senses of phenomenological continuance (Kelly, 1955/1991a).

Role relationships and support

In conceptualizing the personal and the interpersonal, Kelly (1955/1991a) proposes that although meanings are essentially unique (the individuality corollary), they will, in part, be similar to those of another (the commonality corollary). Furthermore, to the extent that people construe the meaning processes of another, they may play a role in a social process involving the other person (the sociality corollary). Role relationships provide a primary source of validation and invalidation (Leitner, 1985), 'our sense of who we are, who we would like to be, and who we feel we are becoming' (Leitner and Dill-Standiford, 1993, p.137), and, potentially, afford the experience of richness and meaning in life (Leitner, 1985; Leitner and Dill-Standiford, 1993). This statement of sociality provides the framework for understanding supportive relationships. When people cannot take an unexpected event in their stride, or when they cannot handle all modes of their reality, Kelly states that 'support minimizes the negative results growing out of their experimentation' (1955/1991b, p. 662/p. 74). As a personal construct concept, support is defined as a broad-based response pattern that permits the receiver to experiment widely and successfully. Unlike reassurance, support does not trap the individual in her own construct system. Furthermore, the supporter, in attempting to see things from the other's point of view, 'is not responding in terms of certainties or outcomes' (Kelly, 1955/1991b, p. 658/ p. 71), but is accepting and acknowledging their construing and their exploratory attempts to communicate their meanings.

The literature on adjustment to breast cancer survival shows that support from the interpersonal environment is an important factor in adaptation to a cancer diagnosis (Bloom, 1982; Dunkel-Schetter and Wortman, 1982; Dunkel-Schetter, 1984; Ell et al., 1989; Mor, Malin and Allen, 1994; Parker et al., 2003), yet, many women report feeling isolated by their diagnosis (Welch-McCaffrey et. al., 1989; Lane and Viney, 2000a; Marlow et al., 2003). Women living with cancer run the risk of driving away potential support if they exhibit high levels of distress, but frequently fail to receive much needed support if they do not display that distress (Silver,

Wortman and Crofton, 1990). Many women find their anticipation that 'others' will understand is disconfirmed and they find themselves bereft of the interpersonal context in which to elaborate a system of meaning (Lane and Viney, 2000b). It appears, therefore, that following a diagnosis of breast cancer, women's prior role relationships may now be 'disrupted' (RA Neimeyer and GJ Neimeyer, 1985) and fail to provide the level of support necessary to construct new meanings. A major task of therapeutic work with women facing the ongoing threat of breast cancer, therefore, is to facilitate supportive interpersonal opportunities in which these women can formulate, test and elaborate their ongoing interpretations and predictions about themselves.

Personal construct group work

The two overarching purposes of personal construct group work are to provide opportunities for clients to maximize their potential for confirmation of their interpretations (Epting, 1984), and to construct alternative understandings of their more problematic meanings (RA Neimeyer, 1985; Fransella and Dalton, 1990; Viney, 1990b, 1996). Unlike many theoretical orientations, personal construct psychology also offers a theoretical rationale for conducting therapy on a group basis (Winter, 1997). In the group, common understandings provide the experience of consensual validation of the individual view of each participant, offering some assurance of the workability of their current meanings. These understandings also provide a psychologically secure context in which to elaborate their new meanings (Koch, 1985). The construction of more helpful meanings provides clients with an opportunity to change their actions to fit their new stories (Viney, 1996). Koch (1985) has suggested that the ability to experience recurring cycles of commonality and sociality is a key feature of psychological well-being. As a base for experimentation, the group, with its range of personalities and experiences among the members, therefore affords more scope for the development of new and more comprehensive roles than might individual therapy (Winter, 1992a).

Therapeutic practice

The group work for women with breast cancer runs with a minimum of eight participants, once a week, for 2 hours, over 8 weeks. The sharing of prior meanings and the testing of new meanings takes place in dyads (Landfield and Rivers, 1975) or small groups of women. Frequent opportunities to share with the larger group are given. Confidentiality and the importance of non-judgemental response are agreed upon as the right and, therefore, the responsibility of each member. The themes and group processes (Lane and Viney, 2001a) for each of the eight sessions are now presented.

Session 1

The theme of the first session is commonality. Activities focus on exploring the experiences and meanings shared by the group members. Emphasizing their commonality provides the foundation on which the members will develop a network of supportive relationships based on an understanding of each other as construers of meaning. Tasks for this session include the identification of other group members who share similar interests, likes, dislikes and experiences.

Session 2

The theme of this session is individuality. Group members examine how different their personal meanings may be from those of others. This lays the foundation for the members to explore alternative constructions of experience. This session also provides the opportunity to discuss how pre-diagnosis future stories might now need to be rewritten.

Session 3

The theme for this session is self construction. Group members begin to identify the important meanings by which they define themselves. A group guided imagery exercise takes the participants back in time. They draw on these reminiscences to explore the constructs by which they define themselves at different life stages, particularly focusing on the qualities they identify in themselves. Participants are also asked to write, at home, a brief personal autobiography choosing from one of the following: 'the history of my family of origin'; 'the history of the family I created'; 'the history of my friendships', or 'the history of my loves' (Botella, 1991).

Session 4

Self-disclosure is the theme for this session. Self-disclosure is a prerequisite for the formation of role relationships. Sharing of their personal stories allows members of the group to make their own meanings explicit. In the context of the supportive relationships formed, group members can then experiment with new meanings, thus widening the range of choices available for action (Lovenfosse and Viney, 1999). The generation of alternative constructions of these histories is also considered to be an essential process in the revision of the individual's system of meaning (Botella, 1991).

Session 5

The major theme of this session is alternative meanings. Stress, for example, is a construct that group members can all identify; yet it may have different meanings to them. The sharing of these differences is anticipated to provide a range of alternative ways of approaching stressors, providing the context in which to explore alternative constructions of other troublesome areas in their lives.

Session 6

This session extends the work of the previous two sessions by examining alternative meanings about self and relationships. The activities for this session are loosely based on RA Neimeyer's (1999) life imprints exercise. First, group members discuss how people, figuratively, have left their footprints on them. They then examine who is helping them to view themselves positively, and who is not. Opportunities are given to test alternative constructions of these 'footprints'.

Session 7

In this session the group members have the opportunity to retell their cancer stories. They often need to go back and recount again their experience of their diagnosis. In the retelling they have the opportunity to recount their stories to a group that has developed a deep understanding of each other. It is also an opportunity to reflect on how the 'meanings' attached to the experience may now be changing.

Session 8

The theme for the final session is choice. The task of the facilitator is to help the participants identify the following:

- The distance they have come, since their experience of diagnosis;
- Their new perspectives;
- Future goals as choices to be made; and
- Making sure that everyone has telephone numbers and contact details for group members and arranging a social follow-up meeting in 3 months.

Case examples

In this section the processes of therapy from the participants' perspectives are reported with examples of five women's experiences, taken from transcriptions of these sessions. To maintain confidentiality, their names have been changed.

In the early sessions, the women felt compelled to offer comforting words to each other and tissues. They offered each other reassurance. Very soon, with a little guidance, they came to understand that support is not solely about giving comfort to others, and to appreciate the subtle distinction between showing support and closing down others' ways of expressing their experiences. With this understanding, group members began to open themselves to the meanings of other group members. By sharing these meanings they experienced 'commonality'. Margaret said: 'It (being part of the group) reinforces the fact, that while we are all different people, in one way, breast cancer has made us "sisters under the skin".' By validating each other as construers of meaning these women experienced 'sociality'. Susan, describing her experience of disclosing her feelings, said: 'I felt someone listened and cared', and went on to say: 'It puts my problems into a different context.' They also came to share the therapist's role in helping each other elaborate their new meanings.

In addition to sharing their experiences, many found the opportunities to write their autobiographies very helpful. Mary said:

> I'm surprised at what I did write down. I won't be able to relate it all because it's too long, so I'll read a little. It was funny when I was writing this, it was just amazing, and I can see that a lot of healing came because I had two times when I really cried. You know, and I can see now where that's coming from, which I will probably share with you.

Anne also found the autobiography helpful. She said: 'I've never been able to say lots of things, but writing them, even writing this, I seem to have come full circle. And I see the bit in the middle that is still cloudy where it is still cloudy and still not clear, but I see that in writing it down that it's getting clearer, I'm getting clarity on who I am.' This sense of clarity was a common theme in their discussions during the groups. Sometimes this understanding came about by the processes of writing and disclosing, at other times group members helped in the process of defining meanings.

Opportunities to talk about their fear of death and dying were also valuable for many of the participants. Interestingly, it was in these discussions that the women first recognized the choices they made. The following extract illustrates how Susan came to clarify the choices she had made:

> It's very hard to make sense of, I mean I am only 32, and I have always been fit, I never smoked. And how can you make sense of that. I have three small kids and a husband, and I am just starting my life. I've just moved into a new home – I'm just starting out in my life. I'm thinking no way - I am determined, I want to see my children grow up and graduate. So I have come to peace with whatever happens. I want to enjoy everything I have with them and be a positive person in their life. I mean I hope I will be here, but if I am not, then they will remember me well.

As the women talked in general about their week between sessions a number of further changes became apparent. Catherine, for example, had talked about her wish to get a job now that her children had grown up but felt she had been out of the work force for too long, so had no confidence that she would be employed. In Week 4, she reported: 'Well I've been offered a part-time job three days a week. I'm quite chuffed with myself.' In the same week, Margaret said: 'I caught up with the ironing.' This, for Margaret, was a major breakthrough. Margaret had been struggling with depression. In the past few months she 'could not be bothered to do the usual tasks'. Two weeks later she made a cake for our coffee meeting. This was the first time she had cooked since before her diagnosis.

Changes also occurred, for some women, in important relationships outside of the group. Several women found they had reassessed their marriages and in coming to understand not only their own but also their husbands' meanings they felt better able to face the future with their partners. In fact, over the weeks, the participants began to feel that they knew each other's husbands as well as they knew each other, even though they never met. Frank was one husband they came to know from his wife Mary's stories. Mary said:

> In the past I'd forego my activities. I'd be running into the waves and he would be walking sedately with his shoes and socks on. And I would forego doing what I loved. And you can imagine the stress. But, things have now improved so terrifically. Last week we were at the grandchildren's place and Frank was left inside and I enjoyed myself outside. What a change, I did exactly what I wanted to do and allowed him to do exactly what he wanted to do. And it worked out fine.

Research

To examine the effectiveness of this group work content analysis scale measures (Gleser, Gottschalk and Springer, 1961; Gottschalk and Gleser, 1969; Gottschalk and Hoigaard-Martin, 1986; Gottschalk and Bechtel, 1998; Gottschalk, 2000) were collected before, on completion of, and three months after the intervention in a randomized controlled study (Lane and

Viney, 2001b). Forty-two women were assigned to either the group work or wait-list control condition. Ages ranged from 33 years to 69 years. The mean age of the participants in the group work sample at the time of the study (n = 20) was 51.3 years (SD 8.82; median 51.5). The mean age for the control sample (n = 22) was 56.5 years (SD 8.64; median 57.5). In Australia, 40% of women diagnosed with breast cancer are under the age of 54 years at the time of their diagnosis, compared to 67% of the women in this sample (New South Wales Cancer Council, 2003). Data were collected before the group work (Time 1), after the group work (Time 2) and three months after the completion of group work (Time 3) from the group work sample and at baseline, eight weeks later and a further three months later for the control sample. Scores were analysed using multiple univariate repeated measures analyses of variance.

Significant interaction effects of time by group were noted on threat (Total Anxiety Scale) scores (F (2,39) = 4.94, p < 0.05), threat to existence (Death Anxiety Subscale) scores (F (2,39) = 4.94, p < 0.05), dislocation (Depression Scale) scores (F (2,39) = 3.74, p < 0.05), and hope (Hope Scale) scores (F (2,39) = 3.91, p < 0.05) (Figure 24.1). Pairwise comparisons, to

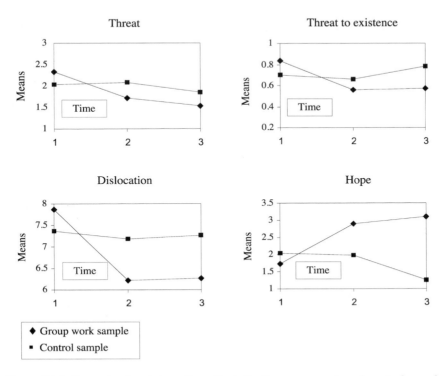

Figure 24.1 Group by time interaction effects for the group work and control samples.

examine between groups across time differences in scores, were then performed. These findings of the study (Lane and Viney, 2001b) showed that, together, the processes of commonality and sociality were effective in reducing levels of threat to both women's psychological and physical integrity. The personal construct group work was also effective in reducing the participants' levels of dislocation from their meanings and increasing their levels of hope. The effect of the group work was clear immediately following the group therapy and was maintained three months after the participants' last group session. This finding is particularly valuable as it suggests that the meanings the participants had elaborated in the context of the group therapy were helpful to them in anticipating events beyond this social context and later in time.

Conclusions

One of the unique aspects of human experience is that people attempt to find meaning, even in incomprehensible events such as life-threatening illness and death (Feifel, 1959). This task can be made harder if the context in which to 'try out new meanings' is unavailable. Survivors of a life-threatening illness face the task of redefining themselves, and giving meaning to their experiences. Unlike many psychological theories, personal construct psychology offers a conceptual rationale for understanding the interpersonal mechanisms of successful adjustment to breast cancer. In this chapter we have shown that the concepts of personal construct theory have much to offer to our understanding of the processes that both help and impede their adjustment to living as survivors.

Adjustment to breast cancer survival consists of dynamic and complex processes that take place in social contexts and are mediated by the unique meanings women place on their experiences. Personal construct concepts of the personal and the interpersonal allow therapists to 'make sense' of these processes. Perhaps the greatest contribution these make to an understanding of women's adjustment to breast cancer survival is that they point to ways in which all those involved in their care can support women in their attempts to adjust to breast cancer survival. In supporting breast cancer survivors, it is essential that we, as their therapists, carers, partners, parents, daughters, sons and friends, respond not only to the content of their communications but also to their attempts to find meaning in their experiences. These women offer themselves as makers of meaning in their communications about their breast cancer experiences, and to have these offers invalidated can be severely damaging (Leitner and Faidley, 1995). As women living with breast cancer attempt to make the unreal real, support that offers validation of their current meanings and of themselves as meaning makers, with opportunities to experiment with alternative meanings, will help these women restore a sense of coherence to their ongoing life stories. In concluding this chapter, the processes of role relationships and support are best described in the following poem, written by one of the participants about her group experience. Gloria gave each member of her group a copy of this poem at the last session:

Strangers we were, friends we've become.

Happily we have spent some time together getting to know one another.
We have shared – laughed a little and shed a few tears.
And in this time we have come to understand what it is that draws us out of isolation,
into seeking a deeper meaning of the transformation taking place in us
through a diagnosis of breast cancer.
I now go forward as I believe you do too
To meet the present moment with an expectation
of a future bright and worthwhile with thankfulness and appreciation.
Life is not passing me by, for I am standing firm to claim its benefit.

Gloria W (December 2000)

Acknowledgement

We acknowledge the invaluable assistance of the many women of the Illawarra, New South Wales, Australia, currently living with breast cancer, who have shared their experiences so generously.

CHAPTER TWENTY-FIVE

Personal construct workshops for women experiencing menopause

HEATHER FOSTER, LINDA L VINEY

The topic of menopause has recently become a staple of the popular media. Scarcely a month goes by without the latest release of controversial data, which receive attention-grabbing headlines in the press and are hotly debated on television and radio. According to the Nexis database (Nexis, 2003), in a two-year period the *New York Times* and *The Times* of London included the word 'menopause' in headlines or the first paragraph of articles 74 and 57 times respectively, an average of two to three citations per month. The figure for *The Australian* newspaper was 27 citations, an average of once a month (Nexis, 2003). Publicity about menopause treatments in the general community has created a climate in which women are now facing the changes of menopause in the face of conflicting information.

In this context, women may find their construct systems of already proven effectiveness inadequate for prediction during the physical changes of menopause. This need for reconstruction may be a particular challenge for menopausal women in paid employment. Menopausal changes, like other changes relating to women's reproductive status, may have an impact on women's wellbeing, but must be accommodated more-or-less invisibly within their working lives. Expectations about the 'normality' of these changes may leave women who experience difficulties feeling they have to hide their perceived failure, often leaving each woman feeling she must face the changes alone. Women managers, at all levels, may experience particular difficulty in reconciling their workplace role and their menopausal experiences.

Women in industrialized societies are in a paradoxical position (Foster and Viney, 2000). In a study of women in Western Europe, it was found that women mainly acquire information about hormone replacement therapy through the mass media (Oddens et al., 1994). Publicity is often given in the media, sometimes dramatically, to conflicting information about menopause, but self-identification as menopausal is still inhibited by taboos and fears, and there are few opportunities for women to develop their own meanings for menopause. Decision making is hard in this context of confusion, and anxiety can be the result (Oddens et al., 1994).

Despite a recognition that women may experience distress at the time of menopause (Coope, 1996; Bosworth et al., 2001; Bromberger et al., 2001), psychologically based interventions for menopausal women are rarely reported. The interventions that are described are predominantly medical (Kenemans et al., 2001; Maartens, Knottnerus and Pop, 2002). The non-medication based interventions reported are most often education programs (Liao and Hunter, 1998; Blalock et al., 2002). Only four group interventions for menopausal women have been reported in the menopausal literature as including a psychologically based component (Anderson et al., 1987; Anarte, Cuadros and Herrera, 1998; Jones, Keene and Green, 1999; Takamatsu et al., 2001). Their outcomes may indicate some benefits for the women but, in general, concerns about the nature of these interventions inhibit the drawing of general conclusions.

The purpose of this chapter is to introduce brief menopause workshops, personal construct workshops for women anticipating or experiencing menopause.

Theory

The workshops were based on the assumption of constructive alternativism (Kelly, 1955/1991a), which provides an optimistic view of a client's potential for change, and a goal for interventions: that of assisting clients to form new constructions, 'reconstruing life' (Kelly, 1955/1991b, p. 830/p. 192), and make choices with more useful predictive power, 'to alleviate complaints' (Kelly, 1955/1991b, p. 831/p. 193). A personal construct approach to psychotherapy is built on the notion that choice, both of meanings and actions, is possible. This is formally stated in the choice corollary (Kelly, 1955/1991a). 'The theme that we are not "victims of our biography", that we can *choose* which direction we take in our lives places great emphasis on this process of choice and the way we make our decisions' (Dunnett, 1985, p 37; italics in the original).

Kelly (1955/1991a) saw that the processes of construing were cyclical (Winter, 1992a). He described two cycles of construction, the circumspection–pre-emption–control (C-P-C) decision-making cycle, and the creativity cycle, consisting of sequences of loosened and tightened construing. The workshops were planned so that the processes provided opportunities for women to engage in these cycles, to assist them in completing the cycles and move to satisfactory prediction and decision-making. Kelly (1970a, pp. 19 and 20) also described an 'experiential cycle', in relation to the experience Corollary, since referred to as the Experience Cycle (RA

Neimeyer, 1985; Fransella and Dalton, 1990; Oades and Viney, 2000). The three cycles form what have been called 'the three cycles of change' (Fransella and Dalton, 1990). The menopausal transition as a whole can be seen as an example of the experience cycle, and the menopause workshops as a means of helping women to successfully complete the cycle.

Throughout life, as circumstances change, people are confronted by challenges to their construct systems. While many transitions may be easily accommodated, others are more difficult. Kelly (1955/1991a) described a set of diagnostic constructs that are relevant to transition. These are threat, guilt, fear, and most importantly in this case, anxiety.

Anxiety is 'the recognition that the events with which one is confronted lie outside the range of convenience of one's construct system' (Kelly, 1955/1991a, p. 489/p. 365). Anxiety has been identified as an issue for menopausal women (Banister, 2000; Goldstein, 2000; Lyons and Griffin, 2003). Kelly (1955/1991b) observed that: 'whereas a "normal" person . . . lives with anxiety' (p. 896/p. 237) and 'anxiety is universal among mankind' (p. 900/p. 240), 'there is a sense in which all disorders of construction are disorders involving anxiety' (p. 895/p. 237).

Kelly (1955/1991a) used the term validation to describe 'the verification of a prediction', even in the cases in which 'what was predicted was something unpleasant' (p. 158/p. 111), distinguishing this concept from the cognitive behavioural concept of reinforcement. The validation of predictions would therefore result in a reduction in anxiety or other emotions associated with transition.

Personal construct approaches to group psychotherapy are characterized by the active position of the therapist (Epting, 1984), and a structured approach to process (RA Neimeyer, 1988a; Viney, 1996). Strategies used to achieve a positive therapeutic outcome for group participants include commonly used therapeutic strategies (Yalom, 1970/1975/1995), as well as those that are informed by a distinctively constructivist approach. Koch (1985), for example, focuses on searching for commonality and validation, and clarifying differences through reciprocal elaboration. Viney (1996) has identified five key group therapeutic processes: developing better discrimination, examining pre-emptive constructs, understanding others, dispersing dependency, and validating or invalidating constructs. These processes were all engaged in the workshop described here.

Therapeutic practice

A recent study of women's meanings of menopause (Foster and Viney, 2001a) found that many women identified a need for an opportunity to talk about, and resolve, feelings of confusion, an inability to predict what was happening, and a need for change. The women did not construe them-selves as ill, and they were not in search of 'therapy' as such. The menopause workshop was designed in response to this need. It was brief and flexible for two reasons: in recognition, first, of the needs of busy women occupied outside the home, who were predominantly in the paid workforce; and, second, the need for low delivery costs for future users of the intervention, such as women's health centres. The workshop, although adaptable to more extended delivery, was based on a core of three sessions of 90 minutes each. These sessions could be offered either on three con-secutive weeks, or, in combination, as a one-day workshop of three sessions. Structured processes were provided: (a) to promote therapeutic movement (GJ Neimeyer and Merluzzi, 1982; Winter, 1992a; Viney et al., 1997); (b) to avoid the dangers of uncontrolled loosening or tightening (Winter, 1996); and (c) to provide processes to ensure group members could provide alternatives for each other (Winter, 1996).

The three workshop sessions were each structured around a major activ-ity (see Table 25.1). It was assumed that constructs relating to menopause

Table 25.1 Menopause workshop

Session 1
1 Welcome and overview. Confidentiality requirements. Introductions. Expectations.
2 'Self-characterization' – a character sketch in relation to menopause. Discussion of strengths.
3 Past experience – discussion.
4 Predictions and strategies – groups.
5 Review expectations. Feedback. Preview next session.

Session 2
1 Review – group discussion.
2 A situation and its opposite – drawing menopause.
3 Choices – discussion.
4 Review expectations. Feedback on unfinished business.
5 Preview next session.

Session 3
1 Review – group discussion.
2 The opposite side of the story – enactment and discussion.
3 Choices – discussion.
4 Control – discussion.
5 Support, resources and sources of information – discussion.
6 Review expectations – discussion. Feedback.

might well be non-verbal, or pre-verbal, as well as verbal (Kelly, 1955/1991a). The sessions were planned as a series of explorations that moved from reflection about the self to engagement in the C-P-C (decision-making) cycle, and dispersion of dependency. It was also assumed that women would 'approach the first session already anticipating some sort of change' (Fisher, 2000, p 436).

The major activity in Session 1 was writing a self-characterization (Kelly, 1955/1991a). In Session 2, the major activity was drawing a situation and its opposite (Ravenette, 1999) in relation to a choice women were facing. In Session 3, the major activity was an enactment (Kelly, 1955/1991a/1991b) in which the women were invited to enact the contrasting choice to that which they identified in Session 2. This final task was designed to provide access to constructions that had been stored as bodily sensations (Epting and Prichard, 1993), a particularly appropriate method for exploration of construing about menopause. The menopause workshop has been described in more detail elsewhere (Foster and Viney, 2001b, 2002).

Case examples

Three case studies illustrate the changes in women's construing as they took part in the menopause workshop. These women were selected as having backgrounds with similarities and differences. All of them worked at a level categorized as 'professional' by the Australian Standard Classification of Occupations (Australian Bureau of Statistics, 1998). Two of the women were employed in offices of a large government department located in different suburbs of Sydney, Australia. The third woman was a health professional in private practice in a rural town in New South Wales, Australia. The women's ethnic and cultural backgrounds were Australian, Chinese-Australian, and European-Australian. Pseudonyms were assigned, using only names that were not held by any woman taking part in the wider research.

The construing of the three women represents some of the themes identified in an earlier study (Foster and Viney, 2001a) as important to women experiencing menopause. The four major themes, identified in 70% or more of women's responses in that research, were physical or psychological changes; distressing feelings such as anxiety; feelings of confusion and an inability to predict what would happen; and an awareness of change and feelings of loss of control. Nancy's construing reflects a concern with menopause as a significant time, childlessness and mortality. Nora focuses on her mother's experience, and taboos about menopause and women's bodies. Margo's construing showed an elaboration of her construct of 'spiritual development'.

Nancy

Nancy was 49 years old, and was starting to experience menopausal changes. Before the workshop, she identified the over-arching meaning that menopause had for her:

> In symbolic terms . . . it is very important. I am a person who wished to have children, but have none . . . This has not been emotional or traumatic, but it has been important in further defining my identity as a non-parent. I have a strong sense of moving into the future without a grown family . . . and I have few role models for this.

During the workshop, in Session 1, Nancy described herself as 'caught in a land between hope and despair'. She seemed to be elaborating and reconstruing these polarities as she took part in the workshop sessions. In Session 3, Nancy commented that she had reflected on decision-making and menopause after Session 2, and said that, prompted by the sessions, she would now 'play with the choices'. At this stage she seemed to have arrived at a more lighthearted construction.

After the workshop she commented on her elaboration of the experience of menopause. Although she referred to mortality, she was able to reconstrue this in terms of actions, a contrast to her previous reference to 'despair'.

> Just being in a room with peers and colleagues, talking about the issue together, had a 'normalizing' effect. Before that, I had not discussed the issue with regard to myself at all . . . It made me determined to 'own' the whole experience as important, and to make sure it was not to be hidden or avoided as a shameful thing . . . I do experience . . . a strong consciousness of my own mortality . . . The menopause is hugely symbolic for me of entering a 'last phase' of life . . . this somehow makes it time to get on with my own life – and to go for the experiences of life that I need . . . Without the workshop I would not have found names for these thoughts and feelings.

Five months after the workshop, Nancy had clearly elaborated the polarities of her meanings of menopause, and reconstrued menopause as a less anxiety provoking and threatening experience. The women's levels of anxiety were measured three times: before and after the workshop, and after 5 months, and Nancy's anxiety was reduced after the workshop, and remained at a lower level. She retained her meaning of menopause as symbolic of another stage of life, and also her references to mortality, made more vivid for her by the events of 11 September 2001.

At this time, however, she was able to elaborate her construing of the future:

> I remain . . . interested in the psychological challenges of this transition, it's so symbolic of moving into the second half of life's bell curve. My identity

is changing . . . I now understand . . . the intense reality that the body has its own clock . . . Bodies wear out – and let our spirits go. Not that death is dangerous or scary, but just that it is inevitable . . . (This week, too, we have seen the World Trade Center come down, and have heard people taking their last breaths with resignation or terror.) These 'intimations of mortality' are enlarged by my knowledge that my tiny branch of the human family ends with me, I am the end of a six million year journey by my genes . . . Your research helped me to be more open about my menopause, to be willing to speak about it occasionally when it comes up – and to move it from the intensely private to the slightly more public arena.

Nancy had clearly been engaged in a continuing process of better discrimination and reconstruction since the workshop. Despite her reference to the disturbing events of 11 September 2001, she seems to have been able to experiment with her construing outside the group, dispersing her dependencies. She arrived at a construction of menopause that was less of a private ending, and that reflected more sense of future possibilities.

Nora

Nora, at 49 years, was starting to experience menopausal changes. Prior to the workshop, Nora said: 'I am very reluctant to talk to people about my own experiences . . . I think it is a bit more of a taboo subject in our society . . . From my own Chinese background it's not talked about at all, I don't broach it with my Mum . . . and with my mother-in-law, I don't talk about it.' She agreed, however, to take part in the workshop, and expressed considerable distress in her response to a standard question inviting her to describe the good and bad things in her life. As responses were written, she was able to indicate her emphasis.

In one word HORRIBLE!!!!! I am moody and emotional. Feelings of inadequacy, hopelessness and alienation invade my thoughts often. I am experiencing constant hot flushes (about 5 in the day and 2–3 times at night sufficient to wake me up). After consulting the FPA [Family Planning Association] I started on [brand of hormone replacement therapy] which sent one side of my face numb. I thought I was having a stroke so have decided to do it without drugs. I've put on weight, about five kilograms, even though I don't think I have increased my food intake. I certainly exercise regularly, playing competition squash twice weekly. My husband and children are unsupportive as they doesn't [sic] understand and/or are uninterested in menopause. He is so busy lately that we haven't the time to really communicate except for the normal daily messages. The good bits – there aren't many!!! I now tell people what I'm going through hoping that by spreading the word, menopause won't be such a 'taboo' subject.

During session 3 of the workshop, Nora was able to share a traumatic experience she had had as a teenager. It is understandable that Nora's construing about menopause showed anxiety, given some of the elements of her construing of this process. Her story also illustrated why Nora might have difficulty in construing herself as menopausal, as her memory was that menopause was associated with a seemingly life-threatening condition:

> I do remember when I was about 12 or 13 . . . my mother just absolutely bleeding, and I thought 'my mother's dying', because I didn't understand . . . she nearly collapsed because of all this blood that was just coming out. And I started . . . to clean, and she said 'no that's my blood don't touch it' . . . nobody was allowed to touch it, and in fact my mother said 'go and lock the door', and so she dealt with her own women's issues, and it wasn't until I started to read more, that I understood that that was what she was going through.

Immediately after the workshop, Nora repeated her themes of physical and psychological changes, concerns about her weight, and difficulty in construing herself as menopausal. After participating in the workshop, however, her distress was noticeably less, and her feelings of alienation seemed to have decreased. Sharing her construing with other women seemed to have alleviated some of her anxiety:

> Menopause partly dominates my life at present. I made the decision to take HRT . . . It has certainly helped my mood swings, and decreased the incidences of hot flushes. I'm still not very accepting of this stage in my life, so my self-image suffers. I am unhappy about my weight increase, and the resultant change in body shape. I have just rejoined the gym to try to address this issue . . . I enjoyed the opportunity . . . to listen to other people's experiences and expectations. What I have learnt is that everyone is different, so there is no definitive answer about how to cope/manage menopause.

Five months later, Nora was much less anxious, and more hopeful than before. Her changed construing was shown in a reduction in her content analysis scale scores for anxiety and feelings of helplessness, and an increase in her scores for hope and positive feelings. Nora had been away on a holiday with her husband, and she had been taking hormone replacement therapy for 7 months, which had helped with her unpleasant physical and psychological changes. She had elaborated, and validated, her construing about bringing discussions of menopause into the open.

> Being able to talk about menopause in our little group has helped. I even talked about it with some well-educated Asian women on our . . . cruise. They were uncomfortable, and initially were horrified that I would bring up

such a 'taboo' subject. Once we got into the conversation they didn't want to stop, even when the men joined us . . . Breaking down barriers is a slow process.

Nora's choices to take hormone replacement therapy and a holiday had been validated, and these decisions had improved her situation. Her construing also showed, however, that participation in the workshop had facilitated her processes of reconstruction and understanding of others. She had been engaged in a continuing process of reconstruction since the workshop. She had carried her experiments outside the group, and from this account, she seems to have felt that they were validated.

Margo

Margo, at 45 years, felt that she was experiencing some changes related to menopause. Before she took part in the menopause workshop, her concerns reflected anxiety, but she also had positive constructions about her time of life.

I feel I am in the early stages, with some symptoms re mood, periods, skin, hair, aging issues. Good: midlife is a happy time for me re personal, professional, philosophical, financial issues. I feel 'settled' and a level of contentment that I have not felt until now. I am comfortable with myself and less self-critical. Bad: the body crumble – aches, pains, not being as fit as I was 10 years ago. Periods are annoying and the PMT stuff is tedious. Memory: it is hard to know whether my poor memory is sleep deprivation or early alzheimers or menopause.

During the workshop, Margo focused on choices between earning more money and a more rewarding, healthy life enjoying activities such as growing vegetables and riding a bicycle. In the workshop, Margo seemed to have found that her more positive construing was validated. Immediately after that, she elaborated her anticipations with a sense that she would be able to achieve control in her decisions.

Menopause – so what! Life exists in so many ways, realities, stages, states and perceptions that menopause is yet another perception . . . I feel great, love life and look forward to the future! The bad is my body doesn't match my thoughts and perceptions of what I want to do and the brief time in which I have to do it.

After 5 months, Margo's construing was still growing more positive. She had continued to elaborate the advantages of her time of life, and was exploring strategies to do what she could to ensure that her positive anticipations would be validated. She was reconstruing her views about life in a thoughtful way:

> Life is good in the perimenopause at age 47. I am not afflicted with the flushes or other symptoms yet. I believe I am more tolerant, relaxed and positive about life, and the world around me, despite the suffering of many souls . . . Aging brings with it physical changes, but I think these are balanced by the philosophical growth and spiritual development that I pursue more these days . . . The more I think about it, the more I realise life is happening NOW and not to be postponed.

After the workshop, Margo's construing became less anxious, and more hopeful, as assessed by content analysis scale scores. It is clear that she also had been engaged in a continuing process of reconstruction since the workshop. Like other women, such as Nancy, she acknowledged that distressing events happen in the world, but she had developed an elaborated bipolar construction of menopause that seemed to be subsumed by a more superordinate construct of spiritual growth, allowing her an ultimately positive outlook.

Research

The major aims of the research reported here were to test whether the menopause workshop could:

- reduce participants' distressing emotions such as anxiety and helplessness, and
- increase participants' feelings of control, hope and positive feelings in relation to menopause.

Thirty-eight women agreed to take part in menopause workshops, and a further 16 women provided two data collections, yielding a contrast sample. Random selection was not used, but rather screening for distress, with each woman's choice providing relationships of trust (Holmes, 2002).

Two sets of content analysis scales were used to assess psychological states:

- the Cognitive Anxiety Scale (Viney and Westbrook, 1976) (anxiety), the Origin and Pawn Scales (Westbrook and Viney, 1980) (control and helplessness, respectively) and the Positive Affect Scale (Westbrook, 1976) (positive feelings); and
- the Hope Scale (Gottschalk and Gleser, 1969) (hope) and the Depression Scale (Gottschalk and Hoigaard-Martin, 1986) (distress).

The last scale was used as a screening and predictive measure of distress, discriminating between women who were unable to revise their constructs about menopause, and were therefore experiencing higher levels of distress than normal, and those who were not. The more distressed women, therefore, were expected to benefit most from the opportunity for reconstruction.

An evaluation study was conducted, using a repeated measures, contrast group design. Data were collected on three occasions: pre-workshop, post-workshop, and after 5 months.

The key measures that distinguished between the two workshop samples and the contrast sample were anxiety and helplessness. For anxiety, results for samples A (above-average distress) and B (normal levels of distress) showed that there was a reduction in Cognitive Anxiety Scale scores between times 1 and 3, significant in sample B and approaching significance in sample A. This was not shown in contrast sample C.

In sample B (normal), a significant reduction was shown in Pawn Scale scores, the measure of helplessness, between time 1 and five months after the workshop at time 3. There was also evidence of a reduction in Pawn Scale scores over time in Sample A (above average). No difference was shown for Contrast Sample C. In summary, these results point to workshop participation as reducing anxiety and helplessness in the workshop samples. An examination of graphs for Cognitive Anxiety and Pawn Scale scores for samples A (above average), B (normal), and C (contrast) makes the direction of the effects clear (see Figures 25.1 and 25.2).

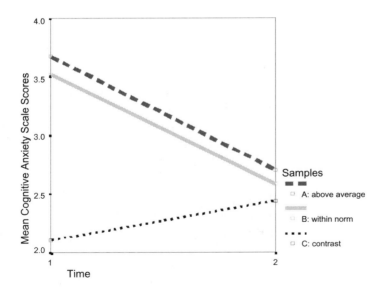

Figure 25.1 Mean Cognitive Anxiety Scale scores for samples A, B, and C at times 1 and 3.

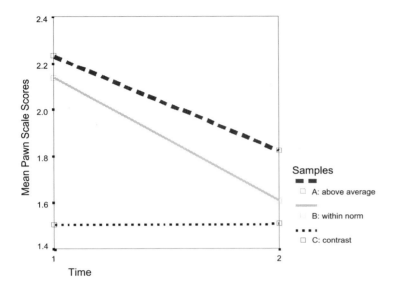

Figure 25.2 Mean Pawn Scale scores for samples A, B, and C at times 1 and 3.

There was a beneficial result for sample A (above average), in that there was a significant long term decrease in feelings of helplessness, and a long-term decrease in anxiety that approached significance, but there was no significant long-term change in relation to positive measures. Participation in the workshop also appeared to produce beneficial results for women in sample B, whose initial distress was within normal levels.

Increases in feelings of control and positive emotions occurred in the short term, immediately after the workshops, but they were not sustained over 5 months. It may, however, be that the brief nature of the workshops was sufficient to assist women to move from anxiety to engaging in decision making, but not adequate to achieve improvements in their perceptions of control, and long-lasting positive feelings. It is important to note that all the women in this study had high initial scores on the Origin and Positive Affect scales, possibly an effect of their predominantly high occupational status. The choice of the non-randomized design, while appropriate for this research, limits the ability to generalize from the findings. Further research with more representative, larger and randomized samples should be undertaken.

Conclusions

The menopause workshop is the first true psychological intervention in its field. In an age of financial restrictions on health services (RA Neimeyer and Raskin, 2000), and increasingly 'time-poor' professionals, brief group interventions are likely to become more important. This chapter offers an application of the personal construct approach, which was helpful to women experiencing, or anticipating, the menopausal transition, regardless of their levels of distress.

Using a personal construct approach in the workshops provided a flexible and creative context for the cooperative exploration of individual non-verbal, pre-verbal, and verbal construing. This approach also provided an orientation to the future, which was crucial for the focus on reconstruction. It facilitated reciprocal elaboration of predictions and actions, with the aim of developing accurate predictions, and was the context for the provision of opportunities for loosening and tightening in relation to gaining understanding and support, and opportunities for the dispersion of dependency. In summary, the processes of the personal construct menopause workshop provided the women with an opportunity to reconstrue their experience of menopause, and achieve long-lasting reductions in anxiety and feelings of helplessness, at a time when menopause and menopausal psychological treatments continue to be hotly debated.

PART THREE
EVIDENCE BASE

CHAPTER TWENTY-SIX

A process and outcome study of personal construct psychotherapy

SUE WATSON, DAVID A WINTER

Introduction

The results of half a century of intensive research on psychotherapy outcomes were aptly encapsulated in Shapiro's (1996, p. viii) metaphor of 'the glass that is either half full or half empty'. Although it is half full, he suggests, in terms of empirical evidence for the effectiveness of psychotherapy, it is half empty in terms of lack of supportive evidence for the many therapeutic approaches claimed by their proponents to be efficacious. Evidence-based practice has long been a requirement of managed healthcare systems in the US (Barlow, 1994) and the same trends are now apparent in the UK. According to the Review of Strategic Policy on NHS Psychotherapy Services (Parry and Richardson, 1996), decisions to fund specific forms of treatment are likely to be taken on the basis of research evidence of their effectiveness. Thus, it follows that under-researched therapies are likely to be particularly vulnerable to the possibility of suffering the same fate as did the dodo, the subject of that other metaphor which is so familiar to psychotherapy researchers. Lewis Carroll's placatory creature, borrowed by Luborsky, Singer and Luborsky in 1975 to describe the ubiquitous equivalence of outcome finding, faces renewed threat in the twenty-first century. Those dodoesque theorists who decline the opportunity to engage in research that demonstrates the validity of their espoused therapeutic approach are in danger of extinction. For this to occur would be unfortunate, since, as Roth, Fonagy and Parry (1996, p. 44) argue, 'the absence of evidence for efficacy is not evidence of ineffectiveness, and valuable approaches that offer appropriate and clinically effective care should not perish for lack of funding.'

Personal construct therapy is one such under-researched and potentially valuable approach, the outcomes of which were conspicuously absent from state of the art reviews of psychotherapy research, such as Bergin and Garfield's magnum opus (Lambert, 2004), and Roth and Fonagy's (1996) seminal volume. This is unfortunate, because the omission of personal construct therapy may induce potential healthcare purchasers and clients consulting these authorities to conclude that this cannot be an efficacious therapy (Watson and Winter, 2000). In fact, there is considerable evidence of the effectiveness of personal construct therapy from single case studies and group studies with homogenous client groups (Winter, 2003b). However, apart from the present study, personal construct therapy has not featured in comparative therapy outcome research with heterogeneous clients.

In addition to the dearth of reported evidence of the effectiveness of personal construct therapy in mainstream publications, there are several other gaps in the psychotherapy research literature. Many therapeutic approaches currently practised are under-researched; there is little agreement regarding the utility of available outcome measures; research on therapy process is piecemeal; few studies have examined the relationships of pre-treatment client characteristics with therapeutic process and outcome; and, most importantly, many existing research findings are based on efficacy trials with dubious relevance to clinical practice with clients who are typically referred to service settings.

The objectives of the present study, designed to bridge some of these gaps, are listed below in order of sequence rather than importance:

- to consider client characteristics in terms of symptomatology and aspects of functioning in a large sample of clients referred to a British National Health Service Clinical Psychology Department for psychological therapy;
- to identify possible differences in process between therapeutic approaches with a view to distinguishing differential change mechanisms;
- to examine the relationship of therapeutic process with both pre-treatment client characteristics and outcome;
- to compare the outcome at post-therapy, 6 months and 1 year later, of individual short-term personal construct, cognitive and brief psychodynamic therapies practised as delivered, in a service setting;
- to investigate the outcome of a hitherto under-researched approach, personal construct therapy, with diagnostically heterogeneous clients;
- to identify pre-treatment client characteristics that are differentially predictive of outcome;
- to assess the utility of the repertory grid as an index of change in psychological distress.

Method

The participants in the study were 80 clients referred for therapy to a British National Health Service Clinical Psychology Department. Mean age was 35.7 years (SD 10.7 years). No alterations were made to usual selection and allocation to treatment procedures within the department; this was truly 'research into psychotherapy as delivered', as recommended by Parry and Richardson (1996, p.10). From the original 80 clients participating in the study pre-therapy, 48 clients remained in the research assessment post-therapy, 40 remained at first follow-up and 38 remained at second follow-up. In terms of the therapy conditions, 23 clients were treated by personal construct therapists, 17 by cognitive therapists, and seven by psychodynamic therapists. Therapy was conducted on the basis of 12-session renewable contracts. Clients participated in a maximum of five research assessments, two prior to therapy, post-therapy and at 6 and 12 month follow up. At each assessment, clients completed a repertory grid in which the 15 elements were the self now, ideal self, self before problems began, self after therapy, parents, partner, child or sibling, therapist, a man and woman who are liked, a man and woman who are disliked, and two other significant people. Triads of these elements were used to elicit 13 constructs. To obtain two final constructs, clients were asked to disclose two self-identified problems and their contrast poles.

Clients also completed a battery of measures tapping various aspects of symptomatology and functioning. These included the Beck Depression Inventory (BDI) (Beck et al., 1961); the Beck Hopelessness Scale (BHS) (Beck et al., 1974); and the Beck Anxiety Inventory (BAI) (Beck et al., 1988). Also used was the Brief Symptom Inventory (BSI) (Derogatis, 1993), which has three global indices measuring global severity (GSI), positive symptom total (PST), and positive symptom distress (PSDI). Other measures of functioning were the Dysfunctional Attitudes Scale (DAS) (Weissman and Beck, 1978), which taps depressogenic assumptions considered to facilitate the onset and maintenance of depression; the Personal Construct Inventory (PCI) (Chambers and O'Day, 1984), which measures various Kellian diagnostic constructs; the Problem Rating Scale (Watson and Marks, 1971), which provides a measure of the severity of clients' two self-identified major problems; the Life Experiences Survey (Sarason, Johnson and Siegal, 1978), a measure of potentially stressful life changes during the past year; the Treatment Expectancies Questionnaire (Caine et al., 1982), which differentiates between a preference for a psychosocial or a medical/behavioural approach to treatment; and the Direction of Interest Questionnare (Caine et al., 1982), which measures the extent to which individuals are inner directed or outer directed in terms of Jung's personality typology.

In the personal construct and cognitive therapy conditions, the fifth therapy session was audiotaped with client consent. Audiotapes and transcripts of the sessions were subjected to content analysis using the Vanderbilt Psychotherapy Process Scale (Strupp, Hartley and Blackwood, 1974; O'Malley, Suh and Strupp, 1983), which measures positive and negative features of the client/therapist interaction likely to expedite or inhibit progress in therapy; the Levels of Client Perceptual Processing scheme

(Toukmanian, 1986), a schematic model based on cognitive and constructivist perspectives of mental operations and mechanisms that mediate client change during therapy; and the Hill Counselor Verbal Responses Modes Category System (Hill, 1986), which measures operationally defined therapist utterances. Treatment integrity was confirmed by the accurate blind identification of the theoretical orientation from fifth session transcripts by prominent cognitive and personal construct theorists (Winter and Watson, 1999).

After the fifth session, clients and therapists completed reciprocal versions of the Barrett-Lennard Relationship Inventory (Barrett-Lennard, 1964), which measures the extent of Rogerian facilitative conditions within the therapeutic relationship. After the twelfth session, clients and therapists completed an amended version of the Helpful Aspects of Therapy questionnaire (Llewelyn, 1988), on which they described and rated events during therapy perceived to have been the most helpful. The helpful events were then coded and subjected to content analysis.

Results and discussion

In the interests of brevity, it is possible only to summarize here the numerous results from this multidimensional study: a detailed account is presented in the first author's PhD thesis (Watson, 1998).

Pre-treatment data

Comparison of clients' mean symptom scores with normative scores from similar populations confirmed the existence of substantial levels of psychopathology in the sample. Characteristics of construing were less easy to interpret in view of both an absence of normative grid data, and, in some instances, relatively untested and therefore moot assumptions regarding the meaning of some grid measures, for example, the percentage of variance accounted for by the problem constructs. However, in comparison with existing literature, on the structural measures, construing in the sample was found to be less tight than might have been predicted for clients referred for psychological therapy. Similarly, on the distance measures, the mean scores for distances between the self and other elements were indicative of higher levels of self-esteem and less construal of the self as different from others than would have been expected for clients who are seeking therapy. The only grid measure appearing to reflect the extent of psychopathology suggested by the questionnaire measures was the low mean score for the average angular distance between the self and problem constructs, which indicated the centrality of clients' problems to their self-constructions.

Test-retest reliability over the waiting time period was acceptable for six grid measures concerning structure and distance, but was inadequate for the remaining five measures. There were also significant differences in mean scores between the two waiting list assessments on two grid measures, the distance between self and problem constructs, and that between self and therapist, and three scales from a symptom questionnaire, the BSI. This may be due to unreliability of these specific measures, and/or statistical noise due to methodological deficiencies. However, for most measures there were no significant differences in scores for the two pre-therapy assessments, indicating that subsequent change could reasonably be attributed to the effects of therapy.

On measures of personal style, as would have been predicted, inner-directed clients exhibited a preference for a psychotherapeutic treatment approach, whereas outer-directed clients demonstrated treatment expectancies favourable to a medical/behavioural approach. Surprisingly, in view of previous research, there were no relationships between personal style measures and symptomatology. However, clients with medical/behavioural treatment expectancies were noted to be more pre-emptive on the Personal Construct Inventory, whereas inner-directed clients scored more highly on its Looseness subscale.

In terms of the relationships between questionnaire measures, it was apparent that the symptom measures were highly inter-correlated, suggesting the existence of substantial redundancy in the dataset. The Problem Rating Scales and some of the Personal Construct Inventory subscales were also significantly related to symptom measures, but with correlation coefficients of lesser magnitude, indicating that these measures may be tapping domains other than mere symptoms. An exploratory principal components analysis of the questionnaire scores confirmed the clustering of symptom questionnaires together with two of the Personal Construct Inventory subscales on a substantial first component.

In view of the high correlations between symptom measures, in order to reduce the risk of Type I error through multiple comparisons of redundant data, a composite measure of psychopathology for use in further statistical analyses was created from aggregated symptom scores on the BDI, BHS, BAI, BSI and DAS.

Comparison of grid measures with questionnaire scores indicated that, consistent with previous findings (Winter, 1992a), tight construing was significantly related to high scores on symptom measures. Large distances between the self and the ideal self, other people and the self after therapy, indicative respectively of low self-esteem, construal of the self as different from others, and high expectation of therapeutic change, were associated with higher levels of symptomatology, as was construal of the self in terms of the problem constructs. Similar relationships were noted between some of these grid measures and scores on the Problem Rating Scale and some of the Personal Construct Inventory subscales. Thus there appeared to be some evidence for the predictive and concurrent validity of these grid measures as indices of psychological distress, issues that are discussed more fully in Watson's (1999) analysis. Principal components analysis of the grid measures indicated that, contrary to previous research evidence (Adams-Webber, 1970), structural measures could be factorially differentiated from measures concerning the self.

Therapeutic process

The distinctiveness of personal construct therapy as compared to cognitive therapy was indicated in a number of ways. There were significant differences in the processes of the two therapies in terms of therapist and client verbal responses, behaviour and attitudes at the fifth therapy session. On the Hill Counselor Verbal Response Modes Category System, personal construct therapists used significantly more of the response modes of silence, open questions, paraphrase and also more interpretation and confrontation than did cognitive therapists, who used more approval, information and direct guidance. On the Vanderbilt Psychotherapy Process Scale, personal construct therapists demonstrated significantly less negative attitude and more exploration, and their clients showed greater participation than did those in cognitive therapy. On the Levels of Client Perceptual Processing measure, clients in personal construct therapy used significantly more of the higher order processing categories such as differentiation, reevaluation and integration than did cognitive therapy clients.

In the personal construct and cognitive therapy groups, there were significant differences on the Barrett-Lennard Relationship Inventory between therapist and client perceptions of the levels of some of the Rogerian facilitative conditions within the therapeutic relationship, clients perceiving levels of regard to be lower and levels of congruence to be higher than did their therapists. There were no such differences in the psychodynamic group, probably due to small sample size. There were also significant differences between the three therapy groups in terms of therapist perceptions of levels of most of the facilitative conditions, levels of perceived regard being higher for personal construct therapists although perceived levels of empathy were higher for cognitive therapists. Perceived levels of unconditionality were higher for both personal construct and cognitive therapists than for psychodynamic therapists. There were no significant differences in client perceptions, indicating that type of therapy is not an important predictor of client perception of the quality of their therapeutic relationship. Clients rated their therapeutic relationship as being generally of higher quality than was their closest relationship outside therapy.

A comparison was conducted of process subscales measuring therapist verbal response modes, client levels of perceptual processing and therapist and client behaviour and attitudes for the complete sample. The results indicated the existence of interactive therapist/client effects, which can be identified by comparing discrete units of client and therapist behaviour both within and between process measures. The comparison of a molar measure, the Vanderbilt Psychotherapy Process Scale, with the molecular measures of Counsellor Verbal Response Modes Category System and Levels of Client Perceptual Processing revealed significant relationships between constructs that appear dissimilar but when considered together are far from counterintuitive. For example, therapist provision of information was associated with less client participation; and client differentiation was related to more therapist exploration.

Personal style was found to be moderately predictive of client behaviour and also, albeit to a lesser extent, of that of their therapists in the fifth session. For example, inner-directed clients used fewer undifferentiated statements and less elaboration and more exploration, whereas their therapists would use more paraphrase and interpretation. Personal style did not differentially predict levels of facilitative conditions in the relationship, as perceived by clients and therapists in the three therapies. However, for the complete sample, although the extent to which clients were inner or outer-directed was not predictive of perceived levels of facilitative conditions, in general, clients with medical/behavioural treatment expectancies tended to rate the therapeutic relationship as lower in levels of facilitative conditions.

There were some significant differential relationships between scores on pre-treatment repertory grid measures and therapist verbal response modes and client levels of processing, but levels of psychopathology were not very predictive of these processes in either personal construct or cognitive therapy. However, levels of psychopathology and repertory grid measures were to some extent differentially predictive of client and therapist behaviour and attitudes. In personal construct therapy, there were few relationships between therapist or client perception of the therapeutic relationship and pre-treatment levels of psychopathology and functioning. Cognitive therapists tended to perceive themselves as offering higher levels of facilitative conditions to the less optimally functioning clients, whereas their clients with high pre-treatment levels of psychopathology and functioning tended to rate the relationship as lower in levels of perceived facilitative conditions. In psychodynamic therapy, therapist-offered regard was related to high levels of pre-treatment psychopathology, but, as in cognitive therapy, such clients rated their therapeutic relationship less favourably.

Surprisingly few significant relationships were apparent between therapist verbal response modes, behaviour and attitudes and therapeutic outcome in either personal construct or cognitive therapy. However, levels of client perceptual processing and behaviour and attitudes regarded as being characteristic of the therapy concerned were, to some extent, differentially predictive of outcome in the two therapies. There were few significant relationships between therapist- or client-perceived levels of facilitative conditions and outcome in any of the three therapy groups.

There were differences between clients and therapists in each type of therapy, and between the therapies, in terms of the categories of events each reported as being most helpful. To some extent, the events reported were consistent with the specific focus of the therapy involved, thus providing further evidence of differences in process. Personal construct clients most frequently reported personal insight, followed by awareness and problem solution, although their therapists reported problem solution and client involvement as most helpful. Cognitive therapy clients reported problem clarification and personal contact, whereas their therapists reported involvement and problem solution as most helpful. Psychodynamic therapy clients reported reassurance and sense of relief, although their therapists reported personal insight as most helpful. It is interesting that the categories of helpful events were consistent with definitions of common factors (Wiser et al., 1996). Results from this study indicate the possible existence of potential differences between therapeutic approaches in terms of the type of event regarded as helpful by clients and therapists. Thus it could be that there are differential change mechanisms across therapeutic approaches that are a function of the interaction between common factors and specific treatment techniques. For the complete sample, the extent to which clients rated their therapy overall as helpful was significantly related to positive change in levels of psychopathology and on some grid measures.

Therapeutic outcome and follow up

The descriptive statistics for the personal construct and cognitive groups at each assessment indicate that, from pre-therapy to second follow-up, there were reductions in mean scores on measures of psychopathology and client self-identified problems; grid measures concerning distance from the self now; and some of the Personal Construct Inventory subscales. In the psychodynamic group, reductions in pre-therapy mean scores were less marked and therapeutic gains appeared to be less well maintained than in the other two therapy groups. In comparison with normative scores, all three therapy groups continued to exhibit some degree of symptomatology on validated measures of psychopathology one year after therapy was completed. For the interest of those familiar with these widely used measures and because norms are available for comparison, descriptive statistics for the measures comprising the psychopathology composite variable are shown in Table 26.1.

A process and outcome study of personal construct psychotherapy   343

Table 26.1 Means and SDs for questionnaire measures of psychopathology in three therapy conditions at four assessment points

Group	Measure		*Pre-therapy mean	SD	*Post-therapy mean	SD	**1st follow-up mean	SD	***2nd follow-up mean	SD
Personal construct therapy (PCT)	Beck Depression Inventory	(BDI)	24.70	11.07	16.09	9.38	17.14	10.66	15.05	11.58
	Beck Hopelessness Scale	(BHS)	12.43	5.20	8.39	5.72	8.05	6.05	7.21	5.53
	Beck Anxiety Inventory	(BAI)	20.43	13.84	13.74	11.46	16.57	14.55	16.16	16.24
	Dysfunctional Attitudes Scale	(DAS)	153.83	42.33	136.70	36.50	133.90	44.84	122.89	37.25
	Global Severity Index	(BSI GSI)	1.70	0.86	1.23	0.85	1.22	0.96	1.09	1.04
Cognitive therapy (CT)	Beck Depression Inventory	(BDI)	19.00	11.39	13.22	12.37	12.69	10.27	13.62	13.04
	Beck Hopelessness Scale	(BHS)	9.61	5.74	7.89	6.09	6.62	6.08	7.31	6.36
	Beck Anxiety Inventory	(BAI)	13.39	10.26	9.44	7.34	6.08	5.22	8.85	10.12
	Dysfunctional Attitudes Scale	(DAS)	141.61	29.04	133.17	40.82	121.85	41.31	123.85	36.03
	Global Severity Index	(BSI GSI)	1.36	0.76	1.01	0.91	0.75	0.68	0.72	0.64
Psycho-dynamic therapy (PT)	Beck Depression Inventory	(BDI)	21.43	16.22	17.57	17.15	18.17	17.95	19.50	17.52
	Beck Hopelessness Scale	(BHS)	10.29	7.50	11.14	7.93	10.67	7.47	10.50	6.35
	Beck Anxiety Inventory	(BAI)	21.86	14.21	18.29	15.13	18.50	16.79	21.00	14.79
	Dysfunctional Attitudes Scale	(DAS)	134.14	41.25	128.71	54.26	132.50	51.49	128.83	55.25
	Global Severity Index	(BSI GSI)	1.69	1.27	1.45	1.25	1.65	1.56	1.61	1.27

* PCT n = 23; CT n = 18; PT n = 7 ** PCT n = 21; CT n = 13; PT n = 6 *** PCT n = 19; CT n = 13; PT n = 6

It was not possible to identify substantial between-groups differences in outcome at post-therapy or at either of the two follow-up points. There were a few significant differences and trends for differences at some assessment points on some grid measures concerned with distance from the self now and the ideal self; the Problem Rating Scale; and some of the Personal Construct Inventory subscales. Within-groups comparisons indicated significant pre- to post-therapy changes on over half the outcome measures in the personal construct and cognitive groups, but on less than one quarter in the psychodynamic group. Effect size for changes in levels of psychopathology and two grid measures are shown in Table 26.2. The greater magnitude of change in psychopathology measures in the personal construct therapy group may be a function of the fact that pre-therapy scores on some symptom measures were higher for this group. Research has shown that clients with high pre-therapy levels of psychopathology are likely to demonstrate greater change (Mintz and Keisler, 1982).

Table 26.2 Effect size calculated from $(M1 - M2)/SD$, where M1 is the pre-treatment mean, M2 is the post-treatment mean and SD is the standard deviation

	PCT (n = 23)	CT (n = 18)	PT (n = 7)
Psychopathology composite	0.74	0.43	0.12
Problem rating A	1.22	0.88	1.33
Problem rating B	1.47[a]	0.60[b]	0.63[c]
Distance *self/ideal self*	0.91	0.51	0.60
Distance *self/others*	0.50	1.06	0.32

[a] n = 20; [b] n = 12; [c] n = 5

To explore possible changes in client construing, the first 10 constructs of clients' pre-and post-therapy grids were categorized using Landfield's (1971) classification system. None of the therapy groups showed major change in the content of construing after therapy. In addition, there were no significant between-group or within-group differences with regard to the number of new constructs produced at any of the assessment points. The formation of new constructs appeared to be largely unrelated to therapeutic input. However, for the complete sample, there were significant associations between the production of new constructs and greater perceived amount and impact of negative and total life change events on the Life Events Survey at each assessment point. High scores on the Treatment Expectancies Questionnaire were also significantly related to the manifestation of fewer new constructs post-therapy.

Pre-treatment predictors of improvement in levels of psychopathology for the complete sample were the threat subscale of the Personal Construct

Inventory, the psychopathology Composite Variable and the Treatment Expectancies Questionnaire. One grid measure, the distance between the self now and others, was predictive of outcome in personal construct and cognitive therapies, although the relationship was in opposite directions in the two therapy conditions: low distance between these elements was related to more improvement in personal construct therapy but less in cognitive therapy. None of the identified predictive variables provided adequate explanations of pre- to post- change in levels of psychopathology, as they accounted for a very limited percentage of the variance in improvement.

In general, attempts to identify both differences in outcome between the therapies on multiple dimensions, and pre-treatment predictors of change were not very fruitful. The robustness of the dodo bird verdict has once again been demonstrated.

Conclusion

Substantive issues arising from the main findings include the acknowledgement of the distinctiveness of the process of personal construct therapy, which should lay to rest the notion that it is a cognitive approach. The equivalent outcomes of the therapies confirm previous findings. Given the weight of invalidating evidence in the psychotherapy research literature, the search for differential outcome should cease. In terms of therapeutic effectiveness, 12 sessions of therapy were enough to elicit improvement but not removal of symptoms for many clients. Longer therapeutic contracts might usefully be offered to the more symptomatic clients. Post-therapy booster sessions might also be made available to help clients cope with temporary crisis or relapse. Additional implications arising from the findings are the suggestion of differential change mechanisms mediated by an interaction between common factors and specific treatment techniques; the possibility that the Rogerian facilitative conditions are not a necessary and sufficient component of change in all therapies; and the potential use of personal style measures at pre-therapy assessment as predictors of client outcome.

Methodological issues arising from the study include the difficulty of interpreting repertory grid scores in view of the obscure meanings of some grid measures and the absence of normative data. Many questionnaire measures of psychopathology appear to be highly correlated, so it may be sufficient in future studies to use a single, multidimensional symptom measure. Aspects of research instrumentation, including audiotaping of the fifth session and completion of repertory grids, may have had an impact on outcome. Numbers of participants in the study were probably too small to ensure adequate power in the statistics. Some clients had extra sessions of therapy after termination, which could cause problems in the interpretation of follow-up data.

Suggestions for further research include improving the psychometric properties of grid measures, collection of normative data, and the compilation of a standard grid, despite the fact that this might elicit considerable personal construct anxiety or threat for some theorists. An examination of the factor structure of a multidimensional symptom measure used in this study might confirm the existence of diagnostic categories, or reveal the existence of a single homogeneous psychopathology variable. The impact on outcome of the use of grids in research should be investigated. Further differences in therapy processes and their possible relationship with outcome may be identified through the sequential analysis of therapist and client verbal interactions. The extent to which therapists make use of both therapy-specific techniques and common factors should be examined.

The study has generated a huge amount of information regarding therapeutic process and outcome in a National Health Service setting. Its limitations in terms of small sample size are acknowledged. Nevertheless, it has provided considerable evidence for the effectiveness of personal construct psychotherapy with diagnostically heterogeneous clients, finding this to be at least as effective as the more commonly used and recommended approach of cognitive therapy. It has also contributed towards our understanding of the relationships between pre-treatment client characteristics and process variables and outcome. Perhaps most importantly, it has demonstrated that it is possible to carry out a study of process and outcome in personal construct therapy with a reasonable claim to ecological validity in a naturalistic setting with authentic clients who, although depicting the researcher's worst nightmare in terms of comorbidity, complexity and levels of motivation, are probably highly representative of clients regularly seen in clinical practice.

CHAPTER TWENTY-SEVEN

The effectiveness of personal construct psychotherapy: a meta-analysis

LINDA L VINEY, CHRIS METCALFE, DAVID A WINTER

Introduction

A substantial body of research on the outcome of psychotherapy has indicated that 'a broad range of therapies, when offered by skilful, wise, and stable therapists, are likely to result in appreciable gains for the client' (Lambert and Ogles, 2004, p. 180) but that 'differences in outcome between various forms of therapy are not as pronounced as might have been expected' (p. 180). The impetus for much of the more recent research in this area has been the demand that therapeutic practice should be 'empirically validated' or 'evidence based'. To quote a review of policy on psychological therapies by the British Department of Health: '. . . it is unacceptable . . . to continue to provide therapies which decline to subject themselves to research evaluation. Practitioners and researchers alike must accept the challenge of evidence-based practice, one result of which is that treatments which are shown to be ineffective are discontinued' (Parry and Richardson, 1996, p. 43).

There has been reluctance by some personal construct psychotherapists to 'accept the challenge' described by Parry and Richardson because the notion of empirical validation has been regarded as incompatible with the constructivist and humanistic assumptions underlying this form of therapy, which is thus in danger of 'empirical violation' (Bohart, O'Hara and Leitner, 1998; Botella, 2000). However, an unfortunate consequence of failure to accept this challenge is that the effectiveness of personal construct psychotherapy may not be appreciated by healthcare purchasers, policy makers, and potential clients (who, it might be argued on purely ethical grounds, should be provided with information on the effectiveness of the treatments which they are offered). As a result, ultimately clients may be denied access to an approach that is not based on the mechanistic assumptions of those that have more readily embraced the ideas of empirical validation and evidence-based practice (Winter, 2000).

347

Nevertheless, there is a growing evidence base for personal construct psychotherapy as a small number of practitioners and researchers, consistent with Kelly's metaphor of the person as scientist, investigate the outcome of this form of therapy. Some of the studies concerned have been described in previous chapters in this volume, and most of the earlier studies have been reviewed by Viney (1998) and Winter (1992a, 2003b). Here we build upon those previous reviews, both by ensuring we conduct a 'systematic review', and by employing the statistical technique of meta-analysis. A systematic review addresses a clearly expressed question through a methodical search aimed at identifying all the relevant existing evidence from high quality empirical research studies (Chalmers and Altman, 1995). The approach was devised in response to increasing discontent with conventional narrative reviews, these commonly being based upon a biased sample of the available evidence.

In some cases it is appropriate to produce a quantitative summary of the results of a systematic review. Meta-analysis synthesizes the results of a number of investigations to give a single pooled estimate of the treatment effect magnitude. Where the measure of the treatment effect varies across studies, the synthesis uses a common metric, usually an 'effect size'. While meta-analysis has had its critics, Eysenck (1995) famously referring to an early attempt as 'adding apples and oranges', discerning use of the method has become widely accepted. So long as the studies under review are addressing much the same research question, the pooled estimate of the treatment effect obtained with meta-analysis can assist the interpretation of the review findings. Meta-analysis has been used to summarize and compare research findings for a number of forms of psychotherapy, even those, such as psychodynamic and humanistic therapies (Crits-Christoph, 1992; Elliott, 2001), which have not been noted for a tradition of empirical research.

Aims

The aim of this systematic review was to identify empirical research studies in which a group of clients undergoing personal construct psychotherapy were compared with either (i) a group receiving no intervention or (ii) a group undergoing an alternative intervention such as another form of psychotherapy. Separate meta-analyses were conducted for comparisons (i) and (ii), with the aim of presenting, for each, pooled estimates of the effect of personal construct psychotherapy.

Methods

Systematic review

The following steps were taken in order to identify outcome studies of personal construct psychotherapy:

- in January 2003, previous review papers were consulted (Viney, 1998; Winter, 1992a, 2003b);
- leading personal construct psychotherapists were contacted to enquire whether they knew of any recent reports of outcome studies;
- Web of Knowledge citation searches were conducted for the references in Viney (1998) and Winter (2003b);
- the University of Wollongong PCP references database and the Fransella Collection at the University of Hertfordshire were searched;
- abstracts of international and regional personal construct psychology conferences were searched;
- the Medline, Web of Knowledge and PsychInfo databases were searched (in January 2003) for abstracts containing any of the following terms: reconstruction and (psychotherap* or counsel*); self characterisation; interpersonal transaction; fixed role; rotating dyad; Kellian; George Kelly; personal construct;
- reference lists for identified papers were examined.

The suitability of papers was assessed according to the following criteria. Where possible this was done by reading the abstract. Where doubt remained, the full paper was obtained and consulted.

Inclusion criteria

- The described study had to compare clients receiving personal construct psychotherapy with other similar clients not undergoing an intervention or undergoing a different intervention which is not personal construct psychotherapy.
- The report had to include the following to allow inclusion in the meta-analysis: (i) number of individuals in each experimental condition; (ii) mean and standard deviation outcome for each experimental condition, or proportion subject to an outcome (such as relapse) for each experimental condition. Equivalently, a study would be included if it reported an appropriate t-statistic and degrees of freedom.

Exclusion criteria

There was no requirement for random allocation of individuals to experimental conditions but the personal construct psychotherapy and comparison groups were required to be composed of broadly similar groups of people.

Outcomes

For simplicity, a single outcome measure was selected for each study. The following sequence was followed until an outcome measure was selected:

1. Where, as recommended by the CONSORT criteria (Moher, Schulz and Altman, 2001), a primary outcome measure was specified or where an outcome measure had been the basis of a sample size calculation, that measure was selected.
2. Where study participants shared a common characteristic that was the subject of the therapeutic intervention, then the outcome measure most specific to that characteristic was selected.
3. In studies of participants with a wide range of problems, the outcome measure sensitive to the widest range of those problems was selected.
4. For a handful of studies there were two measures of equal suitability and in a couple of cases no obvious measure of the key concern. In these cases the outcome first mentioned was chosen.

For all studies, the results with the chosen measure were compared to the full range of results. In no case did the results with the chosen measure diverge markedly from the whole picture.

Comparisons

Where a study included comparisons between more than two groups, all comparisons that satisfied the inclusion and exclusion criteria were used. Separate meta-analyses were conducted for two groups of studies, due to different hypotheses being addressed:

- comparisons of personal construct psychotherapy with standard care or a waiting list control;
- comparisons of personal construct psychotherapy with something additional to standard care, whether this was an alternative therapeutic approach or additional support not conducted within any particular model of therapy or counselling.

Statistics

For each comparison, an effect size was calculated for the effect of personal construct psychotherapy relative to the comparison group. Where means were compared between conditions with adjustment for pre-treatment responses, the effect size was based on that analysis if the necessary statistics were presented. This could be the t-statistic, or the adjusted regression coefficient with standard error from which the t-statistic could be calculated. The effect size was derived as the t-statistic multiplied by the square root of $(1/n_1 + 1/n_2)$. In addition, while the required t-statistics are not presented, they were obtained from reanalyses of the original data for the two studies reported in chapters of this volume (Watson and Winter, 2005; Foster and Viney, 2005).

Otherwise, the effect size was calculated using the post-treatment means, standard deviations and sample sizes. That is, the difference between the means was divided by the pooled standard deviation. Alternatively, where the outcome was measured as a proportion, this was transformed onto an equivalent scale of effect size using Chinn's methodology (2000). That is, the effect of the intervention was calculated as the natural log of the odds ratio and divided by 1.81.

Having so obtained an effect size for each comparison, this was adjusted to obtain an unbiased estimator and its standard error using the approach proposed by Hedges (1981).

As each meta-analysis incorporates information from studies diverse in the nature of the intervention and client group, it is likely that the true treatment effects vary across studies. Random effects meta-analysis accommodates this variation (Kirkwood and Sterne, 2003), and was employed here using Sharp and Sterne's (1997) Stata program (StataCorp, 2003). The contribution of variations in modality (individual and group psychotherapy), treatment allocation (random or otherwise), and publication (peer-reviewed journal or otherwise) to the heterogeneity across studies was investigated. For each of the three factors the two subgroup-specific pooled estimates of the treatment effect were presented, and the null hypothesis of equal pooled treatment effects between the two subgroups tested using Stata's metareg command (Sharp, 1998; StataCorp, 2003).

Results

Table 27.1 presents identified before and after studies that were not included in the meta-analysis because they did not include a comparison group.

Table 27.2 presents identified studies that were excluded from the meta-analysis, either because they failed to meet the eligibility criteria or because they presented insufficient information to be included in the meta-analysis. Moreover, studies that were included in previous reviews but where the intervention was clearly based on another therapeutic model, albeit perhaps employing some personal construct techniques, were excluded from the meta-analysis (for example, Neimeyer, Heath and Strauss, 1985).

Table 27.1 Before and after studies

Reference	Participants
Landfield AW, Rivers, PC (1975) An introduction to interpersonal transaction and rotating dyads. *Psychotherapy: Research and Practice* 12: 365–373.	15
Morris, JB (1977) The prediction and measurement of change in a psychotherapy group using the repertory grid. In F Fransella, D Bannister (eds) *A Manual for the Repertory Grid Technique*. London: Academic Press, pp 120–148.	8
Sheehan, MJ (1985) A personal construct study of depression. *British Journal of Medical Psychology* 58: 119–128.	12
Button, E (1987) Construing people or weight?: An eating disorders group. In RA Neimeyer, GJ Neimeyer (eds) *Personal Construct Therapy Casebook*. New York: Springer, pp 230–244.	8
Viney LL, Benjamin YN, Preston, C (1988) Promoting independence in the elderly: the role of psychological, social and physical constraints. *Clinical Gerontologist* 24: 71–82.	60
Beail N, Parker S (1991) Group fixed role therapy: a clinical application. *International Journal of Personal Construct Psychology* 4: 85–96.	5
Sewell KW, Ovaert L B (1997) Group treatment of post-traumatic stress in incarcerated adolescents: Structural and narrative impacts on the permeability of self-construction Paper presented at the Twelfth International Congress of Personal Construct Psychology, Seattle, WA.	43
Pekkola D, Cummins, P (2005) Evaluating the anger program. To appear in P Cummins (ed.) *Working with Anger*. London: Wiley.	7
Horley J, Francoeur A (2003) Personal construct group therapy with domestic abusers: A program rationale and preliminary results Paper presented at the Fifteenth International Congress of Personal Construct Psychology, Huddersfield.	14

Table 27.2 Studies excluded from the meta-analysis

Reference	Reason for exclusion
Karst TO, Trexler LD (1970) Initial study using fixed role and rational-emotive therapy in treating speaking anxiety. *Journal of Consulting and Clinical Psychology* 34: 360–6.	No standard deviations.
Bannister D, Adams-Webber JR, Penn WI, Radley PL (1975) Reversing the process of thought disorder: a serial validation experiment. *British Journal of Social and Clinical Psychology* 14: 169–180.	Means and standard deviations not given.

Table 27.2 contd

Reference	Reason for exclusion
Landfield AW (1979) Exploring socialisation through the interpersonal transaction group. In P Stringer, D Bannister (eds) *Constructs of Sociality and Individuality*. London: Academic Press, pp 133–152.	Intervention groups (problem drinkers) and control group (students) not comparable.
Viney LL , Clarke AM, Bunn TA, Benjamin YN (1985a) An evaluation of three crisis intervention programs for general hospital patients. *British Journal of Medical Psychology* 58: 75–86.	All three interventions were based upon personal construct psychotherapy.
Viney LL, Henry RM (2002) Evaluating personal construct and psychodynamic group work with adolescent offenders and non-offenders. In RA Neimeyer, GJ Neimeyer (eds) *Advances in Personal Construct Psychology: New Directions and Perspectives*. Westport, CT: Greenwood Press, pp 259–294.	Sample sizes not given for each intervention group.

Where a study was reported in several papers, only those papers presenting information on a comparison of interest were included. Where two or more papers presented information on a particular comparison, the one presenting most information was selected for inclusion in this study. Considering those papers with comparisons between personal construct psychotherapy and a no treatment, standard care or waiting list control, Table 27.3 gives basic details and Table 27.4 gives basic information on the research methodology and results. Figure 27.1 presents the effect size for each comparison with its 95% confidence interval.

Table 27.3 Basic details of studies comparing a personal construct therapy intervention with a no treatment, standard care or waiting list control

First author	PCP	Control	Clients	Modality	Outcome
Lovenfosse (1999)	PCT	Waiting list	Mothers of children with special needs	Group	Quality of life
Botella (1992–3)	PCT informed self-development	No intervention	Elderly volunteers	Group	Change in construing
Nagae (2001)	PCT	Waiting list	Student volunteers with social anxiety	Individual	Fear of negative evaluation
Nagae (MS)	Fixed role therapy	Waiting list	Shy student volunteers	Individual	Shyness
Lira (1975)	Fixed role therapy	No intervention	Snake phobic student volunteers	Individual	Behaviour task with snakes
Malins (MS)	PCP-based guidance	No intervention	Staff in elderly care homes	Group	Sociality

Table 27.3 contd

First author	PCP	Control	Clients	Modality	Outcome
Alexander (1989)	Interpersonal transaction	Waiting list	Adults sexually abused as children	Group	Global symptoms (psychological)
Winter (MS)	PCT + standard care	Standard care	A&E attenders due to self-harm	Individual	Suicidal ideation
Lane (2001b)	PCT	Waiting list	Survivors of breast cancer	Group	Threat
Foster (2005)	PCT	No intervention	Women approaching the menopause	Group	Anxiety
Truneckova (MS)	Interpersonal transaction	No intervention	Troubled adolescents	Group	No. interpersonal constructs
Viney (1989)	PCT	Waiting list	Elderly people with psychological probs	Individual	Anxiety
Haugli (2000)	PCT + standard care	Standard care	Off work due to musculoskeletal pain	Group	Pain in last week
Viney (1985b)	PCP-based counselling	No intervention	Surgical and medical hospital inpatients	Individual	Days on antibiotics
Viney (1985a)	PCP-based counselling	No intervention	Surgical and medical hospital inpatients	Individual	Anxiety

Table 27.4 Basic methodological details and results for studies comparing a personal construct therapy intervention with a no treatment, standard care or waiting list control

First author	Treatment allocation	No. in PCP condition	No. in control condition	Effect size	Standard error
Lovenfosse (1999)	Client choice	6	6	−0.71	0.60
Botella (1992–3)	Client choice	8	10	−1.74	0.56
Nagae (2001)	Randomized	10	10	−1.93	0.54
Nagae (MS)	Randomized	10	10	−1.04	0.48
Lira (1975)	Randomized	12	12	−0.94	0.43
Malins (MS)	According to workplace	13	14	−0.81	0.40
Alexander 1989)	Randomized	16	21	−0.55	0.34
Winter (MS)	Order of referral	20	18	−0.66	0.33
Lane (2001b)	Randomized	20	22	−0.47	0.31
Foster (2005)	Client determined	37	16	−0.30	0.30
Truneckova (MS)	Randomized	26	22	−0.15	0.29
Viney (1989)	Randomized	28	28	−0.78	0.28
Haugli (2000)	Randomized	58	53	−0.09	0.19
Viney (1985b)	Randomized	90	94	−0.28	0.15
Viney (1985a)	Randomized	107	114	−0.46	0.14

Table 27.3 shows that a diverse range of studies are included in this meta-analysis, with respect to the personal construct psychotherapy techniques employed, the client group served, and the outcome measured. Both individual and group interventions are well represented. Table 27.4

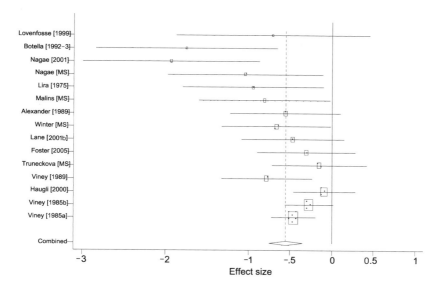

Figure 27.1 Forest plot of comparisons between personal construct therapy and non-active control at post-treatment assessment. The centre of the box indicates the effect size, and the lines the 95% confidence interval. The size of boxes is in proportion to the number of participants. An effect size of less than zero suggests an advantage of personal construct therapy.

shows that treatment allocation was random in the majority of studies. Studies range in size from the very small to the moderately large. As can also be seen from Figure 27.1, effect sizes tend towards showing personal construct psychotherapy to be beneficial over no treatment, standard care or waiting list controls. Eight of the 15 comparisons were significant at the 5% level. The random effects meta-analysis provides a combined estimate of the effectiveness of personal construct psychotherapy compared to no treatment, standard care, or waiting list control: combined effect size = −0.55; 95% confidence interval is −0.75 to −0.35; p < 0.001.

There was evidence of heterogeneity in the estimated effect size across the fifteen comparisons (Q = 25.0, 14 d.f., p = 0.034). Table 27.5 divides the comparisons into two groups according to modality (individual versus group treatment), whether treatment allocation was random or by some other means, and whether the study was published in a peer-reviewed journal or not. As expected, the apparent trends were for stronger treatment effects to be observed in the absence of random treatment allocation (Kunz and Oxman, 1998) and in published studies (Sutton et al., 2000). However, perhaps due to the power of the tests being limited by the small number of studies, in no case was there convincing evidence against the null hypothesis of equal treatment effects between two subgroups.

Table 27.5 Subgroup specific estimates of the pooled treatment effect according to three factors that may contribute to heterogeneity across studies. Meta-regression calculates a *weighted* difference in pooled treatment effects between the two subgroups, and tests the null hypothesis of zero difference

Factor and subgroups	No. of studies	Treatment effect	Subgroup difference	Standard error	p-value
Modality					
Individual	7	−0.67	0.21	0.20	0.30
Group	8	−0.44			
Allocation					
Random	10	−0.50	−0.12	0.11	0.31
Non-random	5	−0.72			
Published					
Peer-reviewed journal	9	−0.62	0.07	0.22	0.74
Other/unpublished	6	−0.48			

Table 27.6 Basic details of studies comparing a personal construct psychotherapy intervention with an active treatment control

First author	PCP	Control	Clients	Modality	Outcome
Nagae (2001)	PCT	Rational emotive	Student volunteers with social anxiety	Individual	Fear of negative evaluation
Nagae (MS)	Fixed role therapy	Self-instructional training	Shy student volunteers	Individual	Shyness
Watson (1998b/2005b)	PCT	Psychodynamic	Clients referred to clinical psychology department	Individual	Global symptoms (psychological)
Lira (1975)	Fixed role therapy	Modelling	Snake phobic student volunteers	Individual	Behaviour task with snakes
Alexander (1989)	Interpersonal transaction	Interpersonal process	Adults sexually abused as children	Group	Global symptoms (psychological)
Winter (in press)	Interpersonal transaction and exposure	Support groups and exposure	Agoraphobics referred to clinical psychology dept.	Group	Agoraphobic symptoms
Watson (1998a/2005a)	PCT	Cognitive behavioural	Clients referred to clinical psychology department	Individual	Global symptoms (psychological)
Evesham (1985)	PCT	Fluency training	Stutterers referred to speech therapy	Group	Relapse

Table 27.6 gives basic details of those papers with comparisons between personal construct psychotherapy and an active treatment control. Table 27.7 gives basic information on the research methodology and results, and Figure 27.2 presents the effect size for each comparison with its 95% confidence interval.

Table 27.7 Basic methodological details and results for studies comparing a personal construct psychotherapy intervention with an active treatment control

First author	Treatment allocation	No. in PCP condition	No. in control condition	Effect size	Standard error
Nagae (2001)	Randomized	10	8	0.03	0.47
Nagae (MS)	Randomized	10	10	−0.14	0.45
Watson (1998b/2005b)	Observational	23	7	−0.35	0.43
Lira (1975)	Randomized	12	12	−0.90	0.43
Alexander (1989)	Randomized	16	20	−0.71	0.35
Winter (in press)	Order of referral	21	19	0.05	0.32
Watson (1998a/2005a)	Observational	23	18	−0.04	0.31
Evesham (1985)	Randomized	22	23	−0.86	0.31

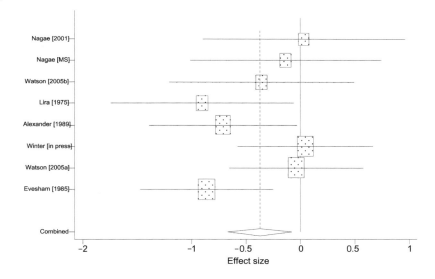

Figure 27.2 Comparisons of personal construct psychotherapy with other active interventions at post-treatment assessment. An effect size of less than zero indicates an advantage of personal construct psychotherapy.

Table 27.6 shows there to be a diverse range of studies comparing personal construct psychotherapy against alternative approaches to treatment. Again there is a range of client groups, approaches to personal construct psychotherapy, comparison treatments and outcome measures. While a minority of studies look at group therapy, Table 27.7 indicates that these are the larger studies. Table 27.7 indicates that three of the eight comparisons were not based on random allocation of participants to interventions, the two studies responsible both being carried out in the same UK National Health Service Clinical Psychology Department.

Table 27.7 also shows that six of the eight comparisons gave results consistent with an advantage of personal construct psychotherapy over an active treatment control. This is clearer in Figure 27.2; for three of the six comparisons suggesting an advantage of personal construct psychotherapy the 95% confidence interval excluded an effect size of zero, indicating statistically significant evidence of a difference at the 5% level. The combined estimate of the effect size for personal construct psychotherapy against an active treatment control was −0.37; 95% confidence interval: −0.66 to −0.08; p = 0.012.

Unexpectedly, there was no evidence of heterogeneity in the estimated effect size across the eight comparisons (Q = 8.82, 7 d.f., p = 0.27). Despite this, Table 27.8 presents modest evidence against equal treatments effects between studies with random treatment allocation and those with allocation by some other means. As already mentioned, two studies conducted in the same UK NHS Clinical Psychology Department account for all three comparisons based upon non-random allocation of treatment.

Table 27.8 Sub-group specific estimates of the pooled treatment effect according to three factors that may contribute to heterogeneity across studies. Meta-regression calculates a *weighted* difference in pooled treatment effects between the two subgroups and tests the null hypothesis of zero difference

Factor and subgroups	No. of studies	Treatment effect	Subgroup difference	Standard error	p-value
Modality					
Individual	5	−0.25	−0.24	0.31	0.44
Group	3	−0.50			
Allocation					
Random	5	−0.60	0.27	0.13	0.043
Non-random	3	−0.07			
Published					
Peer-reviewed journal	5	−0.49	0.34	0.31	0.27
Other/unpublished	3	−0.14			

Returning to comparisons of personal construct psychotherapy with a no-treatment, standard care or waiting list control, Table 27.9 gives summary statistics for those studies in which there was a follow-up assessment, and Figure 27.3 presents the effect sizes with their 95% confidence intervals. The duration of follow-up ranged from 1 month to 12 months across studies. As might be expected, there had been some attrition of participants between post-treatment and follow-up assessments for the Winter et al. and Viney et al. studies, and so there may be some bias in these results. Less expected is the increase in numbers over that period for participants allocated to personal construct psychotherapy in the Haugli et al. study. This appears to be due to the follow-up results being presented in a later paper, which was written after a number of missing assessments had been retrieved.

Table 27.9 Results at follow-up for studies comparing a personal construct psychotherapy intervention with an no treatment, standard care or waiting list control

First author	Follow-up (months)	No. in PCP condition	No. in control condition	Effect size	Standard error
Nagae (MS)	1	10	10	−1.37	0.50
Winter (MS)	6	12	11	−0.30	0.42
Lane (MS)	3	20	22	−0.52	0.31
Haugli (2001)	12	77	44	−0.46	0.19
Viney (1985a)	12	74	84	−0.42	0.16

At the follow-up assessment, again all studies suggested a benefit of personal construct psychotherapy over no treatment, standard care or waiting list control. For three out of five studies the 95% confidence interval excluded an effect size of zero, and again the pooled estimate of the effect size gave strong evidence of a benefit of around half a standard deviation with personal construct psychotherapy: effect size = −0.48; 95% confidence interval: −0.69 to −0.27; p < 0.001.

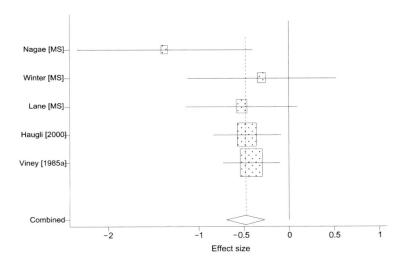

Figure 27.3 Forest plot of comparisons between personal construct psychotherapy and non-active control at follow-up assessment. An effect size of less than zero indicates an advantage of personal construct psychotherapy.

Table 27.10 gives summary statistics for those studies comparing personal construct psychotherapy with an active control, and for which a follow-up assessment was available. The study by Watson and Winter experienced a small loss of participants between post-treatment and follow-up assessments, as did the study by Winter et al., for which imputation of missing values had been employed. Effect sizes and 95% confidence intervals are depicted in Figure 27.4. The Evesham and Fransella (1985) study could arguably have been included here, although it was not, as the primary outcome, relapse, was assessed 18 months after the completion of treatment.

Table 27.10 Results at follow-up for studies comparing a personal construct psychotherapy intervention with an active treatment control

First author	Follow-up (months)	No. in PCP condition	No. in control condition	Effect size	Standard error
Watson (1998b/2005b)	12	19	6	−0.82	0.48
Nagae (2001)	3	10	8	0.41	0.48
Nagae (MS)	1	10	10	−0.07	0.45
Watson (1998a/2005a)	12	19	13	0.09	0.36
Alexander (1989)	6	16	20	−0.31	0.34
Winter (in press)	18	21	19	0.91	0.33

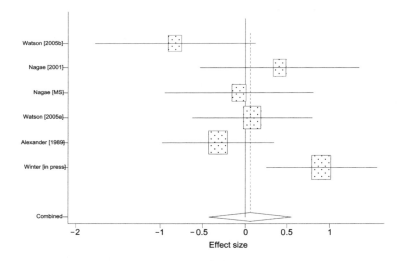

Figure 27.4 Comparisons of personal construct psychotherapy with other active interventions at follow-up assessment. An effect size of less than zero indicates an advantage of personal construct psychotherapy.

Follow-up varied between 1 month and 18 months. Only around half of these studies provided data suggesting an advantage of personal construct psychotherapy over active control, with the 95% confidence interval excluding an effect size of zero in just one study, which favoured the control intervention. There was no convincing evidence that the pooled effect size differed from zero: pooled effect size = 0.06; 95% confidence interval: −0.42 to 0.55; p = 0.80.

Discussion

Exclusion of before-and-after (uncontrolled) studies

In contrast to previous reviews (for example, Viney, 1998; Winter, 2003b), uncontrolled before-and-after studies were excluded from consideration. While such studies are useful in the initial development of an intervention, they are unable to separate the effect of treatment from spontaneous remission of symptoms over time, and so are highly likely to overestimate the effect of treatment (Altman, 1991). They were excluded as the aim of the meta-analysis is to estimate accurately the magnitude of benefit with personal construct psychotherapy.

Inclusion of studies without random allocation to treatment

This review did not include uncontrolled studies but studies with non-random allocation of participants to treatments were included. It would have been difficult to justify their exclusion; while randomized studies of students or highly selected client groups may have better internal validity, the non-randomized studies of clients in health service settings have greater external validity and are considerably more likely to influence practice. We agree with Linde et al. (2002) that the quality of non-randomized studies may be high in other respects.

Statistical analysis for trials of group psychotherapy

A number of studies were of group psychotherapy; the statistical analysis of data from such studies must accommodate the tendency for clients in the same group to have outcomes that are more similar than for clients in different groups. Only the study by Winter et al. (in press) did so, and so it is likely that the standard errors for the other studies of group psychotherapy are underestimated. That said, the problem is avoided by only running one group in each experimental condition but at the expense of obtaining results that are very unlikely to generalize (Botella and Feixas, 1992–3; Lovenfosse and Viney, 1999).

Publication bias

Publication bias is something of a misnomer, given that a number of unpublished manuscripts are included in the meta-analysis, but the general issue is of concern here. Smaller studies will give less accurate estimates of the effect of personal construct psychotherapy due to greater scope for sampling error. Inaccuracy due to sampling error will lead to both overestimates and underestimates of the effect of therapy, but while Figure 27.1 shows smaller studies with evidence of very large (possibly overestimated) positive effects of therapy, there are no small studies which appear to underestimate the effect of therapy. This suggests that data were more likely to be identified for inclusion in this review if they favoured personal construct psychotherapy over a non-active control condition. For this reason it is likely that the benefit of personal construct psychotherapy compared to no treatment, standard care or waiting list control is over-estimated in the present meta-analysis. The three largest studies may present a truer picture, being less subject to sampling error, and these suggest a pooled estimate of the effect size of -0.30 (95% -0.51, -0.10) p = 0.003.

Interpretation

So far as the studies in the two meta-analyses are representative of the practice of personal construct psychotherapy in the context of interest to the reader, then the combined evidence from those studies strongly favours personal construct psychotherapy over no treatment, standard care or waiting list controls at post-treatment (effect size = 0.55; p < 0.001) and supports an advantage of personal construct psychotherapy over other possible interventions at post-treatment (effect size = -0.37; p = 0.012). Only a small number of studies assessed outcome some time after the completion of treatment. The combined evidence from these studies strongly favours personal construct psychotherapy over no treatment, standard care or waiting list controls at follow-up (effect size = -0.48; p < 0.001) but suggests no difference between personal construct psychotherapy and other possible interventions at that time (effect size = $+0.06$; p = 0.80). For comparison, Cohen (1962) distinguished small, medium and large treatment effects as effect sizes of 0.25, 0.50 and 1.00 respectively. Kazdin and Bass (1989) found in their review that the median effect size for comparisons of psychotherapy with no-treatment controls was 0.78 while the median effect size for comparisons between different interventions was 0.47.

Conclusions

Numerous uncontrolled, single case, and/or qualitative studies of personal construct psychotherapy have been reviewed elsewhere (Viney, 1998; Winter, 1992a, 2003b), and some have been described in other chapters in this volume. These studies have been of great value in indicating the richness of the personal construct approach and increasing our understanding of the therapeutic process. By using assessment methods consistent with constructivist psychology (Viney, 1988) and measures that tap the structure and content of the construct system (Winter, 2003d) and construing processes (Viney, 1993b), they have been able to reveal the reconstruction accompanying personal construct psychotherapy. In several of these studies, the use of individualized outcome measures has ensured the personal relevance to the client of the changes that are monitored.

Such investigations have now been usefully complemented by the work of those personal construct practitioners and researchers who have accepted the challenge of evidence-based practice by carrying out traditional quantitative, controlled studies. The current systematic review and meta-analyses indicate that these studies can be considered to have provided encouraging evidence of the effectiveness of personal construct psychotherapy.

Papers included in the review

Alexander PC, Neimeyer RA, Follette VM, Moore MK, Harter SL (1989). A comparison of group treatments of women sexually abused as children. Journal of Consulting and Clinical Psychology 57: 479-83.

Botella L, Feixas G (1992–3). The autobiographical group: a tool for the reconstruction of past life experience with the aged. International Journal of Aging and Human Development 36: 303–19.

Evesham M, Fransella F (1985) Stuttering relapse: the effects of a combined speech and psychological reconstruction program. British Journal of Disorders of Communication 20: 237–48.

Foster H, Viney LL (2005) Personal construct workshops for women experiencing menopause. In DA Winter, LL Viney (eds) Personal Construct Psychotherapy: Advances in Theory, Practice and Research. London: Whurr.

Haugli L, Steen E, Lærum E, Finset A, Nygaard R (2000) Agency orientation and chronic musculoskeletal pain: effects of a group learning program based on the personal construct theory. Clinical Journal of Pain 16: 281–9.

Haugli L, Steen E, Lærum E, Nygaard R, Finset A (2001) Learning to have less pain – is it possible? A one-year follow-up study of the effects of a personal construct group learning programme on patients with chronic musculoskeletal pain. Patient Education and Counseling 45: 111–18.

Lane LG, Viney LL (2001) When the real becomes unreal: an evaluation of personal construct group psychotherapy with survivors of breast cancer. Paper presented at the Fourteenth International Congress of Personal Construct Psychology, Wollongong. (Since the analyses presented in this chapter, this study has been accepted for publication in the *Journal of Consulting and Clinical Psychology* as 'The effects of personal construct group psychotherapy on breast cancer survivors'.)

Lira FT, Nay R, McCullough JP, Etkin MW (1975). Relative effects of modeling and role playing in the treatment of avoidance behaviors. Journal of Consulting and Clinical Psychology 43: 608–18.

Lovenfosse M, Viney LL (1999) Understanding and helping mothers of children with 'special needs' using personal construct group work. Community Mental Health Journal 35: 431–42.

Malins GL, Couchman L, Viney LL, Grenyer BFS (2004) Time to talk: evaluation of a staff-resident quality time intervention on the perceptions of staff in aged care. Clinical Psychologist 8: 48–52.

Nagae N, Nedate K (2001) Comparison of constructive cognitive and rational cognitive psychotherapies for students with social anxiety. Constructivism in the Human Sciences 6: 41–9.

Nagae N, Nedate K. Effects of fixed role therapy and self instructional training for students with shyness. Unpublished manuscript.

Truneckova D, Viney LL (2003) Evaluating personal construct group work with troubled adolescents. Unpublished manuscript, University of Wollongong.

Viney LL et al. (1985b) The effect of a hospital-based counseling service on the physical recovery of surgical and medical patients. General Hospital Psychiatry 7: 294–301.

Viney LL et al. (1985c) Crisis-intervention counseling: an evaluation of long- and short-term effects. Journal of Counseling Psychology 32: 29–39.

Viney LL, Benjamin YN, Preston C (1989) An evaluation of personal construct therapy for the elderly. British Journal of Medical Psychology 62: 35–41.

Watson S (1998) (comparisons a and b). A Process and Outcome Study of Personal Construct, Cognitive and Psychodynamic Therapies in a National Health Service Setting. Unpublished PhD thesis. University of Hertfordshire.

Watson S, Winter DA (2005) (comparisons a and b). A process and outcome study of personal construct psychotherapy. In DA Winter, LL Viney (eds), Personal Construct Psychotherapy: Advances in Theory, Practice and Research. London: Whurr.

Winter D, Gournay K, Metcalfe C, Rossotti N (2005). Expanding agoraphobics' horizons: an investigation of the effectiveness of a personal construct psychotherapy intervention. Journal of Constructivist Psychology.

Winter D, Sireling L, Riley T, Metcalfe C, Quaite A, Bhandari S. A controlled trial of personal construct psychotherapy for deliberate self-harm. Unpublished manuscript, University of Hertfordshire.

An introduction to personal construct theory

Theory

George Kelly's (1955/1991a) personal construct theory is based upon the philosophical assumption of *constructive alternativism*, which states that 'all of our present interpretations of the universe are subject to revision or replacement' (Kelly, 1955/1991a, p. 15/p. 11). In other words, not only do we construct our worlds but we can reconstruct them.

Fundamental postulate

Kelly presented his theory formally in terms of a 'fundamental postulate' and 11 corollaries. The Fundamental Postulate states that 'A person's processes are psychologically channelized by the ways in which he anticipates events' (Kelly, 1955/1991a, p. 47/p. 32). This emphasis on anticipation was further emphasized in Kelly's metaphor of the person as a scientist, formulating hypotheses about his or her world, testing these out, and if necessary revising them.

The corollaries are as follows.

Construction corollary

'A person anticipates events by construing their replications' (Kelly, 1955/1991a, p. 50/p. 35). We search for repeated themes in our experiences of our world, identifying similarities and differences between events.

Individuality corollary

'Persons differ from each other in their constructions of events' (Kelly, 1955/1991a, p. 55/p. 38). No two people are ever likely to construe an event in exactly the same way.

Organization corollary

'Each person characteristically evolves, for his convenience in anticipating events, a construction system embracing ordinal relationships between constructs' (Kelly, 1955/1991a, p. 56/p. 39). *Constructs* may be viewed as 'transparent patterns or templets' that the person 'creates and then attempts to fit over the realities of which the world is composed' (Kelly, 1955/1991a, pp. 8–9/p. 7). They are organized in a hierarchical system in which some are *superordinate* to others.

Dichotomy corollary

'A person's construction system is composed of a finite number of dichotomous constructs' (Kelly, 1955/1991a, p. 59/p. 41). Constructs are bipolar (for example, 'good–bad'), and we therefore construe events in terms of the contrasts between them, although these do not necessarily carry verbal labels.

Choice corollary

'A person chooses for himself that alternative in a dichotomized construct through which he anticipates the greater possibility for the extension and definition of his system' (Kelly, 1955/1991a, p. 64/p. 45). Our choices are essentially elaborative rather than hedonistic, being directed towards maximizing our capacity to anticipate our world rather than maximizing our level of pleasure.

Range corollary

'A construct is convenient for the anticipation of a finite range of events only' (Kelly, 1955/1991a, p. 68/p. 48). Each construct has a *focus of convenience,* the area of its maximum usefulness, and a *range of convenience,* an area in which it can still be applied but less well.

Experience corollary

'A person's construction system varies as he successively construes the replications of events' (Kelly, 1955/1991a, p. 72/p. 50). Our predictions of events may be *validated* or *invalidated,* and this will generally result in either the strengthening or the modification of the constructions concerned.

Modulation corollary

'The variation in a person's construction system is limited by the permeability of the constructs within whose ranges of convenience the variants lie' (Kelly, 1955/1991a, p. 77/p. 54). A *permeable* construct is one that may be readily applied to new elements of the person's experience: 'good–bad', for example, is likely to be a more permeable construct for most people than is 'Theravada Buddhist–Zen Buddhist'.

Fragmentation corollary

'A person may successively employ a variety of construction subsystems which are inferentially incompatible with each other' (Kelly, 1955/1991a, p. 83/p. 58). Construct systems do not have to be entirely logically organized, and inconsistent *subsystems* may be tolerated if the person's superordinate constructs are sufficiently permeable to subsume these.

Commonality corollary

'To the extent that one person employs a construction of experience which is similar to that employed by another, his processes are psychologically similar to those of the other person' (Kelly, 1955/1991a, p. 90/p. 63). Especially within a particular cultural group, there may be similarities within aspects of people's construing and therefore of their 'behaviour'.

Sociality corollary

'To the extent that one person construes the construction processes of another, he may play a role in a social process involving the other person' (Kelly, 1955/1991a, p. 95/p. 66). The essence of social relationships, including the therapeutic relationship, is the attempt to see the world though the other person's eyes.

Dimensions of diagnosis and transition

Kelly provided a set of 'professional constructs' as an aid to clinicians in construing their clients' construction processes (although these constructs are just as applicable to people who are not clients). Some concern *covert construction*, namely that which is at a low *level of cognitive awareness*. They include *preverbal* constructs, which have no consistent verbal symbols; *submergence*, where one pole of a construct is relatively inaccessible; and *suspension*, where a particular construction is held in abeyance.

Kelly's 'dimensions of transition' are particularly associated with emotions, the experience of which essentially reflects the awareness of a transition in construing. Thus, *threat* is the awareness of an imminent comprehensive change in core structures, those that govern the person's maintenance processes and are central to his or her identity. One aspect of core structure is the person's *core role*, those constructions of others' construing that determine the person's characteristic ways of interacting with others. *Guilt* is the experience of an apparent dislodgement from one's core role. *Anxiety* occurs when we find our world largely unconstruable, events being seen to be outside the range of convenience of our construct system. *Aggressiveness* was associated by Kelly (1955/1991a, p. 508/p. 374) with the 'active elaboration of one's perceptual field', whereas *hostility* was defined as 'the continued effort to extort validational evidence in favour of a type of social prediction which has already proved itself a failure' (Kelly, 1955/1991a, p.510/p. 375). The hostile person tries to make the world fit in with his or her constructions rather than vice versa.

Kelly viewed the process of transition in construing as generally being cyclical in nature, and he delineated various cycles of construction. The *experience cycle* (1970a) is the essence of construing, and consists of the anticipation of an event, investment of the person in this anticipation, encounter with the event, confirmation or disconfirmation of the anticipation, and constructive revision if reconstruing is deemed necessary. The *circumspection–preemption–control* (C–P–C) cycle is concerned with decision making. Its circumspection phase involves *propositional* construing, in which a particular construction of an event does not determine how else the event is construed. This type of construing is in contrast with *constellatory* construing, as occurs in stereotypes, and *preemptive* construing, in which the application of a particular construct pole to an event prevents the event from being construed in any other way. In the circumspection phase of the C-P-C cycle, the issues concerning a particular decision are surveyed, in the preemption phase a particular issue, or construct, is focused upon, and in the control phase one particular pole of this construct is applied to an event. The *creativity cycle*, which is concerned with the development of new constructs, consists of the contrasting processes of *loose* and *tight* construing. In the former, the assignment of events to construct poles shifts constantly while in the latter this assignment is fixed and the person's predictions are unvarying. Another pair of contrasting processes, or strategies, that the person may use, in this case to deal with apparent incompatibilities in construing, are *dilation* and *constriction*. In the former, the perceptual field is extended with a view to reorganizing it on a more comprehensive level. Referring to the psychotherapy client who uses dilation, Kelly (1955/1991a, p. 477/p. 352) stated that 'he tends to see everything that happens to him as potentially related to his problem.' In *constriction*, by contrast, the outer boundaries of the perceptual field are drawn in, and the client 'insists that the therapist stick to a sharply delimited version of his problem' (p. 477/p. 352).

Assessment of construing

Personal construct theorists use various methods to assess construing. In the *self-characterization* (Kelly, 1955/1991a), the person is asked to write a character sketch of himself or herself as if it were written by an intimate and sympathetic friend. Kelly's other major assessment method was *repertory grid technique* (Fransella, Bannister and Bell, 2004), in which a set of elements of the person's experience (usually other people and/or aspects of the self) are compared and contrasted in order to elicit a set of the person's constructs. The elements are then sorted in terms of the constructs, usually by rating each of them on each construct. Analysis of the grid, usually by computer, can provide a range of measures, including those concerning the similarities and differences between elements, relationships between constructs, and aspects of the structure (such as tightness or looseness) of construing.

Personal construct theorists after Kelly have developed several other assessment methods. *Laddering* (Hinkle, 1965) was developed to elicit superordinate constructs by successively asking which pole of a construct the person would like to be assigned to and why. A contrasting procedure, *pyramiding* (Landfield, 1971), provides access to subordinate constructs by asking what type of people are described by particular construct poles. The *implications grid* (Hinkle, 1965; Fransella, 1972) involves direct questioning concerning the implications of each of a person's constructs in terms of the other constructs in his or her system. Tschudi's (1977) *ABC technique* identifies the positive and negative implications of particular constructs – for example, those relating to a person's symptoms.

Interviews may also be used to identify processes of construing and Kellian emotions, as in Viney's (1983a, 1993b) use of content analysis scales (see also Viney and Caputi, 2005).

In assessment and in therapy, the clinician who works from a personal construct theory perspective will adopt a *credulous attitude* to the client's construing, 'taking what he sees and hears at face value' (Kelly, 1955/1991a, p. 173/p. 121).

Personal construct psychotherapy

Personal construct psychotherapy may be considered to be a process of reconstruction. It is technically eclectic, using a variety of techniques, the modes of action of which are conceptualized in personal construct theory terms, for example as means of elaborating, loosening or tightening construing. One of the few such techniques specifically developed by Kelly (1955/1991a) is *fixed-role therapy*, in which, largely to facilitate experimentation, the client is asked to take on a new role for a short period of time. However, personal construct psychotherapy is by no means limited to this particular technique, which is only used with a relatively small percentage of clients.

References

Abel GG, Becker JV, Cunningham-Rathner J (1984) Complications, consent, and cognitions in sex between children and adults. International Journal of Law and Psychiatry 7: 89–103.

Abrahamson LY, Seligman MEP, Teasdale JD (1978) Learned helplessness in humans: Critique and reformulation. Journal of Abnormal Psychology 87: 49–74.

Adams-Webber JR (1970) An analysis of the discriminant validity of several repertory grid indices. British Journal of Psychology 61: 83–90.

Adams-Webber J (1977) The golden section and the structure of self-concepts. Perceptual and Motor Skills 45: 703–6.

Adams-Webber J (1978) Personal Construct Theory: Concepts and Applications. New York: Wiley.

Adams-Webber J, Benjafield J (1976) The relationship between cognitive complexity and assimilative projection in terms of personal constructs. Bulletin of British Psychological Society 29: 219.

Adams-Webber J, Davidson DL (1979) Maximum contrast between self and others in personal judgements. British Journal of Psychology 70: 517–18.

Adams-Westcott J, Dobbins C (1997) Listening with your 'heart ears' and other ways young people can escape the effects of sexual abuse. In C Smith, D Nyland (eds) Narrative Therapies with Children and Adolescents. New York: Guilford, pp. 195–220.

Adams-Webber J, Mancuso JC (1983) The pragmatic logic of personal construct psychology. In J Adams-Webber, JC Mancuso (eds) Applications of Personal Construct Psychology. New York: Academic Press, pp. 1–10.

Adams-Webber J, Schwenker B, Barbeau D (1972) Personal constructs and the perception of individual differences. Canadian Journal of Behavioral Sciences 4: 218–24.

Aldridge D (1998) Suicide: The Tragedy of Hopelessness. London: Jessica Kingsley.

Alexander F, French TM (1946) Psychoanalytic Therapy: Principles and Application. New York: Ronald Press.

Alexander PC, Follette VM (1987) Personal constructs in the group treatment of incest. In RA Neimeyer, GJ Neimeyer (eds) Personal Construct Therapy Casebook. New York: Springer, pp. 211–19.

Alexander PC, Neimeyer RA, Follette VM (1991) Group therapy for women sexually abused as children. A controlled study and investigation of individual differences. Journal of Interpersonal Violence 6: 218–31.

Alexander PC, Neimeyer RA, Follette VM, Moore MK, Harter SL (1989) A comparison of group treatments of women sexually abused as children. Journal of Consulting and Clinical Psychology 57: 479–83.

Altman DG (1991) Practical Statistics for Medical Research. London: Chapman & Hall.

American Psychiatric Association (1980) Diagnostic and Statistical Manual of Mental Disorders (3 edn). Washington, DC: American Psychiatric Association.

American Psychiatric Association (2000) Diagnostic and Statistical Manual of Mental Disorders. 4 edn. Washington, DC: American Psychiatric Association.

Anarte MT, Cuadros JL, Herrera J (1998) Hormonal and psychological treatment: Therapeutic alternative for menopausal women? Maturitas 29: 203–13.

Anderson E, Hamburger S, Liu JH, Rebar RW (1987) Characteristics of menopausal women seeking assistance. American Journal of Obstetrics and Gynecology 156: 428–33.

Anderson WT (1990) Reality Isn't What It Used To Be. San Francisco, CA: Harper & Rowe.

Andrews DA, Bonta J (1998) The Psychology of Criminal Conduct. Cincinatti, OH: Anderson.

Andrews DA, Wormith JS (1990) A summary of normative, reliability and validity statistics on the Criminal Sentiments Scale. Unpublished manuscript, Carleton University, Ottawa.

Andrews DA, Zinger I, Hoge R, Bonta J, Gendreau P, Cullen, FT (1990) Does correctional treatment work? A clinically relevant and psychologically informed meta-analysis. Criminology 28: 369–404.

Androutsopoulou A (2001) The self-characterisation as a narrative tool: applications in therapy with individuals and families. Family Process 40: 79–94.

Angus LE, Lewin J, Bouffard B, Rotondi-Trevisan D (2004) 'What's the story?' Working with narrative in experiential psychotherapy. In LE Angus, J McLeod (eds) The Handbook of Narrative and Psychotherapy. Thousand Oaks, CA: Sage, pp. 87–102.

Apfelbaum B (1980) Retarded ejaculation. In SR Leiblum, LA Pervin (eds) Principles and Practice of Sex Therapy. London: Tavistock, pp. 263–96.

Apolinsky SR, Wilcoxon SA (1991) Symbolic confrontation with women survivors of childhood sexual victimization. Journal for Specialists in Group Work 16: 85–90.

Apparigliato M, Ruggiero GM, Sassaroli S (2003) Il criticismo: Un'analisi cognitiva. Unpublished manucript.

Arentewicz G, Schmidt G (1983) The Treatment of Sexual Disorders: Concepts and Techniques of Couple Therapy. New York: Basic Books.

Arsenio W, Lemerise E (2001) Varieties of childhood bullying: values, emotion processes and social competence. Social Development 10: 59–73.

Arthur AR (2000) The personality and cognitive-epistemological traits of cognitive behavioral and psychoanalytic psychotherapists. British Journal of Medical Psychology 73: 243–57.

Attig T (2000) The Heart of Grief. New York: Oxford.

Australian Bureau of Statistics (1998) A Guide to Major ABS Classifications, Occupation. Canberra: Australian Standard Classification of Occupations (ASCO).

Bacal HA, Newman KM (1990) Theories of Object Relations: Bridges to Self Psychology. New York: Columbia University Press.

Badanes L, Estevan R, Bacete F (2000) Theory of mind and peer rejection at school. Social Development 9: 271–83.

Baddeley A (1994) Memory – a User's Guide. London: Penguin.

Bagnara S (1984) L'attenzione. Il Mulino: Bologna.

Bandura A (1977) Self-efficacy: Towards a unifying theory of behavioral change. Psychological Review. 84, 191-215.

Bandura A (1986) Social Foundations in Thought and Action: A Social Cognitive Theory. Englewood Cliffs, NJ: Prentice-Hall.

Banister E (2000) Women's midlife confusion: 'Why am I feeling this way?' Issues in Mental Health Nursing 21: 745–65.

Bannister D (1960) Conceptual structure in thought-disordered schizophrenics. Journal of Mental Science 106: 1230–49.

Bannister D (1962) The nature and measurement of schizophrenic thought disorder. Journal of Mental Science 108: 825–42.

Bannister D (1963) The genesis of schizophrenic thought disorder: a serial invalidation hypothesis. British Journal of Psychiatry 109: 680–6.

Bannister D (1965a) The genesis of schizophrenic thought disorder: re-test of the serial invalidation hypothesis. British Journal of Psychiatry 111: 377–82.

Bannister D (1965b) The rationale and clinical relevance of repertory grid technique. British Journal of Psychiatry 111: 977–82.

Bannister D (1975) Psychology as an exercise in paradox. Bulletin of the British Psychological Society 19: 21–63.

Bannister D (1977) The logic of passion. In D Bannister (ed.) New Perspectives in Personal Construct Theory. London: Academic Press, pp. 21–37.

Bannister D (1985) The psychotic disguise. In W Dryden (ed.) Therapists' Dilemmas. London: Harper & Row, pp. 167–79.

Bannister D, Agnew J (1976) The child's construing of self. In J Cole, AW Landfield (eds) The Nebraska Symposium on Motivation: Personal Construct Psychology. Lincoln, NB: University of Nebraska Press, pp. 99-125.

Bannister D, Bott M (1973) Evaluating the person. In P Kline (ed.) New Approaches in Psychological Measurement. London: Wiley, pp. 157–77.

Bannister D, Fransella F (1980) Inquiring Man: The Psychology of Personal Constructs. 2 edn. Harmondsworth: Penguin.

Bannister D, Fransella F (1986) Inquiring Man: The Psychology of Personal Constructs. 3 edn. London: Croom Helm.

Bannister D, Salmon P (1967) Measures of superordinacy. Unpublished MS. Bexley Hospital.

Bannister D, Adams-Webber JR, Penn WI, Radley PL (1975) Reversing the process of thought disorder: a serial validation experiment. British Journal of Social and Clinical Psychology 14: 169–80.

Barlow DH (1988) Anxiety and its Disorders: The Nature and the Treatment of Anxiety and Panic. New York: Guilford.

Barlow DH (1991) Disorders of emotion. Psychological Inquiry 2 : 58–71.

Barlow DH (1994) Psychological interventions in the era of managed competition. Clinical Psychology: Science and Practice 1: 109–22.

Baron-Cohen S, Tager-Flusberg H, Cohen D (2000) Understanding Other Minds: Perspect- ives from Developmental Cognitive Neuroscience. New York: Oxford University Press.

Barrett-Lennard GT (1964) The Relationship Inventory. Australia: University of New England.

Bartlett FC (1932) Remembering. Cambridge: Cambridge University Press.

Bartol CR, Bartol AM (1999) History of forensic psychology. In AK Hess, I Weiner (eds) The Handbook of Forensic Psychology. New York: Wiley, pp. 3–23.

Basoglu M, Mineka S (1992) The role of uncontrollable and unpredictable stress in post-traumatic stress responses in torture survivors. In M Basoglu (ed.) Torture and Its Consequences: Current Treatment Approaches. Cambridge: Cambridge University Press, pp. 182–225.

Bateson G (1972) Steps to an Ecology of Mind. New York: Ballantyne.

Bateson G (1976) Foreword. In CE Sluzki, DC Ransom (eds) Double Bind: The Foundation of the Communicational Approach to the Family. New York: Grune & Stratton.

Batson C, Ahmad N, Lishner D, Tsang J (2002) Empathy and Altruism. In C Snyder, S Lopez (eds) Handbook of Positive Psychology. New York: Oxford University Press, pp. 485–98.

Beail N, Parker S (1991) Group fixed role therapy: a clinical application. International Journal of Personal Construct Psychology 4: 85–96.

Beck AT (1976) Cognitive Therapy and the Emotional Disorders. New York: International Universities Press.

Beck AT, Epstein N, Brown G, Steer RA (1988) An inventory for measuring clinical anxiety: psychometric properties. Journal of Consulting and Clinical Psychology 56: 893–7.

Beck AT, Rush AJ, Shaw BF, Emery G (1979) Cognitive Therapy of Depression. New York: Guilford.

Beck AT, Ward CH, Mendelson M, Mock J, Erbaugh J (1961) An inventory for measuring depression. Archives of General Psychiatry 4: 561–71.

Beck AT, Weissman A, Lester D, Trexler L (1974) The measurement of pessimism: the Hopelessness Scale. Journal of Consulting and Clinical Psychology 42: 861–5.

Beitchman JH, Zucker KJ, Hood JE, DaCosta BA, Akman D, Cassavia E (1992) A review of the long-term effects of child sexual abuse. Child Abuse and Neglect 16: 101–18.

Bentall RP (1996) From cognitive studies of psychosis to cognitive-behaviour therapy for psychotic symptoms. In G Haddock, PD Slade (eds) Cognitive-Behavioural Interventions with Psychotic Disorders. London: Routledge, pp. 3–27.

Berg I (1994) Family Based Services: a Solution Focused Approach. New York: Norton.

Berzonsky MD (1990) Self construction over the life span: a process perspective on identity formation. In GJ Neimeyer, RA Neimeyer (eds) Advances in Personal Construct Psychology Volume 1. Greenwich CT: JAI Press, pp. 155–86.

Berzonsky M (1994) Individual differences in self construction: the role of constructivist epistemological assumptions. Journal of Constructivist Psychology 7: 263–81.

Bion WR (1961) Experiences in Groups. London: Tavistock.

Biran M (1988) Cognitive and exposure treatment for agoraphobia: reexamination of the outcome research. Journal of Cognitive Psychotherapy 2: 165–78.

Blalock SJ, Devellis BM, Patterson CC, Campbell MK, Orenstein DR, Dooley MA (2002) Effects of an osteoporosis prevention program incorporating tailored educational materials. American Journal of Health Promotion 16: 146–56.

Blatt SJ, Sanislow CA, Zuroff DC, Pilkonis PA (1996) Characteristics of effective therapists: further analysis of data from the National Institute of Mental Health Treatment of Depression Collaborative Research Project. Journal of Consulting and Clinical Psychology 64: 1276–84.

Bloch S, Crouch E (1985) Therapeutic Factors in Group Psychotherapy. Oxford: Oxford University Press.

Bloom JR (1982) Social support, accommodation to stress and adjustment to breast cancer. Social Science and Medicine 16: 1329–38.

Bohart AC, Tallman K (1999) How Clients Make Therapy Work. Washington, DC: American Psychological Association.

Bohart AC, O'Hara M, Leitner LM (1998) Empirically violated treatments: disenfranchisement of humanistic and other psychotherapies. Psychotherapy Research 8: 141–57.

Book H (2004) The CCRT approach to working with patient narratives in psychodynamic psychotherapy. In LE Angus, J McLeod (eds) The Handbook of Narrative and Psychotherapy. Thousand Oaks, CA: Sage, pp. 71–85.

Bosworth HB, Bastian L, Kuchibhatla M, Steffens D, McBride CM, Sugg Skinner C, Rimer BK, Siegler IC (2001) Depressive symptoms, menopausal status, and climacteric symptoms in women at midlife. Psychosomatic Medicine 63 (July/August): 603–8.

Botella L (1991) Psychoeducational groups with older adults: an integrative personal construct rationale and some guidelines. International Journal of Personal Construct Psychology 4: 397–408.

Botella L (1995) Personal construct theory, constructivism, and postmodern thought. In RA Neimeyer, GJ Neimeyer (eds) Advances in Personal Construct Psychology. Volume 3. Greenwich CT: JAI Press, pp. 3–35.

Botella L (2000) Personal construct psychology, constructivism, and psychotherapy research. In JW Scheer (ed.) The Person in Society: Challenges to a Constructivist Theory. Giessen: Psychosozial-Verlag, pp. 362–72.

Botella L (2001) Diálogo, relações e mudança: uma aproximação discursiva à psicoterapia construtivista [Dialogue, relationships, and change: A discursive approach to constructivist psychotherapy]. In Gonçalves Ó, Gonçalves M (eds) Abordagens Construcionistas à Psicoterapia. Coimbra, Portugal: Quarteto, pp. 50–61.

Botella L, Feixas G (1989) The autobiographical group: a tool for the reconstruction of past life experience with the aged. Paper presented at the Eighth International Congress on Personal Construct Psychology, Assissi, Italy.

Botella L, Feixas G (1992-3) The autobiographical group: a tool for the reconstruction of past life experience with the aged. International Journal of Ageing and Human Development 36: 303–19.

Botella L, Herrero O (2000) A relational constructivist approach to narrative therapy. European Journal of Psychotherapy, Counselling and Health 3: 1–12.

Botella L, Herrero O, Pacheco M, Corbella S (2004) Working with narrative in psychotherapy: a relational constructivist approach. In LE Angus, J McLeod (eds) The Handbook of Narrative and Psychotherapy. Thousand Oaks, CA: Sage, pp. 119–36.

Bowlby J (1958) The nature of the child's tie to his mother. International Journal of Psycho-Analysis 39: 350–73.

Bowlby J (1969) Attachment and Loss. Volume 1, Attachment. New York: Basic Books.

Bowlby J (1973) Attachment and Loss. Volume 2, Separation. New York: Basic Books.

Bowlby J (1988) A Secure Base: Clinical Applications of Attachment Theory. London: Routledge.

Bowman KF, Deimling GT, Smerglia V, Sage P, Kahana B (2003) Appraisal of the cancer experience by older long-term survivors. Psycho-Oncology 12: 226–38.

Bridges SK, Neimeyer RA (2005) The relationship between eroticism, gender and interpersonal bonding: a clinical illustration of sexual holonic mapping. Journal of Constructivist Psychology 18: 15–24.

Briere J (1996) Therapy for Adults Molested as Children: Beyond Survival. 2nd Edn. New York: Springer.

Briere J, Runtz M (1993) Child sexual abuse: long-term sequelae and implications for assessment. Journal of Interpersonal Violence 8: 312–30.

Brogna P, D'Andrea T (2000) Therapists' transitions and the risk of suicide. In JW Scheer (ed.) The Person in Society: Challenges to a Constructivist Theory. Giessen: Psychosozial-Verlag, pp. 421–7.

Bromberger JT, Meyer PM, Kravitz HM, Sommer B, Cordal A, Powell L, Ganz PA, Sutton-Tyrrell K (2001) Psychologic distress and the natural menopause: A multi-ethnic community study. American Journal of Public Health 91: 1435–42.

Brown EJ, Heimberg RG, Frost RO, Makris SG, Juster HR, Leung AW (1999) Relationship of perfectionism to affect, expectations, attributions and performance in the classroom. Journal of Social and Clinical Psychology 18: 98–120.

Browne A, Finkelhor D (1986) Impact of child sexual abuse: a review of the research. Psychological Bulletin 99: 66–77.

Bruch H (1973) Eating Disorders: Obesity, Anorexia Nervosa, and the Person Within. New York: Basic Books.

Buber M (1958) I and Thou. New York: Macmillan.

Burnham J (2000) Internalized other interviewing: evaluating and enhancing therapy. Clinical Psychology Forum 140: 16–20.

Burns DD (1980) The perfectionist's script for self–defeat. Psychology Today (November): 34–51.

Burns T, Hunter M, Lieberman S (1980) A repertory grid study of therapist/couple interaction. Journal of Family Therapy 2: 297–310.

Burr V (1995) An Introduction to Social Constructionism. London: Routledge.

Burt JC (1977) Preliminary Report of an Innovative Surgical Procedure for Treatment of Coital Anorgasmia. Bloomington IN: International Academy of Sex Research.

Butler G, Mathews A (1983) Cognitive processes in anxiety. Advances in Behaviour Research and Therapy 5: 51–62.

Butler G, Mathews A (1987) Anticipatory anxiety and risk perception. Cognitive Therapy and Research 91: 551–65.

Butler R (2001) The Self Image Profiles For Children (SIP–C) and Adolescents (SIP–A). London: The Psychological Corporation.

Butler R, Green D (1998) The Child Within. The Exploration of Personal Construct Theory with Young People. Oxford: Butterworth Heinemann.

Butler R, Hardy L (1992) The performance profile; theory and application. Sport Psychologist 6: 253–64.

Button EJ (1980) Construing and Clinical Outcome in Anorexia Nervosa. Unpublished PhD Thesis. University of London.

Button E (1985) Eating disorders: A quest for control? In E Button (ed.) Personal Construct Theory and Mental Health. London: Croom Helm, pp. 153–68.

Button EJ (1987) Construing people or weight?: An eating disorders group. In RA Neimeyer, GJ Neimeyer (eds) Personal Construct Therapy Casebook. New York: Springer, pp. 230–44.

Button EJ (1993) Eating Disorders: Personal Construct Therapy and Change. Chichester: Wiley.

Button EJ (1994) Personal construct measurement of self-esteem. International Journal of Constructivist Psychology 7: 53–65.

Button E (1996) Validation and invalidation. In JW Scheer, A Catina (eds) Empirical Constructivism in Europe: The Personal Construct Approach. Giessen: Psychosozial–Verlag, pp. 142–8.

Button EJ, Warren RL (2002) Self-image in anorexia nervosa 7.5 years after initial presentation to a specialized eating disorder service. European Eating Disorders Review 10: 399–412.

Caine TM, Smail DJ, Wijesinghe OBA, Winter DA (1982) Claybury Selection Battery Manual. Windsor: NFER–Nelson.

Caine TM, Wijesinghe OBA, Winter DA (1981) Personal Styles in Neurosis: Implications for Small Group Psychotherapy and Behaviour Therapy. London: Routledge & Kegan Paul.

Calvo MG, Eysenck MW, Castillo MD (1997) Interpretative bias in test anxiety: the time course of predictive inference. Cognition and Emotion 11: 43–63.

Calvo MG, Eysenck MW, Estevaz A (1994) Ego-threat interpretative bias in test anxiety: on-line inferences. Cognition and Emotion 2: 127–46.

Capps L, Ochs E (1995) Constructing Panic: The Discourse of Agoraphobia. Cambridge, MA: Harvard University Press.

Carlsen MB (1988) Meaning Makings: Therapeutic Processes in Adult Development. New York: Norton.

Carrell S (1993) Group Exercises for Adolescents: A Manual for Therapists. Thousand Oaks, CA: Sage Publications.

Carter BJ (1993) Long-term survivors of breast cancer: a qualitative descriptive study. Cancer Nursing 16: 354–6.

Catina A, Schmitt GM (1993) Die Theorie der Persönlichen Konstrukte. In JW Scheer, A Catina (eds) Einführung in die Repertory Grid-Technik. Band I. Göttingen: Huber, pp. 11–23.

Cashdan S (1988) Object Relations Therapy: Using the Relationship. New York: Norton.

Chadwick P, Birchwood M, Trower P (1996) Cognitive Therapy for Delusions, Voices and Paranoia. Chichester: Wiley.

Chalmers I, Altman DG (eds) (1995) Systematic Reviews. London: BMJ Publishing Group.

Chambers WV, O'Day P (1984) A nomothetic view of personal construct processes. Psychological Reports 55: 555–62.

Chambless DL, Caputo GC, Jasin SE, Gracely EJ, Williams C (1985) The Mobility Inventory for Agoraphobia. Behaviour Research and Therapy 23: 35–44.

Chiari G, Nuzzo ML (1996a) Personal construct theory within psychological constructivism: Precursor or avant-garde? in BM Walker, J Costigan, LL Viney, and Warren B (eds) Personal Construct Theory: a Psychology for the Future. Melbourne: Australian Psychological Society Imprint Series, pp. 25–54.

Chiari G, Nuzzo ML (1996b) Psychological constructivisms: a metatheoretical differentiation. Journal of Constructivist Psychology 9: 163–84.

Chiari G, Nuzzo ML (2001) Penetrating the sphere of between: the adoption of a framework of complementarity and its implications for a constructivist psychotherapy. The British Psychological Society, Psychotherapy Section Newsletter 30: 30–51.

Chiari G, Nuzzo ML (2004) Steering personal construct theory towards hermerneutic constructivism. In JD Raskin, SK Bridges (eds) Studies in Meaning 2: Bridging the Personal and Social in Constructivist Psychology. New York: Pace University Press, pp. 51–65.

Chiari G, Nuzzo ML, Alfano V, Brogna P, D'Andrea T, Di Battista G, Plata P, Stiffan E (1994) Personal paths of dependency. Journal of Constructivist Psychology 7: 17–34.

Chinn S (2000) A simple method for converting an odds ratio to effect size for use in meta-analysis. Statistics in Medicine 19: 3127–31.

Ciuffi G (1989) Direct forgetting: un paradigma per lo studio dell'oblio intenzionale e della memorizzazione accidentale. Ricerche di psicologia. 4: 5–40.

Clarke KM (1993) Creation of meaning in incest survivors. Journal of Cognitive Psychotherapy: An International Quarterly 7: 195–203.

Cloitre M, Koenen KC, Cohen LR, Han H (2002) Skills training in affective and inter-personal regulation followed by exposure: a phase-based treatment for PTSD related to childhood abuse. Journal of Consulting and Clinical Psychology 70: 1067–74.

Cohen J (1962) The statistical power of abnormal – social psychological research: a review. Journal of Abnormal and Social Psychology 65: 145–53.

Cohen J (1988) Statistical Power Analysis for the Behavioral Sciences. Hillsdale, NJ: Erlbaum.

Combs G, Friedman J (2004) A poststructuralist approach to narrative work. In LE Angus, J McLeod (eds) The Handbook of Narrative and Psychotherapy. Thousand Oaks, CA: Sage, pp. 137–55.

Connan F, Treasure J (1998) Stress, eating and neurobiology. In HW Hoeck, JL Treasure, M Katzman (eds) Neurobiology in the Treatment of Eating Disorders. Chichester: Wiley, pp. 211–36.

Coope J (1996) Hormonal and non-hormonal interventions for menopausal symptoms. Maturitas 23: 159–68.

Cordess C, Cox M (eds) (1996) Forensic Psychotherapy: Crime, Psychodynamics and the Offender Patient. London: Jessica Kingsley.

Corr CA (1993) Coping with dying: lessons we should and should not learn from the work of Elisabeth Kübler–Ross. Death Studies 17: 69–83.

Crits-Christoph P (1992) The efficacy of brief dynamic psychotherapy: a meta-analysis. American Journal of Psychiatry 149: 151–8.

Cromwell RL, Sewell KW, Langelle C (1996) A personal construction of traumatic stress. In BE Walker, J Costigan, LL Viney, WG Warren (eds) Personal Construct Theory: A Psychology for the Future. Melbourne: APS Imprint Books, pp. 173–97.

Crosina M (1994–2000) Personal communications to Sandra Sassaroli.

Cullen E (1997) Can a prison be a therapeutic community? The Grendon Template. In E Cullen, L Jones, R Woodward (eds) Therapeutic Communities for Offenders. Chichester: Wiley, pp. 75–99.

Cullen M and Freeman–Longo RE (1996) Men and Anger; Understanding and Managing your Anger for a Much Better Life. Brandon, VT: Safer Society Press.

Cummins P (1993) Engagement in psychotherapy. In LM Leitner, NGM Dunnett (eds) Critical Issues in Personal Construct Psychotherapy. Malabar, FL: Krieger, pp. 85–97.

Cummins P (2003) Working with anger. In F Fransella (ed.) International Handbook of Personal Construct Psychology. Chichester: Wiley, pp. 83–91.

Dallos R (2003) Using narrative and attachment theory in systemic family therapy with eating disorders. Clinical Child Psychology and Psychiatry 8: 521–35.

Dalton P (1985) Remembering as reconstruction. Paper submitted for the Diploma in Personal Construct Counselling and Psychotherapy.

Dalton P (1992) Living in the present: the experience of amnesia. Changes 10: 213–21.

Dalton P, Dunnett G (1992) A Psychology for Living: Personal Construct Theory for Professionals and Clients. Chichester: Wiley.

Damani S, Button EJ, Reveley CH (2001) The Body Image Structured Interview: A new method for the exploration of body image in women with eating disorders. European Eating Disorders Review. 9: 167–81.

Daneman M, Carpenter PA (1980) individual differences in working memory and reading. Journal of Verbal Learning and Verbal Behavior 19: 450–66.

Davidson G, Reser J (1996) Construing and constructs: personal and cultural. In B Walker, J Costigan, L Viney, B Warren (eds) Personal Construct Theory – a Psychology for the Future. Melbourne: APS Imprint Books, pp. 105–28.

Davies P, Thomas P, Leudar I (1999) Dialogical engagement with voices: a single case study. British Journal of Medical Psychology 72: 179–87.

Davis CG (2001) The tormented and the transformed. In RA Neimeyer (ed.) Meaning Reconstruction and the Experience of Loss. Washington, DC: American Psychological Association, pp. 137–55.

Davis CG, Wortman CB, Lehman DR, Silver RC (2000) Searching for meaning in loss: are clinical assumptions correct? Death Studies 24: 497–540.

Deimling GT, Kahana B, Bowman KF, Schaefer ML (2002) Cancer survivorship and psychological distress in later life. Psycho-Oncology 11: 479–94.

Derogatis LR (1977) SCL-90-R: Administration, Scoring and Procedures Manual I for the Revised Version of the SCL-90. Baltimore, MD: Johns Hopkins University Press.

Derogatis LR (1993) Brief Symptom Inventory: Administration, Scoring and Procedures Manual. Baltimore: Clinical Psychometric Research.

Derrida J (1997) Of Grammatology. Trans. Gayatri Chakravorty Spivak. Baltimore, MD: Johns Hopkins University Press. (Original work published in 1967.)

DiGiuseppe R, Linscott J (1993) Philosophical differences among cognitive behavioral therapists: rationalism, constructivism, or both? Journal of Cognitive Psychotherapy 7: 117–30.

Draucker CB (1992) The healing process of female adult incest survivors: constructing a personal residence. IMAGE: Journal of Nursing Scholarship 24: 4–8.

Draucker CB (1996) Family-of-origin variables and adult female survivors of childhood sexual abuse: a review of the research. Journal of Child Sexual Abuse 5: 35–63.

Drysdale B (1989) The construing of pain: a comparison of acute and chronic low back pain patients using the repertory grid technique. International Journal of Personal Construct Psychology 2: 271–86.

Duck SW (1973) Personal Relationships and Personal Constructs: A Study of Friendship Formation. New York: Wiley.

Duck SW, Spencer C (1972) Personal constructs and friendship formation. Journal of Personality and Social Psychology 23: 40–5.

Dugas MJ, Freeston MH, Ladouceur R (1997) Intolerance of uncertainty and problem orientation in worry. Cognitive Therapy and Research 21: 593–606.

Dugas MJ, Gosselin, P, Ladouceur R (2001) Intolerance of uncertainty and worry: investigating specificity in a non clinical sample. Cognitive Therapy and Research 25: 551–8.

Dunkel-Schetter C (1984) Social support and cancer. Findings based on patient interviews and their implications. Journal of Social Issues 40: 77–98.

Dunkel-Schetter C, Wortman C (1982) The interpersonal dynamics of cancer: problems in social relationships and their impact on the patient. In HS Friedman, MR Matteo (eds) Interpersonal Issues in Healthcare. New York: Academic Press, pp. 69–100.

Dunn J (1988) The Beginnings of Social Understanding. Oxford: Basil Blackwell.

Dunnett G (1985) Construing control in theory and therapy. In D Bannister (ed.) Issues and Approaches in Personal Construct Theory. London: Academic Press, pp. 37–46.

Dunnett G, Llewelyn S (1988) Elaborating personal construct theory in a group setting. In G Dunnett (ed.) Working with People: Clinical Uses of Personal Construct Psychology. London: Routledge, pp. 186–201.

Durrant M, Kowalski K (1990) Overcoming the effects of sexual abuse: developing a self-perception of competence. In M Durrant, C White (eds) Ideas for Therapy with Sexual Abuse. Adelaide: Dulwich Centre Publications, pp. 65–110.

Dzamonja-Ignjatovic T (1997) Suicide and depression from the personal construct perspective. In P Denicolo, M Pope (eds) Sharing Understanding and Practice. Farnborough: EPCA Publications, pp. 222–34.

Eccles A, Walker W (2003) Treating offenders in the community: assessment and treatment issues and the special challenges of sexual offenders. In J Horley (ed.) Personal Construct Perspectives on Forensic Psychology. New York: Brunner-Routledge, pp. 143–77.

Ecker B, Hulley L (1996) Depth Oriented Brief Therapy. San Francisco, CA: Jossey-Bass.

Ecker B, Hulley L (2000) The order in clinical 'disorder': symptom coherence in depth-oriented brief therapy. In RA Neimeyer, JD Raskin (eds) Constructions of Disorder: Meaning-Making Frameworks for Psychotherapy. Washington, DC: American Psychological Association, pp. 63–89.

Efran JS, Lukens MD, Lukens RJ (1990) Language, Structure and Change. New York: Norton.

Ell KO, Mantell JE, Hamovitch MB, Nishimoto RH (1989) Social support, sense of control, and coping among patients with breast, lung, or colorectal cancer. Journal of Psychosocial Oncology 19: 3–27.

Elliott R (2001) Contemporary brief experiential psychotherapy. Clinical Psychology: Science and Practice 8: 38–50.

Ellis A (1962) Reason and Emotion in Psychotherapy. New York: Lyle Stuart.

Ellis A (1979) The theory of rational-emotive therapy. In A Ellis, JM Whiteley (eds) Theoretical and Empirical Foundations of Rational-Emotive Therapy. Monterey, CA: Brooks/Cole, pp. 33–60.

Ellis JM (1996) He was big and old and frightening: nursing students' constructs of older people. In BM Walker, J Costigan, LL Viney, B Warren (eds) Personal Construct Theory: a Psychology for the Future. Melbourne: APS Imprint Books, pp. 89–103.

Ellis JM (1997) Nurses' anticipations of caring for elderly patients. In P Denicolo, M Pope (eds) Sharing Understanding and Practice. Farnborough: EPCA Publications, pp. 267–76.

Ellis JM, Scheer JW (1995) Making sense of a long life – construing successful ageing. Paper presented at the 12th International Congress on Personal Construct Psychology, Barcelona.

Emmelkamp PM, Brilman E, Kuiper H, Mersch PP (1986) The treatment of agoraphobia: a comparison of self-instructional training, rational emotive therapy, and exposure in vivo. Behavior Modification 10: 37–53.

Emmelkamp PM, Kuipers AC, Eggeraat JB (1978) Cognitive modification versus prolonged exposure in vivo: a comparison with agoraphobics as subjects. Behaviour Research and Therapy 16: 33–41.

Emmelkamp PM, Mersch PP (1982) Cognition and exposure in vivo in the treatment of agoraphobia: Short-term and delayed effects. Cognitive Therapy and Research 6: 77–90.

Epting F, Amerikaner M (1980) Optimal functioning: a personal construct approach. In AW Landfield, LM Leitner (eds) Personal Construct Psychology: Psychotherapy and Personality. New York: Wiley, pp. 55–73.

Epting F, Neimeyer RA (1984) Personal Meanings of Death. New York: Hemisphere.

Epting F, Prichard S (1993) An experiential approach to personal meanings in counseling and psychotherapy. In LM Leitner, NGM Dunnett (eds) Critical Issues in Personal Construct Psychotherapy. Malabar, FL: Krieger, pp. 33–59.

Erbes CR (2004) Our constructions of trauma: a dialectical perspective. Journal of Constructivist Psychology 17: 201–20.

Erbes CR, Harter SL (2002) Constructions of abuse: understanding the effects of childhood sexual abuse. In JD Raskin, SK Bridges (eds) Studies in Meaning: Exploring Constructivist Psychology. New York: Pace University Press, pp. 27–48.

Eron JB, Lund TW (1993) How problems evolve and dissolve: integrating narrative and strategic concepts. Family Process 32: 291–309.

Eron JB, Lund TW (1996) Narrative Solutions in Brief Therapy. New York: Guilford.

Eron JB, Lund TW (2002) Narrative solutions: toward understanding the art of helpful conversation. In JD Raskin, SK Bridges (eds) Studies in Meaning: Exploring Constructivist Psychology. New York: Pace University Press, pp. 63–97.

Erwin P (1985) Similarity of attitudes and constructs in children's friendships. Journal of Experimental Child Psychology 40: 470–85.

Evans C, Mellor-Clark J, Margisan F et al. (2000) CORE: Clinical outcomes in routine evaluation. Journal of Mental Health 9(3): 244–55.

Essex S, Gumbleton J (1999) 'Similar but different' conversations: working with denial in cases of severe child abuse. Australian and New Zealand Journal of Family Therapy 20: 139–48.

Evesham M, Fransella F (1985). Stuttering relapse: the effects of a combined speech and psychological reconstruction program. British Journal of Disorders of Communication 20: 237–48.

Eysenck HJ (1995) Problems with meta-analysis. In I Chalmers, DG Altman (eds) Systematic Review. London: BMJ Books, pp. 64–74.

Faidley AF, Leitner LM (1993) Assessing Experience in Psychotherapy: Personal Construct Alternatives. Westport, CT: Praeger.

Faidley AJ (2001) 'You've been like a mother to me': treatment implications of non-verbal knowing and developmental arrest. The Humanistic Psychologist 29; 138–66.

Faidley AJ, Leitner LM (2000) The poetry of our lives: symbolism in experiential personal construct psychotherapy. In JW Scheer (ed.) The Person in Society: Challenges to a Constructivist Theory. Giessen: Psychosozial-Verlag, pp. 381–90.

Fairburn CG, Shafran R, Cooper, Z (1998) A cognitive behavioural theory of eating disorders. Behaviour Research and Therapy 37: 1–13.

Fallot RD, Harris M (2002) The Trauma Recovery and Empowerment Model (TREM): Conceptual and practical issues in a group intervention for women. Community Mental Health Journal 38: 475–85.

Fava GA, Rafanelli C, Grandi S, Conti S, Ruini C, Mangelli L, Belluardo P (2001) Long-term outcome of panic disorder with agoraphobia treated by exposure. Psychological Medicine 31: 891–98.

Feifel H (1959) The Meaning of Death. New York: McGraw-Hill.

Feixas G (1995) Personal constructs in systemic practice. In R Neimeyer, M Mahoney (eds) Constructivism in Psychotherapy. Washington DC: American Psychological Association, pp. 305-37.

Feixas G, Cornejo JM (2002) GRIDCOR version 4.0: Correspondence analysis of personal constructs. Internet: www.terapiacognitiva.net/record

Feixas G, Saúl LA (2003) Dilemma project internal report (Database, April, 2003). Unpublished document.

Feixas G, Procter HG, Neimeyer G (1993) Convergent lines of assessment: systemic and constructivist contributions. In G Neimeyer (ed.) Casebook of Constructivist Assessment. New York: Sage, pp. 143–78.

Feixas G, Saúl LA, Sánchez V (2000) Detection and analysis of implicative dilemmas: implications for the therapy process. In J Scheer (ed.) The Person in Society: Challenges to a Constructivist Theory. Giessen: Psychosozial–Verlag, pp. 391–9.

Feixas G, Saúl LA, Avila-Espada A, Sánchez V (2001). Implicaciones terapéuticas de los conflictos cognitivos. Revista Argentina de Clínica Psicológica. X: 5–13.

Ferrans CE (1994) Quality of life through the eyes of survivors of breast cancer. Oncology. Nursing Forum 2: 1645–51.

Finkelhor D (1979) Sexually Victimized Children. New York: The Free Press.

Finkelhor D (1990) Early and long-term effects of child sexual abuse: an update. Professional Psychology: Research and Practice 21: 325–30.

Finkelhor D, Hotaling G, Lewis IA, Smith C (1990) Sexual abuse in a national survey of adult men and women: prevalence, characteristics, and risk factors. Child Abuse and Neglect 14: 19–28.

Fisher J (2000) Creating the future? In JW Scheer (ed.) The Person in Society: Challenges to a Constructivist Theory. Giessen: Psychosozial-Verlag, pp. 428–37.

Fisher LM, Wilson GT (1985) A study of the psychology of agoraphobia. Behaviour Research and Therapy 23: 97–108.

Foa EB, Rothbaum BA (1998) Treating the Trauma of Rape: Cognitive-Behavioral Therapy for PTSD. New York: Guilford.

Foa EB, Zinbarg R, Olasov-Rothbaum B (1992) Uncontrollability and unpredictability in post-traumatic stress disorder: an animal model. Psychological Bulletin 112: 218–38.

Fonagy P (2003) Towards a developmental understanding of violence. British Journal of Psychiatry 183: 190–2.

Foster H, Viney LL (2000) The menopausal paradox: when too much information is just not enough. In Australasian Menopause Society, Fourth Annual Congress. Adelaide: Australasian Menopause Society.

Foster H, Viney LL (2001a) Meanings of menopause: development of a PCP model. In JM Fisher, N Cornelius (eds) Challenging the Boundaries: PCP Perspectives for the New Millennium. Farnborough: EPCA Publications, pp. 87–108.

Foster H, Viney LL (2001b) Menopause: The art of change. Paper presented at 14th International Personal Construct Congress, Wollongong, Australia.

Foster H, Viney LL (2002) Predicting the 'Change of Life': Wellness or weariness? Eleventh Australasian Personal Construct Psychology Conference, Sydney, New South Wales, Australia.

Foster H, Viney LL (2005) Personal construct workshops for women experiencing menopause: reconstruction and validation of non-verbal, preverbal and verbal construing. In DA Winter, LL Viney (eds) Personal Construct Psychotherapy: Advances in Theory, Practice and Research. London: Whurr.

Foucault M (1970) The Order of Things. New York: Pantheon.

Foucault M (1975) I, Pierre Riviere, Having Slaughtered my Mother, my Sister and my Brother . . . Harmondsworth: Penguin.

Foucault M (2000) Power/Knowledge: Selected Interviews and Other Writings, 1972 – 1997. New York: Pantheon Books.

Fransella F (1970) Stuttering: not a symptom but a way of life. British Journal of Communication Disorders 5: 22–9.

Fransella F (1972) Personal Change and Reconstruction. London: Academic Press.

Fransella F (1985) Individual psychotherapy. In E Button (ed.) Personal Construct Theory and Mental Health. London: Croom Helm, pp. 277–301.

Fransella F (1995) George Kelly. London: Sage.

Fransella F (2000) Personal construct psychology by the year 2045. In JW Scheer (ed.) The Person in Society: Challenges to a Constructivist Theory. Giessen: Psychosozial-Verlag, pp. 440–8.

Fransella F (ed.) (2003) International Handbook of Personal Construct Psychology. Chichester: Wiley.

Fransella F, Adams B (1966) An illustration of the use of repertory grid technique in a clinical setting. British Journal of Social and Clinical Psychology 5: 51–62.

Fransella F, Dalton P (1990) Personal Construct Counselling in Action. London: Sage.

Fransella F, Bell R, Bannister D (2004) A Manual for Repertory Grid Technique. 2 edn. Chichester: Wiley.

Frazer H (1980) Agoraphobia: Parental Influence and Cognitive Structures. Unpublished PhD thesis: University of Toronto.

Freedman J, Combs G (1996) Narrative Therapy: A Social Construction of Preferred Realities. New York: Norton.

Freshwater K, Leach C, Aldridge J (2001) Personal constructs, childhood sexual abuse and revictimization. British Journal of Medical Psychology 74: 379–97.

Freud S (1897/1950) Letter 55. Determinants of psychosis. In J Strachey (ed. and trans) Standard Edition of the Complete Psychological Works of Sigmund Freud, Volume I: Pre-Psycho-Analytic Publications and Unpublished Drafts (1886–1899). London: Hogarth.

Freud S (1914/1957) On the history of the psycho-analytic movement. Part I. Early history. Freud working alone. In J Strachey (ed. and trans) Standard Edition of the Complete Psychological Works of Sigmund Freud, Volume XIV: A History of the Psycho-Analytic Movement, Papers on Metapsychology, and Other Works (1914–1916). London: Hogarth.

Freud S (1957) Mourning and melancholia. In J Strachey (ed.) The Complete Psychological Works of Sigmund Freud. London: Hogarth, pp. 152–70.

Friedman S (1996) Couples therapy changing conversations. In H Rosen, KT Kuhlwein (eds) Constructing Realities: Meaning-Making Perspectives for Psychotherapists. San Francisco, CA: Jossey-Bass, pp. 413–53.

Frith U, Happe F, Siddons F (1994) Autism and theory of mind in everyday life. Social Development 3: 108–24.

Fritz G, Overholser J (1989) Patterns of response to childhood asthma. Psychosomatic Medicine 51: 347–55.

Frost RO, Marten P, Lahart C, Rosenblate R (1990) The dimensions of perfectionism. Cognitive Therapy and Research 14: 449–68.

Gardner GG, Mancini F, Semerari (1988) A Construction of psychological disorders as invalidation of self-knowledge. In F Fransella, L Thomas (eds) Experimenting with Personal Construct Psychology. London: Routledge & Kegan Paul, pp. 259–72.

Gendreau P (1996) Offender rehabilitation: what we know what needs to be done. Criminal Justice and Behavior 23: 144–61.

George C, Kaplan N, Main M (1996) The Adult Attachment Interview. Unpublished Manuscript, University of California at Berkeley, 3 edn.

Gergen KJ (1985) The social constructionist movement in modern psychology. American Psychologist 40: 266–75.

Gergen KJ (1992) Toward a postmodern psychology. In S Kvale (ed.) Psychology and Postmodernism. London: Sage, pp. 17–30.

Gergen KJ (1994) Realities and Relationships. Cambridge, MA: Harvard University Press.

Gergen KJ, Gergen MM (1986) Narrative form and the construction of psychological science. In TR Sarbin (ed.) Narrative Psychology. New York: Praeger, pp. 22–44.

Giles L (2004) Use of Drawings and Reflective Comments in Family Construct Development. Unpublished PhD thesis. Milton Keynes: Open University.

Gleser GC, Gottschalk LA, Springer KJ (1961) An anxiety scale applicable to verbal samples. Archives of General Psychiatry 5: 593–605.

Goldstein AJ, Chambless DL (1978). A reanalysis of agoraphobia. Behavior Research and Therapy 9: 47–59.

Goldstein DE (2000) 'When ovaries retire': contrasting women's experiences with feminist and medical models of menopause. Health 4: 309–23.

Goleman D (1985) Vital Lies, Simple Truths: The Psychology of Self–Deception. Simon & Schuster: New York.

Gonçalves OF, Henriques MR, Machado PPP (2004) Nurturing nature: cognitive narrative strategies. In LE Angus, J McLeod (eds) The Handbook of Narrative and Psychotherapy. Thousand Oaks, CA: Sage, pp. 103–18.

Gonçalves OF, Korman Y, Angus L (2000) Constructing psychopathology from a cognitive narrative perspective. In RA Neimeyer, JD Raskin (eds) Constructions of Disorder: Meaning-Making Frameworks for Psychotherapy. Washington, DC: American Psychological Association, pp. 265–84.

Gottschalk LA (2000) The application of computerized content analysis of natural language in psychotherapy research now and in the future. American Journal of Psychotherapy 54: 305–11.

Gottschalk LA, Bechtel RJ (1982) The measurement of anxiety through the computer analysis of verbal samples. Comprehensive Psychiatry 23: 364–69.

Gottschalk LA, Bechtel RJ (1998) Psychiatric Content Analysis and Diagnosis (PCAD 2000). Corona del Mar CA: GB Software.

Gottschalk LA, Gleser GC (1969) The Measurement of Psychological States Through the Content Analysis of Verbal Behavior. Berkeley, CA: University of California Press.

Gottschalk LA, Hoigaard-Martin J (1986) A depression scale applicable to verbal samples. Psychiatry Research 17: 213–27.

Gournay K (1989) Failures in the behaviour treatment of agoraphobia. In K Gournay (ed.) Agoraphobia: Current Perspectives on Theory and Treatment. London: Routledge, pp. 120–39.

Graham J, Cohen R (1997) Race and sex as factors in children's sociometric ratings and friendship choices. Social Development 6: 355–72.

Gray J (2002) Men are from Mars, Women are from Venus: How to Get What You Want in Your Relationships. New York: HarperCollins.

Green D (1997) An experiment in fixed-role therapy. Clinical Child Psychology and Psychiatry 2: 553–64.

Greenberg JR, Mitchell SA (1983) Object Relations in Psychoanalytic Theory. Cambridge, MA: Harvard University Press.

Greenberg LS, Watson JC, Lietaer G (eds) (1998) Handbook of Experiential Psychotherapy. New York: Guilford.

Greenson RR (1965) The working alliance and the transference neurosis. Psychoanalytic Quarterly 34: 155–81.

Greenson RR (1978) The 'real' relationship between the patient and the psychoanalyst. In RR Greenson (ed.) Explorations in Psychoanalysis. New York: International Universities Press, pp. 425–40.

Grieger R (1989) A clients' guide to rational-emotive therapy (RET). In W Dryden, P Trower (eds) Cognitive Psychotherapy: Stasis and Change. London: Cassell, pp. 53–72.

Guidano VF (1987) Complexity of the Self: A Developmental Approach to Psychopathology and Therapy. New York: Guilford.

Guidano VF (1991) The Self in Process. New York: Guilford.

Guidano VF (1995) Self-observation in constructivist psychotherapy. In RA Neimeyer, MJ Mahoney (eds) Constructivism in Psychotherapy. Washington DC: APA Press, pp. 155–68.

Guidano VF, Liotti G (1983) Cognitive Processes and Emotional Disorders. New York: Guilford.

Guthrie AF (1991) Intuiting the process of another: symbolic, rational transformations of experience. International Journal of Personal Construct Psychology 4: 273–9.

Haddock G, Slade PD (eds) (1996) Cognitive-Behavioural Interventions with Psychotic Disorders. London: Routledge.

Hafner RJ (1977a). The husbands of agoraphobic women and their influence on treatment outcome. British Journal of Psychiatry 130: 289–94.

Hafner RJ (1977b) The husbands of agoraphobic women: assortative mating or pathogenic interaction. British Journal of Psychiatry 130: 233–9.

Hafner RJ (1983) Marital systems of agoraphobic women: contributions of husbands' denial and projection. Journal of Family Therapy 5: 379–96.

Hafner RJ (1984) Predicting the effects on husbands of behaviour therapy for wives' agoraphobia. Behaviour Research and Therapy 22: 217–26.

Hafner RJ, Ross MR (1983) Predicting the outcome of behaviour therapy for agoraphobia. Behaviour Research and Therapy 21: 375–82.

Hallam RS (1978) Agoraphobia: a critical review of the concept. British Journal of Psychiatry 133: 314–19.

Hamachek DE (1978) Psychodynamics of normal and neurotic perfectionism. Psychology 15: 27–33.

Hand I, Lamontagne Y (1974) Paradoxical intention and behavioral techniques in short-term psychotherapy. Canadian Psychiatric Association Journal 19: 501–7.

Harker T (1997) Therapy with male sexual abuse survivors: Contesting oppressive life stories. In G Monk, J Winslade, K Cricket, D Epston (eds) (1997) Narrative Therapy in Practice: The Archaeology of Hope. San Francisco, CA: Jossey-Bass, pp. 193–214.

Harré R, Gillett R (1994) The Discursive Mind. Thousand Oaks, CA: Sage.

Harter S (1988) Psychotherapy as a reconstructive process: implications of integrative theories for outcome research. International Journal of Personal Construct Psychology 1: 349–67.

Harter SL (1995) Construing on the edge: clinical mythology in working with borderline process. In RA Neimeyer, MJ Mahoney (eds) (1995) Constructivism in Psychotherapy. Washington DC: American Psychological Association, pp. 371–84.

Harter SL (2000) Quantitative measures of construing in child abuse survivors. Journal of Constructivist Psychology 13: 103–16.

Harter SL (2001) Constructivist psychology of child abuse and implications for psychotherapy. The Humanistic Psychologist 29: 40–69.

Harter SL (2004) Making meaning of child abuse: Personal, social, and narrative processes. In JD Raskin and SK Bridges (eds) Studies in Meaning. Volume 2. New York: Pace University Press, pp. 115–35.

Harter SL, Neimeyer RA (1995) Long term effects of child sexual abuse: toward a constructivist theory of trauma and its treatment. In RA Neimeyer, GJ Neimeyer (eds) Advances in Personal Construct Psychology. Volume 3. Greenwich CT: JAI, pp. 229–69.

Harter SL, Vanecek J (2000) Cognitive assumptions and long-term distress in survivors of childhood abuse, parental alcoholism, and dysfunctional family environments. Cognitive Therapy and Research 24: 445–72.

Harter SL, Alexander PC, Neimeyer RA (1988) Long-term effects of incestuous child abuse in college women: social adjustment, social cognition, and family characteristics. Journal of Consulting and Clinical Psychology 56: 5–8.

Harter SL, Erbes CR, Hart CC (2004) Content analysis of the personal constructs of female sexual abuse survivors elicited through Repertory Grid technique. Journal of Constructivist Psychology 17: 27–43.

Hartley R (1986) 'Imagine you're clever.' Journal of Child Psychology and Psychiatry 27: 383–98.

Harvey JH (1996) Embracing Their Memory. Needham Heights MA: Allyn & Bacon.

Haugli L, Steen E, Lærum E, Finset A, Nygaard R (2000) Agency orientation and chronic musculoskeletal pain: effects of a group learning program based on the personal construct theory. Clinical Journal of Pain 16: 281–9.

Haugli L, Steen E, Lærum E, Nygaard R, Finset A (2001)Learning to have less pain – is it possible? A one-year follow-up study of the effects of a personal construct group learning programme on patients with chronic musculoskeletal pain. Patient Education and Counseling 45: 111–18.

Hawkins DK (1986) Understanding reactions to group instability in psychotherapy groups. International Journal of Group Psychotherapy 36: 241–59.

Hawton K, Arensman, E, Townsend E, Bremner S, Feldman E, Goldney R, Gunnell D, Hazell P, Van Heeringen K, House K, Owens D, Sakinofsky I, Traskman-Bendz L (1998) Deliberate self harm: systematic review of efficacy of psychosocial and pharmacological treatments in preventing repetition. British Medical Journal 3171: 441–7.

Hedges LV (1981) Distribution theory for Glass's estimator of effect size and related estimators. Journal of Educational Statistics 6: 107–28.

Herman JL (1981) Father–Daughter Incest. Cambridge, MA: Harvard University Press.

Herman JL (1992) Trauma and Recovery: The Aftermath of Violence – from Domestic Abuse to Political Terror. New York: Basic Books.

Hermans HJM (1995) From assessment to change: the personal meaning of clinical problems in the context of the self-narrative. In RA Neimeyer, MJ Mahoney (eds) Constructivism in Psychotherapy. Washington DC: American Psychological Association Press, pp. 247–74.

Hermans HJ (2002) The person as a motivated storyteller. In GJ Neimeyer, RA Neimeyer (eds) Advances in Personal Construct Psychology. Volume 5. Westport, CN: Praeger, pp. 3–38.

Hermans HJ (2004) The innovation of self-narratives: a dialogical approach. In LE Angus, J McLeod (eds) The Handbook of Narrative and Psychotherapy. Thousand Oaks, CA: Sage, pp. 175–219.

Hermans HJ, Kempen HJ, van Loon RJ (1992) The dialogical self: Beyond individualism and rationalism. American Psychologist 47: 23–33.

Hess AK (1999) Defining forensic psychology. In AK Hess, I Weiner (eds) The Handbook of Forensic Psychology. New York: Wiley, pp. 24–47.

Hewitt PL, Flett GL (1993a) Dimensions of perfectionism, daily stress, and depression: a test of the specific vulnerability hypothesis. Journal of Abnormal Psychology 102: 58–65.

Hewitt PL, Flett GL (1993b) Perfectionistic self–presentation and maladjustment. Paper presented at the annual conference of the American Psychological Association, Toronto.

Hewitt PL, Flett GL, Ediger E (1995) Perfectionism traits and perfectionistic self–presentation in eating disorder attitudes, characteristics, and symptoms. International Journal of Eating Disorders 18: 317–26.

Hill CE (1986) An overview of the Hill counselor and client verbal response modes category systems. In LS Greenberg, WM Pinsof (eds) The Psychotherapy Process: A Research Handbook. New York: Guilford, pp. 131–59.

Hill EA (1988) Understanding the disoriented senior as a personal scientist. In F Fransella, L Thomas (eds) Experimenting with Personal Construct Psychology. London: Routledge, pp. 287–96.

Hinkle DN (1965) The change of personal constructs from the view-point of a theory of construct implications. Unpublished PhD thesis, Ohio State University.

Hirschman J (ed.) (1967) Antonin Artaud Anthology. San Francisco, CA: City Lights.

Hochschild AR (1983) The Managed Heart: Commercialization of Human Feeling. Berkeley, CA: University of California.

Hoffman IZ (1998) Ritual and Spontaneity in the Psychoanalytic Process: A Dialectical–Constructivist View. Hillsdale, NJ: The Analytic Press.

Hollander MH (1965) Perfectionism. Comprehensive Psychiatry 6: 94–103.

Holmes L (2002) Women in group and women's groups. International Journal of Group Psychotherapy 52: 171–88.

Honos-Webb L, Leitner LM (2001) How using the DSM causes damage: a client's report. Journal of Humanistic Psychology 41: 36–56.

Hopkins NJ (1996) On the Origin of Panic in Agoraphobic Women: Explorations of a Psycho-Social Hypothesis using a Personal Construct Theory Analysis. Unpublished PhD thesis: University of Sheffield.

Horley J (1995) Cognitive-behavior therapy with an incarcerated exhibitionist. International Journal of Offender Therapy and Comparative Criminology 39: 335–9.

Horley J (2000) Cognitions supportive of child molestation. Aggression and Violent Behavior: A Review Journal 5: 551–64.

Horley J (2003a) Forensic personal construct psychology: assessing and treating offenders. In F Fransella (ed.) International Handbook of Personal Construct Psychology. Chichester: Wiley, pp. 163–79.

Horley J (2003b) Forensic psychology and personal construct theory. In J Horley (ed.) Personal Construct Perspectives on Forensic Psychology. New York: Brunner-Routledge, pp. 1–13.

Horley J (2003c) Sexual offenders. In J Horley (ed.) Personal Construct Perspectives on Forensic Psychology. NewYork: Brunner-Routledge, pp. 55–85.

Horley J (2005) Fixed-role therapy with multiple paraphilias. Clinical Case Studies 4: 72–80.

Horley J, Francoeur A (2003) Domestic assault from a PCT perspective. Paper presented at the XVth International Congress of Personal Construct Psychology, Huddersfield, UK, July.

Horley J, Quinsey VL, Jones S (1997) Incarcerated child molesters' perceptions of themselves and others. Sexual Abuse: A Journal of Research and Treatment 9: 43–55.

Horowitz MJ (1997) Stress Response Syndromes. 3 edn. Northvale, NJ: Jason Aronson.

Hosie J (2001) Go let it out. The Psychologist 14: 24–7.

House A, Owens D, Storer D (1992) Psycho-social intervention following attempted suicide: is there a case for better services? International Review of Psychiatry 4: 15–22.

Houston J (1998) Making Sense with Offenders: Personal Constructs, Therapy and Change. Chichester: Wiley.

Houston J (2003) Mentally disordered offenders. In J. Horley (ed.) Personal Construct Perspectives on Forensic Psychology. New York: Brunner-Routledge, pp. 87–119.

Howard GS (1991) Culture tales: a narrative approach to thinking, cross-cultural psychology and psychotherapy. American Psychologist 46: 187–97.

Hoyt MF (ed.) (1994) Constructive Therapies. Volume 1. New York: Guilford.

Hoyt MF (ed.) (1996) Constructive Therapies. Volume 2. New York: Guilford.

Hughes SL, Neimeyer RA (1990) A cognitive model of suicidal behaviour. In D Lester (ed.) Understanding Suicide: The State of the Art. New York: Charles Press, pp. 1–28.

Hughes SL, Neimeyer RA (1993) Cognitive predictors of suicide risk among hospitalized psychiatric patients: a prospective study. Death Studies 17: 103–24.

Humphrey LL (1988) Relationships with subtypes of anorexic, bulimic, and normal families. Journal of the American Academy of Child and Adolescent Psychiatry 27: 544–51.

Jackson J (1992) 'Agoraphobia' as an elaborative choice. In H Jones, G Dunnett (eds), Selected Papers from the Second British Conference on Personal Construct Psychology, York, UK.

Jackson S, Bannister D (1985) Growing into self. In D Bannister (ed.) Issues and Approaches in Personal Construct Theory. London: Academic Press, pp. 67–82.

Jackson SR (1992) A PCT therapy group for adolescents. In P Maitland, D Brennan (eds) Personal Construct Theory Deviancy and Social Work. London: Inner London Probation Service and Centre for Personal Construct Psychology.

James W (1890) The Principles of Psychology. London: Macmillan.

Janoff-Bulman R (1989) Assumptive worlds and the stress of traumatic events. Social Cognition 7: 113–16.

Janoff-Bulman R (1992) Shattered Assumptions: Towards a New Psychology of Trauma. New York: Free Press.

Johnson TJ, Pfenninger DT, Klion RE (2000) Constructing and deconstructing transitive diagnosis. In RA Neimeyer and JD Raskin (eds) Constructions of Disorder: Meaning-Making Frameworks for Psychotherapy. Washington, DC: American Psychological Association, pp. 145–74.

Johnstone L (1989) Users and Abusers of Psychiatry: A Critical Look at Traditional Psychiatric Practice. London: Routledge.

Jones RCM, Keene M, Greene F (1999) The middle years group: a holistic approach to the management of the menopause in primary care. Maturitas 33: 95–8.

Kalogerakis MG. Foreword. In P Kymissis, DA Halperin (eds) (1996) Group Therapy with Children and Adolescents. Washington, DC: American Psychiatric Press, pp xiii–xv.

Kaplan HS (1974) The New Sex Therapy. New York: Brunner/Mazel.

Karst TO, Trexler LD (1970) Initial study using fixed role and rational-emotive therapy in treating speaking anxiety. Journal of Consulting and Clinical Psychology 34: 360–6.

Katzman MA, Lee S (1997) Beyond body image: the integration of feminist and transcultural theories in the understanding of self starvation. International Journal of Eating Disorder 22: 385–94.

Kauffman J (ed.) (2002) Loss of the Assumptive World. New York: Brunner-Routledge.

Kaye J (1995) Postfoundationalism and the language of psychotherapy research. In J Siegfried (ed.) Therapeutic and everyday discourse as behavior change: Towards a micro-analysis in psychotherapy process research. Norwood, NJ: Ablex, pp. 29–59.

Kazdin AE, Bass D (1989) Power to detect differences between alternative treatments in comparative psychotherapy outcome research. Journal of Consulting and Clinical Psychology 57: 138–47.

Keen E (1986) Paranoia and cataclysmic narratives. In TR Sarbin (ed.) Narrative Psychology. New York: Praeger, pp. 174–92.

Kegan R (1994) In Over Our Heads: The Mental Demands of Modern Life. Cambridge, MA: Harvard University Press.

Kellett M, Nind M (2003) Implementing Intensive Interaction in Schools. London: David Fulke.

Kelly GA (1955) The Psychology of Personal Constructs. Volumes 1 and 2. New York: Norton.

Kelly GA (1961) Theory and therapy in suicide: the personal construct point of view. In M Farberow, E Shneidman (eds) The Cry for Help. New York: McGraw-Hill, pp. 255–80.

Kelly GA (1966) Experimental dependency. Unpublished manuscript, Brandeis University.

Kelly GA (1969a) Man's construction of his alternatives. In B Maher (ed.) Clinical Psychology and Personality: The Selected Papers of George Kelly. New York: Wiley, pp. 66–93.

Kelly GA (1969b) Ontological acceleration. In B Maher (ed.) Clinical Psychology and Personality: The Selected Papers of George Kelly. New York: Wiley, pp. 7–45.

Kelly GA (1969c) The psychotherapeutic relationship. In B Maher (ed.) Clinical Psychology and Personality: The Selected Papers of George Kelly. New York: Wiley, pp. 216–23.

Kelly GA (1969d) Personal construct theory and the psychotherapeutic interview. In B Maher (ed.) Clinical Psychology and Personality: The Selected Papers of George Kelly. New York: Wiley, pp. 224–64.

Kelly GA (1969e) Hostility. In B Maher (ed.) Clinical Psychology and Personality: The Selected Papers of George Kelly. New York: Wiley, pp. 267–80.

Kelly GA (1970a) A brief introduction to personal construct theory. In D Bannister (ed.) Perspectives in Personal Construct Theory. London: Academic Press, pp. 1–29.

Kelly GA (1970b) Behavior is an experiment. In D Bannister (ed.) Perspectives in Personal Construct Theory. London: Academic Press, pp. 255–69.

Kelly GA (1977) The psychology of the unknown. In D Bannister (ed.) New Perspectives in Personal Construct Theory. London: Academic Press.

Kelly GA (1986) Transcript of a tape-recorded conversation with Fransella F. In D Bannister, F Fransella (eds) Inquiring Man: The Psychology of Personal Constructs. 3 edn. London: Croom Helm.

Kelly GA (1991a) The Psychology of Personal Constructs. Vol. 1. A Theory of Personality. London: Routledge.

Kelly GA (1991b) The Psychology of Personal Constructs. Vol. 2. Clinical Diagnosis and Psychotherapy. London: Routledge.

Kelly GA (2003) Is treatment a good idea? In F Fransella (ed.) International Handbook of Personal Construct Psychology. Chichester: Wiley, pp. 233–6.

Kenemans P, van Unik GA, Mijatovic V, van der Mooren MJ (2001) Perspectives in hormone replacement therapy. Maturitas 38: S41–S48.

Kirkwood B, Sterne J (2003) Essential Medical Statistics. 2nd edn. Oxford: Blackwell.

Kirsch H, Jordan J (2000) Emotions and personal constructs. In JW Scheer (ed.) The Person in Society; Challenges to a Constructivist Theory. Giessen: Psychosozial-Verlag, pp. 290–302.

Kitwood T (1996) A dialectical framework for dementia. In RT Woods (ed.) A Handbook of the Clinical Psychology of Ageing. London: Wiley, pp. 267–82.

Klass D (1999) The Spiritual Lives of Bereaved Parents. Philadelphia, PA: Brunner.

Klass D, Silverman PR, Nickman S (1996) Continuing Bonds: New Understandings of Grief. Washington, DC: Taylor & Francis.

Koch H (1985) Group psychotherapy. In E Button (ed.) Personal Construct Theory and Mental Health. London: Croom Helm, pp 302–26.

Krohne HW (1993) Attention and avoidance. Gottingen: Hogrefe and Huber.

Kubler-Ross E (1969) On Death and Dying. New York: Macmillan.

Kukil KV (ed.) (2000) The Journals of Sylvia Plath 1950–1962. London: Faber & Faber.

Kunz R, Oxman AD (1998) The unpredictability paradox: review of empirical comparisons of randomised and non–randomised clinical trials. British Medical Journal 317: 1185–90.

Kvale S (ed.) (1992) Psychology and Postmodernism. London: Sage.

Kymissis P, Halperin DA (1996) Introduction. In P Kymissis, DA Halperin (eds) Group Therapy with Children and Adolescents. Washington, DC: American Psychiatric Press, pp xvii–xix.

Laing RD (1960) The Divided Self. London: Tavistock.

Lambert MJ (ed.) (2004) Bergin and Garfield's Handbook of Psychotherapy and Behavior Change. 5 edn. New York: Wiley.

Lambert MJ, Ogles BM (2004) The efficacy and effectiveness of psychotherapy. In MJ Lambert (ed.) Bergin and Garfield's Handbook of Psychotherapy and Behavior Change. 5 edn. New York: Wiley.

Landfield AW (1971) Personal Construct Systems in Psychotherapy. Chicago, IL: Rand McNally.

Landfield A (1976) A personal construct approach to suicidal behaviour. In P Slater (ed.) The Measurement of Intrapersonal Space by Grid Technique. Vol. 1. Explorations of Intapersonal Space. London: Wiley.

Landfield AW (1979) Exploring socialization through the interpersonal transaction group. In P Stringer and D Bannister (eds) Constructs of Sociality and Individuality. London: Academic Press, pp. 133–52.

Landfield AW (1980) The person as perspectivist, literalist, and chaotic fragmentalist. In AW Landfield, LM Leitner (eds) Personal Construct Psychology: Psychotherapy and Personality. New York: Wiley, pp. 122–40.

Landfield AW, Epting FR (1987) Personal Construct Psychology: Clinical and Personality Assessment. New York: Human Sciences Press.

Landfield AW, Rivers PC (1975) An introduction to interpersonal transaction and rotating dyads. Psychotherapy: Theory, Research and Practice 12: 365–73.

Lane LG, Viney LL (2000a) The meanings of a breast cancer diagnosis: the role of others in validating helpful constructions of the cancer experience. Paper presented at Ninth Australasian Personal Construct Psychology Conference, Bendigo.

Lane LG, Viney LL (2000b) The meanings of a breast cancer diagnosis: a model of women's construing. In JM Fisher, N Cornelius (eds) Challenging the Boundaries: PCP Perspectives for the New Millennium. Farnborough: EPCA Publications, pp 121–31.

Lane LG, Viney LL (2000c) The role of others in validating helpful constructions of the breast cancer experience. Paper presented at the 5th World Congress of Psycho-Oncology, Melbourne. [Abstract] Psycho-Oncology 9. S75.

Lane LG, Viney LL (2001a) Role relationships and the restoration of coherence in the stories of women diagnosed with breast cancer: A group intervention. Paper presented at the 14th International Congress of Personal Construct Psychology, Wollongong. [Abstract]. Australian Journal of Psychology 53. S101.

Lane LG, Viney LL (2001b) When the unreal becomes real: An evaluation of the personal construct group psychotherapy with survivors of breast cancer. Paper presented at 14th International Congress of Personal Construct Psychology, Wollongong. [Abstract] Australian Journal of Psychology 53. S102.

Langer EJ (1975) The illusion of control. Journal of Personality and Social Psychology 32: 311–28.

Lawlor M, Cochran L (1981) Does invalidation produce loose construing? British Journal of Medical Psychology 54: 41–50.

Laws DR (ed.) (1989) Relapse Prevention with Sex Offenders. New York: Guilford.

Lazarus AA (1971) Behavior Therapy and Beyond. New York: McGraw-Hill.

Lazarus AA (1980) Psychological treatment of dyspareunia. In SR Leiblum, LA Pervin (eds) Principles and Practice of Sex Therapy. London: Tavistock, pp. 147–66.

Lea M (1979) Personality similarity in unreciprocated friendships. British Journal of Social and Clinical Psychology 18: 393–4.

Leitner LM (1985) The terrors of cognition: On the experiential validity of personal construct theory. In D Bannister (ed.) (1985) Issues and Approaches in Personal Construct Theory. London: Academic Press, pp. 83–103.

Leitner LM (1988) Terror, risk and reverence: experiential personal construct psychotherapy. International Journal of Personal Construct Psychology 1: 261–72.

Leitner LM (1995) Optimal therapeutic distance: a therapist's experience of personal construct psychotherapy. In RA Neimeyer, M Mahoney (eds) Constructivism in Psychotherapy. Washington, DC: American Psychological Association, pp. 357–70.

Leitner LM (1999) Levels of awareness in experiential personal construct psychotherapy. Journal of Constructivist Psychology 12: 239–52.

Leitner LM (2001) Therapeutic artistry: evoking experiential and relational truths. Paper presented at 14th. International Congress on Personal Construct Psychology, Wollongong.

Leitner LM, Celentana MA (1997) Constructivist therapy with serious disturbances. The Humanistic Psychologist 25: 271–85.

Leitner LM, Dill-Staniford T (1993) Resistance in experiential personal construct psychotherapy: theoretical and technical struggles. In LM Leitner, NGM Dunnett (eds) Critical Issues in Personal Construct Psychotherapy. Malabar, FL: Krieger, pp. 135–55.

Leitner LM, Dunnett NGM (eds) (1993) Critical Issues in Personal Construct Psychotherapy. Malabar, FL: Krieger.

Leitner LM, Faidley AF (1995) The awful, aweful nature of role relationships. In RA Neimeyer, GJ Neimeyer (eds) Advances in Personal Construct Psychology, Volume 3. Greenwich CT: JAI Press, pp. 291–314.

Leitner LM, Faidley AJ (1999) Creativity in experiential personal construct psychotherapy. Journal of Constructivist Psychology 12: 273–86.

Leitner LM, Faidley AF (2002) Disorder, diagnoses, and the struggles of humanness. In JD Raskin, SK Bridges (eds) Studies in Meaning: Exploring Constructivist Psychology. New York: Pace University Press, pp. 99–121.

Leitner LM, Guthrie AJ (1993) Validation of therapist interventions in psychotherapy: clarity, ambiguity, and subjectivity. International Journal of Personal Construct Psychology 6: 281–94.

Leitner LM, Pfenninger DT (1994) Sociality and optimal functioning. Journal of Constructivist Psychology 7: 119–35.

Leitner LM, Celentana MA, Faidley AJ (1998) Experiential personal constructivism and the body. Paper presented at the Annual Convention of the American Psychological Association, San Francisco, CA.

Leitner LM, Faidley AJ, Celentana MA (2000) Diagnosing human meaning making: an experiential constructivist approach. In RA Neimeyer, JD Raskin (eds) Constructions of Disorder. Meaning-Making Frameworks for Psychotherapy. Washington DC: American Psychological Association, pp. 175–203.

Lester D (1968) Attempted suicide as a hostile act. Journal of Psychology 68: 243.

Leudar I, Thomas P (2000) Voices of Reason, Voices of Insanity: Studies of Verbal Hallucinations. London: Routledge.

Liao KLM, Hunter MS (1998) Preparation for menopause: prospective evaluation of a health education intervention for mid-aged women. Maturitas 29: 215–24.

Linde K, Scholz M, Melchart D, Willich SN (2002) Should systematic reviews include non–randomized and uncontrolled studies? The case of acupuncture for chronic headache. Journal of Clinical Epidemiology 56: 77–85.

Lindemann E (1944) Symptomatology and management of acute grief. American Journal of Psychiatry 101: 141–8.

Linehan MM (1993) Cognitive-Behavioral Treatment of Borderline Personality Disorder. New York: The Guilford Press.

Liotti G (1987) The resistance to change of cognitive structures: a counterproposal to psychoanalytic metapsychology. Journal of Cognitive Psychotherapy: An International Quarterly 1: 87–104.

Liotti G (1999) Understanding the dissociative processes: the contribution of attachment theory. Psychoanalytic Inquiry 19: 757–83.

Lira FT, Nay R, McCullough JP, Etkin MW (1975) Relative effects of modeling and role playing in the treatment of avoidance behaviors. Journal of Consulting and Clinical Psychology 43: 608–18.

Little M, Jordens CFC, Paul K, Montgomery K, Philipson B (1998) Liminality: a major category of the experience of cancer illness. Social Science and Medicine 47: 1485–94.

Llewelyn SP (1988) Psychological therapy as viewed by clients and therapists. British Journal of Clinical Psychology 27: 223–37.

Logie RH (1999) State of the art: working memory. The Psychologist 12: 174–9.

LoPiccolo J (1992) Post–modern sex therapy for erectile failure. In RC Rosen, SR Leiblum (eds) Erectile Failure: Assessment and Treatment. New York: Guilford, pp. 171–97.

LoPiccolo J (1994) The evolution of sex therapy. Sexual and Marital Therapy 9: 5–7.

Lorenzini R, Sassaroli S (1987) La Paura della Paura: un Modello Clinico delle Fobie. Rome: Nuovo Italia Scientifica.

Lorenzini R, Sassaroli S (1988) Building change in patients with agoraphobic symptoms. In F Fransella, L Thomas (eds) Experimenting with Personal Construct Psychology. London: Routledge & Kegan Paul, pp. 329–41.

Lorenzini R, Sassaroli S (1995) Attachment as an informative relationship. International Journal of Personal Construct Psychology 3: 239–48.

Lorenzini R, Sassaroli S (2000) La Mente Prigioniera. Strategie di Terapia Cognitiva. Milan: Raffaello Cortina Editore.

Loux MJ (1999) Essentialism. In R Audi (ed.) The Cambridge Dictionary of Philosophy. New York: Cambridge University Press, pp. 281–3.

Lovenfosse M, Viney LL (1999) Understanding and helping mothers of children with 'special needs' using personal construct group work. Community Mental Health Journal 5: 431–42.

Luborsky L (1984) Principles of Psychoanalytic Psychotherapy. New York: Basic Books.

Luborsky L, Singer B, Luborsky L (1975) Comparative studies of psychotherapies: Is it true that everyone has won and all must have prizes? Archives of General Psychiatry 32: 995–1008.

Lyddon WJ (1989) Personal epistemology and preference for counseling. Journal of Counseling Psychology 36: 423–9.

Lyddon WJ (1990) First-and second-order change: implications for rationalist and constructivist cognitive therapies. Journal of Counseling and Development 69: 122–7.

Lyddon WJ (1993) Developmental constructivism: An integrative framework of psychotherapy practice. Journal of Cognitive Psychotherapy: An International Quarterly 7: 217–24.

Lyons AC, Griffin C (2003) Managing menopause: a qualitative analysis of self-help literature for women at midlife. Social Science and Medicine 56: 1629–42.

Maartens LWF, Knottnerus JA, Pop VJ (2002) Menopausal transition and increased depressive symptomatology. Maturitas 42: 195–200.

Mackenzie KR (1983) The clinical application of a group climate measure. In R Dies, KR Mackenzie (eds) Advances in Group Psychotherapy: Integrating Research and Practice. New York: International Universities Press, pp. 159–70.

MacLeod C (1999) Anxiety and anxiety disorders. In T Dalgleish, M Power (eds) Handbook of Cognition and Emotion. Chichester: Wiley, pp. 447–78.

MacLeod C, Cohen I (1993) Anxiety and the interpretation of ambiguity: a text comprehension study. Journal of Abnormal Psychology 102: 238–47.

Mahoney MJ (1988a) Constructive metatheory: I. Basic features and historical foundations. International Journal of Personal Construct Psychology 1: 1–35.

Mahoney MJ (1988b) The cognitive sciences and psychotherapy; patterns in developing relationship. In KS Dobson (ed.) Handbook of Cognitive-Behavioral Therapies. New York: Guilford.

Mahoney MJ (1988c) Constructive metatheory II: Implications for psychotherapy. International Journal of Personal Construct Psychology 1: 299–315.

Mahoney MJ (1991) Human Change Processes: The Scientific Foundations of Psychotherapy. New York: Basic Books.

Mahoney MJ (1995) The psychological demands of being a constructive psychotherapist. In RA Neimeyer, MJ Mahoney. Constructivism in Psychotherapy. Washington, DC: American Psychological Association, pp. 385–99.

Mahoney MJ (2003) Constructive Psychotherapy. New York: Guilford.

Mahoney MJ, Albert CJ (1996) Worlds of words: the changing vocabulary of psychology 1974–1994. Constructivism in the Human Sciences 3–4: 22–6.

Mahoney MJ, Gabriel TJ (1987) Psychotherapy and the cognitive sciences: an evolving alliance. Journal of Cognitive Therapy: an International Quarterly 1: 39–59.

Mahoney MJ, Lyddon WJ (1988) Recent developments in cognitive approaches to counseling and psychotherapy. The Counseling Psychologist 16: 190–234.

Mahoney MJ, Marquis A (2002) Integral constructivism and dynamic systems in psychotherapy processes. Psychoanalytic Inquiry 22: 794–813.

Mair M (1977) The community of self. In D Bannister (ed.) New Perspectives in Personal Construct Theory. London: Academic Press, pp.125–49.

Mair M (1988) Psychology as storytelling. International Journal of Personal Construct Psychology 1: 125–37.

Mair M (1989) Kelly, Bannister, and a story-telling psychology. International Journal of Personal Construct Psychology 2: 1–15.

Malekoff A (1997) Group Work with Adolescents: Principles and Practice. New York: Guilford Press.

Malins GL, Couchman L, Viney LL, Grenyer BFS (2004) Time to talk: evaluation of a staff–resident quality time intervention on the perceptions of staff in aged care. Clinical Psychologist 8: 48–52.

Malkinson R, Bar-Tur L (1999) The aging of grief in Israel. Death Studies 23: 413–31.

Mancini F, Semerari A (1985) Kelly e Popper: una teoria costruttivistica della conoscenza. In F. Mancini, A. Semerari (eds) La Psicologia dei Costrutti Personali: Saggi sulla Teoria di G.A. Kelly. Milan: Franco Angeli, pp. 52–72.

Mancuso JC, Adams-Webber JR (1982) Anticipation as a constructive process: the fundamental postulate. In JC Mancuso, JR Adams-Webber (eds) The Construing Person. New York: Praeger, pp. 8–32.

Mann S, Russell S (2002) Narrative ways of working with women survivors of childhood sexual abuse. The International Journal of Narrative Therapy and Community Work 3: 3–22.

Marks IM, Mathews AM (1979) Brief standard self-rating for phobic patients. Behaviour Research and Therapy 17: 263–7.

Marlow B, Cartmeill T, Cieplucha H, Lowrie S (2003) An interactive process model of psychosocial support needs for women living with breast cancer. Psycho-Oncology 12: 319–30.

Marshall W, Anderson D, Fernandez Y (1999) Cognitive Behavioural Treatment of Sexual Offenders. London: Wiley.

Marshall WL, Barbaree HE (1988) An outpatient treatment program for child molesters. In RA Prentky, VL Quinsey (eds) Human Sexual Aggression: Current Perspectives. New York: Annals of the New York Academy of Sciences, pp. 205–14.

Marshall WL, Barbaree HE (1990) An integrated theory of the etiology of sexual offending. In WL Marshall, DR Laws, HE Barbaree (eds) Handbook of Sexual Assault. New York: Plenum Press, pp. 257–78.

Martinson R (1974) What works? Questions and answers about prison reform. The Public Interest 35: 22–54.

Massie MJ, Holland JC (1984) Diagnosis and treatment of depression in the cancer patient. Journal of Clinical Psychiatry 45: 25–8.

Massie MJ, Holland JC (1990) Depression and the cancer patient. Journal of Clinical Psychiatry 51: 12–19.

Masters WH, Johnson VE (1966) Human Sexual Response. Boston, MA: Little, Brown.

Mathews A, Richards A, Eysenck M (1989) Interpretation of homophones related to threat in anxiety states. Journal of Abnormal Psychology 98: 31–4.

Maturana HR (1988) Reality: The search for objectivity or the quest for a compelling argument. The Irish Journal of Psychology 9: 25–82.

Maturana HR and Varela FJ (1992) The Tree of Knowledge: The biological roots of human understanding (R. Paolucci trans. rev. ed.). Boston, MA: Shambhala.

McCoy MM (1977) A reconstruction of emotion. In D Bannister (ed.) New Perspectives in Personal Construct Theory. London: Academic Press, pp. 93–124.

McCoy MM (1981) Positive and negative emotion: a personal construct theory interpretation. In H Bonarius, R Holland, S Rosenberg (eds) Personal Construct Psychology: Recent Advances in Theory and Practice. London: Macmillan, pp. 95–104.

McFayden M (1989) The cognitive invalidation approach to panic. In R Baker (ed.) Panic Disorder: Theory, Research and Therapy. Chichester: Wiley, pp. 281–99.

McKenna PJ (1994) Schizophrenia and Related Syndromes. Hove: Psychology Press.

McNally RJ, Foa EB (1987) Cognition and agoraphobia: bias in interpretation of threat. Cognitive Research and Therapy 11: 567–81.

McNamee S, Gergen KJ (eds) (1992) Therapy as Social Construction. London: Sage.

Mead GH (1934/1977) Self. In A Strauss (ed.) George Herbert Mead: On Social Psychology. Chicago: University of Chicago Press, pp. 199–246.

Meichenbaum D (2001) Treatment of Individuals with Anger-Control Problems and Aggressive Behaviors: A Clinical Handbook. Florida: Institute Press.

Merleau-Ponty M (1964) The primacy of perception. In JM Edie (ed.) The Primacy of Perception and Other Essays on Phenomenological Psychology, the Philosophy of Art, History and Politics. Evanston, IL: Northwestern University Press.

Metcalfe C (1997) The relationship between symptom constructs and social constructs in agoraphobia. In P Denicolo, M Pope (eds.) Sharing Understanding and Practice. Farnborough: EPCA Publications, pp. 188–98.

Miceli M, Castelfranchi C (1995) Le Difese della Mente. Rome: NIS.

Middleton W, Raphael B, Burnett P, Martinek N (1998) A longitudinal study comparing bereavement phenomena in recently bereaved spouses, adult children, and parents. Australian and New Zealand Journal of Psychiatry 32: 235–41.

Milan MA, Chin CE, Nguyen QX (1999) Practicing psychology in correctional settings: assessment, treatment, and substance abuse programs. In AK Hess, I Weiner (eds) The Handbook of Forensic Psychology. New York: Wiley, pp. 580–602.

Millon T, Davis R, Millon C (1997) Millon Clinical Multiaxial Inventory III: Manual. 2 edn. Minneapolis, MN: National Computer Systems Inc.

Mineka S, Kelly KA (1989) The relationship between anxiety, lack of control and loss of control. In A Steptoe, A Appels (eds) Stress, Personal Control, and Health. Brussels: Wiley, pp. 163–91.

Mineka S, Zinbarg R (1996) Models of anxiety disorders: Stress-in-dynamic-context anxiety models. In DA Hope (ed.) Nebraska Symposium on Motivation: Perspectives on Anxiety, Panic, and Fear. Vol. 43. Lincoln, NB: University of Nebraska Press, pp. 135–210.

Mintz J, Keisler DJ (1982) Individualised measures of psychotherapy outcome. In PC Kendall, JN Butcher (eds) Handbook of Research Methods in Clinical Psychology. New York: Wiley, pp. 491–534.

Minuchin S (1991) The seductions of constructivism. Family Therapy Networker 15: 47–50.

Mischel W (1980) George Kelly's anticipation of psychology. In MJ Mahoney (ed.) Psychotherapy Process: Current Issues and Future Directions. New York: Plenum, pp. 85–7.

Moan CE, Heath RG (1972) Septal stimulation for the initiation of heterosexual behaviour in a homosexual male. Journal of Behaviour Therapy and Experimental Psychiatry 3: 23–30.

Mobley MJ (1999) Psychotherapy with criminal offenders. In AK Hess, I Weiner (eds) The Handbook of Forensic Psychology. New York: Wiley, pp. 603–39.

Moher D, Schulz KF, Altman DG (2001) The CONSORT statement: revised recommendations for improving the quality of reports of parallel–group randomised trials. Lancet 357: 1191–4.

Monk G, Winslade J, Crocket K, Epston D (1996) Narrative Therapy in Practice. San Francisco, CA: Jossey Bass.

Mor V, Malin M, Allen S (1994) Age differences in the psychosocial problems encountered by breast cancer patients. Journal of the National Cancer Institute Monographs 16: 191–7.

Moran H (2001) Who do you think you are? Drawing the ideal self: a technique to explore a child's sense of self. Clinical Psychology and Psychiatry 6: 599–604.

Morris C (2001) Working with people: understanding dementia. Journal of Dementia Care 8: 4.

Morris C (2004) Personal construct psychology and person centred care. In GMM Jones, B Miesen (eds) Care Giving in Dementia, Vol 3. London: Brunner-Routledge.

Morris JB (1977) Appendix I. The prediction and measurement of change in a psychotherapy group using the repertory grid. In F Fransella, D Bannister (eds) A Manual for Repertory Grid Technique. London: Academic Press, pp. 120–48.

Morrow SL, Smith ML (1995) Constructions of survival and coping by women who have survived childhood sexual abuse. Journal of Counseling Psychology 42: 24–33.

Mundy P (2003) Annotation: the neural basis of social impairments in autism: the role of the dorsal medial–frontal cortex and anterior cingulate system. Journal of Child Psychology and Psychiatry 44: 793–809.

Murphy JJ (2000) Common factors of school-based change. In MA Hubble, BI Duncan, SC Miller (eds) The Heart and Soul of Change. Washington, DC: American Psychological Association, pp. 361–86.

Nagae N, Nedate K (2001) Comparison of constructive cognitive and rational cognitive psychotherapies for students with social anxiety. Constructivism in the Human Sciences 6: 41–9.

Nagae N, Nedate K (n.d.) Effects of fixed role therapy and self instructional training for students with shyness. Unpublished manuscript.

Najavits L (2001) Seeking Safety: A Treatment Manual for PTSD and Substance Abuse. New York: Guilford.

Nash MR, Neimeyer RA, Hulsey TL, Lambert W (1998) Psychopathology associated with sexual abuse: the importance of complementary designs and common ground. Journal of Consulting and Clinical Psychology 66: 568–71.

Nathanson DL (1992) Shame and Pride: Affect, Sex, and the Birth of the Self. New York: Norton.

Neimeyer GJ (1985) Personal constructs in the counselling of couples. In F Epting, AW Landfield (eds) Anticipating Personal Construct Psychology. Lincoln NB: University of Nebraska Press, pp. 201–15.

Neimeyer GJ (ed.) (1993) Constructivist Assessment. Newbury Park CA: Sage.

Neimeyer GJ, Merluzzi TV (1982) Group structure and group process: personal construct therapy and group development. Small Group Behavior 13: 150–64.

Neimeyer GJ, Morton RJ (1997) Personal epistemologies and preferences for rationalist versus constructivist psychotherapies. Journal of Constructivist Psychology 10: 109–23.

Neimeyer GJ, Neimeyer RA (1981) Functional similarity and interpersonal attraction. Journal of Research in Personality 15: 427–35.

Neimeyer GJ, Neimeyer RA (1993) Defining the boundaries of constructivist assessment. In GJ Neimeyer (ed.) (1993) Constructivist Assessment: A Casebook. Thousand Oaks CA: Sage Publications, pp. 1–30.

Neimeyer GJ, Saferstein J (2003) Personal epistemologies and psychotherapists' preferences. Unpublished manuscript, University of Florida.

Neimeyer GJ, Behnke M, Reiss J (1983) Constructs and coping: physicians' responses to patient death. Death Education 7: 245–64.

Neimeyer GJ, Hagans CL, Anderson R (1998) Intervening in meaning: applications of constructivist assessment. In C Franklin, PS Nurius (eds) Constructivism in Practice. Milwaukee WI: Families International Inc., pp. 115–37.

Neimeyer GJ, Prichard S, Lyddon WJ, Sherrard PAD (1993) The role of epistemic style in counseling preference and orientation. Journal of Counseling and Development 71: 515–23.

Neimeyer RA (1978) The interpersonal transaction group in death education. Unpublished MS. University of Nebraska.

Neimeyer RA (1981) The structure and meaningfulness of tacit construing. In H Bonarius, R Holland, S Rosenberg (eds) Personal Construct Psychology: Recent Advances in Theory and Practice. London: Macmillan, pp. 105–13.

Neimeyer RA (1985) Personal constructs in clinical practice. In PC Kendall (ed.) Advances in Cognitive-Behavioral Research and Therapy. Vol. 4. New York: Academic Press, pp. 275–339.

Neimeyer RA (1987) An orientation to personal construct therapy. In RA Neimeyer, GJ Neimeyer (eds) Personal Construct Therapy Casebook. New York: Springer, pp. 3–19.

Neimeyer RA (1988a) Integrative directions in personal construct therapy. International Journal of Personal Construct Psychology 1: 283–97.

Neimeyer RA (1988b) Clinical guidelines for conducting interpersonal transaction groups. International Journal of Personal Construct Psychology 1: 181–90.

Neimeyer RA (1993) Constructivism and the cognitive psychotherapies: Some conceptual and strategic contrasts. Journal of Cognitive Psychotherapy: An International Quarterly 7: 159–71.

Neimeyer RA (1995a) Constructivist psychotherapies: features, foundations, and future directions. In RA Neimeyer, MJ Mahoney (eds) Constructivism in Psychotherapy. Washington DC: American Psychological Association Press, pp. 11–38.

Neimeyer RA (1995b) Client-generated narratives in psychotherapy. In RA Neimeyer, MJ Mahoney (eds) Constructivism in Psychotherapy. Washington DC: American Psychological Association, pp. 231–46.

Neimeyer RA (1999) Narrative strategies in grief therapy. Journal of Constructivist Psychology 12: 65–85.

Neimeyer RA (2000) Narrative disruptions in the construction of self. In RA Neimeyer, JD Raskin (eds) Constructions of Disorder: Meaning making frameworks for psychotherapy. Washington, DC: American Psychological Association, pp. 207–41.

Neimeyer RA (ed.) (2001) Meaning Reconstruction and the Experience of Loss. Washington, DC: American Psychological Association.

Neimeyer RA (2004a) Fostering posttraumatic growth: a narrative contribution. Psychological Inquiry 15: 53–9.

Neimeyer RA (2004b) Lessons of Loss: A Guide to Coping (2 edn). New York:

Neimeyer RA, Bridges SK (2003) Postmodern therapies. In S Messer (ed.) Essential Psychotherapies. 2 edn. New York: Guilford, pp. 272–316.

Neimeyer RA, Gamino LA (2004) Grief and bereavement. In C Bryant (ed.) Handbook of Death and Dying. Thousand Oaks, CA: Sage.

Neimeyer RA, Jordan J (2002) Disenfranchisement as empathic failure. In K Doka (ed.) Disenfranchised Grief. Champaign, IL: Research Press, pp. 97–117.

Neimeyer RA, Mahoney MJ (eds) (1995) Constructivism in Psychotherapy. Washington, DC: American Psychological Association.

Neimeyer RA, Neimeyer GJ (1977) A personal construct approach to perception of disclosure targets. Perceptual and Motor Skills 44: 791–4.

Neimeyer RA, Neimeyer GJ (1983) Structural similarity in the acquaintance process. Journal of Social and Clinical Psychology 1: 146–54.

Neimeyer RA, Neimeyer GJ (1985) Disturbed relationships: a personal construct view. In E Button (ed.) Personal Construct Theory and Mental Health: Theory, Research and Practice. London: Croom Helm, pp 195–223.

Neimeyer RA, Neimeyer GJ, Landfield AW (1983) Conceptual differentiation, integration and empathic prediction. Journal of Personality 51: 185–91.

Neimeyer RA, Raskin JD (eds) (2000) Constructions of Disorder: Meaning-Making Frameworks for Psychotherapy. Washington, DC: American Psychological Association.

Neimeyer RA, Stewart AE (1996) Trauma, healing, and the narrative emplotment of loss. Families in Society: The Journal of Contemporary Human Services 77: 360–75.

Neimeyer RA, Winter DA (2005) To be or not to be: personal construct perspectives on the suicidal choice. In T Ellis (ed.) Cognition and Suicide: The Science of Suicidal Thinking. Washington DC: American Psychological Association.

Neimeyer RA, Heath AE, Strauss J (1985) Personal reconstruction during group cognitive therapy for depression. In F Epting, AW Landfield (eds) Anticipating Personal Construct Psychology. Lincoln, NB: University of Nebraska Press, pp. 180–97.

Neimeyer RA, Harter SL, Alexander PC (1991) Group perceptions as predictors of outcome in the treatment of incest survivors. Psychotherapy Research 1: 148–58.

Neimeyer RA, Prigerson H, Davies B (2002) Mourning and meaning. American Behavioral Scientist 46: 235–51.

Neuringer C (1964) Rigid thinking in suicidal individuals. Journal of Consulting Psychology 28: 54–8.

New South Wales Cancer Council (2003) Cancer Maps. See www.nswcc.org.au/cncrinfo/research/reports/index.htm [25 February 2003].

Nexis (2003) Nexis Database. University of Wollongong Library access. Vol. 2003.

NHS Centre for Reviews and Dissemination (1998) Deliberate self–harm. Effective Health Care 4: 1–12.

Nisbett RE, Wilson TD (1977) Telling more than we can know: Verbal reports on mental processes. Psychological Review 8: 231–59.

Nitsun M (1996) The Anti-Group. Destructive Forces in the Group and their Creative Potential. London: Routledge.

Norcross JC (1986) Eclectic psychotherapy: an introduction and overview. In JC Norcross (ed.) Handbook of Eclectic Psychotherapy. New York: Brunner/Mazel, pp. 3–24.

Novaco RW (1998) Workshop on Anger. Dublin: Trinity College.

Oades LG, Viney LL (2000) In JW Scheer (ed.) The Person in Society: Challenges to a Constructivist Theory. Giessen: Psychosozial-Verlag, pp. 160–73.

Oddens BJ, Boulet MJ, Lehert P, Visser AP (1994) A study on the use of medication for climacteric complaints in Western Europe II. Maturitas 19: 1–12.

Oei TPS, Llamas M, Devilly, GJ (1999) The efficacy and cognitive processes of cognitive behaviour therapy in the treatment of panic disorder with agoraphobia. Behavioural and Cognitive Psychotherapy 27: 63–88.

O'Hara M, Anderson WT (1991) Welcome to the postmodern world. Family Therapy Networker 15: 18–25.

O'Malley SS, Suh CS, Strupp HH (1983) The Vanderbilt Psychotherapy Process Scale: A report on the scale development and a process-outcome study. Journal of Consulting and Clinical Psychology 51: 581–6.

O'Sullivan B (1985) The experiment of agoraphobia. In N Beail (ed.) Repertory Grid Technique and Personal Constructs: Applications in Clinical and Educational Settings. London: Croom Helm, pp. 75–86.

Padesky CA (1994) Schema change processes in cognitive therapy. Clinical Psychology and Psychotherapy 1: 267–78.

Paley G, Shapiro DA (2002) Lessons from psychotherapy research for psychological interventions for people with schizophrenia. Psychology and Psychotherapy: Theory, Research and Practice 75: 5–18.

Paris ME, Epting FR (2004) Social and personal construction: two sides of the same coin. In JD Raskin, SK Bridges (eds) Studies in Meaning. Volume 2. Bridging the Personal and Social in Constructivist Psychology. New York: Pace University Press, pp. 3–35.

Parker K (1981) The meaning of attempted suicide to young parasuicides: a repertory grid study. British Journal of Psychiatry 139: 306–12.

Parker PA, Baile WF, De Moor C, Cohen L (2003) Psychosocial and demographic predictors of quality of life in a large sample of cancer patients. Psycho-Oncology 12 : 183–93.

Parle M, Jones B, Maguire P (1996) Maladaptive coping and affective disorders among cancer patients. Psychological Medicine 26: 735–44.

Parry G, Richardson A (1996) NHS Psychotherapy Services in England: Review of Strategic Policy. London: NHS Executive.

Patch AR (1984) Reflections on perfection. American Psychologist 39: 386–90.

Pekkola D, Cummins P (2005) Evaluating the anger program. In P Cummins (ed.) Working with Anger. London: Wiley.

Pennings M, Romme M (1998) Hearing voices in patients and non-patients. In M Romme (ed.) (1998) Understanding Voices: Coping with Auditory Hallucinations and Confusing Realities. Cheshire: Handsell Publishing.

Pilch JJ (1993) 'Beat his ribs while he is young' (Sir 30:12): a window on the Mediterranean world. Biblical Theology Bulletin 23: 101–13.

Polinsky ML (1994) Functional status of long-term breast cancer survivors: demonstrating chronicity. Health and Social Work 19: 165–73.

Polkinghorne DE (1992) Postmodern epistemology of practice in S Kvale (ed.) Psychology and Postmodernism. London: Sage, pp. 146–65.

Polkinghorne DE (2004) Narrative therapy and postmodernism. In LE Angus, J McLeod (eds) The Handbook of Narrative and Psychotherapy. Thousand Oaks, CA: Sage, pp. 53–67.

Pollock KM, Kymissis P (2001) The future of adolescent group therapy. An analysis of historical trends and current momentum. Journal of Child and Adolescent Group Therapy 11: 3–11.

Polusny MH, Follette VM (1995) Long-term correlates of child sexual abuse: theory and review of the empirical literature. Applied and Preventive Psychology 4: 143–66.

Prentky RA, Knight RA (1991) Identifying critical dimensions for discriminating among rapists. Journal of Consulting and Clinical Psychology 59: 645–61.

Prigerson HG, Jacobs SC (2001) Diagnostic criteria for traumatic grief. In MS Stroebe, RO Hansson, WS Stroebe, H Schut (eds) (2001) Handbook of Bereavement Research. Washington, DC: American Psychological Association, pp. 614–46.

Procter HG (1981) Family construct psychology: an approach to understanding and treating families. In S Walrond-Skinner (ed.) Developments in Family Therapy. London: Routledge & Kegan Paul, pp. 350–66.

Procter HG (1985) A construct approach to family therapy and systems intervention. In E Button (ed.) Personal Construct Theory and Mental Health. Beckenham, Kent: Croom Helm, pp. 327–50.

Procter HG (1987) Change in the family construct system: therapy of a mute and withdrawn schizophrenic patient. In R Neimeyer, G Neimeyer (eds) (1987) Personal Construct Therapy Casebook. New York: Springer, pp. 153–71.

Procter HG (1996) The family construct system. In D Kalekin-Fishman, B Walker (eds) The Structure of Group Realities: Culture and Society in the Light of Personal Construct Theory. Malabar FL: Krieger, pp. 161–80.

Procter HG (2000) Autism and family therapy: a personal construct approach. In S Powell (ed.) Helping Children with Autism to Learn. London: David Fulton.

Procter HG (2001) Personal construct psychology and autism. Journal of Constructivist Psychology 14: 107–26.

Procter HG (2002) Constructs of Individuals and Relationships. Context 59: 11–12.

Procter HG, Dallos R (2005) Making me angry – the constructions of anger. In P Cummins (ed.) Working with Anger: a Constructivist Approach. London: Wiley.

Rachman S (1998) The nature of anxiety. In S Rachman, Anxiety. Hove: Psychology Press, pp. 1–26.

Rankin PM, O'Carroll PJ (1995) Reality discrimination, reality monitoring and disposition towards hallucination. British Journal of Clinical Psychology 34: 517–28.

Rapee RM, Craske M, Brown TA, Barlow DH (1996) Measurement of perceived control over anxiety related events. Behavior Therapy 27: 279–93.

Raskin JD (2002) Constructivism in psychology: personal construct psychology, radical constructivism, and social constructionism. In JD Raskin, SK Bridges (eds) Studies in Meaning: Exploring Contructivist Psychology. New York: Pace University Press, pp. 1–25.

Raskin JD (2004) The permeability of personal construct psychology. In JD Raskin, SK Bridges (eds) Studies in Meaning 2: Bridging the Personal and Social in Contructivist Psychology. New York: Pace University Press, pp. 327–43.

Raskin JD, Bridges SK (eds) (2002) Studies in Meaning: Exploring constructivist psychology. New York: Pace University Press.

Raskin JD, Bridges SK (eds) (2004) Studies in Meaning 2: Bridging the personal and social in constructivist psychology. New York: Pace University Press.

Raskin JD, Epting FR (1993) Personal construct theory and the argument against mental illness. International Journal of Personal Construct Psychology 6: 351–69.

Raskin JD, Epting FR (1995) Constructivism and psychotherapeutic method: transitive diagnosis as humanistic assessment. Methods: A Journal for Human Science. Annual Edition 3–27.

Raskin JD, Lewandowski AM (2000) The construction of disorder as human enterprise. In RA Neimeyer, JD Raskin (eds) Constructions of Disorder: Meaning-Making Frameworks for Psychotherapy. Washington, DC: American Psychological Association, pp. 15–40.

Råstam M, Gillberg C (1991) The family background in anorexia nervosa: a population-based study. Journal of the American Academy of Child and Adolescent Psychiatry 30: 283–9.

Rather L (2001) The therapeutic and working alliances revisited. See http://www.fort-da.org/spring_01/therapeutic.html [6 January 2004].

Ravenette T (1997) Tom Ravenette: Selected Papers. Farnborough: EPCA publications.

Ravenette T (1999) Never, never, never give advice: an essay on professional practice in personal construct theory. In AT Ravenette, Educational Psychology: a Practitioner's View. London: Whurr.

Ravenette T (1999) Personal Construct Theory in Educational Psychology: A Practitioner's View. London: Whurr.

Richards A, French CC (1992) An anxiety related bias in semantic activation when processing threat/neutral homographs. Quarterly Journal of Experimental Psychology 45A: 503–25.

Rigdon M, Clark C, Hershgold E (1993) A case demonstration of two methods for promoting the credulous approach in personal construct psychotherapy. In LM Leitner, NGM Dunnett (eds) Critical Issues in Personal Psychotherapy. Malabar, FL: Krieger, pp. 157–72.

Rivers PC, Adams J, Meyer J (1978) Research in progress on the use of IT with alcohol counselors. Unpublished manuscript. Lincoln, NB, University of Nebraska.

Robbins S (1993) Facing the future. In LL Leitner, NG Dunnett (eds) Critical Issues in Personal Construct Psychotherapy. Malabar, FL: Krieger, pp. 265–77.

Robbins S, Bender M (2001) Understanding dementia. Paper presented at 14th International Congress on Personal Construct Psychology, Wollongong.

Roesch R (1988) Community psychology and the law. American Journal of Community Psychology 16: 451–63.

Rolland J (1987) Chronic illness and the life-cycle: a conceptual framework. Family Process 26: 203–21.

Romme MAJ (1998) Understanding Voices: Coping with Auditory Hallucinations and Confusing Realities. Runcorn: Handsell Publishing.

Romme MAJ, Escher S (1993) Accepting Voices. London: Mind Publications.

Romme MAJ, Escher S (2000) Making Sense of Voices: A Guide for Mental Health Professionals Working with Voice Hearers. London: Mind Publications.

Rosenberg M (1965) Society and the Adolescent Self–Image. Princeton, NJ: Princeton University Press.

Rossotti NG, Winter DA, Watts MH (2005) Trust and dependency in younger and older people. Paper presented at 14th International Congress on Personal Construct Psychology, Wollongong.

Roth A, Fonagy P (1996) What Works for Whom? A Critical Review of Psychotherapy Research. New York: Guilford.

Roth A, Fonagy P, Parry G (1996) Psychotherapy research, funding and evidence-based practice. In A Roth, P Fonagy (eds) What Works for Whom? A Critical Review of Psychotherapy Research. New York: Guilford, pp. 37–56.

Roth S, Cohen L (1986) Approach, avoidance, and coping with stress. American Psychologist. 41: 813–19.

Rowan RL, Howley TF, Nova HR (1962) Electro-ejaculation. Journal of Urology 87: 726–9.

Rowe D (1971) Poor prognosis in a case of depression as predicted by the repertory grid. British Journal of Psychiatry 118: 297–300.

Royce JR (1964) The Encapsulated Man: an Interdisciplinary Essay on the Search for Meaning. Princeton, NJ: Van Nostrand.

Royce JR, Mos LP (1980) Psycho-Epistemological Profile Manual. Edmonton: University of Alberta Press.

Royce JR, Powell A (1983) Theory of Personality and Individual Differences: Factors, Systems, Processes. Englewood Cliffs, NJ: Prentice-Hall.

Ruggiero GM, Ciuna A, Levi D, Sassaroli S (2003) Stress situation reveals association between perfectionism and drive for thinness. International Journal of Eating Disorders 34: 220–6.

Rush F (1980) The Best Kept Secret: Sexual Abuse of Children. New York: McGraw-Hill.

Ryle A (1979) The focus in brief interpretative psychotherapy: dilemmas, traps and snags as target problems. British Journal of Psychiatry 134: 46–54.

Ryle A, Breen D (1972) A comparison of adjusted and maladjusted couples using the double dyad grid. British Journal of Medical Psychology 45: 375–82.

Safran JD, Segal ZV (1990) Interpersonal Process in Cognitive Therapy. New York: Basic Books.

Salmon P (1985) Living in Time. London: Dent.

Sanderson WC, Rapee RM, Barlow DH (1989) The influence of an illusion of control on panic attacks induced via inhalation of 5.5% carbon dioxide – enriched air. Archives of General Psychiatry 46: 157–62.

Sarason IG, Johnson JH, Siegal JM (1978) Assessing the impact of life changes. Development of the Life Experiences Survey. Journal of Consulting and Clinical Psychology 46: 932–46.

Sarbin TR (1986) The narrative as a root metaphor for psychology. In TR Sarbin (ed.) Narrative Psychology. New York: Praeger, pp. 3–21.

Sassaroli S, Ruggiero GM (2002) I costrutti dell'ansia: obbligo di controllo, perfezionismo patologico, pensiero catastrofico, autovalutazione negativa e intolleranza dell'incertezza. Psicoterapia Cognitiva e Comportamentale 8: 45–60.

Schacht TE, Black DA (1985) Epistemological commitments of behavioral and psychoanalytic therapists. Professional Psychology: Research and Practice 16: 316–23.

Scheer JW (2001) Reconstruing after a change in health conditions. Paper presented at 14th International Congress on Personal Construct Psychology, Wollongong.

Scheer JW, Hundertmark K, Ellis JM (1997) Life satisfaction in young adults and elderly persons. In P Denicolo, M Pope (eds) Sharing Understanding and Practice. Farnborough: EPCA, pp. 166–76.

Schore AN (1994) Affect Regulation and the Origin of Self. Hillsdale, NJ: Lawrence Erlbaum.

Schover L, LoPiccolo J (1982) Treatment effectiveness for dysfunctions of sexual desire. Journal of Sex and Marital Therapy 8: 179–97.

Scully D, Marolla J (1984) Convicted rapists' vocabulary of motive: excuses and justifications. Social Problems 31: 530–44.

Seligman MEP (1975) Helplessness: On Depression, Development, and Death. San Francisco, CA: WH Freeman.

Seligman MEP (1991) Learned Optimism. New York: Knopf.

Semerari A, Mancini F (1987) Recursive self-invalidation in neurotic processes. Paper presented at 7th International Congress of Personal Construct Psychology, Memphis.

Sewell KW (1996) Constructional risk factors for a post-traumatic stress response following a mass murder. Journal of Constructivist Psychology 9: 97–107.

Sewell KW (1997) Posttraumatic stress: towards a constructivist model of psychotherapy. In RA Neimeyer, GJ Neimeyer (eds) Advances in Personal Construct Psychology, Volume 4. Greenwich, CT: JAI Press, pp. 207–35.

Sewell KW (2002) Psicoterapia con clients traumatizados y en duelo: un marco constructivista para el amor y la curacion. (Psychotherapy with bereaved and traumatized clients: A constructivist framework for love and healing.) Revista de Psicoterapia XII: 123–32.

Sewell KW (2003) A personal constructivist approach to posttraumatic stress. In F Fransella (ed.) International Handbook of Personal Construct Psychology. London: Wiley, pp. 223–31.

Sewell KW (2005) The experience cycle and the sexual response cycle: conceptualization and application to sexual dysfunctions. Journal of Constructivist Psychology 18: 3–13.

Sewell KW, Ovaert LB (1997) Group treatment of post-traumatic stress in incarcerated adolescents: structural and narrative impacts on the permeability of self-construction. Paper presented at the Twelfth International Congress of Personal Construct Psychology, Seattle, WA.

Sewell KW, Taber I (2001) Construal disruption following trauma: relations between domains of construction and trauma content. Paper presented at 14th International Congress on Personal Construct Psychology, Wollongong.

Sewell KW, Williams AM (2001) Construing stress: a constructivist therapeutic approach to posttraumatic stress reactions. In RA Neimeyer (ed.) Meaning Reconstruction and the Experience of Loss. Washington, DC: American Psychological Association, pp. 293–310.

Sewell KW, Williams AM (2002) Broken narratives: trauma, metaconstructive gaps, and the audience of psychotherapy. Journal of Constructivist Psychology 15: 205–18.

Sewell KW, Baldwin CL, Williams AM (1998) Multiple self-awareness groups: Format and application to a personal growth experience. Journal of Constructivist Psychology 11: 59–78.

Sewell KW, Baldwin CL, Moes AJ, Ovaert LB (1994) Post-traumatic stress disorder: a symposium on constructivist findings of combat, disaster, and rape survivors. I. Introduction, overview, and discussion. Presented at Sixth North American Conference on Personal Construct Psychology, Indianapolis, IN.

Sewell KW, Cromwell RL, Farrell-Higgins J, Palmer R, Ohlde C, Patterson TW (1996) Hierarchical elaboration in the conceptual structure of Vietnam combat veterans. Journal of Constructivist Psychology 9: 79–96.

Sexton TL, Griffin BL (1997) Constructivist Thinking in Counseling Practice, Research, and Training. New York: Teachers College Press.

Shapiro D (1965) Neurotic Styles. Basic Books: New York.

Shapiro DA (1996) Foreword. In A Roth, P Fonagy (eds) What Works for Whom? A Critical Review of Psychotherapy Research. New York: Guilford Press, pp. viii–x.

Shapiro DA, Paley G (2002) The continuing potential relevance of equivalence and allegiance to research on psychological treatment of psychosis. Psychology and Psychotherapy: Theory Research and Practice 75(4): 375–80.

Shapiro DH, Astin J (1998) Control Therapy: An Integrated Approach to Psychotherapy, Health, and Healing. Chichester: Wiley.

Sharp S (1998) Meta-analysis regression. Stata Technical Bulletin 42: 16–22.

Sharp S, Sterne J (1997) Meta analysis. Stata Technical Bulletin 38: 9–14.

Sheehan MJ (1985) A personal construct study of depression. British Journal of Medical Psychology 58: 119–28.

Shorts ID (1985) Treatment of a sex offender in a maximum security forensic hospital: Detecting changes in personality and interpersonal construing. International Journal of Offender Therapy and Comparative Criminology 29: 237–50.

Shotter J (1993) Cultural Politics of Everyday Life: Social Constructionism, Rhetoric and Knowing of the Third Kind. Toronto: University of Toronto Press.

Shute R, Patton D (1990) Childhood illness – the child as helper. In H Foot, M Morgan, R Shute (eds) Children Helping Children. London: Wiley, pp. 327–52.

Silver RC, Wortman CB, Crofton C (1990) The role of coping in support provision: the self-presentational dilemma of victims of life crises. In BS Sarason, IG Sarason, GR Pierce (eds) Social Support: An Interactional View. New York: Wiley, pp. 397–426.

Skelly A (2002) The psychological effect of stroke and the repertory grid. Clinical Psychology 10: 31–4.

Skene RA (1973) Construct shift in the treatment of a case of homosexuality. British Journal of Medical Psychology 46: 287–92.

Slade P (1982) Toward a functional analysis of anorexia nervosa and bulimia nervosa. British Journal of Clinical Psychology 21: 167–79.

Small MP (1983) The Small-Carrion penile implant. In RK Krane, MB Siroky, I Goldstein (eds) Male Sexual Dysfunction. Boston, MA: Little, Brown, pp. 253–65.

Smucker MR, Dancu C, Foa E and Niederee JL (2002) Imagery rescripting: a new treatment for survivors of childhood sexual abuse suffering from posttraumatic stress. In RL Leahy, TE Dowd (eds) Clinical Advances in Cognitive Psychotherapy: Theory and Applications. New York: Springer, pp. 294–310.

Sobrero AJ, Stearns HE, Blair JH, (1965) Technique for the induction of ejaculation in humans. Fertility and Sterility 16: 765–7.

Soldz S (1993) Beyond interpretation: the elaboration of transference in personal construct therapy. In LM Leitner, NGM Dunnett (eds) Critical Issues in Personal Construct Psychotherapy. Malabar FL: Krieger, pp. 173–92.

Spielberger C (1999) STAXI-2; Psychological Assessment Resources. Florida.

Spindler Barton E, Walton T, Rowe D (1976) Using grid technique with the mentally handicapped. In P Slater (ed.) The Measurement of Intrapersonal Space by Grid Technique. Volume 1: Explorations of Intrapersonal Space. London: Wiley.

StataCorp. (2003) Stata Statistical Software: Release 8.0. College Station, TX: Stata Corporation.

Stearns P (1995) Emotion in Harre R and Stearns P (eds) Discursive Psychology in Practice. London: Sage, pp. 37–54.

Stefan C, Linder HB (1985) Suicide, an experience of chaos or fatalism: perspectives from personal construct theory. In D Bannister (ed.) Issues and Approaches in Personal Construct Theory. London: Academic Press, pp. 183–209.

Stefan C, Von J (1985) Suicide. In E Button (ed.) Personal Construct Theory and Mental Health. London: Croom Helm, pp. 132–52.

Stevens CD (1998) Realism and Kelly's pragmatic constructivism. Journal of Constructivist Psychology 11: 283–308.

Stewart AE, Neimeyer RA (2001) Emplotting the traumatic self: narrative revision and the construction of coherence. The Humanistic Psychologist 29: 8–39.

Stiles WB (1980) Measurement of the impact of psychotherapy sessions. Journal of Consulting and Clinical Psychology 48: 176–85.

Stiles WB (1999) Signs and voices in psychotherapy. Psychotherapy Research 9: 1–21.

Strasser F (1999) Emotions – Experiences in Existential Psychotherapy and Life. London: Duckworth.

Stroebe M (1992) Coping with bereavement: A review of the grief work hypothesis. Omega 26: 19–42.

Stroebe M, Schut H (1999) The dual process model of coping with bereavement: rationale and description. Death Studies 23: 197–224.

Strupp HH, Hartley D, Blackwood GL (1974) Vanderbilt Psychotherapy Process Scale. Unpublished manuscript, Vanderbilt University.

Stuss D, Knight R (2002) Principles of Frontal Lobe Function. London: Oxford University Press.

Suls J, Fletcher B (1985) The relative efficacy of avoidant and nonavoidant coping strategies: a meta-analysis. Health Psychology 4: 249–88.

Surrey JL (1991) The self-in-relation: a theory of women's development. In JV Jordan, AG Kaplan, JB Miller, IP Stiver, JL Surrey (eds) Women's Growth in Connection: Writings from the Stone Center. New York: Guilford, pp. 51–66.

Sutton AJ, Duval SJ, Tweedie RL, Abrams KR, Jones DR (2000) Empirical assessment of effect of publication bias on meta-analyses. British Medical Journal 320: 1574–7.

Sutton J, Smith P, Swettenham J (2001) 'It's easy, it works, and it makes me feel good' – a response to Arsenio and Lemerise. Social Development 10(1): 74–8.

Szasz T (1961) The Myth of Mental Illness. New York: Harper & Row.

Takamatsu K, Ohta H, Makita K, Horiguchi F, Nozawa S (2001) Effects of counseling on climacteric symptoms in Japanese postmenopausal women. Journal of Obstetrics and Gynaecology Research 27: 133–40.

Tarrier N, Haddock G, Barrowclough B, Wykes T (2002) Are all psychological treatments for psychosis equal? The need for CBT in the treatment of psychosis and not for psychodynamic psychotherapy. Psychology and Psychotherapy: Theory Research and Practice 75(4): 375–80.

Taylor K, Marienau C, Fiddler M (2000) Developing Adult Learners: Strategies for Teachers and Trainers. San Francisco, CA: Jossey-Bass.

Taylor L (1972) The significance and interpretation of replies to motivational technique in a clinical setting. British Journal of Social and Clinical Psychology 5: 51–62.

Telfer R, Cummins P (2003) Working Memory and Emotion. Unpublished paper presented to Coventry Psychological Service.

Thienemann M, Steiner H (1993) Family environment of eating disordered and depressed adolescents. International Journal of Eating Disorders 14: 43–8.

Thomas JC, Schlutsmeyer MW (2002) A place for the imaginal in personal construct theory and experiential personal construct therapy. Paper presented at the 10th Conference of the North American Personal Construct Network, Vancouver BC.

Tillitski CJ (1990) A meta-analysis of estimated effect sizes for group versus individual control treatment. International Journal of Group Psychotherapy 40: 215.

Tomarken AJ, Cook M, Mineka S (1989) Fear – relevant selective associations and covaration bias. Journal of Abnormal Psychology 98: 381–94.

Tomm K (1988) Interventive interviewing: Part 111. Intending to ask lineal, circular, strategic, or reflexive questions. Family Process 27: 1–15.

Tompkins S (1992) Affect, Imagery, Consciousness, Volume 4: Cognition: Duplication and Transformation of Information. New York: Springer.

Toukmanian SG (1986) A measure of client perceptual processing. In LS Greenberg, WM Pinsof (eds) The Psychotherapy Process: A Research Handbook. New York: Guilford, pp. 107–30.

Truneckova D, Viney LL (1997) Assessing the effectiveness of personal construct group work with problematic adolescents. Paper presented at 12th International Congress of Personal Construct Psychology, Seattle.

Truneckova D, Viney LL (2001) Can personal construct group work be an effective intervention with troubled adolescents? Australian Journal of Psychology 53 (supplement): 106.

Truneckova D, Viney LL (2002) Personal construct group work processes with troubled adolescents. University of Wollongong. Manuscript in preparation.

Truneckova D, Viney LL (2003) Evaluating personal construct group work with troubled adolescents. University of Wollongong. Unpublished manuscript.

Tschudi F (1977) Loaded and honest questions: a construct theory view of symptoms and therapy. In D Bannister (ed.) New Perspectives in Personal Construct Theory. London: Academic Press, pp. 321–50.

van der Kolk B, van der Hart O (1991) The intrusive past: the flexibility of memory and the engraving of trauma. American Imago 48: 425–54.

Varela FJ (1991) Laying down a path in walking. In W Thompson (ed.) Gaia: A Way of Knowing. Hudson NY: Lindisfarne Press, pp. 48–64.

Vasco AB (1994) Correlates of constructivism among Portuguese therapists. Journal of Constructivist Psychology 7: 1–16.

Vasey MW, Borkovec TD (1992) A catastrophizing assessment of worrisome thoughts. Cognitive Therapy and Research 16: 1–16.

Vincent N, LeBow M (1995) Treatment preference and acceptability: epistemology and locus of control. Journal of Constructivist Psychology 8: 81–96.

Viney LL (1983a) The assessment of psychological states through content analysis of verbalizations. Psychological Bulletin 94: 942–63.

Viney LL (1983b) Images of Illness. Malabar, FL: Krieger.

Viney LL (1988) Which data collection methods are appropriate for a constructivist psychology? International Journal of Personal Construct Psychology 1: 80–92.

Viney LL (1990a) A constructivist model of psychological reactions to physical illness and injury. In GJ Neimeyer, RA Neimeyer (eds) Advances in Personal Construct Psychology (Volume 1). Greenwich, CT: JAI Press, pp 117–51.

Viney LL (1990b) Psychotherapy as shared reconstruction. International Journal of Personal Construct Psychology 3: 437–56.

Viney LL (1993a) Life Stories: Personal Construct Therapy with the Elderly. Chichester: Wiley.

Viney LL (1993b) Listening to what my clients and I say: content analysis categories and scales. In GJ Neimeyer (ed.) Constructivist Assessment: A Casebook. Newbury Park, CA: Sage.

Viney LL (1994) Sequences of emotional distress expressed by clients and acknowledged by therapists: are they associated more with some therapists than others? British Journal of Clinical Psychology 33: 469–81.

Viney LL (1995) Reminiscence in psychotherapy with the elderly: telling and retelling their stories. In BK Haight, JD Webster (eds) The Art and Science of Reminiscing: Theory, Research, Methods and Applications. Taylor and Francis, pp. 243–54.

Viney LL (1996) Personal Construct Therapy: A Handbook. Norwood NJ: Ablex.

Viney LL (1998) Should we use personal construct therapy? A paradigm for outcomes evaluation. Psychotherapy 35: 366–80.

Viney LL, Benjamin YN, Preston C (1988) Constructivist family therapy with the elderly. Journal of Family Psychology 2: 241–58.

Viney LL, Benjamin YN, Preston CA (1989) An evaluation of personal construct therapy for the elderly. British Journal of Medical Psychology 62: 35–41.

Viney LL, Caputi P (2005) The origin and pawn, positive affect, psychosocial maturity and cognitive affect scales: using them in counselling research. Measurement and Evaluation in Counselling Research, in press.

Viney LL, Clarke AM, Bunn TA, Benjamin YN (1985a) An evaluation of three crisis intervention programs for general hospital patients. British Journal of Medical Psychology 58: 75–86.

Viney LL, Clarke AM, Bunn TA, Benjamin YN (1985b) The effect of a hospital-based counseling service on the physical recovery of surgical and medical patients. General Hospital Psychiatry 7: 294–301.

Viney LL, Clarke AM, Bunn TA, Benjamin YN (1985c) Crisis-intervention counseling: an evaluation of long- and short-term effects. Journal of Counseling Psychology 32: 29–39.

Viney LL, Henry RM (2002) Evaluating personal construct and psychodynamic group work with adolescent offenders and non-offenders. In RA Neimeyer, GJ Neimeyer (eds) Advances in Personal Construct Psychology: New Directions and Perspectives. Westport, CT: Praeger, pp. 259–94.

Viney LL, Henry RM, Campbell J (2001) The impact of group work on offender adolescents. Journal of Counseling and Development 79: 373–81.

Viney LL, Truneckova D, Weekes P, Oades L (1997) Personal construct group work with school-based adolescents: Reduction of risk-taking. Journal of Constructivist Psychology 10: 167–86.

Viney LL, Truneckova D, Weekes P, Oades L (1999) Personal construct group work for adolescent offenders. Journal of Child and Adolescent Group Therapy 9: 169–85.

Viney LL, Westbrook MT (1976) Cognitive anxiety: a method of content analysis for verbal samples. Journal of Personality Assessment 40: 140–50.

Vitousek KB, Hollon KB (1990) The investigation of schematic content and processing in eating disorders. Cognitive Therapy and Research 14: 191–214.

Von Glaserfeld E (1984) An introduction to radical constructivism. In P Watzlawick (ed.) The Invented Reality: How Do We Know What We Believe We Know? Contributions to Constructivism. New York: Norton, pp. 17–40.

Von Glaserfeld E (1995) Radical Constructivism: A Way of Knowing and Learning. London: The Falmer Press.

Walker BM (1992) Values and Kelly's theory: becoming a good scientist. International Journal of Personal Construct Psychology 5: 259–69.

Walker BM (1993) Looking for a whole 'mama': personal construct psychotherapy and dependency. In LM Leitner, NGM Dunnett (eds) Critical Issues in Personal Construct Psychotherapy. Malabar FL: Krieger, pp. 61–81.

Walker BM (1997) Shaking the kaleidoscope: dispersion of dependency and its relationships. In GJ Neimeyer, RA Neimeyer (eds) Advances in Personal Construct Psychology. Volume 4. Greenwich, CT: JAI Press, pp. 63–97.

Walker BM (2000) 'We don't call it traveling; we call it living.' In JW Scheer (ed.) The Person in Society. Giessen: Psychosozial-Verlag, pp. 100–13.

Walker BM (2002) Nonvalidation vs. (In)validation: implications for theory and practice. In JD Raskin, S Bridges (eds) Studies in Meaning: Exploring Constructivist Psychology. New York: Pace University Press, pp. 49–60.

Walker BM (2003) Making sense of dependency. In F Fransella (ed.) International Handbook of Personal Construct Psychology. Chichester: Wiley, pp. 171–80.

Walker BM, Ramsey FL, Bell RC (1988) Dispersed and undispersed dependency. International Journal of Personal Construct Psychology 1: 63–80.

Walker BM, Oades LG, Caputi P, Stevens C, Crittenden N (2000) Going beyond the scientist metaphor: from validation to experience cycles. In J Scheer (ed.) The Person in Society: Challenges to a Constructivist Theory. Giessen: Psychosozial-Verlag, pp. 100–13.

Walsh F, McGoldrick M (1991) Living Beyond Loss. New York: Norton.

Wampold BE (2001) The Great Psychotherapy Debate: Models, Methods, and Findings. Mahwah, NJ: Lawrence Erlbaum.

Warren B (1992a) Subjecting and objecting in personal construct psychology. In A Thomson, P Cummins (eds) European Perspectives in Personal Construct Psychology. Lincoln: European Personal Construct Association, pp. 57–66.

Warren B (1998) Philosophical Dimensions of Personal Construct Psychology. London: Routledge.

Warren WG (1992b) Personal construct theory and mental health. International Journal of Personal Construct Psychology 4: 223–37.

Watkins J (1998) Hearing Voices: A Common Human Experience. Melbourne: Hill of Content Publishing.

Watson JP, Marks IM (1971) Relevant and irrelevant fear in flooding: a crossover study of phobic patients. Behaviour Therapy 2: 275–93.

Watson S (1998) A Process and Outcome Study of Personal Construct, Cognitive and Psychodynamic Therapies in an NHS Setting. Unpublished PhD thesis. University of Hertfordshire.

Watson S, Winter D (1999) Use of the repertory grid as a nomothetic measure in psychotherapy research: An example of optimal functioning or of failure to complete the experience cycle? In JM Fisher, DJ Savage (eds) Beyond Experimentation into Meaning. Farnborough: ECPA Publications, pp. 123–45.

Watson S, Winter DA (2000) Towards an evidence base for personal construct psychotherapy. In JM Fisher, N Cornelius (eds) Challenging the Boundaries: PCP Perspectives for the New Millenium. Farnborough: EPCA Publications, pp. 220–47.

Watson S, Winter DA (2005) A process and outcome study of personal construct psychotherapy. In DA Winter, LL Viney (eds) Personal Construct Psychotherapy: Advances in Theory, Practice and Research. London: Whurr.

Weiner B (1992) Human Motivation. Newbury Park, CA: Sage.

Weinreich P, Doherty J, Harris P (1985) Empirical assessment of identity in anorexia and bulimia nervosa. Journal of Psychiatric Research 19: 297–302.

Weisman AD, Worden JW (1976) The existential plight in cancer: Significance of the first 100 days. International Journal of Psychiatry in Medicine 7: 1–15.

Weissman A, Beck AT (1978) Development and validation of the Dysfunctional Attitude Scale: a preliminary investigation. Paper presented at the annual meeting of the American Educational Research Association: Toronto.

Welch-McCaffrey D, Hoffman B, Leigh S, Loescher LJ, Meyskens FL (1989) Surviving adult cancers. II. Psychosocial implications. Annals of Internal Medicine 111: 517–24.

Westbrook MT (1976) The measurement of positive affect using content analysis scales. Journal of Consulting and Clinical Psychology 12: 85–6.

Westbrook MT, Viney LL (1980) Scales measuring people's perception of themselves as origins and pawns. Journal of Personality Assessment 44: 167–74.

Westbury E, Tutty LM (1999) The efficacy of group treatment for survivors of childhood abuse. Child Abuse and Neglect 23: 31–44.

White M (1995) Re-authoring Lives: Interviews and Essays. Adelaide: Dulwich Centre.

White M, Epston D (1990) Narrative Means to Therapeutic Ends. New York: Norton.

Widom CS (1976) Interpersonal and personal construct systems in psychopaths. Journal of Consulting and Clinical Psychology 44: 614–23.

Williams SL, Rappoport A (1983) Cognitive treatment in the natural environment for agoraphobics. Behavior Therapy 14: 299–313.

Winnicott DW (1949) Hate in the countertransference. In Institute of Psycho-analysis Through Paediatrics to Psychoanalysis. London: Karnac.

Winslade J, Monk G (2001) Narrative Mediation. San Francisco, CA: Jossey Bass.

Winter DA (1985a) Neurotic disorders: the curse of certainty. In E Button (ed.) Personal Construct Theory and Mental Health. London: Croom Helm, pp. 103–31.

Winter DA (1985b) Group therapy with depressives: a personal construct theory perspective. International Journal of Mental Health 13: 67–85.

Winter DA (1988a) Constructions in social skills training. In F Fransella, L Thomas (eds) Experimenting with Personal Construct Psychology. London: Routledge & Kegan Paul, pp. 342–56.

Winter DA (1988b) Reconstructing an erection and elaborating ejaculation: personal construct theory perspectives on sex therapy. International Journal of Personal Construct Psychology 1: 81–99.

Winter DA (1989a) Resistance to therapy: stubborn opposition or constructive choice? Paper presented at 3rd European Conference on Psychotherapy Research, Bern.

Winter DA (1989b) An alternative construction of agoraphobia. In K Gournay (ed.) Agoraphobia: Current Perspectives on Theory and Treatment. London: Routledge, pp. 93–119.

Winter DA (1992a) Personal Construct Psychology in Clinical Practice: Theory, Research and Applications. London: Routledge.

Winter DA (1992b) Repertory grid technique as a group psychotherapy research instrument. Group Analysis 25: 449–62.

Winter DA (1996) Psychotherapy's contrast pole. In J Scheer, A Catina (eds) Empirical Constructivism in Europe: The Personal Construct Approach. Giessen: Psychosozial-Verlag, pp. 149–59.

Winter DA (1997) Personal construct theory perspectives on group psychotherapy. In P Denicolo, M Pope (eds) Sharing Understanding and Practice. Farnborough: EPCA Publications, pp. 210–21.

Winter D (2000) Can personal construct therapy succeed in competition with other therapies? In JW Scheer (ed.) The Person in Society: Challenges to a Constructivist Theory. Giessen: Psychosozial-Verlag, pp. 373–80.

Winter DA (2003a) Psychological disorder as imbalance. In F Fransella (ed.) International Handbook of Personal Construct Psychology. Chichester: Wiley, pp. 201–9.

Winter DA (2003b) The evidence base for personal construct psychotherapy. In F Fransella (ed.) International Handbook of Personal Construct Psychology. London: Wiley, pp. 265–72.

Winter DA (2003c) A credulous approach to violence and homicide. In J Horley (ed.) Personal Construct Perspectives on Forensic Psychology. New York: Brunner-Routledge, pp. 15–54.

Winter DA (2003d) Repertory grid technique as a psychotherapy research measure. Psychotherapy Research 13: 25–42.

Winter D, Gournay K (1987) Construction and constriction in agoraphobia. British Journal of Medical Psychology 60: 233–44.

Winter DA, Watson S (1999) Personal construct psychotherapy and the cognitive therapies: different in theory but can they be differentiated in practice? Journal of Constructivist Psychology 12: 1–22.

Winter DA, Gournay K, Metcalfe C (1999) An investigation of the effectiveness of a personal construct psychotherapy intervention. In JM Fisher, DJ Savage (eds) Beyond Experimentation into Meaning. Lostock Hall: EPCA Publications, pp. 146–60.

Winter D, Gournay K, Metcalfe C, Rossotti N (2005) Expanding agoraphobics' horizons: an investigation of the effectiveness of a personal construct psychotherapy intervention. Journal of Constructivist Psychology. In press.

Winter D, Tschudi F, Gilbert N (2005) Psychotherapists' theoretical orientations as elaborative choices. In P Caputi, L Viney, H Foster (eds) Personal Construct Psychology: New Ideas. London: Whurr.

Winter D, Gournay K, Metcalfe C, Newman-Taylor K, Asimakopoulou K, Richards A (1997) Expanding agoraphobics' horizons: an investigation of the effectiveness of a personal construct psychotherapy intervention. Paper presented at 12th International Congress on Personal Construct Psychology: Seattle, WA.

Winter D, Bhandari S, Metcalfe C, Riley T, Sireling L, Watson S, Lutwyche G (2000) Deliberate and undeliberated self-harm: theoretical basis and evaluation of a personal construct psychotherapy intervention. In JW Scheer (ed.) The Person in Society: Challenges to a Constructivist Theory. Giessen: Psychosozial – Verlag, pp. 351–60.

Winter DA, Watson S, Gillman-Smith I, Gilbert N, Acton T (2003) Border crossing: a personal construct therapy approach for clients with a diagnosis of borderline personality disorder. In G Chiari, ML Nuzzo (eds) Psychological Constructivism and the Social World. Milan: FrancoAngeli, pp. 342–52.

Winter D, Sireling L, Riley T, Metcalfe C, Quaite A, Bhandari S (n.d.) A controlled trial of personal construct psychotherapy for deliberate self-harm. Unpublished manuscript, University of Hertfordshire.

Winton EC, Clark DM, Edelman R (1995) Social anxiety, fear of negative evaluation and the detection of negative emotion in others. Behaviour Research and Therapy 33: 193–6.

Wiser SL, Goldfried MR, Raue PJ, Vakoch D (1996) Cognitive-behavioural and psychodynamic therapies: a comparison of change processes. In W Dryden (ed.) (1996) Research in Counselling and Psychotherapy: Practical Applications. London: Sage, pp. 101–32.

Wittgenstein L (1921/1988) Tractatus Logico-Philosophicus (Dr Pears and B. F. McGuinness, trans). London: Routledge.

Wolfsdorf BA, Zlotnick C (2001) Affect management in group therapy for women with posttraumatic stress disorder and histories of childhood sexual abuse. In Session: Psychotherapy in Practice 57: 169–81.

Woolfus B, Bierman R (1996) An evaluation of a group treatment program for incarcerated male batterers. International Journal of Offender Therapy and Comparative Criminology 40: 318–33.

Wortman CB, Silver RC (1987) The myths of coping with loss. Journal of Consulting and Clinical Psychology 57: 349–57.

Wykes T, Tarrier N, Lewis S (eds) (1998) Outcome and Innovation in Psychological Treatment of Schizophrenia. Chichester: Wiley.

Yalom ID (1970/1975/1995) The Theory and Practice of Group Psychotherapy. New York: Basic Books.

Yalom ID (1980) Existential Psychotherapy. New York: Basic Books.

Yehuda R, McFarlane AC (1995) Conflict between current knowledge about posttraumatic stress disorder and its original conceptual basis. American Journal of Psychiatry 152: 1705–13.

Zabora J, Brintzenhofeszoc K, Curbow B, Hooker C, Piantadosi S (2001) The prevalence of psychological distress by cancer site. Psycho-Oncology 10: 19–28.

Zetzel E (1956) Current concepts of transference. International Journal of Psycho-Analysis 37: 369–76.

Zilbergeld B, Kilmann PR (1984) The scope and effectiveness of sex therapy. Psychotherapy 21: 319–26.

Zlotnick C, Shea TM, Rosen K, Simpson E, Mulrenin K, Begin A, Pearlstein T (1997) An affect–management group for women with posttraumatic stress disorder and histories of childhood sexual abuse. Journal of Traumatic Stress 10: 425–36.

Zumaya M, Bridges SK, Rubio E (1999) A constructivist approach to sex therapy with couples. Journal of Constructivist Psychology 12: 185–201.

Author index

Abel, G.G., 235
Abrahamson, L.Y., 134
Abrams, K.R., 355
Adams, B., 238
Adams, J., 275
Adams-Webber, J.R., 30, 74, 272, 340, 352
Adams-Westcott, J., 183
Adroutsopoulou, A., 103
Agnew, J., 272
Albert, C.J., 81
Akman, D., 177
Aldridge, D., 129
Aldridge, J., 179
Alexander, F., 48
Alexander, P.C., 48, 125, 179, 186, 187, 196, 286, 354, 356, 357, 360
Alfano, V., 45
Allen, D., 212
Allen, S., 311
Altman, D.G., 348, 350, 361
American Psychiatric Association, 5, 165, 189, 212
Amerikaner, M., 25
Anarte, M.T., 321
Anderson, D., 267
Anderson, E., 87, 88, 267, 321
Anderson, R., 88
Anderson, W.T., 87
Andrews, D.A., 226, 229, 231
Androutsopoulou, A., 103
Angus, L.E., 13, 69
Apelbaum, B., 288
Apolinsky, S.R., 188
Apparigliato, 41
Arensman, E., 135
Arentewicz, G., 289
Arnold, W., 81

Arsenio, W., 266
Arthur, A.R., 87
Attig, T., 115
Australian Bureau of Statistics, 324
Austin, J., 36
Avila-Espada, A., 137

Bacal, H.A., 44
Bacete, F., 266
Badanes, L., 266
Baddeley, A., 248, 250
Bagnara, S., 38
Baile, W.F., 311
Baldwin, C.L., 272
Bandura, A, 35, 226
Banister, E., 322
Bannister, D., 27, 28, 43, 94, 97, 152, 198, 215, 219, 239, 240, 254, 269, 271, 272, 290, 294, 321, 352, 353, 369
Barbaree, H.E., 226, 238, 272
Barbeau, D., 272
Barlow, D.H., 36, 335
Baron-Cohen, S., 265
Barrett-Lennard, G.T., 338
Barrowclough, B., 223
Bartlett, F.C., 116
Bartol, A.M., 226
Bartol, C.R., 226
Bar-Tur, L., 114
Basoglu, M., 36
Bass, D., 362
Bateson, G., 51, 94, 106
Batson, C., 269
Beail, N., 352
Bechtel, R.J., 316
Beck, A.T., 46, 86, 337
Becker, J.V., 235

Begin, A., 188
Beitchman, J.H., 177
Bell, R., 29, 97, 369
Bender, M., 298
Benjafield, J., 272
Benjamin, Y.N., 107, 308, 352, 353
Bentall, R.P., 212
Berg, I., 102
Berzonsky, M.D., 78, 83, 91
Bierman, R., 238
Bion, W.R., 277
Biran, M., 150
Birchwood, M., 217
Black, D.A., 85
Blackwood, G.L., 337
Blair, J.H., 287
Blalock, S.J., 321
Blatt, S.J., 75
Bloch, S., 155
Bloom, J.R., 311
Bohart, A.C., 75, 76, 347
Bonta, J., 226, 231
Book, H., 69
Borkovec, T.D., 35
Bosworth, H.B., 321
Botella, L., 13, 69, 71, 73, 74, 80, 307, 313, 347, 353, 354, 361
Bott, M., 290
Bouffard, B., 69
Bowlby, J., 44, 45, 114
Bowman, K.F., 310
Breen, D., 290
Bremner, S., 135
Bridges, S.K., 12, 123, 289, 290
Briere, J., 177, 183
Brilman, E., 150
Brogna, P., 131
Bromberger, J.T., 321
Brown, E.J., 40
Brown, G., 337
Brown, T.A., 36
Browne, A., 177
Bruch, H., 40
Buber, M., 51, 55
Bunn, T.A., 353
Burnett, P., 114
Burnham, J., 268
Burns, D.D., 41
Burns, T., 294

Burr, V., 12, 262
Burt, J.C., 287
Butler, G., 35, 261, 262, 263, 264
Butler, R., 261, 262, 264
Button, E., 26, 40, 196, 198, 203, 204, 210, 352

Caine, T.M., 337
Calvo, M.G., 35
Campbell, J., 272
Capps, L., 151
Caputo, G.C., 155
Caputi, P, 26
Carlsen, M.B., 81
Carpenter, 250
Carrell, S., 276
Carter, B.J., 310
Cartmeill, T., 311
Cashdan, S., 9
Cassavia, E., 177
Castelfranchi, C., 38
Castillo, M.D., 35
Catina, A., 239
Celentana, M.A., 8, 58, 67, 219, 248, 278, 286
Chadwick, P., 217
Chalmers, I., 348
Chambers, W.V., 337
Chambless, D.L., 148, 155
Chiari, G., 4, 5, 12, 13, 45, 49, 51
Chin, C.E., 229
Chinn, S., 351
Cieplucha, H., 311
Ciuna, A., 40
Ciuffi, G., 38
Clark, D.M., 35, 61
Clarke, A.M., 353
Clarke, K.M., 88
Cloitre, M., 188
Cochran, L., 28
Cohen, J., 283, 362
Cohen, L., 36
Cohen, L.R., 188
Cohen, R., 267
Combs, G., 69, 184
Connan, F., 39
Cook, M., 35
Coope, J., 321
Cooper, Z., 36, 40

Corbella, S., 69
Corbella, S., 69, 74
Cordess, C., 226
Crofton, C., 312
Corr, C.A., 144
Cornejo, 137
Couchman, L., 353, 354
Cox, M., 226
Craske, M., 36
Crits-Christoph, P., 348
Crittenden, N., 26
Crocket, K., 116
Crofton, C., 312
Cromwell, R.L., 175
Crosina, M., 36
Crouch, E., 155
Cuadros, J.L., 321
Cullen, E., 228
Cullen, F.T., 226–229
Cullen, M., 241
Cummins, P., 238, 239–255, 247, 248, 250, 252, 253, 352
Cunningham-Rather, J., 235

D'Andrea, T., 131
DaCosta, B.A., 177
Dallos, R., 103, 104
Dalton, P., xx, 274, 298, 312, 322
Damani, S., 203
Dancu, C., 188
Daneman, 250
Davidson, G., 239, 272
Davies, B., 118
Davies, P., 223
Davis, C.G., 115, 125
Davis, R., 189
Deimling, G.T., 310
DeMoor, C., 311
Derogatis, L.R., 142, 337
Derrida, J., 82
Devilly, G.J., 150
Diagnostic and Statistical Manual of Mental Disorders, 5
Di Guisseppe, R., 86
Dill-Standiford, T., 25, 32, 66, 311
Dobbins, C., 183
Doherty, J., 210
Dominici, D., 54
Draucker, C.B., 179, 180

Drysdale, B., 308
Duck, S.W., 272
Dugas, M.J., 35
Dunkel-Schetter, C., 311
Dunn, J., 266
Dunnett, N.G.M., 3, 189, 321
Durrant, M., 178, 182
Duval, S.J., 355
Dzamonja-Ignjatovic, T., 133, 308

Eccles, A., 229
Ecker, B., 18, 19, 240, 246, 247
Edelman, R., 35
Ediger, R., 39
Efran, J.S., 81
Eggeraat, J.B., 150
Ell, K.O., 311
Elliott, R., 348
Ellis, A., 86, 231,
Ellis, J.M., 296, 306, 307
Emmelkamp, P.M., 150
Emery, G., xv
Epston, D., 125
Epston, N., 13, 14, 15, 16, 81, 121, 125, 184, 337
Epting, F., 3, 6, 10, 12, 13, 25, 31, 229, 238, 288, 308, 312, 322, 324
Erbaugh, J., 337
Erbes, C.R., 177, 178, 181, 186, 188
Eron, J.B., 13, 16, 17
Erwin, P., 268
Escher, S., 212, 223
Essex, S., 107
Estevan, R., 266
Estevaz, A., 35
Etkin, M.W., 353, 354, 356, 357
Evans, C., 253
Evesham, M., 356, 357, 360
Eysenck, H.J., 348
Eysenck, M., 35

Faidley, A.J., 3, 6, 8, 10, 54, 56, 57, 58, 60, 62, 63, 66, 67, 89, 167, 248, 271, 278, 286
Fairburn, C.G., 36, 40
Fallot, R.D., 188
Farrell-Higgins, J., 175
Fava, G.A., 150
Feifel, H., 318

Feixas, G., 81, 88, 98, 107, 136, 137, 140, 145, 146, 307, 361
Feldman, E., 135
Fernandez, Y., 267
Ferrans, C.E., 310
Fiddler, M., 88
Finkelhor, D., 177, 180
Finset, A., 354, 359
Fisher, L.M., 324
Fletcher, B., 36
Flett, G.L., 39, 40
Foa, E.B., 35, 36, 182, 188
Follette, V.M., 177, 186, 275, 286
Fonagy, P., 243, 247, 248, 335
Foster, H., 189, 320–332, 322, 324, 351, 354
Foucault, M., 82, 122, 128
Francoeur, A., 229, 238, 352
Fransella, F., 3, 13, 30, 32, 97, 102, 129, 136, 149, 162, 198, 238, 271, 272, 288, 290, 291, 312, 322, 349, 352, 356, 357, 360, 369
Frazer, H., 149
Freedman, J., 184
Freeman-Long, R., 241
Freeston, M.H., 35
Freshwater, K., 179
French, C.C., 35
French, T.M., 48
Freedman, J., 184
Freeman-Longo, R.E., 241
Freshwater, K., 179
Freud, S., 44, 114, 165
Friedman, S., 69, 72, 73
Frith, U., 265
Fritz, G., 264
Frost, R.O., 35, 40

Gabriel, T.J., 85
Gamino, L.A., 113
Gendreau, P., 226
George, C., 103
Gergen, K.J. 12, 51, 78, 79, 80, 83
Gergen, M.M., 78
Gilbert, N., 87
Giles, L, 97
Gillberg, C., 41
Gillett, R., 116
Gillman-Smith, I., 189

Gleser, G.C., 316, 329
Goldfried, M.R., 342
Goldney, R., 135
Goldstein, A.J., 148
Goldstein, D.E., 322
Golman, D., 38
Gomez, T., 69
Goncalves, O.F., 13, 69
Gosselin, P., 35
Gottschalk, L.A., 316, 329
Gournay, K., 148, 149, 150, 156, 196
Gracely, E.J., 155
Graham, J., 267
Gray, J., 267
Green, D., 256–270, 261, 270, 321
Greenberg, J.R., 44
Greenberg, L.S., 124
Greene, F., 321
Greenson, R.R., 46
Grenyer, B.F.S., 353, 354
Grieger, R., 246
Griffin, B.L., 3
Griffin, C., 322
Guidano, V.F., 13, 45, 81, 88, 124, 141, 148, 149, 151
Gumbleton, J., 107
Gunnell, D., 135
Guthrie, A.F., 31, 62, 318

Haddock, G., 217, 223
Hafner, R.J., 148
Hagans, C.L., 88
Hallam, R.S., 150
Halperin, D.A., 271
Hamachek, D.E., 41
Hamovitch, M.B., 311
Han, H., 188
Hand, I., 150
Happe, F., 265
Hardy, L., 264
Harker, T., 183
Harré, R., 116
Harris, M., 188
Harris, P., 210
Hart, C.C., 179
Harter, S.L., 177, 178, 179, 180, 181, 182, 183, 186, 187, 188, 190
Hartley, D., 337
Hartley, R., 264, 337

Harvey, J.H., 121
Haugli, L., 354, 358, 359
Hawkins, D.K., 277
Hawton, K., 135
Hazell, P., 135
Heath, A.E., 351
Heath, R.G., 287, 351
Hedges, L.V., 351
Heimberg, R.G., 40
Henriques, M.R., 69
Henry, R.M., 272, 353
Herman, J.L., 177, 180
Hermans, H.J., 71, 77, 78, 88, 117, 120
Herrera, J., 321
Herrero, O., 69, 74
Hershgold, E., 61
Hess, A.K., 226
Hewitt, P.L., 39, 40
Hill, C.E., 338
Hill, E.A., 307, 308
Hinkle, D.N., 92, 138, 369
Hirschman, J., 128
Hochschild, A.R., 242
Hoffman, B., 311
Hoffman, I.Z., 52
Hoge, R. 226, 229
Hoigaard-Martin, J., 316, 329
Holland, J.C., 310
Hollander, M.H., 41
Hollon, K.B., 41
Holmes, L., 329
Honos-Webb, L., 11
Hood, J.E., 177
Hopkins, N.J., 149, 150
Horley, J., 226, 228, 229, 230, 238, 352
Horowitz, M.J., 117
Hosie, J., 242
House, A., 135
House, K., 135
Houston, J., 228, 229
Howard, G.S., 116
Howley, T.F., 287
Hoyt, M.F., 3
Hughes, S.L., 129, 130, 131, 133
Hulley, L., 18, 19, 240, 246, 247
Hulsey, T.L., 179
Humphrey, L.L., 41
Hundertmark, K., 306
Hunter, M.S., 294, 321

Jackson, J., 149
Jackson, S., 269
Jackson, S.R., 272
Jacobs, S.C., 119
James, W., 121
Janoff-Bulman, R., 178, 310
Jasin, S.E., 155
James, W., 121
Johnson, J.H., 337
Johnson, T.J., 10, 24, 289, 337
Johnstone, L., 24
Jones, B., 310
Jones, D.R., 355
Jones, R.C.M., 321
Jones, S., 321
Jordan, J., 120, 121, 239
Jordens, C.F.C., 310
Juster, H.R., 40

Kahana, B., 310
Kalogerakis, M.G., 271
Kaplan, H.S., 103, 295
Karst, T.O., 352
Katzman, M.A., 40
Kauffman, J., 117
Kaye, J., 75
Kazdin, A.E., 362
Keen, E., 78
Keene, M., 321
Kegan, R., 146
Keisler, D.J., 344
Kelly, G.A., 3, 4, 5, 6, 7, 8, 11, 12, 15, 17, 19,
    21, 22, 23, 24, 25, 26, 28, 29, 30, 31, 32,
    33, 34, 35, 36, 37, 42, 43, 45, 46, 47, 49,
    50, 52, 55, 57, 61, 62, 65, 74, 76, 79, 81,
    82, 83, 87, 88, 89, 90, 94, 98, 99, 102,
    105, 107, 115, 127, 128, 136, 137, 141,
    142, 148, 150, 169, 178, 189, 190, 191,
    192, 194, 196, 212, 213, 214, 215, 216, 219,
    225, 226, 227, 228, 229, 230, 232, 239,
    240, 243, 251, 257, 258, 259, 260, 261,
    262, 264, 265, 266, 267, 270, 271, 272,
    273, 288, 289, 290, 291, 293, 296, 297,
    301, 302, 308, 310, 311, 321, 322, 324,
    337, 348, 349, 365, 366, 367, 368, 369
Kelly, K.A,. 36
Kellet, M., 269
Kempen, H.J., 71
Kenemans, P., 321

Kirkwood, B., 351
Kirsch, H., 239
Killman, P.R., 294
Kiltwood, T., 298, 307
Klass, D., 115
Klion, R.E., 10
Knight, R.A., 238, 266
Knottnerus, J.A., 321
Koch, H.C.H., 276, 312, 322
Koenen, K.C., 188
Korman, Y., 13
Kowalski, K., 178, 182
Krohne, H.W., 38
Kubler-Ross, E., 114
Kuiper, A.C., 150
Kuiper, H., 150
Kukil, K.V., 128
Kunz, R., 355
Kvale, S., 71,
Kymissis, P., 271

Ladoucer, K.,35
Laerum, E., 354, 359
Lahart, C., 35
Laing, R.D., 24
Lambert, M.J., 335, 347
Lambert, W., 179
Lamontagne, Y., 150
Landfield, A.W., 3, 25, 35, 133, 151, 192, 196, 238, 275, 276, 286, 312, 344, 352, 353, 369
Lane, L.G., 310–319, 311, 312, 313, 316, 318, 354, 359
Langelle, C., 166, 175
Langer, E.J., 36
Lawlor, M., 28
Laws, D.R., 232
Lazarus, A.A., 238, 288, 295
Lea, M., 272
Leach, C., 179
Le Bow, M., 90
Lee, S., 40
Lehman, D.R., 115
Leigh, S., 311
Leitner, L.M., 3, 6, 8, 10, 11, 19, 25, 27, 30, 31, 32, 51, 54, 55, 56, 57, 58, 59, 60, 62, 63, 64, 66, 67, 89, 167, 219, 248, 271, 278, 282, 286, 301, 311, 318, 347
Lemerise, E., 266

Lester, D., 129, 337
Leudar, I., 223
Leung, A.W., 40
Levi, D., 40
Lewandowski, A.M., 6, 24
Lewin, J., 69
Lewis, S., 223
Liao, K.L.M., 321
Lieberman, S., 294
Lietaer, G., 124
Linde, K., 361
Lindemann, E., 114
Linder, H.B., 128, 129, 130
Linehan, M.M., 182
Linscott, J., 86
Liotti, G., 32, 45, 148
Lira, F.T., 353, 354, 356, 357
Little, M., 310
Llamas, M., 150
Llewelyn, S.P., 189, 338
Loeffler, V., 54
Loescher, L.J., 311
Logie, R.H., 248
Lopiccolo, J., 289, 290, 294
Lorenzini, R., 34, 36, 37, 38, 148, 149
Loux, M.J., 83
Lovenfosse, M., 314, 353, 354, 361
Lowrie, S., 311
Luborsky, L., 48, 69, 335
Lukens, M.D., 81
Lukens, R.J., 81
Lund, T.W., 13, 16, 17
Lyddon, W.J., 81, 82, 84, 85, 90, 91
Lyons, A.C., 322

Maartens, L.W.F., 321
Mackenzie, K.R., 154
Machado, P.P.P., 69
MacLeod, C., 35, 40
Maguire, P., 310
Mahoney, M.J., 3, 9, 12, 50, 74, 81, 82, 84, 85, 86, 88, 93, 123, 124, 246
Main, M., 103
Mair, M., 31, 51, 77, 105, 116, 130, 190, 217
Makris, S.G., 40
Malekoff, A., 271
Malins, G.L., 353, 354
Malkinson, R., 114

Malin, M., 311
Mancini, F., 28, 34
Mancuso, J.C., 30, 74
Mann, S., 182
Mantell, J.E., 311
Marienau, 88
Marks, I.M., 155, 337
Marlow, B., 311
Marolla, J., 227
Marshall, W., 267
Marshall.W.L., 226, 238
Marten, P., 35
Martinson, R., 226
Martinek, N., 114
Marquis, A., 9
Massie, M.J., 310
Masters, W.H., 289
Mathews, A.M., 35, 155
Maturana, H.R., 12, 167
McCoy, M.M., 29, 167, 239, 247
McCullough, J.P., 353, 354, 356, 357
McFadyen, M., 150
McFarlane, A.C., 177
McGoldrick, M., 115
McKenna, P.J., 212
McNally, R.J., 35
McNamee, S., 12, 51
Mead, G.H., 228
Meichenbaum, D., 241, 242, 244, 245
Melchart, D., 361
Mendelson, M., 337
Merleau-Ponty, M., 171
Merluzzi, T.V., 323
Mersch, P.P., 150
Metcalfe, C., 148, 149, 150, 156, 196,
    347–364
Meyer, J., 275
Meyskens, F.L., 311
Miceli, M., 38
Middleton, W., 114
Milan, M.A., 229
Millon, C., 189
Millon, T., 189
Mineka, S., 35, 36
Mintz, J., 344
Minuchin, S., 88
Mischel, W., 74
Mitchell, S.A., 44
Moan, C.E., 287

Mobley, M.J., 226
Mock, J., 337
Moes, A.J., 175
Moher, D., 350
Monk, G., 116, 125
Montgomery, K., 310
Moore, M.K., 186
Mor, V., 311
Moran, H., 301, 305
Morris, C., 298
Morris, J.B., 196, 352
Morrow, S.L., 180
Morton, R.J., 86, 91, 246
Mos, L.P., 85
Mulrenin, K., 188
Mundy, P., 266
Murphy, J.J., 286

Nagae, N., 353, 354, 356, 357, 359, 360
Najavitis, L., 182, 185
Nash, M.R., 179
Nathanson, D.L., 171
Nay, R., 353, 354, 356, 357
Nedate, K., 353, 354
Neimeyer, G.J., 23, 81, 84, 86, 88, 91, 92,
    98, 246, 272, 275, 290, 312, 323, 352
Neimeyer, R.A., 3, 6, 12, 23, 28, 84,
    88, 111, 113, 115, 116, 117, 118, 119,
    120, 121, 123, 124, 127, 129, 130, 131,
    133, 161, 166, 177, 178, 179, 180, 182,
    183, 186, 187, 192, 246, 272, 275, 286,
    290, 305, 308, 312, 314, 322, 332, 351,
    352
Neuringer, C., 134
Newman, K.M., 44
New South Wales Cancer Council, 317
Nexis Database, 320
Nguyen, Q.X., 229
Nickman, S., 115
Niederee, J.L., 188
Nind, M., 269
Nisbett, R.E., 227
Nishimoto, R.H., 311
Nitsun, M., 277, 281
Norcross, J.C., 129
Nova, 287
Novaco, R.W., 241, 242, 243
Nuzzo, M.L., 4, 5, 12, 13, 49, 51
Nygaard, R., 359

Oades, L.G., 26, 272, 322
O'Carroll, P.J., 212
Ochs, E., 151
O'Day, P., 337
Oddens, B.J., 320, 321
Oei, T.P.S., 150
Ogles, B.M., 347
O'Hara, M., 87, 347
Ohlde, C., 175
Olasov-Rothbaum, B., 36
O'Sullivan, B., 149
Ovaert, L.B., 352
Overhoiser, J., 264
Owens, D., 135
Oxman, A.D., 355

Pacheco, M., 69, 74
Padesky, C.A., 99
Paley, G., 223
Paris, M.E., 13
Parker, K., 134
Parker, P.A., 311
Parker, S., 352
Parle, M., 310
Palmer, R., 175
Parry, G., 335, 337, 347
Patch, A.R., 41
Paton, D., 264
Patterson, T.W., 175
Patton, D., 264
Paul, K., 310
Pearlstein, T., 188
Pekkola, D., 253, 352
Penn, W.I., 352
Pennings, M., 212
Pfenninger, D.T., 8, 10, 59
Philipson, B., 310
Pichard, S., 81, 82, 90
Pilch, J.J., 42
Pilkonis, P.A., 75
Polinsky, M.L., 310
Polkinghorn, D.E., 70, 71, 72, 73
Pollock, K.M., 271
Pop, V.J., 321
Poslusny, M.H., 177
Powell, A., 85
Prentky, R.A., 238
Preston, C., 107, 308, 352
Prichard, S., 31, 288, 324

Prigerson, H.G., 118, 119
Procter, H.G., 81, 88, 94, 95, 97, 100, 104, 105, 106, 107, 141

Quinsey, V.L., 230

Rachman, S., 40
Radley, P.L., 352
Ramsey, F.L., 29
Rankin, P.M., 212
Rapee, R.M., 36
Raphael, B., 114
Rappoport, A., 150
Raskin, J.D., 5, 6, 10, 12, 13, 14, 24, 123, 332
Råstam, M., 41
Rather, L., 46
Rau, P.J., 342
Ravenette, T., 101, 257, 259, 260, 261, 268, 324
Raymond, 86
Reser, J., 239
Reveley, C.H., 203
Richards, A., 35
Richardson, A., 335, 337, 347
Rigdon, M. 61
Rivers, P.C., 151, 192, 275, 286, 312, 352
Robbins, S., 296–309, 298, 301
Roesch, R., 229
Rolland, J., 264
Romme, M.A.J., 212, 214, 217, 223
Rosen, K., 188
Rosenberg, M., 204
Ross, M.R., 148
Rossoti, N.G., 308
Roth, A., 36, 335
Roth, S., 36
Rothbaum, B.A., 182
Rotondi-Trevisan, D., 69
Rowan, R.L., 287
Rowe, D., 138, 218
Royce, J.R., 85
Rubio, E., 289, 290
Ruggiero, G.M., 34, 36, 40, 41
Runtz, M., 177
Rush, A.J., 180
Rush, F., 180
Russell, S., 182
Ryle, A., 29, 138, 290

Saferstein, J., 81, 92
Safran, J.D., 44
Sage, P., 310
Sakinofsky, I., 135
Salmon, P., 152, 256, 257
Sánchez, V., 137, 145
Sanderson, W.C., 36
Sanislow, C.A., 75
Sarason, I.G., 337
Sarbin, T.R., 77
Sassaroli, S., 34, 36, 37, 38, 40, 41, 148, 149
Saúl, L.Á., 136, 137, 142, 145, 146
Schacht, T.E., 85
Scaefer, M.L., 310
Scheer, J.W., 296, 306, 307, 308
Schlutsmeyer, M.W., 54
Schmidt, G., 289
Schmitt, G.M., 239
Scholz, M., 361
Schore, A.N., 118
Schover, L., 294
Schulz, K.F., 350
Schut, H., 114
Schwenker, B., 272
Scully, D., 227
Segal, Z.V.,
Seligman, M.E.P., 35
Semerari, A., 28, 34
Sewell, K.W., 117, 165, 166, 167, 169, 175, 178, 179, 182, 272, 289, 290, 352
Sexton, T.L., 3
Shafran, R., 36, 40
Shapiro, D., 38
Shapiro, D.A., 223, 335
Shapiro, D.H., 36
Sharp, S., 351
Shaw, B.F., 374
Shea, T.M., 188
Sheehan, M.J., 352
Sherrard, P.A.D., 81, 82, 90
Shorts, I.D., 237
Shotter, J., 12
Shute, R., 264
Siddons, F., 265
Siegal, J.M., 337
Silver, R.C., 115, 312
Silverman, 115
Simpson, E., 188

Singer, B., 335
Skelly, A., 308
Skene, R.A., 237
Slade, P., 40, 217
Small, M.P., 287
Smerglia, V., 310
Smith, M.L., 180, 266
Smith, P., 266
Smucker, M.R., 188
Sobrero, A.J., 287
Soldz, S., 52
Spencer, C., 272
Spielberger, C., 253
Spindler Barton, E., 218
Springer, K.J., 316
StataCorp, 351
Stearns, H.E., 287
Stearns, P., 242
Steen, E., 354, 359
Steer, R.A., 337
Stefan, C., 127, 128, 129, 130, 131
Steiner, H., 41
Sterne, J., 351
Stevans, G., 26
Stevens, C.D., 13
Stewart, A.E., 117, 124, 179, 183
Stiffan, E., 45
Stiles, W.B., 120, 124, 154
Storer, D., 135
Strasser, F., 239
Strauss, J., 351
Stringer, P., 353
Stroebe, M., 114, 115
Strupp, H.H., 337
Stuss, D., 266
Suls, J., 36
Surrey, J.L., 55
Sutton, A.J., 266, 355
Sutton, J., 266
Swettenham, J., 266
Szasz, T., 24

Taber, I., 166, 175
Tager-Flusberg, H., 265
Takamatsu, K., 321
Tallman, K., 75, 76
Tarrier, N., 223
Taylor, K., 88
Taylor, L., 227

Teasdale, J.D., 134
Telfer, R., 248
Thienemann, M., 41
Thomas, B., 118
Thomas, J.C., 54, 63, 223
Thomas, P., 223
Tillitski, C.J., 271
Tomarken, A.J., 35
Tomm, K., 268
Tompkins, S., 171
Townsend, E., 135
Toukmanian, S.G., 338
Traskman-Bendz, L., 135
Treasure, J., 391
Trexler, L.D., 337, 352
Trower, P., 217
Truneckova, D., 196, 271–286, 272, 283, 354
Tschudi, F., 30, 87, 138, 141, 161, 290, 304, 369
Tutty, L.M., 187
Tweedie, R.L., 355

Vakoch, D., 342
Van der Hart, O., 117
Van der Kolk, B., 117
Vanecek, J., 179
Van Heeringen, K., 135
Van Loon, R.J., 71
Varela, F.J., 12, 47, 167
Vasco, A.B., 89
Vasey, M.W., 35
Vincent, N., 90
Viney, L.L., 3, 84, 89, 107, 166, 189, 196, 239, 271–286, 272, 275, 283, 292, 297, 299, 301, 307, 308, 310–319, 311, 312, 313, 314, 317, 318, 320–332, 322, 323, 324, 329, 347–364, 348, 349, 351, 352, 353, 354, 358, 359, 361, 362, 363, 369
Vitousek, K.B., 41
Von, J., 127, 128, 131
Von Glaserfeld, E., 12

Walker, B.M., 13, 21, 26, 27, 28, 29, 45, 243
Walker, W., 229
Walsh, F., 115
Walton, T., 218
Wampold, B.E., 5

Ward, C.H.
Warren, B., 5, 13, 25
Warren, R.L., 199, 204, 210
Watkins, J., 214
Watson, J.C., 124
Watson, J.P., 337
Watson, S., 89, 146, 189, 231, 246, 335–346, 336, 338, 340, 351, 356, 357, 359, 360
Watts, M.H., 308
Weeks, P., 272
Weiner, B., 38
Weinreich, P., 210
Weisman, A.D., 310
Weissman, A, 337
Welch-McCaffrey, D., 311
Westbrook, M.T., 292, 329
Westbury, E., 187
White, M., 13, 14, 15, 16, 70, 72, 81, 103, 121, 125, 184
Widom, C.S., 29
Wilcoxon, S.A., 188
Williams, A.M., 169, 178, 179, 182, 272
Williams, S.L., 150
Willich, S.N., 361
Wilson, G.T., 324
Winnicott, D.W., 281
Winslade, J., 116, 125
Winter, D.A., 3, 4, 5, 10, 21, 28, 30, 32, 34, 36, 87, 89, 127, 130, 131, 133, 136, 137, 148, 149, 150, 156, 158, 189, 191, 196, 197, 228, 229, 231, 237, 238, 246, 272, 275, 287–295, 288, 308, 312, 321, 323, 335–346, 336, 338, 339, 340, 347–364, 348, 349, 351, 354, 356, 357, 358, 359, 360, 361, 362, 363
Winton, E.C., 35
Wiser, S.L., 342
Wittgenstein, L., 82
Wolfsdorf, B.A., 188
Woolfus, B., 238
Wortman, 115, 312
Wormith, J.S., 235
Wortman, C.B., 115, 311, 312
Worden, J.W., 310
Wykes, T., 223

Yalom, I.D., 55, 131, 155, 278, 322
Yehuda, R., 177

Zabora, J., 310
Zetzel, E., 45
Zilbergeld, B., 294
Zinbarg, R., 36
Zinger, I., 226, 229

Zlotnick, C., 188
Zucker, K.J., 177
Zumaya, M., 289, 290
Zuroff, D.C., 75

Subject index

ABC technique, 92, 138, 141, 147, 161 290, 304, 369

acceptance, 49

adolescents; troubled

case examples, 278–283

developing group work, 272–278

group setting, sessions and structure, 275–276

group work goals, 273–274

group work processes, 276–277

implications for the leaders of the anti-group, 280–282

personal construct work with, 271–286

research, 283–285

themes, 274–275

theory, 271–272

therapeutic practice, 273–28

working in personal construct groups with troubled adolescents, 277–278

ageing, 296–309

agoraphobia

case example, 151–153

manual for PCP for agoraphobia, 158–164

PCP, 148–164

research, 153–157

theory, 148–149

therapeutic practice, 150–151

agreement to differ, 100

analytic dyad, 46

anger

case example, 251–252

constructivist approach to running an anger group, 246–248

experience of, 239–255

extent of illiteracy/dyslexia, 248–251

pain of change, 243–246

PCP and CBT, 241–243

research, 253–254

therapeutic practice, 246–251

theory (PCP and CBT), 239–246

anorexia, 199, 202, 209, 210

attachment, 37–39

avoidance, 38

awareness, levels of, 19, 20, 60–63

borderline personality disorder

case example: the group, 194–196

personal construct group therapy, 189–197

research, 196–197

theory, 189–190

therapeutic practice, 191–194

breast cancer

case example, 315–316

group work with, 310–319

personal construct group work, 312

research, 316–318

role relationships and support, 311–312

theory, 310–312

therapeutic practice, 312–316

bulimia, 199, 209–210

bullying, 266–267

case examples, 7–12, 15, 17, 123–125, 131–133, 142–144, 151–153, 172–175, 184–186, 194–196, 206–209, 219–223, 233–237, 251–252, 259–261, 264, 278–283, 291–294, 302–305, 315–316, 324–329

chief values and views that each holds in particular scenarios, 98–99

child sexual abuse
  case example, 184–186
  personal constructions in therapy,
    177–188
  research, 186–188
  theory, 178–181
  therapeutic practice, 181–184
children
  bullying, 266–267
  case examples, 259–261, 264
  common concerns, 261–268
  friendship networks, 267–268
  growth of sociality, 265
  intensive interaction, 269–270
  interviewing the interalized other,
    268–269
  research, 262
  theory, 256–257, 258, 261–262, 264,
    265
  therapy with, 256–270
client as expert, 15
cognitive psychologist's perspective, 5,
  44, 46, 69
collaborative alliance between client and
  therapist, 45, 75–76
collaborative empiricism, 46
construal, 17, 18, 178, 203
constructionism, 71, 73–75
constructive alternativism, 4–5, 48–53
constructivist therapists, 3, 14–20, 69, 73,
  169–170
constructs
  as bipolar mental structures, 4, 6
  as different areas of a family's universe,
    101–102
  congruent, 137
  core, 214–215
  corporate, 79
  discrepant, 137
  family, 79
construing
  assessment, 369
  changes in, 107
  individual and group, 101
  moving from individual to relational,
    106–107
  range and scope, 101
  research, 186–188
  trauma of sexual abuse, 178–179

contexts
  interpersonal, 103–104
control, 36, 37, 39–42, 207–208
conversation
  constructive, 102
  functional, 102
  topics containing therapeutic lessons, 102
countertransference, 47, 63–65
corollaries, 4, 7–8, 213–214, 261,
  296–297, 311, 365–367
credulous approach, 8, 17, 369

depth-oriented brief therapy
  functionless versus functional
    symptoms, 19
  personal, hierarchically structured
    meaning, 19
  preverbal constructs and levels of
    awareness, 19
  symptom coherence, 18
dilation, 215
dilemmas, resolution of, 136–147
  case example, 142–144
  research, 145–146
  therapeutic practice, 139–144
  theory, 136–138
dimensions of meaning, 4
disorder, 21, 22, 23, 24
divergence, 47

early relational experiences, 44
eating disorders, 198–211
  anorexia nervosa, 209–210
  bulimia nervosa, 209–210
  case example, 206–209
  research, 209–210
  theory, 198–201
  therapeutic practice, 201–205
effectiveness of PCP, 347–363
  aims, 348
  methods, 349–351
  results, 351–362
empathy, 105
epistemological constructivism, 13–14
epistemology
  epistemic and therapeutic orientation,
    84–87
  epistemic match and psychotherapy
    preferences, 90

epistemic style and therapeutic
    practice, 87
nature of, 82–92
practical epistemology, 83–84
experiential personal construct
psychotherapy, 54–68
    creative artistry, 65
        art of therapy, 66–7
        creativity cycle, 65–66
        creativity in ROLE relationships,
            67–68
    diagnosing human meaning making,
        56
        EPCP diagnostic system, 58–60
        role of symptom in EPCP theory,
            57–58
        theoretical basis, 56–57
        using the diagnostic system, 60
    theoretical and philosophical
    background, 55–56
    therapist–client ROLE relationship,
        symbolism, and levels of awareness,
        60–63
    transference and countertransference,
        63–65
experiential therapies, 69
experimenting via behaviour, 15
externalizing the problem, 14

family, 79, 94–108
fixed-role therapy, 11, 12
forensic psychotherapy, 226–238
    case examples, 223–237
    cognitive restructuring, 231
    problem identification, 232
    relapse prevention, 232–237
    research, 237–238
    therapeutic practice, 228–237
    theory, 227–228
functioning, optimal and non-optimal,
    25–30
functionless versus functional symptoms,
    19

grief
    case examples, 123–125
    growing through, 111–126
    theory and research, 113
        constructivist perspective, 115–116

disorganised narratives, 117–119
dissociated narratives, 119–121
dominant narratives, 121–123
loss and narrative disruption,
    116–117
new landscape of loss, 114–115
therapeutic practice, 123
group, 101, 194–196, 271–286

hermeneutic constructivism, 13
holons 289–290, 294
humanistic psychologists, 5

individual, 7, 101, 106
identity, 51
interpersonal understanding, 105
invalidation, 34–37, 39–42, 200, 215

laddering, 140, 147, 252, 369
loss
    case examples, 123–125
    narrative disruption, 116–123
    narratives of, 111–126
love
    from a therapist, 168
    therapeutic, 167–168

meaning and affect of particular
    constructs, 97
meaning in therapy, 4
meaning, personal, hierarchically
    structured, 19
menopause
    case examples, 324–329
    research, 329–331
    theory, 321–322
    therapeutic practice, 322–324
    women experiencing, 320–332
members' concerns and worries and
    changes that would address them, 97
meta-analysis, 347–363

narrative
    dissociated, 119–121
    dominant, 121–123
narrative solutions therapy
    construal, roles and relationships, 17
    preferred view, 16
    the gap, 16

narrative therapy, 14
  common themes with post-modern
    therapy, 69–73
  contribution of PCP, 80
  equated with storytelling, 69

older people
  ageing experience and attitudes, 306
  case examples, 302–305
  clinical research, 307–308
  effecting change, 301–302
  life-experience issues, 300–301
  practical considerations, 299–300
  research, 306–308
  theory, 296–299
  therapeutic practice, 299–302
  working with, 296–309
orthogonal psychotherapeutic
  relationships, 52–53

personal change and the
  psychotherapeutic relationship, 51
personal construct family therapy,
  94–108
  areas of the family's universe, 101–102
  commitment by negoating agreed
    therapy goals, 99–100
  developing understanding, empathy
    and sociality, 105
  differences in viewpoint as a resource,
    94
  enhancing 'agreement to differ', 100
  individual and group construing, 101
  involving different subsystems and
    subgroups, 104–105
  meaning and affect of particular
    constructs, 97–98
  members' concerns, worries and
    changes, 97
  members' values and views, 98–99
  moving from individual to relational
    construing, 106–107
  reflecting on changes in construing
    and making sense of the original
    concerns, 107
  steering conversation and topics,
    102–103
  unique preferences, interests and
    choices, 95–96

widening interpersonal contexts,
  103–104
personal construct theory
  an introduction, 4–12, 365–370
  assessment of construing, 369
  constructive alternativism, 4–5
  core constructs, 214–217
  corollaries: choice 366, commonality
    367, construction 365, dichotomy
    366, fragmentation 367, individuality
    7, 365, modulation 366–367,
    organisation 213–214, 366, range 366
  dimensions of diagnosis and transition,
    367–368
  fundamental postulate, 4, 213, 365
personal construct psychotherapy: a
  meta-analysis of its effectiveness
  aims, 348
  comparisons, 350
  conclusions, 362–363
  discussions, 361
    exclusion of before-and-after
      (uncontrolled) studies, 361
    interpretation, 362
    inclusion of studies without random
      allocation to treatment, 361
    publication bias, 361–362
    statistical analysis for trials of group
      psychotherapy, 361
  introduction, 347–348
  methods, 349
    exclusion criteria, 349–350
    inclusion criteria, 349
  outcomes, 350
  results, 351–360
  statistics, 350–351
personal construct psychotherapy: a
  process and outcome study
  introduction, 335–336
  method, 336–338
  results and discussions, 338
    conclusion, 345–346
    pre-treatment data, 338–340
    therapeutic outcome and follow up,
      345–345
    therapeutic process, 340–342
personal identity and sociality, 51
personal construct psychotherapy
  as a process of reconstruction, 369–370

diverging from the medical model, 5
evidence base, 333–364
experience, 6, 7
fixed-role therapy, 11, 12
general principles, 1–108
individuality, 7, 8
meaning construction as agentic
  process, 5, 6
sociality, 8, 9
specific clinical problems, 109–332
transference in PCP terms, 9, 10
transitive understanding, 10, 11
personal construct psychotherapy
for agoraphobia, 148–157
for anger, 239
for borderline personality disorders, 189
for child sexual abuse, 177
for children, 256
for dilemmas, 136
for eating disorders, 198
for families, 94–108
for forensic problems, 226
for loss, 111
for older people, 296
for people who hear voices, 212
for psychosexual problems, 287
for self-harm, 127
for trauma, 165
for troubled adolescents, 271
for women experiencing menopause,
  320
for women living with breast cancer, 310
PCP: epistemology and practice, 81–93
epistemic match and
psychotherapeutic
preferences, 90–92
epistemic style and therapeutic
  orientation, 84–87
epistemic style and therapeutic
  practice, 87–90
practical epistemology, 83–84
the nature of knowledge, 82–83
PCP and constructivism, 3–20
case examples, 7, 8, 9–10, 11, 12, 15, 17
three examples of constructivist
  therapies:
  narrative, 14–16
  narrative solutions, 16–18
  depth-oriented brief, 18–20

types of constructivism, 12–14, 73–75
post-modern therapy
common themes with narrative
  therapy, 69–73
contribution of PCP, 80
constructivism, 71
definition, 70–72
foundationlessness, 71
fragmentariness, 71
neopragmatism, 71
synthesis, 72–73
postulate, fundamental, 4, 365
posture
psychotherapeutic, 71
preverbal constructs, 19
psychoanalytic perspective, 44
psychodynamic psychotherapists, 69
psychological disorder and
reconstruction, 21–33
limitations of Kellian disorder, 23–24
non-optimal functioning, 27–30
optimal functioning, 25–27
'resistance' to therapy, 32
therapeutic process, 30–32
psychotherapeutic relationship
in psychoanalytic, cognitive and
  constructivist perspectives, 43–48
elements of convergence, 44–47
elements of divergence, 47–48
reconstructive relationship, 48–53
pyramiding, 369

realism, 13, 14
reconstruction
and constructive alternativism, 48–53
and deliberate self-harm, 127–135
of self-identity, 76–80
psychotherapy as, 123
reconstructive relationship, 48, 49
relapse prevention, 232–233
relationships, therapeutic, 17, 44
repression, 38
resistance, 32
ROLE relationship, 8, 17, 54, 60–63,
scotomization, 38
SELFGRID procedure, 204,210
self harm, deliberate, 127–135
case examples, 131–133
research evidence, 133–135

theory, 127–129
therapeutic practice, 129–131
sex therapy
   case examples, 291–294
   personal construct, 287–295
   research, 294
   theory, 288–289
   therapeutic practice, 289–294
sociality, 8, 105
subsystems and subgroups, 104–105
symbolism, 60–63
symptom coherence, 18

therapeutic role relationship, 8
transference and countertransference, 9,
   46, 47, 63–65
transitive understanding, 10

trauma
   case example, 172–175
   constructivist psychotherapy, 165–176
   research, 175–176
   theory, 165–166
   therapeutic practice, 166–172

voices, hearing them
   case example, 219–223
   commonality and sociality, 216
   research, 223–224
   theory, 212–217
   therapeutic practice, 217–219
   the self and the community of selves,
      216
   working with people who hear voices,
      212–225